A Chronicle of Echoes: Who's Who in the Implosion of American Public Education

By

Mercedes K. Schneider

INFORMATION AGE PUBLISHING, INC.
Charlotte, NC • www.infoagepub.com

Library of Congress Cataloging-in-Publication Data

The CIP data for this book can be found on the Library of Congress website (loc.gov).
Paperback: 978-1-62396-673-7
Hardcover: 978-1-62396-674-4
EBook: 978-1-62396-675-1

CONTENTS

ACKNOWLEDGEMENT

MY MENTOR, DIANE RAVITCH

On September 13, 2013, I was having dinner following an advisory board meeting of a research group associated with Arizona State University, and the conversation drifted toward both my completing this book and other issues related to the education climate, including Diane Ravitch's 2006 change of position on education reform issues. I was surprised to learn that a number of people continue to equate Ravitch with the pro-privatization bent that I expose in this book.

I decided that my dinner companions needed to know how indebted I am to Diane for both the popularity of my blog and the production of this book. Thus, I told them a version of the story that follows.

On January 2, 2013, fellow blogger Jason France suggested that I send a paper I had written critiquing Louisiana's value-added modeling pilot study to Diane Ravitch. She posted my work on her blog, and I was grateful. It did not immediately occur to me to keep writing. However, Diane asked if I had written any analysis on the Louisiana charters. And so, I found myself writing more about Louisiana education issues. Needing a place to store my writings, I followed the advice of another Louisiana blogger, Lee Barrios, and started my own blog on January 25, 2013.

A Chronicle of Echoes: Who's Who in the Implosion of American Public Education,
pages vii–ix.

On January 26, I began a series of posts investigating the National Council on Teacher Quality's (NCTQ). I emailed Diane to let her know; she committed to posting the series on her blog after reading my first entry. In the end, from January 26 to February 20, I wrote a 17-post series on NCTQ, primarily focused on its advisory board. Diane carried the entire series, as promised.

On February 9, Diane first mentioned the idea of my writing a book on education reform. She included it as a single statement in our email correspondence on the NCTQ series: "There is a book here if you can find a publisher." Her comment was the planting of an idea in my mind. However, I still did not view myself as a writer of books. Despite my lack of vision, I asked Diane if she had an idea for a publisher. I don't know why I asked. She responded with some names and added, "Very few publishers take chances." That I understood. Besides, who was I, anyway? An unknown who had just started a blog only weeks before.

Nevertheless, the wheels in my mind were turning. I was encouraged because Diane Ravitch had read my work and thought me capable of writing a book. It's a strange place to be: doubting and hopeful simultaneously. I offered, "…Perhaps over summer break I can work on turning [my expose on a number of corporate reform boards] into a book proposal. I would like your guidance on this as I have never written a book before."

Diane's response: "A book: the tiny number of people who want to take control of the nation's education system. Read Arthur Bestor on the "interlocking directorate" that controlled education on the 50s."

And so, the mentoring began. Though I did not see myself capable of writing a book, I was willing to change my mind about myself based upon what Diane saw, both in me and in the focus of the book.

On March 20, 2013, Information Age Publishing CEO George Johnson contacted Diane about possibly publishing her next book. Her response to him:

Thanks, George,

Knopf is publishing my next book.

However, I would like to alert you to a talented writer who is profiling organizations and individuals involved in the privatization movement.

It should be an important and controversial book. I have posted parts of it on my blog.

Her name is Mercedes Schneider and her email is deutsch29@aol.com.

Diane

That same day Johnson contacted me about my book. Fortunately, despite fear of the unknown, I recognized his offer for the opportunity it was. Johnson also had encouragement from Gene Glass to offer me a contract. At that point, I had a framework in mind for this book; I had a number of blog postings that could inform the content of the book, but I had no written proposal. When Johnson asked me to send my proposal to him that weekend, I sent him an email assuring him I would, then I immediately emailed Diane asking what exactly Johnson expected to receive. Never having written a book, I had no idea what to send. Diane told me to draft a table of contents and offer a brief summary of the book's message. This I did.

The next week, I was on vacation in Roanoke, Virginia, when George Johnson and I had a telephone conference; in the end, he agreed to publish my book.

I phoned Diane with the news. Then, I went rollerblading in the crisp, wintery Roanoke air to celebrate.

Johnson emailed the paperwork, which I mailed back following my vacation. As of March 31, 2013, I was officially under contract to write this book.

As a public school teacher, I was well aware that for this book to happen, I would have to spend my ten weeks of summer vacation in a book-writing marathon. This I did, at seven to twelve hours a day. I finished writing the body of the book—24 chapters—on July 29, 2013. I rested for a day then began proofreading and writing endnotes.

Diane has been readily available to me during my writing, which speaks volumes to her commitment given the demands of her schedule. She has offered invaluable suggestions regarding my navigating the writing and publication processes, including suggesting numerous books that I should read in order to inform my writing—just as her mentor, Lawrence Cremin, did for her.

And like Lawrence Cremin did for her, never once did she try to alter my writing voice.

In early April, she even sent me the file for her unpublished book so that I might solidify the direction for my own—a remarkable demonstration of commitment and trust.

So, when I sit at academic dinner tables and hear talk of the "old" Diane Ravitch, the one who supported privatization, I can contribute little except to say that I do not know her. The Diane Ravitch I know not only fights for the democratic institution of American education but also has invested much of herself in me to carry on that fight.

I am both honored and grateful for Diane's assistance and her friendship. She owed me nothing yet tirelessly gave me so much. Thank you, Diane, for your investment in me. I hope this book does you proud.

ADDITIONAL ACKNOWLEDGEMENTS

Thank you, George Johnson, for offering me a contract to write this book.

Thank you, Gene Glass, for your confidence in my writing for IAP.

Thank you, my friends, colleagues, and fellow "righters of reformer wrongs" who have assisted with proofing my writing and offering valued opinions and suggestions: Jennifer Berkshire, Anthony Cody, Susan Muchmore, Gary Rubinstein, Patrick Sullivan, Susan Ohanian, and Brant Osborn.

Thank you, my friend in neighbor, Michael Badon, for often cutting my lawn and freeing up more of my time for my writing.

Thank you to numerous well-wishers who celebrate with me as my book is now published.

And thank you, Jesus Christ, for providing all I needed in order to bring this book to successful completion, including the wonderful people who graciously guided and assisted me.

A special acknowledgment in memory of my colleague, Carrie Speer, who exemplified the beauty that is the dedicated, lifelong public school teacher and counselor.

A Chronicle of Echoes: Who's Who in the Implosion of American Public Education,
page xi.
Copyright © 2014 by Information Age Publishing

INTRODUCTION

As I was writing this book, the detailed image of an abandoned building being imploded and collapsing upon itself often came to mind. Even now the vision is before me: A white building, about ten stories tall, not ornate, not without need for repairs, but sturdy. Men in yellow hard hats watching the building, knowing what is about to transpire because they have orchestrated it from the inside. Though these men are responsible for the impending structural failure, they themselves are outside and distant from it. They have planned the failure but are removed from its consequences.

Seconds later, the collapse begins. The left side begins to fall; then the middle. The rest happens quickly as what was once a study structure yields to a condemnation it could not control. A pile of rubble; a cloud of dust.

The men are satisfied. Their work is done.

This is how I see it every time.

The building is American public education.

The men in yellow hard hats—they represent the individuals and organizations in the twenty-four chapters to come. Their dynamite: the echoes of American education "failure."

I am a public school teacher, and for several years, I have been told that American public education is failing. I have been told that the "data-driven" solution is to privatize. I have been told that those primarily outside of education hold this solution.

I notice that these education outsiders enter the building and plant destructive devices. They assure me that it is For the Good of the Country. They assure me that this is The Solution.

I notice evidence of collapse. They tell me that this proves they were right: American education is failing.

I hear their echoes in my ears. I realize that the unassuming listener might mistake their echoes for the truth, and I want to expose the lie. That is why I have written this book. I want to reveal and dismantle the echoes. I want to halt the implosion.

The individuals and organizations in the subsequent chapters truly are a Who's Who in the destruction of American public education. I reveal their ulterior (often profit-driven) motives; their clandestine arrangements; their strings of corporate reform failures reshaped into twisted versions of "success." In order to do so, I have researched books, newspaper articles, blog entries, email exchanges, interviews, webpages, advertisements, income tax forms, dissertations, conference materials, meeting minutes, video presentations, legislation, and formal testimony.

In writing this book, my purpose is to dismantle the dismantlers. As such, my words are not kind. My words expose, and that exposure is harsh. The individuals and organizations profiled in this book have declared war on my profession, and I take that personally.

This book reflects the factually-grounded consistency of my outrage.

In the end, readers will see that this reform-bent group is the new, traditional-education-destroying Status Quo. By revealing their self-serving histories, I hope to ruin their game, whether it be to corporately run their own schools, districts, states, education companies, or the country.

CHAPTER 1

JOEL KLEIN: THE MAN FROM WHOM NOTHING GOOD COMES

My first opportunity to write about Joel Klein was as part of a National Council for Teacher Quality (NCTQ) series I authored on my blog.[1] In some sections of this chapter, I borrow from my blog entry. It was in writing my blog post on Klein that I began to learn just how devious and self-serving he is. I also began to understand Klein's influence in training others who are effectively propagating reformer destruction in other states. These emerging realizations led me to dub Klein "the viral host of the corporate reform agenda."

Klein's deleterious involvements could easily yield a book, let alone one chapter.

I'll keep it to one chapter, but know that it was a task to trim down the information.

BLOOMBERG AND KLEIN

Joel Klein was appointed chancellor of NYC schools in 2002 by Mayor Michael Bloomberg. Bloomberg assumed mayoral control of NYC schools

A Chronicle of Echoes: Who's Who in the Implosion of American Public Education,
pages 1–18.
Copyright © 2014 by Information Age Publishing

in 2002,[2] and he continues to promote what has become "the usual" for hard-core corporate reformers, the party line that traditional public school closures are good (to be replaced with charters), unions are bad, and student test scores are the ultimate measure of teacher and school "success."[3] (Bloomberg has even decided to fund his own charter schools.)[4] Klein followed suit regarding Bloomberg's education "vision":

> *As chancellor of New York City's 1.1 million-pupil public school system from 2002 through the end of 2010, Klein championed policies like increasing the number of charter schools and closing schools deemed to be failing.*[5]

As is true of many corporate reformers posited in power over education, Bloomberg has no background in education, and Klein has no formal training as a teacher, though he did "teach" for part of one year in a middle school math class.[6] Still, Klein had to have the education background requirements waived[7] in order to become chancellor. Yet according to the *New York Times,* they both believe in a "bottom line" of test scores:

> *While the test scores have been a major source of pride for Mr. Bloomberg and Mr. Klein, they have also become a lightning rod, with many people questioning the validity of the results, and others complaining about the single-minded focus of test preparation in schools.*[8]

It is a hallmark of those with no educational training to promote such the narrow, "scores are everything" focus.

Klein is a lawyer, not a teacher. In fact, during the Clinton administration, Klein served as assistant attorney general, antitrust division, a role in which Klein served as lead prosecutor against now-comrade-in-privatization, Bill Gates. The US Department of Justice won the case; Microsoft was found to have violated the Sherman Antitrust Act 1890 in creating a monopoly.[9] As a result, Microsoft was required to share its application programming interfaces with third-party companies. However, the settlement actually enabled Microsoft to proceed with even less regulation.[10,11]

In September 2000, during the time that Microsoft was appealing the above finding, Joel Klein resigned as assistant attorney general.[12] He offered no explanation.

Education Experience: Who Needs It?

Klein was successful as an antitrust lawyer:

> *Serving one of the longest tenures ever as head of the 700-lawyer division, Mr. Klein led landmark cases against Microsoft, WorldCom/Sprint, Visa/Mastercard, and General Electric, prevailing in a large majority of cases. Mr. Klein was widely credited with transforming the antitrust division into one of the greatest successes of President Bill Clinton's administration. His appointment to the U.S. Justice Department came after Mr. Klein served two years (1993–95) as deputy counsel to President Clinton.*[13]

Certainly this qualifies Klein to run the education system for all of New York City.

A major problem with the modern privatization movement is that reformers promote the faulty view that persons successful in professions outside of education are automatically suited to assume positions of authority in education. Consider this telling information promoted by the Broad Foundation "Manifesto," co-authored by Eli Broad and Chester Finn. The following is from the foreword written by Broad:

> *We're told to improve the quantity and quality of school leadership by adding more formal training and certification requirements to those already in place. We're advised that one must first teach before one can possibly lead teachers. And we're cautioned, therefore, that the best if not the only place to look for tomorrow's leaders is within the ranks of today's educators.*
>
> *As happens far too often in American education, however,* **this conventional wisdom turns out to be wrong,** *or at least incomplete. We will undoubtedly find some of tomorrow's great education leaders in the usual places, trained and licensed in the old, familiar ways. But we won't find enough of them there.* **And there's no reason to confine our search to the usual places.**
>
> *The alternative approach—* **open more gates, welcome people from many different directions to enter them, minimize the hoops and hurdles and regulatory hassles, look** *for talent rather than paper credentials—***has already taken root in public-school teaching (where it's often termed "alternative certification"). It's taken root in America's private and charter schools. And in a dozen or more communities it's begun to take** *root in the superintendent's office,* **as leaders with such unconventional (i.e. non-education) backgrounds as New York City's Joel Klein....Why not simply seek the best leadership talent for our schools wherever it can be found?**[14] [Emphasis added.]

Eli Broad, who himself has no background in education,[15] believes that "conventional wisdom" (common sense?) that says before one can lead in a field, one must first gain experience in the capacity of those one would lead, is "wrong," or "at least incomplete." And Broad offers Joel Klein as an example of one having "talent" rather than "paper credentials."

POOR KLEIN, EXCEPT NOT REALLY

Perhaps in order to draw attention away from his utter lack of education experience, Klein has promoted his own personal history as being one of "overcoming poverty via 'great teachers.'"

Klein's "history" is a lie. However, the impact of poverty upon the classroom is not.

One of the great arguments of corporate reform is that poverty is used as an excuse for maintaining "the status quo," which is, of course, "failing" public schools. Corporate reformers ignore studies such as those demonstrating the strong positive correlation[16] between their labeling schools as "failing" and the proportions of students receiving free and reduced lunch. Joel Klein has taken the "poverty doesn't matter" stance further by offering his own life as proof that it wasn't his poverty that was the problem; it was that he needed an effective teacher to come along and usher him into the world of educational success.

US Secretary of Education Arne Duncan has used Klein's story to promote the idea of "effective teacher as savior":

> *"Klein knows, as I do, that great teachers can transform a child's life chances—and that poverty is not destiny. It's a belief deeply rooted in his childhood, as a kid growing up in public housing. … Joel Klein never lost **that sense of urgency** about education as the great equalizer. He understands that **education is … the force that lifts children from public-housing projects to first-generation college students**. … In place of a culture of excuses, Klein sought [as chancellor] **to build a culture of performance and accountability**."[17]* (Emphasis added.)

Joel Klein helped sell the "urgency" concept as co-chair of the Council on Foreign Relations committee (fellow co-chair, former Secretary of State Condoleeza Rice) that determined it is the public schools that are "threatening national security."[18]

Together, Klein and Rice promoted the unsubstantiated view that domestic security hinges on the schools.

I can think of no other country that has ever promoted such a view.

Interestingly, others believe that the real threat to national security rests in the crisis of the middle class. People in the American middle class earn less than they did decades ago, and they are less likely to be upwardly mobile since corporations began their "disruptive restructuring," which saves companies but all too often dispenses of the permanent corporate jobs upon which the middle class depends.[19] This "bottom line" business model is the same one being promoted as the "no excuses answer" to the fabricated crisis of American education.

In order to effectively sell himself as one suited to remedy the homeland security crisis that he and Rice declared, Klein needs a good story. Like other reformer mantras, the idea that a good teacher is all that is needed to rescue children from the debilitating grasp of poverty certainly sounds appealing. Thus, Klein offers himself as proof that exposure to an effective teacher is all that is needed to combat childhood poverty. After all, who could argue against the firsthand experience of a man who was himself rescued?

Klein promotes this story, but it is not his story. He was middle class, and his achievements are what one might expect from someone of his actual economic upbringing.

Consider this first excerpt, representative of what Klein promotes about his history. The writer is a contemporary of Klein's. The second excerpt is a clarification Klein's contemporary provides regarding the contradictions in Klein's self-styled story:

Here is Klein's autobiographical account in his own words, faithful to original context…:

I grew up in public housing in Queens…. I always like to think of myself as a kid from the streets, and education changed my life. … I stood on the shoulders of teachers to see a world that I couldn't have seen growing up in [my] family….

My father had dropped out of high school in the tenth grade during the Great Depression. My mother graduated from high school and never went to college. No one in my family had attended college … or knew about college. … By most people's lights, we were certainly working-class, poor. … I grew up in a pretty unhappy household. …

Teachers set expectations for me that were not commensurate with my background or my family's income. …

Nobody in [my] school said to me, 'Well, you grew up in public housing, your parents don't read, you've never been to a museum, so we shouldn't expect too much from you!' … Mr. Harris, my physics teacher at William Cullen Bryant High School, saw something that I hadn't seen in myself. … I realized, through him, that the potential of students in inner-city schools is too often untapped. …Demography need not be destiny.

From the day I took the job as chancellor of the New York Public Schools, friends told me that I would never fix education in America until you fix the poverty in our society. … I'm convinced now more than ever that those people have it exactly backwards—because you'll never fix poverty in America until you fix education.

I reject categorically the principle that poverty is an insurmountable impediment….

I never forget and never will forget …where I came from, and what public education did for me. I am still the old kid from Queens.[20]

And now, the challenge by Klein's contemporary, Richard Rothstein:

*…As it turns out, Klein and I grew up in similar circumstances—third-generation, educationally ambitious, Queens, New York, Jewish households, with parents who had nearly identical jobs and incomes. …We attended neighboring schools; I even had the same physics teacher, Mr. Sidney Harris, whom Klein credits with his rescue. **We both attended Ivy League colleges** (he went to Columbia, I to Harvard)…. Educational values were not absent from Klein's family. His father, Charles Klein, like many of his generation, left high school during the Depression, **but the notion that his parents couldn't read or didn't know about college is misleading.** His mother, Claire Klein, was a bookkeeper. With fierce competition for scarce jobs, Charles did well enough on a civil-service exam to land work at the post office, remaining for 25 years in a secure job*

*he hated to ensure he could send his children to college. **This was not the commitment of semi-literate parents with little knowledge of higher education.** … Klein's family was also **not poor by any reasonable criteria.** Charles Klein's annual post-office salary in the 1950s was about **equal to the national median household income.**[21] [Emphasis added.]*

As for Klein's savior teacher, Mr. Harris: It's hard to argue that a student needs "saving" if the student is already excelling in school. Before Mr. Harris came along, Klein was already a member of the National Honor Society, math team, editor of his school newspaper, and student body president.[22]

The most misleading information in Klein's fabricated, my-teacher-saved-me-from-my-poverty success story is in his reference to "living in public housing." As his contemporary notes:

*…**As Klein must know, the words "public housing" evoke an image of minority unemployment, welfare dependence, unwed motherhood, truancy, gangs, drug dealing, addiction, and violence.** Klein, though, grew up in racial privilege, dramatically different from the segregated world of most youngsters in public housing today. … Klein did live in public housing after his family moved to Queens in 1955 when he was nine years old. **But he fails to say… that some public housing in New York in the 1940s and 1950s, including the Woodside Houses project where his family resided, was built for white, middle-class families. The poor and the problems poverty causes were unwelcome.** This distinction is critical to understanding Klein's history **and why it undermines his current policy prescriptions.**[23] (Emphasis added.)*

As another article reveals:

*If my suspicions were correct, rather than proving, as Klein would have it, that 'demography need not be destiny,' **his life story would actually support the opposite claim— that Joel Klein's academic and professional success fulfilled conventional demographic predictions for children of his middle class upbringing.**[24] [Emphasis added.]*

Like many reformers, Klein "shapes the truth" to promote his agenda. He is even willing to "reshape" his own story. However, the truth is that Klein's lie places undue pressure on public education institutions to "save" children from all societal ills, the most pervasive being childhood poverty.

STUDENTSFIRST AND ASTROTURF REFORM

It is a well-documented fact that poverty affects test scores.[25,26] Still, the reformer push to raise those scores continues. In 2012, Klein joined with Michelle Rhee to form StudentsFirstNY. Their mission was to place the responsibility for overcoming the effects of poverty squarely on the schools, the same place that Klein and Rice heaped the responsibility for national security:

StudentsFirstNY is bringing together parents, children, educators and political leaders who know that great schools can help students overcome the challenges of poverty— and who together will build a grassroots movement to fight against a failed status quo which, if left unchanged, will ultimately shatter the people's faith in the importance, power and possibility of public education.[27] [Emphasis added.]

Again, the agenda sounds good: We're going to overcome poverty, and we're going to do so through the schools. Not only that: We're going to "come together" and form a "grassroots movement." The irony here is that a political group is promoted as the foundation for a "grassroots" movement:

StudentsFirstNY, the new political group formed by leaders of the education reform movement like Joel I. Klein and Michelle Rhee, officially announced its arrival on Wednesday morning.

In a news release, the group gave the full line-up of its board members, who include Mr. Klein, the former city schools chancellor, and Ms. Rhee, the former Washington chancellor, as well as charter school and reform advocates like Eva Moskowitz, who runs a chain of charter schools in New York City, and Geoffrey Canada, the founder of the Harlem Children's Zone.[28] [Emphasis added.]

Though Klein and Rhee attempt to package StudentsFirstNY as a "grassroots" organization, emerging from locals and directed by locals, it is anything but. StudentsFirst is a fraudulent "grassroots" movement; such groups are sometimes referred to as "astroturf" movements. Those driving the "movement" are not community members. They are not the parents of children enrolled in local schools. They are financiers of a privatization machine:

There are also a number of people from the hedge fund and investment banking world, many of whom have been long-time supporters of the reform agenda.[29] [Emphasis added.]

It should come as no wonder why hedge fund managers and investment bankers would fit the category of those "long supporting" the "reformer agenda." The current reform agenda is a privatization agenda. Michael Bloomberg endorses this agenda, and he brought Klein on board as NYC schools chancellor because in reality, privatization has little to do with education. A successful antitrust lawyer would do just fine in promoting the systematic dismantling of traditional public education in favor of business interests:

The group supports the expansion of charter schools, merit pay for teachers and the firing of teachers who are found to be ineffective. It is opposed to granting teachers tenure and conducting layoffs based on employees' seniority.[30] [Emphasis added.]

THE KLEIN PROTÉGÉS

Perhaps his most destructive reformer "accomplishment" is that Joel Klein, through his connections with reformer-philanthropist Eli Broad, has been responsible for the grooming of Broad graduates to usurp educational leadership positions around the nation, including Baltimore Schools Chief Andres Alonso, New Orleans Superintendent-gone-state-superintendent John White, Chicago Superintendent Jean-Claude Brizard, New Haven, CT, Assistant Superintendent Garth Herries, and Newark Superintendent Cami Anderson. In the next several paragraphs, I shall briefly note a few of the "accomplishments" of this fine Klein-Broad brood in the undermining of (or, at best, the noncontribution to) quality public education.[31]

While serving as deputy superintendent under Klein, White was connected via emails obtained by the *New York Daily News* to Klein and New York City Charter School Center Executive Director James Merriman on an Albany charter school campaign in 2010. These communications included fundraising specifically aimed at increasing the number of charter schools in New York.[32] White has been in Louisiana since 2011, with a six-month stint as superintendent of New Orleans' Recovery School District (RSD); then, he was fast-tracked as state superintendent, where he has continued to be implicated in questionable dealings based upon Freedom of Information releases of his emails.[33,34]

As for former Klein deputy superintendent Andres Alonso: In 2011, a year plagued with school budget cuts, Alonso paid his chauffer $154,000, including $78,000 in overtime pay. In fact, Alonso paid $14 million in overtime to Baltimore City school employees over a four-year period.[35,36] Also, even as basic repairs were needed for school buildings, Alonso and Baltimore City Schools paid for a $500,000 renovation of the central office, including a $250,000 renovation of the chief of information technology's executive suite.[37,38]

Concerning Chicago's Jean-Clade Brizard, also a former Klein deputy: He resigned following the Chicago teachers strike; in a *Chicago Tribune* interview, Brizard compares his relationship with Mayor Rahm Emanuel to marriage, and he notes that he resigned because he believes Emaunel was, as the article notes, "not happy with him."[39] Brizard lasted only six months as Emanuel's hand-picked superintendent.[40] Funny how he resigned in the month following the teachers' strike and a month prior to Obama's reelection hitting the polls.

As for New Haven Assistant State Superintendent Garth Herries, who says that he wants to bring to New Haven the same reforms that Bloomberg instituted in NYC,[41] consider this quote from a news story about the first "turnaround" school in which, unknown to parents, a New Haven school was being "tapped" by a for-profit company, Renaissance School Services, LLC:

*Since they launched in 2009 a citywide school reform campaign to close the achievement gap, **the mayor and superintendent have declared the process would be transparent.** Hoffman said Thursday the district cannot disclose any details on the turnaround now because the plans have not been made official. **That means no public debate on the plans or the ideas behind them is to take place until an agreement is reached. "When this process is complete, at that point we will be transparent, "** Hoffman said.[42]*

Not until the takeover has been decided will there be parental input and "transparency." Until then, all is "hush hush" behind closed doors. This is not transparency. This is top-down control with a veneer of public inclusion.

In considering Klein's protégés, let us finally attend to Newark's Cami Anderson. Anderson closed down Global Village Schools, a partnership between Newark's schools and New York University (NYU), in favor of an all-too-familiar, "nouveau status quo" reform model:

*Anderson's administration said **foundations will work directly with the renewal schools** to fund the services they need without NYU taking a cut as middleman. And those services will be provided against **a backdrop of much stronger principal and teacher accountability for academic outcomes,** including the **new teacher performance bonuses** included in a historic contract ratified in mid-November.[43] [Emphasis added.]*

Unlike Global Village and NYU, Anderson completely ignores the effects of poverty upon lower performing schools. Note the position on poverty of the NYU administrator overseeing Global Village:

*Beyond bureaucratic complications is the difficulty of tackling education in tandem with poverty. **The philosophy behind Global Village was that poverty is inextricably linked with academic performance, a force more than schools are able to handle on their own.***

*"**If you want to really build sustainable school reform then you have to take into account poverty, the conditions of communities, and you have to work intentionally and systemically to weave all kinds of relationships and supports,"** Lauren Wells, who administered Global Village for NYU, told WNYC last spring.[44] [Emphasis added.]*

It should come as no surprise that Anderson's reform efforts include school closings. In addition, her method of operation regarding such closures does not include informing the public of her plans prior to a public meeting. In a meeting were she planned to announce the closing of seven Newark schools, Anderson did not hold the planned question and answer session. Anderson said that she wanted to avoid prior public announcement n order to inform the public "at once," and not in "dribs and drabs."[45] This is what Anderson calls "transparency," not unlike Herries' transparency, in which the decision has been made and the public is then allowed to "weigh in." Yet the public is not stupid. In Anderson's situation, she neglects to recognize that schools belong to communities; the public has a vested interest in and a connection with its schools. The school is not some business acquisition to its neighborhood. The school is not an object. It is an integrated and valued component of the community. This is lost on would-be reformers like Anderson and Harries and Klein, who work to deliver a public institution into the hands of disinterested, community-unvested corporations.

These five—White, Alonso, Brizard, Harries, and Anderson—have accomplished little on behalf of public education. What I have offered in a few paragraphs does not cover these five individuals in depth, but it does offer a glimpse into Klein's legacy, which appears to be lies, manipulations, self-service, and blind, unyielding promotion of an education reform agenda scripted and designed to benefit an increasingly privatized education market.

KLEIN'S LEADERSHIP ACADEMY: THE JOKE IS ON NYC

I would be remiss in concluding this discussion of Klein protégés without offering a word about Klein's Leadership Academy. Created in 2003 under the direction of Bloomberg with Klein as board chair, the Leadership Academy purports to train principals. Its first CEO, Robert Knowling, was not an educator. He was, however, CEO of an internet business with a plummeting stock value, Covad.[46] The second CEO, Sandra Stein, wrote about principals but was not one herself. It was not until 2011 that the Leadership Academy was actually led by a former principal.[47]

In 2008, the NYDOE reviewed contracts for an organization to train principals. In this case, Klein's Leadership Academy "won" the contract, with Klein playing the same, "but-I-removed-myself-from-the-board" game that he would play again a couple of years later when he quit NYDOE to join Murdoch's ranks. So, Klein basically appointed himself overseer of the five-year, $50 million contract for "training" principals. Consider how the *NYC Public School Parents* blog writes it:

> *That the Leadership Academy—created by Joel Klein, with Joel Klein chair of the board, Joel Klein who had selected the other board members, Joel Klein who had appointed the director, Joel Klein who had raised $75 million in private money to start it through the Fund for Public Schools, an organization which is also chaired by Joel Klein....had now been awarded a $50 million contract by Joel Klein, went mostly unreported. (see partial correction below)*

> *News update and partial correction:*

> *A savvy reporter informed me that Joel Klein took himself and [New Jersey Commissioner of Education] Chris Cerf off the board at the Leadership Academy about a month*

ago—just before awarding them the $50 Million competitively bid contract. Not that this would fool anyone, but…

Sure enough, when you go to the Academy's website…, you see the original board listed; but **the links are missing for the bios for Klein, Cerf and Robert F. Arning, who is head of the NYC office of KPMG and has a huge contract with DOE as well. And when you go to another page listing the board, their names are omitted. Wonder if any of this is legal.…since Klein stepped off the board right before granting the contract,** *presumably he thought there might be a problem.*

UPDATE (July 27); the DOE's Truth Squad at work has made sure that the first of these links has been removed, **eliminating any trace of Joel Klein's previous leadership of the Board, as well as Cerf's participation.**[48] [Emphasis added.]

If I remove my name from my blog, have I really been there? If I expunge my school email address, am I excused from any acts I committed while in my district's employ?

If an ethically-suspect tree falls in a forest of $50 million dollars, can it stir up enough ignored wind to make the money fly without question into a well-connected cheat's pocket?

In Klein's case, apparently so.

Now, let us take a moment to consider who benefits from becoming a principal though Klein's academy. Completers of Klein's academy tend to be younger, have less classroom experience, and have fewer students enrolled at their schools. They also tend to be paid higher salaries than traditionally trained principals and have more freedom in how they lead—including choosing their own staff and training them—provided they make a high school letter grade. And according to the *New York Times*, Leadership Academy principals

> *…were less than half as likely to get A's as other principals, and almost twice as likely to earn C's or worse. Among elementary and middle-school principals on the job less than three years, Academy graduates were about a third as likely to get A's as those who did not attend the program. …The Times's analysis shows that experience counts—at least on school report cards. Forty-three percent of principals with at least a decade at their schools received A's last fall (including Mr. Weinberg), compared with 30 percent of those who had been at their schools up to two years.*[49]

So, if the final assessment of the principal's value is the school letter grade, then Klein's principals are not only not much of a story but also arguably a waste of money by the standard that he set for them—millions of taxpayer dollars that Klein managed to funnel to his own company via NYDOE.

And what of Leadership Academy completers whose obvious lack of ability for the job leaves any appreciable program rigor in question? Consider, for example, Leadership Academy graduate Andrew Buck. Now there's a story. Buck, who appears to have materialized out of nowhere, somehow managed to "complete" Klein's Leadership Academy without knowing how to write. Buck became principal of Brooklyn's Middle School for Art and Philosophy in 2007. The Brooklyn teachers union voted him "least trustworthy principal" in 2008.[50] He refused to provide textbooks to students,[51] forcing teachers to resort to either using materials on the web or Xeroxing books for class use.[52] Buck sent a email dated October 16, 2010, in which he alternately argues for and against textbooks in what is summarily best described as an incoherent ramble. His email included such erroneous and/or incoherent statements as, "First, just because student have a text book, doesn't mean she or he will be able to read it. ...Additionally, students can't use a text book to learn how to learn from a textbook. ...So, are text books necessary? No. Are text books important? Yes. Can a teacher sufficiently teach a course without them? Yes, but conditionally."[53]

Buck was also a poor disciplinarian; his middle school garnered headlines for the violence at his school, including a sexual assault by a student to a teacher in a darkened classroom as she showed her class a film. Another student punched a teacher in the chest after being told to report to the cafeteria. Students also engaged in sexual acts at school in places such as stairwells.[54]

Despite his utter lack of leadership and substandard email ramblings, in 2011, Buck appealed to parents and staff to write letters of endorsement in order to help him secure tenure. One year earlier, in June 2010, Buck had been denied tenure.[55] He was finally fired in July 2011.[56]

Andrew Buck is a product of Joel Klein's efforts to bring noneducators into education and fast-track then into principalships by way of the overpriced-yet-Klein-benefiting Leadership Academy.

In a 2005 interview with PBS' Headrick Smith, Klein says the following regarding accountability and sound leadership. Once one is able to set aside Klein's ego, his words really do sound so noble:

> *First and foremost, is accountability.* **This (New York schools) is a system that has had no accountability. And very few systems that we know that work well have zero accountability.** *Basically whether you perform well or you perform poorly, you're fundamentally treated the same. And that's been an organizing principle.*
>
> *The second thing, I think, that's been critical is the focus on leadership.* **You know, I ... created probably the most dynamic and certainly the largest Leadership Academy for training principals in the United States.** *We raised close to $75 million from the private sector to support this effort. ...A great principal is critical ....*[57] [Emphasis added.]

Now, as one digests that bit of self-aggrandizing-yet-duplicitous pap, one should keep in mind Klein's maneuverings to position his Leadership Academy as financial beneficiary of public funds, and one should consider the likes of Andrew Buck. If one does so, one can unequivocally conclude that Klein is nothing more than a self-serving liar.

THE BIG IDEA OF SMALL SCHOOLS

Even though Klein and Gates have a rocky history due to Klein's former prosecution of the Microsoft monopoly, in 2003, Bill and Melinda Gates Foundation contributed $51 million dollars to NYC schools to create 67 "small public high schools."[58] The general idea is that the atmosphere of a smaller school would encourage bonding between students and their teachers, thus leading to improved student performance. However, NYC small schools appear to have fallen victim to the reformer mindset that controlling the appearance of an outcome equals true change. In the NYC small schools, one measure of success is a low number of suspensions. Sadly, this "great result" can be achieved by refusing to acknowledge the need for consequences. Consider this situation recorded by a teacher at NYC's Campus Magnet:

> *The day before 17 fights broke out and one student's arm was broken. One student threatened a principal after one of the fights and told her she would "f— her up." She took no action because she both feared the student who threatened her and possible retribution from her superiors who might accuse her of being excessively harsh if she suspended the culprits. ...*
>
> *So if you look at the latest citywide suspension numbers you'll see that they've been reduced by an astounding 30 percent over the past 18 months! These numbers might be music in the ears of the mayor, the editorial boards, and the city council but they actually mask a worsening condition in the schools.*
>
> *The discipline code has been revised to ensure that insubordination is merely a word in the dictionary and not an act of improper student behavior. Last week a student told me to "shut the f— up" three times. I finally called for a dean who promptly returned the student to my room and told me he understands the consequences of his actions. He promptly returned to the same pattern of behavior.[59]* [Emphasis added.]

Some NYC small schools are rough, but not all. Some boast of high test scores and above-average graduation rates. What of the small schools' scores and selection? The process and "stellar" results follow a now-common reformer pattern: These "transformed" schools are able to appear better than they are because they are not the schools that must accept all students— that role continues to belong to the traditional public school:

> *Overall the new small schools Bloomberg created have boosted test scores and graduation rates. But they cannot accommodate all the students the big schools once did.*
> *So, the small schools select their students. This does not mean all kids at small schools*

are top students. But it does mean that they applied to schools, filled out a form and were assigned somewhere, courtesy of New York's opaque high school choice process.

The small schools do not have as many students with serious disabilities *as many schools slated for closing.* **Most do not accept the city's most challenging students—so-** *called "over-the-counter" kids who are not assigned to any high school.*[60] [Emphasis added.]

In the end, the Bloomberg-Klein-Gates "small schools" do not appear to justify the disruption they create. The real measure of small school success would be success in the absence of any traditional public school serving as a catch-all for small school "undesirables." So long as any reformer alternative school is not required to accept all students, any success should rightly be met with skepticism. Also, small school "success" should be measured by the quality of education evident in a site visit and not just based upon easily-manipulated statistics.

KLEIN AND MURDOCH ROB NEW YORK

In 2010, Klein left NYC to work for news mogul Rupert Murdoch.[61]

It should come as no surprise that Klein and Murdoch share an interest in corporate reform.[61] Both Murdoch and Klein want to expand charter schools, neutralize unions, and remove teachers found to be "ineffective." And, of course, there was the power of Murdoch's *New York Post* in promoting Klein's education agenda while he was chancellor, including eliminating statewide caps for charter schools.

Murdoch donated one million dollars to Education Reform Now, an organization chaired by Klein and that promotes an anti-LIFO ("last in, first out") faculty seniority message.[62] Its board of directors is made up of executives at the hedge funds Hawkshaw Capital, Gotham Capital, SAC Capital and Maverick Capital, all pro-charter.[63]

Following the Chicago teachers strike in Fall 2012, Education Reform Now paid for Chicago Mayor Rahm Emmanuel's commercial about the strike where he promotes reform "for the kids."[64] Education Reform Now also involved itself in school board elections in Buffalo, NY, and Milwaukee, WI.[65]

Indeed, Murdoch's money influences NYC even beyond Klein's departure:

Combined with the increased scrutiny of Klein's role in the DOE's recent proposal[66] *to renew a $4.5 million contract with Murdoch's Wireless Generation (which Klein himself now oversees in his work as head of the Education division at News Corp.) and the State Education Department's decision*[67] *to award a $27 million no-bid contract to the same company, it's likely that this web of connections will be important to keep an eye on as Klein settles into his new position at Murdoch's side.*

This NYC no-bid contract to Wireless Generation (not owned by Murdoch at the time) was awarded in November 2010.[68] This is the same month that Klein resigned as NYC chancellor effective the end of the year and accepted a position with Wireless Generation.69 Two weeks after Klein announced his upcoming resignation, Murdoch purchased 90% of Wireless generation for $360 million.[70] Apparently, when big money is involved, the ethics of a situation really do not matter. Klein was the head of NYC schools; through the Murdoch acquisition of Wireless Generation, Klein is now the head of a company benefitting in the millions off of NYC schools. Reformers can do this, folks, because they are so firmly allied and well-funded:

> *Conflict-of-interest rules set strict limits for city employees, both during and after their tenure, which could make Mr. Klein's transition a tricky one. City employees are never allowed to disclose confidential information about the city's business dealings or future strategy, **and they cannot communicate with the agency for which they worked for one year after they leave. The rules also bar them from ever working on matters they had substantial involvement in as city employees.***

> *A spokeswoman for the Education Department, Natalie Ravitz, said that **Mr. Klein recused himself from all business dealings between the department and Wireless Generation "as soon as we learned that News Corp had acquired" Wireless Generation.** He will also "continue to follow the advice of the conflicts board on this matter" and abide by all applicable rules once he starts work at News Corporation, Ms. Ravitz said.[71]* [Emphasis added.]

Let us consider what is not written above. Solely based upon the power and influence of his position as chancellor, a position Klein continued to hold even as Murdoch purchased Wireless generation, Klein should not be connected to Wireless Generation. Period. Not only is there a conflict of interest because of a connection between Klein's employ with both NYC schools and Murdoch; there is another entire layer based upon the fact that Klein is in fact benefitting from the millions NYC schools spent (and continue to spend) on Wireless Generation because Klein is in charge of Wireless Generation.

In July 2011, City Comptroller John Liu halted a $1.3 million payment to Wireless Generation based upon Klein's conflict of interest. One project given to Wireless Generation replaced IMB in operating the ARIS system.

In 2007, Klein and his DOE awarded IBM a five-year contract to develop the Achievement Reporting Innovation System (ARIS).[72] The system cost over $80 million, and it did not even work correctly. A 2011 audit (released January 23, 2012) of ARIS[73] found the system wanting:

> *What's more, the audit concludes, the city can't show that ARIS is leading to higher student performance—something that former chancellor Joel Klein signaled would be a result when he rolled out the system in 2008.*

*"This costly tech program was much-touted by the DOE to help principals and teachers track progress and thereby improve student learning, even as long-time educators questioned its cost and effectiveness," Liu said in a statement today. "**$83 million later, there is little discernible improvement in learning and many principals and teachers have given up on the system.**"*[74] [Emphasis added.]

One month prior to expiration of the lucrative-yet-unproductive contract with IBM, NYCDOE decided to transfer the final month of the ARIS contract to—no guessing needed—Wireless Generation—for an additional cost of $10 million. Comptroller Liu objected,[75] yet Wireless Generation won in the end, albeit briefly. In July 2012, NYDOE began "quietly transitioning" from the now-obsolete ARIS to a new statewide data system, DNAinfo, funded via USDOE grant monies.[76] DNAinfo was to be in place in 2013.

Klein and NYDOE managed to waste approximately $100 million on ARIS. Klein authorized $80 million to IBM, and his company, Wireless Generation, took the rest.

ALVAREZ AND MARSAL: YET ANOTHER NO-BID RIP OFF

Joel Klein really likes the no-bid contract. It allows him to freely choose to whom he bequeaths loads of taxpayer money. The no-bid contract easily converts public money into Klein's own amply-funded financial tap. Klein (and Bloomberg, all via NYDOE, of course) is able to wield their "no-bid" power because mayoral control removes a school system from being classed as a "city agency." Were the schools designated a city agency (which is the usual course), then competitive bidding would be required prior to contract issuance, as would comptroller oversight. Instead, NYCDOE views itself as a state agency; city oversight cannot touch Bloomberg, or Klein, or NYCDOE spending of taxpayer money.[77]

Reformer ecstasy: Unfettered power. Freedom to spend sans oversight.

Klein's brazenness with awarding himself the Wireless Generation contract was not his first no-bid dealing. Far from it. Klein was NYC schools chancellor for just over eight years (2002–2010). According to ParentAdvocates.org, by the time he was halfway though his stay (2006), his penchant for the no-bid was hardly unnoticed:

*…In the past four years the DOE has awarded hundreds of millions of dollars in no-bid contracts; for instance, **on the same day the Alvarez deal was approved, the DOE okayed $42 million in other no-bid deals.** While the no-bids are a very small percentage of its overall spending, **the DOE is doing no-bid deals way more than it used to.**[78]* [Emphasis added.]

One duo that benefited from Klein's public money largesse is Alvarez and Marsal (A&M). In the summer of 2006, NYDOE awarded A&M a contract worth approximately $17 million.[79] One of the tasks given A&M by Klein was to "restructure the Office of Pupil Transportation to obtain annual cost savings."[80] Thus, the goal of spending this $17 million was, ironically, to cheapen the transport of NYC children. In fact, A&M were tasked with shaving off $200 million in the cost of running NYC schools.

In the process of A&M's "saving money" on student transportation, in early 2007, they inadvertently contributed to mass confusion in their restructuring of bus routes. Children were left out in winter weather, with no busses arriving to take them to school. This created a dangerous situation for scores of students, requiring the school system to set up a hotline to deal with the issue:

> *Closing out a week of confusion in New York, officials said, a special hot line set up to handle bus problems had received 2,043 calls as of 4:30 p.m. yesterday [February 2, 2007], down somewhat from the day before.*[81]

Two years later, in a 2009 interview, Klein admits responsibility out of one side of his mouth and then excuses himself by noting that his decision to hire A&M "did cut costs":

> *Schools Chancellor Joel Klein admitted Friday some things have not gone as smoothly as they could have under his watch.*
>
> *Among them was **the bungled school bus overhaul two years ago aimed at squeezing out cost savings that ended up stranding thousands of kids and enraging parents.***
>
> *"I made the mistake, and I'm responsible for it," Klein said at the Assembly's second public hearing on mayoral control.*
>
> ***He was quick to add, though, that the high-priced consulting firm behind the fiasco did help cut costs.***[82] [Emphasis added.]

Again with the sad irony of a "high priced firm cutting costs."

Before A&M had arrived to scoop up millions in NYC, they had been in St. Louis "cutting costs" for a year (2003–04) to the tune of $5 million. In the end, the St. Louis schools faced state takeover due to their facing bankruptcy.[83] Here is evidence of A&M's St. Louis "success" prior to its "restructuring" transportation in NYC:

> *…In St. Louis—which had about 40,000 students at the time, a fraction of New York's nearly 1.1 million—some parents, politicians and school board members said things were not so simple. They said **the firm erred by eliminating needed positions, and ignored the human cost behind decisions like closing 16 schools with little notice. Today, they point out, the St. Louis system remains near bankruptcy, and student performance is abysmal.***
>
> *"I think they [A&M] made things far worse," said William Purdy, the St. Louis school board vice president. "There were many, many protests, and people were angry."*

In fact, one of the firm's controversial moves involved eliminating bus stops, changing routes and enforcing a policy that only children living within a mile of school should receive yellow bus service.

Peter L. Downs, a St. Louis school board member, **described the changes as a "disaster,"** **saying "assignments were made without regard to highways, bus routes were drawn** **without regard to one-way streets or streets that had been blocked off."**[84] [Emphasis added.]

Sure sounds a lot like the "restructuring" A&M "accomplished" in NYC.

A&M had also racked up more than $17 million for its "fiscal restructuring" of New Orleans' schools following Hurricane Katrina in 2005. In overseeing modular campus construction, A&M's supervision resulted in the project costing an extra $29 million, with $6 million being designated as questionable costs. A&M did not provide the necessary verification to show that work supposedly completed had actually been done.[85]

In 2012, the DC Public Schools, under Kaya Henderson, also hired A&M to "investigate" charges of cheating during Michelle Rhee's time as chancellor. Rhee had previously hired A&M in 2007 to audit DC schools finances. Never mind that A&M has no experience in investigating test security breaches, nor is the firm experienced in erasure analysis. As the *Washington Post* observes:

It is not known how much experience Alvarez and Marsal has in test security. Its Web site says it offers "turnaround and restructuring advisory, crisis and interim management, performance improvement, business consulting, global forensic and dispute services and tax advisory.[86]

So much for A&M's resolving the DC cheating scandal. As of 2013, the scandal continues full force.[87] However, A&M did garner $236,000 for less than two months' work.[88]

Reformers like Rhee and Klein really seem to like paying A&M for at best nothing and at worst, running school systems into the ground.

TIME TO WRAP IT UP

Joel Klein is a reformer's reformer. First, he is willing to lie about his history in order to deny the effects of poverty upon the whole child. Next, as he passes, he leaves a trail of destruction that just happens to also place millions of taxpayer money in his hands and the hands of his corporate-policy-friendly cronies. Third, in a truly amazing feat of high-order corruption, he is even able to direct public money beyond his official time as a chancellor. Finally, Klein even takes his reformer talents a step further by training other empty adults to destroy what should be "for the children."

If Dante had thought of the likes of Joel Klein, he might have added more levels.

CHAPTER 2

EVA MOSKOWITZ: STAGE MOTHER OF CHARTER SCHOOL "SUCCESS"

If Mama Rose had forsaken Vaudeville and instead had focused upon a career establishing and running charter schools, she might have been mistaken for Eva Moskowitz. And just as Mama Rose did whatever she needed to do in order to propel her daughter Gypsy Rose Lee's career, Moskowitz is equally as pushy and controversial in the charter school arena.

Moskowitz is the founder and chief executive officer of what was originally Harlem Success Academy Charter Schools, later changed to Success Charter Network.[1] Moskowitz holds a Ph.D. in history and has taught at the university level (Vanderbilt, University of Virginia, and City University of New York). She has also taught civics at a New York school for gifted children, Prep for Prep, and served as a New York City Council member from 1999 to 2005.[2]

Since 2006, Moskowitz has been building for herself a charter school empire.

Moskowitz might try to promote herself as an educator, but she is first and foremost a shrewd business mind. One can know so not only from her

A Chronicle of Echoes: Who's Who in the Implosion of American Public Education, pages 19–37.

driven behavior but also from those appointed to the Success Charter Network Board of Directors, not one of whom has a primary, lifelong career in education. The following board of directors information is from the Success website:

Joel Greenblatt is a managing partner of Gotham Capital, a hedge fund.

John Petry is the founder and managing principal at Sessna Capital. Previously he was with Gotham Capital.

Gideon Stein is the co-founder and president of Future Is Now Schools, a national non-profit focused on building sustainable school models. Mr. Stein is also a partner with Argyle Holdings LLC, a real estate development company in Northern Manhattan.

Ms. Mary G. Berner serves as the president & CEO, MPA, of the Association of Magazine Media. She has extensive global experience in both publicly traded and private companies ranging in size from less than ten million to more than three billion in revenue.

Jay Bryant is a managing director at BlueMountain Capital Management.

Steve Galbraith was a partner at Maverick Capital prior to forming Herring Creek Capital in November 2012.

David Greenspan is founder and president of Slate Path Capital, a New York based global investment firm. He founded the firm in 2012. Prior to Slate Path, Mr. Greenspan was partner and managing director at Blue Ridge Capital in New York.

Kevin Hall is the president and CEO of the Charter School Growth Fund. Before joining CSGF, Mr. Hall served as the Chief Operating Officer of The Broad Foundation

Yen Liow is a principal of Ziff Brothers Investments.

Daniel S. Loeb is the founder and chief executive officer of Third Point LLC, a $12 billion event—driven hedge fund headquartered in New York.

Rich Pzena is the founder and co-chief investment officer and a member of the executive committee of Pzena Investment Management.

John Scully is a founding partner of SPO Partners & Co., a private investment firm. He is also a director of Plum Creek Timber Company and chairman of the board of Advent Software, both public companies.

Regina Kulik Scully is a premier public relations and brand marketing expert and founder of Rpr Marketing Communications.

Kent A. Yalowitz is a litigation partner at Arnold & Porter LLP.[3]

If I had read this information without knowing these people were sitting on a board of directors for a network of schools, I would have never guessed it.

Neither would I have guessed it by Moskowitz' salary, which topped $475,000 based upon a September 2013 *New York Daily News* report.[4]

Moskowitz insists that her obsession is "for the children." Yet she has chosen to surround herself with career financiers and pays herself handsomely. She is a driven, controlling woman running a business in education.

Nowhere is Moskowitz' drive clearer than in the 125, now-public emails between her and former New York Schools Chancellor Joel Klein and, to some extent, then-deputy Chancellor John White.[5] In one notable exchange, Moskowitz writes her own gratulatory recommendation supposedly from Klein to Jennifer Sneed of the Charter School Institute and actually emails the draft to Klein as a prompting for his support of her opening additional charters. This is quintessential Moskowitz—very bossy. Below is the text of the August 16, 2007, email "instructing" Klein as to what he should do to assist her securing approval for three additional charter schools:

> *We just received CSI's [Charter Schools Institute's] requests for amendments to our application for 3 charters in Harlem.... As you know, I met with Ed Cox about the replication effort so I think it's looking very favorable. One of CSI's main concerns is facilities. They explicitly state that we are required to submit a letter of commitment from your office... (and that we must get them this letter by Monday).* **To save time, I drafted a quick letter. If you could put some variation of this letter on letterhead and sign and fax back to me at [phone number], I would really appreciate it. If there's anything more I can do to make this happen,** *please let me know. Thanks so much Joel and look forward to hearing from you soon.*[6] [Emphasis added.]

And now, an excerpt from the letter, which immediately follows the above email:

> *I know Eva Moskowitz and the Success Charter Network founders Joel Greenblatt and John Petry very well. They have put together an incredible operational team, and Eva and her staff have been focused since day one on replication. Iris Nelson, a gifted educational leader and Chief Instructional Officer of the Network, was responsible for turning around PS65Q. I also know many prospective board members for the new schools and am confident of their ability to govern the new schools.*

> *When Eva Moskowitz and I sat down to discuss replication I told her that effective Charter Management Organizations with ambitious replication plans are precisely what we need to transform the educational landscape in New York City. I wholeheartedly support the Success Charter Network's plan and am committed to securing space for 3 Harlem Success Academy Charter Schools in Harlem in the 2008–09 school year.*

> *Sincerely,*

> *Joel Klein*
> *Chancellor*[7]

There you have it: Moskowitz telling Klein what she wants of him.

In his fashion typical of the email exchanges whereby Moskowitz sends a lengthy, detailed request to him, Klein responds to this brazen directive in only a few words:

garth will be in touch—he's managing lots of requests in harlem—joel[8]

Not the response Moskowitz wanted. Based upon previous email exchanges regarding public school building access, Deputy Superintendent Garth Harries is not moving quickly enough for Moskowitz. So, she sends another lengthy email (also dated August 16, 2007) noting that she wants to open the schools in Harlem, that she has already scouted out space in five Harlem public schools for her charter schools, and that if Klein or Harries want her to open schools elsewhere after next year (but not next year, mind you), she will do so. She ends this email with, "Am very concerned that with Garth's full plate that we will not meet CSI's Monday deadline. Is there anything more Joel Greenblatt or I can do to move foreward?"[9]

Again, Klein offers a brief response:

yeah but so do other charters in harlem—you should review the schools w garth and let's try to make it work—just can't say from where i sit that the five you want are fine. jk[10]

In an April 2011 *New York Times* article, Klein is quoted as saying that "at times, she (Moskowitz) was a complete pain in my neck."[11]

I'm thinking that this might be one of those times.

"Pain in the neck" or no, Moskowitz did get her CSI recommendation letter, not from Klein, but from Harries, and one not so "obviously Eva."

In the previous email exchange, Klein is giving away free public school space to privately-operated charter schools. Furthermore, neither Klein nor Moskowitz mentions any consultation with the public school administration or staff regarding charter school squatting.

As of 2011, Moskowitz had started seven charters, all housed rent-free in public school buildings. (The five Harlem Success Academy schools had been opened: one in 2006; three in 2008, and one in 2010, as had two SAs in the Bronx).[12] The relinquishing of free public school space is the charter-friendly custom in NYC:

*Rent is not something charter chains worry about. KIPP, the nation's biggest (99 schools) and richest ($160 million in corporate grants over the last four years) chain, pays no rent for its seven charter schools in the city. **Nor does Eva Moskowitz, who has opened seven Success Academy charters in Harlem and the Bronx.** ...Citywide, 67 percent of chain charters receive free space in public school buildings....*[13] [Emphasis added.]

The Bloomberg/Klein practice of offering free space in public school buildings to privately-managed charters is a cause for contention, as is Moskowitz's behavior towards those with whom she is expected to work and negotiate. Consider this email, dated June 4, 2009, from NYCDOE Panel for Educational Policy member Patrick Sullivan to Klein[14] regarding several issues: Harlem Success Academy presence in the PS123 building; Klein's decision to hand over public school space, free of charge, to charter schools, and Moskowitz' alleged unwillingness to meet with the community education council (CEC) representative:

Joel,

As you probably know, there has been much publicity about an Eva Moskowitz charter school, Harlem Success Academy 2 expanding within PS 123. I include below a link to an article by Juan Gonzalez on the issue.[15] *I would appreciate it if you could intervene in what is clearly a deteriorating situation in the building.*

I spoke to Diane Johnson of CEC (Community Education Council) D5 today who has been working with PS 123. She's been trying to open up a dialogue… only to be repeatedly rebuffed. Moskowitz has refused requests to meet… and, in blatant violation of Chancellor's Regulation A-660 has even barred the HSA2PTA from meeting with the PS123 PTA.

*In my conversation with Diane, as in similar conversations with Hector Nazario of CEC D4 and Lisa Donlon of CEC D1, I found a CEC member who is very pragmatic and is seeking to forge a working relationship in an effort to address the needs of her community. **I don't see Eva Moskowitz reciprocating here or in other situations were people who deal with her report she is disrespectful of the very communities she is trying to help.***[16] [Emphasis added.]

In his email to Klein, Sullivan alleges that Moskowitz has instructed the charter school parent teacher association (PTA) of HSA2 to not attend meetings with the PS 123 PTA. He references Chancellor's Regulation A-660.[17] The following is an excerpt from the regulation:

*To foster strong and effective parent representation in every school, PA/PTA members must be treated fairly by the PA/PTA executive board and school officials, **without fear of penalty or retaliation.***

*Self-determination must be the rule … when it comes to the governance of PA/PTAs. … **They are not to be run by the principal or other school officials.*** [Emphasis added.]

Sullivan continues and asks Klein to "help arrange a meeting between Diana and Eva"; to "require a meeting of the PTAs as required by A-660," and to "work collaboratively with both PS 123 and CDEC [Community District Education Council] to revie w (sp) the needs of PS 123 and help them continue their [thoroughly impressive] good work." Sullivan candidly states,

*I read the PS 123 quality review online. It is a thoroughly impressive school doing great work with children and families, **many of whom would never be accepted into HSA2.*** [Emphasis added.]

Following this, he notes that Klein's decision to give public school space to charter schools is poorly viewed:

*...I have been involved in many discussions about the future of mayoral control. ... [New York State Assembly Member] Cathy Nolan asked me to come to Albany where I spent talking to electeds including [State Assembly Member] Shelly Silver. **In almost every conversation, this high-handed manner in which you force charter schools into neighborhood schools was mentioned.** Many parents and electeds oppose the renewal of mayoral control **simply because the way you dictate to schools and the CDECs** (same as CECs) **without consultation confirms that you have abandoned the community schools you are supposed to be championing.** [Emphasis added.]*

Sullivan brings home his point directly and powerfully:

*This case at PS 123 is just one more example. There is no obligation for any of us at the Board of Education to provide any charter school with free facilities, food, maintenance, transportation and other services. If we will give them to Moskowitz we must demand the requisite amount of cooperation and decorum. **Otherwise she should be told to take her school elsewhere.**[18] [Emphasis added.]*

The following morning, Klein forwarded Sullivan's email to Moskowitz and included the brief note, "FYI."[19] Moskowitz responds within the hour:

Thanks. Simply not so. I have received one letter (without any contact info) from ps123 parents I responded in writing, saying happy to meet and proposed a date. Bc [because the letter included] no contact [I] sent [my reply] to [the PS 123] principal and asked her to forward. She responded she knew nothing about [this letter]. So we tracked down address. Anyway, one of several lies in letter.[20]

This is an unusually brief reply from a woman whose emails are often lengthy. In essence, Moskowitz is saying that only a single PS 123 parent tried to contact her. She attempts no detailed defense of any other charges against her made by named people in Sullivan's email, including Sullivan himself. This is not like Moskowitz, who is aggressive, even in email, even with people on her side, like Klein.

In his email, Sullivan refers to a *Daily News* article written by Juan Gonzalez[21] regarding a number of issues, including a cap set on PS 123 enrollment to apparently make room for Moskowitz' expanding Harlem Success enrollment. Gonzalez even notes that NYCDOE is assisting Harlem Success Academy in an enrollment drive by using its automated phone system to encourage parents to apply to Harlem Success.

On December 21, 2007, Moskowitz presses Klein for NYCDOE assistance in handling multiple mailouts advertising Harlem Success. Klein contacts

NYDOE Charter School Office Director Michael Duffy and allows NYCDOE to assist Moskowitz with sending multiple mailouts (Moskowitz: "..to make market share a reality we need to be able to mail 10–12 times to elementary and pre-K families").[22]

There is no question that the decision is biased in favor of Moskowitz' schools. As Duffy writes on December 26, 2007:

> *Hey Eva,*
>
> *The Chancellor asked me give you an update... with getting mailing labels **to you and other charter schools** so that you can begin the process of **recruiting for new applicants**.*[23] [Emphasis added.]

"Recruitment" comes from the very schools that Moskowitz seeks to invade by declaring declines in enrollment as her excuse to exercise her "charter squatter's rights." Throughout the emails, Moskowitz is fixated on finding the next "failing" public school to house her next Success Academy. In insisting upon the need for these "multiple mailouts," Moskowitz reveals the mystery to the demand for her charters—a market saturated with charter propaganda. Meanwhile, forcibly-competing public schools retain their single-mailout status, placing them at a predetermined disadvantage to Moskowitz' (and others') charters.

In his email to Moskowitz, Duffy comments that the reason for this marketing "high priority to Harlem Success" is to "empower parents... who are looking for an alternative." The truth is that parental awareness and "choice" are being shaped by NYCDOE's bias toward charters. If parents prefer for their community schools to flourish without facing charter invasion, they must fight for that option. Sometimes they win—sort of:

> *Public School 194 and Public School 241 were failing schools, [Moskowitz] said, and should have been closed.*
>
> ***Both received a "D" in 2008 on the DOE's performance evaluation.*** *The closing announcement drew the ire of parents* and political leaders.
>
> *That's because they were the only zoned public schools for their respective neighborhoods, **and Klein had not submitted the closings to a vote of the community district education councils, as required by state law.***
>
> *His action led the United Federation of Teachers to sue, after which the DOE suddenly withdrew its decision and let the schools stay open.*
>
> *Amazingly, both PS 194 and PS 241 received "A" ratings from Klein's evaluators later in the year, contradicting the DOE's claim the schools could not be turned around.*
>
> *The Harlem Success academies had to find other space....*[24] [Emphasis added.]

Note that the parents wanted the community schools to remain open despite the low letter grades—evidence that there is more to school quality than is captured by a capricious rating system.

Note also that the unions stood up for what the parents wanted. Moskowitz hates unions. She views them as the ultimate foe and herself as the aggressive hero willing to combat them. Consider this email excerpt from Moskowitz to Klein, dated June 20, 2008:

> *Unions are problem. Not about teaching and learning. Anyone who takes em on deserve credit and support. Our children have suffered long enough.*[25]

I wonder what it would take for Moskowitz to overcome her arrogant blaming of unions and actually ask parents what they want for *their* children. I wonder if it has ever crossed her mind to ask a community for permission to open one of her schools.

Ironically, the community often views Moskowitz as the ultimate foe, one who with Klein's assistance and blessing is allowed to usurp the power belonging to the community and to parents, usually via "surprise attack":

> *They are calling it the invasion of the charter schools.*

> *It seems to work this way:*

> *Parents at a neighborhood public school suddenly learn Chancellor Joel Klein has decreed they must surrender scarce classroom space in their building for a new charter school.*

> **No parent or faculty meeting to gauge whether anyone wants the new school.**

> **No official vote of the local Community Education Council.**

> *Some young bureaucrat from the city Education Department's Office of Portfolio Development arrives one day with a bunch of maps under his arm and promptly orders a new allocation of rooms.*[26] [Emphasis added.]

The "space-sharing" tactic of NYCDOE's installing a charter school inside of an existent public school is to have only one school survive. Consider this email excerpt from then-Deputy Chancellor John White to Moskowitz. It is part of a greater exchange in which Moskowitz is demanding another classroom for her school, a short-term outcome according to White, who is attempting to refocus Moskowitz on a longer-term "strategy" to "play nice for now" in order to possibly gain the entire facility in the future:

> *Going back to the school and reopening the space allocation process... is not an advisable course of action **when a longer-term discussion about how all students in this zone are served** looms. It doesn't take much investigation to realize that Harlem Succcess's very place... in the P.S. 7 facility **implies a question for 2009–2010: one school has to***

move or one school has to phase out or close. Given the immediacy of **that very large question**... *I do not think that starting a dispute... about an individual classroom at this stage in the process is prudent.*[27] [Emphasis added.]

White is telling Moskowitz to let the single classroom issue go so as to not stir up the people who will likely lose their entire school to Moskowitz if all goes as planned. The "one school" to "phase out or close" is supposed to be the public school. This is the NYCDOE plan, and parents and community members such as those of PS 194 and PS 241 know that they risk losing their schools to Moskowitz if she is allowed to enter.

Moskowitz doesn't want to hear of "strategy" for the "long term" from White. She wants her single classroom now; she focuses her next lengthy email on arguments about fairness in sharing space—space handed to her for free and usurped from an existing school that she has determined is among the "forces that are harming children, everyday (sic), in a fundamental way, 007 is doing just that."[28]

If it's a public school, to Moskowitz, it is wrong. If it's a charter—her charters, for sure—it's right. Note this in her response to White:

> *Kids will only win in the end if our side has the courage to decrease harm being done by status quo and unabashedly support schools that truly put children first.*[29]

One cannot "truly put children first" of one does not respect the rights of their parents and their communities to choose to support their community public schools.

Moskowitz, Klein, and White all clearly choose to support expansion of charter schools at the expense of public schools.

As to Sullivan's accusation that Klein has "abandoned the community schools" he is "supposed to be championing," consider this email from Klein to Dan Katzir, senior director of the Broad Foundation— Education. The subject line reads, "eva moskowitz" and leads into the following text:

> *mentioned that she is seeking support and suggest you might have concerns re alignment of our work.* **i'm a big supporter of what she's doing, not just in terms of her charters (which appear to be very strong) but also in terms of the political sophistication she brings to the overall effort. she's done more to organize parents and get them aligned with the overall reforms than anyone else on the outside.**[30] [Emphasis added.]

Klein obviously favors Moskowitz' charters enough to put a word in with Katzir, who influences Eli Broad, who has the millions Moskowitz desires to fund her charter expansion. Also, Klein supports Moskowitz's "work" with parents because Moskowitz takes control and "aligns" parents with the reforms (making parents akin to objects to be placed "in line" with the agenda Moskowitz endorses).

It is clear from White's email to Moskowitz that the "strategy" is to not make too much fuss upon charter entry into the public schools so as to seem to quietly get along— with the ultimate goal of answering "that very large question" of "one school" "phasing out" or "closing." It is also clear that Klein supports Moskowitz's efforts to build her charter empire. Not only does he write as much in his emails; he also provides for her extra help from NYDOE in promoting her schools over the public schools. And yet, in the face of a lawsuit accusing NYDOE of purposely closing public schools with the intent of replacing them with charters, Moskowitz denies that such is the goal and brazenly instructs both White and Klein to "correct mistakes" in the March 25, 2009, *New York Times* article[31] on the situation:

> *You must call and correct mistakes.*
>
> *There were public hearings. N case of 194 not one byt (sp) 2. Hundreds and hundreds from the community attended. Even the uft came out in force.*
>
> *These schools are not being "wholly replaced"*
>
> *This is what i mean by pr and how we can get killed. I will call Hernandez. But you can't let him get a way (sp) with it.*[32]

That email was sent at 10:42 a.m. Later that evening (8:26 p.m.), Moskowitz sent to Klein one of her longer missals on the issue. Here are some notable excerpts:

> *Have been pondering extensively. ...**The trick** in my view to coming out ahead is to be extremely disciplined on the messaging and **not let this be portrayed as a legal issue** but as an issue against change and against kids. **We need to make this about special interests and the political class.** Finally we have hope and this is about squashing opportunity. **Your pr people (in my not so humble view) don't always do a good job of this.***[33] [Emphasis added.]

Well. There you have it, Joel. Another bossy Moskowitz moment.

The *New York Times* article entitled, "Suit Challenges City Plan to Replace Three Schools," is an article about the lawsuit.[34] Yet Moskowitz doesn't want this "to be portrayed as a legal issue." The suit concerns not seeking school board approval before closing schools. Moskowitz wants to reframe this issue as being "against change." The actual lawsuit[35] charges Klein and NYC-DOE with attempting to erase PSs 150, 194, and 241 from the zoning map instead of supporting them. The suit further alleges that upon erasure, no public schools would be provided in place of the removed schools but that charters would be installed in existing buildings. The suit notes that it is the CECs that have the authority to approve zoning changes. In the suit, Klein is quoted as saying in a 2003 senate task force meeting, "I want to underscore that nothing in the school system reorganization will affect established attendance feeder patterns and zoning of schools."[36]

Moskowitz wants to frame the argument that the lawsuit is "against kids." Yet the suit includes information from a letter sent to the parents of PS 150 students offering no local traditional public school option, only three out-of-zone choices or the charter school to be located in the former PS 150 school building. Too, the charter cannot be considered a zoned school since it must take applicants via lottery and by law cannot restrict application to a specific zone. (However, in an October 3, 2008, email to Klein in which Moskowitz delivers her sales pitch for "2 schools most interested in" that "got ds and fs," PSs 194 and 241, Moskowitz adds, "Will give students preference" and that she wants to "move quickly."[37] If applicants apply by lottery, how is it that Moskowitz can make such a promise to "give preference"?)

In her evening email, Moskowitz laments, "Finally we have hope and this is about squashing opportunity."[38] The question is, who are "we"? The displaced students who would be provided no zoned school alternative for their closed public school? Or are "we" the reformer set, including Moskowitz, who would replace any traditional public school with a charter no matter what the community wants or needs?

Despite Moskowitz' push to "not let this be portrayed as a legal issue," it was indeed a high-profile legal issue. Klein and NYCDOE acquiesced, and the following week, the lawsuit was dropped. No closing of any of the three community public schools. However, like a tumor, the charters were allowed to continue to "expand inside DOE space."[39] Here is then-Deputy Chancellor John White's on-the-record response for the DOE's "uncharacteristic about face":

> *White said the department made its decision* **because the lawsuit left parents unsure of which schools would be open next year.** *"Rather than continue to confuse them through this lawsuit, which is hanging over the process, we know that they will be given all of these options [and can]* **choose the one** *that will be best for them," he said.*[40] [Emphasis added.]

White's response has layered meaning. First, if there had been no lawsuit, parents would have been "sure" that they would have no zoned school to which to send their children, and they would have also been "sure" that they had no say in the closure or the decision to hand public school buildings over to charters that were required by law to determine enrollment by lottery. Now that there was a lawsuit, parents might not have been "sure" of the outcome, but they were "sure" that they were being given legal recourse instead of an unanswered, top-down, charter-friendly usurping of their schools.

John White also paints the outcome as one in which parents can "choose." Not necessarily true. Parents can "choose" the charter only insofar as entering a child's name into the lottery for a limited number of seats. The "choice" to automatically attend the charter is an illusion, just as the "choice" to keep the zoned schools open without legal recourse is also an illusion.

Moskowitz advocates for "choice"—so long as it isn't the choice in favor of community public schools.[41]

Keep in mind also White's "strategy" email to Moskowitz: Quietly invade public school space: then, wait it out for the eventual takeover. Not all involved in the lawsuit are satisfied with the charter-sharing arrangement:

> *"As far as we're concerned, [charter space sharing is] still problematic, [plaintiff Jennifer] Freeman said,* **because the DOE did not involve the elected parent council in the decision to site the school there,** *she said. She said her purpose in joining the lawsuit was* **to push the DOE to follow state laws requiring community input in decisions about school siting....**[42] [Emphasis added.]

In avoiding court, NYCDOE avoided having a judge rule regarding the DOE's practice of offering charters public school space at will, without input from community authorities. Thus, NYCDOE's decision to "uncharacteristically" fold remains one of self-benefit.

In the competition between Moskowitz' charters and the traditional public schools, Moskowitz often wins because she is relentlessly controlling. Such is also obvious in her solicitation of funds from billionaire privatization sympathizer Eli Broad in this November 5, 2008, email to Klein. Moskowitz has in mind an amount that she wants from Broad: five million over two years:

> *Am hearing good things thanks to you and others re Broad. Am very grateful.*
>
> *Am also hearing that he may give me* **considerably less than asked for (admittedly alot—5 million over 2 years)**
>
> *The next two years are critical for us.* **For me to grow this aggressively and maintain exceptionally high quality I need upfront funds.** *...Am... planning on opening up 4 schools simultaneously for next decade. ... Planning on doing 3 more [in Harlem]and with a few others growing we will be at market share and I believe have a formidable education/political base* **from which to demand high levels of accountability.** *...*
>
> **Any advice for me on how to ensure getting closer to amount need? Am actually not too familiar with philanthropic politics and how to play/not play.**[43] [Emphasis added.]

I wonder what "accountability" Moskowitz wishes to "demand." She is accountable to no one.

Moskowitz wants to know how to "play the game" in order to get that five million out of Broad. Klein's response is to the point: "Candidly, knowing [Broad] that well, I don't think he will give you that kind of money...."[44]

Klein was right. Broad gave Moskowitz one million.

She did not rush to her email to communicate the news to Klein.

That was February 2009. Moskowitz indicated that she would use the money toward the "plan to open the last 3 in Harlem in august 2010 and then move to Bronx."[45]

The UFT lawsuit on behalf of PSs 150, 194, and 241 was filed one month later.

There are those who believe that Moskowitz should be called a success because her schools produce high test scores.[46] However, Moskowitz' success is not good for children. When students of HSA1 scored phenomenally well on state standardized tests in reading and math, it is obvious from this *New York Magazine* article that Moskowitz instituted her own signature version of obsessive test prep towards producing those "phenomenal" scores:

> *...Moskowitz says her teachers prepped their third-graders a mere ten minutes per day ... plus some added time over winter break, she confides upon reflection, when the children had but two days off: Christmas and New Year's.* **But the holiday push wasn't the only extra step that Success took to succeed last year.** *...[Director of Instruction]* **Paul Fucaloro** *kept "the bottom 25 percent" an hour past their normal 4:30 p.m. dismissal—four days a week, six weeks before each test. "The real slow ones," he says, stayed an additional 30 minutes, till six o'clock: a ten-hour-plus day for 8- and 9-year-olds.* **Meanwhile,** *much of the class convened on Saturday mornings from September on. ...*
>
> *The day before the scheduled math test, the city got socked with eight inches of snow. Of 1,499 schools in the city, 1,498 were closed.* **But at Harlem Success Academy 1, 50-odd third-graders trudged through 35-mile-per-hour gusts for a four-hour session** *over Subway sandwiches. As Moskowitz told the Times, "I was ready to come in this morning and crank the heating boilers myself if I had to."*
>
> **"We have a gap** *to close, so I want the kids on edge, constantly," Fucaloro adds.* **"By the time test day came, they were like little test-taking machines."**[47] [Emphasis added.]

If Shirley Jackson had written a modern day horror story about the idolization of test scores produced by the sacrificing of children, her text could not have surpassed the true horror that is Moskowitz. In her self-centered fixation on consuming public education via charters, Moskowitz is more than willing to transform children into "little test taking machines." Anything to secure first place.

In an April 27, 2013, article, "Eva Moskowitz's sin," the *New York Post* lauds Moskowitz' test scores:

Eva Moskowitz has committed the ultimate sin in public education: Her charter schools are wildly successful.... At Success Academy Harlem 4, some 98 percent of third-graders passed the state math exam, while just 9 percent did at its unionized neighbor. In English, 87 percent passed at Moskowitz's charter, while no one did at the union school.

The figures are likewise lopsided citywide: 96 percent of Moskowitz's kids passed math and 88 percent passed English, versus 30 percent and 20 percent respectively at union schools. Wouldn't it be nice to have a New York where it was a sin for a school to fail rather than succeed?[48]

All that matters is the test score. It does not matter how the score is achieved. It does not matter that children are being trained to produce test scores in sweatshop, assembly-line fashion: High test scoresà automatically and unquestionably evidence of good teaching. Low test scoresà automatically and unquestionably evidence of poor union-backed teaching.

Those unions. With them out of the way, Moskowitz can demand her teachers to forfeit their personal lives for the sake of higher test scores. She can demand that they put in a six-day work week[49] at 11 hours a day;[50] she can insist that they be available in the evenings via cell phone;[51] she can even require that they eat lunch with their students.[52]

No wonder "star teachers... often burn out and quit, saying they have to save their marriages and their health."[53]

Let's get something clear, *New York Post*: Schools do not join unions. Teachers join unions, and they do so to guard against the very abuses Eva Moskowitz characteristically demands of her faculty who are purposely denied the option to join a union.

Among the 125 publicly-released emails is an exchange in which Moskowitz reveals her feelings about union contracts. In the exchange, she is negotiating with Broad via Dan Katzir (with Klein's assistance) for the five million Moskowitz hoped to obtain over two years. Klein comments that Broad is close to then-UFT President Randi Weingarten. Moskowitz next discusses a brief negotiation between Weingarten and herself over possibly exchanging union contract usage for giving Moskowitz access to "half of your [Klein's] schools" or "500 schools of yours [Klein's]." "Otherwise," writes Moskowitz, "nfw—no f**king way."[54]

Moskowitz has big plans, and she will not allow humane behavior to get in her way.

Herein lay "Eva's sin," *New York Post*. Shame on you for missing it.

As for her plan following opening "the last 3 Harlem in august 2010," Moskowitz did move "then to Bronx," where by January 2013, she had installed her third Bronx charter. And in Bloomberg-promoted, charter-friendly fashion, the Department of Youth and Child Development (DYCD) had paid Moskowitz start-up funding in 2011 for Harlem 5, Bronx 1, and Bronx 2, at $121,380 per school.[55] In fact, in March 2011, DYCD paid a total of $2,876,811 to 27 charters, and that amid continued budget cuts for youth services.[56,57]

Moskowitz et al. are able to move in with both free room and financed board.

What a deal.

Not to worry, Moskowitz is soliciting ample money.[58] In 2010, her Success Charter Network hauled in $12 million, $3 million of which was public money. And Moskowitz' salary of $336,402 rivals that of a public school state superintendent. By May 2013, The State of Eva had only 14 schools with another 6 set to open in fall 2013,[59] and yet another 6 slated for fall 2014.[60] Moreover, despite her only having had 10 functioning schools in 2012, Moskowitz garnered a per-pupil management fee raise from $1350 to $2000. That's public funding, folks. To the State University of New York's (SUNY's) Charter School Institute (CSI), Moskowitz cried "budget shortfall" even as Network financial records indicated it had received $28 million from foundations and investors over the six years since its inception in 2006.[61]

Moskowitz' "power support" is set; in fact, she held the first gala for Success Academy Schools in New York's Mandarin Oriental in May 2013. The attendees were corporate reform elite, including billionaire hedge-fund manager Daniel Loeb of Sony Corp., billionaire hedge-fund manager David Einhorn of Greenlight Capital, billionaire hedge-fund manager Paul Tudor-Jones of Tudor Investment Corp., multi-millionaire investment banking CEO Rich Handler, billionaire hedge-fund manager John Griffin od Blue Ridge Capital....

I should stop.

However, if I stopped now, then readers would not know that former Florida Governor Jeb Bush, New Jersey Governor Chris Christie, and New York State Board of Regents Chancellor Meryl Tisch were also present.[62]

There's money to be made in children.

Characteristic of Moskowitz' public-school-space intrusions, parents have no say in the matter. In the name of "doing it for the children, Moskowitz moved into PS 146 and planted Bronx 3. No need for parents of PS 146 to attend the so-called "public hearing" when the decision to allow charter "replication" to occur in PS 146 had been made months earlier:

> A controversial charter school network **aggressively expanding under founder Eva Moskowitz** is slated to add a third school in the Bronx this September **with little parent feedback.**
>
> **There were no parents or community members at a public hearing Tuesday night to discuss opening Success Academy Charter School—Bronx 3** in Morrisania, which was originally proposed to open in East Harlem.
>
> It's a departure from sharp outcries in Brooklyn and Harlem, opposing the charter schools and claiming they take away space from other needed programs. Six more are

slated to open in September [2013] throughout the city. [Hell's Kitchen, Crown Heights, Fort Greene, Union Square, Prospect Heights, Bronx 3]

Though the hearing was held on Tuesday, Success Academy Charter School—Bronx 3 was already approved to share space with Public School 146 on Cauldwell Ave. in a December Department of Education panel vote.[63] [Emphasis added.]

Here is the twist regarding lack of parental presence at the token, cosmetic "public hearing":

Kerri Lyon, spokeswoman for the charter network, said the lack of parent presence at the hearing is a positive sign.

She said the school has already received about 500 applications for fewer than 200 spots in the new Bronx charter.[64]

Note that the "500 applications" are not exclusively from PS 146; by law, New York charter schools cannot restrict enrollment to a single district. In fact, none of these 500 need be PS 146 students. So, for Lyon to imply that "lack of parent presence" translates to those parents' applying for the incoming Success charter is misleading. What Lyon doesn't mention is that Bronx 3 will only enroll kindergarten and first grade for the 2013–14 school year.

Success Academy cannot possibly accommodate the volume of students displaced by an SA takeover.[65] This massive displacement of children cannot possibly promote community stability. Then I remind myself that reformers like Moskowitz endorse "aggressive, disruptive reform." In fact, billionaire hedge-fund manager Daniel Loeb lauds Moskowitz by saying the following ironic statement at a Success gala:

Success is a completely disruptive business model.[66]

Let that one sink in.

Success Academy seldom loses. If "lack of parental presence" is "a positive sign," for Bronx 3, lack of Bronx 1 parents at an expansion hearing is also a foregone conclusion in favor of Moskowitz' SA1. Consider this February 2013 public hearing regarding the closure of MS 203 and the attendant expansion of Bronx 1:

*District 7 parents and teachers said they worry that if the city closes "failing" public schools and allow charter schools to expand, **local students won't have good educational options in their neighborhoods if they don't win spots in charter school enrollment lotteries.**...*

*Often, the Success Academy charter school network has supporters turn out in droves for public hearings about their schools' bids for space. **But no one from Success Academy*** *spoke at the hearing, and representatives of the Bronx Success Academy 1 declined multiple requests for comment.*[67] [Emphasis added.]

It appears that Moskowitz is finally following White's suggestion to quietly wait for her moment as part of "long-term strategy" in light of the "really large question."

The article continues:

*The Panel for Educational Policy… is set to vote on the changes to the South Bronx building and dozens of other schools next month. **A majority of panel members serve at the will of Mayor Bloomberg, and the panel has never rejected a city proposal.***

*"**The decision to close M.S. 203 has already been made,**" said Rich Farkas, vice president of the United Federation of Teachers, who represented the union's central leadership at the hearing. "**[Success Academy] is going to expand at the cost of M.S. 203.**"*

*Kyesha Christopher, a junior at Bronx Academy of Letters [another charter in the MS 203 building], offered the same sentiment. "**I have a feeling that nothing we do is going to change it,**" she said.*[68] [Emphasis added.]

Moskowitz' Bronx 3 opened August 2013 and initially serve grades K-1 and add one grade per year.[69] It seems that many of those "500 applicants" are likely to be parents of children who had not yet attended school and thus had no established relationship with MS 203.

As to those displaced middle school students: If Bronx 3 adds a grade per year, the current middle schoolers will be out of high school by the time Bronx 3 could possibly "serve" them.

Being conspicuously absent from a public meeting connected to SA presence has served Moskowitz in the past. In 2011, at a PTA meeting in advance of the public hearing about Moskowitz' proposed SA Cobble Hill in Brooklyn, Moskowitz also decided not to show:

***Community concerns have been building for weeks against the school,** which is part of former Councilmember Eva Moskowitz's Success Charter Network.*

*Roughly 30 people from schools across the district attended…, **but there were no representatives present from Success Charter Network**. Many voiced their frustration with **a system they see as serving charter schools at the expense of public schools.** Some said they weren't opposed to charter schools in general, **but did take issue with charter schools co-locating within public school buildings.***

*"This particular proposal for the charter co-location…is not going to work out in this building without really damaging what we have here already," said building librarian Judy O'Brien. "**We don't want any charter school in public school space in District 15.**"*[70] [Emphasis added.]

The article provides examples of how SA presence will crowd the school, especially if SA reaches its projected capacity:

> *The building at 284 Baltic St. is underutilized by DOE standards. The capacity is listed as 1,615 and there are currently 924 students enrolled there, according to the DOE.*
>
> *But O'Brien said the School for International Studies currently occupies 35 classrooms with an average class size of roughly 25 students. The current proposal suggests that if co-location were approved there would be 20 classrooms for the roughly 520 students.* **The DOE proposal also notes that if Success Academy Cobble Hill reaches its full capacity, 600 students, the building will then be at 108 percent capacity.**[71] [Emphasis added.]

By the spring of 2013, Moskowitz' Success Academy Network was comprised of 14 existing schools and 6 schools set to open August 2013. SA Cobble Mill opened as Moskowitz planned, rent-free as an unwelcome intrusion at 284 Baltic St.[72] She has also apparently forsaken her mission to save disadvantaged children from "failing" public schools and seized the opportunity to move up to the Upper West Side:

> *Opening a charter on the upper West Side—preferably somewhere between 96th and 120th Sts., says Success Academy CEO Eva Moskowitz—signals that* **charter operators are willing to compete in neighborhoods that already boast outstanding public and private schools,** *and* **preparing to make their schools the norm** *in all sorts of communities rather than a specialized response in our most underserved neighborhoods.*[73] [Emphasis added.]

And notice Moskowitz' attempt to move into Williamsburg, a far cry from the likes of Harlem, as noted in this January 20, 2013, *Village Voice* excerpt:

> *Success Academy Williamsburg opened this past fall. Citizens of the World was approved in December to open in the fall of 2013—unless* **a lawsuit by local parents,** *who have taken their campaign from the hui (community group for parents and parents-to-be) to City Hall, manages to stop it.*
>
> **This isn't some "Waiting for Superman" scenario wherein charters swoop in to save a broken, overcrowded public school system.** *Quite the opposite. As a rule,* **Williamsburg's schools are neither overcrowded nor broken.** *With Hispanic and Italian families priced out* **and white families moving in,** *the number of children in District 14 is actually dropping....* **So there is plenty of room in the local schools, and parents aren't obliged to send their kids to the one they're zoned for—they essentially have their pick of the neighborhood. ... "Several district schools in the neighborhood received an 'A' or a 'B' on the 2012 Progress Report,"** *notes Devon Puglia, a Department of Education spokesperson.*
>
> **The flip side of under-enrollment, however, is that it opens up a vacuum in the district school buildings.** *Charter elementary schools... save money by "co-locating" in existing*

school buildings; **they see the depopulated hallways in a place like Williamsburg as an empty niche waiting to be exploited.**

...The issue at stake in Williamsburg is not the virtues or the evils of charter schools. **This is about the basic American democratic principle of local control, the notion that families should have meaningful input in determining their own educational needs** *and that* **a few entrepreneurial carpetbaggers pulling down six-figure salaries—with the backing of an unabashedly free-marketeering, union-hating mayor—shouldn't be allowed to trample parents' rights in order to advance their own philosophies and agendas.**[74] [Emphasis added.]

Thus, the true Moskowitz goal comes to light: Success Academy (it was once Harlem Success Academy before Moskowitz moved it beyond Harlem with Klein's and NYCDOE enablement) is not about rescuing children from failing schools in poor neighborhoods. Success Academy's goal is to replicate.

And Moskowitz does not want to be held to any required quota of "high needs" students.[75] In fact, she says that any law requiring quotas of high needs children would force charters to purposely misclassify students.

As of 2013, Success Academy Citizens of the World was not listed on the Success Charter Network website. However, Success Academy Upper West opened its doors to K-1 in 2011.[76]

Moskowitz' first love is an ever-expanding Success Academy. Whether or not the receiving community wants her school is irrelevant. Until she is stopped by concerned individuals union or otherwise, she will continue to relentlessly scope out those under-capacity, free-to-charter public school buildings in order to turn as many New York children into efficient "test-taking machines" as she can.

CHAPTER 3

WENDY KOPP, THE LEADER IN TEMP AGENCY EDUCATION: TEACH FOR AMERICA (TFA)

Wendy Kopp is not an educator. And unlike her product, the Teach for America (TFA) temporary-teacher-ideally-gone-administrator, Kopp has not even spent the customary TFAer's two years in the classroom. Yet in 1989, she was willing to settle on teaching following college in light of having no job offers in her chosen field, as I detail in this chapter.

I first wrote about Wendy Kopp as an entry on my blog.[1] I have taken that piece and expanded upon it considerably in this chapter. After studying Kopp, I have learned that she is driven. Had she really wanted to become a teacher, even an "eleventh hour" teacher, I think she could have accomplished as much. But I don't believe Kopp wanted to be a teacher. I believe she wanted to be in charge.

Though Kopp's vision began with having college graduates from fields other than education spend a two-year stint in the American classroom, there is today an additional layer to TFA, that of systematically replacing the traditional education administrator with former TFA recruits—and garnering salaries unknown to most classroom teachers. This second purpose

A Chronicle of Echoes: Who's Who in the Implosion of American Public Education,
pages 39–57.
Copyright © 2014 by Information Age Publishing

of TFA threatens more than the first to not only destroy teaching as a profession but also to bankrupt American education via unbridled corporate greed.

Despite its seeming altruistic beginnings, Kopp's TFA— with its turnstile teaching and out-of-field, education leadership usurping— is dangerous to our democracy's pillar of public education.

KOPP, PRIVILEGE, COLLEGE, AND QUESTIONABLE ETHICS

Having grown up in Dallas' Highland Park/University Park area, a locale boasting some of the highest per capita incomes in the state of Texas,[2] Wendy Kopp was a child of privilege. Thus, both her view of the impact of poverty upon public education and her willingness to improve the education conditions of the poor are from the "outside in," a perspective absent any firsthand experience. Kopp even admits that her formative experience was "extraordinarily isolated from reality and the disparities in education and opportunity."[3] Indeed, the high school Kopp attended, Highland Park High,[4] boasts a 95% graduation rate for its predominately white student body (as of 2013: 1848 students,1782 of whom are white[5]). Yet even at this high school of privilege, white students consistently score higher than Hispanic students on the Texas Assessment of Knowledge and Skills (TAKS).[6] Furthermore, whereas the dropout rate for Highland Park High's white students is 3.4%, for Hispanic students, the rate is 14.3%.[7]

Even among the affluent public school students, there is a "gap" in which white students tend to outscore minorities.

Following high school, Kopp attended another elite school, Princeton, where she majored in political science. While a Princeton student, Kopp became editor-in-chief of *Business Today*, originally named *Princeton Business Today* when it was created in 1968. By its second issue, *Princeton Business Today* had a readership of 200,000, the largest student-run magazine in the US. By the time Kopp became editor-in-chief in 1987, the magazine had become *Business Today* and had a multi-university readership with a goal to "bring students and the business world together." By the time Kopp ran it, *Business Today* was wholly funded by advertising, which, in 1987, cost advertisers $5000 per year. In 1971, the Foundation for Student Communication was created to fund students as they traveled soliciting ads for the magazine.[8]

Kopp belongs to the elite. Not too many undergraduates run magazines in which businesses pay five grand per year to advertise (this is decades ago, mind you) and which have a foundation to cover student expenses as they travel selling ads.

The Foundation also expanded its role to include a national Business Tomorrow conference. Wendy Kopp was also in charge of this foundation as its president.

So, what we have in 1987 is college sophomore Wendy Kopp's running a widely-circulated, well-funded magazine and leading the foundation that funds both student travel for ad sales and a national-level, business-student-to business-world conference.

Certainly this power and influence could go to someone's head.

On April 22, 1987, *The Daily Princetonian* published an article entitled *Business Today Fabricates Own "Letters to the Editor"; Publisher Says Magazine Will Revise Policy*. I found this title interesting, for it implies that perhaps those in charge of *Business Today* (i.e., Kopp) did not know it was fraudulent to fabricate news and needed to create some policy that says clearly, "News items cannot be created by the staff." Sure enough, Kopp and her staff created letters and attributed them to other students. In a poor show for someone in charge of a major (if student-run) publication, Kopp tries to explain the process she and her staff followed in violating journalistic ethics:

> *Kopp said that although the Business Today staff wrote the letters, "We called the people, read them the letters, and asked if we could use their names." In one case, however, a student said he had no knowledge that his name was used in the magazine until he was informed yesterday by The Daily Princetonian. Other students said that while they had approved the use of their names, they never knew the contents of the letters prior to publication.*[9]

Apparently, Kopp and her staff initiated contact with former classmates and friends to ask if these friends would allow their names to be posted on letters they themselves did not write. Furthermore, the *Business Today* staff wrote some letters and published them without consent of those whose names appeared on the letters. And just as Kopp lightly excuses the deceptive practice as "just doing" what is "slightly questionable," so her staff also refuses to admit to the careless breach of trust created between publication and readership:

> *[Former Business Today publisher David] Frank said that* **Business Today wrote a letter consisting of "what (Lee) (a student) was going to write in about." Frank admitted that Business Today "did not read the text to him."** *In all, at least six of the 15 letters to the editor in the two issues were not written by the alleged student authors. Five could not be reached for comment. In addition,* **Kopp confirmed that the four students polled in the spring issue's "Student Poll" section all went to her high school, Highland High School outside Dallas, TX.**[10] [Emphasis added.]

If news is what they need, Kopp and her staff simply create it—a useful skill for her future in corporate reform.

Even though *Business Today* was overseen by two boards of directors,[11] neither board took action against Kopp or any other staff. Princeton University also took no action. The closest faculty or staff came to any sort of publicized sanction appears to be this quote by one Princeton professor:

Wilson School professor Richard Ullman, formerly a member of The New York Times edi-
torial board, said that "if these allegations are true, it demonstrates that the magazine
has very little standing as a publication. It shows it's lacking in credibility."[12]

Kopp does not care. She was insulated from consequences of lying to the public and abusing her position as editor-in-chief. She also continued in lies that directly contradicted the stories of a number of students whose names appeared on letters that they did not write. Notice the delusional reasoning that would come to serve Kopp as leader of her well-funded corporate reform substitute for qualified classroom teachers:

> **Wendy Kopp, last year's [1987] publisher [of Business Today] said that** *she "just*
> *didn't feel there was a need for a retraction."* **She did add, however, that** *all the letters*
> *last fall were legit.* She also explained that *BT's readership changes every year, that*
> *those 200,000 students across America are simply names a huge computer spits out to*
> *make up a mailing list. She reasoned that if different people read the magazine each time*
> *it comes out, a retraction and apology would serve no purpose.*[13] [Emphasis added.]

No need to publicly apologize for a publicly-perpetrated fraud since public readership changes.

The author of the *Daily Princetonian* article quoting Kopp's casual attitude towards her and her staff's deceit reflects upon the implications such an attitude holds for the integrity of *Business Today* as a whole:

> *If BT's (Business Today's) attitude toward its readers is: "What they don't know won't*
> *hurt them," then maybe the entire magazine is full of half-truths that simply go unno-*
> *ticed because it's just not worth anyone's time to find them. We'll just have to wait to see*
> *what the next issue holds in store. After all, maybe someone will write a letter in about*
> *it. But don't hold your breath.*[14]

Another student offers this tongue-in-cheek response in the *Daily Princeton-*
ian opinion section:

> *To the Chairman: It's good to know that after all those Business Today issues about*
> *ethics in business that the magazine decided to provide an example of ethical behavior*
> *for the university as a whole. What with our alumni's antics, I've long believed that the*
> *business community is the real purveyor of ethics in this country and this latest incident*
> *only reaffirms my belief that on a university level, the business school hopefuls should*
> *dictate our ethics.*
>
> *Pierre Gentin '89 Princeton University (or maybe University of Honolulu)*[15]

In the same opinion section as the letter above, Kopp did acknowledge that her actions were wrong... sort of. She begins by writing that the *Business Today's* staff was wrong but immediately frames her response to justify hers and her staff's actions:

A shortage of material prompted us to solicit opinions *from students we know at other schools. In some cases,* we wrote the letters, *called friends, and asked them if we could use their names. The letters did not represent our opinions: they represented a variety of viewpoints and included many criticisms of Business Today. To my knowledge, every writer, with the exception of one, had agreed to allow his or her name to appear on the letters. That one exception was a mistake on our part. In the shuffle of editorial copy,* we accidentally *matched a wrong name* with *one of the letters.*[16] [Emphasis added.]

Kopp refers to students who did not write their own letters as "writers." Also, she never explains how a person's name came to be included "in the shuffle of editorial copy" given that this student wrote no letter in the first place.

The remainder of Kopp's letter is essentially an attempt to separate *Business Today's* actions from those of the business world in general and of turning an accusation on a *Daily Princetonian* reporter whom Kopp alleges lied about his identity in order to solicit the truth from a student whose name appeared on one of the letters. In other words, the remainder of Kopp's letter steers responsibility away from her and her staff.

Kopp never takes responsibility for her deceit. In justifying her actions, Kopp hopes to sell readers on the idea that defrauding them with fake news isn't so bad after all.

Kopp's sliding ethics take a turn, however, when her behavior is not in the spotlight. When Princeton President Harold Shapiro was in the news for his late-night visits to a "mystery woman" after being followed by reporters, Kopp replied,

"I'm outraged," said Wendy Kopp, publisher of Business Today. *"That man has no ethics, and neither do those 'journalists.'* "[17]

Her exact words less than a year after her own scandal.

One-face, two-face. No loss for Kopp. She was moving on. She might no longer have been editor-in-chief of *Business Today*, but she still had the resume padding such a title offers to an ambitious student like her. Besides, she had a thesis to write, and it would be on education, though, ironically, she missed a major opportunity to learn how to behave ethically and responsibly in her own personal education. No problem for one willing to impose her views upon the unsuspecting traditional public education masses. Kopp is a reformer, and for reformers, what is right and good is what they say is right and good.

In November 1988, Kopp and twelve other members of the Foundation for Student Communication organized a conference for 50 business people and 50 students to discuss education. The Business Tomorrow conference was entitled, *Education: Key to American Competitiveness.*

The conference included no classroom teachers. It did include numerous business and industry presidents and chairmen; a foundation executive director; two university professors as moderators, and a featured address from former US Secretary of Education William Bennett. Thus, this conference was a Mount Olympus discussion of the issue of education without inclusion of those actually educating the majority of American students.[18]

I wonder if any in attendance thought to raise the concern that this group was too far removed from public education to do anything other than "act upon" education.

Perhaps that was the goal: a top-down, business imposition upon American education.

An eerie precursor to Kopp's TFA and corporate reform in general.

Despite her demonstrated lack of ethics in journalism, Kopp earned a B.A. in 1989 as a member of Princeton's Woodrow Wilson School of Public and International Affairs. Though she talked about education, Kopp did not graduate in the field of education; she planned to secure employment in the business world. Kopp applied for but "had been rejected for jobs at an investment bank, two consulting companies, a food products company, and a commercial real estate venture."[19] Desperate for a job, Kopp considered teaching and investigated the teacher licensure program at Princeton; however, she had waited beyond the deadline. Given its timing in her life, it seems that this experience occurred concurrently to her undergraduate thesis ideas about a Peace-Corps-like teaching force.[20]

In a 1993 interview with the Philadelphia *Inquirer*, Kopp does not mention her failed attempt to secure a last-minute, out-of-field public school teaching position and instead attributes the idea for TFA to her "extracurricular" time writing for *Business Today* run by the Foundation for Business Education.[21] This experience, more befitting that of a business or journalism career than a career in the public school classroom, is arguably connected to public school teaching by a thin and long-stretching thread.

If Kopp had had an interest in a teaching career, she could have majored in education and earned licensure. As it was, Kopp had not demonstrated a commitment to the field of education by investing her time in a major in education. On the contrary, she was simply desperate for a job; so, she tried to turn to teaching.

Kopp's desperation in turning to teaching also betrays the attitude, "If I can't find a job elsewhere, I'll just teach," as though education is a default for the "entitled jobless" and not a field in its own right. Kopp spins this entitlement into a seeming altruistic bent that those "from her generation" want to "make a difference" and that "top college students would choose teaching over more lucrative opportunities if a prominent teacher corps existed."[22] But don't ask for a permanent commitment to the classroom from these cream graduates because in the end, the lucrative job search wins, even if TFA must manufacture such lucrative positions in education leadership for these non-educator "top students."

Initially, Kopp's TFA focused on temp teaching without the added education administrative usurping.

Initially.

TEMP AGENCY TFA

Kopp first wrote about her "Peace Corps teaching force" concept in her 1989 undergraduate thesis at Princeton.[23,24] She envisioned TFA as a temporary teaching force composed of recent, top college graduates who would commit to provisionally enter the teaching field and agree to serve for two years in order to offset teacher shortages. In order to create such a noble organization, Kopp needed financial backing. So, she contacted prospective funders with the following message:

> *I graduated from Princeton this past June and have been working to put my senior thesis into action ever since. I proposed the creation of an organization that would use the Peace Corps model—active recruitment on a national scale, a selective application process, lots of publicity, a short initial time commitment, and a centralized application, training and placement mechanism—to attract top recent graduates into teaching in the United States. With the help of a number of business and education leaders, I have created the organization as a privately funded nonprofit called TEACH AMERICA Inc. I am writing to request your help.[25]*

Using this strategy, Kopp garnered 2.5 million dollars in order to manage the initial, 500-member cohort of TFA recruits in 1990.

Following her securing money from Mobil and office space from Union Carbide,[26,27] the honeymoon was on. As one writer puts it: "By making the case that the organization would prove the 'feasibility' of 'educational equality,' Kopp and her staff tapped into powerful wells of sentiment. … The TFA message was designed to appeal to potential participants…. But Wendy Kopp also carefully crafted the organization's image with major donors and grant makers in mind."[28]

Nevertheless, the honeymoon ended as TFA staff became aware of Kopp's seeming unwillingness to delegate authority. Kopp is not a delegator; she is a top-down, authoritarian leader:

> *She began to hear criticism of her solo style of controlling the organization. At one of the meetings during the 1991 summer training institute, staff members threatened to quit en masse unless Kopp agreed that decisions would be made by vote of the entire staff. Not sure what to do, Kopp adjourned the meeting without taking action. The next morning, she circulated a memo indicating that decisions would not be made by a vote of the staff. "No one left," Kopp recalled, "but it was hardly a victory."[29]*

As the years passed, TFA continued to struggle. By 1995, Kopp faced mounting debt to the tune of 1.2 million dollars, and this despite TFA's receiving its first federal grant of $2 million in 1994.[30] Initial funders were backing out. Internally, TFA suffered from "undeveloped management systems "and shortages in teacher recruitment in spite of Kopp's plan to "recruit as aggressively on campuses as the corporate recruiters."[31] Kopp lacked the experience necessary for structuring and maintaining an organization the size of TFA, and the cracks were becoming caverns. She did not know how to hire recruiting staff; her initial staff of twelve had trouble managing the work load associated with informing recruits and organizing training. The second year, the TFA staff had grown to 55, but Kopp lacked the training to manage such a large staff. And aside from managing the growing TFA was the burden of incessant fundraising.[32]

Adding to Kopp's troubles was Linda Darling-Hammond's 1994 critique of TFA, printed in the *Phi Delta Kappan* and excerpted here:

> *When TFA first began, the brash idealism of its founders sold funders on what is actually a very old approach to recruiting teachers during times of shortage. Though similar initiatives failed to prepare and retain teachers in previous decades, the recent political climate persuaded many funders to take a gamble on TFA.... **However, the evidence now shows that TFA has fared no better than past emergency routes to teaching and much worse than many of today's alternatives. Extremely costly, plagued by questionable fiscal practices, exhibiting continuing problems with training and management, and unable to prepare most of its recruits to succeed in the classroom, TFA demonstrates once again why quick fixes don't change systems.***
>
> *A former TFA board member states that **it may never be possible to subject the program to a rigorous analysis because Kopp will not allow scrutiny and pushes out those who raise questions.** He notes that, during his association with the organization, staff turnover was extremely high, the **"financial numbers never added up"—the books were not audited despite the board's queries and continue to be unaudited**—and "the retention numbers [for recruits] were totally unreliable."*
>
> *Worse than TFA's organizational shortcomings, however, is the trail of failure with their young students that so many TFA recruits have left behind them. **While TFA has some success stories, which it touts widely, these are far outnumbered by the problems.** Such failures are especially pronounced among recruits who are placed in elementary and middle schools **but have had no training in child development, learning theory, or such essential skills as how to teach reading.** [Former TFAer] Schorr's concern about the effects of TFA recruits on the students they serve is a credit to his teaching sensibilities. He is one of the few who went on to earn a teaching certificate, and he was still in the classroom after three years. This places him in the minority of those who entered TFA with him: of the 489 original corps members who entered classrooms in the fall of 1990, **only 206 (42%) were still teaching after two years—an attrition rate nearly twice that of other new teachers.**[33] [Emphasis added.]*

Darling-Hammond continues by questioning who TFA is "for."; the lack of teacher training contributes to the idea that TFA serves the "bright, young college students" who use TFA as a career stepping stone. According to

Darling-Hammond, Kopp was unconcerned about the TFA recruit "not succeeding" because "most of them would not stay in teaching anyway. And they would have had an important experience that would affect their future lives. She never mentioned the children's lives."[34] Recall that Kopp's conceptualization of TFA is as a temporary teacher service. As Heilig et al. note, "By requiring only a two-year commitment, TFA validates 'the conception of teaching not as a profession but as a short-term stopover before graduate school or employment in the "real world."'"[35] Indeed, one of Kopp's recruits echoes the issue of teacher training not being worth the effort as she comments, "I never would have gotten into teaching otherwise…. I wasn't interested in the traditional teacher-training programs. They didn't seem academically interesting and they seemed like a big commitment."[36]

Darling-Hammond herself was recruited in the early 1970s to a quick and alternative teacher "training" program and even told Kopp of the limitations of trying to train qualified teachers in seminar style. Darling-Hammond notes, "Kopp maintained that she was sure she could do in a few weeks whatever it was that universities took much longer to do (though she had never examined a teacher preparation program)…."[37]

Though Kopp did not believe this single article could have a detrimental impact on TFA, it apparently did, as funders and the media began to contact Kopp regarding article assertions. In addition, educational experts and financial backers wanted proof regarding TFA claims of higher student achievement resulting from TFA presence in the classroom.[38]

I could locate no studies supporting TFA efficacy conducted and published in the years surrounding the Darling-Hammond study (1994). The TFA website offers studies of efficacy between the years of 2009–12,[39] but these results are not undisputed.[40] A major issue of TFA research is that TFA longevity studies cannot be conducted since TFA recruits are temporary.

Despite the financial and organizational issues and bad press, Kopp managed to scrape by and carry TFA with her into the new millennium. TFA faced insolvency a number of times—until corporations and foundations began funneling money into the struggling organization.[41] In 2001, TFA's net assets totaled over $35 million.[42] By 2005, TFA's net assets totaled over $105 million.[43] Finally, by 2010, TFA's net assets had increased almost tenfold from 2001 to almost $350 million.[44] And in 2011, the Walton Family Foundation gave TFA $49.5 million "to help double the size of Teach for America's national teaching corps over the next three years."[45]

PERMANENT TAKEOVER TFA

Corresponding to its newfound financial popularity, TFA experienced a "mission shift":

Acknowledging retention issues, the organization began to promote itself as being equally **committed to leadership development as it was to recruiting top college students into teaching. "The program was never intended to solve the teacher shortage problem or even to fix public education simply by preparing bright college students to teach for two years,"** *argued TFA advocate Julie Mikuta in 2008. "Instead,"* she contended, *"TFA intends to transform public education by exposing these talented people to the challenges of public education...."* **TFA's impact will only be seen in the future, once "alumni take on more visible and influential roles."** [Emphasis added.]

Why did this shift take place? From its earliest stages, TFA has framed itself for funders, taking care to promote the legitimacy of its model even if volunteers did not stay in the teaching profession.[46]

Mikuta says that TFA doesn't expect to "solve the teacher shortage problem or even fix public education." Compare this to Valerie Strauss' take on a Kopp's words regarding a Kozol book critique:

As for a "fully fledged movement dedicated to ensuring educational opportunity for all kids," [Kopp] is clearly referring to her own organization, Teach for America, and the public charter school movement as if both were the answer to the issues that ail public education.[47]

And consider Kopp's view of TFA in 1993. Notice there is no mention of "taking on more visible and influential roles":

These days (1993), Kopp is mulling grander schemes. Though the organization is seeking federal funding to augment its corporate donations, she feels as if Teach for America in its current form has reached its limits.

"I'm just not sure that expanding Teach for America would get us where we want to get," she says. "First of all, I hope that Teach for America can have a fundamental impact on the way that all beginning teachers are recruited, selected and trained and certified.

"And I actually don't think that the answer is for Teach for America to expand and provide more teachers.

"One potential is for us to get into the field much more broadly, through a different organization entirely, through a spinoff organization," she says, "actually **recruiting and selecting teachers for specific school districts on more of a revenue-generating basis."**

The idea, she says, is **to be a for-profit contractor** *that can patch up school districts just as private contractors patch up the highways.*[48] [Emphasis added.]

Though the TFA website notes that Kopp's organization has "aggressively worked to grow and deepen [TFA] impact,"[49] Kopp's initial push had nothing to do with placing former TFAers in educational leadership positions. By 2001, TFA began to clearly publicize its now-twofold mission: Yes, to continue to place "top talent" in the classroom in two-year, Peace-corps style. However, in addition, TFA would enable those "teacher leaders" to "force systemic change to ensure educational equity."[50]

The "shift" is evident in this feature page about Kopp on Echoing Green's website. The site notes Kopp's "bold idea":

> *Eliminate educational inequality by recruiting outstanding recent college graduates of all academic majors to commit two years to teach in urban and rural public schools* ***and to become lifelong leaders in expanding educational opportunity.***[51] [Emphasis added.]

In his pro-corporate reform book, *Class Warfare*, Steven Brill refers to this "shift" as "TFA's greatest contribution" (p. 54). Contrary to Kopp's description prior to 2001 of the TFA recruit's role as that of Peace Corps-type temporary teaching, in Brill notes that in Kopp's book, *One Day All Children* (published in 2001) that

> *...she stated that she had thought **from the start** that 'beyond influencing children's lives directly' for the two years they taught, her recruits would be so sensitized by their experience that 'many corps members would decide to stay in... education." ...Twenty years later, 67 percent of all of TFA's 21,000 alumni would be working in public education.*[52] [Emphasis added.]

Note that the phrase, "working in public education" does not mean "continuing as classroom teachers." As of 2001, what TFA clearly advocates is the systemic usurping of leadership roles in both education administration and educational policy. This opportunity to seize and command power over education in the United States has not been lost on corporate money. Wendy Kopp declared that she had a force of young, predominantly-Ivy-League idealists for sale, and Big Money arrived on the scene to make the purchase. No more insolvency issues for Wendy Kopp and TFA.

This reframing of the TFA mission attracted names now synonymous with corporate education reform funding. In the early 2000s, TFA listed as its major donors the four $10-million gifts from the Broad Foundation, the Dell Foundation, Don and Doris Fisher (founders of the Gap), and the Rainwater Charitable Funds. Furthermore, in 2010–2011, the following were among the TFA corporate donors ($100,000—$999,999 category):

> *Anheuser-Busch, ATT, Bank of America, Blue Cross/Blue Shield, Boeing, Cargill, Chesapeake Energy, Chevron, Emerson, Entergy, ExxonMobil, Fedex, Fidelity Investments, GE, Marathon Oil, Monsanto, Peabody, Prudential, State Farm, Symantec, Travelers, Wells Fargo.*[53]

All of the above-listed mega-donors are American Legislative Exchange Council (ALEC) companies.[54] ALEC is a corporate bill mill whereby corporations write and promote legislation to their liking and benefit. Having read hundreds of pages of ALEC education legislation model bills[55] mailed to ALEC legislators, I can say with certainty that the current educational reform push, including letter grades for schools, "parent trigger" laws promoting charter schools, "parent choice" (voucher) legislation, and "data driven" teacher evaluation and resulting "ineffective" quotas are all ALEC promotions.

Other 2010–11 donors include foundations such as Walton, Gates, Dell, Carnegie, Casey, Kauffman, and Rodell. (We're talking anywhere from 10 to 50+ million. In fact, in 2013, Waltons awarded TFA another cool 11.5 million.)[56]

But let us not forget Eli and Edythe Broad. They are listed as 2010–11 $25k-49.9k donors. As this TFA promo all-too-clearly notes,

> *"Ultimately, we're working to develop a leadership force that will work to bring about the systemic changes that are necessary to really fulfill our vision," Ms. Kopp says. That message ... appeals to donors interested in overhauling the nation's schools. Mr. Broad, who has committed more than $400-million to improving public education, sees Teach for America alumni as a source of talent for his other projects....[57]*

What "other projects" might those be? To give some idea, consider this triage:[58]

> *...In 2010, Arne Duncan, through the Department of Education, provided Ms. Kopp with a $50M grant to help her teach the most impoverished children in our country. To explain this a bit, Wendy Kopp is on the Broad Foundation board.[59] Arne Duncan[60] who has close ties with Eli Broad from his days in Chicago as CEO of the Chicago school district,[61] keeps the "Broad Prize" in the offices of the Department of Education,[62] are you starting to see how this all works?*

There is apparently a lot to TFA, Chicago, and "Broad involvement."[63] Take our Louisiana Department of Education as an example. Superintendent John White is a former TFAer with a "credential" from the Broad Superintendents Academy. He hires other TFAers, and sometimes, the media shines the reality light a bit too brightly on them, like former TFAer Molly Horstman,[64] who made the media for her being a "director" of teacher evaluation with only the Peace-corps-like two years of teaching experience and an expired teaching certificate. In order to solve the credential problem, John White brings in Hannah Dietsch,[65] a former TFAer with three years of teaching but also a masters degree in education from the Harvard Graduate School of Education (HGSE).[66,67] A Harvard masters degree in education sounds above question–except that the HGSE is already known to "partner" with TFA in order to "fast track" former TFAers as principals in Chicago.[68]

The HGSE is not the only graduate school "partnering" with TFA to promote education reform. On its website, TFA is very open concerning the benefits offered former TFAers not only for graduate school but for "leadership across many other professions and sectors":

> As a Teach For America corps member, you'll develop strengths that are critical to being a successful teacher in a low-income community. **These skills are also essential to leadership across many other professions and sectors.** We see our corps members' talent and resolve play out in the classroom **and beyond**, and so do the exceptional **graduate schools and employers that actively recruit second-year corps members and alumni.**
>
> In addition, **many graduate schools and employers offer special benefits to our corps members and alumni.** These range from two-year employment deferrals to application fee waivers and special scholarships once you've completed your two-year commitment. Explore these opportunities below. The graduate school benefits listed here are opportunities for second-year corps members and alumni.[69]

Wendy Kopp and TFA are working hard to place "bright young minds" with minimal classroom experience in education leadership "and beyond." Their website invites former TFAers to choose from among 265 graduate programs or employment opportunities in the areas of business and finance, education, law, medicine and dentistry, policy, STEM (science, technology, engineering, and mathematics), and social services. This is profound. Most have agreed to offer deferment to those accepted to TFA—that is, a student can put off enrolling if the student is accepted and serves TFA for two years. However, a number also offer preferential acceptance to former TFAers and financial assistance.

Here is the advertisement on the TFA Graduate School and Employer Partnerships page:

> I took advantage of the graduate school partnership between Teach For America and the Gerald R. Ford School of Public Policy at the University of Michigan. **I received a full fellowship including tuition, living stipend, and health insurance.** [Emphasis added.]
>
> —**Brandy Johnson**, Las Vegas Valley Corps '05[70]

All for teaching for two years after having five weeks of training. Not a bad deal for these young "talented ones." It is not the TFAers who lose in this game of turnstile teaching. It is their students: TFA presence in a district keeps that district in a constant churn of inexperienced teachers—for two years—it the TFAer remains that long.[71] TFA is careful to guard the numbers of those recruits who do not fulfil their two-year careers. However, according to one TFA recruit who quit following one year,

> Jessica said that after she notified local TFA leadership of her decision [to not return for a second year], the reaction was severe. "They chewed out my character and made per-

sonal allegations," she said. She was told, she recalls, that she would "personally have to deal with remorse and regret."[72]

Why the push to guilt TFA recruits into remaining for two years? Answer: TFA has lucrative contracts with school districts. Despite the millions in corporate funding, TFA continues to operate like a temp agency in its collecting fees for a district's using it recruits. For example, aside from paying each TFAer a teacher salary, the Louisiana Department of Education pays as much as $9000 per TFA recruit to Kopp's organization.[73] The constant churn of biennial TFAers keeps the temp fees rolling in; the contract for a certain number of TFA recruits assures that TFA will not "lose out" to replacement by traditional classroom teachers.

TFA pulls in the cash; the recruits are able to pad their resumes and move along in pursuing a more lucrative, "real" career—including a possible career in privatizing public education—hence, the Broad investment in grad school for former TFAers.

Of course, one might expect from the Broad investment noted above that Harvard is inclined to offer TFAers either deferment (Harvard Business School; Harvard Law; Harvard University Graduate Program in Physics) or deferment plus a full-tuition fellowship (Harvard John F Kennedy School of Government). But the real jackpot comes from—you guessed it—the Harvard Graduate School of Education—both on the masters and doctoral levels:

> *Harvard University Graduate School of Education, Doctorate in Education Leadership (Ed.L.D.), Massachusetts*
> * *Collaboration with faculty from the Harvard Business School, John F. Kennedy School of Government, and Graduate School of Education*
> * *Three-year program; two years on campus in classes, modules, and practice-based experiences and third year in a residency in a partner education organization*
> * **Cohort of 25 people, all receiving full-tuition fellowship and stipend support**
> * *Contact: askedld@gse.harvard.edu;www.gse.harvard.edu/edld*
> * Graduate School Harvard University Graduate School of Education, Massachusetts
> * **Provides two Leadership in Education Awards annually for Teach For America alumni enrolling in the full-time masters program. The Leadership in Education Awards cover approximately one-half year's tuition.**[74] [Emphasis added.]

This "collaboration" between Harvard John F. Kennedy School of Government and the Graduate School of Education promotes a "partnership" that bespeaks the "business of education." To people like Kopp, education is a business.

I find this hypocrisy stunning: TFA des not believe any education credential is necessary for classroom teaching, but it promotes education credentials beyond the TFAer's classroom time in order to advance the TFAer's career.

How about those TFAers who have served their two years and wish to proceed directly into business? Never fear. These Bright Lights have opportunities waiting with a number of companies, including Mitt Romney's once-claimed Bain and Company, GE, Goldman Sachs, Google, and JP Morgan.

And what about the TFA "cream"—the ones who are the real "movers and shakers"—who can wield the wand to produce real privatization magic in elected offices, or policy or advocacy positions?

They deserve their own TFA spinoff—Leadership for Educational Equity (LEE). LEE is classed as a "social welfare nonprofit," or a 501(c)4, which means it can funnel money into elections (in an attempt to position people and influence outcomes, of course) and can claim their "donations" as "public welfare."[75] Except for some general statements on its home page, LEE website access is restricted.[76] However, *American Prospect* writer James Ceronsky offers this insight into LEE:

> *LEE functions in part as a network for TFA alumni. In the restricted section of its website, to which I gained access through an existing member, you can find job postings ranging from government relations at the National Education Association to Web Editor for the Heritage Foundation. Members are also encouraged to connect with each other: "[P]erhaps you want to bring some of your fellow LEE members to an education rally in Houston. You could cast a wide net, and search for all LEE members within 100 miles of zip code 77001. Your search returns about 240 LEE members—that's quite a rally."*

> *…Though LEE's 990 filings are missing from the IRS' online database and chronically allergic to press attention, executive director Michael Buman says that its budget this year is $3.5 million. While Buman maintains that elections constitute the "minority" of LEE's work, some portion of that sum has gone toward electing TFA alums to office.[77]*

What an incredible privatization machine this TFA has turned out to be. It should come as no surprise that one can actually earn an Ed.D. in Leadership and Education Equity (University of Colorado Denver [CU Denver]). Notice where this degree is designed to take the promising graduate:

> *Careers for EdD degree holders include senior positions inside school districts, community colleges, higher education policy or community-based education organizations. Roles may include that of director, deputy, superintendent or president.[78]*

Straight to the top, where Kopp expects LEEers to perch. None of this "first become an assistant principal, then principal" nonsense. Even classroom teaching experience is not a requirement for acceptance into the CU Denver Ed.D. in Leadership and Education Equity program.[79] Although the TFA website does not list a partnership between CU Denver's School of Education on the TFA website, CU Denver's School of Education and Human Development has a cozy relationship with TFA, to the point of hosting a TFA dinner in the school of education (??). A panel discussion even included former TFAer and Colorado Senator Michael Johnston.

It might appear that TFA is unstoppable. As of 2013, and TFA was well financed by pro-reform funders like the Broad Foundation, and it has joined forces with other agencies, including once-reputable, degree-offering institutions like the Harvard Graduate School of Education, in order to push the reform agenda down the public education digestive tract.

As former TFAer Gary Rubenstein notes: "Twenty years ago TFA was, to steal an expression from the late great Douglas Adams—'mostly harmless.' Then about ten years ago they became 'potentially harmful.' Now, in my opinion, they have become 'mostly harmful.'"

Rubinstein continues:

> Leaders [like Michelle Rhee, John White, and Kevin Huffman] are some of the most destructive forces in public education. They seem to love nothing more than labeling schools as "failing," shutting them down, and blaming the supposed failure on the veteran teachers. The buildings of the closed schools are taken over by charter networks, often with leaders who were TFA alums and who get salaries of $200,000 or more to run a few schools.

> Rather than be honest about both their successes and their failures, they deny any failures, and charge forward with an agenda that has not worked and will never work. Their 'proof' consists of a few high-performing charters. These charters are unwilling to release the data that proves that they succeed by booting the 'worst' kids—the ones that bring down their test scores. See this recent peer reviewed research paper[80] from Berkeley about KIPPs attrition.

> TFA and the destructive TFA spawned leaders suffer a type of arrogance and overconfidence where they completely ignore any evidence that their beliefs are flawed. The leaders TFA has spawned are, to say this in the kindest way possible, "lacking wisdom."[81]

This is what Broad, and Walton, and Dell, and Gates, and others like them, including those under the ALEC veil, are purchasing and calling "educational reform." Yet the question remains as to whether TFA has reached a point of unemployable saturation regarding its "talented leadership" alumni. There simply are too many of them for the few education administrative positions they would usurp from true educators. As one alumnus notes,

> With an "alumni network" of nearly 28,000 it's difficult to see how pumping in several thousand additional corps members each year won't lead to diminishing returns. Indeed, when I was considering jobs in education policy, multiple interviews mentioned how often they interview many TFA alumni for a single spot. In the educational world, TFA alumni have become a dime a dozen.[82]

The former TFAer cited above believes that TFA has run its course but that some well-intentioned alumni still have something to offer public education. However, as a traditional career educator, I do not advocate the view that former TFAers, no matter how enthusiastic, should conveniently assume highly paid leadership roles in education following a paltry couple of years in the classroom—costly years for the teacher turnover inherent in the temp agency nature of TFA. The author does note that the cost of TFA turnover outweighs its usefulness:

> *...I am extremely skeptical that TFA is whatsoever cost-effective. Needless to say, this is important because money is scarce; money spent on education is even scarcer. If TFA is crowded investment into more effective organizations, then its money could be better spent.*

> *TFA is now massive, with annual expenses at $220 million in fiscal year 2011. According to the charity site Give Well, TFA's budget 2009 budget came to a stunning $38,046 spent per corps member who started teaching; this was a more than twofold increase from 2005. (Corps member spending by TFA does not include corps members' salaries, which are paid for by their respective school district. School districts also pay TFA a fee for each corps member hired.) Admittedly, a per-corps-member measurement is imperfect because it accounts for recruiting a new and ever-larger corps, as well as a ballooning alumni base. The question remains: if you have money to donate to education causes, is TFA your best investment?*

> *Consider some of the main items in TFA's budget: recruiting and selecting corps members (18%), management and general (9%), alumni support (8%). None of these makes corps members effective teachers. "Corps member development" (39%) and institute training (17%), on the other hand, purportedly do. Reality, as is its wont, is not so simple.*

> *For many corps members, the required five-week summer training "institute" is close to useless. Why? Not, as some have argued, because it's so short. Rather, it's because for many of us the training doesn't come close to simulating what it's like to be teaching during the real school year.*[83]

In a sad yet predictable way, school districts dependent upon TFA recruits remain dependent as the TFA turnover from one year to the next leads to need to immediately fill positions left vacant by TFA—and like one offering the next fix to an addict, TFA is there to once again "fill" the vacancies. Unfortunately, the quality of the replacement TFAers does not always guarantee TFA can even fulfil the two-year commitment:

> *The other problem is the wasted investment a school makes in a teacher who leaves after just a few years. Sadly, I'm a poster child for this. I remember my last day at my school in Colorado, as I made the rounds saying goodbye to veteran teachers, my friends and colleagues who had provided me such crucial support and mentorship. As I talked of my plans for law school in Chicago, and they bade me best wishes, I felt an overwhelming*

wave of guilt. Their time and energy spent making me a better teacher—and I was mas-
sively better on that day compared to my first—was for naught. The previous summer
I had spent a week of training, paid for by my school, to learn to teach pre–Advanced
Placement classes. I taught the class for a year; presumably, I thought, someone else
would have to receive the same training—or, worse, someone else would not receive the
same training. All that work on classroom management and understanding of the cur-
riculum, all the support in connecting with students and writing lesson—it would all
have to begin again with a new teacher. (Indeed, my replacement apparently had a ner-
vous breakdown and quit after a few months. She was replaced by a long-term substitute
who one of my former colleagues must write lesson plans for.)[84]

TFA is too temporary to be a viable solution to the issues facing the American classroom. And rather than retire the TFA organization, Kopp chose a predictably reformer course of "retiring" herself as a means of moving on to bigger and better things: promoting her TFA organization on an international scale.

"RETIRED" WENDY

Wendy Kopp has fashioned and financed an educational ideology that undeniably benefits from the death of all things educationally "traditional." And effective March 1, 2013, she "retired" from TFA[85] (well, kind of—she is still chair of the board[86]) only to head a global organization, Teach for All. (I believe "all" is a bit of a stretch. I am hard pressed to envision the temp agency teacher concept thriving in either the hardship of such locales as Calcutta, India, or teacher-revering countries such as Finland.) Kopp was in charge of both TFA and Teach for All for five years. And with board control of TFA still in hand, she has shifted her focus "to infinity and beyond":

> *As CEO of Teach For All, Kopp leads a growing global network of independent organi-*
> *zations that, like Teach For America, are enlisting their countries' most promising future*
> *leaders to become lifelong advocates for educational excellence and equality. Now in its*
> *sixth year, the Teach For All network includes organizations in 26 countries worldwide.*
> *In the coming years, Teach For All aims to build support for the growth of the network*
> *and its partners.... "It has been my privilege to serve as CEO of both Teach For America*
> *and Teach For All for more than five years," said Kopp.*[87]

Nothing like taking an expensive yet temporary solution with mixed results global. As of February 2013, Teach for All has a presence in Argentina, Australia, Austria, Bangladesh, Bulgaria, Chile, China, Columbia, Estonia, Germany, India, Israel, Japan, Latvia, Lebanon, Lithuania, Malaysia, Mexico, Nepal, New Zealand, Pakistan, Peru, Philippines, Spain, Sweden, and the United Kingdom.[88] Whether or not a country is more or less advanced, and whether or not its education system is more or less rigorous and stable, the teacher-churn produced by Teach for All can only introduce an education credentialing instability that serves no one but the recruits who would later assume the powerful, lucrative education leadership positions in similar fashion to the education leadership usurpation in the United States.

Wendy Kopp is no visionary. She is a well-financed conduit for worldwide education destabilization designed to serve a privileged few.

CHAPTER 4

MICHELLE RHEE: SOCIOPATHY FINDS A HOME IN ED REFORM

By May 2013, the National Council of Teacher Quality (NCTQ) had apparently—and rather quietly—removed Michelle Rhee from its advisory board. Since that time, Rhee has been the center of a revived DC testing scandal that she cannot seem to shake. Nor should she, given the unanswered questions and shoddy investigation surrounding the cheating incident. More on that to come.

WHO IS MICHELLE RHEE?

In short, Rhee is one of the more famous (infamous?) former TFAers who was catapulted into well-financed education reform fame as the inexperienced chancellor of DC schools at the appointment of then-DC Mayor Adrien Fenty. Rhee was ruthless in her smug execution of punishing teachers and administrators who did not meet their test score targets. Once Fenty lost his bid for re-election, Rhee lost her appointment as chancellor. She turned her attention to her pro-reform group, StudentsFirst, a well-funded organization known for pumping money into elections in selected states in

A Chronicle of Echoes: Who's Who in the Implosion of American Public Education,
pages 59–77.

order to advance the education privatization agenda but an organization nonetheless that Larry Cuban writes is "all Michelle."[1]

During her time as DC chancellor, test scores soared. Once she left, scores dropped.

As of this writing, Rhee's reformist career appears to be waning, particularly due to her inability to distance herself from what is the DC testing scandal.

That is the "very short" of it. But of course, it goes much deeper.

HARLEM PARK MIRACLE TEST SCORES

As is true for other reformers in this book, I first wrote about Rhee due to her association with NCTQ and have built upon that post in creating this chapter. Before Rhee was expelled from NCTQ, this pro-privatization, self-proclaimed police force of traditional teacher training programs advertised Rhee's presence as follows:

> *Michelle Rhee CEO of StudentsFirst, formerly served as Chancellor of D.C. Public Schools. Ms. Rhee is a change agent who had already transformed many urban public school systems through her work with The New Teacher Project (TNTP) which she founded in 1997, and is now a nationally recognized leader in understanding and developing innovative solutions to the challenges of new teacher hiring. As Chief Executive Officer and President, she partnered with school districts, state education agencies, non-profit organizations, and unions, to transform the way schools and other implemented widespread reform in teacher hiring, improving teacher hiring in Atlanta, Baltimore, Chicago, Miami, New York, Oakland, and Philadelphia. Thanks to TNTP, 23,000 new, high-quality teachers were placed in these schools across the country. Ms. Rhee's commitment to excellence in education began in a Baltimore classroom in 1992, as a Teach For America teacher. the right teacher, students in urban classrooms can meet teachers' high expectations for achievement, and the driving force behind that achievement is the quality of the Educator who works inside it. Chancellor Rhee currently serves on the Advisory Boards for the National Council on Teacher Quality (NCTQ); the National Center for Alternative Certification (NCAC); Project REACH of the University of Phoenix's School of Education. She is an Ex-Officio Member of the Kennedy Center Board of Trustees. Chancellor Rhee's expertise on education is also informed by a Bachelor's degree in Government from Cornell University, and a Master's degree in Public Policy from the Kennedy School of Government at Harvard University.[2]*

Rhee views herself as an "expert educator," yet her classroom experience is even more restricted than the three years it appears to be on the surface. Like many former TFAers, she spent only token time in the classroom as a teacher. For one known for pushing test scores as a means of gauging "success," Rhee's students' scores on Maryland's Comprehensive Test of Basic Skills (CTBS) hardly evidenced such. In fact, the scores were so low as to warrant her own firing by the standard she would later enforce as DC chancellor.[3]

Rhee taught from 1992–95 at Harlem Park Elementary in Baltimore City, a school that was being run by education management companies Edison/EAI/Tesseract during Rhee's time there.[4] Edison et al. provided no notable innovation:

> *At a minimum, it is probably fair to say that Edison's has provided little pedagogical and curricular innovation, choosing instead to adopt successful approaches largely developed elsewhere and that are widely employed by other public schools.... As a viable quasi-market alternative to hierarchical control, it is also probably fair to say that Edison and other education management companies that have followed in its wake have yet to prove themselves.[5]*

Also, consider this excerpt from an evaluation of academics (i.e., test scores) of Tesseract schools in Baltimore:

> *The Tesseract Schools in Baltimore City are nine public schools operated by The Alliance for Schools That Work, an association of for-profit businesses. ... The [Tesseract] program was effective in raising Comprehensive Test of Basic Skills (CTBS) test scores in some schools but not in others. Maryland School Performance Assessment Program (MSPAP) scores for 1993–94 were similar for both groups of schools [Tesseract and Baltimore City Schools]; however, they (Tesseract scores) were below the results for Baltimore City and well below the results for Maryland. In 1994–95, class size was similar for both groups. Also, ratings of overall effectiveness were similar for both groups. The per-pupil cost for 1995–96 in Tesseract schools will be 11.2 percent higher than for comparison schools. Over 3 years, scores for Tesseract students decreased and then increased to about the pre-program level.[6]*

If it is test scores that are supposed to distinguish education management schools from community public schools, then Tesseract/Edison did not deliver in Baltimore.[7] Neither did Michelle Rhee.

During her three years at Harlem Park Elementary, Rhee's students' CTBS test scores were nothing remarkable. At the end of her first year, Rhee's students' scores fell to around the 20th percentile in both reading and math. At the end of her second year, Rhee's students' reading scores were around the 15th percentile, and math scores, around the 38th percentile. Finally, at the end of Rhee's third year, students' CTBS scores were the best they have been during her time as teacher: reading scores were around the 45th percentile; math, 55th percentile[8] (the number of test takers in Rhee's third year [1994–95] was lower than in other Baltimore schools: only 64%)[9]. However, Rhee advertised that by the end of her third year, 90 percent of her students scored at the 90th percentile. Her statement has not been validated.[10]

In a more tempered note, another article refers to "some students [in the class originally at the 13th percentile] soaring to the 90th percentile."[11] "Some students" is much less spectacular than "90 percent." However, even "some students" remains invalidated.

It is worth repeating that in her first two years as a TFA teacher, Rhee's students' CTBS scores were seriously low in comparison with the scores of other test takers. This is certainly not an argument for the five weeks of training that placed Rhee, a woman with a bachelors in government,[12] in the public school classroom. It is important to add that Rhee was not teaching alone for three years; she was part of a teaching team for her second and third years.[13,14] Thus, the idea that student test scores can be directly connected to a single teacher, for better or worse, is immediately foiled by the complexities inherent in modern American education. I noted as much in my review of the Louisiana TFA "success" study.[15] The question of whether or not other teachers were present in the classroom with TFA recruits is an important one for assessing TFA "effectiveness."

Model TFAer Michelle Rhee had assistance in the classroom.

By her own admission, Rhee had a terrible first year. I am not surprised that her second and third years involved "combined classes with another teacher, and together they taught the same children for two years."[16] So, Rhee, who later became chancellor of DC schools, only taught alone for a single year. And she fared badly. Then, she taught with assistance for the next two years. Then she taught no more.

A 2007 *New York Times* article notes, "…Ms. Rhee speaks directly and confidently." I am not impressed with Rhee's ability to "speak directly and confidently." Politicians can do so. Narcissists can do so. Pathological liars can do so. Even serial killers can do so. So in and of itself, the ability to "speak directly and confidently" means little. What does matter is Rhee's undemonstrated ability to effectively run a classroom without assistance and the media's willingness to overlook Rhee's dangerous lack of experience combined with obvious cockiness. Consider this pre-pontification of Rhee on the first day of her job:

> *Says Rhee:* **"The war is won in the classroom.** *It's all about leadership."* **This is where Rhee lives—in the classroom,** *making the connection between the teacher and the student.*[17] [Emphasis added.]

Did I really just cite this? What irony. Rhee "lives" in the classroom? Only when exercising power over teachers. Not as a teacher herself.

This is a woman literally placed into power with a view to "win" no matter what it takes. This is not admirable. This is red flags waving:

> *At first, Ms. Rhee said, she plans to "push more money to the classroom" and give teachers ample support. Then,* **she will demand** *they raise achievement.*[18] [Emphasis added.]

This attitude of "demanding achievement" would lead to scandal in Rhee's future.

According to Rhee's own self report, she earned a teacher certification.[19] Certification or not, Rhee did not continue in the classroom beyond three years but instead pursued the interest in which she invested most of her own education: government and public policy. Rhee is not a teacher. She is a controversial political figure whose stage happens to be education. There is certainly a difference.

Much of Rhee's controversy involves the manner in which she conducts herself with those of lesser rank: teachers and students.

RHEE: IDEAL PRIVATIZER

Rhee has introduced incredible "disruption" into the lives of those in public education, a valued trait by TFA "talented leadership" standards. Thus, it should come as no surprise that Rhee is the ideal TFA privatizer:

> **No organization has been more complicit than TFA in the demonization of teachers and teachers' unions,** *and no organization has provided more "shock troops" for education reform strategies which emphasize privatization and high-stakes testing.* **Michelle Rhee, a TFA recruit, is the poster child for such policies**....[20] *[Emphasis added.]*

As previously noted, Rhee's TFA stint was hardly the "commitment to excellence in the classroom" stated in her now-deleted NCTQ bio. She glorifies her "effectiveness" as one who miraculously raises test scores, yet her self-aggrandizing remains unsubstantiated. Even still, there is a more sinister side to Rhee's "effectiveness." As noted on my blog,

> *If corporate reform bred with sociopathy, it would produce the likes of Michelle Rhee.*[21]

Rhee has become known for not only her cruelty to others, but also for the twisted ease with which she discusses such cruelty. Consider these stories Rhee openly recounts to a group of new DC teachers:

> *"[My first year of teaching was] the worst and in many ways definitely the toughest year of my entire life," she said.*[22]

So, let's get this straight: Potentially one half of the time a TFA recruit spends in the classroom could be "the worst in one's life?" Forget the teacher recruits: What does that say about the quality of the experience for their students? Rhee speaks to this "quality" as she admits perpetrating an abuse on her students and then attempts to excuse herself because of her ignorance:

> *Rhee had poor class management skills, she said, recalling that her class "was very well known in the school because you could hear them traveling anywhere because they were so out of control." On one particularly rowdy day, she said she decided to place little pieces of masking tape on their lips for the trip to the school cafeteria for lunch.*

"OK kids, we're going to do something special today!" she said she told them.

Rhee said it worked well until they actually arrived at the cafeteria. "I was like, 'OK, take the tape off. I realized I had not told the kids to lick their lips beforehand... **The skin is coming off their lips and they're bleeding. Thirty-five kids were crying.** *"*

Rhee said in an e-mail Friday that the students' mouths weren't covered. "I was trying to express how difficult the first year of teaching can be **with some humor.** *My hope is that our new teachers will bring great creativity and passion to their craft while also learning from my own challenges." Still,* **it's difficult to imagine a DCPS instructor, first-year or tenth-year, surviving the masking tape stunt without suspension at a minimum.**[23]
[Emphasis added.]

There is no record of Rhee's being suspended for her actions. Nevertheless, keep in mind that Rhee's second and third (final) years in the classroom were not ones in which she was teaching without another teacher present.

In Rhee's case, it is good for the children that she left the classroom.

The second story Rhee decided to tell a group of new teachers involves Rhee's not having emergency contact information on a field trip and thereby her being unable to verify that she actually sent a child home, to the correct home, with an approved guardian:

"I start to panic...my heart is beating 100 miles a minute," she said. Then the other three children, sensing her worry, chimed in. She recalled one little boy saying:

"Lawwwd Ms.Rhee whatchu gonna do!!!!??" Rhee boomed, drawing a big laugh. "Lawwwd Ms. Rhee whatchu gonna do!!!!??"

Rhee said she eventually found a neighbor who was able to take the girl home.[24]

Let's just take a moment to digest: Rhee ignorantly handed a child over to potential danger. That child could have been harmed. And all Rhee could do many years later in her role as chancellor (!!) is make light of the incident and not even realize her own emotional disconnect.

In her former NCTQ bio, Rhee is described as a "change agent."

In an article detailing her first day as chancellor, Rhee describes herself as a "change agent."[25]

A wrecking ball is also a "change agent."

Both Rhee's involvement with suspicious DC test scores and her crass, divisive actions have diminished her 2013 value to privatizers; in this blog post, Larry Cuban states that the public can "kiss Rhee goodbye"...

Because she is a divisive figure and damaged goods as an educator. Both mean that her celebrity-hood as a school reformer–on the cover of Time magazine, chatting with Oprah and Jon—will give her visibility in 24/7 news cycle but not lead to any substantial elected or appointed political or educational office.

No President will appoint her Secretary of Education; no governor will appoint her state superintendent of education and no school board will appoint her as their school chief. She is a polarizing, radioactive figure who will set off Geiger counters and create instant political turmoil and organizational instability—outcomes that may be good for media attention and garnering large speaker fees but disastrous for those responsible for making schools better and improving student performance.[26]

In the anti-community-school, anti-union, charter-promoting film, *Waiting for Superman*, Rhee comments that her time as chancellor in DC will be her only time in such a position. Cuban notes that her brief three years as chancellor has halted her propulsion as a career reformer. But he adds that she might save herself if she returns to the classroom for several years:

> **But there is something that Rhee can do to reduce the radioactivity, remove suspicions about her motives, and regain a pinch of credibility that she carried as a school reformer when the mayor of Washington, D.C. appointed her in 2007.**
>
> *That something is for her to return to the classroom and teach for three to five years.*[27]

There is one glaring problem with such a suggestion: Rhee revels in fast-track fame. She enjoys inflicting pain on others and even regards the resulting stories as worth repeating, with lightness and humor, both to novice teachers and film crews. Rhee believes she is "effective," and she also believes that she is qualified to assess "effective" in others. Yet for Rhee, "effective" is confused with "cruel."

According to her NCTQ bio, Rhee sees herself as "improving teacher hiring." Perhaps she meant, "improving teacher firing." Rhee doesn't stop with callous perverseness in harming children. She is versatile and can even take pleasure in harming adults, as well. As reporter John Merrow notes:

> *"We were totally stunned [when Rhee asked if his crew wanted to watch her fire a principal]," Mr. Merrow said. She let them set up the camera behind the principal and videotape the entire firing. "The principal seemed dazed," said Mr. Merrow. "I've been reporting 35 years and never seen anything like it."*[28]

CHANCELLOR RHEE: CLEANING HOUSE

Michelle Rhee became DC's first school chancellor in 2007. Up to that point, DC's board of education had executive powers; however, the District of Columbia Public Education Reform Act of 2007[29] changed the board of education into a "cabinet-level agency subordinate to the Mayor," and it created "a Chancellor of the District of Columbia Public Schools," among other changes. When Adrian Fenty won the election for DC mayor, Rhee was living in Denver and running her TNTP. New York reformist chancellor Joel Klein advised Fenty to consider Rhee. In short, Fenty offered Rhee the job, and she accepted.[30]

During her three-year tenure as chancellor (2007–10), Rhee was known for "measuring teacher quality by students' test scores, firing underperforming instructors (also tied to test scores), and pushing merit pay (also tied to test scores)."[31] So, it seems that the reforms Rhee advocates can be reduced to test scores.

And Rhee pressured DC teachers to produce those scores—and, ironically, proper teacher credentialing. But Rhee, whose own "certification" dies with self-report,[32] began teaching with only the five-week preparation of TFA. In 2008, Rhee fired 75 probationary teachers for "receiving negative recommendations from school principals," but they were reinstated because Rhee failed to provide them with a reason for termination.[33] This wrongful firing took three years to resolve:

> [Independent Arbitrator] Feigenbaum ordered the District to make a 60-day good-faith effort to find the fired teachers and offer them reinstatement in an appropriate job. **He also ordered that they be made financially whole. Union officials estimate the back-pay award could amount to $7.5 million—a considerable sum for the cash-strapped District.** [Emphasis added.]

So much for any argument that Rhee's aggressive actions are "cost saving."

> [DC Schools spokesman]Lewis said the cash awards would be offset by any earnings since the day of termination.

> Nathan Saunders, president of the Washington Teachers' Union, said the arbitrator's decision is affirmation that Rhee's aggressive approach to firing teachers was counterproductive and illegal.[34]

In June 2009, Rhee fired 250 teachers; 60 were first- or second-year teachers who had been placed "on probation"; an additional 80 for "low performance" (low test scores), and the remainder, for improper credentials.[35] Only months later, in October 2009, she laid off 229 teachers (6% of the DC teaching force), offering leave with pay only until November 2, 2009. The *Washington Post* painted this Rhee/Fenty decision in a favorable light:

> The combination of events, which included a skirmish between students and police at McKinley Technology High School that resulted in two arrests, highlighted the challenges faced by Schools Chancellor Michelle A. Rhee and Mayor Adrian M. Fenty (D) as they struggle to reform the troubled system in lean economic times. The layoffs were the deepest cuts for the school system since 2003.

> In all, 388 school employees received separation notices, the latest jolt to a system that has seen broad and sometimes wrenching change under Rhee. The schools chief has

rolled out a tough evaluation regimen that links some instructors' job security to stan-
dardized test scores and raised the bar for other educators with an elaborate set of class-
room requirements and guidelines.[36]

It sounds so noble—the mayor and chancellor battling rough economic times—and "raising the educational bar." But to qualify such immediate and drastic cuts as "progress" without any reservation as to the devastating impact they have on individuals and communities reads as propagandistic.[37]

In 2010, Rhee fired six percent of DC teachers. Ironically, of the 241 teachers fired, 76 were terminated for not having "proper teaching credentials." The remainder were fired due to "poor performance"—low test scores.[38] A 2011 *Washington Post* article includes this summary of Rhee's firing storm during her three-year stint as DC's first mayor-appointed chancellor:

> *The 75 teachers [fired in 2008 and reinstated in 2011] were part of the approximately*
> *1,000 educators fired during Rhee's 3 1/2-year tenure, which ended with her resigna-*
> *tion in October [2010]. Of the total, 266 were laid off in October 2009 for budgetary*
> *reasons, about 200 were dismissed because of poor performance, and the rest were on*
> *probation or did not have licensing required by the No Child Left Behind law.*[39]

In short, during her brief time as chancellor, Rhee fired approximately one-fourth of DC's teachers.[40] Given this fact, it seems illogical to assume that DC teachers (and administrators) under Rhee would not feel intense pressure to meet student test score quotas.

CROSBY S. NOYES EDUCATION CAMPUS

If there were a single DC school that Rhee promoted as a model of reformer success, that school would be Noyes.[41] Noyes serves pre-kindergarten through eighth grade,[42] though during Rhee's tenure, the school went only to sixth grade in 2007–08, later adding the seventh (2008–09) and eighth (2009–10) grades.

In 2009, Noyes was named a National Blue Ribbon School by the US Department of Education. It comes as no surprise that a chief criterion for this distinction is a remarkable rise in student test scores. And the scores were indeed rising overall for a few years, though not consistently for given cohorts of students. For example, 55.3% of Noyes third graders were proficient in math in 2006–07. This same group of students had a proficiency rate of 83.8% the next year (fourth grade). But the proficiency rate dropped to 72.1% in 2008–09 (fifth grade) and further still—to 49.0%— in 2009–10 (sixth grade).[43] Some scoring differences could be attributed to students leaving Noyes and still others enrolling. But these score jumps are too erratic to attribute to any unremarkable student turnover.

These number jumps remind me of what I expect to see in groups of completely unrelated students.

And it is no better for this same group of students' reading scores: Third grade (2006–07): 57.9% proficiency; fourth grade (2007–08): 67.6% proficiency; fifth grade (2008–09): 90.7% proficiency, and sixth grade (2009–10): 7.3% proficiency.[44]

These results indicate some "nonrandom interference" in scores.

Indeed, eyebrows were raised at the unusual score jumps at Noyes:

> **Michelle Rhee, then chancellor of D.C. schools, took a special interest in Noyes. She touted the school, which now serves preschoolers through eighth-graders, as an example of how the sweeping changes she championed could transform even the lowest-performing Washington schools. Twice in three years, she rewarded Noyes' staff for boosting scores:** In 2008 and again in 2010, each teacher won an $8,000 bonus, and the principal won $10,000.

> **A closer look at Noyes, however, raises questions about its test scores from 2006 to 2010. Its proficiency rates rose at a much faster rate than the average for D.C. schools. Then, in 2010, when scores dipped for most of the district's elementary schools, Noyes' proficiency rates fell further than average.**[45] [Emphasis added.]

Notice the awkward duality of test scores as the goal: Firings if scores are not up to expectations, and "merit pay" (in this case, a federally-funded Together Everyone Achieves More [TEAM] stipend) if they exceed.

Pressure to succeed and corresponding high erasures.

It was the erasure rate that drew attention to Noyes and over one hundred other DC schools:

> A USA TODAY investigation, based on documents and data secured under D.C.'s Freedom of Information Act, found that for the past three school years (2007–10) most of Noyes' classrooms had extraordinarily high numbers of erasures on standardized tests. **The consistent pattern was that wrong answers were erased and changed to right ones.**

> Noyes is one of 103 public schools here that have had erasure rates that surpassed D.C. averages at least once since 2008. That's more than half of D.C. schools.[46] [Emphasis added.]

This examination of erasure issues covers Rhee's entire time as DC chancellor. And as for Noyes, the Blue Ribbon school, erasure issues abounded:

> **In 2007–08, six classrooms out of the eight taking tests at Noyes were flagged by McGraw-Hill because of high wrong-to-right erasure rates. The pattern was repeated in the 2008–09 and 2009–10 school years, when 80% of Noyes classrooms were flagged by McGraw-Hill.**

*On the 2009 reading test, for example, seventh-graders in one Noyes classroom aver-aged 12.7 wrong-to-right erasures per student on answer sheets; the average for seventh-graders in all D.C. schools on that test was less than 1. **The odds are better for winning the Powerball grand prize than having that many erasures by chance,** according to statisticians consulted by USA TODAY.[47]* [Emphasis added.]

THE EMAILS

In 2011, *USA Today* obtained emails between the DC Office of State Super-intendent of Education (OSSE) and DC Public Schools (DCPS) regarding the DCPS erasure issue. What is amazing is that this situation continues to be unresolved.[48]

DCPS Communications Director Anita Dunn, formerly Obama's com-munications director, actively discouraged DCPS from honoring *USA To-day's* requests for information. Dunn advised DCPS Assistant Press Secretary Safiya Simmons to "disengage" and to "just stop answering [Jack Gillum's] emails."

In November 2008, then-DC State Superintendent Deborah Gist emails Rhee the results of an independent analysis by McGraw Hill regarding the high number of erasures on standardized tests in DC Public Schools. The memo is marked "action required."

In an interesting note at the end of the memo, Gist writes,

It is important to note that these analyses do not suggest reasons for the high erasure rates. There are many reasons that a class could have more erasures than other classes. However, it is important that we can ensure that all procedures available to us are employed to guarantee the validity of the state assessment system. Therefore, please take appropriate steps to investigate the results enclosed and provide a report to the Office of the State Superintendent of Education (OSSE) within 60 calendar days.[49]

The suggestion that there are "many reasons" for an erasure rate that ri-vals winning Powerball in its likelihood of occurring is ludicrous. Gist does ask Rhee to explain herself, but the wording of the above paragraph makes it sound like OSSE is rather open regarding the explanations it will accept.

Two weeks prior to the deadline, DC Chief of Data and Accountability Erin McGoldrick requests an extension until February 28, 2009. On Janu-ary 10, 2009, OSSE Deputy Superintendent Kimberly Stratham approves of this extension.

On February 29, 2009, McGoldrick (DCPS) sends OSSE Assistant Super-intendent of Assessment and Accountability Alex Harris not an explanation but a request for additional information, including which erasure analysis tests to interpret and how; examination of original answer sheets, and an erasure pattern analysis.

Then, in March 2009, comes an apparently unanswered mystery memo from McGraw Hill to OSSE advising that even though certain schools were "flagged... for possible cheating," "we advise against concluding that cheating behavior may have occurred...." McGraw Hill offers as its reasoning that its analysis did not extend to a sufficient number of standard deviations from the mean. McGraw Hill determines that it should have used 4+ standard deviations as the criteria for cheating when it only used 2—4 standard deviations.

On April 1, 2009, OSSE's Harris sends DCPS's McGoldrick a list of 13 classes to investigate based upon erasure results of three procedures, including two that employed 2.5 standard deviations from the average number of erasures. Harris includes a statement that the data alone provide no reasons for the results but that the results must be investigated. Harris notes that the investigation of these classes should occur given the "proximity to 2009 DCCAS [standardized test] administration."

McGoldrick responds on May 8, 2009, to tell Harris that DCPS has taken steps to ensure test security and includes an extensive test security plan manual. McGoldrick makes no mention of investigating any classes for excessive erasures.

The next memo is from Victor Reinoso, Deputy Mayor of Education. It is dated September 3, 2009, and is directed toward no specific individual. Reinoso declares the results of the 2008 erasure analysis "ultimately inconclusive" and ensures "clear and consistent test security policies" for 2009 and "continuous improvement" for 2010. The memo appears to be an effort to leave a paper trail declaring the 2008 erasure situation "closed." There is no mention of any detailed investigation into the 2008 erasures. In fact, Reinoso justifies not investigating specific schools.

Despite Reinoso's assurances, in February 2010, eight teachers were interviewed regarding erasure issues on the 2009 test by a group called Caveon. No administrator interviews are included with these documents. Note that this is not an investigation; it is simply an interview. The interviewer asked teachers how the testing proceeded, and the teachers' responses were recorded. Caveon concluded "[no] test security irregularities that require further investigation." Yet this was no "investigation." It was a summative interview report.

Regarding its 2010 investigation (yes, this is the song that never ends), the *Washington Post* notes that Caveon did "exactly what his client, DCPS, asked. Had it asked for more, he said, more could have been done."[50] So much for any investigation.

And this is very telling regarding what one might mean when one says that he/she "brought in an independent investigator." It is possible that this "independent investigator" was paid to do a very restricted job.

To its credit, Caveon did include this recommendation following the interviews of teachers with flagged 2009 scores at one particular school:

Increase classroom monitoring of teachers in question. Run specialized data forensics analysis on suspected teachers for a more in-depth analysis of unusual gains and erasure patterns. … Don't allow the teachers in question to participate in DC CAS testing. Analyze test data and interview teachers immediately following 2010 DC CAS testing.[51]

OSSE agreed with Caveon's recommendations for this school and sent a memo to Rhee on March 16, 2010, regarding their decision.

Given the fact that erasure issues had been present across two school years, OSSE appears to be rather shortsighted in advocating restrictions at a single DCPS school.

This appears to be little more than a token response on the part of OSSE.

SEEKING A RHEE INTERVIEW ON ERASURE ISSUES

According to *USA Today,*

*Rhee had agreed to an in-person interview with USA TODAY [in 2011], **but later declined after her representatives believed USA TODAY's questions would focus too much on erasures during her tenure as DC schools chancellor.***[52] [Emphasis added.]

Rhee is a woman in control. She does not want to answer for the shoddy "investigation" into erasure issues that span her entire time as chancellor. But she wants to offer the illusion of cooperation. Mafara Hobson of StudentsFirst was the liaison between Rhee and *USA Today's* Marisol Bello. Bello emailed Hobson to let her know that the *USA Today* piece on Rhee would "reflect that Rhee agreed to a sit-down interview but backed out because she did not want too many erasure-related questions and instead would only answer questions by email."

Hobson responds, "We are absolutely interested (and have always been) in fully cooperating with you to ensure you can write a comprehensive story" and that Rhee's "backing out" over erasure-related questions was "simply untrue," that it is "Michelle's …extraordinarily tight" schedule." But then she writes that Bello "mischaracterized the thrust of [the] piece." Hobson continues, "We were comfortable about any number of questions you wanted to ask about any topic." But in subsequent emails in which Rhee offers responses to Bello's questions, the ones related to the cheating scandal are left blank.

In March 2011, *USA Today* did publish an article on the DC Board of Education hearing to be held regarding the "irregularities" in student test scores. Keep in mind the "Powerball" probability noted above while reading Rhee's comment regarding the hearing (offered via email):

It isn't surprising that the enemies of school reform once again are trying to argue that the earth is flat and that there is no way test scores could have improved for DCPS students unless someone cheated.[53,54]

But the question is not one of simple "score improvement." The question is one of score continuity—of score consistency. And there is the practical question of whether or not the students perform daily in a manner that bespeaks high test scores. It seems that Noyes students did not.

Adell Cothorne noticed as much.

NOYES GETS A NEW PRINCIPAL

Wayne Ryan was the principal at Noyes under whose watch the test scores jumped erratically during most of Rhee's time as DC chancellor. Ryan is the one who reaped two $10,000 bonuses[55] for the amazing rise in test scores. And Ryan was Rhee's advertisement for DC principal "success":

> *Ryan became a literal poster boy for D.C. school reform under former Chancellor Michelle A. Rhee after DC CAS scores spiked dramatically at Noyes from 2007 to 2009. The District ran principal recruitment ads with his picture asking "Are you the next Wayne Ryan?" Rhee promoted Ryan in 2010 to instructional superintendent, where he supervised a group of principals.[56]*

In 2010, Ryan was promoted to instructional superintendent, a job from which he abruptly resigned in 2011 amid the *USA Today* investigation into the 2009 erasure issues. In the emails previously discussed, *USA Today* reporters Gillum and Bello probed DCPS for information on the erasures—and particularly on two schools— one of which was Noyes.[57]

Formerly an assistant principal in Montgomery County, Maryland, Adell Cothorne was hired in 2010 as a DCPS principal of another school[58] but became Ryan's replacement at Noyes.[59]

Via his promotion, Ryan became Cothorne's immediate supervisor.[60]

On October 26, 2010, DCPS Assistant Press Secretary Simmons sent this email to Cothorne regarding Gillum's request to visit Noyes and interview staff concerning testing issues:

Hi Prin. Cothorne:

I hope this email finds you well.

I wanted to reach out to you to give you a heads up about a reported I've had an exchange with.

Jack Gillum, a writer for USA Today, has expressed interest in visiting Noyes to interview staff about testing procedures, erasure, and other related issues.

I've told him very clearly that he is not to contact you or any of your staff, but I wanted to let you know. He probably won't present an issue or show up or anything, but if he does, please redirect him to me and decline him any other access or answers.

Thanks in advance for your assistance. Let me know if you have any other questions.

Safiya Jafari Simmons
Assistant Press Secretary
District of Columbia Public Schools
Office of the Chancellor

Cothorne responded the same afternoon:

Thank you SO much for this "heads up".

Adell Cothorne, Principal
THE CROSBY S. NOYES EDUCATION CAMPUS
"Where Excellence is the Expectation"
A 2009 National Blue Ribbon School[51]

Cothorne was only a couple months into her first (and only) school year at Noyes. But October was also the month in which Cothorne met with Rhee "to set goals," which, for principals, included a written guarantee.[62]

One can see the pressure mount on these DC principals and, by extension, their faculties.

In an interview with John Merrow of *Frontline*, Cothorne was candid about her "goal setting":

[Cothorne] told Frontline that meeting, which took place early in school year 2010–2011. "You are to 'goal set.' You are to tell her, you know, 'I will raise math scores by 5%. I will raise reading scores by 6%.' And so, yes, she and I had that conversation. And I said to her in early October, 'I'm very comfortable with a 6% gain in math and a 7% gain in reading.'"

JOHN MERROW: But ... if you make the commitment for 6%, 7%, is it understood that if you don't make it you are not going to be around?
ADELL COTHORNE: Yes.
JOHN MERROW: Produce or else?
ADELL COTHORNE: She—yes, she said that to me. Yes.
JOHN MERROW: She said—
ADELL COTHORNE: In a joking fashion, absolutely joking fashion, but she did say, 'You know, Cothorne, if you don't make this, don't be upset if you get a pink slip.' Those were her words to me. In a joking manner.
JOHN MERROW: Did you take it as a joke?
ADELL COTHORNE: No. (LAUGH) That's my livelihood. No I did not.[63]

By the time Cothorne had made her agreement with Rhee, she had already experienced the dissonance between student test scores and observed student ability. Cothorne visited classrooms. She observed Noyes teaching and learning in action. And she already had experience working at Blue Ribbon schools. Cothorne "saw students struggling to read, which is absolutely what does not happen at a Blue Ribbon school. ... I just really saw a lack of instruction across the board."[64]

Cothorne apparently did not know about the erasure questions surrounding her supposedly "Blue Ribbon school." But she did see troubling evidence of faculty wrongdoing:

> *Cothorne told Frontline that she inadvertently discovered a possible explanation for the discrepancy between the high test scores and the students' daily performance: Adults were changing answers on the tests. She had stayed late one night and heard noises coming from one classroom.*

> **"So I walked into the room and I saw three staff members. There were test books everywhere, over 200 test books spread out on desks, spread out on tables. One staff member was sitting at a desk and had an eraser. And then there were two other staff members at a round table and they had test books out in front of them. And one staff member said to me, in a light-hearted sort of way, 'Oh, Principal, I can't believe this kid drew a spider on the test and I have to erase it.' ... That was a little strange to me. I mean, the whole situation of all of these test books, over 200 test books being spread out in this room after school hours with three staff members. It's not the way a testing situation is supposed to happen."**

> **This was not an isolated incident, Cothorne told Frontline.**[65] [Emphasis added.]

There were other issues, as Cothorne notes in her *Frontline* interview, including teacher efforts to "frontload" information to students—that is, teachers offering students information as the test booklets were open.

Jobs are on the line. And again, there's the possibility of a substantial monetary reward for raising scores. But not for Cothorne.

Like an ethical and responsible principal, Cothorne wanted to ensure the security of the tests. Cothorne appealed to her now "higher up," Wayne Ryan; the word from him was to "respect the legacy at Noyes" by, as Cothorne notes, "being quiet."[66]

In March 2011, Cothorne filed a whistleblower complaint with the US Department of Education (USDOE),[67] but the USDOE Inspector General reported finding no cheating among adults. (This amazes me given what Cothorne observed firsthand.) At Noyes, Cothorne chose to increase test security. In the short term, DCPS cooperated, Cothorne notes, given the recent press from *USA Today*. Cothorne asked for and received DCPS test security assistance:

> *...At that point, downtown was more willing to help because the USA Today article had come out, and so Noyes had gotten lots of publicity about an erasure scandal. So when CAS came around in 2011, I did have two extra people from downtown to help monitor to—the test, and then I had another two extra people who helped with, you know, having the test checked in to make sure all the tests came in. We had locks changed on doors so that myself and my assistant principal were the only two people that had the key to the room to get in to testing. No one–the test coordinator did not have it. No one else had the keys.*

JOHN MERROW: So are you convinced that that DC-CAS in the spring of your year there, that that was a secure test?
ADELL COTHORNE: I would honestly say that was a secure test.
JOHN MERROW: So you–you're certain there were no erasures on that test?
ADELL COTHORNE: Now, I cannot be certain because I did not stay at the school 24 hours (LAUGH) a day. But while I was there, and what I saw, I do think it was a secure test.[68]

I believe Cothorne is correct about the security of the 2010–11 DCCAS, for the DCCAS scores in reading and math dropped noticeably from 2009–10 to 2010–11. Percentages of students achieving "proficient" fell roughly 20 points or more for grades 3 through 8 in math, with all grades having between 11.9 and 44.2% proficiency. In reading, the proficiency rates declined noticeably for all grade cohorts except grade 6 (2009) to grade 7 (2010), with the percentage rising from 7.3% to 52.9% proficiency. For grades 3 through 8, the percentage of students proficient ranged from 16.7% to 52.9% in 2010–11.[69]

Merrow includes summative information regarding Noyes' test scores, as well as information on test score drops in other DC schools flagged for erasures:

With heightened security, Noyes' DC-CAS scores dropped 52 points in reading (from 84.21% in 2009 to 32.40%) and 34 points in math (from 62.79% to 28.17%). In fact, in 2010–2011 Noyes performed below its 2007, pre-Rhee, level.

JOHN MERROW: How do you explain the drop?
ADELL COTHORNE: Those were the true test scores.
JOHN MERROW: I'm sorry?
ADELL COTHORNE: Those were the true test scores, in my opinion. Those were what the students in that school actually were able to produce.

Take note, readers. The decline at Noyes was not an exception among 'high erasure' schools. At the 14 schools with erasure rates of 50% or higher, scores declined at 12, often precipitously, after security was tightened.[70]

By the time the 2010–11 DCCAS was administered, Rhee had resigned. In fact, Rhee's resignation came within weeks of her "goal setting" meeting with Cothorne and prior to the email from Simmons about Gillum's denied visit to Noyes. Cothorne herself resigned from Noyes and sued the district for false claims, including funds owed back to the US government from DCPS.[71]

THE RHEE-CREATION AND HER FUTURE

Even though Rhee resigned as DC chancellor years ago (October 2010), the cheating scandal follows her—as it should. As of this writing, Merrow continues to pursue the facts regarding Rhee's cheating scandal.[72] However, in his post asking, "Who created Michelle Rhee?"[73] Merrow does not offer himself as a chief contributor, yet he presented Rhee in a *Frontline* special that failed to pursue the then-familiar issue of Rhee's erasure issues.[74] Of course, Merrow is certainly not alone in promoting Rhee's popularity and power. Rhee has some serious financial backing, as previously noted in her TNTP and StudentsFirst funders. And she has connections to Arne Duncan, and connections to President Obama via former White House communication director Anita Dunn, who was "privately funded" by Katherine Bradley to "help tell the school reform story more effectively."[75] Rhee has also been oft protected in the reporting of the *Washington Post.* And let's not forget the promoting of members of both political parties of Rhee's propagandistic film, *Waiting for Superman.*[76-78]

Will Rhee eventually answer for the erratic test scores during her time as DC chancellor? Only time will tell. Players, including Rhee successor Kaya Henderson, continue to evade the issue.[79] Yet documents are surfacing. Consider excerpts from this 2009 memo, newly publicized by Merrow in 2013. It is from an external analyst, Sandy Sanford, and it has "Project Brief Sheet for Erin" (McGoldrick)[80] at the op, as well as "Sensitive Information—Treat as Confidential" written both at the header and footer of all of its four pages.

I have been working furiously on the Erasure Study. It is common knowledge in the high stakes testing community that one of the easiest ways for teachers to artificially inflate student test scores is to erase student wrong responses to multiple choice questions and recode them as correct. ... There are 191 teachers representing 70 schools that are implicated in possible testing infractions by the[erasure] study. The degree of possible teacher infraction varies, but most of the teachers identified are <u>possibly</u> *culpable at some level.*

Further along in the four pages, Sanford asks,

What happens to the TEAM money paid to teachers if infractions are confirmed?

The outcome of Cothorne's lawsuit should answer that question. Sanford asks yet another powerful question:

How does the "teacher contract" language impact possible actions against teachers guilty of testing infractions?[81]

In other words, could DCPS be held responsible for putting teachers in some position of duress that propelled them to pursue cheating? Could "we the administration" be held responsible?

Rhee denies seeing the memo; and anyway, she gets "countless reports," so why would she remember had she read it?[82] Yet consider that when it came to issues of credentials or low test scores, Rhee fired approximately

25% of DC's teaching force during the years 2007–10. Thus, it is an established fact that when Rhee wants to pursue "unfit" teachers, she does so relentlessly. And yet glaringly—undeniably—obviously—Rhee offers a feeble excuse that she saw no such memo but even if she did, she somehow forgot because, you know, so many memos came across her desk.

For now, those in a position to require Rhee to answer for the DC cheating scandal appear to be inactive. Nevertheless, Rhee appears to be bracing for the impending storm; in January 2013, Merrow reports that Rhee has retained criminal attorney Reid Weingarten.[83]

Being born and raised on the Gulf Coast, I never thought a time would come when I would desire for a storm to arrive, but in the case of Rhee's ultimately accounting for those DC test scores, I must say, I am looking forward to the storm.

CHAPTER 5

ERIK HANUSHEK: EXPERT WITNESS FOR "LESS DOING MORE" IN THE CLASSROOM

Eric Hanushek is a return-on-investment man with a profound influence upon a classroom in which he has never taught. He is an economist and a senior fellow of Stanford University's Hoover Institute, a pro-free-market, pro-federalism "think tank" formed in 1959 reminiscent[1] of the corporation-fattening American Legislative Exchange Council (ALEC).[2] For the past three decades, Hanushek has served as an expert witness in education cases in which education financial sufficiency is in question. He graduated from the Air Force Academy in 1965 and earned a PhD in economics from MIT in 1968. His research on education is that of an economist performing education research— research in which cost is the ultimate consideration. Never having been a classroom teacher, Hanushek's firsthand awareness of the reality of the classroom is conspicuously absent from his financed-based focus.

Hanushek doesn't see schools in terms of children. He sees schools in terms of fewest dollars spent.

A Chronicle of Echoes: Who's Who in the Implosion of American Public Education, pages 79–95.

As a result of his fiscal vision, Hanushek advocates for the financial "bottom line" in education. And given the contemporary push to privatize public education, it should come as no surprise that his work has landed him on many advisory boards and committees where the cost of education (and return on investment) is of primary concern, a position of particular interest to those in "the business of education." Since 2003, Hanushek has chaired the executive board of the Hoover Institute's Texas Schools Project, a mystery-funded front for advancing pro-corporate reform views such as value-added modeling and removing caps on class sizes.[3] Since 2007, he has been a member of the review board for the Broad Prize (as in the education privatizers Eli and Edythe Broad Foundation) for Urban Education. In 2010, Hanushek became a member of the Education Reform Advisory Group at the George W. Bush Institute (George W.— the man who gave the US No Child Left Behind with its focus on the standardized test score). In 2010 Hanushek also became director of the reform-minded group Great-Schools, whose funders include the Gates and Walton foundations.[4,5] Finally, in 2011, he became a member of the US Department of Education's Equity and Excellence Commission, a commission funded by the Big Three in pro-privatization, education reform: the Broad, Gates, and Walton Foundations.[6,7]

Hanushek is undeniably of the corporate education reformer set. Former Florida Governor and ALEC BFF Jeb Bush even identifies him as a "reformer."[8] However, Hanushek's mindset complemented the modern push for the privatization of public education even before privatization of public education even had its formations in ALEC (1973). To appreciate Hanushek's "education bottom line" mindset, one must consider his first notable education publication: his 1968 Ph.D. thesis.

WAY BACK IN '68, CLASS SIZE DIDN'T MATTER

In 1968, Hanushek completed his doctoral thesis, entitled, *The Education of Negroes and Whites.*[9] In it, he performs separate regression analyses on two groups, white and black sixth-grade students in the metropolitan Northeast and Great Lakes region (Michigan), in order to determine variables that influence students' mean scores. (This analysis is not value-added modeling [VAM], but it is an ancestor of the VAM concept). Regarding limitations, Hanushek notes

> *Because of data limitations, the analysis centered on mean achievement test scores for a school, rather than on individual achievement. The estimates are necessarily rather crude and cannot be used to answer detailed questions about specific policies. ... The survey itself is plagued by nonresponse and faulty response. Analysis of the raw data indicated that many items could not be used... because of the severity of the nonresponse*

problem. ...For the modeling of the educational process, the most severe problem with the data sources arises from a basic weakness, or incompleteness, in the questionnaires.[10]

Hanushek's study has these and other limitations that are important to know as one attempts to weigh study outcomes. Thus, this study's conclusions must be tempered by Hanushek's acknowledged data collection issues. I will note other limitations as such pertain to specific outcomes and recommendations.

Keep in mind that Hanushek is an economist; as such, his next statements offer insight into his view of an economist investigating the classroom:

The major vectors of inputs (major variable groupings investigated) are family backgrounds, attitudes, schools factors, and racial composition of the school. **For policy purposes all of the inputs are not equally as interesting. Family backgrounds and attitudes exhibit a significant relationship with achievement. However, their role is generally deemphasized in the analysis since they are not very useful for policy applications.**[11] *[Emphasis added.]*

Let's pause here for a moment. Hanushek notes that factors outside of the control of the school (and classroom) "significantly" affect student achievement. Nevertheless, since policy cannot readily shape these outside factors, he immediately discounts them. They "are not equally as interesting."

What is of interest is that which can be controlled via policy.

What the above perspective produces is a narrowing of all that influences student achievement to a restricted subset of what Hanushek determines is "useful for policy applications." By disregarding major factors external to the school yet significantly impacting student achievement, those factors that are deemed "useful for policy applications" are accorded greater influence and importance: school quality and racial composition of the school.

As a result, this view places a disproportionate burden of responsibility on the schools.

It is also a precursor of the reformer mantra that those pointing to influences outside of the classroom—including child poverty—are merely trying to avoid responsibility.

Hanushek's thesis was published more than four decades ago, and his views might have changed on certain of his assertions. However, some of the points represented in his thesis remain influential in corporate education reform circles, not the least of which is "if it can be measured and controlled, it is important; if it cannot be measured and controlled, it is not important." Consider this information from the discussion section of Hanushek's thesis:

...The models provide information relevant to education policy. In particular, they emphasize the importance of distinguishing between teacher quality and teacher quantity. Educational programs are often designed to increase teacher quantity (reduce pupil-teacher ratios). Experience has shown that, in addition to being extremely expensive, these programs tend to be ineffective. This is precisely what the previous modeling efforts emphasized. The returns to schools are found in quality changes, not quantity changes. (This holds at least within the fairly wide range of school inputs found in the sample.) When costs are considered, the case for purchasing quality instead of quantity becomes even stronger. It is simply cheaper to buy significant changes in the quality sphere.[12] [Emphasis added.]

I bolded the two statements above for their importance to current issues of education reform. The first statement is associated with Hanushek as impetus for a popular privatization view: Class size doesn't matter; if the teacher is "effective," then her/his class size irrelevant.

This finance-focused view assumes that teacher quality is static—that classroom circumstance and teacher ability do not interact. Whereas Hanushek does not state as much directly, those whose chief aim is the privatization of education have taken this "class size doesn't matter" and exploited it for the sake of maximizing financial profit.

The second statement bolded above is an aside in which Hanushek alludes to the limitations of this study. His sample is limited to a specific region of the country and to a specific type of school (elementary school). Also, keep in mind the survey incompletion issues previously noted, which do affect the quality of study outcomes. Unfortunately, limitations rarely receive the same publicity as the "remarkable" finding that "class size does not matter."

Here is the popularized message, intended or not: Pack as many students in the class as one can. If the teacher is truly a "good" teacher, he/she can perform just as well (as indicated by student standardized test scores) no matter the number of students he/she must serve. A corporate reformer's dream, for it is "cost effective"—it leads to the endgame of money.

Hanushek publishes his belief in class-size irrelevance in concise form in his thesis introduction:

...The rewards in education come from better quality teachers, not from increased quantity (reduced class size).[13]

The rewards = increased standardized test scores.

IN 1999, CLASS SIZE STILL DOESN'T MATTER

Over thirty years later, Hanushek continues his work on the "fiscal waste" of districts' setting overall class size limits. In 1999, he published a longitudinal work in which he noted the following regarding the "cost effectiveness" of reduced class size as determined by student test scores:

> *The available evidence suggests some uncertainty about the underlying relationships among families, school organization, class size, and achievement. Allowing for changes in family and special education, however, it remains difficult to make a case for reduced class size from the aggregate data. … The aggregate data are, however, quite limited, restricted to a small number of performance observations over time, and it has been difficult to rule out conclusively other fundamental changes that might affect school success.*[14]

That is, from the generalized data, an "argument" for across-the –board, class-size reduction is not supported… but the generalized data are too "general" and do not conclusively support ruling out class size as an influence.

Hanushek then proceeds to examine numerous individual studies. He concludes the following:

> *The extensive investigation of the effects of class size on student performance has produced a very consistent picture. There appears to be little systematic gain from general reductions in class size. This story comes through at the aggregate level.… But since the aggregate analyses could be misleading for a variety of analytical reasons, more weight should be put on school-level analyses and experimental data. … Across several hundred estimates of the effects of reduced class size, **positive and negative effects almost balance each other out**, underscoring the ineffectiveness of overall class size policies such as those being currently advocated.*[15] [Emphasis added.]

Hanushek offers a jump in logic: Since the effects of reduced class size demonstrate positive effects on standardized test scores in some cases but not in others—since the outcome demonstrates a complexity of seeming benefit in some cases but not "the majority"— then overall reductions in class size are "ineffective." If the study results are mixed, it is possible that removing overall class size limits will remove the "protections," so to speak, on classes such that the standardized test scores decline in classes with previously-noted "positive effects."

In a subsequent word, Hanushek appears to renegotiate his position:

> *None of this says that smaller classes never mattered. Indeed, the micro-level evidence, which shows that differences in teacher-pupil ratios appear to be important, suggests just the opposite.*
>
> *Much of the case for reduced class size rests on common sense. With fewer students, teachers can devote more attention to each child and can tailor the material to an individual child's needs.*[16]

After a slight concession, he returns to protection of the "bottom line":

But consider, for example, a change from classes of twenty-six students to twenty-three. This represents an increase of over 10 percent in teacher costs alone....[17,18]

Such logic can lead to dangerous ends. First of all, this assessment of "cost effectiveness" presumes that the outcome—student test scores—is the ultimate measure of academic success. Yet even as far back as 1968, Hanushek admits that other possible outcome measures aside from test scores should be considered:

The use of test scores is profitable for it does measure a significant dimension of scholastic output. Nevertheless, it is not the only possible measure of output, and analysis of alternative measures would both provide additional information for policy purposes and supply perspective to the test score analysis.[19]

Given the current adulation of the Almighty Test Score, "alternative measures" of student outcomes—those that are not merely seemingly sophisticated attempts to create some "value added" outcome still heavily dependent upon test scores—remain largely uninvestigated. (Other quantifiable student outcomes used in previous research[20] have also found their way into the value-added and school-letter-grading arenas, including graduation rates and attendance rates.) Furthermore, it seems that corporate reformers dismiss the idea that valuable education outcomes might not be quantifiable immediately—or ever. Issues such as responsible citizenship and life satisfaction are qualities indispensable to stable, productive societies, yet these cannot easily be quantified. Nevertheless, given the time students spend in school and with teachers and peers, life quality issues such as these are necessarily interwoven into the American classroom experience. In a previous study, Hanushek admits that "measuring student outcomes" is not interchangeable with "using student test scores":

...The variety of potential outcomes of schooling suggests that the educational process may have multiple outputs, some of which are very poorly measured by test scores. Moreover, how effective test scores are in measuring the contribution of schooling to subsequent performance probably varies at different points in the schooling process. ... In postsecondary education, few people believe that test scores adequately measure outputs.[21]

Assessment of educational outcomes is complex. The corporate reform attempt to reduce this complex process to the two-dimensional, misguided "application" of standardized test scores betrays the ignorance of those who insist time and again on adhering to such a crippled process.

A second danger in focusing on the "cost effectiveness" of overall class size involves the exploitation of teacher effectiveness for the sake of maximizing profits. If states or districts do not set maximum class sizes, or if they do not consider the "common sense" behind class size or teacher-to-pupil ratios, then effective teaching can become difficult or even impossible. And in this era of worship of the business model for running public entities, the short-term gain of decreases in initial capital outlay due to hiring fewer teachers squanders the longer-term quality of educational experience afforded to students whose teachers continue to be pressured to do more with less.

THE FAMOUS 1986 "MONEY DOESN'T MATTER" STUDY

Doing more with less. If there is one single concept with which Hanushek's name has become connected in this age of education privatization, it is this concept. In 1986, Hanushek published a paper entitled, "The Economics of Schooling: Production and Efficiency in Public Schools," in which he examines 147 "qualified" studies in an attempt to determine what "school effects" (teacher education, teacher experience, and teacher-to-student ratio) impact student outcomes (96 of these studies use student standardized test scores as the outcome measure).[22] In Hanushek's results, written in 1986, one can witness the contemporary corporate reformer stance that neither teacher education, nor teacher experience, nor teacher-student ratios "matter":

> *The results are startlingly consistent in finding no strong evidence that teacher-student ratios, teacher education, or teacher experience have an expected positive effect on student achievement. According to the available evidence, one cannot be confident that hiring more educated teachers or having smaller classes will improve student performance. Teacher experience appears only marginally stronger in its relationship.*[23]

Now here comes the often-cited statement italicized in the original report, the one for which Hanushek is primarily known:

> **There appears to be no strong or systematic relationship between school expenditures and student performance.**[24] [Emphasis added.]

There it is. Money doesn't matter. Cut the funding; expect the same test scores, for they are what matters.

I am not certain why Hanushek did not also italicize the limitations that immediately follow this Stellar and Amazing Finding that Money Doesn't Matter. Here are the cautions regarding the above findings. (Though study limitations should receive as much press as the findings themselves, this rarely happens):

> *There are several obvious reasons for being cautious in interpreting this evidence. For any individual study, incomplete information,* **poor quality data, or faulty research could distort a study's statistical results.** *Even without such problems, the actions of school administrators could mask any relationship. For example,* **if the most difficult to teach students were consistently put in smaller classes, any independent effect of class size could be difficult to disentangle** *from mismeasurement of the characteristics*

of the students. ***Finally, statistical insignificance… also can reflect a variety of data problems….***[25] [Emphasis added.]

So many cautions, not the least of which is the possibility of administrators' intentionally grouping at-risk students into smaller classes. One could see how such intentional groupings might interfere with a crude assessment of the relationship of class size to test scores.

If smaller class sizes "are common sense," as Hanushek previously notes, then according a more prominent emphasis to the limitations of this 1986 paper would also have been "common sense." Instead, the "finding" that school expenditure is "not related" to school performance has been publicized as The Truth. As Bruce Baker of the Shanker Institute reports in "Does Money Matter In Education?",

> *The primary source of doubt to this day remains the above-mentioned Eric Hanushek finding, in 1986, that "There appears to be no strong or systematic relationship between school expenditures and student performance." (p. 1162)* ***This single quote, now divorced entirely from the soundly-refuted analyses on which it was based, remains a mantra for those wishing to deny that increased funding for schools is a viable option for improving school quality.***
>
> ***Most generally, however, using the simple juxtaposition of two trends—spending and average test scores—to draw causal inferences about how one affects the other is irresponsible and not at all compelling. The "true effect" of funding on educational outcomes is extremely difficult to isolate, which is precisely why the research discussed above is so complex.***[26] [Emphasis added.]

Baker offers the following words in conclusion:

> *It is certainly reasonable to acknowledge that money, by itself, is not a comprehensive solution for improving school quality. Clearly, money can be spent poorly and have limited influence on school quality. Or, money can be spent well and have substantive positive influence. But money that's not there can't do either.*[27]

An excellent final point, one that ought to not require a direct statement.

What insanity is modern education that researchers must prove that schools need money?

Baker also raises an important question about responsible education spending. Money available at the state level does not readily translate into money available at the school level. That is, education funding does not necessarily funnel from top administration into the classroom:

> *Most funding for public education comes from state and local sources, and is under the jurisdiction of state school finance systems. Therefore, states have the greatest control over whether local public schools have access to sufficient levels of resources, and whether those resources are distributed equitably across children and settings. Furthermore, constitutional protections for children's access to adequate and equitable public schooling*

exist in state constitutions, but not in the U.S. Constitution. Finally, as indicated at the outset of this brief, **it is at the state level where the most raucous rhetoric is occurring around these questions of whether money matters in education. State legislatures and governors can make or break public schooling, and they have.**[28,29] [Emphasis added.]

The idea that money available to the "states" might not be reaching the classroom is a crucial consideration for tempering any finding that says funding has "increased over time" but student test scores "have not." I do not agree that the principal measure of effective education spending should be the standardized test. I see this as a shallow, short-sighted measure of intellectual growth. As Baker notes,

...Not only does money matter, but reforms that determine how money is distributed matter too, and more equitable funding can improve the level and distribution of outcomes.[30]

ERIC HANUSHEK, EXPERT WITNESS FOR THE STATE

Unfortunately, the common sense issue that money affects education quality and opportunity has required reinforcement in the courts. In 2003, the Kansas case of *Montoy vs. State* involved the educational funding inequity of almost 300% resulting from removal of provisions from a 1992 funding act. Haushek testified as an expert; here is the text from the actual memorandum decision regarding the proceedings of the trial and Hanushek's contribution:

In their effort to prove that "money doesn't matter," the Defendants produced a series of experts. Those experts, and the court's assessment of their testimony, follows:

[skip to] Dr. Eric Hanushek, Stanford

Dr. Hanushek was billed as the expert who would demonstrate that "money doesn't matter." What he actually said was that money, foolishly spent, would not close the significant "achievement gap" which exists between the vulnerable and/or protected students who have brought this action and their majority counterparts. **In fact, Dr. Hanushek testified that money spent wisely, logically, and with accountability would be very useful indeed. He concluded by agreeing with this statement: "Only a fool would say money doesn't matter."**

By the way of summary, the Court was persuaded, as a matter of fact, by the evidence that there is a causal connection between the poor performance of the vulnerable and/or protected categories of Kansas students and the low funding provided their schools. **Except for a few expert opinions vaguely to the point that "money doesn't even matter" the causal connection was uncontroverted by those who actually work with students on a daily basis.**[31] [Emphasis added.]

The statement, "only a fool would say money doesn't matter," is a reference to another case in which Hanushek testified, *Hoke County vs. State (North Carolina)*, an case with a complaint similar to that of the Kansas case: funding inequity:

> *The poor school districts allege that the children in their districts are not receiving a sufficient education to meet even the minimum standard for a constitutionally adequate education and that those children, because of disparities in funding between poor and wealthy school systems.... **The plaintiffs complain about a myriad of things, including,** but not limited to, inadequate school facilities, outdated media centers, lack of computers and technology, lack of ability to compete for high quality teachers because of low salary supplements, and **higher student teacher ratios in the classroom.**[32]* [Emphasis added.]

Here are some excerpts regarding Hanushek's testimony from the *Hoke County vs. State* memorandum decision (apostrophes and quotation marks added):

> *While he does not discount the possibility that there are effective practices that enhance student achievement, he is convinced that merely spending more money on education is unlikely to result in improved student performance. Hanushek, Nov. 30, 1999, at 217–36. This Court understood Dr. Hanushek quite clearly. Although plaintiff's counsel described Dr. Hanushek as the witness who was going to testify that "money does not matter" the Court finds Dr. Hanushek to be very credible. His testimony was logical and full of common sense. Put in plain English, the thrust of Dr. Hanushek's opinion is that throwing money at an educational problem without having goals in place for the spending and a system of accountability to measure the effectiveness of the spending is wasteful and not likely to result in improving student performance. The Court is of the same opinion. Dr. Hanushek believes that money matters provided the money is spent in a way that is logical and the results of the expenditures measured to see if the expected goals are achieved. ... Dr. Hanushek is of the opinion the most likely kind of program or policy that will enhance student achievement is one based upon incentives for better student performance. **Typically in the United States neither teachers' careers nor principals' careers are dependent upon student success. Without incentives, merely adding resources is unlikely to make a difference.** Hanushek, Nov. 30, 1999, at 236. This does not mean that "money does not matter." Only a fool would find that money does not matter in education. The point is that money should be spent with specific goals in mind and with a method of accountability in place to measure whether or not the money that is spent is being appropriately spent **to obtain the results desired.**[33]* [Emphasis added.]

I have bolded two statements that I find troubling in this excerpt. The first highlights a common reformer mindset that student outcomes (i.e., test scores) can and should be directly connected to "teachers' and principals' careers" and that the financing of public education should include financial "incentives" contingent upon teacher and principal "success" as such is defined by student "success" (again, test scores). The second statement betrays another corporate reform mindset, one of spending on education "to obtain a desired result," as though humans are objects to be manipulated via money and schools, personnel, and students are little more than resulting test scores or counts in some funding formula. Baker comments on the lack of research supporting such reformer mindsets:

> *Specifically, while many talk of more efficient or cost effective options for spending money, information on these options is sorely lacking.* **Rhetoric abounds regarding current approaches to public schooling—such as spending on class size reduction—being the most inefficient or least cost-effective options. But proposed alternatives, such as restructuring teacher pay around indicators of "effectiveness" rather than seniority or credentials, are not backed by solid research, and include no serious evaluations of cost. Accordingly, they provide no legitimate basis for comparing cost-effectiveness.**[34]
> [Emphasis added.]

It is difficult to "seriously evaluate" the long-term costs to society (i.e., long-term consequences) of focusing so much attention on short-term financial output. In order to effectively do so, researchers must forsake the popular fixation on student test scores.

Hanushek also testified in 2011 in a Colorado case filed in 2005, *Lobato vs. State*, which also alleged the underfunding of public education. In 2011, the plaintiff won in district court.[35] The state appealed the case to the Colorado Supreme Court, where the judges found in favor of the state in 2013.[36] Nevertheless, notice what Colorado's governor admitted following the 2013 judgment:

> *Governor John Hickenlooper admits the state is underfunding education, but he believes a court case is not the way to increase funding. ... "Even after adding extra funding this year for the construction of school buildings and the state education fund, clearly—I think most people would agree—that we are underfunded in education."[Hickenlooper said.]*[37]

Clearly money matters. And it is not just "how money is spent." As Baker writes, "money that's not there" cannot be "well spent."

During the 2011 hearing, Hanushek testified on behalf of the State of Colorado. Here are some key excerpts from Judge Sheila Rappaport's Findings of Fact and Conclusions of Law, with focus on the judge's thoughts on Hanushek's contribution:

1. *The State introduced testimony from several members of the State Board of Education and other witnesses for its case-in-chief. However,* **the Court notes that much of the State's testimony actually bolstered Plaintiffs' arguments in this case [alleging the State's underfunding of education], and certain other contrary testimony lacked factual support.**

[skip to]

C. Important Weaknesses in the Testimony of Defendants' Witnesses

1. *Although some of the State's witnesses' testimony could at first blush suggest support for the State's case, much of that testimony was questionable.* **Many of the State's witnesses offering such testimony are unfamiliar with the funding or programs available in the Plaintiff School Districts or the districts where the Individual Plaintiffs reside.** *... 8/25/11* **Trial Testimony of Dr. Erik Hanushek** *("Hanushek Trial Tr.") 5155:18–5156:10.*

2. **Not one State witness was able to identify specific inefficiencies in the Plaintiff School Districts or any school district in the State that is wasting money.**

[skip to]

12. **Defendants' national expert, Dr. Erik Hanushek, has testified for the defendants in approximately nineteen school finance cases and never on behalf of the plaintiffs.** *In each of the cases, he has testified that there is no consistent relationship between spending on schools and student achievement. In many of the cases, the courts disagreed with Dr. Hanushek's expert opinion and found for the plaintiffs.* **In some of the cases, the courts actually found the data underlying Dr. Hanushek's opinions to be questionable or problematic and found him to lack credibility.** *Hanushek Trial Tr. 5069:4-5, 5106:3-5114:14, 5115:3-5; Ex. 7702, Curriculum Vitae of Eric A. Hanushek, at 24; Ex. 7721,* **Claremont School District v. Governor;** *Ex. 7722,* **Committee for Educational Equity v. State of Missouri;** *Ex. 7723,* **Opinion of the Justices of the Supreme Court of Alabama;** *Ex. 7724,* **Campaign for Fiscal Equity v. State of New York;** *Ex. 7726,* **Montoy v. State;** *Ex. 7729,* **McCleary v. State of Washington.**

13. **Dr. Hanushek arrived at his conclusion that achievement across Colorado school districts bears little relationship to spending differences before he did any review or statistical analysis of Colorado data and before he spoke to any education officials in Colorado. In fact, his expert opinion in this case is essentially the same as the one he rendered for the State of Colorado in a public education case ten years ago.** *Hanushek Trial Tr. 5058:5-5059:6, 5059:23-5060:3, 5160:9-21.*

14. **Dr. Hanushek did not visit any Colorado school districts or speak with any administrators, school board members, teachers, students, or family members in any school district in the State in connection with his work in this case. Nor did he review any Colorado school district budget or specific district policy.** *Hanushek Trial Tr.5048:13-5050:2*

[skip to]

The Defendants offered no evidence or even information to rebut the conclusion that the finance system is completely divorced from the reality of the education system enacted by the General Assembly in the name of the Education Clause. *It is not this Court's function to determine at this time the amount necessary to provide adequate funding for public education. However,* **the Court does find that public education is very significantly underfunded** *and that any legislative response of necessity must address the level of funding necessary to meet the mandate of the Education Clause and the standards-based system and should provide funding consistent with that standard.*[38] [Emphasis added.]

Again, though Judge Rappaport's finding was overturned by the Colorado Supreme Court in 2013, Governor Hickenlooper openly admits that public education in Colorado lacks sufficient funding.

Apparently, Hanushek did not investigate sufficiency of public school funding before agreeing to testify in favor of the state. This bespeaks adherence to ideology over practicality. Furthermore, it is important to note that Hanushek has never testified for a plaintiff. His expert testimony always favors the state, and it is at the state level that privatization has organized its feeding frenzy on public funding.

Whether he intends to or not, Hanushek is assisting in the destruction of public education. As seasoned researcher and professor Gene Glass observes,

> *Eric Hanushek testifies in school finance cases. Again, and again, and again. Thirty-some years ago in the Maryland (Hornbeck) case and most recently in the Colorado (Lobato) case. And each time, Hanushek, an economist at the Hoover Institution, testifies to the same position: increased funding for K-12 schools will not improve their effectiveness; court-ordered remedies that cost money will not improve the lot of poor students or English Language Learners or anyone else for that matter.*
>
> *Hanushek is nothing if not a believer in the unconditional truth emanating from his regression equations.*[39]

Glass continues by discussing the nonsense in Hanushek's "lumping together" a number of categories to "[create] an impression of no effect of teacher experience. ...My reading of these results is much different from Hanushek's. Regression studies have generally shown a positive relationship between teacher experience and student achievement. Period."[40]

Glass then turns his attention to Hanusheks' competence as an expert witness. He alludes to Hanushek's testimony in the *Lobato* case:

> *...If Hanushek's performance in reviewing the research on teacher experience and student achievement is as shaky as this, how does he perform in court on matters closely related? Aaron Pallas, in his blog "A Sociological Eye on Education" recently wrote on that question.*[41]
>
> > *I was reminded of a school finance court case in Maryland some 30 years ago [Hornbeck; I testified in that case on the role of class size and student achievement ~GVG] for which I served as a consultant. ... The poorest districts in the state, including Baltimore City, were suing the state to force it to equalize school funding. The state ... hired noted economist Eric Hanushek to testify that money doesn't make a difference in student outcomes. I was hired to prepare questions for cross-examination that might discredit Hanushek's testimony.*

> *A friend ... suggested a novel line: If, as Hanushek argued, spending more money wouldn't increase achievement, wouldn't spending less money have no effect on achievement either? "Brilliant!" I thought.*
>
> *The time came for the cross-examination, and, among many other questions, the plaintiffs' attorney asked this question.*
>
> *"That—that almost follows," Hanushek replied....It wasn't the Perry Mason moment I was hoping for, but it was enlightening nevertheless.* **The reality is that Hanushek's claim that money doesn't matter was based on natural variations among districts in their spending patterns, and wealthy districts spent more and had better educational outcomes than poorer districts that spent less. There were no studies showing what would happen if spending were to increase or decrease precipitously over time ....**

Now thirty years later, Hanushek is still telling courts that money doesn't matter. (Linda Darling-Hammond probably made the most incisive comment on the "money doesn't matter" position when she said, "If money doesn't matter, why are the rich trying so hard to hold onto it?") **He testified in the recent Colorado school finance case (Lobato vs State of Colorado) once again that money doesn't matter. Only this time, a Colorado judge had little sympathy for counter-intuitive social science stuff.** *In her 189-page ruling deciding in favor of the plaintiffs, Judge Sheila Rappaport commented thusly on Hanushek's testimony:*

> *Dr. Hanushek's analysis that there is not much relationship in Colorado between spending and achievement contradicts testimony and documentary evidence from dozens of well-respected educators in the State, defies logic, and is statistically flawed.*[42] [Emphasis added.]

The judge wrote as much and more in this section of her sum-total 189-pages of *Lobato* findings. At one point, Hanushek attempted to compare Colorado to neighboring state, Wyoming. Judge Rappaport was quick to note the ill fit:

> *Dr. Hanushek believes that examination of achievement and expenditure levels in Wyoming demonstrates that more money does not make a difference. However, Wyoming is not comparable to Colorado.* **Colorado has 800,000 students compared to Wyoming's 80,000** *and has significantly more African-American and Latino students.* **Wyoming is extremely sparse. It has to spend significant amounts of its education money on transportation just to get kids to school.** *Darling-Hammond Trial Tr. 3931:1-23; Hanushek Trial Tr. 4994:4-4995:15; Ex. 7735, Trial Exhibits for Lobato et al. vs. State of Colorado, Eric A. Hanushek, July 2011, at "Colorado versus Wyoming Expenditure and Population Characteristics (2008)."*[43] [Emphasis added.]

The comparison between these two states illustrates an important point: States with extreme differences in overall numbers of students face differing challenges in providing public education to its students, and these differences should be carefully accounted for before passing judgment on the "sameness" of outcome test scores. Apparently Judge Rappaport considered the limitations of a study that superficially presents neighboring states as worthy of underqualified comparison on educational outcomes. And she does indeed declare that Hanushek's work is "statistically flawed." Here are her words on that regard in sum:

> *Dr. Hanushek's analysis that there is not much relationship in Colorado between spending and achievement contradicts testimony and documentary evidence from dozens of well-respected educators in the State, defies logics, and is statistically flawed. Dr. Hanushek's analysis relies on median growth percentiles rather than proficiency levels, which are not a straightforward measure of achievement.* **Median growth percentiles are just a measure of the change in achievement from year to year, not the actual achievement of the students in the district. When Dr. Darling-Hammond used the number of students who score proficient on CSAP from the data set provided to Dr. Hanushek by the State, she found a very strong statistical relationship between achievement in reading and math and spending, measuring expenditures in four different ways.** *Moreover,* **Dr. Hanushek's analysis relies on the existence of huge inefficiencies within school districts.** *However, after over 180 depositions and the production of hundreds of thousands of pages of documents,* **including budgets from almost every school district in the State,** *the State has been unable to point to any specific inefficiencies or waste in the school districts involved in this case.* **The only general inefficiency Dr. Hanushek cites is salary schedules, for which there is contrary evidence.** *Hanushek Trial Tr. 5006:6-5007:16, 5024:8-14, 5050:12-15; 8/29/11 Rebuttal Trial Testimony of Dr. Darling-Hammond ("Darling-Hammond Rebuttal Trial Tr.") 5723:23-5727:9, 5729:6-5731:1, 5736:12-25; Ex. 10,488, Relationship between Expenditures and Achievement (Per pupil Expenditures); Ex. 10,491, Table 1. Estimated OLS Coefficients for the Percent of Students Proficient in Mathematics on Student Characteristics and Expenditures, by Colorado Districts.*[44] [Emphasis added.]

It seems that Hanushek has a penchant for making sweeping conclusions from data that is not specific to the purpose and for not declaring the "inconclusive" as such.

He promotes himself as an expert, and his shaky conclusions feed into the privatization rage that is tearing across American public education state by state.

GREATSCHOOLS: CLASS SIZE DOESN'T MATTER BUT IT DOES

Hanushek believes that schools can and should do more with less. Yet his attempts to promote such a position are riddled with contradiction. For example, consider information offered to the public on the GreatSchools website. In 2010, Hanushek became the director for GreatSchools, a site purportedly available for "involved parents" and "successful kids." GreatSchool partners include a number of powerful corporate reform names, including 50CAN, Dell Foundation, KIPP, Rocketship Education, Stand for Children, Microsoft, and Walmart;[45]

It should be no surprise that at GreatSchools, the primary rating is the school's principal standardized test.[46] The GreatSchools site offers parents advice on class size, "How Important is Class Size?",[47] an article that downplays issues of class size by beginning with a section entitled, "Why small class sizes aren't enough." After all, underfunded districts might have to hire uncertificated teachers in order to meet class size reduction requirements; overcrowding might force a district to "cannibalize" other facilities (a justification to keep class sizes larger). The site tells parents, "class size reduction... is not the answer to all the problems in education." The "downplay" on a site for an organization whose director is famous for his position that money itself doesn't matter; it is how the money is spent that matters.

If this were true, then why use the term, "underfunded" on the GreatSchools site? Why not another term, such as "misappropriated," or "poorly budgeted"?

The article continues with other issues to consider, including team teaching and volunteering, both of which speak to the need for ensuring teacher availability to meet individual student needs. If class size does not matter, then why should parents consider the availability of an additional teacher or other adult volunteers in the room? In the end, however, the ultimate responsibility for each child in the classroom falls on the teacher of record. Class size is an issue. So is money—otherwise, why broach the subject of nonpaid persons (volunteers) in the classroom?

The GreatSchools website offers parents a second article on class size, "Making the Most of Larger Class Sizes."[48] Let's begin with the title. If class size is not an issue, why offer an article to help parents "make the most" of their child's being enrolled in a larger class? One need not "make the most" of an ideal situation; thus, the article admits that larger class sizes are not ideal. Notice how the article opens:

> **Come fall 2009, public school classrooms may look remarkably different, especially in kindergarten through third grade.** Word among administrators throughout the country has it that state budget cuts **will cause those class sizes to balloon** from 20 students, the maximum allowed presently, to a new headcount of 25 or 30 in some states. And, yes, you've done the math correctly: **That's a 25 % increase in students per class.**[49] [Emphasis added.]

Class size matters. So does money.

This article also includes a reference to the Gates study on dropouts, a reference that definite undermines both the "class size doesn't matter to cost effectiveness" argument:

> Research proves what parents already assumed: Smaller classes are better environments for learning. In the 2006 Bill and Melinda Gates Foundation report, "The Silent Epidemic: Perspectives of High School Dropouts,[50] 75 % of surveyed drop-out high school

students stated that smaller class sizes with more individualized instruction might have helped them stay in school.[51] [Emphasis added.]

This citation raises questions about the wisdom of using standardized test scores as the ultimate test of "cost effectiveness." It seems that the potential contribution to quality society is enhanced when citizens complete high school, thereby increasing the likelihood for gainful employment in adult life. In a separate article, Hanushek alludes to this connection between educational level and "positive attributes after schooling."[52] The Gates finding cited above also raises questions regarding the accuracy of a popular view (promoted on this website) that class size matters more in lower grades.

This "making the most" article continues by advising parents to

Be proactive in determining where your child sits in the class. Make sure he is sitting where he can see the board, especially if he has any vision or hearing impairment. What's more, ask that he be seated next to a student who complements—not battles—his own temperament.[53]

Scarcity of resources forces competition. The above advice includes the tacit admission that in larger classes, not all students will have "the best" access to the teacher. Better give your child "the edge" and secure a prime seat before some other child gets it.

Even though Hanushek attempts to promote views to the contrary, class size does matter. Money does matter. His own GreatSchools organization admits as much.

HANUSHEK'S CONTRIBUTION TO PUBLIC EDUCATION

Unfortunately, a man whose career has spanned several decades in best known for two destructive ideas: "class size doesn't matter" and "money doesn't matter." Hanushek advocates that setting overall class limits is not "cost effective"; thus, he opens a wide door for privatizers who wish to spend less and profit more at the expense of both students and teachers. He also has testified in court, "money doesn't matter" so much as how money is spent. Again, this view benefits corporate reform, for it maintains that no amount of money is too small for the operating of a school district. And to what outcome are these two statements tied? Why, standardized test scores, of course.

Hanushek is undoubtedly contributing to the chokehold already plaguing the community public school: the expectation to do ever more with ever less. Such a lie profoundly defies common sense and stuffs increasingly larger amounts of that "non-mattering" money into the bank accounts of cheering, so-called education corporations.

CHAPTER 6

THE CHICAGO CONNECTION:
THE DALEY-VALLAS YEARS

If any single city exemplifies the bipartisan scope of corporate reform, it is Chicago. It is through Chicago that the predominately-Republican push to "free-marketize" the public sector finds its notable Democratic strain via several well-positioned individuals. Three of these reformers have exited the Windy City to promote the privatization of American public education from the White House. Two remained in Chicago (for a time), and one who returned to Chicago from DC continues to wreak unprecedented havoc on Chicago's public schools. They are former Mayor Richard Daley, former Chicago Public Schools CEO Paul Vallas, former Chicago Public Schools CEO Arne Duncan, Mayor Rahm Emanuel, and President Barack Obama. They are the focus to varying degrees of three chapters on Chicago's bearing the heavy, decades-spanning burden of corporate reform. All five are interconnected in the damage they are or have propagated in the name of Improving American Education.

As to this chapter, let us consider the beginnings of Chicago corporate reform propagated by former Chicago Mayor Richard Daley and his first appointee to run Chicago's public schools, CEO Paul Vallas.

A Chronicle of Echoes: Who's Who in the Implosion of American Public Education,
pages 97–110.

RICHARD DALEY

A November 1987 *Chicago Tribune* article carried then-US Secretary of Education William Bennett's proclamation that Chicago Public Schools were "the worst in the nation" based upon the dropout rate and ACT scores. He continued by saying that Chicago schools were "an educational meltdown." Bennett then stated his oft-noted support for vouchers.

Then-Chicago Mayor Harold Washington took offense at Bennett's calling out Chicago Public Schools and criticized Bennett for his association with President Ronald Reagan, who, in Washington's opinion, "literally dismantled public education in this country." Then-Chicago Board of Education President Frank Gardner admitted that the dropout rate and low ACT scores were true.

Eighteen days after the *Tribune* published the above article, Mayor Washington died of a heart attack.[1] In a special election held in 1989, Richard Daley was elected to complete Washington's term.[2] One year earlier, in 1988, the Illinois legislature passed the Chicago School Reform Act of 1988, which created "school councils" at each Chicago public school. The school council's duties include devising an annual budget; primary control approximately $500,000 in annual state funds, and hiring and evaluating the school principal.

The 1988 law also altered the Chicago Board of Education:

> *The 1988 law also abolished the existing 11-member Board of Education. The law expanded the Board of Education to 15 and created a School Board Nominating Commission, composed of 23 parent and community representatives from LSCs (local school councils) across the city and five members appointed by the mayor.* **The Commission screened candidates and gave the mayor a slate of three candidates for each vacant position on the 15-member board. The mayor had 30 days to choose the 15 board members from the list submitted by the Nominating Commission. If the mayor rejected all three slated candidates for a particular slot, the commission had to come up with three more. The mayor's choices had to be approved by the City Council.**[3] [Emphasis added.]

One immediately sees the power that the mayor, a single individual, holds over the appointment of this 15-member Chicago School Board, especially in the face of a "rubber stamp" City Council.[4] Nevertheless, in his years as mayor prior to 1995, Daley apparently rushed in with "no nonsense" solutions that only revealed his lack of knowledge regarding public education in Chicago. As a February 1996 *Chicago Tribune* observes:

> *Unfamiliar with the complexity of educating poor children, Daley and his team early on set about promoting quick-fix solutions-year-round schools, a "no-baloney" back to basics curriculum district-wide. They soon learned, however, that due to the vast differences in student learning levels and teaching know-how, the problems could not be*

fixed that easily. Daley, for one, appears to have learned a lesson; he hasn't ventured to promote any more new educational approaches.[5]

The *Gale Encyclopedia of Biography* notes, "Daley wanted to run Chicago like a business."[6] Businesses are not led collaboratively, but in top-down, one-individual-answering-to his/her-superior, format. This characteristic appears to have been a catalyst in a Republican-dominated legislature granting a Democratic mayor ultimate control over Chicago public education in 1995 in the form of the Chicago School Reform Amendatory Act. Key points of the 1995 Amendatory Act include the following:

This act reversed the decentralized, local governance trend of the 1988 law. It concentrated power in the office of the mayor, giving him/her sole authority over CPS including:

Eliminated the School Finance Authority (SFA) and the School Board Nominating Commission

Mayoral appointment of Board members and top administrators.

Mayor, rather than the Board, selects the Board president

Created position of Chief Executive Officer (CEO) to oversee CPS administration.

The 1995 law gave the mayor sole authority to appoint a five-member School Reform Board of Trustees to serve through 1999. Thereafter, the mayor was to appoint a seven-member board with staggered, four-year terms.[7]

The mayor is the person in charge. No need to fuss with decentralization or shared decision-making. And notice the new name of the board: the School Reform Board. Apparently, collaboration does not reform the schools fast enough or well enough. Throwing the democratic process inherent in the negotiated school board to the wind, the corporate business model of a boss (the mayor) appointing another boss (the CEO of schools) became the new model that would save the Chicago public schools.

If Daley's goal was to run Chicago like a business, he achieved his goal. If his goal were to actually improve public education in Chicago, well, that's a different story.

This is what Chicago education "received" in 1995:

*The management structure of the CPS was transformed into one that closely resembled a corporate-style management system. The top positions within CPS were eliminated, and were replaced with corporate titles. **The superintendent position was eliminated, and replaced with the "CEO" distinction. Daley was given the complete authority to appoint the CPS CEO. In addition, the system would now be managed by a chief financial officer, a chief educational officer, a chief operating officer, and a chief***

purchasing officer, none of which were required to have educational credentials.[8]
[Emphasis added.]

The person in charge of Chicago Public Schools was no longer required to have education credentials. No education degree required. No teaching certification. No classroom experience necessary. This is corporate reform. Credentials do not matter, only "results," which almost always means standardized test scores.

The general Assembly gave Daley four years to prove that mayoral control of education works.[9] Daley must have convinced them; mayoral control of Chicago schools continues to this day.

During his remaining years as mayor, Daley appointed two Chicago Public Schools CEOs; the first was Paul Vallas.

The rest is counterproductive history.

PAUL VALLAS

Daley initially offered the schools CEO position to his Chief of Staff Gery Chico, who declined yet became president of the newly-created, Daley-appointed School Reform Board—and technically, the school CEO's boss. Vallas was Daley's next choice; as the City of Chicago's budget director, Vallas had a reputation for managing budgets and for reconciling with those upset by Vallas' budget cuts.[10] In the newly-created position of CEO, Vallas was indeed part of a top-down, business model of management. Though he is credited with some "experience" teaching "in Downstate schools and on an American Indian reservation in Montana,"[11] Vallas is not an educator. He neither holds degrees in education nor is he certified. Vallas has a B.A. in history and a masters in political science. He has been a revenue analyst, a public finance instructor, an aide to senate president, and executive director of the Illinois Economic and Fiscal Commission.[12]

Vallas is a businessman. A February 1996 *Chicago Tribune* article on Vallas notes his "education as a business" model in the following changes to "managing" education:

> ...Some of the individual decisions Vallas and his team have made [include]-the idea of putting 40 schools in remediation and allowing principals to suspend teachers without pay or a hearing.... ...

> Under the law, the new schools bosses essentially can hire and fire employees as they see fit, move out of the high-overhead Pershing Road headquarters, and use teacher pension money as well as funds once set aside for poor children to make ends meet in the district's general operating fund.

> They can swoop into non-performing schools, take out adults they believe are causing problems-which they have done-and shift difficult students to one of several alternative schools planned.[13]

A major push (and issue of controversy) in Vallas' remediation of public schools involves his declaring schools to be "in educational crisis." In September 1995, the School Reform board passed a nebulous school intervention plan hinging on criteria including a principal's failing to implement the school improvement plan, develop a "reasonable" budget, ensure safe school facilities or complete school opening-day paperwork. Given the Amendatory Act of 1995 that already granted Vallas carte blanche in the running of Chicago's schools, the School Reform Board was now merely offering a formality of agreement. Parents and community leaders were not included in any discussions of this "intervention" that could lead to principal and local school council member removal.[14]

Vallas also had the power to make budget cuts as he saw fit, which he did:

Weeks after taking the reins as schools CEO, Vallas ushered in a new era of austerity where once there had been rampant waste in city schools. He banned all out-of-town trips by central office staff and clipped funding for catered meals after board meetings.

This insulted many, including some of Vallas' own staff. [Chief Education Officer Lynn] St. James and one of her top aides were called on the carpet for outfitting their offices with new furniture.[15]

Vallas' budget cuts also included sale of surplus property; lowering the amount of funds paid to the teachers' pension fund; moving funds into the general fund that were formerly earmarked, and canceling a program for networking district computers.[16] Indeed, he proclaimed not only a balanced budget but also a surplus. As a 1995 *Chicago Tribune* article reports:

Vallas, while directing the bulk of the surplus to balance the budget over time, would use $35 million to: help schools extend the class day and year; move violent students from regular classrooms into several new alternative schools; send armies of tutors and mentors into schools to help students who consistently fail; and establish apprenticeship programs for high school students prone to dropping out.

"Student performance improves when schools are better organized, when you have a longer school year and when you get violent students out of the schools," Vallas said. "Failure is not an option for us; we have to deliver."[17]

In truth, the question on which Vallas' perceived "effectiveness" hinged was one raised by Bennett in 1987—dropout rates and test scores. To corporate reformers, such numbers—especially the test scores—are the primary indicator of education "success." As the 1996 *Chicago Tribune* article continues:

Conrad Worrill, professor at Northeastern Illinois University and head of the National Black United Front, said, "At this point in time [February 1996], it's very difficult to judge this new school team. I think Mr. Vallas is projecting himself as the great savior of Chicago public schools, when in fact what he really is a master of public relations.

"He seems to deal well with people. He speaks well and he has good presence. But the jury is still out. I haven's seen test scores rise."[18]

Vallas believes that the business model is the solution for achieving the ends of lower dropout rates and higher test scores:

In line with his corporate style, Vallas said he soon will create a new position-local school business manager-so that principals can spend less time doing tedious jobs such as checking bus schedules and school cleanliness and more time trying to boost students' test scores.

Within a year, he said, more city high schools and elementary schools will merge into "corporate campuses," united by a common academic theme and funded by adoptive local corporations. One such site, at Wendell Phillips High School Academy, already is in the making.

"This district has got to evolve and become more like a corporation. *This is essentially a $3 billion business,"* Vallas has said, *"and we've got to learn how to leverage our buying power."*[19] [Emphasis added.]

Vallas' idea of the "corporate campus merger" was supposed to yield higher test scores. Always it is about higher test scores. "Leveraging buying power" must lead to this end; otherwise, the "company" "goes under." It could go bankrupt. It could be sold and dismantled. Executives could be fired in yet another "takeover."

Public schools are not businesses. Students, faculty and communities become casualties.

In June 1996, the first standardized test scores were available to gauge Daley's and Vallas' school reform efforts: While elementary school scores rose on the Iowa Test of Basic Skills (ITBS), the high schools showed the lowest reading scores in six years: 18.2% of ninth graders and 24.6% of eleventh graders scored at or above the national norms. High school math scores dropped but not to the point of being the worst in the 1990s.[20] Of course, Vallas credited the elementary test score increases to the rigor of his reforms, including "toughened standards," personnel "changes," and the "threat" of summer school for eighth graders.

There is more to Vallas' retention methods with elementary school students. Specifically, elementary students in grades three, six, and eight were required to meet a certain scoring standard in order to pass to the next grade. Students who did not meet the standard were required to attend a six-week summer session focused on ITBS passage. At the end of these six weeks, students tested again. Those who did not meet the standard were retained. In the fall of 1997, approximately 20 percent of third graders and between 10 and 15 percent of sixth and eighth graders were not promoted. In addition, if a school had fewer than 15 percent of student scoring at or above national norms, it was placed on "probation"—which meant a looming possibility of faculty firings and/or reassignment.[21] In October 1996, 109 out of 557 of Chicago's public schools were placed on probation.[22] The standard for passing the eighth grade ITBS was raised for each year from 1997 to 2000, and in 2000, the standard for six graders was raised for ITBS.[23]

As to the high schools' low scores in 1996, one of the issues Vallas said was to blame was the size of the high schools. Notice the shift in focus from the "corporate merger" to the "small school":

> *Vallas blamed the poor high school scores on the vast size of most high schools, noting his plans to decrease size, create separate programs for freshmen, impose a standard curriculum and expand mandatory summer school for freshmen and sophomores who are behind.*[24]

As the years passed, schools yielding low test scores became the focus of increasingly drastic "reforms." In addition to "probation," the looming threat of state involvement, there was "intervention," the actual state involvement. The June 28, 2000, *Catalyst* (independent news magazine focused on Chicago Public Schools) notes the use of "intervention" on six (later amended to five) high schools based upon low test scores:

> *Board of Education officials announce plans to use sweeping powers for the first time in an attempt to upgrade six high schools with low test scores. Under state law, a process called "intervention" allows board officials to replace the principal, order new local school council elections and fire any school employee after an evaluation. The six schools initially slated for intervention are Bowen, Collins, DuSable, Juarez, Orr and South Shore; however, the board later decides not to use intervention at Juarez.*[25]

One month later, the "intervention" is approved by the board, excepting Juarez. Apparently the Juarez parents influenced the outcome:

> *The School Board approves the start of intervention, its latest attempt to shake up some of the city's poorest-performing high schools. At a board meeting today, the Academic Accountability Council recommends intervention at all 11 high schools with 15% or fewer students scoring at or above national norms. Due to limited resources, the board approved only five. Board President Gery Chico wants Juarez High School, which is not among the 11, to be included but pulls back after parents and staff from Juarez ask the board to reconsider.*[26]

Due to low test scores, time and again a principal is fired and a local board removed. If the state board "had more resources," it could have disrupted more schools, all for the shallow focus of test scores. As many hours as I have spent researching and reading on this reformer-lauded "disruptive innovation," the fact that so many seemingly intelligent people promote disruption as a means of promoting student achievement continues to astound me.

In 1997, test scores appeared to rise; a *Chicago Tribune* headline proclaimed that test scores "soar[ed] at schools on probation." However, upon closer scrutiny, such was not the case.[27] Vallas credited rising test scores to the system of placing schools on probation and "imposing curriculum" onto these schools; however, Donald Moore of Designs for Change refuted this connection. In the 1997 article, Moore notes a trend in improvement over "the last seven years" (1990–1997); thus, the overall trend predated mayoral control. Three years later, Moore presented evidence to show that schools placed on probation in 1996–97 still had roughly 80 percent of students scoring below the national average in reading in the spring of 2000.[28] Based upon his examination of the scoring trends over a decade (1990–2000), Moore makes a strong statement in opposition to Vallas' "disruptive reform":

> ... *The current evidence indicates that the school board's methods for carrying out probation did not work and **should not** serve as the basis for future improvement efforts.*
>
> *Based on DFC's research, one key priority... should be to invest in improving the **core educational program** during the regular school day, not to expand after school and summer school programs. More broadly, there should be a **vigorous public debate** about what has worked, based on independently verified research and open access to information.*[29] [Emphasis added.]

Moore considers the 84 schools that made notable, consistent, sustained gains on the ITBS not only during the period of Vallas' reforms (1995 to 2000) but also in the five years prior to mayoral control and Vallas' appointment (1990 to 1995). As a group, these schools improved ITBS reading scores from 23% of students scoring at or above national norms in 1990 to 32% in 1995, and they continued the increase throughout the reforms at a higher rate than other schools: 38% in 1997, to 45% in 2000. Moore notes that in 1990, none of the 84 schools had ITBS reading scores above the national average, but that by 2000, 29 of the 84 schools surpassed the national average. Certain qualities are associated with these "substantially up schools." Despite the high percentage (83%) of low income students, these notably improved schools included "effective" local school councils as rated by teachers; teachers who were vested in decision making, who felt that their own innovation was encouraged, and who felt collectively responsible; greater community outreach to families; students who felt safer at school. In addition, Moore notes the following comparison between these "substantially up schools" and those placed on probation:

> *Cooperative Adult Development was* <u>*vastly higher*</u> *in the Substantially Up Schools than in elementary schools that were placed on probation in 1996. Therefore, low achieving*

schools need intervention and support that rebuilds <u>the school as a human organiza-</u>
<u>*tion*</u>.[30]

Moore asserts that the probation schools, which still had 78% of students scoring below the national average in reading on the ITBS in spring 2000, need to be nurtured in the qualities of community and collaboration evident in the "substantially up schools." In short, punitive, top-down-instituted policies do not effectively improve public schools. Top-down procedures contribute to antagonistic relationships between those wielding power and other stakeholders, such as local school councils. Moreover, lower performing schools do not benefit from the weight of "bureaucratic procedures and paperwork to prove they are carrying the [shortlist-selected] curriculum out."[31] This finding directly contradicts Vallas' declaration, "Studies have indicated that the schools where we go in and dictate curriculum are the schools that seem to be doing the best."[32] Finally, mayoral control, with its narrow focus on increasing test scores "or else," leads to "a growing crisis in the city because many teaching positions are unfilled or have uncertified teachers in them, especially in inner city schools."[33]

This is a truth worth repeating: Test scores were notably higher in the Chicago schools fostering both collaboration and community than they were in the schools cowering under Vallas' punitive "probation."

In an interesting turn of events in fall 2000, Vallas relaxed the eighth grade promotion criteria of scoring at least at the 50th percentile on ITBS in math and reading; students below the cutoff could be promoted based on "classroom grades, attendance, completed homework, and good conduct."[34] This modifying of criteria for passing corresponded to the US Justice Department's dismissing allegations that the policy of promotion solely on test scores discriminated against minority students. It seems that common sense practice of using multiple criteria to gauge student academic success had to be coerced from the leadership of Chicago Public Schools.

Ironically, in December 2000, the School Reform Board voted to raise the credentialing criteria for Chicago Public Schools principals. It seems that credentials are important for principals but not for the schools' CEO, who simply must be appointed by the mayor. That same month, the board approved three new charter schools even though a slot existed for only two. In order to circumvent the law capping the number of charters, one of the schools was declared to be an extension of an existing school.[35] So, here one sees what has become a national phenomenon of charter school preference via rule bending even as the traditional public schools face "no excuses" punishment measures erroneously labeled as "reform."

Throughout his first few years as Chicago's CEO, Vallas demonstrated a publicly united front with Daley regarding reform decisions. However, in 1998, Vallas voiced a public opinion contrary to Daley's. This situation appears to have been "the crack that was to become a cavern" and would arguably lead to Vallas' exit. The issue at hand concerned whether or not to refuse promotion to students who did not pass ITBS after having been retained once already. Daley declared that he would indeed refuse promotion to such students:

> *"I will not socially promote children to high school, to allow them to drop out and go on,"* added the mayor [Daley], who had been lauded at the conference by other educators for Chicago's get-tough policy on social promotions—the passing of underperforming students to the next grade out of concern for students' self-esteem among peers.

> *"You want to promote them? You go promote them. And then you'll see them in the criminal justice system, and you'll be complaining about your taxes,"* he said.[36] [Emphasis added.]

The *Chicago Tribune* notes that such a policy could result in "segregat[ing] chronically failing students in what amounts to a separate school system."[37]

In his response, Daley makes some interesting extensions in logic. First, he assumes that refusing to promote students who do not meet the standard for ITBS will somehow prevent students' dropping out of school. However, research shows that students who are retained are more likely to drop out than their equally-low-performing, socially-promoted peers.[38] As Jimerson notes in the *California School Psychologist*:

> Several state and federal politicians have sought to end what is known as "social promotion," where a student is automatically advanced to the next grade with his or her peers.... This political trend has been perceived by many involved in education as a directive to retain students who do not meet or who fall below state performance standards. **However, research from the past century fails to demonstrate the effectiveness of grade retention for improving either academic achievement or socio-emotional adjustment....**[39] [Emphasis added.]

Next, Daley not only assumes that retention will prevent students from becoming involved in the criminal justice system; he assumes that retention will not increase taxes. Yet someone must bear the cost of requiring students to repeat a grade—possibly multiple times—until the student passes a standardized test. One might think of the immediate cost in terms of the amount of funding required to educate one student for one year.[40] In essence, the district retaining the student just added that cost. And the issue becomes more complex if so many students are retained that they require additional facilities. Even still, there is no guarantee that the retained students will automatically escape the criminal justice system.

Apparently, by the time that Daley's views were printed in the May 1998 *Chicago Tribune* article, Vallas had already publicly disagreed with Daley's views on mandatory, unlimited retention:

Earlier this week [of May 7, 1998], though, Vallas indicated a reluctance to hold kids back twice, saying the decision would be made by principals and regional officials who would have to carefully weigh the academic benefits versus the social downside.

"After the first retention, the social aspects of the retention are less of a concern," Vallas said. "But when you are talking about flunking for a second consecutive time, then obviously the social aspects have a much greater impact.

"The first retention is more automatic. On the second retention, we want to make a more deliberate decision. We want a collective decision because obviously retaining one student (the first time) . . . is not as draconian as retaining a student a second time."[41]

Vallas was willing to negotiate a second retention. He conceded the need to collaborate and the potentially negative social ramifications for the students. Daley was not willing to negotiate. The distinction is clear in the May 7, 1998, *Chicago Tribune* article cited above. In fact, Vallas refers to a second retention as "draconian," which likely did not reflect well on Daley. Two days later, the *Chicago Tribune* published a piece in which Vallas clearly backpedals:

Chicago Public Schools chief Paul Vallas denied Friday that he was in conflict with Mayor Richard Daley over remarks about whether the school system will continue to hold back students who fail a grade two years in a row.

"I was pretty clear over and over again that I did not feel that the mayor's statement was in any way inconsistent with the policy. But you can take the mayor's strongest statement and take our weakest statement and imply that there is some sort of contradiction," *Vallas said during a taping of WBBM-AM 780's "At Issue" program, to air Sunday at 9:30 a.m. and 9:30 p.m.*[42] [Emphasis added.]

Vallas is really reaching here, and the *Chicago Tribune* knows it:

As nearly all 430,000 Chicago schoolchildren took a nationally standardized exam this week to determine whether they will pass to the next grade, **Daley was asked if the board would flunk 3rd, 6th, 8th and 9th graders two consecutive times. "You better believe it," he replied. "We'll do that. You want to promote them? You go promote them."**

But Vallas said separately that before a student is flunked a second time there would be a review *by the teacher, principal and a board regional officer to weigh the potential social harm of the action against potential academic benefits.*

Older students who flunk elementary grades two or more times will be placed in one of the school board's transition centers at age 15 while trying to show they can do high school class work.[43] [Emphasis added.]

In an arguable demonstration of loyalty to Daley, Vallas states in a *Chicago Tribune* article one month later, in June 1998, that the gains made on tests are "due in large part to the initiatives that were done since the mayor took responsibility of the schools, pure and simple."[44] Vallas does not publicly credit himself with the improvements. He places the glory at the feet of Daley.

One must wonder upon reading the August 22, 1998, *Chicago Tribune* piece detailing the number of students retained twice whether Vallas continued his efforts to openly appear to support Daley's hard line on retention. So much for Vallas' earlier words about the "greater impact" of "social aspects" of retention on the students twice retained:

> *In a dramatic gesture to emphasize their intention not to soften a ban on automatically promoting failing pupils, Chicago school board officials will "double flunk" more than 1,300 3rd graders and 6th graders who failed to pass summer school two years in a row, officials said Friday.*
>
> *The decision means that those students, will in effect, be enrolled in their respective grades for the third consecutive year when school begins Tuesday.*[45]

As to Daley's May 1998 comment about "complaining about the taxes" if retention were not enforced a second time, it seems that the financial responsibility for attempting to have students who failed the ITBS twice to pass a third time would incur a high cost anyway, including $10 million for tutors and teachers. Vallas says "we" are "hanging tough" and not "compromising our standards."[46] In 1999, Vallas decided not to retain students who did not pass ITBS a third time. Astoundingly, amazingly, he made the declaration that these students would likely end up in special education:

> *Schools chief Paul Vallas told the Tribune the system will not hold back any student a third time in the same grade; the student will be promoted. But those students also will be screened for placement in special education, **and Vallas predicted that virtually all screenings will result in such placements.**[47]* [Emphasis added.]

Nothing like a timely screening and adherence to privacy rights. This is an incredible travesty. A student should never be required to fail for three years before a district investigates whether or not the student requires special education services. And to publicly announce that this would be the likely outcome for all who fail the ITBS three times—is this supposed to be the solution to keep students in school? Apparently Vallas has no concept of students' legal rights to privacy.

If there were a rift between Daley and Vallas before August 2000, it was likely widened by the opening lines of this *Chicago Tribune* article:

> **When Chicago Mayor Richard Daley speaks, city employees listen—but apparently not the city's schoolchildren.**
>
> *Although Daley gave his employees time off to walk their kids to their first day of classes this week—and urged the private sector to do the same—attendance was only 76 percent*

of the system's 435,000 kids. That means more than 100,000 students were absent.[48] [Emphasis added.]

And here comes Vallas' perhaps unknown disagreement with Daley's views on prompt arrival for the first day of school:

> *"...I think the major factor is the very early start,"* schools chief Paul Vallas said of the principals' explanations. "We have to figure out a way to have a three-week break instead of a two-week break."[49] [Emphasis added.]

The article continues by declaring the low turnout a "public relations embarrassment"—not exactly a sympathetic response.

Clearly Daley was not pleased with either the negative press nor Vallas' possible explanation for the low attendance. Three days later, the Chicago Tribune broadcasts Daley's public displeasure with Paul Vallas:

> **Mayor Richard Daley on Thursday ridiculed Chicago schools chief Paul Vallas' plan to start school later next year after the district was embarrassed this week with its worst first-day turnout since Daley took over the system in 1995.**
>
> **Daley scoffed at excuses** that a short vacation after summer school led to 103,000 student absences Tuesday.[50] [Emphasis added.]

In response, Vallas decidedly and publicly contradicts Daley:

> Vallas said Thursday he still feels a longer break between summer and fall sessions is needed and said he plans to start school later next year.[51]

It was the beginning of the end for Vallas as CEO of Chicago Public Schools. Aside from his public disagreements with Vallas, Daley was not pleased with the reading scores; he contended that reading is the basis for other subjects. Daley was also not pleased with the fact that reading scores continued to be notably lower than math scores. The September 2000 *Catalyst* did not offer any information to quell Daley's concerns, for it mentions a Brookings Study demonstrating a "flattening out" of elementary reading scores.[52] In February 2001, Daley called for educators to "think outside the box"; Vallas immediately responded with three new-yet-increasingly-controlling "initiatives": Even greater control of curriculum; expansion of summer school, and a program for high schools to focus on reading and algebra.[53]

Despite his plans to ramp up reforms, in June 2001, Vallas officially released the news of his departure as CEO of Chicago Public Schools. For weeks, rumors of Vallas's departure were alive and well in public places. Daley said nothing to dispel them.

Time for Vallas to go. He chose to resign.

In the June 7, 2001, *Chicago Tribune* piece detailing his departure, Vallas was to the point:

"Am I going? Yeah, I'm going, OK? Simple as that," Vallas said. "I don't want to play these games for another year. ... I've tried not to respond to the anonymous this and the anonymous that or the high-level sources close to the mayor this and the close to the mayor that ...

"So you want to know if I'm leaving? Yeah. I'm leaving. Yeah, I'm gonna be gone. End of story. So put it in the paper tomorrow."[54]

Four days before Vallas' resignation, the Chicago Teachers Union elected a new president, eighth-grade teacher Deborah Lynch-Walsh, largely on an anti-Vallas ticket. Lynch-Walsh was also vocal regarding the union's complicity with Daley's reforms. Though Vallas "downplayed any potential conflict with the new union leadership, as has Daley,"[55] it is clear that Lynch-Walsh meant business:

> *...Lynch-Walsh is expected to unleash labor's most vocal assault yet on initiatives originally designed to bring more accountability to teachers and their schools: academic probation, re-engineering and intervention. These crackdowns put the worst teachers in the worst schools on notice, if not the chopping block.*[56]

When Vallas left Chicago, he was facing news of flattened test scores, a new union leadership poised to resist his and Daley's increasingly punitive reform agenda, and public displeasure from Daley, the sole individual in charge of his employment as CEO.

Arguably, it was not a successful departure. Yet Vallas' career as an education reformer was far from over. Next, however, the story of Chicago reform continues with Vallas' successor, Arne Duncan.

CHAPTER 7

THE CHICAGO CONNECTION: DUNCAN (WITH OBAMA IN THE MIX)

In 1995, the Illinois legislature altered the manner in which public schools were governed by shifting power from the school board to the mayor. As mayor, Richard Daley appointed Paul Vallas as CEO of Chicago's public schools; Vallas was known for his work with managing budgets, and this quality initially endeared him with Daley. However, the top-down methods Daley and Vallas attempted to use in order to "improve" Chicago's schools yielded only years of chaos and controversy. By the time that Daley and Vallas were openly contradicting one another as to the management of the schools, coveted test scores had not risen nearly enough to quell Daley's displeasure with Vallas and his publicly disagreeing with the only man who held Vallas' job in his hands.

As is always true in the tightly-knit, corporate-reformer world, all that really matters is the veneer of improvement via the Almighty Test Score. In true reformer fashion, Daley did not consider that the top-down attempts at school reform could be the greater problem. Instead, he focused on Vallas' "resignation" and appointed as CEO another reform-minded individual

A Chronicle of Echoes: Who's Who in the Implosion of American Public Education,
pages 111–121.

who could draw from the privatizers' standard set of pressure-cooker tactics in the name of Improving Education: Arne Duncan. It is through Duncan and Daley's successor Rahm Emanuel that the President himself would become closely identified not only with a national educational reform agenda, but also with the storminess of dysfunctional reform in the Windy City. This chapter concerns Duncan; the third Chicago Connection chapter concerns Emanuel.

ARNE DUNCAN

On June 25, 2001, Daley announced his selection of Arne Duncan as Paul Vallas' successor for CEO of Chicago's public schools.[1] Like Vallas, Arne Duncan is not an educator. That is quite the statement to associate with the man who was appointed US Secretary of Education in 2009 by President Obama. Duncan graduated with a degree in sociology in 1987 and was a professional basketball player in Australia from 1987 to 1991.[2]

In 1992, Duncan's childhood friend John W. Rogers, Jr., chairman and founder of Ariel Investments, appointed Duncan as "director" of the Ariel Education Initiative, a program described on the Ariel Investments website as follows:

> *In 1989, John W. Rogers, Jr. chairman and founder of Ariel Investments, created the Ariel Foundation. In 1991, the Ariel Foundation "adopted" forty sixth grade students at William Shakespeare Elementary on the south side of Chicago and promised to make college affordable for every student who graduated from high school. Through these efforts, the Foundation attempted to create a program that could serve as a model for serving inner city youth involving academic enrichment, mentoring, family support, leadership development and community service opportunities. The experience with the sixth grade class encouraged the Ariel Foundation to do more, starting with changing its name to Ariel Education Initiative (AEI) to better reflect its focus and mission. Today, AEI's primary focus is Ariel Community Academy and its investment curriculum.[3]*

As to the "investment curriculum": Ariel Community Academy offers students a financial curriculum based in the stock market. Each first-grade class is given a $20,000 grant to invest through eighth grade. The profit is split equally between a class gift to the school and money for individual college funds for the students. The idea is for one eighth-grade class to return the original $20,000 to the school for the incoming first grade class.[4]

"Adopting" inner city youth is certainly admirable, especially since a successful investment company investing in a small number of children is able to contribute more money per child than is afforded per pupil by public schools. And from listening to interviews with Rogers, I believe his interest is genuine in helping these children succeed. Nevertheless, the competition between Ariel and "other" schools is part of the Academy's promotional information on the Ariel Investments website. In 1996, Chicago's mayoral-controlled reforms closed William Shakespeare Elementary, and Ariel Investments reopened it as Ariel Community Academy. According to Rogers, the Academy is not a charter;[5] Chicago did not get charter schools until 1997.[6] Although the Harvard article refers to the Academy as a charter,[7] Ariel Community Academy is not listed as such on the June 2013 Chicago Public Schools website.[8] Ariel Investments compares its school to other district and state schools and notes how much "better" the Academy is. Ariel makes no mention of funding advantage its Academy has, particularly compared to traditional public schools. Rogers' Academy is supported by public funds (and still billed as a public school[9] for its drawing upon public funding) as well as any additional funds Ariel and "several friends"[10] choose to devote to the school. The New Public Schooling (i.e., nontraditional vs. traditional public school) has become a competition in which "our school" must be "the best." Privatization is a competition, not a collaboration; it is, as Duncan promotes from the White House, a "race to the top"—and a chance to point out that others are "on the bottom." The "urgency" promoted by corporate reform (and by Duncan himself)[11] is an ironic contrast to the Ariel Investment company logo, "Slow and Steady Wins the Race."[12]

I noted that Duncan was the "director" of the Ariel Education Initiative. The term "director" is in quotes since the only cited article I could find with Duncan as "director" is the Wikipedia article on Duncan;[13] however, the Harvard citation associated with the article does not include such a title,[14] and Duncan's own US Department of Education also includes no reference to Duncan as being "director" of Ariel Education Initiative.[15] Both the Harvard and USDOE references merely note that Duncan "ran" the Ariel Education Initiative. In an interview discussion between Rogers and Duncan, Rogers talks of Duncan's and Duncan's sister Sarah's "vision" for the Ariel Education Initiative, but again, no use of any specific title for Duncan.[16] Thus, even though he was involved with the Ariel Education Initiative, there is no evidence that Duncan held a formal position with a clearly defined job description. If a man becomes US Secretary of Education, he ought to make the comprehensive details of his professional experience public. The record of Duncan's professional life has its vagaries.

The Ariel Investments website includes no detailed account of Duncan's role with either the Ariel Education Initiative or Ariel Community Academy. A *Smart Money* article on Rogers notes that Arne Duncan was "instrumental" in establishing this quasi-public-private school via "providing funding and support,"[17] a rather nebulous description for Duncan's involvement, especially involvement that led to his being placed in Obama's cabinet. Furthermore, though the Harvard article on Duncan promotes the view that Duncan "pursued" education as a career, Duncan never formally taught in a classroom setting. As a Duncan "puff piece," the article fails to expose this amazing truth.[18] Another fluff article, this one in the *Washington Post*, also ignores Duncan's nonexistent professional teaching career:

> *Education has always been a personal crusade for Duncan, who grew up tutoring kids (and being tutored by others) at his mother's after-school program on the South Side of Chicago. He wrote his undergraduate thesis on America's underclass and mentored children while playing professional basketball in Australia. At the press conference when Obama announced Duncan as his pick for education secretary, Duncan called schooling "the civil rights issue of our generation." He has spent most of this decade as the CEO of the Chicago Public School system, the third-largest in the country.*[19]

Duncan's "personal crusade" led him to a degree in sociology and the basketball court, not the classroom. Then, voila, Duncan became celebrated as a great educational leader. Strangely, Duncan's official USDOE bio does not account for 1998 through 2001.[20] However, a *Time* article on Duncan notes that in 1998, he was "hired to run Chicago's magnet schools program."[21] This information is confirmed in this January 2009 usnews.com article:

> *Duncan took a job with the Chicago public school system in 1998. He headed the system's magnet school program and served as the deputy chief of staff of the system. Three years later, he was chosen to lead the system. He has been Chicago Public Schools CEO since 2001.*[22]

So. Duncan played basketball, "ran" a single school, then "took a job" *heading* the magnet schools for an entire school system, then he was "chosen" to *lead the entire city system...* and then... and, why not?... "chosen" to "lead" the nation in education.

Rod Serling should be narrating this.

Duncan has no accredited, credentialed training in education. He never held a formal, licensed teaching position. He holds no degrees in educational history or pedagogy or policy. He did help his childhood friend with a community initiative and then a quasi-public school. Where did that take Duncan?

To the piece missing from Duncan's USDOE bio: Deputy Chief of Staff for former-Daley-Chicago-Schools-CEO Paul Vallas.

Perhaps Duncan omitted from his USDOE bio his time as deputy superintendent since that was first-ever Chicago education CEO Paul Vallas' time in the reformer spotlight. After all, Duncan's really destructive impact upon Chicago's public schools did not occur until 2001, the year that Vallas resigned as CEO.[23] Once Vallas was gone, Duncan became CEO. During his time "leading" Chicago education, Duncan's "achievement" involved choreographing a chronic disruption of school closures. Duncan's promoters try to present closing schools as a positive move:

As CEO, Duncan pursued a mix of programs—some system- wide, some fine-grained. The centerpiece is Renaissance 2010, an ambitious effort to shut down 60 troubled schools and create 100 new state-of-the-art schools across the city. As part of that plan, Duncan pushed to expand the city's roster of charter schools—it now stands at 67—and embraced the turnaround concept, in which a school is temporarily shut down, staff members fired, transferred, or asked to reapply, and a new staff built from the ground up.[24] [Emphasis added.]

Pause and consider the incredible spin placed upon Duncan's role in school closures: an "ambitious effort to shut down 60 troubled schools." No mention is made of the incredible community upheaval school closure causes, the ripple effect to the lives of all involved, all of the firings, the employment uncertainty, the upset to students from knowing their school is "gone," and the utter foolishness behind the entire idea of reformer-promoted "disruptive innovation." Instead, this article downplays the entire traumatic event as "temporary" shut-down.

Duncan's uses his own USDOE bio attempts to place a halo on his head for his role in disrupting the lives of numerous Chicago students and their families. The tactic used in this case is to sandwich the ugly truth between reframed "happy facts," including leading with Duncan's "opening more than 100 new schools" before hitting the reader with the slanted statement, "closing down underperforming schools":

Before becoming secretary of education, Duncan served as the chief executive officer of the Chicago Public Schools (CPS), a position he held from June 2001 through December 2008. **In that time, he won praise for uniting education reformers, teachers, principals and business stakeholders behind an aggressive education reform agenda that included opening more than 100 new schools, expanding after-school and summer learning programs, closing down underperforming schools, increasing early childhood and college access, dramatically boosting the caliber of teachers, and building public-private partnerships around a variety of education initiatives.**[25] [Emphasis added.]

Like many would-be-noneducators-gone-reformers, Duncan's "reform" is described as "aggressive." That it is: Invading communities to both declare and enforce school closures is certainly "aggressive," a term associated with bullying behavior.

(Since I have written and read extensively on the current well-financed obsession with the privatization of public education, the words "urgent," "bold," "sweeping," and "aggressive" are beyond clichéd therefore rendered empty of meaning for me, perhaps forever.)

Via former Mayor Daley, Duncan disguised his ill-informed, bullying behavior "Renaissance 2010." Here is the short word on the "program" as per the Chicago Public Schools website:

In June 2004, Mayor Richard Daley launched Renaissance 2010, a bold initiative whose goal is to increase the number of high-quality educational options in communities across Chicago by 2010. New schools are created through a competitive, community-based selection process which establishes a set of high standards to which every new school will be held accountable. In 2005, Chicago Public Schools opened the first "cohort" of Renaissance 2010 schools.[26]

In order to have students for these "new schools," other schools must first be closed. Of course, the "set of high standards" is inextricably connected to student standardized test scores. In a June 2009 report by the Civic Committee of the Commercial Club of Chicago, a group that initially supported mayoral control of schools,[27,28] the supposedly amazing improvements in the Chicago Public Schools during Duncan's tenure are brought into question—and rightly so. Consider these excerpts from the Civic Committee report, aptly titled, "Still Left Behind." Keep in mind that these were the most recent data on the Chicago Public Schools at the time that Duncan breezed into his USDOE position:

The 2008 test data show that most students in the Chicago Public Schools continue to fail. Roughly half of CPS students drop out before graduation or fail to graduate with their class. Of those who are left to take the PSAE test in the second semester of 11th grade, over 70% fail to meet State standards. The ACT test results show the percentages of 11th graders who meet "college readiness" benchmarks (as established by ACT) in math and science are tiny: 16% in math, and 9% in science; and most of these are in Chicago's few "selective enrollment" high schools. When one looks at the nonselective enrollment high schools—those which serve the neighborhoods of Chicago—the percentages of 11th graders ready for college are even lower: 6.4% in math, and 2.3% in science. In many high schools, not one 11th grader is on track to succeed in a college-level math or science course.

CPS has suggested that the schools have dramatically improved. It reached this conclusion by largely ignoring the high schools and focusing on the elementary grades, where it is true that ISAT scores have jumped remarkably over the past seven years. As recently as January 2009 [The month of Duncan's USDOE appointment], CPS distributed brochures showing that 8th grade reading scores improved from 55% of students meeting/

exceeding standards in 2004—to 76% in 2008. And 8th grade math scores improved from 33% in 2004 to 70% in 2008. But these huge increases reflect changes in the tests and testing procedures—not real student improvement.

And now, a zinger tied to the Civic Committee report title:

> **The reality is that most of Chicago's students are still left far behind. Real student performance appears to have gone up a little in Chicago elementary schools during the past few years–and even those gains then dissipate in high school.**[29] [Emphasis added.]

These are the results of seven years of Duncan as CEO of Chicago Public Schools. These are the results of mayoral control of schools initially supported by the group conducting the report. And these are results that Barack Obama openly and selectively cited[30] *in favor* of Duncan's appointment as reported in *USA Today*:

> *In December [2008], Obama said that during a seven-year tenure, Duncan had boosted elementary school test scores "from 38% of students meeting the standards to to 67%"—a gain of 29 percentage points. But the new report* [the Civic Committee report cited above] *found that, adjusting for changes in tests and procedures, students' pass rates grew only about 8 percentage points.*

> *Obama also said Chicago's dropout rate "has gone down every year he's been in charge." Though that's technically true, the committee says it's still unacceptably high: About half of Chicago students drop out of the city's non-selective-enrollment high schools.* **And more than 70% of 11th-graders fail to meet state standards, a trend that "has remained essentially flat" over the past several years.**

> *Even among those who graduate, it says, skills are poor: An analysis of students entering the Chicago City Colleges in fall 2006 showed that 69% were not prepared for college-level reading, 79% were not prepared for writing, and 95% were not prepared for math.*

> **"Performance is very bad, very weak,"** *says Civic Committee president Eden Martin.*[31] [Emphasis added.]

I am willing to allow Duncan to take full credit for the "results" highlighted in the Civic Committee report. He deserves nothing less.

The failure of Duncan's school closure "innovation" is no better illustrated than in the situation at Dodge Elementary. Dodge was a school supposedly "turned around" as the result of Duncan's closure of the school in 2002.

Dodge Elementary was the site where Obama chose to announce Duncan's appointment. And Obama used the occasion to feature Duncan's "success" at "school turnaround":

> *In 2008, Dodge was where then president-elect Barack Obama announced Duncan as his pick for U.S. Secretary of Education.*
>
> *"He's shut down failing schools and replaced their entire staffs, even when it was unpopular," Obama said at the time.* **"This school right here, Dodge Renaissance Academy, is a perfect example. Since this school was revamped and reopened in 2003, the number of students meeting state standards has more than tripled."** [32] [Emphasis added.]

Obama is certain of this "success," just as he was certain of the "boost" in elementary test scores and the reduction of the dropout rate disputed by the June 2009 Civic Committee report.

Obama sees Dodge as the picture of Duncan's "turnaround" success. That was June 2009.

In 2013, under direction of Chicago Mayor Rahm Emanuel, Dodge has been closed.

The "turned around" Dodge apparently needs another "turn." It is being "relocated from its building" due to under enrollment. The same private operator of Dodge has just lost its right to run another "turnaround" school, Bethune. As WBEZ education reporter Becky Vevea reports:

> *Dodge is closing its doors.*
>
> **In fact, all three of the schools that would eventually help to launch Duncan's signature Renaissance 2010 initiative are getting shaken up by the current CPS administration.** *Williams Elementary and Middle School will close. (Drake Elementary will take over the building.)* **The Dodge building will close. (Dodge will technically continue to operate but will move 1.3 miles west to share a building with Morton Elementary.)** *The school that now operates in the old Terrell building, ACE Tech Charter School, was placed on an academic warning list in February, and district officials have warned if it doesn't improve they will close it down.*
>
> *And for the first time, CPS is pulling the plug on a "turnaround" school, Bethune Elementary. Just four years ago* [on Duncan's watch], *all Bethune staff was fired and the privately run, nonprofit Academy for Urban School Leadership took over—another example of the school reform strategy that says a clean slate can lead to better schools. AUSL also operates Dodge and Morton.* [33] [Emphasis and commentary added.]

Vevea then asks the Question of the Age:

All these changes raise a much bigger question. Does the idea that closing down bad schools and opening new ones actually work? Does it lead to better schools?[34]

Notice the incredibly weak response from Greg Richmond, former head of the Chicago Public Schools Office of New Schools until 2005. Richmond is currently president and CEO of the National Association of Charter School Authorizers and chair of Illinois State Charter School Commission:

> *"I think we have to keep trying until we find some things that work and these are very difficult circumstances and even the most talented people or some of the most talented schools may not work for some reason," says Richmond. "Does that mean we were wrong to try it? I don't think it means we were wrong. It was a very promising program and we tried it. But it didn't work. Then you recognize it and then you move on. I would rather see that attitude than an attitude that keeps trying something that's failing year after year."*[35]

What? Closing a school, firing the entire faculty, handing the school over to a private provider—all of this didn't work—after it was forced on Chicago as The Solution? Well, we just need to keep trying—keep closing the same schools over and over, keep firing faculty, keep shifting students around. Just don't ask about long-term costs, both financial and psychological. Just keep trying.

Duncan landed in DC. Renaissance 2010 definitely benefited him.

Perhaps he could celebrate by earning a teaching credential and earning actual classroom teaching experience. I know. It's a lot to ask. After all, he is busy promoting Race to the Top, promoted as "real time competition state by state,"[36] the whitewashed tomb of No Child Left Behind, with its continued emphasis on test scores, including the use of test scores in teacher evaluation (i.e., value-added modeling); its promoting of the never-piloted Common Core State Standards, its requiring the removal of caps on charter schools and the "turning around" of "low performing" schools (as determined by test scores), its requiring that states build data systems, and its offering states what appears to be a lot of money until one considers the costs of implementing RTTT.[37] The $75 to $700 million a state receives for "opting out" of NCLB and into RTTT is dust blowing across a deserted street. Illusory. And in keeping with the true spirit of competition, most states that applied received no money. A few "winners"; mostly "losers."[38,39]

Not everyone is happy with Obama's choice of Arne Duncan as US Secretary of Education and of Obama's actively promoting the test-score-centered, education privatization agenda. The group MoveOn.org started an online petition directed at President Obama for Duncan's removal and replacement with Linda Darling-Hammond, "a teacher." (Darling-Hammond does document several years of teaching experience aside from her years as a university professor.) [40] The petition includes this request regarding the quality of public education made available to all students:

> *The three most trumpeted and simultaneously most destructive aspects of the united "school reform" agenda are these:*
> 1. *turning over public assets and spaces to private management;*
> 2. *dismantling and opposing any independent, collective voice of teachers; and*
> 3. *reducing education to a single narrow metric that claims to recognize an educated person through a test score.*
>
> *While there's absolutely no substantive proof that this approach improves schooling for children, it chugs along unfazed. **Race to the Top is but one example of incentivizing bad behavior and backward ideas about education: It's one state against another, this school against that one, and my second grade in fierce competition with the second grade across the hall. Arne Duncan attended the University of Chicago Laboratory Schools...; you [Obama] sent your kids to Lab, and so did your friend Rahm Emanuel. There students found small classes, abundant resources,** and opportunities to experiment and explore, ask questions and pursue answers to the far limits, **and a minimum of time-out for standardized testing.** They found, as well, **a respected and unionized teacher corps,** people who were **committed to a life-long career in teaching** and who were **encouraged to work cooperatively** for their mutual benefit **(and who never would settle for being judged, assessed, rewarded, or punished based on student test scores).** In a vibrant democracy, whatever the most privileged parents want for their children must serve as a minimum standard for what we as a community want for all of our children. **Every child deserves the type of education your children receive.** [41] [Empha-sis added.]*

A powerful observation: Duncan promotes the idea that his children attend "public school," yet a lab school is a higher-order public school, one associated with a university. The request that all students be afforded the same quality of public education as Duncan and Emanuel experienced is a reasonable one.

I realize this next statement might sound humorous, but there is serious-ness behind it:

> *I wonder if Obama chose Duncan over Darling-Hammond since Darling-Hammond did not play basketball with him in his youth.*

The connections are just too close to ignore.

For anyone who doubts the power of the "Chicago connection" between Obama and Duncan, consider this admission in the CBS report announc-ing Duncan's US Secretary of Education appointment:

A 44-year-old Harvard graduate, Duncan has played pickup basketball with Mr. Obama since the 1990s. Duncan co-captained the Harvard basketball team.[42]

Prior to Obama's slighting Darling-Hammond and appointing Duncan as US Secretary of Education, Duncan, basketball player-gone-education-administrator, had just completed a seven-year stint as placed CEO of Chicago Public Schools. He closed and reopened schools for seven years, and there were no "remarkable" gains, as one can see even from the excerpt of the Civic Committee report cited previously. But President Obama *did* play basketball with Duncan, so that must be enough for this Cabinet appointment. Duncan's credentials certainly cannot recommend him; neither can close scrutiny of his Chicago Public Schools CEO legacy.

CHAPTER 8

THE CHICAGO CONNECTION: EMANUEL (WITH OBAMA STILL IN THE MIX)

Chicago and reform have a long and complicated relationship, not the least of which concerns Chicago reformer connections to the White House via Arne Duncan. However, Duncan is not Obama's only Chicago connection to grace the Oval Office. Obama also has ties to current Chicago Mayor Rahm Emanuel, who is wreaking his own brand of havoc on the Chicago Public Schools. In January 2009, both Duncan and Emanuel headed for DC and Obama appointments. Emanuel left DC and returned to Chicago in October 2010 to run for mayor. In 2011, Emanuel garnered 55% of the vote and replaced Daley, who had been Chicago's mayor for over two decades and who decided not to run.[1]

In 1989, Emanuel worked as a fundraiser for the Daley campaign.[2]

Here it is again, evidence of a mighty tight Chicago group.

Emanuel had been to the White House before, from 1993–98, as former President Bill Clinton's senior advisor. He resigned from that post, too, that time to become an investment banker. In true reformer style, Emanuel had no prior banking experience and "just thought he would try his hand" at

A Chronicle of Echoes: Who's Who in the Implosion of American Public Education,
pages 123–136.

banking. Two years later, Clinton appointed Emanuel to the board of directors of the Federal Home Loan Mortgage Corporation, better known as Freddie Mac. In short, the books were manipulated, and Obama declined release of public records of Freddie Mac minutes and correspondence during Emanuel's time as director.[3] In its 2003 report, the Office of Federal Housing Enterprise Oversight (OFHEO) accused the entire board, Emanuel included, of "complacency," "failure to ensure the hiring of qualified executives for key positions," and "ineffective oversight of management and operations and condition of Freddie Mac."[4] The auditors concisely summarize the issue from the outset of the OFHEO investigative report:

> In the early 1990s, Freddie Mac promoted itself to investors as "Steady Freddie," a company of strong and steady growth in profits. During that period the company developed a corporate culture that placed a very high priority on meeting those expectations, **including, when necessary, using means that failed to meet its obligations to investors, regulators and the public. The company employed a variety of techniques ranging from improper reserve accounts to complex derivative transactions to push earnings into future periods and meet earnings expectations. Freddie Mac cast aside accounting rules, internal controls, disclosure standards, and the public trust in the pursuit of steady earnings growth.** The conduct and intentions of the Enterprise were hidden and were revealed only by a chain of events that began when Freddie Mac changed auditors in 2002. This report describes the **circumstances leading to Freddie Mac's $5 billion restatement** [necessary correction to the numbers] and makes recommendations on corrective and preventative measures.[5]

The mismanagement of Freddie Mac was tied to the housing crisis still very much alive and well (and publicized for the Emanuel-Obama connection) in 2009. As the *Chicago Tribune* observes in March 2009:

> As gatekeeper to Obama, Emanuel now plays a critical role in addressing the nation's mortgage woes and fulfilling the administration's pledge to impose responsibility on the financial world.

> Emanuel's Freddie Mac involvement has been a prominent point on his political résumé, and his healthy payday from the firm has been no secret either. **What is less known, however, is how little he apparently did for his money and how he benefited from the kind of cozy ties between Washington and Wall Street that have fueled the nation's current economic mess.**[6] [Emphasis added.]

Chicago Tribune blogger Eric Zorn summarizes information contained on subsequent pages of the OFHEO report:

> On Emanuel's watch, the board was told by executives of a plan to use accounting tricks to mislead shareholders about outsize profits the government-chartered firm was then reaping from risky investments. The goal was to push earnings onto the books in future years, ensuring that Freddie Mac would appear profitable on paper for years to come and helping maximize annual bonuses for company brass....[7]

Emanuel was never formally charged with wrongdoing in the Freddie Mac scandal; however, it is certainly interesting that he announced "abruptly" his resignation as Obama chief of staff in October 2010. The official word from Obama was that Emanuel was leaving in order to pursue his "dream job" as Chicago mayor given that longtime Mayor Daley announced his decision to not run for re-election in 2011.[8] So, here one witnesses a convenient exit for Emanuel and his questionable Freddie Mac involvement.

Again with that tight-knit Chicago connection.

Perhaps it was merely a gift of timing—for Emanuel, not for Chicago.

Daley's decision to not seek another term marked the end of an era in which the mayor's office was steeped in scandal, including shady financial connections between one childhood friend of Daley's who was employed by the city offering city contracts to another childhood friend; Daley's friends and neighbors winning an exclusive city contract; other individuals' directing city contracts to family members; the purposive directing of city contracts to specific companies, including those that contributed to the Daley mayoral campaign; a continuing scandal regarding abuses of power in the Chicago Police Department; high-ranking individuals' manipulation of blue-collar jobs and promotions, and Daley's son and nephew conducting business with the city while concealing their connection to its mayor. Daley was never implicated in any of these numerous scandals. In 2009, the mayor's approval rating was the lowest it has even been: 35%. His 22-year tenure ended May 16, 2011.[9]

Mayor Emanuel assumed office that same day: May 16, 2011. Prior to his assuming office, Emanuel discussed his education reform plans for Chicago, including a longer school day and disabling teachers' right to strike. He offered no details regarding how the city would pay for the extended school day. Chicago Public Schools already expected an $820 million deficit.[10]

It seems Emanuel's plan was just to force teachers to comply. As it was, Emanuel was going to have to renegotiate the teachers' contract—set to expire June 2012—with the union. The 2011 Illinois legislature approved of Emanuel's reform requests:

> *The changes would require that* **75 percent of union members approve a strike** *and allow Chicago Public Schools leaders to lengthen the time kids are in school without having to negotiate.* **Unions still could bargain over additional pay or benefits if more time is added.**

> *Emanuel has advocated for a longer school day and year, tying teacher tenure to performance evaluations, requiring that layoffs not rely strictly on seniority, and raising the threshold for strikes.*

> *The mayor-elect largely got what he wanted in the legislation. Emanuel has never specified how much longer the school day or school year should be, just that they be extended.*[11]
> [Emphasis added.]

Though the Chicago Teachers Union (CTU) generally agreed with the longer school day and the strike threshold, CTU President Karen Lewis notes Emanuel's offering no additional pay up front:

> *"Mr. Emanuel came to Springfield looking to tack on two hours to the school day and two weeks to the school year without pay," Lewis said in a statement. "But all he got was language."*[12]

In his appointment of the seven-member School Reform Board and his selection of the next schools' CEO, Emanuel's intention to continue to "reform" Chicago's public schools was clear. Emanuel's board appointees included director of Denver Public Schools' Office of School Reform and Innovation Noemi Donoso, whose department manages the district's charter schools; former businessman and Academy of Urban School Leadership Managing Director of Finance Tim Cawley, whose :"Academy" is comprised of "turnaround" schools, and USDOE Special Assistant to the Assistant of Vocational and Adult Education Andrea Saenz, whose position includes "data-driven performance management for the Philadelphia Public Schools."[13]

Finally, New Chicago CEO Jean-Claude Brizard hailed from the skirts of New York Chancellor Joel Klein; as superintendent of schools in Rochester, New York, Brizard promoted the usual corporate reform menu of increasing charter schools, instituting merit pay, and advocating for test-based teacher evaluation.[14] Two months prior to his Chicago appointment, in February 2011, the Rochester Teachers Association voted "no confidence" in Brizard—with a notable 80% teacher turnout and a 95% "no confidence" vote.[15]

Regarding Emanuel's hiring Brizard, CTU President Karen Lewis commented, "This is going to be a hot, buttery mess."[16] However, the "mess" was nothing new. Following Arne Duncan's move to DC, Daley appointed two other CEOs. The first was Chicago police officer Ron Huberman, who resigned on November 29, 2010[17] and who made news earlier in 2010 for having two cars paid for by the so-broke-we-must-close-schools district. Huberman's cars cost "at least $1800 a month, not including driver's salary."[18] Following Huberman's departure, Daley appointed Chicago Community Trust CEO Terry Manazy as interim schools CEO.[19] Manazy was only schools CEO for five months when Emanuel hired Brizard.

Vallas, Duncan, Huberman, Manazy, Brizard. A reformer revolving door.

Brizard was Emanuel's kind of reformer, and Emanuel, yet another corporate-reform-minded Chicago mayor:

> *In naming Brizard, Emanuel was sending a clear signal: He was going to push the same kind of aggressive reform agenda as Mayor Michael Bloomberg had in New York. And Emanuel has—lengthening Chicago's notoriously short school day, backing charter schools and promoting tougher evaluations of teachers. He has not done this with any particular finesse. The move to extend the school day had even many parents complaining about how it was handled. Then again, neither did Bloomberg.*[20]

Extending the school day did not happen as a uniform policy in Chicago for the 2011–12 school year. What did happen, however, was that Emanuel's newly-appointed school board voted to rescind the teachers' annual four-percent raise. So, not only was Emanuel asking for a longer school day without offering compensation; he removed the current pay raise teachers were expecting. AND he knew he must negotiate a new contract with CTU at the end of what would be his first school year as mayor. The legislature had approved the longer school day, and it was to take effect for certain once the union contract was renegotiated—and regardless of what teachers thought.[21]

I think Emanuel believed he had the union in a corner; after all, CTU would now need for 75% of union members to agree in order to have a strike. Surely that would not happen.

In late August 2011, Brizard offered elementary teachers a 2% raise in exchange for adding 90 minutes to the school day and 2 weeks to the school year. The union declined.[22]

A major question involved whether the Chicago Public Schools really had a much shorter school day when compared to other Chicago districts. It doesn't appear to be the case:

> *The tongue-lashings Chicago Public Schools has endured in the last several weeks over its short school day—**U.S. Education Secretary Arne Duncan called it a "disgrace"**— have overshadowed the fact that that many suburban students aren't receiving much more instruction time than CPS.*
>
> ***Affluent Glen Ellyn's two elementary districts both offer five hours, 15 minutes of instruction daily, only seven minutes more than CPS reports.***[23] [Emphasis added.]

It's heartwarming to know that Duncan remains supportive of Chicago Public Schools—especially since the issue he broadcasts nationally as a "disgrace," the shorter day, was an issue not addressed in his seven years as CEO. I suppose it is only a "disgrace" now that he has been distanced from the responsibility.

In addition, as CTU President Karen Lewis has said, the question is not one of a "longer" school day but a "better" school day.[24] She is not alone:

> *Ultimately, it's not about how long the day is but how the time is used, said Jennifer Davis, co-founder and president of the National Center on Time & Learning, a Boston-based advocacy group for longer school days.*
>
> *"There is mounting evidence about the impact when the time is used well; that is the key, of course," Davis said. "If you look across the country at schools and districts that have experimented with more time, there have been some mixed results. That's why it has to be more time, thoughtfully used with quality teaching.*[25]

Reformers like their numbers, however. Emanuel continued to push for a longer school day, and some elementary schools accepted the deal—for up to $150,000 per school and a one-time stipend of $1200 per teacher. The union filed a grievance regarding this practice of schools choosing independently to accept the terms of a longer day.[26]

In March 2012, the issue of the longer school day was still unresolved, with parent groups pressing for input on the length of the day. The reform-pushing group Stand for Children—a group that pushed for the legislation supporting a longer day regardless of CTU support—ran a telephone campaign[27] promoting the reform "as pleases Emanuel"—meaning no parent negotiations.

In April 2012, Brizard pushed the now-common reformer idea of "empowering principals"—a term that means nothing more than instituting the business model of principal as the sole power in making key decisions about school and faculty minus any required input. Brizard wanted to give principals jurisdiction over the planning of the minutes added to the school day as well as "greater control over school funds"—though the principals get no commitment on exactly how much those funds will be.[28] Given the incredible deficit of the Chicago Public Schools, stakeholders realize "extra money" will translate into cuts to current programs.

Of course, the principal will be the first one fired if those test scores fail to rise as a result of this "increased flexibility."

Such a culture of pressure and fear. Indeed, in January 2010, the Illinois legislature passed the Performance Evaluation Reform Act,[29] the primary goal of which is to connect principal and teacher evaluations to "student growth"—test scores, of course. Though the legislation required 300 Chicago public schools to implement the Act by September 2012, Emanuel wanted to begin the process sooner. In March 2012, a group of 88 academics[30] petitioned Emanuel to pilot the evaluation system first. The group, Chicagoland Researchers and Advocates (CReATE), was concerned about a number of issues, including the instability of value-added evaluation, excessive influence of unpiloted "student growth" on teacher evaluation outcomes, and the excessive focus on test scores.[31] Their message was clear:

> We, *Chicago-area university professors and researchers* **who specialize in educational research,** *conclude that* **hurried implementation of teacher evaluation using student growth will result in inaccurate assessments of our teachers, a demoralized profession, and decreased learning among and harm to the children in our care.** *It is wasteful of increasingly limited resources to implement systemwide* **a program that has not yet been field-tested. Our students are more than the sum of their test scores, and an overemphasis on test scores will not result in increased learning,** *increased well-being, and greater success. According to a nine-year study by the National Research Council,* **the past decade's emphasis on testing has yielded little learning progress, especially considering the cost to our taxpayers.**[32] [Emphasis added.]

Not only does Emanuel ignore the researchers' request to pilot the teacher evaluation; in a display of utter ignorance, in an April 2012 article, the *Chicago Tribune* praises Chicago Public Schools administration for implementing the untested evaluation. Moreover, the *Tribune* suggests that the "student growth" (test score) component be raised from an initial 25 percent (gradually to 40 percent) to 50 percent of a teachers' total score:

> For the first time, Chicago teachers will be evaluated in part on their students' academic growth. That's a seismic shift, great news for students, parents—and teachers, who finally should get an honest evaluation.
>
> Student academic growth will count for 25 percent of many elementary school teachers' assessments, a figure that will rise to 40 percent in five years. High school teachers start at 10 percent and rise to the same level over five years.
>
> That's good, but we urge CPS to reach higher. Some states already count student growth as half of a teacher's evaluation. That's where CPS needs to be.[33]

The foolishness of an uninformed press. The *Tribune* assumes the evaluation will be "honest" and that this is "great news" for all involved. The paper continues by noting how good it would be when in 2013, student feedback was added to the teacher evaluation at 10 percent. Never mind the association between student approval and lax grading or student anticipation of a satisfactory grade.[34] Students can easily rate a teacher poorly simply because the teacher IS doing his/her job well.

The article concludes that value-added measures will work, period.[35]

Never mind the fact that the entire process had not been piloted. Never mind that no one knows the damage that this untested evaluation method might inflict. It is not "what we had," so it must be good.

The union was not vested in the new teacher evaluation process. Even though CTU met with CPS 35 times over the course of 90 days, the stalemate clearly pointed to trouble, with "the specter of a teachers' strike hover[ing] over negotiations."[36] Here is the point of contention:

> A CPS-endorsed teacher survey released last fall found **the greatest group of respondents, about a third, thought student performance should count for about 15 percent in a teacher's evaluation.**
>
> **The CTU argues that the statistical methods the school district plans to use to measure student achievement are not reliable and don't adequately gauge a teacher's contribution.**[37] [Emphasis added.]

Two days after the above article was printed, another *Tribune* article announced that a CTU poll indicated teachers were willing to strike. The article further focuses on teacher salary as the issue at hand.[38] However, the salary increase requested by CTU (30%) corresponds to the percentage of classroom time to be added to the school day (29%).

One month later (mid-May 2012), CTU conducted a more formal polling of its members in preparation for a strike. One of the issues on the ballot involved the resignation of CEO Brizard.[39]

In an astounding show of arrogance, Stand for Children, the reform-focused "out-of-town" group that inserted itself in the support of the 2011 legislation to extend the school day, once again placed itself in Chicago teachers' affairs by "urging" teachers to avoid a strike only weeks (late May 2012) before renegotiation of the CTU contract. Stand for Children was joined by yet another reform-pushing group, Democrats for Education Reform (DFER), "a Washington, DC-based group that came to Chicago four months ago."[40]

On June 6, 2012, even though talks between CTU and CPS continued, CTU members officially voted regarding their support of a strike should contract negotiations fail:

> …*Lewis reiterated to reporters why the union was calling for a strike authorization vote while negotiations for a new contract were ongoing.*

> *"It's important to take now because we need to make some movement at the table," Lewis said. "(CPS) needs to understand that now we have the voice of 30,000 people at the bargaining table with us. It has to be now."*[41]

By law, CTU needed 75% of its members to approve in order to call a strike.

It got 89.7%, or 23,780 out of 26,502 of its members voting to strike.[42]

As the new school year began, on August 2012, the strike appeared to be a certainty.[43] And the fact that Emanuel had connections with Obama was not lost on the press:

> …*While both private- and public-sector unions are taking a pounding across the U.S. with layoffs, pay cuts and pension rollbacks, **the CTU is gearing up for a showdown with America's most politically connected mayor, Rahm Emanuel**—and it will come to a head in September.*[44] [Emphasis added.]

And "come to a head" it did. On September 10, 2012, the Chicago teachers officially went on strike. Lewis told the media that CTU was "committed to staying at the [bargaining] table until a contract is in place."[45] Of course a national issue involved the upcoming presidential election. Barack Obama counted upon union support for re-election; the two major teachers' unions boast a combined membership of 4.5 million.[46] Then again, Obama was also allied with Emanuel.

Definitely a tight spot for the President.

So what did Obama choose to do? Nothing publicly. As the *Washington Post* notes, the Obama administration "has taken a hands-off approach to the dispute."[47] The *Post* then makes a keen observation regarding Obama's "playing both sides." By supporting the privatization of education while courting the public sector:

> *For most of his first term, President Obama has managed to have it both ways on educa-*
> *tion reform.*
>
> **He has received steadily, if not effusive, support** *from politically potent* **teachers unions**
> **while promoting an agenda that is hugely unpopular with many educators,** *including*
> *evaluations that hold them accountable for student test scores.*[48] [Emphasis added.]

There was not much more that a Democratic president with a traditionally Republic privatization agenda could do. There are those who write that Obama's not telling Emanuel to "back off" was a way to "push—however gently—for more accountability and choice in education."[49] In truth, Race to the Top was Obama's agenda (sort of; some refer to RTTT as "a more severe extension of former President George W. Bush's No Child Left Behind policy, which for the first time, held schools accountable for their students' performance on standardized tests"),[50] and Emanuel was enforcing that agenda. Yet Obama was also a politician facing an election; so, I am not surprised at all that publicly he said nothing, either for or against, the Chicago teachers' strike.

Once the strike headed into its second week, Emanuel went to the courts for an injunction to end the strike based upon CTU's allegedly not adhering to Illinois law, which prohibits striking except for wages and benefits.[51] The court did not impose the immediate injunction Emanuel requested on Monday, September 17, 2012. Instead, Judge Flynn of Cook County Circuit Court responded that he would not act until Wednesday at the earliest.[52] Lewis was to meet with teachers on Tuesday, September 18, to vote upon the negotiated contract. As it turns out, most (98%) of the 700 delegates representing the approximately 29,000 teachers[53] voted to end the strike and return to school on Wednesday, September 19.[54] One of the conditions of the contract is its length— three years—just in time for Emanuel's 2015 re-election bid.[55]

Even though the media (and the Chicago Public Schools headed by Emanuel) did not recognize the strike as focused on the "usual" economic issues, the Chicago teachers' strike was highly "economic." For example, connecting teachers' livelihoods to student test scores is indeed an economic issue. Insisting upon a longer school day while refusing to compensate teachers for the extra time spent in the classroom (a 29% longer day bespeaks 29% more pay, and this aside from regularly-scheduled raises, which Emanuel cut the year before) is an economic issue. Understaffed schools and programs is an economic issue. Merit pay is an economic issue, as is increased health insurance costs and cancellation of seniority-based pay. All of these are issues prompting the Chicago teachers' strike.[56] Details regarding negotiations were clearly economic. For example:

> *An arbitrator earlier this year [2012] recommended a pay increase of 14.85 percent, much closer to the union's initial demand for a 30 percent raise to cover the additional hours teachers were expected to work in the new longer school day. CPS, however, has offered only a 2 percent raise, which doesn't even make up for the teachers' previously negotiated 4 percent raise that was cancelled by the board last year.*[57]

One of the concessions negotiated did involve teacher pay—raises that would cost the already-broke Chicago Public Schools $295 million over four years: A three-percent raise in Contract Year One, and two-percent raises in years two and three.[58] Teachers also gained ground regarding issues of layoffs and rehiring following layoffs:

> *The contract also changes the rules governing layoffs: when a school cuts teachers, teachers in the bottom evaluation category will be the first to go, followed by new teachers who have not yet been rated. **According to the new contract, laid off teachers who score "proficient" or higher will be placed on a hiring list. The district must staff half of all open positions with laid-off teachers, a change that for the first time imposes hiring limits on principals.***[59] [Emphasis added.]

And what of the CTU request for Brizard's removal as Chicago Schools' CEO?

Concerning strike negotiations, Brizard made a statement in that demonstrates just how out of touch he was with the plight of Chicago's teachers:

> *"We [CPS]didn't understand the relationship that existed" between the teachers and the administration, he said. **"The distrust among teachers goes back several school chiefs."***[60] [Emphasis added.]

What Brizard failed to recognize in making such a statement is that Lewis' "hot buttered mess" observation was meant for him, not just the "school chiefs" that came before. Brizard was clearly of the reformer set, trained by New York's Joel Klein. He is not simply "a casualty of previous school chief mistrust."[61,62] But he was to be a casualty of the strike. The October 11, 2012, *Chicago Sun-Times* notes that Brizard was "out by mutual agreement," to be replaced by Barbara Byrd-Bennett.[63]

Meanwhile, many issues producing tension between the privatizing Emanuel and the public schools as represented by CTU remained unresolved, lending credence to *Huffington Post's* education writer Joy Resmovits' observation, "Chicago's education scene remains a powder keg, ready to erupt at the smallest provocation."[64] Issues of class size limits remained unresolved. Unresolved issues of merit pay and use of student surveys to rate teachers were "off to committee." And though the evaluation issue was slowed down—with no negative ramifications in the first year for tenured teachers—and test scores were to count for only 30% of the evaluation—the issues of erratic or punitive evaluations—and particularly the details of the appeals process—were by no means settled.

It is important to note that the negotiations also did not address issues of imminent school closures. The reformer-promoted view of school closures is that it is done for economic reasons—not enough money to support schools with low enrollments. So, one the one hand, class size limits are not observed, leading to overcrowded classes. Yet on the other, those promoting the "clean up" of "sweeping" reform advance the argument that schools with low enrollment are too expensive to keep open.

Of course, there is also the "third person in the marriage": the reformer-beloved charter school.

What is increasingly obvious is the irreconcilability between the public school deficit and the hedge-fund and foundation-backed donations expressly earmarked for advancing education privatization. Both Lewis and Alderman Bob Fioretti recognize this duplicity in this November 2012 *Chicago Tribune* article:

> ...*Chicago Teachers Union President Karen Lewis said... that the wealthy backers of Mayor Rahm Emanuel's efforts to overhaul the city's troubled schools should donate money to support public education but otherwise butt out.*

> *"I think they should do what they do when they give money to the Lyric Opera," Lewis said during a City Club of Chicago lunch. "I don't believe they give money to the Lyric Opera and then go tell the singers how to sing. ... Give your money and walk away, buddies. When you don't know something, don't dilettante your way into it."*

> *Lewis' criticism was directed at people like school board member Penny Pritzker, a member of one of Chicago's richest families and a supporter of education reform, and Bruce Rauner, a retired private equity executive who has helped lead the drive for privately run charter schools.*

> ...

> *Lewis criticized "the top-down decision-making that places the views of corporate leaders and hedge fund managers over the voice of parents and communities."*

> ...*The nation's third-largest school system confronts a massive restructuring. Faced with a $1 billion budget deficit in the coming year, CPS officials say they need to close dozens of underused schools. Up to 140 schools are 50 percent underenrolled, according to the district.*

> ...

*Ald. Bob Fioretti... said **eight privately run charter schools moved into his ward over the past six years, while five schools have closed.** The teachers union has long argued that **CPS promotes and funds charters at the expense of neighborhood schools.***

*"It is clear to me that **CPS has created its (school building) utilization problem** with **many of the charter and contract schools that have opened over the last 10 years,"** Fioretti said.[65]* [Emphasis added.]

The situation in Chicago is becoming increasingly familiar in districts across the nation: Declare the community public schools failures. Starve them of resources. Meanwhile, favor the charters and contract schools, but especially the charters. Solicit private funders to pour money and resources into charters. Allow charters to move in on "under-enrolled" community public schools. This produces an inescapable spiral of doom for the community public schools as enrollments continue to fall. Eventually, the favored charter schools are able to take over. This is the climactic dream of privatization.

Recall that Obama and Duncan's RTTT awards points to states that remove the cap on the number of charter schools allowed by law.[66] In doing so, the Obama administration enables the artificial creation of "low enrolled" community schools via charter school encroachment. Furthermore, in upcoming months, Emanuel would certainly do his part to ensure the removal of scores of bothersome community schools, leaving a desolation ripe for "capless" charter school growth.

These reform-bent Chicago boys are "in it to win it."

In a document released to the *Chicago Tribune* in December 2012, Emanuel's planning of the details for upcoming public school closures was made public. One of the details on the document is its date—September 10, 2012—the official start date of the Chicago teachers strike.

Coincidence?

Notice this detail:

*While schools are not listed by name, one section of the document contains a breakdown for closing or consolidating 95 schools, most on the West and South sides, as well as targeting other schools to be phased out gradually **or to share their facilities with privately run charter schools.**[67]* [Emphasis added.]

The encroachment of the charter schools. This "sharing of facilities" will forever remind me of New York's charter school queen, Eva Moskowitz, who is ever on the hunt for the next "low enrollment" community public school into which she might insert her viral charter, Success Academy. Moskowitz worked closely with former New York Chancellor Joel Klein, who trained Jean-Claude Brizard, whose hire Lewis called a "hot buttered mess."

Corporate reform is an undeniably a well-connected, national phenomenon.

New CEO Bennett insisted that the plans dated September 2012 predated her term and therefore did not reflect her decisions. However, the initial list released under Bennett's term included an astounding 330 schools, a list that she "reduced" to 129 schools in February 2013. Bennett noted that she was still "vetting" the list. Parents and community leaders attended "hearings" in which they were required to present their case for keeping their community schools. The state legislature passed a law requiring hearings prior to schools closures after Emanuel closed schools in 2010 without sufficient community input. Emanuel publicly admitted as much—after the passage of the law forcing him to have community hearings.[68] However, the public was skeptical of the seeming good intentions to reduce the list; the idea of beginning with such an incredibly large number was viewed by some as a ploy to make the final list appear "reasonable."[69]

Bennett's view of the outcome of these meetings differed from that of the stakeholders. Whereas Bennett is quoted as saying that "everybody got it, that we really needed to close schools,"[70] others, including Lewis, openly disagreed with her assessment:

> *"People feel like they're being messed with," Lewis said. "Everyone knows Rahm had a number he wanted. I think people feel good that they had the opportunity to speak, but if you continue to do things that they don't want, then how is that changing the problem that exists with trust?"*[71]

State legislators extended the December 1, 2012, deadline for the closure list to March 31, 2013; Bennett's commission on school closings reported that up to 80 schools could either be closed "safely" or "overhauled."[72] Nevertheless, it is not clear what the commission considered in determining "safely" closing a school:

> *Bishop Tyrone Harrington of Greater Morning View Missionary Baptist Church in South Chicago, testified at a hearing last month.* **He said students from Lawrence Elementary on the Far South Side would have to cross three parks, each controlled by a rival gang, if the school closed. He said CPS staff took notes and wrote down his name.**

Harrington said he expected the district to call him back for additional input, but he never heard from anybody.

> *"You need to at least experience it from a child's point of view," Harrington said.* **"These gangs are rivals and they have been for some time. My thing is what's the solution for that? It's just a matter of time before there's an incident."**[73] [Emphasis added.]

In researching this chapter, I have seen numerous photos of the pleading, the begging, the tears of frustration and anger of parents, teachers, and students at hearing that theirs was a school to be closed. The chanting, the marching, the signs, in protesters' hands and posted on freeways, including, "School closings = one term mayor." The police presence. The sit-ins, the arrests, the fights, both physical and emotional. No help coming to save their school. No hedge-fund managers. No foundations. No mayor. Only judgment.[74]

A SAD ENDING

In June 2013, fifty was the number of Chicago public schools slated to be closed for the 2013–14 school year. To the thousands of students affected by the closures, Chicago Public Schools made the promise to "ensure safety for students displaced by the closings and move them to a better performing school."[75] Moreover, the "moving" of children to "better performing schools" was showing itself as a hollow promise given the $74 million in cuts scheduled for 100 of the remaining schools and leading to parent protests in the summer of 2013:

The CPS school funding crisis has reached a crisis point and students face a disastrous reduction in the quality of their educations. This multi-school parent-driven protest will illustrate the devastating reality of next year's school budgets. Hundreds of parents, students and other supporters of many Chicago Public Schools will bring their outrage and their voices for change, to those who need to hear it most. At issue for many schools may be:

- *Slashing of teacher and assistant principal positions*
- *Elimination of Magnet Cluster status funding*
- *Increases in class size to 30 and above*
- *Cuts in bi-lingual education*
- *Elimination or drastic reductions in music, art, physical education, foreign language, technology and other ESSENTIAL programming*[76]

This, dear readers, is the result of almost two decades of mayoral control in Chicago. The legislature, mayor, and school CEOs wanted to run education "like a business." That they did—right into the ground, with lots of community school casualties.

As noted in a previous chapter, Arne Duncan's own "turnaround" schools are some that are taking the hit; so much for Duncan's school closure success. His successor Emanuel has enforced the largest public school closure in US history. But where are these mysterious "better performing schools"? Daley didn't produce them. Neither did Vallas, nor Duncan. Almost 20 years of mayoral control in Chicago, purportedly to give a single person the authority required to Turn Chicago's Schools Around. Until these power-wielding, corporate-reform-minded individuals examine the true issues at hand—beginning with poverty and gang violence—and continuing with the misappropriation of funding to empty promises such as costly standardized tests—Chicago's public schools never will "turn around."

CHAPTER 9

PAUL VALLAS BEYOND CHICAGO

Wrecking Philadelphia

By spring 2001, the Daley-Vallas honeymoon was undeniably over. This reformer duo squabbled publicly via the press concerning their different views on such issues as retaining students multiple times for failure to pass ITBS and approaches to addressing the embarrassingly low first-day attendance rates at Chicago's public schools. Add to that the not-so-amazing-and-astounding improvements in the public schools as a whole, and, well, that leads to a Chicago schools CEO who becomes the former Chicago schools CEO.

Paul Vallas did not "reform" Chicago's public schools. He did promote an atmosphere of pressure and fear.[1] Perhaps he though he might do so statewide; following his exit as Chicago schools CEO, Vallas made a bid for Illinois governor but lost in the primary.[2] The winner, Rod Blagejovich, would end up in prison for trying to sell Obama's vacant senate seat, among other crimes.[3]

In need of employment and now with experience in disrupting public education, Vallas was a candidate for the position of chancellor of New York City's schools; NYC's Mayor Bloomberg was granted mayoral control of schools in June 2002, and he was searching for his first schools chancellor appointee. However, Vallas instead accepted the appointment as Philadelphia schools CEO.[4] The School District of Philadelphia (SDP) had just been taken over by the state for both its low test scores and financial deficit.[5]

The year was 2002. Paul Vallas was going to save Philadelphia's schools. But first, a smidge of Philadelphia education background.

> *In desperation over the prospect of spending over budget, in February 1998, Philadelphia Public Schools Superintendent David Hornbeck told the state that if they did not contribute additional funds to enable the district to end the year with a balanced budget, he would close schools early. In response, in April 1998, the state approved funding that also included state takeover if the district were "financially distressed" and unable to keep the schools open for the entire school year due to financial reasons. Notice also the all-too-familiar, corporate reform direction to which SDP would be subjected:*

> *If financial distress is declared, **the powers of the existing school board would be suspended, the superintendent would be suspended or dismissed, a five-member School Reform Commission would be established, and a Chief Executive Officer would be appointed to run the district. The CEO could hire non-certified staff, suspend compliance with state mandates, reconstitute troubled schools by reassigning or firing staff, hire for-profit firms to manage some schools, convert others to charter schools, and reallocate and redistribute school district resources.***[6] [Emphasis added.]

A terrible and looming prospect for Philadelphia, the appointed Philadelphia CEO could do exactly what the appointed Chicago CEO could do. Of course, there were additional restrictions on collective bargaining:

> *The Philadelphia Federation of Teachers did not see the new law making things better for its 30,000 members, **who would be forbidden to strike under a state takeover. Teachers who failed to show up for work or perform their jobs would not only be disciplined but also would lose their teaching certificate for a year and would be barred from taking advantage of early retirement options.***

> *The new law also prohibits the extension of current collective bargaining agreements beyond their expiration in the year 2000, **even without a declaration of financial distress. After that date, the school district is no longer required to bargain or negotiate** with the union over contracts with third parties; staffing decisions, **including staff reductions; creation of charter or magnet schools; issues related to the academic program;** the use of pilot and experimental programs; and the use of technology.*[7] [Emphasis added.]

In 2000, the Illinois legislature passed the Education Empowerment Act, a piece of legislation that was fiercely reformer-minded. However, it was also obviously biased against districts with higher concentrations of minority students:

> *Last year [2000] the legislature passed the Education Empowerment Act **giving the governor the power to take over 11 out of a total of 501 underachieving Pennsylvania school districts. At least half of the students in these 11 districts scored in the bottom 25 percent on state math and reading tests. Sixty percent of Pennsylvania's black students and 53 percent of its Latino students are concentrated in these 11 districts.***

> *Under the Education Empowerment Act, school officials could be given **the power to dismiss or lay off staff without adhering to seniority, hire uncertified teachers,** and could **privatize services,** educational and otherwise. School officials could **also create charter schools which would not be obligated to follow state civil rights, environmental and labor regulations; could run existing schools as if they are charter schools, and close or reorganize schools.** Currently [2001] , 14,000 of the Philadelphia's 210,000 public school students attend charter schools. Also part of the Act was **$30 million in tax breaks to corporations that offer to pay private school scholarships and invest in new programs in public schools.**[8] [Emphasis added.]*

Philadelphia's public schools did not stand a chance. In "the most radical reform ever undertaken in a large, urban school district,"[9] Philadelphia schools were to be privatized. Philadelphia Governor Mark Schweiker announced his plan to turn over management of SDP to Edison Schools, Inc. approximately 67% of SDP's 264 schools were to be partially or completely privatized. The privatization plan had begun in August 2001 under then-Governor Tom Ridge and was passed on to Schweiker. Interestingly, the privatization process was postponed until after Ridge's appointment as secretary of the newly-created Office of Homeland Security under G. W. Bush.[10,11]

Appearances?

The projected cost of privatization: In excess of SDP's $1.7 billion budget, $150 more per year over five years. In 1998, Superintendent Hornbeck, who resigned in June 2000 for lack of fiscal support,[12] appealed to the state because he did not have sufficient funds to end the school year with a balanced budget. Never mind that SDP received a disproportionately low per-pupil funding as compared to other Pennsylvania districts:

> *An analysis of district finances in 1999 by Moody's Investor Service, a financial rating agency, determined that **increased district spending was limited by a state system which relies heavily on property taxes for local school funding. As a result, wealthier school districts with proportionately more property owners and more expensive real estate have more funds for schools.***

> *The result is great disparities in school system expenditures per student. Last year, the **Philadelphia school district spent $6,969 a year per student. Seventy percent of Philadelphia's students are at or near the poverty line.** This contrasts with expendi-*

tures per student in wealthier suburban school districts: Jenkintown, $12,076; Radnor, $13,288; and Upper Merion, $13,139.[13] [Emphasis added.]

As to the Edison Schools place in the takeover, Edison was selected via no-bid contract to conduct its own study on running SDP without increasing required state funding. The study was not widely publicized. Edison's effectiveness was already in question:

> **Despite raising $265.5 million in three public offerings, Edison reported on March 31 [2001] that since November 1996 it has accumulated a total debt of $144.8 million. It has never recorded a profit.** *It lost $38 million in fiscal year 2000 and $36.6 million in fiscal year 2001. On February 8, Edison stock hit an all-time high of $38.75. By mid-August it had fallen to $18.85 in trading on Nasdaq.*[14] [Emphasis added.]

As of June 30, 2001, Edison's accumulated debt had increased to $153.6 million. In their 2001 Annual report, Edison excused its excessive debt in a single sentence:

> *Because of our rapid growth, and in view of the evolving nature of our business and our limited operating history, we believe that period-to-period comparisons of our operating results may not be meaningful.*[15]

There you have it: "We're is a serious fiscal pit, but don't judge us."

Edison Schools, Inc., is a privatization company that is itself drowning. However, that did not stop it from making promises and claims:

> *Edison's business model is based on the premise that it can take the same amount of money the public schools receive and use it more effectively by reducing administrative costs. It has its own curriculum and preferred teaching methods.* **On September 26, Edison released a report claiming test scores had improved at 84 percent of its schools. Critics pointed out that the figures are based on comparisons to Edison schools only and not to non-Edison schools in the same districts.**[16] [Emphasis added.]

It sure sounds good for Edison to say, "We'll solve your school problems for the same amount of money you're currently spending, and then we'll compare our scores with our scores." However, Edison itself was failing on both counts. Furthermore, contrary to its "premise," Edison was going to require more finances to "reform" the already-fiscally-drowning SDP.

This is the company that two Philadelphia governors agreed to hire to "solve" SDP financial and achievement problems. Why no one seriously considered that SDP achievement and fiscal problems are interwoven with urban poverty is any sane person's guess. Nevertheless, Edison offered suggestions appealing to reformers' desires:

> *Edison's 32-page report calls for* **abolition of the school board, which is appointed by the mayor, and for the management of the school district to be turned over to Edison. A five-member School Reform Commission appointed by the governor would**

replace the board. In a move that outraged Philadelphia city and school officials, the Republican controlled state legislature passed legislation to appoint the commissioners to five- to seven-year terms, thus making them unaccountable to anyone.[17] [Emphasis added.]

Just as the Edison study was kept quiet, so the legislation that handed control of SDP over to Edison was also not only properly publicized but also shadily connected to and passed with unrelated legislation. In addition, those voting for the legislation stood to financially benefit from the new law:

The legislation was passed on October 23 [2001] in a late-night session, prior to Edison's report being made public—with one minute of notice and 30 seconds of debate—as an amendment to a bill that would provide loan assistance to nursing students. The bill would also allow the nullification of current contracts with school district employees, except teachers whose contacts expire in three years. The law gives the new board the authority to impose local taxes exclusively on Philadelphians to implement the plan. State officials indicated they want the commission to replace the 50 top administrators in the school district in order to "change the culture" of the district.

The Edison plan also calls for 45 of the lowest performing schools to be operated directly by Edison, 15 of these low performing schools to be operated by community groups and universities; 170 schools to get teacher training to implement a standardized math and science curriculum developed by Edison, and the remainder, primarily competitive admissions magnet schools, to be monitored but left alone. Edison proposes to save money by eliminating 500 teaching positions by attrition and selling the school district administration building. Several Democratic legislators from Philadelphia supported the plan because they want to expand the operations of the charter schools they now operate.[18] [Emphasis added.]

Newly appointed in 2002, Vallas did not want Edison's help in reorganizing Philadelphia's schools. He said his staff could do the job without Edison's leading, yet Edison could take over 20 schools.[19] In 2002, Vallas also proposed budget cuts amounting to $640 million over five years, including reducing general operations; cutting of overtime and workers compensation; the cutting of "nonessential" positions, and the closing of schools.[20] By 2003, Vallas wanted to cut in half the $20 million in fees paid to outside companies and organizations to run 45 of Philadelphia's 265 schools. As is so often the case when privatizers are brought in to run schools, these fees are in excess of operating budgets.[21] After all, privatizers enter the school reform arena in order to turn a profit.

Remember, the reformer goal is to spend less and require more—usually in the form of higher student test scores and lower dropout rates. It is one issue to have to cut education and then to move forward. However, it is another issue altogether to cut, and cut, and still have a deficit and have to cut more. Perhaps Vallas' worst moment as a budgeter occurred on December 11, 2006, when he had to face the Philadelphia City Council and justify not just more budget cuts, but more cuts in an attempt to solve a deficit mid-school-year to the tune of $73.3 million.[22] Keep in mind that the Philadelphia public school budget was already problematic in February 1998 when then-Superintendent Hornbeck appealed to the state that the $1.7 billion budgeted would not suffice for the entire school year. Fast forward to December 2006, when the budget was set at $2.04 billion, and Vallas was now lacking $73.3 million to balance it. This means that Vallas' error set the actual available funding at approximately $1.3 billion—almost nine years after Hornbeck voiced his concerns and was met by punitive legislative action—and with the added burden of paying privatizers fees for their "services." And what of those "services"? Did the dropout rate remarkably improve given the four years that Vallas had been CEO? Consider this excerpt of the heated December 11, 2006, City Council meeting:

> *...It was from Councilman W. Wilson Goode Jr. that Vallas took the most heat. Goode began by asking who sat in on Vallas' final job interview and whether he remembered talking about the dropout rate then.*
>
> *Vallas said the entire School Reform Commission interviewed him and discussed the dropout rate.*
>
> **"How are young black males performing in the district and how has it changed during your tenure?"** *Goode asked.*
>
> **Vallas said that most were still failing** *but that strides had been made.*[23] [Emphasis added.]

This is not the promising response one wishes to offer when also acknowledging that the budget is incredibly in the red.

More cuts, more cuts:

> **The School Reform Commission made more cuts** *last week and* **"conditionally authorized" Vallas to trim an additional $20 million,** *which would get the district the $73.3 million it needs to close the deficit.*[24] [Emphasis added.]

Once again, Vallas was on his way out from a schools CEO position with displeasure toward him hanging in the air:

> *The beginning of the end of his tenure happened when,* **just four months after he had told the Philadelphia City Council that the budget was balanced and a month after the SRC, by a 3–2 vote, had renewed his contract until 2010, the district suddenly was revealed to have a $73 million deficit.**
>
> ...

*Embarrassed SRC members, led by Whelan and James Gallagher, the president of Phila-delphia University, pushed for Vallas's ouster. In the spring of 2007, they took him to lunch at the Four Seasons Hotel **and told him that they had lost confidence in him**.*[25]
[Emphasis added.]

Four months later (April 2007), Paul Vallas would resign from yet another schools CEO position,[26] but not before drawing a handsome salary and benefits for several years.

The budget slashings incurred by Philadelphia's schools were not evident in Vallas' own earnings. His initial salary was $275,000, and it increased to $285,000 in 2007. Interestingly, Vallas' raises in 2008 and 2009 were tied to teachers' raises in the collective bargaining agreement. Vallas was also eligible for annual performance bonuses up to 20% of his salary and 30 days a year of paid vacation. However, he did not remain in Philadelphia long enough to garner his $100,000 per year retention bonuses (effective July 2007).[27]

Vallas made an incredible budgeting blunder in Philadelphia. However, Philadelphia was not the only district suffering from Vallas' budgeting decisions. By 2006, Vallas' 1995 Chicago "miracle" budget "surplus" had begun to unravel.[28] His 1995 decision to "trim" the budget by paying $83 million less into the Chicago teacher pension fund came home with a fury by 2008:

> **The political horse-trading** *that has diminished all of the city's pension funds* **can be viewed most dramatically through the recent history of the Chicago Teachers' Pension Fund.** ...

> *This predicament can be* **traced to decisions made in the wake of Mayor Richard Daley's takeover of the public school system in 1995.**

> *With help from allies in Springfield,* **the Daley administration pushed to have the pension code rewritten so property tax money that normally went to pensions would go to Chicago Public Schools coffers.** *Under the old law, the district's pension bill was slated to be $93 million in 1995. Instead, it paid just $10 million.*

> **CPS officials** *went back to Springfield the following year and* **had the law changed again. This time, the district would have to put money into the pension only if the fund's level fell below 90 percent.**

> **For the next decade, the district's contribution to the retirement of tens of thousands of public school teachers was zero. In all, the pension holiday cost the teachers fund more than $1.5 billion from 1995 to 2009,** *according to fund documents. The state was supposed to help soften the blow by contributing to the fund, but that never happened.*

> *In 2004, it dipped below 90 percent for the first time,* **but because funding is based on results from two years earlier, that milestone didn't affect the district until 2006.** *That year the school system had to contribute* **$36 million** *to the pension fund.* **The bill nearly**

tripled to $90 million in 2007, and by this year it was $340 million—an 844 percent increase in just four years.[29] [Emphasis added.]

This, dear readers, is the long-term result of Vallas Budget Management in Chicago: Short-term gain for long-term fiscal chaos. Paul Vallas initiated this Chicago budget crisis by shaving off pension funding. Apparently, Philadelphia SRB members did not know of the Chicago Vallas Effect even as they were being publicly humiliated by the Philadelphia Vallas Effect.

Amazingly, some count Vallas as a success despite the embarrassing Philadelphia budget deficit. After all, test scores went up, and that is the goal, is it not? During Vallas' time as Philadelphia schools CEO, state standardized test scores in general did rise. Graphs of the Pennsylvania System of School Assessments (PSSA) for students overall can serve as an advertisement for Vallas reform success (just be sure to downplay the awful budgeting decisions Vallas made in both Chicago and Philadelphia). However, the more telling story about "success" as measured by test scores concerns considering test score specifics of certain groups. (Testing grades until 2006 included fifth, eighth, and eleventh; third grade was added in 2006.)[30] Recall that Philadelphia schools likely to qualify for closing were those with higher concentrations of black and Latino students. On Vallas' watch, PSSA reading scores for Latino students rose from 18% scoring proficient or above in 2002 to approximately 33% in 2007 and for black students, from 17.8% scoring proficient or above (2002) to approximately 35% (2007). The overall reading scores were pulled upward by the averages for white students (46.6% in 2002 to ~60% in 2007) and Asian students (40.1% in 2002 to ~63% in 2007). Furthermore, both PSSA reading and math scores for the economically disadvantaged students consistently pulled the average down. As such, the overall PSSA reading percentage of 23.9% scoring proficient or above in 2002 (and approximately 38% in 2006) masks the differences between students more likely to live in poverty (black and Latino students) and those less likely (white and Asian students).[31]

PSSA reading and math scores for both English language learners (ELL) and students with disabilities also pulled the average down. That is, schools with higher concentrations of ELL students, students with disabilities, and the economically disadvantaged were more likely to have lower average PSSA scores and were therefore more likely to be declared "failing."[32]

One of Chicago Mayor Daley's issues with Vallas at the time of his resignation as Chicago schools CEO in 2001 involved low reading scores, especially as compared to math scores. In Philadelphia, it is interesting to note that on Vallas' watch, PSSA reading scores for the percentage of students scoring proficient or above leveled off for Latino students and white students from 2005 to 2007 (Latino: ~31% to ~33%; white: ~58% to ~60%); black students' PSSA reading scores increased modestly (~30% in 2005 to ~36%

in 2007), with the scores of Asian students evidencing the greatest gains, from ~53% in 2005 to ~63% in 2007. However, there are no consistent, across-the-board gains for all ethnic groups during Vallas' final two years in Philadelphia, a time when scores were the highest they had been but were still far from remarkable.[33] Even the highest scoring ethnic group, Asian students, is just past 60% scoring proficient or above on the PSSA. A more telling perspective involves the percentage of students overall scoring below basic in reading on PSSA during Vallas' tenure. In 2002, 49.4% of Philadelphia's students scored below basic; in 2003, the percentage dropped slightly to 48.0%. In 2004, another drop: 43.8%; in 2005, a slight rise to 44.7%; in 2006, another drop to 41.9%, and in 2007, a drop to 37.2%. Thus, from the 2002 PSSA test to the 2007 test, the percentage of students scoring below basic dropped modestly, from 49.4% to 37.2%.

Is this corporate reform success: A reduction of 12.8% in Philadelphia students scoring below basic in reading over the course of six testing years? All of that fear and pressure and focus on standardized test results in Philadelphia's classrooms for five out of every twelve students to be labeled "failing"—and, by extension, their teachers also labeled "failing—for the inability to pass a standardized test.

With such pressure would come cheating. Stay tuned.

Another area for closer scrutiny concerns high school PSSA scores, and the lack of relationship between test scores in general and dropout rates. PSSA reading scores for juniors (11th grade) remained unimpressive across Vallas' tenure as CEO. From 2002 to 2007, the percentages of eleventh graders scoring proficient or higher in reading were 28.7% (2002), 30.1%, 27.0%, 30.6%, 33.2%, and 34.9 (2007). For math, percentages were 23.6% (2002), 21.6%, 22.9%, 23.1%, 26.9%, and 30.9% (2007). Even though eighth- and ninth-grade student attendance is a powerful predictor of dropping out of school, 20% of Philadelphia students late in their high school careers would still drop out. Though Philadelphia's eleventh-grade PSSA scores remain below the 50th percentile even as late as 2012, PSSA scores have not been shown to predict which students are at risk for dropping out. Out-of-school factors are the predictors, not test scores. In latter grades, powerful predictors for dropping out include involvement in the juvenile justice system; substantiated child abuse and neglect; involvement in the foster care system, and giving birth during high school years.[34]

In addressing Philadelphia's high dropout rates, focusing on ever-higher test scores is clearly wrong and accomplishes nothing. In general, insisting upon unbalanced emphasis on standardized test results places undue pressure on administrators, teachers, and students, and invariably leads to cheating. Indeed cheating was discovered in the PSSA tests between 2009 and 2011 involving high numbers of wrong-to-right erasures, and tighter test security was instituted for the 2012 PSSA test.[35] Interestingly, the percentages of students scoring proficient or above on the PSSA in 2012 in reading dropped to either at or below the 2008 percentages, this further illustrating the potential leveling off of scores. The same was true for the percentages of students scoring below basic on both PSSA reading and math; once cheating was addressed in the 2012 test administration, percentages of students scoring below basic rose to between 2007 and 2008 levels.[35]

On the national Terra Nova test, administered to grades 3 through 10 in Philadelphia in 2006, scores were not impressive. And when national scores do not emphatically support the ideology of corporate reform, those national scores receive more of a silenced, sour reformer reception, if such scores are released at all:

> *Results from the spring 2006 TerraNova showed a decline in performance compared to the prior year in most grades and subject areas—the first time that happened on a major standardized test here (Philadelphia) since 2002.*
>
> *Only in grade 10 did students show slight gains across the board in the percentage of students scoring above the national average.*
>
> **Compared to spring 2005, more students in spring 2006 scored near the bottom on the TerraNova. The number of students who scored in the lowest quartile grew by two to four percentage points in each of the tested subjects for grades 1, 2, and 9.**
>
> *The District held onto the spring TerraNova scores for more than six months before posting them without fanfare on the Web in early 2007. ...*
>
> **Mixed results were seen again on the fall 2006 TerraNova scores,** *released in February.* **Significant gains in some grades were balanced by declines in others.** *Combining all the fall 2006 results from grades 3 through 10, scores were up slightly in reading compared to 2005, but were down slightly in math and language arts.* **Science scores, which have generally been the poorest, were not released by the District with the other subjects.**
>
> **Release of the fall 2006 scores also came late.** *According to District assessment experts, the results led to a review and* **determination by the District and its testing company that the previous fall's scores—the point of comparison—were not valid.**[37] [Emphasis added.]

The Terra Nova is a nationally-normed test. As such, national tests like Terra Nova and the National Assessment of Educational Progress (NAEP) provide a more objective perspective regarding student progress than do state tests. According to Philadelphia's Terra Nova results, Vallas' reforms did not produce those ever-rising test scores reformers are quick to say will happen if the top-down, corporate model is imposed upon public education. Rather than admit as much, the results were released in part, and "late" and "without fanfare"; moreover, Philadelphia school administration declared comparisons with earlier administrations "invalid." Reform is not about using test results to better educational opportunities. Reform is about using test results to punish public education while supporting a seeming-unstoppable privatization machine.

Even though I address the issue of test score gains as related to reformer "success," I only do so to illustrate the emptiness of tying educational success to criteria so dimensionless as a standardized test score. I do not endorse the test score as an end-all measure of student learning, or teacher or CEO effectiveness. Higher test scores do not make teachers teach or students learn, but their rising values often do represent back-door efforts to avoid the corporate-reform-induced punishments for not achieving higher test scores.

Administering tests does not address the complex issues in the lives of Philadelphia students at risk for dropping out of school. Administering tests is a shallow, misplaced reformer reaction to the unwillingness to acknowledge and address the greater societal issues plaguing students, families, and communities, not the least of which is childhood poverty.

In 2008, Vallas commented that reforms can have a lasting effect, even after a superintendent leaves[38] —ironic words given the Philadelphia schools cheating scandal that would begin with the next set of PSSA scores—and especially ironic given the frightening fiscal crisis in Chicago schools directly related to Vallas' 1995 budget decisions.

Philadelphia did not benefit from six years of Vallas, his never-ending budget cuts, his high salary, his empty promises to address the dropout rate, and his veneer of testing "success."

In fall 2007, Philadelphia still had education-related problems, but they were no longer Vallas' problems. Vallas had moved on to the Big Easy, where he continued his legacy of digging deeper fiscal ditches in the name of Vallas-brand educational "success."

CHAPTER 10

PAUL VALLAS BEYOND CHICAGO

No Good for New Orleans or Bridgeport

Vallas has been in the education reform business since 1995 with his appointment as CEO of Chicago schools. That didn't work out; so, Vallas left for Philadelphia, where that didn't work out, either. So, as reformers do when their time runs out in a city, he moved on. The next stop for the Vallas Education and Budget Disruption Plan was New Orleans, with its massive infusion of federal aid following Hurricane Katrina, where he would remain for several years before moving on to Bridgeport, where he ended up in the courts for lack of proper credentials.

Let me not get ahead of myself. Before Bridgeport, there was New Orleans. And before there was Vallas in New Orleans, the reformer bent was already fashioning preferred outcomes. Let us therefore first consider education reform New Orleans style—the years preceding the Big Easy arrival of the ongoing "success" myth that is Paul Vallas.

A Chronicle of Echoes: Who's Who in the Implosion of American Public Education,
pages 149–164.
149

NEW ORLEANS PRE-VALLAS

While Vallas was collecting over a quarter of a million dollars as CEO of the financially-stressed, quasi-privatized Philadelphia school district, New Orleans was facing its own reformer legislation. In 2003, both the Louisiana legislature and public vote formed the Recovery School District (RSD), designed to take over "chronically low performing" Louisiana public schools in order for either the state board of education (BESE) or contracted charter operators to run the assumed schools. Prior to Hurricane Katrina, only a handful of schools had been taken over by the state. Not all citizens were in agreement with the takeover plan and viewed it an attempt to specifically take over Orleans Parish Public Schools. As a 2011 Cowen Institute report notes,

> *In New Orleans, significant opposition existed. Local opponents of the amendment were worried about allowing state officials to control local tax dollars.* **Others were concerned about the lack of detail regarding how schools would be improved under state control. Many viewed the takeover strategy as experimental** *and contended that* **state takeovers had not been proven effective elsewhere in the nation.** *The Bureau of Governmental Research, an independent research organization in New Orleans,* **echoed concerns about the lack of evidence supporting takeovers** *and claimed that the amendment was "weak" because it allowed rather than required the takeover of failing schools.* **Most viewed the amendment as a thinly veiled attempt to take over the Orleans Parish school system.**[1] [Emphasis added.]

Senate President John Hainkel confirmed that Act 9 was aimed at Orleans schools. The determination for school takeover was a school performance score (SPS) rating of Academically Unacceptable School (AUS) for four consecutive years. The situation with Orleans Parish Schools was complicated by corruption, mismanagement, and leadership instability:

> *The OPSB (Orleans Parish School Board) and the district central office continued to be considered ineffective and corrupt, so much so that* **in 2004 a special FBI task force was assigned to investigate the school system and 11 district employees were indicted.** *The* **high turnover of the superintendent's position,** *with two regular and six interim superintendents between 1998 and 2005, and the* **lack of steady leadership in the administration's central office departments, allowed corruption, graft, and incompetence to persist. Extensive and long-running financial mismanagement,** *and the* **refusal to confront and rectify it,** *had also taken its toll, and* **by early 2005 the public school system in New Orleans was declared effectively bankrupt.** *Weeks later, beleaguered OPSB Superintendent Anthony Amato resigned. Under threat of total district takeover by the LDE (Louisiana Department of Education), an outside accounting firm was hired in July 2005 to overhaul the system's finances.*[2]

The following incident illustrates the degree of financial crisis that OPSB faced in the months prior to Hurricane Katrina:

...[Orleans Parish Superintendent] Amato "fell on the sword of his inability to fix the finances" a week after it was disclosed, in the face of Amato's denials, that the system had edged dangerously close to failing to make payroll. **In one stark example, one of his administrators rushed to City Hall on April 1 to pick up a check for millions of dollars in tax revenue and hand-delivered it to the bank, minutes before the deposit deadline, state Legislative Auditor Steve Theriot said. If that check would have been late, thousands of payroll checks would have bounced.**[3] [Emphasis added.]

Then in August 2005 came Hurricane Katrina, a massive storm rendering most schools unusable and driving the 65,000-member student body down to 12,500 by June 2006. And with Katrina came widespread state takeover of the public schools in New Orleans. In November 2005, Louisiana Governor Kathleen Blanco approached the legislature with the idea for "rebirth" of New Orleans schools—involving a much-expanded Recovery School District:[4]

Almost as profound as the storm damage, what followed was **a radical decentralization.**... *The central office shrank from about 1,000 employees to 57, and* **most of the 7,500 teachers got pink slips. [The corporate turnaround firm] Alvarez and Marsal got a new, $29.3 million contract**—*this time to oversee the rebuilding.*

The state school board had already swept 112 of New Orleans' 128 schools into something called the Recovery School District; *of those,* **12 reopened as independent charter schools, with five-year contracts and little oversight.** *Thirteen schools were left to district management, but 11 of those are charter schools;* **in the end, two are overseen by the parish.**[5] [Emphasis added.]

Specifically, the 2005 legislation altered the 2003 definition of "failing school" to be any school "below the state average" SPS, which was 87.4 in 2004–05. Prior to the 2005 change, the SPS threshold for state takeover was 60.[6]

New Orleans is the first and perhaps the best example of "disaster capitalism"[7] on American soil. The rushed establishment of post-Katrina RSD is the quintessential corporate reformer opportunity for "orchestrated raids on the public sphere... by capitalists seeking exciting new markets to exploit [and that] take place when disaster is viewed as an economic opportunity."[8]

In the blink of a devastated eye, the approximately 500,000 New Orleans citizens[9] dispossessed and displaced had in hostile-yet-calculated fashion foisted upon them a state-run system ironically promoted as "education choice."

As to leadership of the "new and improved" RSD, Vallas was not the first RSD superintendent. RSD was formed in late 2005; Vallas arrived in the fall of 2007. Even when Vallas came, he made known his intention to remain in New Orleans for only a couple of years. Rumors of a possible second run for Illinois governor circulated, which "Vallas neither confirm[ed] nor denie[d]."[10]

Prior to his arrival, and upon his RSD successor, Robin Jarvis' resignation following "a tumultuous year,"[11] Vallas was portrayed as the Solver of Problems in both Chicago and Philadelphia:

> *Urban-education observers credit Vallas with* **restoring the financial stability in Chicago.** *In Philadelphia, he spearheaded a movement to develop smaller high schools and* **forged partnerships with nonprofit organizations and corporations and implemented a standardized curriculum.** *Under Vallas, Philadelphia has seen growth in standardized test scores in reading and math, though a large number of students still fail to meet standards, according to the system and news accounts.*[12]

No mention of how Vallas' 1995 Chicago schools budget "solution" of paying less into the teacher pension fund contributed to Chicago schools' ballooning fiscal crisis in 2006. Cutting the pension fund contributions was "a short term fix."[13] No mention of the "forged partnership" Philadelphia had with fiscally-failing Edison Schools. No mention of the continued high dropout rate and how Vallas did not address issues research shows to be related to Philadelphia students' being at risk to drop out.

The article, which speculates on Vallas' hire even as Jarvis resigns, does note Vallas' $73 million deficit in Philadelphia and recognizes such as the reason for Vallas' likely departure come June 30, 2007.

NEW ORLEANS BEGINS "THE VALLAS YEARS"

It truly astounds me that State Superintendent Paul Pastorek hired Vallas to run RSD given that one primary reason for state takeover of Orleans schools in 2003 involved fiscal mismanagement. But hire Vallas Pastorek did. As long as corporate reformer ideology matches (As to corporate reform entrenchment, Pastorek continues to be listed[14] as a lawyer with the New Orleans firm, Adams and Reese, an ALEC player).[15]

In 2008, Vallas' "nearly unchecked administrative power" included the following reforms:

> *...Vallas has changed pretty much everything, all at once, with little opposition. He lengthened the school day and year, adding seven weeks of instruction, including two more hours of math and 1.5 hours of reading each day. He started a "credit recovery" program for students who fail core classes. He has remade RSD's high schools into career-themed academies and opened a school for "overaged underachievers."*

> *He is standardizing the curriculum and brought in Read180, a computerized program for older, struggling readers. He installed Internet-linked whiteboards in fourth- through 12th-grade classrooms and last year began handing out laptop computers to every high-school student.*[16]

As a "placed" corporate reform CEO, Vallas answers to no stakeholders in the newly-washed-away New Orleans. Actually involving the community in decisions affecting the community is a complex business, and Vallas prefers a dictatorial role, one where he gets to make the people's decisions for the people and answer to no groups representing the people. Consider this 2008 exchange with *New York Times* reported Paul Tough:

> *When I asked Paul Vallas what made New Orleans such a promising place for educational reform, he told me that it was because* **he had no "institutional obstacles"—no school board, no collective bargaining agreement, a teachers' union with very little power.** *"No one tells me how long my school day should be or my school year should be,"* he said. *"Nobody tells me who to hire or who not to hire. I can hire* the most talented people. **I can promote** people based on merit and based on performance. **I can dismiss people** if they're chronically nonattending or if they're simply not performing."*[17]
> [Emphasis added.]

It sure is easy to run a district by use of unchecked power.

Despite his carte blanche activity in RSD, Vallas continued to promote the idea that he would leave by 2010:

> *Whatever happens, it's clear Vallas won't stick around too long—he has said as much. After Vallas left Philadelphia,* **his wife and three of his four sons returned to their native Chicago. Vallas spends four or five days there each month,** *and he has coyly suggested he might run for governor of Illinois in 2010—he narrowly lost the Democratic nomination in 2002 to Gov. Ron Blagojevich.* [Emphasis added.]
>
> *Vallas openly admits to grooming his chief of staff to take over, saying two years are sufficient to get his reforms in place.*[18]

About those trips to visit his family in Chicago: Apparently, Vallas developed a habit of using his Louisiana-taxpayer-funded automobile. This information was disclosed in the 2009 Louisiana Legislative Audit of RSD: 31 trips, with the state paying $974 for fuel and $776 for damages in an auto accident Vallas was faulted with while driving his Louisiana vehicle to a press conference in Chicago. Furthermore, Vallas did not maintain the required vehicle use log.

State Superintendent Paul Pastorek verbally approved of Vallas' using his state vehicle for personal trips despite the state administrative code that notes use of state vehicles is limited to state business. Pastorek said he thought Vallas had only taken six trips. Apparently Pastorek never asked Vallas to account for use of his state vehicle.[19]

Vallas had made it clear that he would not remain in Louisiana, yet he was more than willing to use Louisiana to support his already-well-paid lifestyle, and his boss was willing to allow it despite the clarity of the administrative code on the issue.

Vallas was the privileged Golden Boy; it seemed that in New Orleans following Katrina, Vallas couldn't lose. Arriving in New Orleans two years after Katrina, Vallas missed the real mess. Plus, he had federal funding flowing in for rebuilding. For the first time in his schools CEO career, Vallas wasn't in a position where he had to cut budgets. He wasn't in a position where he had to deal with a forceful teachers union. He didn't have to close schools. He didn't have to fire teachers; the post-Katrina mass firing had happened prior to his arrival. And by 2008, he had more teacher applicants than he had positions.

To top it all off, he had already made clear that he had no intentions of staying.

Vallas made it known that he was not invested in New Orleans. He was simply a "temp employee" in a district seriously in need of a leader who would stay. Consider this scenario between Vallas and ninth grade students as reported in the 2008 *USA Today*:

> *One recent morning, he and [former police chief Eddie] Compass deliver what amounts to a tag-team commencement speech at the end of a week-long Ninth Grade Nation program for new high schoolers.* **The students, distracted and wanting little more than to go home for the afternoon, listen as he offers a pep talk.**

> "These are all brand-new high schools," he says. "It's not the Reed of old, it's not the Douglass of old, it's not the John Mac (short for John McDonogh) of old. If you come to school every day and try real hard, we will not let you fail. You will succeed."

> *The students shift in their chairs. He is the sixth superintendent they have seen since their school careers began.*

> *"Nobody fails," Vallas says. "Everybody succeeds! Are you with me on it?"*

> **Silence.**

> *It doesn't seem to discourage Vallas,* **who says many kids haven't been paying attention the past few months.**[20] [Emphasis added.]

This scene makes me sad. I feel for the students, who have experienced incredible disruption, not the least of which is the loss of pre-Katrina community. I feel for them as they listen to someone who continues with a supposed "pep talk" despite the obvious lack of connection. I feel for them because this superintendent is talking at them, not with them.

An interesting note regarding the USDOE cohort graduation rates (2007–08 to 2010–11) of the high schools Vallas mentioned in his pep talk: Sarah Towles Reed Senior High School had a 49.6% graduation rate; John McDonough Senior High School, a 45.6% graduation rate, and Douglass was no longer listed as a school. In fact, five of the eight RSD high schools included in the USDOE 2007 cohort graduated less than 68% of their students.[21]

So much for the New Orleans Vallas Effect on high school graduation rates.

Paul Vallas remained in New Orleans until the summer of 2010. He is credited with "leaving a legacy of charter schools." RSD was already on the road to charter takeover before Vallas arrived. In 2009, as part of Louisiana's bid for Race to the Top funding, the Louisiana legislature removed the cap on the number of charter schools allowed in the state. By the 2009–10 school year, New Orleans in general (RSD and the much smaller OPSB) had 51 charter schools. Not all were open enrollment. Eight had selective admission criteria, which made them the subject of discussions about "cream skimming," or selecting students most likely to make test scores soar.[22] As Barbara Ferguson of Research on Reforms notes,

> *According to NCLB (No Child Left Behind), each student is to have an "equal opportunity" to attend Charter schools.* **When the opportunity is conditioned, the school is a Magnet school, not a Charter school. Only in New Orleans have Magnet schools wrongfully been converted into Charter schools**.[23] [Emphasis added.]

An additional issue shaping charter "success" as compared to traditional public schools is the issue of "dumping out"—of the charter school's ability to expel students for any "infractions," a practice prohibited by law in the traditional public schools. Ferguson argues that such a practice is a "misuse of the charter school concept":

> *...While some charter schools try new ways to educate historically low performing or misbehaving students, others simply dump them out.* **Dumping kids out improves the scores, but it does so at the expense of the other charter and traditional schools,** *which educate all students.*[24] [Emphasis added.]

Yes, during Vallas' time in New Orleans, the number of charter schools increased dramatically. Yet is this a measure of reformer success for Vallas? Not if one measures "success" using the same standard applied to originally determining "failure." The criteria for state takeover of a school was an SPS below the state average. Based upon 2010 SPS, handing a school over to state control only propagated a "failing school" holding pattern:

> *In 2010–11, there were approximately 74 RSD schools in Orleans that received MFP funding for the 2010–11 school year. Of these schools approximately 50, or 68%, had 2010 baseline SPSs reported: 30 charter and 20 direct-run schools.*

> *...Using the current state performance labels (from 2010), over 74% of the schools in the RSD are labeled either as failing (AUS) or in danger of failing (AW).*[25] [Emphasis added.]

Notice that 32% of RSD schools in New Orleans did not even receive an SPS so that the school's "success" might be assessed.

In 2010, BESE instituted a letter grade system to correspond with the SPS. The determination of a "F" school in 2011 was an SPS lower than 65; in 2012, an SPS lower than 75 indicated an "F" school according to BESE's determination. Applying the 2011 criteria to the RSD schools that were given an SPS in 2010, Charles Hatfield of Research on Reforms concludes the following:

> *..If the new letter grade standards were applied to the 2010 baseline SPSs, **only 4 schools (6%) would receive an A, B or C (.i.e., Kipp Central and Primary, Dr. MLK, and** Berhman). **However,** 93% would receive a D or an F.*[26] [Emphasis added.]

Hatfield then extends his analysis to the RSD schools taken over by the state in 2005:

> *Of the 93 schools taken over [by the state in 2005], 73% would be labeled with an F and 27% would be labeled with a D. Therefore, in 2005 100% of the schools would be labeled with either an F or a D. **In 2010, 92% of the schools would be labeled with either an F or a D.** This represents a[n] **eight percentage point decrease. Can that really be considered significant progress over five years?**[27] [Emphasis added.]

Vallas might have added to the number of RSD charter schools, but he contributed nothing of note to RSD school improvement as defined by the reformers' own criteria for determining school reform "success."[28] Vallas did manage to pull a $320,000 per year salary from the Big Easy, including housing and car allowances.[29]

At least he didn't slaughter RSD's budget. No, wait... he did.

Four consecutive audits of RSD finances during Vallas' time as superintendent yielded a lack of diligent fiscal oversight, at best. Vallas assumed superintendency of RSD in July 2007. In June 2008, the Louisiana Legislative Auditor Audit Management Letter included numerous mismanagement issues. In short, the corruption for which OPSB had become known pre-Katrina continued on Vallas' watch. First, RSD employees had been overpaid $427,695 as of September 30, 2007. Furthermore, 34 laptops paid for with federal funds ($56,128) had been stolen in February 2007 (pre-Vallas); however, as of October 2007, RSD had notified in writing neither the district attorney nor the legislative auditor. Third, RSD charged the federal School Breakfast Program and National School Lunch Program for students not eligible to receive subsidized meals. The list continues.[30]

In an audit conducted in 2013 concerning modular campus construction for the period of January 2007 through September 2009 regards $6.1 million in "questionable payments for services beyond the scope of firms' contracts, materials that were never provided, and unreasonably high rates":

The audit found that Arrighi-Simoneaux charged the RSD $170,571 for fuel for temporary generators that was never provided and $37,843 for 16 light pole foundations that were never built. An additional $472,852 that was charged for foundations "appears to be unreasonable for the service provided," according to the audit. The firm billed at least $139,000 in work beyond the scope of the contract.

Arrighi-Simoneaux's unit pricing may also have been too high. For instance, the company charged $110 to drill each of 180 four-inch holes in wooden floors, though the task takes less than 30 seconds, auditors say.

As for LH&J [Linfield, Hunter & Junius], the audit found that the company billed a number of basic design services under a higher rate reserved for special services. Those fees also seem to be high, according to the audit, citing a $560,000 charge to increase the width of buildings by 8 feet.[31] [Emphasis added.]

The information presented above is only an excerpt. What is clear is that fiscal oversight was seriously lacking on Vallas' watch to the tune of millions upon millions of dollars in missing or stolen property, overpayments to employees, overpayments for goods and services, and payments for goods not purchased and services not rendered. Notice also that such gross fiscal mismanagement occurred year after year. Consider this excerpt from the legislative auditor's report of RSD for fiscal year 2010:

For the fourth consecutive year, RSD did not tag and report equipment as required by state equipment management regulations and did not maintain accurate information in the state's movable property system, Protégé. As reported in a Louisiana Property Assistance Agency (LPAA) report on RSD, RSD failed to enter 13,247 assets into the asset management system within 60 days of receipt and 1,262 items valued at $2,141,347 could not be located. In our test of 10 equipment purchases and a physical check of 18 property items, we identified items that were not located, not tagged within 60 days, and tagged but not recorded in the property system. In addition, RSD reported 35 incidents involving 380 movable property items with an approximate value of $188,600 as missing or stolen in fiscal year 2010.

For the fourth consecutive year, RSD identified overpayments made to employees, did not ensure that employee separation dates were accurate or timely, and did not have adequate documentation to support certain payroll charges. Payroll overpayment claims identified by RSD during fiscal year 2010 totaled $18,206. ...

For the third consecutive year, RSD did not ensure that certifications for payroll expenditures charged to federal programs were completed as required by federal regulations. ...[32] [Emphasis added.]

Apparently when billions in federal disaster relief are pouring in, there is no need to account for the money. The issues mentioned above were also mentioned in the RSD audit for fiscal year 2011:

*For the fifth consecutive year, RSD did not ensure that movable property was safeguarded against loss including loss, arising from unauthorized use and **misappropriation.** RSD's annual certification of property inventory identified **403 unlocated items totaling $553,385.** Of the 403 unlocated items, 346 items were computers. In addition, RSD reported **194 movable property items totaling $168,375 as missing or stolen in** fiscal year 2011.*

For the fifth consecutive year, RSD identified overpayments made to employees, did not ensure that employee separation dates were accurate or entered timely, and did not have adequate documentation to support certain payroll charges.

Payroll overpayment claims identified during fiscal year 2011 totaled $8,507. ...

For the fourth consecutive year, RSD did not ensure that certifications for payroll

expenditures charged to federal programs were completed as required by federal regulations. ...[33] [Emphasis added.]

During the course of his time as RSD superintendent, Vallas mismanaged RSD's finances. In his first and perhaps only superintendency in which funding was amply available, Vallas failed to monitor the funds. He did manage to make dozens of car trips to Chicago, and he did manage to consult abroad, missing a total of six weeks of work away from RSD to do so.

HAITI, CHILE, BUT STILL RSD

While still superintendent of RSD, Paul Vallas began advising an international development bank in Haiti on rebuilding a school system following widespread natural disaster.[34,35] Vallas did not run for Illinois governor or for any other political post, citing his "need to finish what he started" in New Orleans.[36] If his goal was to leave most RSD schools as still within the "failing" designation as determined by the state while not adequately supervising RSD spending, then he accomplished his goal. However, his physical presence in Louisiana leaves room for doubt about Vallas publicized dedication to RSD. Despite his noble words, Vallas missed 48 full days of work in Louisiana from February to October 2010 due to his traveling to Haiti. Whereas he did not collect pay for his time away, he was not present to serve in the capacity for which he was hired, as former BESE member Linda Johnson observes:

"I think it was a misuse of his services," Board of Elementary and Secondary Education member Linda Johnson said. "We pay him to do work in New Orleans. Until New Orleans no longer needed help, he should have stayed in New Orleans... Of course I want Haiti to return to a robust country with great education. However, I feel New Orleans is still in the state of recovery and needed him there," she said. "Large companies loan their people to help when disasters occur. However, I am certain they would not loan their people if they were also in need."[37]

In 2011, Vallas also "consulted" in Chile, where his privatization efforts were met with clear understanding from Chilean students:

> *Dramatic student protests increased in the streets of Chilean cities as the Race To The Top style reforms increasingly tighten corporate control over Chile's public schools less than a generation after the South American nation escaped the grip of the first round of reforms brought by the "Chicago Boys" during the dictatorship of Augusto Pinochet. On July 14, [2011,] an estimated 20,000 people, mostly students, too[k] to the streets of Santiago to protest the neoliberal attacks on public education and higher education, only to be met with water cannons and tear gas, as well as police beatings which were caught on dramatic video. …*
>
> *According to a report from Reuters, more than 20,000 people demonstrated against the USA style reforms in Santiago, the capital, while being attacked by speeding military vehicles, some of which were equipped with water cannons and tear gas sprayers. Squads of heavily armored Chilean soldiers also attacked individual protesters who became isolated from the groups, but generally shied away from the main large group protests.*[38] [Emphasis added.]

American education privatization efforts appeal to those abroad wishing to exercise continued control over institutions rightfully belonging to the public. The so-called "reforms" do not appeal to those who wish not to be lorded over by dictatorial-style education mandates.

Recall Vallas' preference for "nobody" telling him "what to do" as chief reformer in post-Katrina New Orleans. It seems that a dictatorship lacks appeal to the "dictated." However, the massive protest against American-style corporate reform in Chile holds no detriment for Vallas. As for Paul Vallas, adding "international benevolence" to his reformer resume certainly could not hurt his future earning potential in the business of reform. Never mind what disenfranchised people think, whether in America or abroad.

Vallas' "consulting" did not end with Haiti and Chile. Despite Vallas' delayed crash-and-burn "contribution" to the fiscal devastation of Chicago's public schools; despite his $73 million "uh-oh" in Philadelphia, and despite his gross fiscal and property mismanagement in New Orleans, Vallas partnered with Cambium Learning to market "the Vallas model of reform':

> *The Vallas reform model includes not just improving academic performance, as other turnaround systems do,* **but also stabilizing districts by balancing their budgets** *and reorganizing their administrations. "We are committed to* **affordable change,** *" Vallas says.* **"You will be amazed at the efficiencies and cost savings you can bring to a district."**[39]

I wonder if Chicago Public Schools views its required payment increase into the teacher pension system of 844 percent over four years (2006–2010) as "affordable change" initiated by Vallas' "budget-balancing" hand in 1995.

Corporate reform cannot even recognize its own foolishness.

If one deliberately ignores any contrary evidence, there is always a market for reform.

Vallas' consulting practices via the Vallas Group, Inc., would draw criticism even as he garners yet another education CEO title in Bridgeport, Connecticut.

VALLAS MOVES ON YET AGAIN: BRIDGEPORT

The education system in Bridgeport has become yet another entity embroiled in corporate reform. According to Connecticut law, the state designated Bridgeport schools as a low performing district based upon low test scores sustained over the course of seven years; failure to achieve state benchmarks, and failure to achieve Adequate Yearly Progress in fulfillment of NCLB requirements for two consecutive years. In July 2011, certain members of the Bridgeport Board of Education called for a special vote asking the state to intervene and take over the Bridgeport Board of Education. Then-acting State Commissioner of Education George Coleman appointed a new board. A lawsuit was filed alleging that the state takeover was illegal since certain local board members had not undergone training that those members wishing to deliver the board over to the state had noted all members of the board had undergone.[40]

Meanwhile, the state-appointed board hired Vallas as interim superintendent. On January 1, 2012, Vallas was to officially assume the role of interim superintendent of Bridgeport's schools and solve issues of Bridgeport's $6 million budget deficit.[41] Vallas' pathway into Bridgeport comes via the new Connecticut State Commissioner of Education, Stefan Pryor, who worked with Vallas in during a time that Pryor volunteered in both New Orleans and Haiti.[42]

The Connecticut Supreme Court found in favor of plaintiffs and agreed that the state-appointed board was illegal since the state should have mandated board certification training prior to instituting a takeover. Both Bridgeport Mayor Bill Finch and Connecticut Governor Dannel Malloy wanted the takeover.

Vallas' appointment as interim superintendent was not affected by the Connecticut Supreme Court's decision. However, Vallas did not possess the required credentials to become Bridgeport superintendent, even interim superintendent. Nevertheless, as reformers operate, pushing forward with the illegal in order to get a "foot in the door" and be excused later appears to operate well.

In March 2013, both Vallas and newly-appointed Commissioner of Education Stefan Pryor as well as the Bridgeport school board were sued over Vallas' lack of proper credentials. Pryor granted Vallas a probationary certificate to hold the position of Bridgeport superintendent—extended to two years—and supposed to expire in December 2013. Those filing the suit against Vallas saw Pryor's largesse as nothing more than use of his position to enable Vallas to escape the certification requirement.[43]

Vallas was supposed to complete a certification program at the University of Connecticut:

> *A new state law allows an acting superintendent who successfully completes a school leadership program approved by the state and offered at a public or private institution of higher learning in the state to receive a certification waiver. A semester long program, created just for Vallas, has been developed at the University of Connecticut. Vallas is in the program this spring.*[44]

There was only one problem with Vallas' completion of the school leadership program: He did not meet the prerequisites for enrollment in the program:

> *Earlier this spring [2013], in order to fulfill this education requirement, Vallas went to UConn to apply for UConn's respected Executive Leadership Program, **a 13-month, $25,000 intensive education program** that provides students with the background necessary to get their Connecticut superintendent's certification.*

> *But Vallas couldn't get into the program since, among other things, **he didn't have the required 15 graduate credits beyond his Master's Degree**. In fact, Vallas didn't have any credits past his Master's Degree.*[45] [Emphasis added.]

Vallas already has the job—foot in the door. The governor wants him. The mayor wants him. And the state commissioner wants him. That's all of the "certification" he would need. Besides, corporate reformers don't believe in certification, anyway.

Well, okay. Maybe Vallas should have some sort of token certification:

> *...Somehow, miraculously, the 13-month, $25,000 program morphed into a 3 credit, $3,000 independent study. Despite it being the middle of the semester, Vallas started his "course."*

> *A month later, the State Board of Education "approved" the student leadership program, as required by the statute, but rather than approving UConn's Executive Leadership Program, it approved the independent study "program" that Vallas was enrolled in... calling it a school leadership program.*

> *When all was said and done, less than ninety days after Vallas started his "program," he completed his class and his UConn advisor announced that he was good to go.*[46]

Credentialing is nothing more than a parking lot cone around which reformers drive. Following his completing the "program" and a year of "probationary hire," on June 14, 2013, the state-appointed board of education chairman wrote to Commissioner Pryor recommending Vallas' permanent hire. Pryor agreed.

The issue of the legality of all of this "waiving" of credentials was in Superior Court,[47] and on July 10, 2013, Judge Barbara Bellis ruled that Vallas was not a "properly credentialed superintendent" and that he needed to vacate his positon.[48] However, true to that "foot in the door" reformer ploy, the illegally-state-run school board was in a rush to approve of Vallas' permanent contract.[49] On July 26, 2013, the Connecticut Supreme Court ruled that Vallas can remain as superintendent pending his appeal.[50]

In their devoted haste to hand Bridgeport schools over to the state, business leaders set up a "fund" to pay for Vallas' employment, the Bridgeport Education Reform Fund. Educational "consultants" are also paid out of this fund. The public does not get to know the secrets of the fund, including who the donors are or what the balance is. Vallas also noted the creation of a fund, Good Schools Bridgeport Foundation," to assist in the cost of reforms to Bridgeport schools. One of the declared roles of the mayor-endorsed fund involves "identifying high quality Bridgeport schools for duplication and franchising." Sounds like quite the business deal—the marketing of what one might loosely call "public" education. Even though the Foundation notes that it will have a "process" for "community input," make no mistake—the community has no power in deciding how this money will be spent. The monitoring of the money is to be given to the Bridgeport Regional Business Council, and the evaluation of education progress is to be handed over to the newly-created Bridgeport Academic Accountability Council, misnamed in that it is to be comprised of "national researchers" who will swoop in to judge the locals. And let's be clear: The use of the term "franchising" of education has next to nothing to do with community collaboration and much to do with top-down-directed education privatization.

The Bridgeport community is to be "acted upon," not "involved.

The hidden yet questionable financial dealings of reformers in Bridgeport are undeniably connected to Vallas. Not only has he participated in creating a "public education" funding entity open to neither public view nor public discussion; recall that he is marketing his reform finesse via the Vallas Group, Inc. Apparently he is also hiring Bridgeport Board of Education employees as "consultants" via his company.

We once again enter the shady area of corporate reform's allowing for educational businesses to engage in practices that appear to present undeniable conflicts of interest—such as a school superintendent running an educational business even as he is being paid public money as an education employee and boss.

Vallas has also been in the spotlight in Bridgeport for his "fiscal ingenuity" regarding employee status. One of Vallas' questionable practices involves hiring employees at the Bridgeport Board of Education and paying them via 1099s as opposed to W-2s. It is illegal to pay employees as consultants; W-2 forms are required for employees, and the use of W-2 "would end up costing the district about $25,000 more for each [employee] in benefits."[51] Thus, it is no surprise why a man known for shaving money off of budgets would prefer the 1099 to the W-2.

Vallas is everything good for corporate reform and bad for traditional public education. Within months after his arrival in Bridgeport, in April 2012, Vallas decided that Bridgeport students needed not one but two rounds of standardized tests. And forget planning ahead; Vallas announced his dictatorial decision for the second round approximately six weeks before he expected the tests to be administered: June 4. To students in grades 3 through 11. Top-down decisions are easy for the one at the top. Just say the word.

It doesn't matter if the decision is foolish. It's Vallas' to make. After all, Vallas IS public education, right? As blogger Jonathan Pelto keenly observes:

The new regime's interpretation of how the world works is:

*"**Traditionally, instruction wanes after the administration of the state tests. Unfortunately, this "lull" in teaching and learning deprives our students of much-needed academic support."***

In other words—let's face facts—the only time teachers are capable of teaching (and children are capable of learning) is when they have a gun to their heads—and that gun is called the standardized tests.

Not only are standardized tests the vehicle to make teachers do their jobs (while making kids learn), it is standardized tests that Governor Malloy and his fellow "reformers" say MUST be used in the evaluation process so that government can determine whether teachers are or are not doing their job.

*The memo highlights the directive by stating—in bold—"ALL ELEMENTARY AND HIGH SCHOOLS ARE **REQUIRED TO REFOCUS THE INSTRUCTIONAL DAY TO INCLUDE 90 MINUTES OF LITERACY/ELA INSTRUCTION AND 90 MINUTES OF MATHEMATICS INSTRUCTION EFFECTIVE IMMEDIATELY**.*

Hooray for Education Reform![[52]

Pelto continues by noting the number of "chiefs" and "directors" copied in the "you will do this" email. No collaboration. No consideration of teachers' own plans for their students. Just do it because I said so.

No wonder Chile protests Vallas-style, American corporate reform.

One year later, in May 2013, Vallas "trimmed" the Bridgeport budget by eliminating positions such as department heads and literacy and math specialists. He also removed the special education support system, sending such individuals into classrooms of their own.[53]

Also in May 2013, Vallas was sued by the Connecticut Education Association for not including stakeholders in education decisions. Recall that one of the "benefits" Vallas spoke of in storm-ravaged New Orleans was that he had no powerful teachers union with which to contend. Not so in Bridgeport. These folks sought to inhibit his preferred dictatorial powers. They actually expected to be included in the education decision-making process:

> *According to the complaint, state laws were violated because the following happened with members of School Governance Councils. The councils:*
>
> • *were not given an opportunity to review the fiscal objectives of the draft budget for the school and provide advice before it was submitted to the superintendent*
> • *did not participate in the hiring process of administrators*
> • *did not work with school administration to develop and approve a school compact*
> • *were not involved in developing and approving a written parent involvement policy outlining the role of parents in the school*
> • *had no involvement in analyzing school achievement data and school needs relative to the improvement plan for the school*
> • *did not assist the principal in making programmatic and operational changes for improving the school's achievement*
> • *have not been made aware of their authority, nor have they been given opportunities to exercise this authority*

> *"These are just some of the examples of the flagrant disregard Bridgeport Public Schools Superintendent Vallas has shown for School Governance Councils and state law," said Connecticut Education Association President Sheila Cohen.*[54] [Emphasis added.]

Corporate reform leads to multiple lawsuits, for corporate reformers view themselves as above the law, forcing stakeholders to sue for what used to be unheard-of issues, including public input into public education decisions.

PAUL VALLAS: CAREER REFORMER

For almost two decades, Paul Vallas has sold himself as a corporate reformer. He is willing to slash tight budgets, and he is willing to mismanage ample budgets. He is willing to privatize districts, close schools, and fire teachers. He is willing to sacrifice all of those below him in a given district for the test scores, graduation rates, or school performance scores that he cannot seem to consistently raise. He has, however, managed to consistently collect fine salaries with benefits based on the unfounded reputation he has as a reforming miracle man.

He never seems to be out of a job for long, for someone with the cash, influence, and interest in promoting the shadow of corporate reform success is always at his door.

CHAPTER 11

DAVID COLEMAN AND HIS COMMON CORE STATE STANDARDS

David Coleman is one more in a long line of "educators" who skip credentialed classroom training and any notable classroom experience to become "leaders in education reform." In Coleman's case, his "leading" led to an unprecedented effort for the federal government to surreptitiously promote a set of national standards that drives curriculum while denying that it was doing such. However, the document that Coleman is credited with as "architect," the Common Core State Standards (CCSS), became a required component of state consideration for Obama's Race to the Top (RTTT) funding. Whereas the federal government was not directly imposing CCSS on the states, it was requiring states to agree to CCSS in order to escape the pan of NCLB for the fire of RTTT.

An article ironically entitled "The Schoolmaster" details non-educator David Coleman's narrow plan to force public school students onto what Coleman has determined to be a college-prep track from kindergarten onward.[1] Coleman sees no need to accommodate the reality that not all students will desire futures connected with four-year colleges and universities,

A Chronicle of Echoes: Who's Who in the Implosion of American Public Education,
pages 165–183.

nor does he consider that no society can exist where all enter professions requiring college degrees. In an era in which reformers are quick to cry for "choice," Coleman makes the choice for all of America via "his" (he is at the helm) decided standards. But it sure does sound impressive to say that one's goal is for all students to attend a four-year college or university. Still, to the critical thinker, it sounds naïve and disconnected from education reality.

The dual realities that more than one in five American children lives in poverty and that what affects children outside of the classroom affects children inside the classroom are completely dismissed as Coleman pushes CCSS: All students learning at the same rate and mastering each learning level before proceeding to the next.

A factory model of American education.

Why should anyone expect Coleman to be grounded in the reality of American public education? Coleman is no schoolmaster. He has spent no time teaching in a public school classroom. He has no practical sense regarding whether his dictated standards could work there. Coleman is a businessman who has packaged what he believes should be standards applied to a classroom setting in which he possesses no firsthand professional experience. Furthermore, his proffered standards have never been piloted, which means Coleman has no evidence that they work in the modern public school classroom. Rest assured, however; the CCSS assessments will require up to ten hours for students to complete.[2] No assessment of the program itself, but heavy assessment of the students exposed to the as-of-yet-untested CCSS.

The hypocrisy astounds me.

These two key issues—Coleman's lack of classroom experience and his standards' lack of supporting evidence regarding implemented effectiveness—remain amazingly unanswered as Coleman's CCSS becomes the Duncan-endorsed, "not a federal" non-curriculum "voluntarily adopted" by any states wanting out of NCLB.

COMMON CORE'S BREAK WITH REALITY

CCSS is labeled as a "set of voluntary standards" and not a "curriculum." It is designed to focus student academic development (kindergarten thru grade 12) in two areas: English Language Arts (ELA) and math. What CCSS truly is, is a mammoth, pervasive education experiment. Below is what CCSS declares itself to be, a set of college and career readiness (CCR) standards first, and what CCSS proclaims it will do, definitely prepare students for college and beyond. Consider this excerpt from the CCSS ELA standards, intended to invade other subject areas, as well:

> *The CCR standards anchor the [CCSS ELA] document and define general, cross-disciplinary literacy* **expectations that must be met for students to be prepared to enter college and workforce training programs ready to succeed.** *The K–12 grade-specific standards define end-of-year expectations and a cumulative progression designed to enable students to meet college and career readiness expectations* **no later than the end of high school.** *The CCR and high school (grades 9–12) standards work in tandem to define the college and career readiness line.…*
>
> **Students advancing through the grades are expected to meet each year's grade specific standards, retain or further develop skills and understandings mastered in preceding grades, and work steadily toward meeting the more general expectations described by the CCR standards.**[3] [Emphasis added.]

An indelible signature of corporate reform is the use of public education as an arena for massive experimentation. No unhurried, small-scale studies first. No careful reconsiderations, adjustments and, if necessary, readjustments prior to overall implementation. Coleman is the credited architect of this program that is just supposed to work because he and others intend it to. They are quick to proclaim that they "based" their assumptions "in research"—but not on research on their own product, CCSS. The CCSS ELA document continues:

> **By emphasizing required achievements, the Standards leave room for teachers, curriculum developers, and states to determine how those goals should be reached and what additional topics should be addressed.** *Thus, the Standards do not mandate such things as a particular writing process or the full range of metacognitive strategies that students may need to monitor and direct their thinking and learning.* **Teachers are thus free to provide students with whatever tools and knowledge their professional judgment and experience identify as most helpful for meeting the goals set out in the Standards.**[4] [Emphasis added.]

Sounds like pedagogical freedom—teachers have autonomy—right?? Except that in the end, CCSS has not been tested. However, the teachers will be, through their students. At the time that this document was published, June 2, 2010, the CCSS assessments had not been written, much less tested themselves. But CCSS and its unwritten assessments would work—they had to work—because It Was Decided.

Teachers did not develop CCSS.

Teachers did not vote to adopt CCSS.

Teachers will not design the assessments to CCSS.

Thus, to be told that teachers "have freedom" in choosing the materials (is this not what CCSS proponents mean when insisting that CCSS is "not a curriculum"?) is like telling the middle of a jump rope that it has "freedom to move however it pleases" despite the fact that both ends are under the control of children at play.

The CCSS ELA standards note that for grade 12, the reading passages on the 2009 National Assessment of Educational Progress (NAEP) were 70 percent informational text and 30 percent literary text. Thus, Architect Coleman concludes that across curricula, by grade 12, students should be exposed to these percentages of these types of texts in the classroom:

> *The percentages on the [NAEP Reading Passage] table reflect the sum of student reading, not just reading in ELA settings. Teachers of senior English classes, for example, are not required to devote 70 percent of reading to informational texts.* **Rather, 70 percent of student reading across the grade should be informational.**[5] [Emphasis added.]

I cannot express how foolish this supposed extension of logic is. If students are exposed, for example, to half literature and half informational text in the senior year does this mean that their experience is not sufficient to score well on the grade 12 NAEP? And if students are exposed to exact percentages of certain types of writing, is this some guarantee that the students will do well on NAEP or other standardized tests? Yet this naïve and rigid logic is being promoted as indisputable truth. Could it be that by the senior year, student coursework lends itself to such 70–30 percentages without CCSS interference? Has anyone On High considered as much? And what of examining the arguable counterproductivity of advising states to micromanage the percentages of classroom instruction devoted to literature versus informational text?

Coleman has not investigated such questions.

What we are witnessing, dear readers, is the insanity of quantification. If a student is exposed to informational texts in a single senior class, that student arguably could complete a senior exam comprised of 100 percent informational texts. Somehow common sense has been lost on a misguided effort to cosmetically match CCSS with a test that will not be regularly used (and neither is designed) to assess CCSS.

Yet Coleman promotes "his" (yes, he slipped up and called them that in New York but caught himself and referred to "the authors'") standards as "the flex of the masteries" allowing students to be "more ready" so that it is "no longer a question of what's on the test."[6]

Corporate reform worships tests. Pay no attention to the Coleman behind the curtain.

CCSS extends this superficial, NAEP-quantifying lunacy to writing, as well. In 2011, the NAEP writing tasks for grade 12 included those that were persuasive (40%), explanatory (40%), and experiential (20%), Of course, this clearly (tongue in cheek) converts to suppressing writing tasks that draw upon student experience. And as to writing, Coleman has become popular for his vulgarity in expressing exactly why he decided that American education needed to move from having students write about themselves to writing about those enlightening examples of nonfiction noted above. In a series entitled "Bringing the Common Core to Life," Coleman offers his rather tacky opinion on the value of personal writing:

> ...*[The two most popular forms of writing in the American high school today] [are] either the exposition of a personal opinion or it is the presentation of a personal matter. The only problem... with those two forms of writing is **as you grow up in this world you realize people really don't give a shit about what you feel or what you think.** What they instead care about is can you **make an argument with evidence,** is there **something verifiable behind what you're saying or what you think or feel....** It is rare in a working environment that someone says, "Johnson, I need a market analysis by Friday but before that I need a compelling account of your childhood."*[7] [Emphasis added.]

In an ironic twist, in the training offered to those teachers who have been recruited to "sell" CCSS to reluctant colleagues that what teachers "think and feel" about CCSS is dismissed. Therefore, this teacher decides to "verifiably" express her feelings on why she has chosen to decline a leadership role in promoting CCSS:

> ...*One of the most offensive statements on the self-study [for CCSS Instructional Coach] was the following, **"In what ways have you already started recognizing and rewarding the "early adopters" of the CCSS at your school? In what ways have you dealt with the "NoNos or naysayers?"** As educators, we should be models of critical thinking for our students in order to better prepare them to solve the complex problems they will be and are facing. I strongly feel that **this statement discourages us from thinking deeply about the CCSS and encourages us to blindly accept this document without questioning the motivations behind it.**[8] [Emphasis added.]

Without having pilot tested CCSS and its associated assessments, Coleman's confidence that it will work is based upon nothing more than that he "thinks" it will and he "feels" it will.

As to motivation: An unwillingness to consider how a program affects its recipients always bespeaks a self-serving agenda on the part of the one promoting the program.

The CCSS ELA standards have been criticized for being weak and for not being "internationally benchmarked"—clearly comparable to international standards. In her testimony before the Texas legislature in April 2011, developer of the Massachusetts education standards and former member of CCSS' Validation Committee, Sandra Stotsky, voiced the following concerns:

> *Common Core's "college readiness" standards for English language arts and reading **do not aim for a level of achievement that signifies readiness for authentic college-level work. They point to no more than readiness for a high school diploma (and possibly not even that,** depending on where the cut score... is set). **Despite claims to the contrary, they are not internationally benchmarked.***

States adopting Common Core's standards will damage the academic integrity of both their post-secondary institutions and their high schools precisely because Common Core's standards do not strengthen the high school curriculum and cannot reduce the current amount of post-secondary remedial coursework in a legitimate way. Their standards may lead to reduced enrollment in advanced high school courses and to weakened post-secondary coursework because Common Core's "college readiness" ELA/R standards are designed to enable a large number of high school students to be declared "college ready" and to enroll in post-secondary institutions that will have to place them in credit-bearing courses. These institutions will then likely be under pressure from the USDE (US Department of Education) to retain these students in order to increase college graduation rates.[9] [Emphasis added.]

In Stotsky's expert opinion, CCSS ELA standards might get students out of high school and into college; however, students would likely lack the quality of learning necessary for college success. This could enable those playing a numbers game to claim success since many students could be enrolled in colleges and universities as a result of having been subjected to CCSS ELA standards, yet such success would amount to no more than veneer as students could lack the grounding indispensable for post-secondary success.

Stotsky offered the same testimony before the Indiana Senate Education Committee in January 2012.[10]

Unlike Coleman's opinions, Stotsky's are rooted and established in educational experience in formulating and evaluating standards:

…I was the senior associate commissioner in the Massachusetts Department of Education from 1999–2003 where, among other duties, I was in charge of the development or revision of all the state's K-12 standards. I have reviewed all states' English language arts and reading standards for the Fordham Institute in 1997, 2000, and 2005. I co-authored Achieve's American Diploma Project high school exit test standards for English in 2004. I co-authored the 2008 Texas English language arts and reading standards. Appointed by then Secretary of Education Margaret Spellings, I served on the National Mathematics Advisory Panel from 2006–2008. Finally, I served on Common Core's Validation Committee from 2009–2010.[11] [Emphasis added.]

Incredibly, Stotsky's advice on the CCSS Validation Committee was ignored, as were her inquiries into the supposed "body of research" in support of CCSS:

Another seemingly important committee, a Validation Committee, was set up with great fanfare on September 24, 2009. The 25 members of this group were described as a group of national and international experts who would ensure that Common Core's standards were internationally benchmarked and supported by a body of research evidence. Even though several of us regularly asked to examine this supposed body of research evidence, it became clear why our requests were ignored.

*In December 2009, the Parent Teacher Association indicated the real role of this committee—**more like that of a rubber stamp.** The PTA predicted that: "both sets of standards will be approved simultaneously in February 2010 by members of the Validation Committee." Why did it think so? Why did the Gates Foundation think so, too?*

***Vicki Phillips and Carina Wong [both from the Gates Foundation] published an article in the February 2010 issue of Phi Delta Kappan talking about Common Core's standards as if they had already been approved.** The final version of these standards didn't come out until June 2010. **After submitting many detailed critiques from October 2009 to May 2010 in a futile effort to remedy the basic deficiencies of Common Core's English/reading standards, I, along with four other members of the Validation Committee, declined to sign off on the final version.**[12] [Emphasis added.]*

Gates wanted these standards, and Gates has what he wanted. Legitimate investigation has been reduced to the appearance of scholarship for the sake of selling CCSS to the public.

Let us briefly consider the Gates push for CCSS via that February 2010 Phillips and Wong Phi Delta Kappan article. In their biased promotion of CCSS, Phillips and Wong characterize the development of CCSS more honestly than they might have realized:

*After more than 20 years of messy thinking, mistakes, and misguided direction, **policy makers have finally given teachers and students** a solid set of standards in mathematics and literacy.[13] [Emphasis added.]*

Those outside of the public school classroom—including David Coleman—created CCSS.[14] Not teachers. CCSS was *given to* teachers. Certainly this parallels Stotsky's experience; her concerns were overwhelmingly ignored. The policy makers had already made their decision. Her committee involvement was a mere formality, a front necessary for presenting the image of collaboration to those who might take a quick glance at the CCSS "process."

The Phillips and Wong article also openly promotes Gates Foundation funding for implementation of the "we know it's already approved" CCSS; this "policymaker-led" initiative was also unmistakably "Gates-led" to the expected tune of $354 million over five years (2010 to 2014).

Genuine quality has nothing to do with CCSS. In the months prior to its suspect finalization, Gates, though Phillips and Wong, had already made yet another major decision for American education, and it was Common Core. Furthermore, as Stotsky realized and testified, the CCSS ELA sparkle is all in the packaging and advertising. American education is set up for a breakdown just beyond CCSS' grade 12 warranty expiration.

On to the CCSS math standards.

Unlike the CCSS ELA standards, the CCSS math standards are not designated as cross-curricular. They are designated by grade level from kindergarten through grade 8, then by math area (e.g., algebra, geometry) or domain (e.g., measurement and data, the number system). Like the ELA standards, the math standards are untested. Moreover, the single math content specialist reviewing the standards did not approve of them for their lack of rigor:

> *[Stanford mathematics] Professor [R. James] Milgram was* **the only math content expert on the Validation Committee reviewing the [CCSS math] standards,** *and he concluded that the Common Core standards are, as he told the Texas state legislature,* **"in large measure a political document that . . . is written at a very low level and does not adequately reflect our current understanding of why the math programs in the high-achieving countries give dramatically better results. "**[15] [Emphasis added.]

Milgram's testimony of his experience advising CCSS continues in his testifying before the Indiana Senate Education Committee (January 23, 2012):

> **The Common Core standards claim to be "benchmarked against to international standards" but this phrase is meaningless.** *They are actually* **two or more years behind international expectations by eighth grade, and only fall further behind as they talk about grades 8—12. Indeed, they don't even fully cover the material** *in an (sp.) solid geometry course, or in the second year algebra course.*

> *...***As someone who was at the middle of overseeing the writing process**—*my main duty on the CCSSO Validation Committee*—**it became clear that the professional math community input to CCSSI [Common Core State Standards Initiative] was often ignored.**.... *A particularly egregious example of this occurred in the sixth and seventh grade standards and commentary on ratios, rates, proportion and percents,* **where there are a number of serious errors and questionable examples.** *But the same issues are also present in the development of the basic algorithms for whole number arithmetic—the most important topic in grades 1 -5.*

> *It was argued by some people on the Validation Committee* **that we should ignore such errors and misunderstandings as they will be cleared up in later versions,** *but I didn't buy into this argument,* **and currently there is no movement at all towards any revisions**.[16] [Emphasis added.]

Technically, Coleman can claim that educators did indeed provide input into the development of CCSS standards. What Coleman fails to mention is that only a single individual advised on math content, and his advice was ignored.

Recall that Stotsky's concerns regarding CCSS ELA standards were also ignored.

Neither state in which Milgram and Stotsky testified currently adheres to CCSS. Texas never did, and Indiana Governor Mike Pence suspended CCSS in May 2013.

"IF I TELL TEACHERS AND PARENTS THEY WROTE CCSS, THEY'LL BELIEVE ME"

The official, CCSS-endorsed word is that CCSS is the creation of the National Governors Association (NGA), and the Council of Chief State School Officers (CCSSO);[17] Coleman is credited as CCSS' "lead architect"[18] In truth, NGA and CCSSO hired Coleman's company, Student Achievement Partners, "to lead the process in researching, writing, and disseminating" CCSS.[19] In 2007, Coleman just happened to form a company, Student Achievement Partners, to design and market a set of national standards, and that company just happened to be hired for that very purpose. Prior to this, Coleman owned (and sold, to McGraw-Hill in 2004) Grow Network, a company that allowed Coleman to profit from NCLB via test score analysis.

By the way, McGraw-Hill just so happens to endorse CCSS.[20]

The very presence of Student Achievement Partners as the company hired to compose and promote CCSS flies in the face of Coleman's efforts to promote CCSS as emerging from the "demanding voices" of teachers.

Privatization demonstrates the theme of Astroturf Disguised as Grassroots yet again. On its website, CCSS insists that teachers and parents "developed" the standards and that the federal government kept its distance. First, the claim that teachers developed CCSS:

> *States across the country collaborated with teachers, researchers, and leading experts to design and develop the Common Core State Standards. Each state independently made the decision to adopt the Common Core State Standards, beginning in 2010. The federal government was NOT involved in the development of the standards. Local teachers, principals, and superintendents lead (sp) the implementation of the Common Core. … The Common Core State Standards Initiative was and will remain a state-led effort.*[21] [Emphasis added.]

CCSS was not a multi-state-collaboration effort. It was a project handed over to Coleman's company, Student Achievement Partners, by two organizations, NGA and CCSSO. The only "state leading" was in the secret collaboration among NGA, CCSSO, and Coleman.

In the CCSS memorandum of understanding states were required to sign in applying for Race to the Top funding, NGA and CCSSO acknowledge two assessment companies, ACT, College Board, and one educational standards-promoting nonprofit, Achieve, Inc., as the "developers" of CCSS. David Coleman and his Student Achievement Partners were also present—yet unacknowledged.[22]

Though Coleman is referred to as the CCSS "architect" and is the clear spokesman for CCSS, he is quick to broadcast that CCSS was developed "by teachers," mostly via formal organizations:

> *There is no voice in these standards stronger than the voice of teachers.... That includes formal organizations like the UFT* [United Federation of Teachers] *in New York City and the AFT* [American Federation of Teachers] *statewide and NYSUT* [New York State United Teachers], *who are deeply involved in this work, the professional organizations of teachers and the disciplines like NCTE* [National Council of Teachers of English] *and NCTM* [National Council of Teachers of Mathematics] *and several others that you know of. But it also involved... in developing these standards [is]of course the NEA and other groups. But if there's one voice that is loud and clear here, it is the voice of teachers.*[23] [Emphasis added.]

Nevertheless, Coleman's insistence that as "lead architect" he was merely doing the bidding of teachers and parents offers problems. First, Gates (via Phillips and Wong) has already publicly acknowledged that "policy makes" "gave" CCSS to teachers and students. Second, one should consider the results of AFT's own survey regarding teacher investment in CCSS. Even though AFT President Randi Weingarten promotes the idea that "75% of AFT teachers overwhelmingly support Common Core," most teachers surveyed expressed hesitation and caution by noting that they "somewhat approve" of Common Core. The percentage of the 800 predominately-New-York teachers surveyed who indicated the choice of "strongly approve" of Common Core was small, with AFT reporting a graphic with not only collapsed categories but also color-coded, non-labeled categories also absent actual percentages of respondents for each and every category.[24] Others and I have publicly requested that AFT release complete survey results, but AFT refuses to do so.

Most of the AFT teachers surveyed were New York teachers (36%, or 288 out of 800 teachers). Most of the teachers surveyed expressed caution regarding CCSS. Yet Coleman notes that New York teachers were those most involved in "contributing to" CCSS. Consider this address he gives in Albany, NY, in April 2011:

> *..The core standards stand on the shoulders of the work New York State has done. ...They stand on the shoulders of many individual people in this state who contributed to them. That involves most of all the teachers of this state who are heavily involved....*[25] [Emphasis added.]

Those Coleman credits for their involvement in CCSS are the very ones expressing hesitancy and caution regarding CCSS implementation, a sensible course of action for a nationwide program never piloted.

A third issue concerns the protections afforded the "work groups" composing CCSS. Notice that "states and national education associations" are excluded from the initial process according to this 2009 NGA press release. Teachers, via professional organizations, are relegated to the CCSS fringes. Indeed, "confidentiality" of deliberations allows for no accountability regarding whose input is being utilized and whose is being disregarded:

*The **Standards Development Work Group** is currently engaged in **determining and writing the college and career readiness standards in English-language arts and mathematics**. This group is composed of **content experts from Achieve, Inc., ACT, and the College Board**. This group will be **expanded later in the year to include additional experts to develop the standards for grades K-12 in English language arts and mathematics**. Additionally, CCSSO and the NGA Center have selected **an independent facilitator and an independent writer as well as resource advisors to support each content area work group**…. **The Work Group's deliberations will be confidential throughout the process. States and national education organizations will have an opportunity to review and provide evidence-based feedback on the draft documents**….[26] [Emphasis added.]*

CCSS is not a "state-led," "teacher-developed" set of standards. It is the product of a secretive corporate-centered coup. Bluegrass Institute's staff education analyst, Richard Innes, testified as much before the Kentucky Legislature's Interim Joint Committee on Education on June 10, 2013:

*Because the major decisions about the Common Core State Standards were made by workgroups operating under confidential conditions…**the lack of transparency precludes us from knowing anything about the processes actually followed. We don't know if comments solicited from the public, our teachers and even the Kentucky Department of Education actually received fair and appropriate consideration**.*

*We do know that NGA and the Council of Chief State School Officers (CCSSO) documents **don't show anyone from Kentucky on the various Common Core workgroups**. Thus, **thanks to the lack of transparency, claims that Kentuckians had significant input into the Common Core State Standards simply cannot be confirmed, but appear unlikely**.[27] [Emphasis added.]*

The lack of transparency guaranteed CCSS development renders any assurance of "teacher input" as empty words. Initially, even the members of the CCSS work groups were kept secret. In July 2009, the public learned that 22 of the 27 members were associated with ACT, College Board, or Achieve. Another two (Coleman and co-founder Jason Zimba) were associated with Student Achievement Partners. Only two members were not affiliated with an education company or nonprofit.[28]

In her testimony before both the Texas legislature in April 2011 and the Indiana Senate Education Committee in January 2012, Stotsky commented on NGA's and CCSSO's intentional lack of openness regarding CCSS activity:

*After the Common Core Initiative was launched in early 2009, the National Governors Association and the Council of Chief State School Officers **never explained to the public what the qualifications were for membership on the standards-writing committees or how it would justify the specific standards they created**. Most important, it never explained why Common Core's high school exit standards were equal to college admission requirements without qualification, even though this country's wide ranging post-secondary institutions use a variety of criteria for admission. Eventually* *responding to the many charges of a lack of transparency, the names of the 24 members (I counted 27) of the "Standards Development Work Group" were revealed in a July 1, 2009 news release.* **The vast majority, it appeared, work for testing companies. Not only did CCSSI give no rationale for the composition of this Work Group, it gave no rationale for the people it put on the two three-member teams in charge of writing the grade-level standards.**[29,30] [Emphasis added.]

Those "at the top" of this CCSS "initiative" intended to promote an agenda leading to national (via state-by-state) adoption of a set of not only untested standards, but unquestioned standards, prematurely announced by Gates mouthpieces and indeed "rubber stamped" by most members of the sadly-named "validation" committee. Those "designing" CCSS were associated with two major testing companies, ACT and College Board, and one non-profit whose funders include a number of American Legislative Exchange Council (ALEC) companies, Achieve, Inc.[31]

Coleman would become president of one of those testing companies, College Board—yet another instance of reformer "back scratching."

Speaking out of both sides of his mouth, Coleman is willing to accept the title of architect of CCSS while also proclaiming that the standards were a collaboration.[32] In addition to claiming teacher contribution, the CCSS website maintains that parents "provided input into the development of the standards."[33] Nevertheless, the phrase "providing input" means nothing in the absence of details. Truly, in its reading like a billboard advertisement, the CCSS website is short on details regarding actual CCSS stakeholder (or profiteer) roles. However, NGA's own press release revealed that the "heavily involved" individuals were almost exclusively associated with ACT, College Board, Achieve, and Coleman's Student Achievement Partners. Even the "inside," seemingly-educator-comprised group, the Validation Committee, was an ignored committee. Teachers (via organizations such as AFT) were on the fringes, at best—their predetermined position, intentionally distanced from anything remotely resembling CCSS key contribution. Thus, one might ask, where were parents in this "collaboration"?

Coleman, whose company created this never-piloted program, so eloquently stated that he is "scared of rewarding bullshit."[34] Common language notwithstanding, absent piloting his (it is his, as he is the public figurehead) CCSS, Coleman deals in this very expletive. Unfortunately, one of the first groups to experience the effects of the untested CCSS assessments was the parents in The Big Apple.

This appears to be the extent of "parental input" into CCSS: surprised reaction.

In spring 2013, New York parents and students were exposed to the CCSS assessment. If parents were involved in CCSS, an idea promoted by National PTA,[35] this assessment should have been no surprise to them:

As New York this week became one of the first states to unveil a set of exams grounded in new curricular standards, **education leaders are finding that rallying the public behind tougher tests may be more difficult than they expected.**

Complaints were plentiful: the tests were too long; students were demoralized to the point of tears; teachers were not adequately prepared. Some parents, long skeptical of the emphasis on standardized testing, forbade their children from participating.[36] [Emphasis added.]

David Coleman's response to parental resistance to the CCSS assessments:

David Coleman, **president of the College Board** *and an architect of the Common Core standards, said he did not understand skepticism about the tests.*

"When the alternative is shallower passages and shallower questions, what are we debating here?" *he said.*[37] [Emphasis added.]

This is the same man who spoke about "adults being informed by data."[38] Yet he pushes these untested assessments upon parents, who are offering what should be utilized feedback regarding initial (unpiloted, mind you) assessment issues, and he disregards it with a word.

Either do what I planned for you to do, or be publicly dismissed.

CCSS: THE NOT-FEDERAL NON-CURRICULUM

True, the federal government cannot force the states to adopt CCSS. States that never opted for CCSS, like Texas, and states that opted yet suspended implementation, like Indiana, are within their rights. Nevertheless, the actual, barely-disguised goal of CCSS development is a national curricular agenda:

(Common Core standards are recommendations. . . .) **The hope was that if enough states opted in, the standards would effectively become national—and that is essentially what happened** *(though Alaska, Texas, Minnesota, Nebraska, Virginia, and a few territories* **have yet** *to sign on). Beginning in the 2014–15 school year, participating states will test their students using standardized exams designed to match the Common Core standards.*[39] [Emphasis added.]

The "national" education agenda that is "not national" for its not originating with the federal government. Yet it is precisely the federal government that holds funding hostage via RTTT requirement for states agree to adopt CCSS. If such were not enough, US Secretary of Education Arne Duncan has made it his personal mission to defend CCSS. As Valerie Strauss of the *Washington Post* notes:

It seems that a big part of Education Secretary Arne Duncan's job now is giving im-
passioned defenses of the Common Core State Standards, which he did Tuesday (June
25, 2013), to a convention of American news editors....

A few months ago, Duncan told Chamber of Commerce leaders that they had to be
more supportive of the Common Core because it was coming under withering attack
from the left and right, and some states were reconsidering implementing the standards.
...

There is some irony in the fact that Arne Duncan keeps saying that the Core is not
the work of the federal government while he, the federal secretary of education, goes
around attacking its critics.[40] [Emphasis added.]

Here more word play enters; CCSS proponents are quick to note that CCSS is not a "curriculum" since districts still select their own materials. Nevertheless, in promoting a set of standards (which are not voluntary to those wishing for RTTT funding), Coleman and others are promoting in the broadest sense a curriculum, a set of standards that define the interaction of teachers and students in the educational process. Furthermore, federal policy (ESEA Subpart Two, section 9527) expressly prohibits CCSS adoption as a condition for RTTT funding:

> *Notwithstanding any other provision of Federal law,* **no State shall be required to have**
> **academic content or student academic achievement standards approved or certified**
> **by the Federal Government, in order to receive assistance under this Act.**[41] [Emphasis added.]

Thus, the federally-promoted focus that CCSS "is not a curriculum" diverts attention from the truth that RTTT funding should not be connected to a "common" set of "student academic achievement standards."

Returning to the "not a curriculum" declaration: Even in "selecting their own materials," districts are restricted by the standards as to what materials might be used. For example, the CCSS ELA for grades 9 and 10 include standards that specify reading "seminal US documents of historical... significance"[42] and "a wide reading of world literature."[43] The decision to include both historical documents and world literature in the tenth-grade classroom is a curricular decision—one dictated by the standards. Thus, the CCSS line between "standard" and "curriculum" is blurred.

Insistence that CCSS is "not a curriculum" (and "not national") is also problematic given the stated intention of individuals like Bill Gates to spend millions on translating CCSS into classroom implementation specifics. Below is one of Gates' goals for the teachers at the mercy of his millions invested in CCSS, including the disclaimer of teachers' "using their own creativity" despite the fact that Bill is inserting his will directly into the nation's classrooms:

> **The Gates Foundation will spend** *an estimated $354 million between 2010 and 2014* **to: Develop syllabi that lay out a course that connects the standards, assessments, and instruction** *but depends on teachers using their own creativity in the classroom.*[44] [Emphasis added.]

Even the CCSS website barely skirts the "national curriculum" designation in its own attempt to define the CCSS goal:

> *The Common Core State Standards will not prevent different levels of achievement among students, but* **they will ensure more consistent exposure to materials and learning experiences through curriculum, instruction, and teacher preparation** *among other supports for student learning.*[45] [Emphasis added.]

Just remember: CCSS is not federal, and it is not a curriculum, and it is especially not a federal curriculum, but it is promoted by the US secretary of education, and it does significantly define what teachers are to teach their students as ultimately determined by CCSS standardized tests.

COLEMAN'S COLLEGE BOARD PROMOTION

CCSS and standardized testing are inextricable. More than any other stakeholders, the Big Business of Standardized Assessment was amply represented at the CCSS planning table. My referring to the assessment companies as stakeholders was intentional, for the incredible profits to be drawn from public coffers by the likes of ACT, College Board, and others is certainly not lost on the testing industry.

A company like College Board would never miss a lucrative opportunity to form a royal marriage between itself and the Architect of the Common Core. Imagine the continued opportunity for profits that admittedly began in the planning of CCSS:

> **The College Board... helped design the standards—an outline of what students should learn in English and math from kindergarten through high school—meant to ensure that all high school graduates are prepared for college.**[46] [Emphasis added.]

Every student is going to college. The profiteers have decided as much for virtually the entire nation.

> *Mr. Coleman's new position [as College Board president] will involve a continued focus on college readiness.* **"We have a crisis in education, and over the next few years, the main thing on the College Board's agenda is to deliver its social mission,"** *he said in an interview on Tuesday.* **"The College Board is not just about measuring and testing, but designing high-quality curriculum."**[47] [Emphasis added.]

We're here to help "you people." And even though I, David Coleman, the Voice Behind CCSS, have insisted that CCSS is not a curriculum, now We, the College Board Social Missionary Society, are going to give You People in Crisis The Curriculum You Need.

Coleman's arrogance and hardly-subtle admissions concerning the true goals of College Board's connection to CCSS do not stop here. In a speech in Boston on May 17, 2013, Coleman seeks data. As is large-scale data collection.

Nothing is so valuable to education privatization as the details of student identities. Personal information is what has made identity theft a booming black-market industry,[48,49] and businesses that store personal information are realizing that they can profit handsomely by selling the details of people's lives.[50] But to directly state as much would be foolish, so privatizers must convince the public of some altruistic motive—that the data is needed in order to improve education.

Do not be fooled. Organizations storing data realize the potential for huge profits. For example, the Texas Department of Motor Vehicles is making $2.1 million per year selling Texas driver information; in 2012 alone, the Texas DMV sold personal information to almost 2500 entities. Furthermore, because of the way the laws are worded, there appears to be little that Texas drivers can do to prevent the sales from transpiring.[51]

In education, data can be used to exploit students, tracking their lives to follow paths that financially benefit specific entities, including but certainly not limited to testing companies and post-secondary institutions.

In his Boston speech, Coleman names a number of well-known people and organizations associated with data collection, including the Gates Foundation's Strategic Data Project, Harvard University's Center for Education Policy Research, and Erin McGoldrick, former DC Chancellor Michelle Rhee's chief data analyst.[52]

In an effort to argue for the indispensability of collecting and using data to inform decision making, Coleman conveniently forgets that he has promoted standards that were never tested. Thus, his statement as recorded below is truer than he realizes and causes him to appear as one lacking in self-awareness:

> *...If evidence did not inform the development of standards they would inevitably be vast vague and useless. Now why is that true?*[53] [Emphasis added.]

As a member of the CCSS Validation Committee, Sandra Stotsky asked to see the research upon which CCSS standards were based. She was ignored.

Consider also Coleman's simplistic characterization of the mystery groups assigned to write the standards. Coleman implies that the standards were written by groups at the state level; such contradicts the NGA press release of almost exclusive ACT and College Board involvement:

> *So what happened in states is they got together committees to write standards and they got into groups,* you'd have your geometry team, your statistics team, your data, your algebra team, right, a math meeting or you know the ELA *not knowing that you know just get everyone together and had a nice big old happy thing. And the only way to end the meeting is what, to include everyone's stuff; I'm not leaving here until you put in all my stuff and I'm not leaving till you put in my stuff and everyone's like cool let's put in your stuff with my stuff; we are done here.*[54] [Emphasis added.]

No serious deliberation necessary, dude. We just included everything everyone wanted to include, and everyone was happy, and we had us some standards.

Wow.

Here is what Coleman maintains regarding the rigor of the CCSS math standards:

> *...Overwhelmingly based on evidence* there is a relatively focused portion of mathematics that is extremely important to your future in math. ... *There are only three topics in common in high performing countries—they are addition and subtraction and the qualities they measure. The common core standards adopted by 45 states in mathematics are the first American standards to dare to follow this tight focus.* The American math curriculum as you know has in the past been a mile wide and an inch deep, *but that data that evidence* allowed us to turn back the tide.[55] [Emphasis added.]

Coleman never produced any evidence to Validation Committee member Stotsky, period. Consider also Validation Committee member Milgram's concerns that the CCSS math standards lacked rigor and would leave students a couple years behind by eighth grade on international standards and that there were uncorrected errors in the standards. Concerns ignored.

In the next excerpt, Coleman inadvertently contradicts his earlier statement of the states planning the standards; he does not clarify who "we" is; according to the 2009 NGA press release, "we" is most likely the predominately-ACT and College Board "math work group." It appears that their own conducted "research" involved surveying an unknown number of individuals who taught first-year college math and asking them what they thought students needed to know in order to be successful in the first-year math courses then ranking the identified content based on survey info as well as some poorly defined information from "international" and "domestic" studies.

This is at best crude science, and certainly not substantive enough as a foundation for what is effectively a national set of "standards":

> *...We had evidence from international examples of what the best countries did. We had data from domestic studies early mathematics and of what, what things predicted later success. We had surveys from college professors first-year college professors about what math made the difference in their courses and what did not. What we did differently is we used it to force rank; that is, we didn't just have all this data we*

decided that based on that data you could decide what was critical and what was not and make it that.[56] [Emphasis added.]

We decided. End of story.

Next, Coleman makes his clearest statement concerning the truth about "state-led, voluntary" CCSS: He was sent to push these standards onto the states, and what a glossy-brochured, no-loose-ends sales job it was:

> **When I was involved in convincing governors and others around this country to adopt these standards,** *it was not "Obama likes them"; do you think that would have gone well with a Republican crowd?*
>
> **It was instead, "there's a focused set of math with an overwhelming amount of data that will predict success and your standards have teachers all over the place."**[57] [Emphasis added.]

Keep in mind that in 2007, Coleman formed a Student Achievement Partners, a company with the primary aim of formulating and marketing a set of national standards—exactly what he is admitting to having done in this 2013 speech in Boston.

The "we" Coleman continually refers to in this speech could easily be Student Achievement Partners.

For the next several minutes, Coleman promotes the use of data in making "personnel decisions," namely, using student test scores to grade teachers. His words are nothing new to those accustomed to the current corporate reformer rhetoric: The need to grade individual teachers using "data"; the importance of that "upper quartile" of teachers; the influence of a "great" teacher on overcoming the seeming excuse of poverty ("to ignore the data about the differences between teachers is to make public schools helpless to change the outcomes of poor children"); of the need to "increase the concentration of demonstrated effective teachers in our schools."

The final shift in Coleman's speech is eerily Orwellian in his stated desire to use data to identify students he believes should go to college but who are at risk for not attending college and to use College Board as a vehicle to "care" for students by contacting data-identified students and their parents to attempt to direct such students into college (in other words, to force the outcome of college attendance):

> *You know it's interesting watching Sarah Glover [of the Gates-funded Strategic Data Project at the Harvard Center for Educational Policy Research] summarize the findings and she's like* **we got to find these kids now; that they're certain kinds of data we're just, like, this goes beyond a number like, who are these people? I'm gonna go find them. I wanna go talk to them; I'm going to talk their parents. What's their names?** *Right, that's a certain kind of data in life and it's, it's not just a number it's like, whoa, how could this be happening in this generation?*

The College Board—our philosophy is it's not just that we can see this data, but these students are within our care. That is as the College Board. We cannot stand that these students who can go do not go. It is our obligation and responsibility to do everything in our power to change this result. That means we shall not rest until these inequities go away.[58] [Emphasis added.]

We need data on students so that we can tell them what we intend for their lives.

Coleman's arrogance has serious ramifications.

When it comes to corporate reform's grading teachers, it is okay if students are represented by nothing more than their test scores. When it comes to data on the high percentage of children living in poverty and the unfair comparisons of their international test scores with the scores of students who live at greater levels of financial stability and comfort, such data are ignored and all is placed on the heads of their teachers. But when it comes to seeing the high test scores of students at risk for not attending college, the mission becomes to somehow exert influence on the lives of these students and their parents in order to force a preconceived agenda of mandatory college attendance upon them—never stopping to ask about the appropriate boundaries—and getting lost in objectifying human beings to suit the now-vogue, singular, enforced goal of College Attendance for All.

More than in any other time in the history of the world, human beings have a tremendous amount of data literally keystrokes and seconds away. With this ease of information availability comes an incredible burden of responsibility for how information is used. The speed of communication via an assortment of technologies only complicates the issue; just as we can access information with a single computer, so we can damage and destroy lives the same way. Those in power over others can all too easily use information ("data") to impose their own wills upon others without careful thought to human decency and appropriate boundaries. This is the direction I see repeatedly in Coleman's speech in Boston: The creation of CCSS by a secretive, privileged few and the resulting imposition of this creation upon the many; the misuse of student data for the grading of teachers; the attempted force-fit of post-secondary institution attendance upon all students, and the dangerously unregulated collecting of data that might easily feed privatizers' profit motives.

David Coleman is a dangerous man; he has the ability to both direct a massive course of action in education policy and financially profit tremendously from doing so. Like many privatizers, Coleman is accountable to no one. No data is collected on him and handed over to some agency holding his livelihood and his future in its hand. No one is attempting to impose some predetermined course of action over his life.

In concert with a handful of other powerful individuals via CCSS, Coleman has made American public education into a national puppet.

CHAPTER 12

CHESTER FINN AND FREDERICK HESS: PUSHING REFORMS "JUST BECAUSE"

The two reformers included in this chapter are not in reform in order to make quick money or wield their own power. They hold no political offices whereby they might seize school districts. They have neither frozen nor cut any education budgets. They have closed no schools. They have fired no teachers. They have altered no test scores. Nevertheless, in their speaking, writing, and overall support for and involvements with corporate-reform-driven institutions and financiers, these two men form a very visible face and audible voice for the tenets of privatization. They are indeed powerful promoters and protectors of the damaging ideal that is corporate reform, and that is why I have included them in my book.

The unassuming public should be aware of these men and their often intertwined influence upon the privatization message. In this brief writing, I do not examine the entire careers of these men. My goal is simply to leave readers with a heightened awareness of their reform positions and select involvements.

They are Chester Finn and Frederick Hess.

A Chronicle of Echoes: Who's Who in the Implosion of American Public Education, pages 185–203.
185

CHESTER FINN

I first learned of Chester Finn in January 2013 as I was writing my blog series on the National Council of Teacher Quality (NCTQ), a controversial advocacy group that rates teacher training programs based upon program artifacts—no site visit necessary. Finn was one of the creators of NCTQ in 2000 as president of NCTQ's parent organization, the Fordham Institute. Finn also continues to sit on the NCTQ board of directors.[1]

By the time of NCTQ creation in 2000, Finn had a decades-long career in education, including that of professor, education policy analyst, and former US Department of Education Assistant Secretary of Education for Research and Improvement.[2,3]

Like many who promote corporate reform, Finn was never a classroom teacher. And like many who promote corporate reform, he exerts his influence upon the classroom though his many associations, not the least of which are the Fordham and Hoover Institutes.

The Thomas B. Fordham Institute was created in 1959 in Finn's childhood hometown of Dayton Ohio. Thelma Fordham Pruett, Fordham's widow, funded the Institute, which was not education-specific until Mrs. Pruett's death in 1997. In 2007, the Institute was combined with the Fordham Foundation. The Fordham Institute website describes the Institute as the "public face of nearly all that Fordham does."[4]

What exactly does Fordham do?

In short, Fordham is a "think tank" that promotes a corporate reform agenda in education. It operates via donations from some highly influential funders who endorse (and often, actively promote) the same push for privatization as does the Finn-directed Fordham. Finn and others promote their views via publications and endorsements. Fordham also presents awards in recognition of individuals it believes best exemplify the privatization agenda.

I mentioned previously that in 2000, Fordham created NCTQ, a group with a purpose to supposedly advance "teacher quality." In 2001, then-Secretary of Education and current Fordham board member[5] Rod Paige gave NCTQ a $5 million grant despite the NCTQ application's being rejected by the review panel. This and other capricious grant-awarding actions brought Paige censure from the Government Accountability Office.[6] Moreover, a quick glance at the NCTQ website reveals that NCTQ has a clear agenda to alter, not assist, public education:

> *Based in Washington, D.C., the National Council on Teacher Quality was founded in 2000* **to provide an alternative national** *voice to existing teacher organizations and to* **build the case for a comprehensive reform agenda that would challenge the current structure and regulation of the profession.**[7] [Emphasis added.]

In true modern reformer fashion, most of the members of NCTQ's advisory board are not and never have been classroom teachers. However, most do own and/or run education businesses that stand to profit from an atmosphere of corporate reform.[8] Despite NCTQ's lack of grounding in the very area it purports to evaluate for "quality," Fordham considers NCTQ a partner.[9]

Fordham and NCTQ funding noticeably overlaps. NCTQ receives much of its money from major pro-reform foundations, including the Gates, Broad, Joyce, and Arnold foundations (each funding NCTQ for $200,000+) and Walton, Dell and Bradley (funding between $75,000 and $200,000).[10] Fordham's list of 2010–2013 funders includes all of the reform-friendly NCTQ funders listed above except Dell. In addition, Fordham's funders include Bloomberg Philanthropies, College Board, Education Reform Now, Fisher Fund, the Hoover Institution on War, Revolution, and Peace (Hoover Institute), the Koret Foundation, and School Choice Ohio. The goal for each of these funders is not to improve but to replace traditional public education with a market-driven model.

Under the direction of Chester Finn, the Fordham Institute is a well-financed privatization force. On its website, Fordham lists as its "policy priorities" three issues: "standards-based reforms," "quality choices," and a "reform-based system." First, concerning Fordham's (and Finn's) priority of standards-based reforms:

> *... We press for the full suite of standards-based reforms...* **including (but not limited to) careful implementation of the Common Core standards (CCSS) for English language arts (ELA) and mathematics... rigorous, aligned state assessments and forceful accountability mechanisms....**[11] [Emphasis added.]

One of Fordham's funders is College Board, whose current president is David Coleman, the "architect" of the Common Core State Standards (CCSS). College Board was one of two major testing companies that drafted CCSS. Thus, the so-called "state-led initiative" to design a standardized set of "standards" was actually designed by Coleman, College Board, and ACT. (See Coleman chapter for details on CCSS.)

Common Core is listed as a partner with Fordham.[12]

Even though CCSS has never been piloted, and even though members of CCSS's own Verification Committee expressed concerns about the lack of rigor and unavailability of the research upon which CCSS was purportedly structured, Finn endorses CCSS. Consider his views in this piece, written for the Hoover Institution (another privatization think tank and Fordham funder), where Finn serves as a senior fellow of the Koret K-12 Task Force (Koret: yet another Fordham funder). In this article, Finn refers to CCSS as a "promising education initiative," one that he cannot grasp "conservatives stoutly resisting":

> *Though few Americans have ever heard of the "Common Core,"* it's causing a ruck-
> us.... *Prompted by tea party activists, a couple of influential talk-radio hosts and
> bloggers, some disgruntled academics, several conservative think-tanks, and a couple
> of mysterious but deep-pocketed funders, the Republican National Committee recently
> adopted a resolution blasting the Common Core as "an inappropriate overreach to
> standardize and control the education of our children."* Several red states that previ-
> ously adopted it for their schools are on the verge of backing out. **Indiana has already
> hit the "pause" button.**[13] [Emphasis added.]

"Few Americans hearing of the Common Core" is hardly enticement to
embrace an initiative supposedly not only state-led but also designed by
teachers and parents and officially approved in June 2010, three years prior
to Finn's article. Moreover, his list of the individuals and groups opposing
CCSS is a bit long for one trying to dismiss these "few" as manipulating eas-
ily-duped Republicans. And Indiana did indeed "hit the pause button"—
after hearing testimony of individuals on the CCSS Verification Committee whose recommendations were ignored, including recommendations to
correct content errors, and whose requests to view the research upon which
CCSS was supposedly constructed were also dismissed. (See Coleman chapter.) As though he pilot tested CCSS himself, Finn continues his endorsement, adding that CCSS is the undisputed solution for solving the problem
of varied rigor in state standards nationwide:

> *...Beginning five years ago, the National Governors Association and Council of Chief
> State School Officers... launched **a foundation-funded project** called the "common core
> state standards initiative," **which gave birth to a set of commendably strong standards
> for English and math from kindergarten through high school. Fordham Institute re-
> viewers found them superior to the academic expectations set by three-quarters of the
> states—and essentially on par with the rest.**[14] [Emphasis added.]

Since Fordham finds the standards "commendable," they must be. What
Finn fails to acknowledge is that the Fordham-funding College Board held
a huge role in designing CCSS, and "architect" David Coleman later became president of College Board. In addition, as of March 2013, former
Gates Foundation advocacy chief Stefanie Sanford is employed with College Board. Finn downplays Gates' role in promoting CCSS—he calls it the
"heavy artillery" against CCSS—those who believe Obama is "in cahoots
with the Gates Foundation."[15] Nevertheless, these interconnections present undeniable conflicts of interest that render any Fordham review and
endorsement of CCSS meaningless.

Finn does not detail exactly who "gave birth" to CCSS. Let me assure you,
it was not "the locals."

Like others do who endorse CCSS, Finn insists that their implementation is "voluntary" and that "states unserious about implementing it are bet-

ter off not pretending to." Why, then, worry about the states "on the verge of dropping out"? Is it not their choice?

After all, Finn advocates choice.

As an additional selling factor, Finn offers that states with rigorous standards such as Massachusetts contributed to the process of formulating CCSS. He fails to note that Sandra Stotsky, who testified against CCSS both in Texas and Indiana, assisted with the Massachusetts standards. She was never provided with the purported research upon which CCSS was supposedly based. (See Coleman chapter.)

While high on pro-CCSS rhetoric, Finn's article is low on critical details. Furthermore, the declaration that Fordham "presses for… forceful accountability mechanisms at every level" is amazingly ironic given Finn's willingness to disregard both NCTQ's superficial process of grading traditional teacher training programs as well as CCSS' implementation across virtually the entire Unites States absent any piloting of either the program or the CCSS assessments.

The second priority of Fordham's website is "quality choices":

> *…We strive to develop policies and practices leading to a lively,* **accessible marketplace of high-quality education options**…*(including* **charter schools, magnet schools, voucher programs, and online courses***), as well as families empowered and informed so that they can successfully engage* **with that marketplace**.[16] [Emphasis added]

Finn not only approves of charter schools; he approves of selective admission processes for "public schools," which encompasses both privately-run charters and district-run magnet schools.[17] However, successful district-run magnet schools do not receive the same laudation by reformers as do successful privately-run charter schools. In the current reform environment, charter schools are promoted as superior to traditional public schools; charters are part of the sales package of "school choice" that is supposed to introduce the market element of competition, thus forcing the public schools to "do better." Selective admission charters further propagate the myth of charter success over traditional public schools; the traditional public school is the lowest rung on the compulsory education ladder and the selective charter, the highest. As a result, students whom the selective admission charter rejects must attend elsewhere—the "final option" always being the traditional public school. Finn alludes to the selective admission charters in New Orleans that "were selective before they were charters" and notes disapprovingly that a charter advocate (Howard Fuller) spoke against them.[18] In fact, Fuller did say, 'There should not be any reason to have any charter schools that can select children."[19] The New Orleans selective admission charters were magnet schools prior to converting to charters following Hurricane Katrina. These magnet-become-charter schools are not the state-associated, failing-school-"takeover" charters; therefore, they escape the mandate of open enrollment. Nevertheless, the selective admission charter schools are labeled a New Orleans Miracle of charter success and often confused for the state-associated, continuously-failing, open enrollment charters.[20] Thus, Finn is perpetrating a caste-type education system with multiple tiers: 1) selective admissions schools, including charters and magnets; 2) open enrollment charters, able to still set retention criteria to "weed out" undesirable students via harsh discipline policies, and, at the bottom, 3) traditional public schools, which remain the default "catch all" for students rejected by tiers 1 and 2.

Finn views charter schools as "choice," as "exit options" that "allow many families [to] vote with their feet and move their kids out of district-operated schools."[21] In his ideal, Finn presumes that charters will be better than the district-operated schools. However, in New Orleans, the May 2013 effort of parents to "vote with their feet" has yielded a preference for the Orleans Parish district-run schools despite the fact that the number of open enrollment charters outnumbers the OPSB direct-run schools ten to one. Furthermore, the "cream" schools, the selective admission charters (also connected to OPSB and not the state) are off limits to most students by virtue of their selectivity—no "voting with feet" allowed.[22]

Another "choice" that Finn endorses is the voucher. In his book, *Troublemaker*, Finn speaks approvingly of the Milwaukee voucher program.[23] However, he does not discuss the number of students who forsake vouchers to return to their original schools. In assessing voucher "success," Patrick Wolf et al. of the University of Arkansas use "intent to treat" analysis to gauge voucher success, which means that voucher attrition is ignored in favor of voucher "exposure" (i.e., use of vouchers even for a brief period then returning to the public school). The result:

A student accepting a voucher for a freshman year and returning to public school for the remaining three years and graduates is considered a voucher "success" since she graduated and used a voucher at some point. In the Wolf et al. study, only 25% of students (or maybe 44%— there is some discrepancy in Wolf's et al. reporting) who accepted vouchers actually followed through using vouchers until graduation.[24]

A final "choice" that Finn endorses is the online course. Finn notes that the "enormous potential" of online learning "will require a wholesale reshaping of the reform agenda itself, particularly in the realms of school finance and governance."[25] He writes of "exploiting the potential" of digital learning; however, if online education in Louisiana is any indication, it seems that the true exploitation will likely be perpetrated on the consumer, not the online education businesses.[26] In his focus on impediments to digital learning, Finn views school districts, school boards, and unions as the "self-absorbed and self-serving groups that do their utmost either to capture the potential of technology to advance their own interests or to shackle it in ways that keep it from messing with those interests."[27] To Finn, even teacher certification requirements could "hamper" the "innovation" of online learning. He is also against union efforts to ensure that teachers are not replaced with online vendors and that class size limits apply to digital learning.

Finn calls for national governance of online learning—or "at least, the states." Just bypass the cumbersome districts, with all of their bureaucratic, self-serving regulations. Sure, digital learning requires regulation—but let larger government do so since online learning is not restricted by locale. He cites the perils of regulation encountered by charters: caps on enrollment, lack of "proper" charter funding ("almost nowhere are charters properly funded").[28] Finn does not wish for digital learning to suffer the same fate as these "not properly funded" charters that "in many places…remain shackled by myriad regulations."

He lost me with discussion of the "poor charters." I am from Louisiana, home of the New Orleans Miracle, where the FY 2012 charter audit found gross under-regulation, including failure to follow up on previously identified financial issues at charters on probation, failure to verify school-level data, failure to administer student pretests until spring of the following year (four semesters late), and failure even to conduct site visits. The superintendent of Louisiana's schools, John White of Teach for America and the Broad Superintendents Academy (as in the Broad Foundation, the same one that funds both Fordham and NCTQ), has responded that he believes site visits are not necessary due to "budget restrictions"; the state board also altered the charter regulations following LDOE negligence *in order to justify* the negligence regarding both the pretest issue and checking on charter schools on probation.[29]

This is state-level regulation of Louisiana charters.

"State regulation" of Louisiana vouchers has produced an ongoing scandal whereby White included uninvestigated schools as voucher schools; the school approved for the largest number of vouchers, already known to lack sufficient space, instructional materials, and qualified teachers. A voucher school audit revealed that the school in question overcharged the state $378,000. Most of the audits (49 out of 51) could not be completed due to schools' not having a separate checking accounts for state funding.[30]

"State regulation" of Louisiana online vendors has resulted such a "rigorous approval process" that one vendor of Louisiana's online education initiative, called Course Choice, FastPath, signed up 1100 students from Caddo and Webster parishes without parental consent. Often students were "enrolled" in grade-inappropriate courses; some students were enrolled in courses they had already passed:

[High school junior Randall] Gunn was called into a counselor's office and told he was enrolled in three Course Choice classes—all of which he already had passed standardized tests with exceptional scores.

"I had no clue what was going on," Gunn said. "I have no reason to take these classes and still don't know who signed me up."

*According to parents, students, and Webster and Caddo education officials, **FastPath Learning is signing up some students it shouldn't—in many cases without parent or student knowledge. A free tablet computer is offered to those who enroll ....***

"I have graduating seniors signed up for math classes," Roberts said. "I have even seen kids, sophomores, enrolled in second-grade math and reading classes. There's no rhyme or reason to who these companies are signing up or for what classes." One example is freshman Shakelvin Calhoun. Calhoun was signed up for junior- and senior-level classes, and said he still is unsure how he was enrolled. " It was a complete surprise to me," he said. "We still can't figure out how I was signed up or why I was put in those classes, but I don't want to have anything to do with it. "[31] [Emphasis added.]

Here is something worth knowing: FastPath is an Austin,TX, firm headed up by none other than former US Secretary of Education and Fordham board member Rod Paige.[32,33]

Finn suggests that online education needs to be freed of cumbersome local regulations. In Louisiana, FastPath, a company whose chairman of the board just happens to also sit on the Fordham board, had enrollment freedom, and it grossly abused such underregulation before the program could even be fully implemented.

Do not believe that these overlapping power structures will serve "the children."

FastPath and other online course vendors stand to make a lot of money in Louisiana, with little of it contingent upon student outcomes:

*FastPath, as with all course choice providers, charges $700 to $1250 in tuition and like all providers, receives 50 percent of that ($350 to $625) up front. **Only 10 percent of the final 50 percent (or 5 percent of the overall tuition) is contingent upon students' showing only an increase, not a "significant" increase. Thus, if a FastPath student failed to show gains, FastPath would lose only $62.50 of a total tuition of $1250 or $35 of a $700 tuition.***

Some penalty.[34] [Emphasis added.]

Following discovery of FastPath's shady enrollment practices, the Louisiana legislature filed a resolution requiring LDOE and BESE to formally report on Course Choice on September 30, 2013, including providing enrollment information. The focus of legislative interest was centered on the actions of FastPath's known exploitation of online course enrollment:

Several state legislators and superintendents said FastPath Learning, which accounted for 88 percent of the state's initial enrollees, blanketed neighborhoods and apartment complexes offering students free tablet computers if they signed up for Course Choice.

*State Rep. Patrick Jefferson, D-Arcadia, vice chairman of the House Education Committee and chief sponsor of the resolution, said it was prompted in part by reports **that children in his area were being approached about the courses, which alarmed parents.***

"It was my understanding that if the kids signed up, they promised them computers," Jefferson said.

*State Rep. Gene Reynolds, D-Dubberly, **whose House district included more than 20 percent of initial enrollees, criticized FastPath's earlier enrollment methods.***

"They were offering incentives like devices to do the courses and they were signing them up and they never really contacted the schools," Reynolds said.

"And these people would just sign up, whether they needed the course or not," he said. "They just wanted names. They got paid by names."[35] [Emphasis added.]

The legislature's attention to online course enrollment exploitation coupled with the Louisiana Supreme Court finding that redirecting funds earmarked for public schools to either non-public voucher schools or online providers is unconstitutional contributed to a substantial enrollment drop for FastPath—zero confirmed enrollment requests as of June 16, 2013. Regarding their situation, FastPath "declined several requests for interviews."[36]

Before Finn publishes articles promoting modified regulation of the privatizing of public education, he should investigate the current results of underregulation, especially as such relates to companies run by individuals directly connected to him.

The final "policy priority" on the Fordham website is a "reform-based system":

*... We seek to deepen and strengthen the K–12 system's capacity to deliver quality education to every child, **based on rigorous standards** and **ample choices**, by ensuring that it possesses the **requisite talent, technology, policies, practices, structures, and nimble governance arrangements to promote efficiency as well as effectiveness.***[37] [Emphasis added.]

Finn approves of an unpiloted CCSS. He dismisses the concerns of those seasoned educators involved in (and yet also ignored in) the process, a process unduly influenced by two major testing companies, one of which that happens to be a Fordham funder. He speaks of "choices" yet disregards the reality that is charter inequity, voucher ineptness, and online vendor exploitation as discussed in this chapter, with voucher exploitation connected to a Fordham board member. Indeed, based upon the few powerful examples presented here, readers can easily conclude that when education privatization comes to town, there will likely be no "nimble governance," no "efficiency," and little, if any, "effectiveness."

FREDERICK HESS

Frederick Hess is unusual for the corporate reform crowd; he has much more classroom teaching experience: two full years, and not with Teach for America. Hess graduated from Brandeis the same year that TFA founder Wendy Kopp graduated from Princeton: 1989. Both Hess and Kopp had the same major: political science. While Kopp was attempting to launch her teacher temp agency, Hess was enrolled in a masters program at Harvard and graduated one year later with a degree in teaching and curriculum. The Harvard program requires no previous experience in classroom teaching and is tailored to those with liberal arts degrees who are to become "leaders and agents for organizational and social change in classrooms, schools, and society."[38]

Hess had no plans of staying in the classroom. He is not a classroom teacher; he is a promoter of corporate reform policy who is now able to write that he is a "former high school social studies teacher." Given that Hess' bachelors and PhD (also from Harvard) focus on political science/government, it is easy enough to see that he wanted to be that "agent for social change." Unfortunately, the corporate reformer set spends little time in the classroom before fancying themselves as leaders in education. Even though he taught for only two years, Hess advertises that he has even "supervised student teachers."[39] Again, heavy on the leadership; light on the trenches.

And Hess is heavy on corporate reform leadership. He is the executive editor of *Education Next*, a reform publication where Chester Finn and Eric Hanushek sit on the board. *Education Next* is published by the Hoover Institution and funded in part by the Fordham Foundation. An influence on Hess was noted voucher proponent, Harvard professor and editor-in-chief of *Education Next*, Paul Peterson, who also influenced other *Education Next* editors, including executive editor and Fordham Institute Senior Editor Marci Kanstoroom,[40] contributing editor and University of Arkansas Department of Education Reform Chair Jay Greene,[41] editorial board member and Stanford University professor/Hoover Institute Senior Fellow Terry Moe,[42] and editorial board member and former EdisonLearning CEO John Chubb.[43–45] A number of the individuals associated with *Education Next* also currently serve or have served on the advisory board of Fordham-created NCTQ, including Hess, Hanushek, E.D. Hirsch, and Paul Hill.[46] In its mission statement, *Education Next* purports to "go where the evidence points";[47] however, like Finn, Hess endorses CCSS despite the lack of evidence for and the mounting evidence against it (see Coleman chapter). In June 2013, Hess wrote a two-part series advising those who are pro-CCSS. One of Hess' suggestions for those combatting resistance to CCSS is to read the wriritngs of Chester Finn,[48] who endorses CCSS enough to have CCSS as a partner listed on the Fordham website.

Here is some interesting advice Hess offers to pro-CCSS individuals: Admit the federal government's role in CCSS:

> *Sec. **Duncan needs to give a speech in which he pleads "mea culpa"** and acknowledges that **federal involvement and money** played a nontrivial... role in the early stages of the Common Core.*[49] [Emphasis added.]

Tell the public the truth: The federal government was involved in (and financed) this "state-led" initiative, after all. (Duncan's public defense of CCSS makes federal involvement obvious enough, already.)

More advice from Hess for the appearance of state-initiated support:

> *Jeb Bush, Bobby Jindal, and Chris Christie ought to pen an op-ed in which they unapologetically repeat their support for the Common Core project.... They should demand an acknowledgment from Duncan (making it easier for him to deliver that essential mea culpa), insist on **safeguards regarding data collection and federal involvement**, and seek clarity as to how governance of the Common Core and the assessments are going to be ordered so as to respect state sovereignty....*[50] [Emphasis added.]

Admit that the federal government is indeed involved in CCSS, but stage op/ed concerns from governors—a sort of "good cop, bad cop" in which the pro-privatizing governors get to play "good cop." It is not about addressing the truth behind CCSS concerns; it is about setting the stage in order to cause the public to forget that the federal government lied about its involvement in CCSS and to successfully push the untested standards on the unconvinced "fringes."

As for the data collection issue, David Coleman is clear about his intentions to focus efforts on using student data to contact students and their parents in order to convince them of the need for the students to attend college. In his public acknowledgement of this intention that he views as part of his role as College Board president, Coleman does not consider the rights of individuals to their own decision-making and privacy. Hess wants pro-reform governors to calm the fears of constituents regarding improper usage of personal data while at the same time, powerful individuals like Coleman are publicly expressing their intentions to use that data in ways they determine are "good for the students" (see Coleman chapter).

The hand that the federal government had in CCSS development, the potential for inappropriate use of student data collected in the name of "what is good for students—both are part of the CCSS package.

I wonder if Hess would volunteer to return for another two years to the Baton Rouge, Louisiana, high school classroom and demonstrate implementation of CCSS, complete with having his inflated reputation depend upon the results of CCSS assessments.

It was just a thought. Then I remembered that Hess is a "change agent leader," not a classroom teacher. I remembered that Hess is blindly and blissfully disconnected from the confusing and incredibly stressful reality that the nation's teachers will face under CCSS and its marathon assessments.

In his proliferation of advice to pro-CCSSers, Hess next attempts to enlist the assistance of a cadre of corporate reform notables. Not once does he suggest a serious re-examination of the issues of CCSS. Halting CCSS implementation is not an option. Hess' goal is merely to help his fellow reformers "make the medicine go down" with CCSS doubters:

> **The stellar state superintendents who make up Chiefs for Change** *should make clear that they're willing to take the lead on addressing serious concerns with an open mind.* **Rather than merely voicing support for the effort, as they've done of late, they should explain how they're addressing key concerns and signal an openness** *to weighing questions....*[51] [Emphasis added.]

Chiefs for Change is a Jeb-Bush-directed group of superintendents. Jeb Bush wants CCSS, so these superintendents will want it, too. Again, opting out of CCSS is not a question. The question is whether Chiefs for Change will offer enough head-nodding and concerned-appearing visages to take the public's mind off of not wanting CCSS and to refocus it on "proper implementation."

As for his next suggestion, that key individuals openly admit federal involvement in CCSS, I cannot say why Hess believes this admission will quell CCSS dissidents, but he apparently believes it will:

> *Key leaders of the Common Core effort need to ...show some evidence that they're listening to concerns and taking critics seriously. Those who could be especially influential here are CCSSO chief Chris Minnich; Achieve honcho Mike Cohen; NGA's Richard Laine;* **Student Achievement Partner's Jason Zimba; and David Coleman, president of the College Board** *and the dynamo* **who played the critical role in pushing the Common Core.** *They need to do more than keep insisting on the urgency of the exercise, praising the standards,* **and saying that the feds weren't involved. ... They should publicly concede that the feds played a significant facilitative role...** *that reasonable people may be nervous about the power seemingly being wielded by unaccountable associations, and that advocates...* **may have focused too much on the ambition of the project and not enough on allaying practical concerns.** *Such concessions would... reassure nervous parents and teachers..., and permit* **a reasonable back-and-forth** *to start emerging.*[52] [Emphasis added.]

Hess admits quite a bit here concerning his view of CCSS. First, he notes that David Coleman is the "pusher" of CCSS and that CCSS implementation was less "state-initiated" and more of a sales job on Coleman's part. Hess is fine with the sales job. As previously noted, he knows about the federal involvement; here, he tacitly admits that he is fine with it, for his goal is not to question the "significant facilitative role" of the federal government in CCSS but to sell the idea that "the power being wielded by unaccountable associations" isn't so bad. The "ambition of the project" certainly encompasses the millions (if not billions) of dollars College Board, ACT, and other education corporations stand to make from CCSS, yet Hess believes that this handful of individuals who kept their actions secret in the devising of CCSS can calm their detractors with a few well-placed pseudo-apologies. Finally, the "back and forth" to which Hess alludes is not a reconsideration of CCSS but only discussions about smooth implementation.

Hess is all in for offering advice on how to sell the CCSS product.

Let us shift to another of Hess' contributions: That of a board member of the Broad Prize in Urban Education,[53] as in Broad Foundation, a funder of both the Fordham Foundation, which funds *Education Next*, and NCTQ, another board on which Hess sits. Former and current NCTQ advisory board members Deborah McGriff and Eric Hanushek also sit on the Broad Prize board, as does the CEO of Jeb Bush's Foundation for Excellence in Education, Patricia Levesque. Moreover, this is not the only Broad board. NCTQ also has representation in former and current advisory board members Michelle Rhee and Wendy Kopp, and NCTQ board of directors member Paul Pastorek, on the Broad board of directors.[54]

If it seems that the same reformer names keep coming up, it is that they do. The key reformers are a tight group having many board membership overlapping connections and allegiances.

It should come as no surprise that Hess supports Kopp's TFA, especially in its efforts to usher "dynamic, impassioned, and entrepreneurial education leaders" into education administration and policymaking roles and TFA's having "created a corps of change agents like Rhee...."[55]

If by "change" Hess means "perpetrating a fraud on the American public by promoting fraudulent test score gains," then yes, Rhee is a "change agent."

Hess names other TFA alumna, including those who have begun charter schools, such as KIPP's Mike Feinberg and Dave Levin, and YES Prep's Chris Barbic. He also names Sarah Usdin, who started New Schools for New Orleans and sits on the Orleans Parish school board.

Hess assumes that one can run a school without having had an established classroom teaching career. Yet Hess takes his views regarding Fine Young Talent a couple steps further: In a viewpoint that he shares with corporate reform financier Eli Broad and Chester Finn, Hess believes in "deregulating the path to school leadership." Even though the endorsers of this manifesto note that leadership recruitment should happen "both inside and outside the education field," the focus is clearly on removing regulations so that non-educator or token-educator reformers might more easily gain access to influential leadership positions. Notice also that the position that Hess, Finn, Broad, and others (Hanushek, Hirsch, McGriff, and John Walton, to name a few) assume follows a top-down, results-based model:

> *Conventional certification requirements for public-school principals and superintendents should be radically reduced, and replaced by criteria that stress leadership qualities rather than simply an education background. **Candidates for school-leadership positions** should **be recruited** from inside **and outside the education field**, trained as necessary, **and evaluated according to the results they achieve. Principals and superintendents should be well compensated..... Superintendents and principals need sweeping authority..... Principals and superintendents who fail to produce the needed results after a reasonable period of time should not be retained.*[56] [Emphasis added.]

This manifesto includes the tacit assumption that corporate reformers are the recruiters. After all, this is their model—put one person in charge, giving him or her carte blanche and ultimate responsibility for producing outcomes. And who better to decide what "talent" is than the ones who have of late overused the word?

The manifesto Hess signed also reeks of worship of the business model—management is paid higher salaries, makes all key decisions, and values only quantifiable results. Yet the manifesto completely ignores issues previously and repeatedly documented in this book, not the least of which are abuses of power to financially serve one's own ends at the expense of the masses. Reformers cry for a single individual to be placed in charge, unfettered by rules yet somehow held accountable for outcomes. The reality is that many of those individuals placed in charge with few if any restrictions misspend incredible amounts of money and leave schools and school systems in disarray without having to account for their damaging actions. They simply move on to the next lucrative reformer venture. In his defense of CCSS, Hess also neglects to suitably address actual abuses of power perpetrated by reformers upon the public, all in the name of "bold initiatives" and "urgent change."

Hess never addresses the problem that the business model objectifies students by reducing their value to test scores. Children become numeric outcomes, with the dangerous yet all-too-real potential to be manipulated, disguised, and shifted about in an effort to make teachers, administrators, and schools appear to be above termination.

In addition, via his connection to the manifesto, Hess promotes a dichotomous professional system in education, one that clearly favors administration over classroom teachers. For example, as to the freedom afforded leaders in the manifesto document to select their own staffs since their performance is based upon the work of those of lesser rank, I noticed that there is no extension of such logic to the traditional classroom teacher, who cannot choose his or her own students on the basis that these are the individuals on whom teacher performance outcomes are based.

As he and others attest to in their manifesto, Hess believes that educational leaders need not have even been teachers; in fact, Hess advocates that teachers who move out of the classroom to assume administrative positions are often overreaching their own talent, so to speak. In other words, leave the leading (and the higher salaries that accompany such leadership) up to the "talented" non-classroom "leaders."

In a January 2013 speech Hess gave before the American Enterprise Institute, where he holds the position of director of education policy studies, he talked of what he considers to be "cage busting leadership," based upon his recently-released book of the same title. In his speech, Hess says, "If we trust in educators, and otherwise leave the system largely untouched, nothing is going to change." The "we" appears to be education reformers. Hess offers four tips for reformers, including the "healthy and constructive role" that lawyers have in advancing reforms, for attorneys can help reformers "figure out exactly what is prohibited." What districts need, according to Hess, is "in addition to general counsel, they need help from lawyers on the outside." Next Hess makes his TFA connection—lots of TFAers "went through law" and are "hugely interested in educational issues. But districts are doing little or nothing at all to tap this pool of free labor."

Let me add that TFA is anything but "free." In Louisiana, districts pay fees to TFA for each of the "temp teachers" to whom the district must also pay a salary." And TFA expects (and receives) millions in funding from states utilizing their temp teachers. In June 2013, former TFA superintendent John White and his primarily Jindal-controlled state board approved $1.2 million in funding for TFA.

Back to Hess' speech: Enlisting lawyers in the education reform effort was his first point. What Hess is not saying, but what I have found true particularly true in Louisiana education reform, is that the legal system might require circumventing, and lawyers are able to advise on these ends. Whereas Hess' advocating that lawyers be brought in for the sake of determining the boundaries of legality certainly sounds noble, the sheer number of Louisiana lawsuits centered on education reform issues attests to the fact that education reformers will push the bounds of law to see how much they might get by with.

For that, it certainly is helpful for the reform-minded to have a number of lawyers on hand.

For his second point, Hess talks of the need to bring in talent from outside of education since, apparently, the expectation that teachers have of rising in the ranks of their own profession often raises them above their abilities. I commented on this speech in my 2013 NCTQ series on my blog:

> ...*[Hess]... notes the need for "an increased mix of people going in" to reform education*, including *"great financial minds" to be involved (**Gates? Walton? Broad?**), and "smart technology leaders who are excited about this work" (**online education companies? testing companies?**). **Hess also advocates** "bringing in" HR people, as opposed to having teachers go back to school to earn administrative degrees and rise through the ranks. ...**The teachers are rising above their training... and likely do not make good administrators. It is the same logic as is reflected in [the] 2003 Broad education leadership manifesto on which Hess advised.**[57] [Emphasis added.]

At this point, Hess is clearly walking a fine line. He is all but saying that teachers should stay in their place, which is not one of matriculating into education leadership positions. He does not assume that time in the classroom contributes to development of leadership skills necessary for education leadership, not the least of which is a thorough and grounded knowledge of the classroom. Hess does extend a cursory acknowledgement of the need for "career paths" for the classroom. But "career paths" for classroom teachers is not the focus of "busting the cage." "Busting the cage" involves positioning business in the key (and more lucrative) positions in public education.

Consider in this next blog excerpt Hess' body language as talks of the classroom versus the "talent":

> **Hess says, "We need to figure out how to get people who are great in managing talent... in district and state offices."**
>
> **"Talent" is another TFA/Broad/reformer catchword. In Louisiana, we now have an Office of Workforce Talent, a Talent Policy Director, and a Talent Statute....**
>
> *(An aside: I don't think Hess realized what he was doing with his left hand as he was comparing the "place" of the classroom teacher to the "place" of this "new HR talent."* **When talking of the classroom teacher, Hess moved his hand back and forth, in a pushing-away motion, at chest level. In contrast, when speaking of the "new HR talent," Hess moved his hand up more to shoulder/head level, and his hand made more of a fist pointing.** *Very telling.*[58] [Emphasis added.]

Hess' own body language dismisses classroom teachers as potential leaders within their own profession. "Talent" must come from outside.

Now, I understand that my assertions regarding Hess' view might appear to contradict the Broad manifesto that Hess signed, for the manifesto urges promotion of " candidates... recruited from inside and outside the education field."[59] However, the "education field" is not equivalent to "the school." A person entirely lacking in classroom experience could still be part of the "education field."

Notice that TFA never advises its recruits to pursue careers as a classroom teachers. It does, however, promote the idea of this "TFA talent" moving into key leadership roles.[60]

The bottom line is that classroom teaching is not lucrative enough for this "fine young talent." For TFA, teaching truly is temporary, a resume padder as one looks toward more fiscally promising career ventures.[61] The Broad manifesto enforces the idea of classroom teaching as "less than" in its section entitled "Paying the Price": As a signatory, Hess asserts that principals should have starting salaries at least 150% of the highest-paid teacher's salary since principals spend "at least a 60-hour week and an eleven month year" working.[62] In such a statement, Hess and other supporters of this manifesto reveal their ignorance regarding the number of hours a classroom teacher must devote to the running of the classroom, not the least of which involves lesson planning, grading, and before- and after-school meetings and extracurricular supervisory responsibilities. No "paying the price" for the incredible work teachers do. Based upon the manifesto, it is clear that any Hess-suggested "career paths" for those who remain in the classroom are not valued as are the price-paying career paths of those descending upon education from the outside as the profession's business-modeled new leaders. Hess himself was once in the classroom—but that was over 20 years ago, only as a TFA-like, temporary stop on the way to "cage busting leadership."

In concurrence with the manifesto, Hess agrees that this "leadership talent" requires money to keep it around:

> *...Hess goes on to say that state departments of education... need to "**rethink their salary caps**" because "if your maximum salary in the state department of education is 130,000 dollars... **you can't even bid good talent away from big school districts in your state**."*[63] [Emphasis added.]

Reformers like to remove caps. No caps to the number of charters competing with traditional public schools for state-allocated, per-pupil funding. No caps on the number of voucher students, also with the potential of bankrupting traditional public schools as such vie for funding. No caps for the number of online courses or the number of students in the courses. Again, forget the survival of the community school. And here, Hess advocates removing salary caps for the administrators brought into the state from outside of traditional public education without a word regarding where he believes this extra money will be taken from (because it will be taken from somewhere, likely from schools, teachers, and students).

Hess' third suggestion involves leadership training:

...Hess continues by saying that these talented new leaders need **mentorships "outside of K12"** *so that the talent can model "corporate re-engineering or total quality management" to "find out what worked and what didn't work... outside of ed and leadership"; that what is needed* **is the establishment of "leadership institutes" nationwide.**[64] [Emphasis added.]

As part of their leadership training, Hess suggests "buying out two or three weeks"[65] of the contract that might be restricting the talented-leader-in-training. Yet another money issue. However, as concerns the training of these up-and-coming reform leaders, Hess offers a financial solution, and it is his fourth and final point: Convince the philanthropies (the foundation purse strings of corporate reform, such as Broad and Gates and Walton) to fund a nationwide network of leadership institutes.

Hess actually refers to his fourth point as "the philanthropy business." Hess sees the "philanthropy business" as already occurring:

[Philanthropies provide] *...***a huge impetus** *to invest in policy to line up behind making sure* **that we're doing away with social promotion,** *or to make sure* **that we're promoting, ahh, good charter school laws....**[66] [Emphasis added.]

All too often, the role of contemporary education philanthropy is to advance the corporate reform agenda. Foundations like Gates, Broad, and Walton openly express their intentions for their giving; in the end, it is the community school that pays the greater price for the billions in supposed-philanthropic monies pouring in to promote privatization.

Hess approves of this philanthropic role in purchasing education policy to "make sure" the end result of market-based reform. Nevertheless, Hess believes that the philanthropies can and should do more:

But we also need these guys *to invest and push* **in making sure that states are launching upstanding leadership institutes.... We've need to build and cultivate these kinds of talent, these networks and these ideas across the country,** *and business and philanthropy have got to play a big role in doing that,* **and so far it's not been something on their radar."**[67] [Emphasis added.]

Hess' words reveal the role he views foundation funders as playing in corporate reform: Those who wield the money and "push" the agenda. This is the same word that Hess used in referring to David Coleman's role in promoting CCSS—that of "pushing" CCSS. Reform is not "grass roots." It is purchased and pushed by the few who have the power, prestige, and bank accounts to do so. And now, Hess is calling for a push to establish a national network to train reform leaders. He notes that such a network is crucial, and he is right: For corporate reform to completely and thoroughly annihilate all that is democratic and truly "public" about public education, reformers must network in order to successfully construct a reform web from which no district, school, teacher, or student can escape.

Yes, it is true that Hess is not pocketing state money by running an unregulated charter school chain. He is not on the board of a major testing company that stands to profit well from so-called "data-driven" outcomes. He is not vying for mayoral control of any public school system. He has neither hidden nor altered student test scores than might make or break his career as a corporate reformer. However, Hess promotes an agenda that serves well the driven ideologues and petty opportunists who benefit from the privatization of traditional public education, and he does so in the face of monumental mounting evidence as to the fraud that is modern education reform. For these reasons, Hess has earned his place in this book among others in the echo chamber.

CHAPTER 13

JEB BUSH AND HIS FLORIDA MIRACLE (WELL, MOST OF IT)

When Florida Governor Jeb Bush spoke before the Minnesota legislature in April 2011 regarding his agenda for educational reform, House Speaker Kurt Zellers made the following remark[1]:

> *Governor Bush took on the status quo. There was no political gain in it. He's no longer governor. He's not running for Senate. He's just trying to help kids.*

That, readers, is a short-sighted comment.

True, Bush had not committed to running for president in 2016.[2] He was also not denying it.[3]

Bush has certainly connected his name with educational reform in a manner that has become all too familiar across the United States, particularly since 2012. Bush's "secret" agenda involves applying business principles to the realm of public education. Even though I believe that the overall goal of corporate reform is to access and exploit the half a trillion dollars spent on US public education per annum, it is worth noting that Bush could also use his personal reform agenda, particularly his education reform plan, to propel himself into the White House.

A Chronicle of Echoes: Who's Who in the Implosion of American Public Education,
pages 205–221.
Copyright © 2014 by Information Age Publishing

Bush has an elaborate plan for remaking American public education into that which serves his own political goals. In the next two chapters, I offer a detailed examination of this plan and demonstrate just how flawed a plan it is. As such, I use a number of lengthy block quotes. In an effort to make the Bush chapters more "reader friendly," I was tempted to reduce the quoted information. After careful thought, however, I decided to leave the extensive block quotes for those readers who require such detailed information in order to combat corporate reform in statehouses across the country.

And now, let us examine the Wonder That Is Jeb.

Bush's first run for governor was in 1994. The year after he lost that race—1995—he formed his first organization, Foundation for Florida's Future (FFF). The current mission statement of this organization is "To make Florida's education system a model for the nation."[4]

It is important to not miss the emphasis on "national model" here. It shadows Bush's national ambitions. As Bush writes,

> *Our [Florida's] success was built on a foundation of core principles. Starting with the A+ Plan in 1999 and continuing today, our reforms combine high expectations, standardized measurement, a clear and achievable system of accountability, rewards and consequences for performance, effective teaching in the classroom and more choices to customize education to each student.*[5]

By the end of his letter to readers of the FFF website, Bush declares Florida education reform a success:

> *While Florida is now a model for the nation, our job is far from done. We must continue to reform education to keep the promise of a quality education for all Sunshine State students.*[6]

Bush considers Florida "now a model for the nation." Indeed, some credit Jeb Bush's Florida reforms as being the model for Race to the Top (RTTT)[7]— President Barack Obama's repackaged substitute for George Bush's No Child Left Behind (NCLB)—and an idea that illustrates the bipartisan, odd-bedfellow nature of the current reform climate.[8] Around 2007, the pro-corporate-reform Hoover Institute lauded Bush's Florida reforms while highlighting the deficiencies in NCLB.[9] The reform-sympathetic Heritage Foundation also issued a paper in 2009 comparing the Florida educational reforms to NCLB and finding in favor of Jeb Bush's version of education reform. The author of the Heritage Foundation paper, Matt Lauder, now works for Jeb Bush.[10] (Both the Hoover and Heritage papers are interesting as both pit the reforms of one Bush brother against the other.)[11] Furthermore, US Secretary of Education Arne Duncan solicited input from a Bush-connected state education superintendent regarding RTTT before releasing RTTT criteria to the public. This superintendent turned to a Bush organization for advice on what to send to Duncan. More on this in the Chiefs for Change (C4C) chapter.[12]

What, exactly, does the Bush education reform plan include?

In sum, six points:[13]

1. Grading schools on an A through F scale based upon student standardized test scores.
2. Using of high-stakes testing.
3. Preventing student social promotion.
4. Basing teacher pay upon student performance on standardized tests.
5. Using non-traditional avenues for teacher credentialing.
6. Supporting charter schools, vouchers for private schools, and on-line schools ("parent choice").

One could consider Bush's statement, that Florida education reforms are "now a model for the nation," from two different perspectives. First, one might view such a statement to mean that the Florida education reforms actually work, and are therefore "a model to the nation." Second, one might consider that, regardless of the efficacy of these Florida reforms, model legislation has been written and is being actively marketed to states across the nation as the panacea to "reform" education.[14] Bush himself promotes both views. I examine each of these perspectives in the next two chapters; my primary focus in this chapter is the first perspective— reforms supposedly do work—according to points 1 through 5 above. I refer to Point 6 in the next chapter.

The second focus—that of the active marketing of Bush's education reform agenda—is discussed later in the book along with two additional, Bush-agenda-promoting organizations, Foundation for Excellence in Education (FEE) and C4C.

Bush's educational reforms are a colossal failure, yet they are being pushed nationwide as The Answer for American education.

The Answer is a calculated lie designed to obliterate the American community school.

SCHOOL LETTER GRADES

Let's begin with school letter grades. The school letter grade is a means of narrowly defining school "success" chiefly based upon student standardized test scores in select subjects. This narrowness is illustrated in the declared purpose of school letter grades according to Bush's FFF:

School grades reflect whether students are learning a year's worth of knowledge in a year's time, which is the leading indicator of a quality education.... Parents use school grades to understand the quality of education their child is receiving so they can make informed decisions for their family.[15]

As a statistician, professional researcher, and classroom teacher, I cannot emphasize just how naïve and limited the above statement is. For one, learning is not linear. Learning is complex and cannot be partitioned "a year at a time." Nor can it be partitioned "by subject." Nor is it reasonable to conclude that learning occurs at some standardized rate for all learners. Finally, it is foolish to believe that student test scores are clearly and singularly connected to the school the student attends.

School letter grades are supposed to provide parents with a means of "understanding the quality of education their child is receiving." The Hoover Institute refers to the letter grading of schools as an "intuitive" system.[16] However, immediately following this stated purpose is information noting that the school letter grades are dependent upon standardized tests in only certain subjects. How "intuitive" is that?

School grades are based on FCAT (Florida Comprehensive Assessment Test) scores in reading, writing, math and science. Half of the grade is based on performance, which is the percentage of students who have the knowledge and skills required for their grade level. Half of the grade is based on progress, which is the percentage of students who gained knowledge and improved their skills from one year to the next even if they are not yet on grade level.[17]

Thus, Bush and the State of Florida discount untested subjects, including all social studies, fine arts, and physical education. If testing is the end-all, then these courses simply do not matter to a well-rounded, "quality" education. Since such courses (and others, especially at the high school level) are not measured using standardized test scores, their contributions to student education are in effect declared useless.

According to the same FFF information, there are also other factors that contribute to school grade calculation:

First, schools must test at least 90% of their students to earn a grade and 95% of their students to be eligible for an A. Schools that test fewer than 90% of their students are given an Incomplete, or "I."

*Second, at least **half** of the students who score in the lowest 25% must show progress from one year to the next. Schools who fail to meet this requirement lose a letter grade (from an A to a B, from a B to a C, and so on).*[18]

Such obvious capriciousness in school letter grade calculation. For example, setting threshold values requiring the "testing at least 90%" is an arbitrary practice. The practice of calculating letter grades is far from consistent from one year to the next. Consider this explanation of school letter grade calculation changes from 1999 up to 2011:

The purpose of this technical assistance paper is to provide a description of the procedures used to determine school grades for the 2011 school year. In 2011, all school grades include four measures of student achievement and four measures of student learning gains plus several non-FCAT-based components for high schools. Florida's current school accountability system originated with state legislation passed in 1999 (the "A+ Plan") and has been revised periodically to reflect increased standards and expectations for student performance. Florida is the first state to track annual student learning gains based on the state's academic standards.

School grades have been issued since 1999, *with the Florida Comprehensive Assessment Test (FCAT) being the primary instrument in calculating school grades.* ***In 2002, significant improvements were made in how school grades were calculated*** *to fully implement the intent of Florida's original plan. The most noteworthy improvement was the inclusion of student learning gains. Additionally, a measure was added to determine whether the lowest performing students are making annual improvements in specified subjects. Florida's accountability system allows the improvement of individual students to be tracked from one year to the next based on FCAT developmental scores in reading and mathematics in grades 3 through 10.* ***In 2010, Florida's school grading system was further revised*** *to include several additional measures for high schools, including the four-year graduation rate, the graduation rate for at-risk students, participation and performance in accelerated curricula, and postsecondary readiness, as well as a component for measuring annual growth or decline in these measures.* ***In 2011, the Grade 9 FCAT Mathematics Assessment was discontinued*** *with the phase-in of the state's Algebra 1 End-of-Course (EOC) Assessment (which will not be used in school grades until the 2011–12 school year).* ***Also in 2011, the "percent proficient" criterion for the FCAT Writing component was changed*** *to the percent scoring at 4.0 and above (from the percent scoring at 3.5 and above).*[19] [Emphasis added.]

If school letter grade calculation is "revised," it is a tacit admission that the grade calculation was not as "good" as it should have been in previous years, yet schools were still subjected to the consequences of the "not as good" system. Furthermore, there is the issue of the inability to compare school letter grades from one year to the next. If the criteria for calculation are in constant flux, then comparisons from one year to the next are meaningless.

Bush doesn't talk too much about such issues. And the Hoover Institute, in its promoting of the Bush 1999 A+ Plan, did not anticipate the potential chaos that floating criteria could make of the school letter grading system. According to Hoover:

The grading system under A+ (Bush's 1999 Florida education reform package) does a satisfactory job of identifying higher quality schools and an even better job of identifying those that are the least effective.[20]

Notice the change of exam in 2012 from the FCAT to the EOC (End of Course Test):

*The purpose of this technical assistance paper is to provide a description of the procedures used to determine school grades for the 2012 school year. School grades include four measures of student achievement and four measures of student learning gains plus several components for high schools that are based on measures other than state assessments, **as well as a new measure for middle schools that measures participation in and performance on high-school-level end-of-course (EOC) assessments.** Florida's current school accountability system originated with state legislation passed in 1999 (the A+ Plan) and has been revised periodically to reflect increased standards and expectations for student performance. Florida is the first state to track annual student learning gains based on the state's academic standards.*

***Additional substantive changes** to the school grading system were adopted by the State Board of Education in 2012, **including new assessments and achievement level cut scores, expansion of performance measures to include students with disabilities and English language learners, implementation of a new middle-school component measuring participation in and performance on high-school level end-of-course (EOC) assessments, and a more rigorous graduation rate formula for high school grading.**[21]*
[Emphasis added.]

"Substantive changes" translates to "the school letter grades are no longer comparable from year to year, but we will continue to compare, anyway." The press certainly does so.

So many revisions to the now-tedious Florida school letter grade formula bring increased opportunities for calculation errors. In 2012, the Florida Department of Education forgot part of the formula in the calculation of school letter grades for 213 Florida schools. This omission did not inspire confidence in an already-capricious school letter grade system:

State education administrators, who are in charge of grading schools and students, failed to follow their own formula.

In fact, they forgot part of it.

The error means 48 schools in South Florida will get higher, revised grades: 31 in Miami-Dade and 17 in Broward.

The mistake has piled more doubt on the state's accountability system.

"A flawed accountability system that forgets to embed a critical element in its formula ... is an accountability system that needs reform," said Miami-Dade Superintendent Alberto Carvalho Monday. "And those that lead it need to consider the implications of their actions."

The state's accountability system has come under fire by parents who think their children take too many tests; by teachers whose evaluations now depend in part on test scores; and by educators who believe the state has made too many policy changes, too fast. The state Department of Education announced the revision of letter grades at 213 schools statewide —with the most in Miami-Dade—in a news release late Friday night. All had their grade raised one letter grade.

Carvalho joined the chorus of criticism, even though Miami-Dade schools benefited from the correction. **"I have lost confidence in an accountability system that is not only ever-changing but fails to accurately depict student learning and the effectiveness of teachers," he said.**[22] [Emphasis added.]

Doesn't sound like much of a "miracle," does it?

HIGH-STAKES TESTING

One cannot separate high-stakes testing from the assigning of school letter grades. That is, the "stakes" (consequences, particularly the negative consequences) are "high" (substantial; life altering) to the schools receiving letter grades based upon the results of standardized tests of its students. Moreover, the use of high-stakes testing extends beyond the school letter grade arena. The use of standardized tests is the fuel of the Bush educational reform machine. It is what makes Bush education reform function… or dysfunction:

> **FCAT is a high-stakes test. It is a single, defined assessment** *that draws a clear line between those who pass and those who fail and delivers direct consequences to students, teachers and schools. …* **Florida third graders, who fail FCAT are held back and labeled failures in the eyes of the state regardless grade point average. Failure impacts the entire system. Serious consequences for schools include loss of funding, accreditation, lowering of overall school grade, changes to school management and teachers face loss of pay and dismissal.**

> *Although test scores might improve when teachers spoon-feed students a steady diet of test prep review,* **the long term consequences are concerning.** *Professional educators faced with high-stakes consequences are robbed of the chance to practice the art of teaching* **leaving students deprived** *of acquiring the deep understanding of full, broad curriculum needed to compete in college.*[23] [Emphasis added.]

The logical byproduct of high-stakes testing is system dysfunction. Earning high scores on the high-stakes test will become the end-all of survival for the school and/or teacher whose professional life is connected with the scoring outcomes. Gone is "learning for learning's sake." Gone are the joy of teaching and the freedom of discovery.

And what exactly is achieved when the high-stakes test scores are deemed favorable? Since high-stakes testing promotes a culture of fear, favorable scores mean "purchased time" to keep one's job or one's school. Moreover, high scores do not necessarily translate into learning. Consider this comparison of FCAT on-level percentages to National Assessment of Educational Progress (NAEP) on-level percentages for Florida eighth graders in 2008–09:

FCAT Reading: 54 percent on level; NAEP Reading: 32 percent on level FCAT Math: 66 percent on level; NAEP Math: 29 percent on level.[24]

The NAEP is not under the control of the State of Florida, making NAEP scores more objective measures of actual student achievement.

Florida has had other issues of FCAT test score inflation.[25] In 2010, the FCAT writing test scores for Florida's middle schoolers did not match the reading scores. Reading test scores were noticeably lower than corresponding writing scores, with 72 percent the average score for fourth grade reading, and 55 percent, the average for eighth grade reading. However, on the FCAT writing test, the average score for fourth graders was 94 percent, and for eighth graders, 96 percent. As it turns out, Pearson, the company responsible for FCAT, was delinquent in delivering its writing test results. Furthermore, the Florida Department of Education changed the writing test grading criteria from two readers to one. A single reader graded each test. There was no system in place for multiple reads and even a third, "tiebreaker" read. (I was once a writing exam grader in Colorado for the tenth grade writing assessment, and this is the procedure we used: two raters if agreement, and a third if not. This process leads to a more objective assessment of student writing than does a single rater.)

The score inflation caused by capricious grading practices has serious ramifications for schools, teachers, and students. First, students receiving inflated scores could be exempted from extra assistance and unduly classified as more capable than they actually are. This only sets a student up for future failure when his/her score "drops" if the inflation is remedied in subsequent years. A similar plummeting effect holds true for teachers; if student scores are inflated one year and not the next, the scores appear to "drop," and the classroom teacher of record could have his/her livelihood in jeopardy as a result. Finally, the school letter grade is so heavily influenced by student standardized test scores that an artificially-induced "drop" from one school year to the next could mean state (or charter) takeover of what might be deemed a "failing" school.

Jeb Bush is proud of his reliance upon high stakes testing. It is part of the "reform" Bush writes about so fondly. In fact, he uses the terms "reform" and "quality education" interchangeably.[26]

Not everyone in Florida considers of Bush's reliance upon high-stakes testing as part of a "quality education." Consider this June 2012 *Bradenton Times* article:

> **A rising tide of protest is emerging**, *as growing numbers of parents, teachers, and administrators are lobbying against high-stakes testing. The Manatee [Florida] School District joined the movement this week…*

The [National Resolution on High Stakes Testing] calls for a system "which does not require extensive standardized testing, more accurately reflects the broad range of student learning, and is used to support students and improve schools."

*In Florida, more than a dozen countywide school committees serving three-quarters of a million students endorsed the National Resolution, according to FairTest. Early supporters included Broward County, the nation's sixth biggest district, and Palm Beach County, the 11th largest. Then, the state association of school boards annual convention voted to endorse a state-specific version. **Dozens of newspaper editorials, opinion columns, and letters to the editor have called for a reduction in testing and an overhaul of the state's assessment system.***[27] [Emphasis added.]

If "more than a dozen countywide school committees serving three-quarters of a million students" are dissatisfied with the Bush plan for educational reform's reliance upon high-stakes testing, I would say that there is no miracle here. Moreover, if FCAT scores do not approximate the more objective and established NAEP scores, then the "miracle" is once again suspect. Finally, if the Florida Department of Education produces inflated writing scores as the result of a questionable decision to reduce the number of writing test raters from the more-stable two to a highly-subjective one, I would agree that the smoke has subsided and the mirrors can be seen—the high-stakes magic trick has been effectively exposed.

NO STUDENT SOCIAL PROMOTION

In 1999, as part of Bush's A+ Plan, Florida legislation called for social promotion (the promoting of a student to the next grade regardless of academic achievement) in third grade to stop.[28]

However, the social promotion continued; the Orlando Sentinel published a number of stories addressing the issue of Florida school districts' circumventing the law. In December 2001, the legislators vowed to take action:

Angry lawmakers Monday called for "tightening the vise" on school districts that ignore a state law requiring teachers to fail fourth-graders who can't read.

The Orlando Sentinel reported Sunday that ***districts widely ignore the 1999 law that Gov. Jeb Bush and lawmakers vowed would end "social promotion."*** Instead, the newspaper found that most schools promote poor readers anyway—***issuing "good cause" exemptions to thousands of students each year.***[29] [Emphasis added.]

Therefore, it was back to the drawing board for Bush and the Florida legislature:

The bill (the 2002 revision of the original 1999 social promotion portion of the A+ Plan), the result of a series of stories published in the Orlando Sentinel, is intended to clean up and strengthen a 1999 law that Gov. Jeb Bush and legislators once touted as the end of social promotion.

*But the Sentinel found that **districts were ignoring the law.** Currently, **about 33 percent of Florida's fourth-graders should be retained under state law, but only 3 percent are held back.***[30] [Emphasis added.]

So, a total of 33% of students were being passed from third grade to fourth socially. Remember this number.

In 2002, the Florida legislature passed a law ending social promotion for third graders (actually, the "law" was an improved version of the 1999 A+ Plan's section on social promotion). In order to be promoted to fourth grade, Florida's third graders were now required to score Level 2 or higher on FCAT Reading in order to be promoted to fourth grade.

The law had exceptions. Notice the exemptions from this 2004 study on Florida social promotion legislation. Notice also the percentage of students eligible for exemption:

*A child who misses the FCAT benchmark **can be exempted from the policy and promoted to fourth grade** if he meets any one of the following criteria: 1) he is a **Limited English Proficiency student** who has received less than two years of instruction in an English for Speakers of Other Languages program; 2) he has **a disability sufficiently severe** that it is deemed inappropriate for him to take the test; 3) he **demonstrates proficiency on another standardized test;** 4) he demonstrates proficiency through **a performance portfolio;** 5) he has **a disability and has received remediation for more than two years;** or 6) he has already been held back for two years.*

*Of third-grade students in 2002–03 who scored below the Level 2 threshold and were thus subject to retention under the new policy, **21.3 percent were reported as having received one of these exemptions.***[31] [Emphasis added.]

Bush claims to have ended social promotion... sort of. Note his words to Minnesota legislators in 2011:

*"**We're the only state to have eliminated social promotion in the third grade in a robust way,**" Mr. Bush said Tuesday in an appearance in the Capitol here [in St. Paul, MN], urging the Legislature's new Republican majorities to be bold.*[32] [Emphasis added.]

How does one "eliminate... in a robust way"? To "eliminate" means to "completely remove." "In a robust way" means "firmly." Thus, it seems that Mr. Bush is saying that in Florida, social promotion in third grade has been "firmly and completely removed."

Not according to the history of the 1999 A+ legislation that many Florida districts ignored. And certainly not according to the 2002 law with its numerous exceptions, the most interesting of which amounts to, "Okay. We tried retaining you twice. It didn't work. So we're going to promote you socially."

Before the 2002 law specifically addressing social promotion, many Florida districts continued to socially promote students from third to fourth grade. As noted previously, 30 percent of third grade students promoted despite not meeting the FCAT Reading test criteria. With the 2002 law, a list of exemptions was added so that 21.3 percent of students met the exemption criteria and were still socially promoted.

If originally (before the 1999 legislation) 33 percent of third graders were being socially promoted, and now, under the 2002 law, 21.3 percent were, that means that instead of only 3 percent being held back under the 1999 statute (as reported in the Orlando Sentinel), with this "bold new reform," 11.7 percent were being retained (33—21.3 = 11.7). (This 11.7 percent retained is confirmed in a 2012 study examining Florida's gains on the NAEP in fourth grade. The question in this study is whether removal of this 11.7 percent has contributed to an artificial NAEP score "jump.")[33,34]

One in three of Florida third graders were being socially promoted prior to Bush's reform. Now it is only just over one-five.

One in five is not "elimination."

Is there a miracle here? Has social promotion been eliminated in Florida?

Not hardly.

Teacher Pay Based Upon Student Standardized Test Performance

Bush's 1999 A + Plan included no teacher evaluation plan.[35] The evaluating of teachers based upon student standardized test scores became effective in Florida on July 1, 2011, under Governor Rick Scott, with the passage of Florida's Senate Bill 736.[36] However, Jeb Bush supports connecting teacher employment to the standardized test scores of their students. He wrote as much in the Chicago Tribune in September 2012, in the throes of the Chicago teachers' strike:

> *We must make children the priority by identifying and rewarding great teachers and weeding out ineffective ones who fail to improve.* ***This can be done by including student test data in job reviews.***[37] [Emphasis added.]

Jeb Bush believes that using student test data will rid school systems of "bad" teachers. Keep that in mind.

Florida law states that teachers are to be rated using a four-category system: highly effective, effective, needs improvement, and unsatisfactory. Fifty percent of a teacher's rating is to be based upon "student gains," with the clarification that "one measure of student gains will be testing. Teachers parents, and students should anticipate an increase in FCAT-style tests." Even though each district is to develop its own evaluation system, all districts must incorporate the stipulation that 50% of an FCAT teacher's evaluation must be based upon three years of data using a value added modeling system that had not been developed prior to passage of the teacher evaluation law.[38]

That right there deserves pause. Florida rushed to set up an arguably punitive teacher evaluation plan. (Not only could two unsatisfactory ratings lead to termination; the legislation offered no guarantee that a teacher rated effective or highly effective would "avoid non renewal.") Florida did not bother to create the measurement system by which teachers would be measured, much less pilot test such a system.

Teachers not tested using FCAT must still incorporate some form of student scores into the evaluation, and such must count for at least 40% of the teacher's annual evaluation score.

Now, here's more confusion: Though the districts have until 2014–15 to create and implement their teacher evaluation systems for FCAT-untested subjects, an evaluation must be implemented for the 2011–12 school year "based on the Commissioner's formula" for FCAT-tested subjects. Districts are instructed to develop assessments for teachers of other subjects; DOE must approve what districts devise.[39]

Top-down and out-of-balance from inception.

It just so happens that the 2011–12 Florida teacher evaluation results made national news,[40] not for its stellar implementation or striking results, but for its brevity of release. The December 5, 2012, Tampa Bay Times headline says it all: State Botches Release of New Data on Teacher Evaluations:

Florida's Department of Education on Wednesday rolled out the results of a sweeping new teacher evaluation system that is designed to be a more accurate, helpful and data-driven measure of how well teachers actually get students to learn.

*And then, **within hours of releasing the data, the department pulled the numbers off its website** and sheepishly admitted that much of it was wrong.*[41] [Emphasis added.]

In the handling of teacher reputation and livelihood, the Florida Department of Education apparently did not proof its results before release; thousands of Florida teachers were duplicated in the system due to their having multiple computerized job codes.

The real shame is that the error is glaring to anyone who knows how many teachers were employed in each district. Hillsborough County was the first district to notice that its 15,000 teachers were recorded as 23,970 on the state teacher evaluation release. Regarding Florida's embarrassing predicament, Bob Schaeffer of FairTest offered the following comment: "When you rush to put a shoddy system into place, you get ludicrous results."[42]

The *Tampa Bay News* article also reminds readers that the Florida Department of Education also issued more than 200 incorrect school letter grades earlier that same year. In their "urgency" to incorporate "bold, sweeping reforms" the state education agency forfeited careful planning, both in the high-stakes areas of school and teacher performance.

These errors ought not to be. Certainly they undermine any national promotion of a "Florida miracle."

And yet, perhaps there may be some miracle here after all. Once the "glitch" was corrected, an astounding 97 percent of Florida teachers were rated as either effective or highly effective.[43] Indeed, out of 157,000 teachers, not even 500 were rated as unsatisfactory. That is approximately three one-thousandths of one percent.

Is this another "glitch," or are Florida teachers actually competent in fulfilling their duties?

In Charlotte county, every single teacher was rated as effective. How is this possible?

That depends upon whom one asks. A December 5, 2012, *Herald Tribune* article notes, "the grading system may not be as punitive as critics feared."[44] However, there seems to be the expectation that schools with lower letter grades should have teachers with lower evaluation ratings and vice-versa. Consider this excerpt from a January 2013 Tallahassee article:

> Late last year, [Florida Senate President] Gaetz and other legislative leaders were dismissive of calls by the Florida Education Association to halt the teacher evaluations, which are part of a 2011 law designed to tie teacher pay more closely to student performance. But lawmakers and **new Education Commissioner Tony Bennett have talked openly in recent weeks about tweaking the law**. . . .
>
> One common source of concern is that teachers' grades do not always dovetail with a school's grade—there might be a low number of teachers rated highly at "A" schools, for example, or a high number of reportedly effective teachers at a "C" or "D" school.
>
> '**I think we have to start with drawing a line that connects those data points,**" Gaetz **said.** "And if we can't do that, then I think we're going to have a hard time explaining this to teachers and explaining it to parents."[45] [Emphasis added.]

In a January 2013 Jacksonville article, Gaetz responds,

"How can you have a C or D ranked school in which 85 percent, or 90 or 95 percent of the teachers are classified as effective or highly effective? ... It seems to me that those two data points have to have some relationship to each other."[46]

I hold a Ph.D., in statistics, and I have no idea what Gaetz means by "connecting those data points." It sure does sound fancy, though. Does he expect to take a pencil, connect the dots, and proclaim, 'There! It all makes sense now!" Gaetz might be able to connect the dots; however, I do not believe the result will be a nice, neat, clean line. As for his wanting "some relationship," he may well be seeing that, albeit a weak relationship for attempting to connect the complex by way of the simple.

There are three issues for consideration regarding Gaetz's desire to "connect" teacher evaluation results with corresponding school letter grades. For one, Gaetz's view fails to consider additional factors that are related to schools but not to teachers. For example, school zoning has nothing to do with the quality of teaching. If zoning and quality of teaching were directly related, then schools zoned to receive students from more affluent neighborhoods would have the "good" teachers and those zoned in poorer sections of town would have the "bad" teachers. If this simplistic view were true, Gaetz could "connect the dots" and produce a line (i.e., a perfect relationship between teacher rating and school grade).

Next, the premise inherent in Gaetz's view is that the two systems, school grades and teacher ratings, should automatically relate; never mind that no one thought to develop these systems concurrently and use measurement techniques and pilot testing to ensure that school letter grades coincided with teacher evaluation measures. In order to accomplish this, the school letter grading criteria must be stable—the criteria cannot change from year to year. Additionally, the time and effort must be devoted to development and assessment of the two systems concurrently prior to implementation of each system.

Finally, one must consider the incredible assumption that teacher ratings drive the school letter grade system (or vice-versa). A school is a sophisticated, complex entity; teachers are only one component of the school environment. It seems that Senator Gaetz is expecting a simple answer to a complex issue. Rushing forward with trying to answer the complex using the simple appears to be a corporate reform trademark.

No miracle material here, Mr. Bush. Sure is a lot of confusion and embarrassment, though.

NON-TRADITIONAL AVENUES FOR TEACHER CREDENTIALING

As part of its efforts at non-traditional teacher credentialing, the Florida Department of Education currently offers ABCTE (American Board for the Certification of Teacher Excellence) certification.[47] Information on the history of ABCTE is available on their website:

> *Founded in 2001 via a grant from the U.S. Department of Education, the American Board addresses the need for knowledgeable and dedicated teachers in every classroom. We offer a flexible and cost-effective certification program designed for career changers. The American Board opens new pathways into the classroom, helping states, districts and communities meet the needs of their students.*[48]

Curiously, the USDOE grant for initial ABCTE funding was approved for this program despite two of the three reviewers expressing disapproval. The

USDOE was cited for this and other erratic funding practices in a 2006 Government Accountability Office (GAO) report:

In the case of the grant to NCTQ [National Council on Teacher Quality] in 2001, Education awarded $5 million to the council, despite the fact that its proposal was not recommended for funding by two of three reviewers. The council's award was based on an unsolicited proposal to create a new national accreditation program for teachers—the American Board for Certification of Teacher Excellence (ABCTE).[49]

California Congressman George Miller called for the GAO investigation into the ABCTE finances; NCTQ posted a response on its website criticizing Miller's request as simply "digging up reviews and looking for nefarious behavior" (an argument that could be equally applied to NCTQ's own manner of operating in its review of traditional teacher training programs).[50] NCTQ noted that ABCTE was "nothing more than a sincere effort to provide a practical, sorely needed, meaningful teacher credential."[51]

As noted in the NCTQ commentary on Miller, the GAO report includes a footnote stating that in 2003, NCTQ applied for a $35 million grant to cover five years of ABCTE, and this grant was approved unanimously. However, this latter approval does not nullify the fact that the initial funding of ABCTE was not in line with established USDOE funding protocol. Furthermore, in 2006, Education Leaders Council, the corporate-reform-leaning organization responsible for managing ABCTE finances, was labeled a "high risk grantee" by the USDOE Office of Inspector General (OIG) for its mismanagement of federal grant monies for a number of its programs, including its 2004 deficit of $501,595 for ventures including ABCTE.[52]

In summary, in 2006 two powerful reports were released regarding questionable fiscal management of ABCTE.

Prior to the release of these reports, in September 2005, the founder and president of ABCTE, Kathleen Madigan, resigned. In the same month, NCTQ President Kate Walsh also resigned from the ABCTE board.[53] In short, when it came time for a financial reckoning, leadership fled the scene.

The ABCTE definitely has something for sale. It offers a "free trial" and advertises, "Become a certified teacher now for less than the cost of one college class." It the site also offers "$100 off" of its "Math and Science Plus +" program.[54] The "plus" program appears to be the "make that a meal" version of the course, with the "premium" program being the "supersized" version.[55] Drive-thru certification. I'm sure this is "for the children." ABCTE's site even follows the "fast-food-produced meals" analogy:

> *In the near future **we will be rolling out** other workbooks and quizbanks for subject areas that a few people have requested. Rather than raise the cost for everyone, especially those who do not need the extra materials, we will continue to make these separate offerings **a la carte**.*[56] [Emphasis added.]

Is ABCTE an example of the "high standards" Bush spoke about at the 2012 Republican national Convention?[57] I am not sure how I would feel about my child being taught by someone who clipped a coupon or used a fast-tracking "menu" to become a teacher. Apparently Jeb Bush is fine with such "alternative" certification. How meaningful is such a certification, one that allows a person with a bachelors degree in any area to complete one course to teach in any number of subject areas? Note that the bachelors degree need not be in the subject area taught.

And why is this ABCTE alternative certification "sorely needed" (NCTQ's words) in Florida? Is it due to teacher shortages? In that case, one would expect ABCTE certification in Florida to align with identified critical need areas in Florida. Surely Jeb Bush and the Florida Department of Education would not promote a shortcut certification program in teaching areas where the number of traditionally certified teachers is sufficient....

Based upon a report released by the Florida Department of Education regarding 2011–12 teacher shortage areas, the following are critical areas of teacher need:

- *middle and high school level mathematics*
- *middle and high school level science*
- middle and high school level English/language arts
- *reading*
- *all exceptional student education programs*
- *English for speakers of other languages (ESOL)*
- *foreign languages*
- *technology education/industrial arts*[58]

The ABCTE program offers single-year certification in all of the above areas except foreign language and technology education/industrial arts.[59] However, ABCTE also offers certification in elementary education—not a critical need area in Florida. This means that traditionally-trained, elementary education teachers could lose jobs to alternatively-certified counterparts. Furthermore, the offering of an ABCTE "certification" in elementary special education in a single year (and a little more training for secondary level) to a person with no related four-year degree could be highly problematic. Working with special needs populations often requires more of the teaching professional (i.e., ability to tailor general curriculum to meet individualized ability/need; greater ability to handle crisis situations; increased paperwork load) than does the regular classroom experience.[60]

I must also emphasize that a person receiving an alternative certification in a critical area in Florida is not required to teach in a given district registering a critical need. Thus, traditionally trained teachers could still lose jobs to individuals holding alternative certifications. *The 2010–11 Florida House of Representatives Alternative Certification Fact Sheet* [61] includes statistics for both traditionally trained teacher employment and alternative certificated employment. The shocking piece is that only 43 percent (2,616 of 6,093) of the traditionally trained teacher completers in 2008–09 were employed "in an instructional position" for the 2009–10 school year. Aside from a recognized teacher shortage in certain areas, there is apparently a teacher overage in others. Surely 57 percent of those graduates did not purposely forego the classroom; surely such a high percentage did not willingly leave Florida to teach.

Of the 3,612 alternative certification completers in 2008–09, only 68 percent (2,474) were employed "in instructional positions" in 2009–10. That is still a low percentage, which speaks again to overall teacher overages.

Why promote an alternative teacher certification program when certified teachers are apparently unable to secure employment "in instructional positions"? It seems that it would make better fiscal sense to cancel alternative certification in favor of provisional certification for teachers unable to secure teaching positions specifically in their fields of study.

An interesting requirement of the alternative certification program is that entrants must hold bachelors degrees or higher in fields "other than education," preventing a teacher with a certification in an overage area from using ABCTE to quickly recertify in a critical area while ABCTE fast-track-funnels non-education-degreed individuals into fields for which they have no established formal training.

Alternative teacher certification that promotes ABCTE is no miracle. It is, however, yet another sad commentary on the apparent bias of Bush-promoted, so-called education reform against the traditionally trained classroom teacher.

NO MIRACLE HERE, FOLKS

So. Bush's education reform plan has six points, five of which fell apart in this chapter. Jeb Bush is working really hard to promote his so-called Miracle Reforms nationwide. Is it possible for the man to so staunchly ignore the evidence of failure of what I can assume will be his presidential platform?

Every voter should read this book.

Let me not get ahead of myself. We still have one last Bush-promoted reform to go: The multiplicity of school options, those Florida charters, vouchers, and online education opportunities.

CHAPTER 14

JEB BUSH AND HIS MIRACLE REFORMS (THE REST OF IT)

The last of the Bush-promoted educational package involves his attempt to sell the American public on "alternatives" to the ""failing" traditional public schools: Charters, vouchers, and online schools. As the evidence reveals, this last reform fares no better than did the first five.

The handle has been pulled, and the water is swirling around the bowl.

Let us first consider Bush's push for charters.

CHARTER SCHOOLS

If anyone believes that Jeb Bush does not wish for his education agenda to become THE national education agenda, that person needs to ask the question, "Why would a former Florida governor bother to visit Arkansas in January 2013 in order to push for an independent authorizer of charter schools? Isn't Arkansas governor Mike Beebe against such an authorizer?"[1] Is there no "governor-to-governor etiquette"? It is not the first time Bush has used his influence to promote his agenda nationally; indeed, his organizations Foundation for Excellence in Education (FEE) and Chiefs for

A Chronicle of Echoes: Who's Who in the Implosion of American Public Education,
pages 223–237.

Change (C4C) are notorious for such "Bush interventions." (See FEE and C4C chapter.)

Like many self-declared education reformers, Bush is connected to education business ventures,[2] including the charter school. (See FEE and C4C chapter.) As such, Bush is a member of an increasingly popular club. Modern education reformers view themselves as exempt from conflicts of interest arising from promoting legislation that supports their own business ventures—even as they sit on organizational boards and hold public offices where they purport fairness in carrying out the noble tenets of education reform.

(A few notable examples of education venture conflicts of interest immediately come to mind. First is NCTQ, that listed 33 advisory board members in February 2013. On the NCTQ advisory board webpage, 15 of these 33 advertised their positions as "Partner," "President," "CEO," "Vice President," "Director" and/or "Founder" of some education business.[3] Next is a Louisiana example, Caroline Roemer Shirley, Executive Director of the Louisiana Association of Public Charter Schools, whose brother, Louisiana Board of Elementary and Secondary Education President Chas Roemer, openly advocates for more charter schools.[4] Finally, there is the Arizona ethical stipulation that so long as nine others benefit from a venture that also benefits a public official, the venture is not considered a conflict of interest. So, if ten people benefit, then Arizona school board members can do business with the very same charter schools they supposedly oversee.[5] The world of the corporate reformer is a world in duality: reform advocate/reform fiscal beneficiary.)

Though fiscal conflicts of interest abound in the "business of education," I do not believe Bush co-founded a charter school for the money. I believe he did so for the leverage it provided in securing him the 1998 Florida governor's race.

Bush promoted charter legislation in the Florida legislature; it passed in 1996.[6] The same year, Liberty City Charter School in Miami was the first charter school to open in Florida. It was co-founded by Bush and Willard Smith and publicized under the umbrella of Bush's education reform organization, FFF. In their announcement of the school, Bush and Smith declare Liberty City as a "public" school, "open to all, without tuition." In truth, the school is not "open to all"; Bush and Smith promise , "the total student body and class sizes will be small." Thus, not all who wish to attend can be selected to attend. They also declare that "parents will be involved," that there will be "active and constant parental involvement"; that parents "will be required to put in 30 work hours at the school." And what if parents are not involved? What if parents do not meet the 30-work-hour requirement? Bush and Smith note that even though the contract parents sign regarding their involvement "has no legal force, it's (sic) force will be moral, which is good enough for us."[7]

So utopian. Let's consider a timeline: In 1994, Bush runs for governor. He loses. In 1995, he forms FFF. In 1996, Bush promotes charter school legislation that passes. That same year, Bush co-founds the first Florida charter. That's sure to get some press coverage. In 1998, Bush runs for governor and wins. He resigns from the Liberty City Charter board.

Did Bush get what he was after—a platform for his 1998 gubernatorial run?[8] As Paul Moore of the Miami Carrol City Public High School notes:

Liberty Charter would be the shining school of choice on the hill for inner-city victims of the public schools. ***Turns out it was just an electoral device and the African-American children inside were just props in a campaign photo-op.*** *You see in 1994 Jeb Bush ran for governor for the first time. He came very close but Lawton Chiles bested him by less than two percentage points.* ***The fact that Bush got only 4% of the Black vote was probably the difference. Jeb realized that when asked during the campaign what a Bush Administration would do for Black Floridians it was unwise to have answered, "Probably nothing."***

So in his second run for Florida's top job, ***Jeb set out to polish up his image with the Black community.*** *He got together with T. Willard Fair and established the first charter school in Florida in 1996. They set their school up near Liberty City and called it Liberty Charter School.*[9] [Emphasis added.]

And what happened to Liberty City Charter School, the FFF's "new lease on learning"? The lease expired in 2008. The school was closed. According to financial statements for the 2007 fiscal year,[10] the school's cash flow had decreased by 53% ($37,000) due to pending litigation with the school's landlord (the school had to cut two grade levels due to facility use restrictions; unexpected legal costs were $106,000). Capital assets decreased by 12%, ($103,000) and liabilities increased by 80% ($219,000). Total revenue decreased by 14% ($320,000).

In short, the school was in both a financial and litigious bind, and it would not survive. From Liberty City Charter School's FY2007 Audit:

As shown in the accompanying financial statements, the Charter School has incurred a significant loss for operations for the fiscal year ending June 30, 2007, and as of June 30, 2007, ***the Charter School's current liabilities exceed its current assets by approximately $400,000 and its total liabilities exceeded its total assets by approximately $216,000.*** *These factors raise substantial doubt about the Charter School's ability to continue as a going concern.*[11] [Emphasis added.]

In speaking to a visiting North Carolina group in 2012, Bush referred nostalgically to his and Smith's founding Liberty City Charter School. What he failed to mention was that the school closed in 2008, and that by the time this happened, Bush had been disassociated from Liberty City for ten years.

The *Education Next* article reporting this North Carolina delegation's visit includes the following note:

> *Mediocre results, as Bush sees it, only embolden those who oppose reform and make the next reform effort harder.*[12]

So, let's not discuss those "mediocre results," if closure of the first Florida charter school could be described as "mediocre" for the students and, by extension, the community affected by the school's closure. Let's just proceed to tell the crowd the threadbare reformer phrase, "Be bold!"

And what of other Florida charter schools?[13] By 2010–11, approximately 156,000 students in 42 school districts attended roughly 459 Florida charter schools.[14] An April 2013 *Palm Beach Post* article has the number of Florida charters at 575.[15]

Even though by law the charter schools are to "increase learning opportunities for all students,"[16] racial and economic imbalances persist in Miami-Dade County, location of the original charter school. There the charter schools serve noticeably fewer minority students and fewer lower-socioeconomic students than do the traditional public schools. This disparity between the overall student population and the charter school attendees promotes an atmosphere of education inequity, a system whereby charters "skim the cream," the higher performing students in a district or region:

> *Florida school districts are not required to monitor charter schools' admissions lotteries or marketing methods, **and they seldom do—even with millions of dollars in taxpayer money on the line** . But in 2009, Miami-Dade school district researchers looking at enrollment patterns found that the Mater and Doral academies, two popular charter school networks managed by the same company [Academica], **had admitted a disproportionately high percentage of advanced students**. The findings raised the possibility "that **specific students were targeted in some way**," according to the report.*[17] [Emphasis added.]

And what do those advanced students get for the Zululeta brothers who run Academica? Incredible wealth. Here is how it works: One brother starts a charter chain, but it is not the brothers' only business venture. The two also control millions in real estate—real estate on which many of the schools in their South Florida charter empire sit—real estate that is all tax free because it is leased to "public" schools. Thus, the Zululeta brothers run the charters and act as landlords to the same charters. In 2010, the Zuluetas collected $19 million in charter rent and $9 million in "management fees."[18]

But wait: There is more. The Academica principals at one school act as board members for other Academica schools. As board members, these principals approve the management contracts and leases. In other words, this tight-knit group of administrators hands its employer more money. And what do these faithful principals get? Why, a trip to the Bahamas.[19]

No kidding. Other board members include a charter school lobbyist, and one school approved a construction contract that happened to be awarded to a contractor currently serving as a board member. Even the "outside attorney" who negotiates board contracts sits on one of the Academica school boards.

So, as one can see, there really are successful charter schools in Florida. The Zululeta brothers are pulling in Miami-Dade and Broward County public school money hand over fist, and their schools do not face closure.

And it all rests on the backs of those exploited, high-performing children.

It's a good thing for the Zulueta brothers that there is a traditional public school system to catch all of those "other" kids who prove to not be such ROI (return on investment), unable to feed into shining test scores and school letter grades. In fact, the Florida House just passed a bill allowing "high performing charters" to expand without further school board approval. And there is the added possibility of the charter's gaining access to unused district space.[20] It's all in the "high performance"—student test scores and school letter grades.

Not that all Florida charter schools receive a letter grade. Many do not. In 2006, 43% of Florida's charter schools received no letter grade. However, a 2006 *Orlando Sentinel* investigation found the FCAT scores of the ungraded schools to be very low. Furthermore, the *Sentinel* found that "a disproportionate number" of charters are among "the worst performing campuses in Florida," receiving almost 25% of the "failing" school grades even though these schools enroll only 3% of Florida students. As for FCAT performance, the *Sentinel* found that students in the charter schools performed similarly to those in traditional public schools.[21]

In 2011, the *Sentinel* reported that half of the state's 31 "F" school grades went to charters.[22]

In 2012, a higher percentage of charter schools than traditional public schools earned an A; and a higher percentage of charter schools than traditional public schools earned an F. Keep in mind that one cannot compare letter grades from one year to the next due to changes in the grading criteria from year to year (discussed in the previous chapter). In fact, a National Public Radio (NPR) report noted that school officials "expected grades to drop" due to changes in the grading criteria.[23]

What, then, is the purpose of grading? Why bother to grade if the grades are "expected to drop," not because of a drop in performance, but as an artifact of a capricious grading system?

Regardless of the whimsical changes in scoring criteria, one notable issue about the Florida charters is that they do not consistently outscore or outperform the traditional public schools.[24] In addition, the charters are arguably less stable than are the traditional public schools (i.e., charters are more prone to fiscal mismanagement), with some charter operators capitalizing on both higher performing students and lack of any substantive fiscal oversight (Academica), while other, independent, charters fail financially (Liberty City).

For some failed charters, the payout to self-serving administration is shorter lived, but it is still an unfortunate possibility. One charter school in Orange County paid its principal $519,000 after closing its doors. Moreover, the principal's husband also "earned" $460,000 over a five-year period for "management services." And as a final kick, the same school paid at least two of its board members $48,000 for clerical/administrative work.[25]

Regarding Bush-promoted charter school "success": The only "miracle" here is that the entire Florida public school system has not yet been bankrupted by the parasitic, under-regulated charter succubus that has been allowed to feed from public funds for over 17 years. A September 2012 report from the Office of the Inspector General examined the degree and effectiveness of charter school oversight in three states: Arizona, California, and Florida. Charter oversight in all three states was found wanting. For example, the USDOE Office of Innovation and Improvement (OII) waited 29 months before even placing a phone call to investigate deficiencies in Florida's charter school monitoring report. Moreover, once the phone call was made, it was after the second site visit, and that just to say, "Yeah, everything is okay here.":

> *In addition, by the time OII made its documented followup phone call to the Florida SEA [State Education Agency] to address deficiencies identified in 2008, WestEd (US-DOE contractor for charter school site visits and data collection) had already conducted its second monitoring visit of the Florida SEA in February 2011. In fact, according to OII documentation, WestEd's February 2011 monitoring visit was mentioned during that followup phone call. WestEd went on to issue its second report in July 2011.* **We concluded that OII waited for WestEd to conduct its second monitoring visit of Florida, almost 3 years after the first one was conducted, before following up with deficiencies noted on the first monitoring report. The revisit monitoring report did not note any serious deficiencies in Florida, finding that "Florida has demonstrated the necessary program management and fiscal controls to meet the application's objectives." Our audit work in the Florida SEA found the contrary.**[26] [Emphasis added.]

Note the list of unaddressed, uncorrected deficiencies observed in Florida charter schools—deficiencies overlooked not only by the Florida Department of Education, but also by USDOE:

> *...OII could not provide support for any corrective actions to rectify the significant deficiencies noted...[including] (1) Federal definition of a charter school was not met; (2) parents and other members of the community were not involved in the planning, design, and implementation of the school; (3) lack of a high quality strategy for assessing the achievement of the non-SEA grant objectives;* ***(4) uses of Charter School Program***

funds were not allowable, allocable, and reasonable; (5) lack of fiscal control and fund accounting procedures; and (6) financial and programmatic records related to the Charter School Program funds were not adequately maintained. OII did not have documentation in its files to support adequate followup to the non-SEA charter school grantees. OII did not require any of the charter schools to develop corrective action plans in response to the WestEd monitoring reports.[27] [Emphasis added.]

So, adequate oversight of Florida charters is lacking, and the USDOE turns its head. This is not "charter success." This is not a Bush-induced "miracle." This is mass fraud perpetrated on the American public, a quintessential, pocket-lining snow job that Bush is actively promoting in other states as "education reform, Florida style"—including "parent trigger" legislation[28] that allows parents to vote to hand over a "failing" school to charter operators. Such legislation operates under the guise of parent empowerment. However, once the "trigger" is "pulled," parents have no say in the outcome:

*[Palm Beach County PTA President] Martinez said PTAs and other public school advocates are wary of what they foresee developing under the[parent trigger] bill: **Private companies paying petition gatherers to collect parent signatures—and positioning themselves to draw taxpayer dollars running the new schools.***[29] [Emphasis added.]

In short, opportunities abound for those wishing to make steep, arguably unmonitored money off of charter school "(mis)management" in Florida (and, according to OIG, elsewhere, as well). What is all too obvious is that charter school success in Florida is a lie. The "miracle" is a two-bit parlor trick.

Next, let us consider vouchers.

FLORIDA VOUCHERS

Part of the original A Plus legislation signed into Florida law in 1999, the "opportunity Scholarship" program allows students at "failing" public schools to either change public schools or attend participating private schools.[30] "Opportunity Scholarships" is the privatizer-preferred term for what is a school voucher program. The question of legality was raised almost immediately following the passage of A Plus.[31] The use of vouchers to divert public education dollars to private schools was found unconstitutional in the lower court and then again in the judgment handed down from the First District Court of Appeals. Finally, in 2006, the Florida Supreme Court declared vouchers unconstitutional:

*In its ruling, the Florida court cited an article in the State Constitution that says, "Adequate provision shall be made by law for a **uniform**, efficient, safe, secure and high quality system of free public schools."*

The Opportunity Scholarships Program "violates this language," the court said.

"It diverts public dollars into separate private systems parallel to and in competition with the free public schools that are the sole means set out in the Constitution for the state to provide for the education of Florida's children," the ruling said. "This diversion not only reduces money available to the free schools, but also funds private schools that are not 'uniform' when compared with each other or the public system."[32] [Emphasis added.]

Since the Florida vouchers use no federal money, the case cannot be appealed to the US Supreme Court.

Following the unconstitutional ruling on the Opportunity Scholarship program, Jeb Bush and the Florida legislature created two other voucher entities, the Corporate Tax Credit Scholarship Voucher and the John McKay Scholarship for Students with Disabilities program.[33] The Corporate Tax Credit Scholarship allows corporations to bypass paying taxes directly to the state and instead to pay such money into a privately-run Scholarship Funding Organization. Thus, the tax money never becomes "public," so proponents of the Corporate voucher maintain that there is no violation of the Florida Supreme Court decision regarding the Opportunity Scholarship program. In addition, the Florida legislature has constructed the tax shelter such that names of participating corporations are kept secret:

The Legislature also set up specific laws to shield many details about the program, including which businesses participate, how much they give and how well schools are performing. However, two consecutive annual studies ordered by lawmakers showed the scholarship students are performing no better than public school students.

The program allows companies to divert up to 75 percent of corporate income taxes to one of two Florida nonprofits administering the program. The program's popularity resulted in the Legislature expanding it this year, authorizing it to grow annually by 25 percent.[34] [Emphasis added.]

That sure makes for a lot of secret money from hidden companies to fund a venture that demonstrates no marked gain over the traditional public schools. The Florida legislature has definitely undergone substantial trouble in making sure the public, who has a "choice," really has no clue where this "scholarship" money is coming from or whether the schools receiving the money are delivering any education at all to their children.

But for Jeb Bush and the Florida legislature, one such shady voucher program wasn't enough. Time for some real fraud.

The McKay Scholarship program is open to Florida public school students who have an IEP (Individualized Education Plan) or 504 accomodations[36] (not as pervasive or severe as disability requiring an IEP).[37] As is true of Florida charter schools, Florida vouchers are a "cash cow" begging for exploitation. For example, in Alachua County, Florida, 217 McKay Scholarships totaled $1.15 million in 2013, or approximately $5300 per student. Moreover, the Corporate Scholarships are serving 40,200 Florida students in 2013 for a cost of $229 million. That equals approximately $5600 per student.[38] Now, $5300 to $5600 per student isn't much if the money is actually being spent on a quality education. And that is a big "if" given the scandals surrounding the use of voucher monies in Florida.

The lack of voucher money regulation has led to McKay voucher students' being "educated" in substandard facilities, "including a dingy strip mall space above a liquor store and down the hall from an Asian massage parlor."[39] It has led to non-certified "teachers" popping video tapes in a machine in place of a curriculum. It has led to music classes with not one instrument. It has led to questionable discipline practices, including corporal punishment.

So-called "choice" has led to a Tallahassee "school" being paid six figures for educating students who were not enrolled in a school apparently staffed with "teachers" who just happened to be relatives. How was this fraud able to happen in the first place?

An Education Department investigation found that the school was receiving scholarship money for students who were enrolled in Polk County public schools, not the Faith Christian Academy.

A bill that would have provided more accountability in the state's voucher program died during the legislative session that ended April 30. At the time, Senate President Jim King said the programs were "a disaster waiting to happen" without greater state oversight.[40] [Emphasis added.]

Let us consider once more what "choice" is getting for parents:

Mike Kooi, the director of the [Florida] state's school choice office, confirmed to lawmakers that schools that receive McKay scholarships face minimal regulation. The schools have to fill out paperwork claiming to have a physical location and are supposed to be subjected to background checks, but the department never learns the results of that background check.

McKay schools are also not required to be accredited and only three site visits are permitted each year. ...

Kooi said the schools found to engage in fraud through McKay are a "small percentage." While acknowledging there could be a need for greater oversight, he was cautious about protecting the "independence of private schools."

"We don't want to get into (telling them) how to do their jobs," Kooi said.[41] [Emphasis added.]

The great irony here is the same corporate machine that King laments and Kooi represents—the Bush machine—is smothering the traditional public schools, not only by telling them "how to do their jobs," but by insisting that they are not doing their jobs, by insisting that public education is in some fantastic crisis that removal of both regulation and common sense will miraculously solve.

Consider the double standard of voucher school freedom versus traditional public school oppression as noted in this 2010 Jacksonville article:

> *If the goal of Florida's Corporate Income Tax Scholarship program is simply to reduce state spending on public education, it's graded an A.*
>
> *If the goal of the program is to improve education for low-income students, it scores an incomplete.*
>
> **But if the goal is to ensure the same educational accountability Florida politicians demand of public schools, then the program gets an F.**[42] [Emphasis added.]

The constitutionality of diverting tax money in order to "keep it private" for the unregulated costs of the Corporate and McKay vouchers is the subject of a suit filed in 2013 by a group of Florida parents represented by Southern Legal Council and Jon Mills of the University of Florida Law School.[43]

Let's see: Vouchers are tied up in litigation for years and finally declared unconstitutional by the Florida Supreme Court. To circumvent this ruling, Jeb Bush and the Florida legislature create a means for corporations to not pay most of their taxes but instead to participate in this educational tax shelter in order to fund vouchers anyway. The corporations' identities are kept secret, as is the voucher schools' performance. But performance leaks out, and it is not good. And numerous frauds are perpetrated by so-called voucher "schools" and their "teachers." Yet the legislature continues to open more doors to ensure more money is available for vouchers.

So this is the Florida voucher miracle, eh?

ONLINE EDUCATION

Jeb Bush promotes online education. In his op/ed for CNN, Bush says that digital learning (in other words, a child's school experience as one where the child is connected to a computer) is "not for everyone" but that it is "one important element in the overall school choice movement."[44] I have to admit, "digital learning" does sound appealing.

The question becomes, How many children are being subjected to an ill-fitting "online education"? Is digital learning really a matter of choice, or is it being craftily marketed and forced upon districts in lieu of a superior traditional, person-to-person education?

Who is making money off of this digital education venture?

In 2010, Jeb Bush and former West Virginia governor Bob Wise announced the creation of 10 Elements of High Quality Digital Learning.[45] In this announcement, Bush and Wise note that they already have already "learned that a comprehensive roadmap to reform yields success." Thus, it is a "given" that other Bush-endorsed and –promoted reforms have succeeded. (Perhaps Bush and Wise ought to read the preponderance of evidence to the contrary previously noted in these two chapters.)

The press release includes a link to a Digital Learning Now! The page has been removed from what is Bush's FEE website.[46]

Hmm.

I finally found a document on the Alliance for Excellent Education website.[47] In it,[48] Bush and Wise make some bold declarations. For example, they state, "Digital learning can transform education." For evidence, they note that technology has transformed "corporations, the military, and higher education." So, let's get this straight: Digital education has not been pilot tested on public school students, yet these two former governors proclaim that widespread online education "will" work in with public school students?

If Jeb Bush says it, it must be true—as true as the previously-noted efficacy of his other reforms.

Why "Digital Learning Now!"? Why not "Digital Learning After We Have Pilot Tested It and Carefully Examined the Results!"?

In their Digital Learning Now! manifesto, Bush and Wise also state, "Digital learning is the great equalizer." Keep in mind that Bush and Wise also say that digital learning is "not for everyone." Does it stand, then, that the "great equalizer" will automatically be utilized by those needing "equalizing"? Will it "close the gap"? Again, faulty logic to sell their goods.

Will digital learning "close the gap" by reducing educational rigor for those who would otherwise soar? There is, after all, more than one way to "equalize" two groups: The lower group can be raised—but the higher group can also be lowered.

Hmm, again.

Despite a lack of evidence, Bush and Wise's 10 Elements is featured in Forbes, where it is promoted as "a disruptive innovation."[49] It is interesting how "disruption" is packaged as somehow good for educating children. Those trained as teachers know that a principal educational goal should be to minimize disruption in student learning. Students are not automobiles to be jump-started or laundry to be agitated in a washer. They are developing human beings, and anyone knowledgeable about child and adolescent development knows that stability is critical to healthy human development, not disruption.

But modern reformers like Jeb Bush are politicians and businessmen, not teachers. It shows in what they package and sell.

In 2011, Bush and Wise began promoting their digital learning program nationally under the name of Roadmap for Reform: Digital Learning.[50] The 10 Elements sound rather noble:

1. Student access.
2. No barriers to access.
3. Personalized learning.
4. Advancement (according to progress achieved).
5. Quality content.
6. Quality instruction.
7. Quality choices (access to multiple digital learning providers).
8. Assessment and accountability.
9. Funding.
10. Infrastructure.

As of September 2011, ALEC has also officially adopted Bush's 10 Elements and promotes this "model legislation" nationally.[51]

In 2012, the Florida legislature passed the Digital Learning Now Act,[52] which requires all students to complete one online course in order to graduate high school. In 2013, Jeb Bush notes that digital learning is "not for everyone," but apparently in Florida, it is, and parents and students have no "choice" regarding the issue.

I love the reformer twist: Tell parents they have a "choice," then mandate what their children must do.

Indeed, students can be placed in Florida Virtual School without parental consent.[53]

The Digital Learning Now Act includes virtual charter schools, under-regulated opportunities for charter providers to seat children in front of computers, clicking all day long. In 2012, the virtual charter chain K12 was investigated for using uncertified teachers and asking certified teachers to sign rosters as a means of concealing the practice.[54] This investigation of K12's practices has yet to be resolved and might never be since former Florida Education Superintendent Tony Bennett accepted campaign contributions from K12[55]—in other words, "arrangements have been made." In other news, charges against K12 for allegedly misleading claims of academic performance, student-to-teacher ratios, and student recruitment resulted in lawsuit with its investors and was settled in March 2012 with K12 paying plaintiffs $6.75 million. K12 maintains that it has done nothing wrong.[56]

The K12 situation bespeaks the need for a level of regulation that does not exist when it comes to education vendors in Florida.

Prior to passage of the Digital Learning Now Act, in January 2012, the Tampa Bay Times published an article examining the outcomes of the then-15-year-old Florida Virtual School.[57] Florida Virtual School educates students for approximately $2500 less per student,[58] so one might easily see how students could be put, not "first," but "second" to state financial considerations. Furthermore, as is so often true of the mandates of corporate reform, Florida Virtual School is held to a different, more lenient (and nebulous) standard than are the traditional public schools. Even though its 2007 promotional literature boasts of outperforming "counterparts" (other virtual schools? traditional schools?) on the FCAT, the school could not produce scores for students across its 15 years and instead offered the Times partial scores for a single year. (These scores should be readily available since the law stipulates that all Florida Virtual School students should return to their respective traditional schools in order to take the required assessments, yet Florida Virtual School maintains that the state system does not allow easy access to students' scores.)[59] In addition, Florida Virtual is not held to the "graduation rates" standard of traditional public schools; instead, Florida Virtual reports "completer rates" in which students are offered multiple opportunities to pass. "Advancement according to progress achieved" looks pretty swell from the perspective of numerous "do-overs." Perhaps unlimited opportunities to "get it right" also qualifies as "personalized learning" or even "no barriers to access" (where "access" is a virtually guaranteed passing grade)?

Most do not stay enrolled long enough to reach any opportunity to "do over" if need be. There is a 28-day period at the beginning of each term when students can opt to drop a course. An astounding 66% choose to drop. Of those who remain, 81% pass.[60] Thus, only 28% of those originally enrolled will pass a given course.

This slight figure does indeed support Bush's statement that "digital learning will transform education"—for worse, not better.

Where is that "assessment and accountability" Bush and Wise promised?

Florida Virtual School has no definitive evidence of its success, and yet it operates using state funding of $166 million and enrolls 130,000 students. As Lee Fang of the Nation notes,

The rush to privatize education will also turn tens of thousands of students into guinea pigs in a national experiment in virtual learning....[61]

Compare the information above regarding unsubstantiated digital learning success to what Michael Horn of Forbes writes about the promise of digital learning:

There are many reasons to be optimistic. This is a proposal that is not in search of more funds; ultimately there are many reasons to believe this will cost less money. The technology is improving rapidly, as technology always does. And we have good people everywhere working together to put students first—where they need to be. Digital learning can take us there.[62]

Note: $166 million, 130,000 students, a $2500-per-student state incentive to promote digital learning at the expense of traditional classroom learning, and no definitive outcomes that Florida Virtual School is delivering on its promises. It cannot even deliver the data necessary to support its assertions of higher FCAT scores. In March 2013, the Florida legislature proposed a funding cut that would make Florida Virtual School no more fiscally attractive to the traditional public schools than would be other, possibly out-of-state, online education providers.[63] The legislators do not cite the lack of outcome data as a reason for the proposed funding cuts.

If the funding changes pass, Florida Virtual School will no longer be Florida's digital learning monopoly. I suppose "access to multiple digital learning providers" is fine just so long as one school is connected to a marketing edge.

Is Bush's idea of online education working? Is it effective? Is it good for children?

It's good for business. But whose?

Florida Virtual, as a matter of statute, is required to "aggressively seek avenues to generate revenue for its future endeavors"[64] In 2010, the Florida Virtual School Board of Trustees "voted unanimously to enter into a profit-sharing contract [45/55, respectively] with Pearson Education, Inc., to market the school's products globally."[65,66] The arrangement was supposed to garner $800,000 for Florida Virtual in the first year, ultimately reaching $44 million by 2015. However, Pearson is a business, and the bottom line is the top priority. Though Pearson was supposed to market Florida Virtual School's "products," it seems that Pearson was distracted from its commitment to Florida Virtual as it set out to woo Florida Virtual competitor, Connections Academy. In September 2011, Pearson purchased Connections; however, according to the Tampa Bay Times, Florida Virtual's profits via Pearson might have been in trouble prior to Person's Connections acquisition. [67,68]

Why would legislators approve a bill that requires a school funded by millions in public money to also "aggressively" fundraise?

Because the "bottom line" is the bottom line.

The miracle here is that despite digital learning's unmistakable allegiance to the bottom line, Jeb Bush not only continues to promote it in other states; he grades the states on how well they conform to his 10 Elements.[69]

IGNORING THE OBVIOUS

In promoting his reforms, Jeb Bush offers the nation two choices: Stay the same (i.e., the well-worn status quo accusation), or "Do as I say." No other options. Except the "Do as I say" reform option consistently yields poor results, or questionable results, or even illegal results. Bush's education reform plan draws public attention and even makes it into the news, but there is nothing good at the bottom of it. And the whole scene is chaos and up-heaval for the children involved.

Jeb Bush is not an educational reformer. He has no miracle. He is a ca-reer politician who is using education as his platform to "move ahead in the family business"—nothing more.

CHAPTER 15

JEB BUSH'S FOUNDATION FOR EXCELLENCE IN EDUCATION AND CHIEFS FOR CHANGE

A man wielding serious reformer power must create organizations to serve him in his ambitions. The Foundation for Excellence in Education (FEE) and Chiefs for Change (C4C) are vehicles for advancing Jeb Bush's career—nothing more.

On its website, FEE clearly states that its purpose is to further corporate reform. Bush founded FEE in 2008, the year after his two terms as Florida's governor had ended.[1] FEE sees as its "unique contribution" that of "working with decision makers on developing, adopting, and implementing reform policies."[2] FEE also describes itself as a "hands-on, how-to organization that provides model legislation, rule-making expertise, implementation strategies, and public outreach."[3] FEE has it all for the would-be reformer:

> *We are building **a one-stop shop** for those working to reform education. It includes **a depository of policies from all 50 states, model legislation, research papers, academic data, and media reports.**[4]* [Emphasis added.]

A Chronicle of Echoes: Who's Who in the Implosion of American Public Education, pages 239–258.

The FEE site includes links for model legislation via its policy library. In 2013, the links were not functioning. Not to worry, however. Model legislation promoted by FEE can be found elsewhere: the American Legislative Exchange Council (ALEC).

FEE sounds a lot like the ALEC, and it should. ALEC has borrowed extensively from Florida reforms clearly associated with and still promoted by Jeb Bush.[5] FEE is directly cited as the source for information and assistance with the menu of reforms in this 2010 ALEC Education Task Force agenda:

> *In passing their comprehensive, linked reforms* **beginning in 1999,** *Florida lawmakers embraced a comprehensive, multifaceted approach to improving academic achievement....*
>
> **The central Florida reform involved increasing transparency: assigning all schools and districts a letter grade of A, B, C, D, or F.** *The other reform elements combined to spur improvement as well.* **Parental choice programs** *(vouchers) for children attending failing schools, low-income students and children with disabilities gave potential exit power for the least advantaged children.* **A strong charter school law** *and* **virtual education statutes** *provide universally available options. Florida embraced far-reaching* **alternative teacher certification** *paths to improve teacher quality, and* **curtailed the social promotion** *of children.*
>
> **Florida lawmakers have continued to update their reforms over time. Those interested in the latest policy innovations in Florida can contact the Foundation for Excellence in**
>
> **Education. The Foundation can assist with technical issues, provide sample rules created by the Florida State Board of Education and other assistance.**[6] [Emphasis added.]

Both ALEC and FEE lobby for the corporate reform agenda. ALEC is more than willing to assist FEE in marketing Florida reforms nationwide, and vice-versa. And both Bush and ALEC present a united front. Originally, ALEC was against the Common Core State Standards (CCSS), viewing it as an attempt for the federal government to impose curriculum on the states. But Bush wanted CCSS and convinced ALEC to move from its position of opposition to one of neutrality.[7] (See ALEC chapter.) Notice Bush's words regarding his "intervention" on behalf of CCSS:

> *"Whether it's Common Core standards or other issues," Bush said, "****where you're trying to force change to yield a greater chance for students to learn—which is the ultimate objective here****—and put pressure on the system, there are those that are uncomfortable about that.*
>
> *"As that debate began, I did get asked to intervene," he said.*[8] [Emphasis added.]

Reform is aggressive. I have already written on the "pushing" David Coleman has done in promoting CCSS. Now Bush is "forcing." But the aggression is necessary say reformers, for we know what is good for "you people."

Bush says he was "asked to intervene." This should come as no surprise; on the FEE website, CCSS "architect" David Coleman is a featured "reformer," as are Arne Duncan, Chester Finn, Frederick Hess, Michael Horn, Mike Petrilli, and former Gates right-hand Stefanie Sanford,[9] all of whom are active and influential in their promoting CCSS.

FEE offers this public statement on ALEC's decision to follow Bush, written on November 19, 2012, by former ALEC Education Task Force Director and current FEE state policy director for FEE's Digital Learning Now!:

> *...**The American Legislative Exchange Council (ALEC) rejected an anti-Common Core bill.....** This action reaffirmed ALEC's position that states should be in charge of their education standards and supports the option for states to freely adopt Common Core.*
>
> *By rejecting the bill, **which would have tied the hands of state legislators,** ALEC made clear its support of states raising student expectations through higher standards...... ...... **The decision to work together to improve academic standards is a choice all 50 states have freely made,** with 46 states adopting Common Core so far, and four states choosing not to adopt the standards.[10] [Emphasis added.]*

It is important to note that ALEC's approving or rejecting model legislation does not "tie the hands of legislators," for ALEC is not a governing body, and its model legislation holds no power of law. Legislators who are able to think for themselves and who are not dependent upon prefabricated legislation know as much. Furthermore, no matter the outcome of the ALEC vote, the line, "This action reaffirmed ALEC's position that states should be in charge of their education standards" could be played to fit the situation. Why does ALEC not oppose CCSS? ALEC is pro-state. And, had it happened, Why does ALEC oppose CCSS? ALEC is pro-state.

Publicized spin is not contingent upon outcomes. Idealized hype never is.

In publicizing the rejection of ALEC model legislation opposing CCSS, FEE refocuses on the "freedom of states to choose CCSS." There is no word about CCSS adoption being a requirement for states to receive federal, Race to the Top money. There is also no addressing of prior ALEC member concerns that CCSS has not been pilot tested. Jeb Bush promoted CCSS, and ALEC followed Jeb, just as ALEC promotes Bush's Florida reform package and advertises for FEE among ALEC members.

Indeed, there is more here than just the "Bush influence" on ALEC: Staunch advocate of CCSS, billionaire Bill Gates, is well represented on both the Bush and ALEC sides. Even though the Gates Foundation publicly dropped ALEC in April 2012, their funding contract continued for another 17 months.[11] FEE also receives Gates money[12] and includes former

Gates employees Stefanie Sanford and Tom Vander Ark among its notable reformers.[13]

On to other FEE reformer ventures.

Considered its "flagship initiative,"[14] FEE's Excellence in Action National Summits provide a venue for those driving educational reform to meet and coordinate their collective reform "push." Jeb Bush and FEE host these summits, with Bush clearly in charge as the opening speaker. The 2012 FEE summit was sponsored by some notable reformer names and reform-benefitting entities, including Amplify, the Bradley Foundation, Educational Testing Service, the Fisher Fund, Bill Gates' Microsoft, Pearson, Alvarez and Marsal, Connections, and Charter Schools USA.[15]

Another "one stop shop":

> On October 17–18, 2013, Governor Jeb Bush and the Foundation for Excellence in Education will host the Excellence in Action National Summit on Education Reform in Boston, MA. ....**Attendees will be immersed in briefings, discussions and debates on the latest research, pilot programs and proven policies for raising student achievement.**

> ...The Excellence in Action National Summit on Education Reform **annually convenes the best and brightest from around the world to share strategies to improve the quality of education for all children, everywhere.** This **one-stop shop of policies and practices offers an opportunity for lawmakers, policymakers and advocates** to learn the nuts and bolts of reform.[16] [Emphasis added.]

In other words, the focus of this summit is to determine how to promote the ALEC-endorsed package of Bush reforms in order to benefit the corporations endorsing Bush and FEE. There is little here to do with "quality education." The superficial outcome of interest is the test score, but the less-publicized outcome of interest is the dollar.

The FEE summit is powerful for its networking and for promoting reformer cohesion. The summit promotional admits as much:

> Attendees leave the National Summit armed with the knowledge **and networks to advance bold education reform in their states.** This uncommon conference **annually serves as a catalyst** for energizing and accelerating the reform movement across the nation.[17] [Emphasis added.]

Jeb Bush uses the FEE summit to grow the cult of privatizing education reform. In 2010, Bush and FEE added another layer to their power by scheduling the FEE summit to occur in Washington, DC, in the days immediately preceding the ALEC national meeting.[18,19] Such a concentration of corporate reformers able to meet together to solidify their movement by way of beneficial financial arrangements. Traditional public education wouldn't know what hit it.

FEE advertises its summit as for the "best and brightest." Often FEE attendees are individuals in positions influential for promoting reform, such as National Council on Teacher Quality (NCTQ) President Kate Walsh, *US News and World Report* Chairman and Editor-in-Chief Mortimer Zuckrman, Success Charter Network CEO Eva Moskowitz; any number of reform-minded state superintendents, including former Louisiana State Superintendent Paul Pastorek and Rhode Island Commissioner Deborah Gist; former Gates Deputy Director Stefanie Sanford (now with College Board[20])[21] and Gates Senior Data and Economic Advisor, Marguerite Roza. The list is filled with highly interconnected people, sitting on any number of reform-promoting foundation, agency, or company boards together and actively assisting one another in pushing forward their collective reform agenda.

But let us not forget the legislators. A number of FEE emails released to the public in early 2013 reveal that FEE has been writing and promoting education reform legislation that benefits its corporate sponsors,[22] Another conflict of interest involves the "summit reimbursement" option for attending FEE summits;[23] as a lobbying organization, FEE is not allowed to pay trip expenses for state officials (such as public school superintendents) or lawmakers to attend its summits, where FEE corporate donors who stand to benefit from education laws enacted by these attendance-financed state officials and legislators are not only in attendance but also financiers of reimbursement monies. As the *Huffpost Miami* reports on March 3, 2013:

> **In recent years, several Florida Department of Education officials and legislators have attended the conferences,** *and in some cases, their flights, hotel stays, meals and incidentals were paid for with money that came partly from the foundation's corporate donors.*

At these events, the state officials attended meetings, panel discussions, meals and receptions also attended by those donors.

> **The donors include companies that sell testing services, high-tech learning products and charter school services to the state and to Florida school systems, or that would like to.**[24] [Emphasis added.]

FEE summits are designed to benefit the reform set, whether state official or corporate sponsor. For example, the 2011 FEE summit in San Francisco featured as a speaker Rupert Murdoch of Amplify (the company that won the contract in 2013 to develop CCSS formative assessments, run by former NYC schools chancellor and FEE member Joel Klein).[25] The same summit also included a fundraiser for Indiana school superintendent and FEE featured reformer Tony Bennett, who lost the election but (amazingly) landed on his feet with an offer to become superintendent in (such a coincidence) Florida.[26] (In July 2013, Bennett resigned as Florida superintendent after emails revealed his allegedly influencing Florida's letter grades to favor a charter school run by hefty GOP donors.)[27]

Jeb Bush has created more than one nonprofit. He has three: FEE, Foundation for Florida's Future (FFF), and Chiefs for Change (C4C). He also was connected to Meridian Strategies, a lobbying group that until March 6, 2012, was registered with FFF. What this arrangement allowed Bush to do was use the FFF-registered Meridian lobbyist, Patricia Levesque, to influence outcomes favorable to FEE, and get by with it—even though Levesque also holds the position of FEE chief executive officer.[28] Technically this ethically-questionable activity is legal even though all four entities share the same address.[29–32] The fact that the organizations were established separately is enough to allow Bush to skirt the law. It becomes a game on paper. Yes, the lobbyists are pushing for the Bush education agenda, but if the summit is an FEE event and the lobbyists are not technically registered with FEE (which has no lobbyists registered), then Bush can have his corporate-sponsored FEE pay for trips for state officials and legislators.[33]

Within days of the *Huffpost Miami* publicity, Meridian Strategies pulled its lobbying registration with FFF. In an email to the Florida Center for Investigative Reporting, Levesque provided the following as her reason:

> *At our annual board meeting last November the board expressed an interest in having me work full-time as an employee of the foundation because of our growing work on education reform in Florida and across the country.*[34]

A safe response.

The revealing component of this Bush-Levesque-lobbying story involves the content of the released emails. Even though its website identifies its two-day, annual summit as the "flagship initiative" of FEE, Bush's behind-the-scenes powers of manipulation play themselves out via the Bush-created reform group for state superintendents, Chiefs for Change (C4C). Much of the remainder of this chapter includes content originally posted on my blog under the title, *Like Spokes to a Hub: Chiefs for Change in Bush's Service,*[35] in which I detail the involvements of the 11 members with FEE and, ultimately, Jeb Bush.

It makes for very enlightening reading.

Bush's FEE created C4C, "to rally behind a common agenda,"[36] highlighted in short form on the C4C member page:

> **Chiefs for Change is a program operated by the Foundation for Excellence in Education, a national 501(c)(3) nonprofit, nonpartisan organization, focused on education reform, state-by-state.**[37] [Emphasis added.]

Bush created Chiefs for Change, an organization for state school superintendents, so that he could control reform efforts through those superintendents. Bush wants these superintendents to promote the previously-mentioned reform agenda lauded by ALEC in Washington, DC, in 2010:

> *The new policies have many champions, but **a little-known common denominator behind sweeping measures in nearly a dozen states is Jeb Bush**, the former Florida governor, **who has re-emerged as an adviser to governors and lawmakers, mostly Republicans, who are interested in imitating what he calls "the Florida formula" for education.***
>
> ***Mr. Bush, for example, has been closely involved in new education bills and laws in Arizona, Florida, Indiana, Minnesota, Missouri, Nevada, New Mexico, Oklahoma and Utah.** One out of five state school superintendents have joined a group that his national foundation created, Chiefs for Change, to rally behind a common agenda.*[38] [Emphasis added.]

Bush's power is demonstrated in his influence over the decision making of the C4C superintendents. In her role as FEE CEO, Patricia Levesque often serves the liaison between Bush's instructions and the superintendents' implementing Bush's wishes.

The remainder of this chapter is devoted to examining the details of Bush's influence over the ten superintendents who have chosen to align themselves with Bush and his reform machine via C4C. Through this handful of well-positioned-yet-compliant education leaders, Bush is able to steer reform efforts across the nation to suit his will.

The first member— already mentioned for his convenient placement as Florida commissioner of education following his FEE-funded defeat in Indiana— is Tony Bennett.

Following his defeat in Indiana, Bennett commented that he planned to remain in education policy. Regarding such plans, Bennett chose the following, highly professional metaphor:

> *Driving education reform policy is probably my drug of choice.*[39]

Stellar.

In Indiana, both Bennett and Indiana Governor Mitch Daniels followed Bush closely:

> ***The most complete adoption of Mr. Bush's approach has been in Indiana,** where **Gov. Mitch Daniels's education talking points in his State of the State speech closely echoed a mission statement of Mr. Bush's foundation.***
>
> ***"We were able to really use many of their policy positions and implement many of their policies to drive pieces of our reform agenda,"*** *said Tony Bennett, Indiana's schools superintendent.*[40] [Emphasis added.]

Bush's FEE fundraiser for Bennett's Indiana reelection should come as no surprise given Bennett's obedience to the Bush agenda. Given that loss, Bennett could now enforce Bush reform in Bush's backyard:

> *The State Board of Education voted unanimously Wednesday to hire Bennett to oversee the Florida's public schools and colleges.* **Bennett is expected to carry over his school reform agenda from Indiana....**
>
> **Bennett's time in Indiana was defined by a number of initiatives that mirror Florida's school reform efforts,** *including* **grading schools on an A-F scale, expanding charter schools and voucher programs, evaluating teachers based on student performance and pushing for turnaround efforts in failing schools.**[41] [Emphasis added.]

C4C member Tony Bennett: Simply another arm of Jeb Bush and an ALEC-paralleled privatization agenda—until Bennett's Indiana letter grade machinations were made public in July 2013. Changing an Indiana donor's school's letter grade[42] leads to exit from Bush's graces via resignation.[43]

Looks like time for "education policy detox" for Bennett.

Bush does not necessarily wait for an individual to become superintendent. Sometimes he engineers the appointment, and he does so via Levesque and FEE. Such is the story for Louisiana Superintendent John White. The following email was part of a 2011 public records request by Donald Cohen of In the Public Interest. The email is from FEE Chief Executive Officer Patricia Levesque to Chiefs for Change members and staff:

> *Chiefs,*
>
> *An article on Louisiana state board of education (BESE) races–that will impact selection of the next chief in Louisiana.* **Gov. Jindal wants John White as next state chief. Governor Bush is lending his support/endorsement to the candidates Gov. Jindal is supporting for the State Board of Ed.** [Emphasis added.]
>
> *Patricia*[44]

Attached to the above email is a Baton Rouge *Advocate* article regarding the fundraising of the BESE candidates. C4C members were being instructed by Bush through Levesque to financially influence the BESE outcome.[45]

Jeb Bush wanted John White as state superintendent in Louisiana. He used his influence to make it happen. As it turns out, the 2011 Louisiana BESE election was a monumental example of the power of reformer money; the education reform candidates raised $2,368,786, compared to the $199,878 raised by the remaining candidates.[46]

John White is not the only Louisiana "Chief" on the Chiefs for Change roster. Former Louisiana State Superintendent Paul Pastorek is an emeritus member of Chiefs for Change. Pastorek, still listed as a lawyer with ALEC-member law firm Adams and Reese,[47,48] was appointed Louisiana state superintendent by the state board of education in 2007

This Chiefs for Change bio on Pastorek is laden with Bush-promoted propaganda:

> *Paul Pastorek fought for a vast amount of education reforms while Louisiana Superintendent of Education, but transforming K-12 education in New Orleans after Hurricane Katrina is arguably his most significant accomplishment.* **After the disaster, Pastorek created the Recovery School District (RSD)** *to reimagine and revamp the schools under its control, more than 100 of which were failing. In March 2007, while the RSD was working through the aftermath of Katrina and unable to reopen schools,* **Pastorek worked relentlessly to create more charter schools, increase private funding in education and keep control over state-run schools that other leaders argued should be returned to local control.** *His efforts to strengthen school accountability have* **led to a decrease in the dropout rate and the number of schools labeled as academically unacceptable in Louisiana.**[49] [Emphasis added.]

Pastorek's C4C bio is an amazing example of propaganda. RSD was created pre-Katrina, in 2003, by legislative action and public vote, and according to the law, RSD was never intended to retain schools. Pastorek did manage to mismanage millions in federal aid by paying firms such as FEE-sponsor and so-called "turnaround firm" Alvarez and Marsal millions over contract for work they did not complete rebuilding schools. (This is the same shady firm discussed in the Klein and Vallas chapters.) As to the dropout rate decline, the definition of "dropout" was changed to exclude students attending adult education programs; such has nothing to do with Pastorek's "strengthening accountability." Finally, seven full school years later, the predominately-charter RSD continues to be 90% D and F schools.[50-54]

Only one month before resigning as state superintendent,[55] Pastorek positioned John White to have his "foot in the door" as the next RSD superintendent, so much so that White's hire was announced by Jindal, Pastorek, and others before the BESE vote had been taken. In an April 7, 2011, hearing before the Louisiana House Appropriations Committee, Pastorek feigned ignorance as to his own publicizing that White had already been hired despite the announcement being widely circulated in the news.6[5] Six months later, Levesque sent her email on Bush's behalf to position White for yet another politically-engineered education leadership position.

Bush's influence via Levesque emails continues. In the set of emails dated October 2011 and obtained by In the Public Interest, Bowen solicits and receives Bush's and other FEE assistance in promoting the reform agenda. Also included in this set of emails is Patricia Levesque's giving Bowen the "heads up" on October 7, 2011, about "requiring new chiefs" to "participate in Partnership for Assessment for Readiness for College and Careers (PARCC) assessment":

Steve,

I am guessing that Maine was part of Smarter Balanced prior to your becoming state chief. Just wondering if you have had any thoughts about moving to PARCC?

I'm asking because there are some Chiefs for Change members who want to pose the issue in your 2012 planning meeting on whether or not PARCC participation has to be a requirement for new Chiefs for Change members.

Just giving you a heads up.

Patricia[57]

Translation: If you want to be a part of our club, know that we plan to dictate even the assessments your state administers. And the test being not-so-subtly promoted, PARCC, has as of March 2013 become its own nonprofit.[58] No money-making, potentially ALEC-connected[59] testing monopoly here....

The benefit of Chiefs for Change membership is its offering of canned legislation for the corporate reform agenda. Bush and FEE are happy to run Maine's education system for Bowen. Note the following emails. First, one from Bowen dated October 18, 2011:

Hi, Patricia.

*I am... a bit daunted by what we have coming–the governor wants to do a major push on teacher effectiveness and on school choice as well. **I want to do the ABC grading as well this time around, but I don't know that we can pull all of this off. When you suggested that there might be a way for us to get some policy help, it was all I could do not to jump for joy.** I have one person here on policy, and she really does more in the way of bill drafting, etc. I have no political policy staff who I can work with to move all this stuff through the process.*

*So please keep me posted as you move forward **and if you need help with a donor or anything, let me know.***

Thanks!

Steve[60]

It's like ordering from a drive-thru menu. But Bowen offers something interesting in his last statement: "If you need help with a donor...." To what would Bowen need to "donate"? To those Bush wants "on board." (Reread the section on John White for an example of Bush solicitation.)

On October 20, 2011, Bush emails Bowen. Here is an excerpt (obtained by In the Public Interest):

*During the last year, Digital Learning Now! developed the Roadmap for Reform: Digital Learning, a comprehensive policy guide that provides **specific steps for states to sys-***

tematically and systemically transform education. Our goal is to provide you with… model policies, research, and expert advice from a national network of advocates–that will allow you to advance and accelerate reforms.[61] [Emphasis added.]

And as to that extra FEE assistance, Patricia Levesque is there to offer help in this October 19, 2011 email:

Let us help.

Matt Ladner can assist with drafting school choice legislation–we should already have model legislation depending upon what type of choice you want to do (e.g. scholarships for kids with disabilities).

Our team can reach out to Sandi Jacobs with NCTQ to see if they have model legislation on teacher quality. Just let us know what you want to put in the bill.

Re: school grading. We already have two versions of model legislation depending upon how much you want to put in statute vs. administrative rule.

Nadia Haberg is our point person on the state of Maine. I'll let her work with your assistant to set up a time for us to have a team call you and hear your thoughts before we start work.

Patricia[62]

Reading emails like the one above galvanizes for me the idea that corporate reform is in it for the approximately half of a trillion dollars in annual public education dollars, nothing more. Recall that the FEE website advertises itself as a "one stop shop"[63] for reformers—and reform designed to benefit education companies.

Bush's influence in Maine extends to its governor:

*Gov. Paul LePage plans to host a conference this month [March 2013] **showcasing the controversial education reforms developed by former Florida Gov. Jeb Bush and promoted nationwide by a foundation that Bush founded.***

*The daylong Governor's Conference on Education March 22 at Cony High School in Augusta **gives senior officials at Bush's Foundation for Excellence in Education prominent billing, including executive director Patricia Levesque, a registered Florida lobbyist for digital education companies who has helped shape LePage administration policies in ways favorable to that sector.***

The foundation has played an influential behind-the-scenes role in shaping the governor's education agenda, a Portland Press Herald/Maine Sunday Telegram investigation found last year.[64] [Emphasis added.]

Via the maneuverings of FEE and C4C, Maine's education agenda belongs to Bush. So does New Mexico's, where former Florida education department hire Hanna Skanderra has been positioned as New Mexico's latest secretary of education:

> *It seems obvious,* **given [Skandera's] complete lack of educational credentials** *and her political background, that* **Hanna Skandera is a foot soldier in an ideological war** *taking place right now against working people—teachers and other unionized workers.* **This is the national agenda of the organizations she is and has been affiliated with.** … …*Ms.* **Skandera can offer absolutely no professional qualifications to be New Mexico's or any other state's secretary of education.**

> **She has no background in curriculum and instruction,** *yet she feels competent enough to suggest a policy of assigning letter grades to classroom teachers as a solution.* **Skandera has never had the day-to-day experience of being in charge of a classroom**

> *with elementary school children herself, yet she feels competent to evaluate trained, experienced teachers.*

> *So, then, why is she being vetted as the New Mexico secretary of education? Most likely the answer is* **because she was recommended to our new governor by people outside the state who are fronting a national political agenda** *that is antithetical and indifferent to the needs of the people and children of New Mexico.*[65] [Emphasis added.]

What "political agenda" is Skandera "fronting"? Why, Jeb Bush's:

> **Hanna Skandera "served as the deputy commissioner of education under (Florida) Governor Jeb Bush,** *where* **she promoted and implemented middle and high school reforms** *that instituted greater accountability, incentives for high performance and the end of social promotion….* "[66] [Emphasis added.]

In the reformer mind, qualifications for securing leadership positions are simply not necessary. Skanderra hasn't the credentials for her current education leadership post. Though the New Mexico constitution requires that the state superintendent be a "qualified, experienced educator,"[67] Skandera tentatively holds the position, and amid much controversy.[68] If one follows the money, one again lands at the feet of Jeb Bush:

> *Skandera has been a contentious figure for her educational reform ideas. But this week, a different issue came up:* **Skandera's frequent out-of-state trips, many of which are funded by nonprofits that contract with PED.**

> *Travel vouchers—obtained from the state Department of Finance and Administration via a public-records request by the union-funded Independent Source PAC—show that Skandera has traveled to various locations around the country and internationally during her two years in office.*

> **Often, her travel is paid for by groups like the Foundation for Excellence in Education,** *a nonprofit founded by former Florida Gov. Jeb Bush, which advocates for the*

> *same education reforms—charter schools, third-grade retention and A-F school grad-*
> *ing—that Skandera is pushing through in New Mexico.*[69] [Emphasis added.]

Below is the September 7, 2011, email in which FEE's Patricia Levesque agrees that Chiefs for Change should foot Skandera's DC trip to testify before congress in favor of relaxed restrictions[70] for use of federal funding of virtual education:

> *Hanna has been asked to testify in front of congress. She needs us c4c [Chiefs for Change] to pick up costs. I told her we would. Can you reach out to her and her Asst to help with whatever she needs.*[71]

Levesque, Bush's right hand, lobbies for the groups Skandera promoted before Congress.[72]

This is what corporate reform does: It promotes itself. Not children. Not schools.

Skandera was doing Levesque a favor by testifying on behalf of virtual education. It was the least Levesque could do to pay Skandera's way.

But FEE/Chiefs for Change is not the only group reimbursing Skandera. The FEE-promoted,[73] newly-nonprofit, PARCC, also reimbursed Skandera:

> **Skandera also serves on the board of the Partnership for Assessment of Readiness for College and Careers,** *a consortium of 22 states "working together to develop a common set of K-12 assessments in English and math"—online evaluations Skandera plans to implement in New Mexico in 2015.* **Travel vouchers show PARCC paid a total of more than $2,000 for Skandera to attend board meetings in Washington, DC, and Alexandria, Va.**
>
> **PARCC, too, has ties to state money:** *It's run by Washington, DC-based nonprofit Achieve, Inc., which last year landed a $39,660 contract with [New Mexico's] PED, according to the Sunshine Portal.*[74] [Emphasis added.]

In short, Hanna Skandera has no background in education, but she is willing to promote Bush's education reform agenda. In turn, Bush's FEE is more than willing to offer Skandera the same type of educational policy "assistance" that it offered Bowen. Here are some excerpts of emails between Skandera and FEE's Bragg obtained by In the Public Interest:

> Skandera: *Hello! Are you working for the Foundation?*
>
> Bragg: *Yes! Just started on Tuesday, working with Mandy on State Initiatives–the implementation side.*
>
> (Four days pass.)
>
> Bragg: *Hey! What's the timeline for rollout of A—F grading?*

Skandera: *We are developing rules late summer. We are providing baseline data to districts sometime this fall. We are still finalizing dates. Any chance I can get you out here this fall to help advise us on our literacy initiative?*

Bragg: *I'm at your beck and call.*

Skandera: *Sweet.*[75]

"Sweet," indeed, for Skandera, who reaps the benefits of appearing to know how to do a job for which she has zero credentials. And sweet for Bush and his effort to promote nationwide his version of educational reform. In May 2013, on the C4C website, Skanderra decided to call herself secretary of education rather than secretary-designee even though she has yet to be confirmed.[76] Without confirmation, Skanderra has held the position since December 2010.[77]

Let us now consider Rhode Island's Deborah Gist. In an email obtained by In the Public Interest, Gist solicits assistance from FEE's Fonda Anderson to secure a donor for Rhode Island's Advanced Placement (AP) project. Anderson assures Gist that the donation was already approved. AP is a product of the Educational Testing Service (ETS),[78] and ETS just so happens to be an FEE corporate sponsor.[79] By promoting AP, Gist is promoting Bush. Gist admits that ETS is costly for her state, and for guidance, she seeks assistance from her friendly FEE advisor, Fonda Anderson:

Gist: *After I received John's email about Teachscape, I discovered that they're one and the same with **ETS, who we'd identified as "the only game in town."** … The problem is that it is expensive.… …. **So, the need remains. … Any thoughts?***

Anderson: *Deborah, let's schedule a phone call so that I can focus on all it is you need, **and how we can work to make that happen.***[80] *[Emphasis added.]*

Chiefs for Change and FEE form a mutual favor society. Gist receives the perks of a Chiefs for Change member, such as those "donations", and, in turn, Chief Gist can promote the previously-mentioned, Bush-pocket-lining Virtual Education Act.[81] Gist's reform agenda is quintessential FEE/Chiefs for Change: Virtual education; school grades; comprehensive student data collection system, and an "academy" for "transformative" leaders.[82]

Time to focus on New Jersey's Chief, Chris Cerf. What a story we have here between Cerf and Bush. In 2001, Cerf became president of a company called Edison Education. As blogger Jersey Jazzman notes, Edison "couldn't produce the results it claimed it could." Edison had gone public in 1999 and was in deep trouble by 2003; not wanting corporate reform to ever appear to fail, Jeb Bush used the vast resources of the Florida teachers retirement system to bail out a company that ironically was trying to shut out public school teachers:

Whittle and Cerf needed a buyout; someone with pockets deep enough to take the company private and protect the value of their own shares. Ironically, their white knight turned out to be funded by none other than the Florida teachers pension fund.[83]

Yes, you read that right: Florida teachers paid for Whittle and Cerf to take their company private—a company that advocated for the continuing corporatization of public schools. *Understand that the fund itself was being run by a firm that was engaging in some questionable practices.*

… The deal was approved by the three trustees of the FL pension: CFO Tom Gallagher, then-Attorney General and future-Governor Charlie Crist, **and then-Governor Jeb Bush.**

… So the pensions of Florida teachers were used to rescue a failing company that advocated education policies counter to those of the teachers unions. ***This buyout saved the contract of an investment firm that was doing a lousy job managing the pension by playing to the ideological predilections of a powerful governor, who just happened to***

be the brother of a president who ushered in No Child Left Behind, the law that set the stage for "school choice."[84] [Emphasis added.]

Jeb Bush used teacher pension money to enable a company to go private. Anything to offer the appearance of success to corporate reform. So, it seems that Cerf "owes" Bush. And why not return the favor and benefit yet again by becoming New Jersey's education superintendent and channeling the Bush agenda into yet another state?

Next, let us travel to Tennessee, where "Chief" Kevin Huffman promotes the same demoralizing, Bush-nodded reforms as his fellow chiefs, including a flawed teacher evaluation system and a pay-for-performance model that has already failed in his state. As educational historian Diane Ravitch notes:

The Tennessee Education Association sent out this bulletin today. **State Commissioner Kevin Huffman, whose only classroom experience was two years in Teach for America,** *has plans to adopt every evidence-free, demoralizing tactic in the corporate reform playbook.*

Huffman is a purveyor of zombie policies. Nothing he advocates has any evidence behind it. ***"Pay for performance" has been tried repeatedly for a century and never succeeded. So he wants more of it. It failed in 2010 in Nashville, where teachers were offered a bonus of $15,000 for higher scores.*** *But Huffman either doesn't know or doesn't care. It's not his money he's wasting.*

He knows that the state's teacher evaluation system is badly flawed, but he wants to push ahead with it anyway. *Apparently, he wants to break the spirit of the state's teachers.*[85] [Emphasis added.]

In 2012, following Jeb Bush's keynote speech at the November 2012 FEE Summit[86] in Washington, DC, the message was to grade the teachers using student test scores.

It doesn't matter that value-added assessments have a terrible track record.[87] Declare them useful:

> But [Tennessee] state education department spokeswoman Kelli Gauthier said **it's reasonable to expect teachers who do well on observations to also post high value-added scores.**[88] [Emphasis added.]

The previous statement is in response to the failure of Tennessee's teacher evaluation system to "identify bad teachers and provide them more training":

> *The data revealed:*
> - *More than 75 percent of teachers received scores of 4 or 5—the highest possible—from their principals, compared with 50 percent scoring 4 or 5 based on student learning gains measured on tests.*
> - *Fewer than 2.5 percent scored a 1 or 2 when observed, while 16 percent scored a 1 or 2 when judged by learning gains.*
> - *Of teachers who received the learning gains score of 1, the average observational score was, on average, 3.6.*
>
> *In this first state review of evaluations—launched last summer—**the education department suggests some principals will need to be trained again on how to observe teachers.** It's one of numerous recommendations in a 45-page report that captures thousands of teacher and administrator responses to the evaluation program.*[89] [Emphasis added.]

It couldn't possibly be a fundamentally flawed measurement system.[90] It must be that the administrators are wrong about the colleagues they work closely with every day. Despite the evidence, and because he is Jeb Bush, Bush continues to promote the broken reforms in Tennessee:

> *"What you are doing right now is leading the country," Bush told [Tennessee] Governor Haslam in the forum titled "Improving Student Achievement."*
>
> **He cited Tennessee's legislation in the past few years that has loosened tenure-driven teacher pay, and moves toward tying it more to student achievement.**
>
> *Many credit the former Florida governor… with raising student achievement in his state student choice programs such as vouchers and charters, along with teacher pay tied to student performance. (Consider the chapters on Bush in this book.)*
>
> *"Without the legislature, none of the things we did in Florida were possible, and it required a lot of courage for them to do this because I was all in already in," Bush said before the forum.*

The former Florida governor minced no words about what to do with both good and bad teachers.

"Pay for successful transfer of teaching to learning, this is what it's all about," *said Bush in his closing remarks. "I would argue for teachers who fail, who are not doing that,* **get them out of classroom** *as soon as possible after remediation hasn't worked. "*[91] [Emphasis added.]

The Bush Conceptualization of Teaching as it is tied to Pay for Performance: Open a kid's head. Pour in the required measure of learning. Close the kid's head. Get paid.

In addition to pay-for-test-results, Huffman also believes in charter schools, so much so that he is willing to withhold funding from districts wary of charters:

Huffman recently withheld $3.4 million from the Metro Nashville school system **because the school board refused to bow to state demands and approve a charter school in West Nashville.** *The board claimed* **the proposed charter school could not guarantee a diverse student population in the mainly white area of town,** *and black community activists claimed* **the school would become a publicly funded school only for affluent white children.**[92] [Emphasis added.]

Why, this sounds like the kind of chief Bush is after: One who not only pursues reforms but who punishes those who oppose his plan, as well.

Like other Chiefs for Change members, Oklahoma's Janet Barresi relies upon FEE members such as Patricia Levesque for "help" with promoting Bush-styled reform. (And it will be Bush-styled, since Chiefs for Change was created by Bush's FEE for the purpose of promoting Bush reform.) Below is Barresi's August 10, 2011, request for assistance with Oklahoma's NCLB waiver:

Patty:

Sec. Duncan called the governor and asked that Oklahoma send **the framework document** *to him next week prior to USDE releasing guidelines.* **I assume other C4C folks received the same call.** *I have a meeting tomorrow with gov staff to discuss.* **I am putting together my ideas but want to bounce some things off of you or anyone working on this.**

Thanks,

Janet[93] [Emphasis added.]

In her email, Baresi indicates that Duncan is asking for a "framework" for an arguably illegal policy (Can Duncan alter federal law by simply saying, We'll let you states out of the federally-mandated NCLB?) on which he has yet to release guidelines. It seems highly questionable to seek input from a select group (Chiefs for Change) "prior to" general release of guidelines for states in general. However, Duncan is a member of FEE, an indication of Bush allegiance. Furthermore, in her own Bush allegiance and as a loyal member of C4C, Baresi is asking for direction (and it seems, approval) of her plans for Oklahoma education.

Certainly Barresi's composed response to Duncan (dated August 12, 2011) received FEE/Chief nods in its including the following stipulation:

> *The [waiver] plan should* **grant flexibility only to those states that have demonstrated bold reforms, an effort to implement rigorous standards and an emphasis on account-ability.**[94] [Emphasis added.]

Wait. It gets better:

> *In addition,* **the plan should adhere to guiding principles provided by Chiefs for Change** *in its Statement for Principles of Reauthorization of the Elementary and Secondary Education Act (May 19, 2011).*[95] [Emphasis added.]

Translation: We have the answer. We are Chiefs for Change. You want out of NCLB? Do what we say. Grant it, there really is no "out" of NCLB; we've only changed the letters from NCLB to RTTT. But we will benefit handsomely from being The Answer.

What if corporate reform is embarrassed by the truth? What if, for example, a report is issued by faculty from two major Oklahoma universities criticizing the capricious school letter grading system of which Bush is so proud? Well, that means that his Chief for Change Barresi might have to go the campaigning to spread the lie that the authors of the report "privately recanted." And Bush is there to assist with the cover-up:

> **The Legislature approved the A-F grading system** *but* **Barresi's department wrote the rules and imposed them with virtually no input from local school officials.** *Most local superintendents and principals don't oppose a grading system,* **but they want it to be consistent,** *fair and transparent.*
>
> *A report by senior researchers at OU and OSU concluded that the grading system is "neither clear nor comparable."*
>
> *With revelations that the Bush foundation would provide to Barresi "air cover—op eds, tweets, letters to the editor, and even expert testimony at the board meeting if you need it," it's not a stretch to conclude they'd be advising Barresi on talking points, too. ...*
>
> *Wherever Bush's Chiefs for Change have set up shop—like Florida and Oklahoma—Bush's foundation drives policy. And* **in the event policy goes bad, they orchestrate the spin campaign, too.**[96] [Emphasis added.]

Sometimes the truth inconveniently makes itself known and Bush Himself must assist in spreading a concentrated version of the lie. In corporate reform, truth is definitely bad for business.

If reality breaks through and corporate reform is really embarrassed, well, one might have to "take one for the team." That seems to be the case for former Florida "Chief" Gerard Robinson, who continues his time with Chiefs for Change as an emeritus member.[97] Even though Robinson resigned "for family reasons," his departure as Florida's state education superintendent occurred amid national humiliation:

> *...Robinson's tenure had been dogged in recent months by the **public-relations pounding the department took after FCAT scores collapsed, followed a few months later by the school grades mix-up.***
>
> *The Florida Board of Education was forced to lower passing grades for the statewide writing tests in May **after the passing rate plunged from 81 percent to 27 percent for fourth graders and showed similar drops in eighth and 10th grades.***
>
> ***Then, in July, the department had to reissue grades for 213 elementary and middle schools and nine school districts as part of a "continuous review process."***
>
> *That came **after the number of schools receiving an "A" had plummeted from 1,481 in 2011 to 1,124 this year.** The new grades showed 1,240 schools getting the highest mark—a jump of 5 percentage points from the first cut of the numbers.*[98] [Emphasis added.]

The article cited above seems to try just a little too hard to steer focus of Robinson's departure away from the chaos that was Florida school and teacher performance under his watch to "he wants to be with his kids." However, according to this *Orlando Sentinel* article, Robinson raised FCAT passing score thresholds in response to Bush's own wishes:

> *Robinson's decision [to raise FCAT passing scores] bucks the recommendations of Florida's school superintendents as well as other public school and college experts asked to weigh in on the new scoring system.*
>
> *But it meshes with the wishes of some State Board members, who said they worry the state's high school standards are too weak, given how many graduates ended up in remedial classes in college. **It also follows the suggestions of two politically influential groups, former Gov. Jeb Bush's education foundation** and the Florida Chamber of Commerce.*[99] [Emphasis added.]

Another source adds:

> *...Bush and the Chamber are so far dodging accountability for the FCAT Writing nightmare. **It was they who served as Robinson's backers on increasing FCAT stakes. Their***

silence on the three-day old story is telling as they've thrown Robinson under the bus.[100] [Emphasis added.]

At least Robinson gets to stay in the Chiefs for Change and to continue to associate with those who chose him to sport their tread marks.

The final member of Chiefs for Change is another former Florida education commissioner, Eric Smith. This April 4, 2012, *Tampa Bay Times* article openly notes the (undemocratic?) influence Bush wields in promoting what Bush wants by way of educational reform:

> *Smith, a founding member of Chiefs for Change (an offshoot of Jeb Bush's education foundation), has found a new roost to promote his view on education reform, **again under the auspices of a Bush organization**. Now, he's an education policy fellow at the George W. Bush Institute.*
>
> *It's a post he shares with other ed reform notables including Sandy Kress and Jay P. Greene.*
>
> *Smith's reemergence came on the Huffington Post today,*[101] *where he urges education policy makers to build upon the core principles of No Child Left Behind and not abandon "accountability, transparency and equality."*
>
> *Smith is not the only former Florida education department leader to **hold a high profile position nationally, furthering the views of the Jeb Bush accountability model**. Others still out there include **Cornelia Orr, now head of NAEP; Hannah Skandera, New Mexico's education chief;** and John Winn, who has worked with several education groups including the National Math and Science Initiative.*
>
> *Longtime Bush confidante and BOE chairman Phil Handy also remains in the mix, **advising on education issues with the Stanford's Hoover Institution and Harvard's JFK School of Government.***
>
> ***No wonder why ideas like school grading and third grade retention continue to gain traction nationally.***[102] [Emphasis added.]

No wonder, indeed. C4C is Bush's own cult of would-be reformers who are nothing more than yes-men and -women to a powerful man with an oversized ego and no true interest in those whose lives he manipulates *en masse*. And **FEE** is the machine behind C4C, via its ALEC-like ability to network reform-intentioned corporate interests with the very individuals who create education policy—enabling Jeb Bush to effectively run US education into the ground of a skewed and self-serving ideology.

Jeb Bush's concerted efforts to control American public education are pavement for his continued political climb.

CHAPTER 16

MICHELLE RHEE'S TNTP AND STUDENTSFIRST

When reformers are out of a job, they create nonprofit organizations that promote reform. Wendy Kopp did it after graduating from Princeton without offers for employment. Jeb Bush did it upon losing a bid for the Florida governor's mansion. And Michelle Rhee did it after her DC chancellor stints. In this chapter, I examine Rhee's two efforts at destabilizing the American institution of traditional public education: Her Rheeform teacher corps, The New Teacher Project (eventually reduced to TNTP) and her aggressive, privatizing misnomer, StudentsFirst.

These folks might lose jobs, shuffle jobs, or be between jobs, but one truth holds: The reform never leaves them.

"JUST CALL US TNTP"

Michelle Rhee "started" The New Teacher Project (now TNTP) in 1997 and seemingly was appointed CEO after teaching for only three years of questionable quality in Baltimore as a Teach for America (TFA) recruit. The wording on the TNTP website is obscure. It does not say that Rhee founded

A Chronicle of Echoes: Who's Who in the Implosion of American Public Education,
pages 259–274.
Copyright © 2014 by Information Age Publishing
All rights of reproduction in any form reserved.

TNTP; just that TNTP "was formed."[1] Former TFAer-gone-career teacher Gary Rubinstein explained to me in an October 22, 2013, email:

> *The way it worked was that TFA was looking to expand and was making something called 'Teach!' which eventually got renamed The New Teacher Project, and Rhee was hired to run it. Rhee was working for TFA as one of the directors of the institute at that time. So it* (TNTP) *was a spinoff of TFA.*

Rhee believed herself competent to lead her own version of TFA "with the aim of giving poor and minority students equal access to effective teachers."[2] Unlike TFA, TNTP purports to send teachers into needy areas for "long-term contributions… in key subjects."[3] An individual wishing to become a teacher via TNTP can apply for a "teaching fellowship" (or "residency") in one of 14 locations nationwide. The TNTP website advertises that "nearly 35,000 candidates apply each year, and 1,500 begin teaching—an acceptance rate on par with top US universities."[4] Such a description is misleading in that TNTP neither reports its attrition rate nor states that the 1,500 were the only ones accepted from any given year's "nearly 35,000" applicants.

TNTP trains its teachers via its TNTP Teacher Academy, where it uses a curriculum called "Teaching for Results," a curriculum that emphasizes "student achievement," a reformer euphemism for student test scores:

> *TNTP's unique Teaching for Results curriculum helps **people without a traditional education background** translate their professional experience and content knowledge into rich and focused classroom instruction. TNTP's evening seminars, led by outstanding teachers, **emphasize proven approaches to improving achievement in schools** where students lag several grade levels behind. Teachers learn to manage a classroom, understand and deliver the content their students must master**, and use assessment tools and data to constantly check** for learning and refine instruction.*

> *Just as teachers set high standards for their students, TNTP Academy sets a high bar for earning certification: **a proven track record of success in the classroom. Once participants complete Teaching for Results and their first year teaching, TNTP Academy staff determine whether to recommend each candidate for state certification.** TNTP's holistic evaluation reflects multiple measures of performance—including principal observations and program completion—**but places the greatest weight on student academic growth. Only teachers who are at least as effective as the average new teacher in their district** will earn certification, and remain in the classroom.*[5] [Emphasis added.]

Since Michelle Rhee started TNTP, it is no surprise that the student test score is the outcome of primary interest. TNTP's board of directors is also biased towards the "data driven," privatizing reformer set, including John Arnold of the Arnold Foundation, FEE Chief Emeritus and ALEC-associated-lawyer-gone-former-Louisiana State Superintendent Paul Pastorek,

Chris Bierly of Bain and Company,[6] and Kati Haycock, president of the Education Trust.[7] (Education Trust funders include the Broad, Gates, Joyce, and Walton Foundations.)[8]

Like TFA, TNTP is a "revenue generating nonprofit." That is, TNTP both accepts philanthropic contributions and charges for its services. Notice what TNTP offers as its reasons for charging "needy" districts for TNTP teachers:

> *The majority of TNTP's revenue comes from its work with clients on a fee-for-service basis. This approach incentivizes TNTP to meet the needs of its clients while continually assessing the value and cost-effectiveness of its services. The fee-for-service model also encourages TNTP's clients to be motivated, active collaborators by literally "investing" them in the success of their partnerships with the organization.*[9] [Emphasis added.]

Districts with low test scores (the outcome of focus for TNTP) tend to also have higher poverty.[10] Such districts are also more likely to suffer from unequitable distribution of state and local funding[11] even as they tend to serve more minority students. (TNTP board member Kati Haycock even did an article on such funding discrepancies.[12]) So, what does TNTP do to "serve" these "poor and minority students" who, according to TNTP, are "receiving a second-rate education"?[13]

TNTP charges the districts that employ and pay salaries to TNTP teachers.

TNTP has something to sell: Itself. Former TFAer Gary Rubinstein observes that like TFA, TNTP has become a "brand name":

> *TNTP is short for The New Teacher Project, though the TNTP doesn't officially stand for that anymore. It is just TNTP. It is like when Kentucky Fried Chicken changed their name to just KFC. I guess that they are now so much more than just new teachers. They have gotten into research and policy advising, beginning with their report 'The Widget Effect' a few years ago which is often quoted when reformers discuss the potential of merit pay and of ending LIFO* ["last in, first out"]. *Then they wrote something recently called 'The Irreplaceables' about how schools are retaining their bad teachers and losing their good ones. A few days ago they came out with a new report called 'Keeping Irreplaceables in D.C. Public Schools.*[14]

As a revenue-generating non-profit TNTP benefits for grants and private monies:

> *Some TNTP initiatives also benefit from the support of federal grant programs and/or private funding. In 2010, TNTP was one of 49 organizations and institutions nationwide to win a **federal Investing in Innovation (i3) grant. Approximately 30 percent of TNTP's annual revenue comes from the generous support of a diverse group of leading philanthropies.** With philanthropic support, TNTP is able to expand its impact,*

*develop a top-quality staff **and play an unbiased, active role in policy and research.***[15] [Emphasis added.]

Unbiased? Not hardly. Note the now-familiar reformeresque language in the Investing in Innovation grant:

*The purpose of this program is to provide competitive grants to applicants with a record of improving student achievement and attainment in order to expand the implementation of, and investment in, innovative practices that are demonstrated to have an impact on **improving student achievement** or student growth, **closing achievement gaps, decreasing dropout rates, increasing high school graduation rates, or increasing college enrollment and completion rates.***[16] [Emphasis added.]

For reformers, it's all about the numbers, not the people. "Improving student achievement" = higher test scores. "Closing the achievement gap" = again, higher test scores, but higher scores for everyone despite the impossibility of all being "above average" on normed tests. "Decreasing dropout rates" = traditionally graduate in four years with your "cohort" or you don't count (and no GEDs, please). "Increasing college enrollment" = numbers of graduates enrolled in college is all that matters, not trade apprenticeships or specialized training programs. Only losers fail to attend college, and only loser teachers and schools "settle" for "second-rate," "non-college" program completion as evidence of human success.

Here's a hard-hitting thought: Are the TNTP "23,000 new, high quality teachers" of the same "effective" caliber as their founder? The memory of children with bleeding lips is humorous to Rhee, nothing more than a light story on which to happily reminisce, a mere "challenge" in her past. "Twisted" doesn't begin to describe such a response to the pain of others.

In 2008, TNTP produced a report called the "Widget Effect,"[17] in which it examined twelve school districts in four states to determine whether these districts assessed teacher performance in a way that allows for the categorizing of teachers into "great, good, fair, and poor." The report declares that "a teacher's effectiveness" is " the most important factor in schools for improving student achievement." The report also proclaims that teacher effectiveness "is not measured, recorded or used to inform decision-making in any meaningful way."

This from a former temp teacher who made students' mouths bleed and kept her job.

The title of the report comes from this statement: "The Widget Effect describes the tendency of school districts to assume classroom effectiveness is the same from teacher to teacher," that teachers are viewed as "interchangeable parts."

I have been teaching full time for 18 years, and part time for 2 additional years, from grade 7 to graduate school, in four states, in regular education and alternative settings, and never have I believed that my administration viewed me as "interchangeable" or that my "effectiveness" had not been assessed "in any meaningful way."

Of course, the "meaningful way" has become none other than the student test score.[18]

Not until 2013 has any administration been forced to reduce my value in the classroom to a set of student standardized test scores. This is the narrow reformer view of "effectiveness," the same view of "effectiveness" that Rhee promoted about herself at Harlem Park yet failed to validate.

One of my teaching colleagues, Susan Muchmore, is a former TNTP New Orleans teacher. She writes that the "Widget Effect" destroyed her efforts to truly teach TNTP recruits:

> *I was employed by the non-profit The New Teacher Project (TNTP) for three years to instruct new teachers how to teach so they could be awarded a Louisiana teaching certificate. When I began the program, I was convinced that there was none better. ...[The TNTP recruits] were hungry for ...all of the knowledge of that an experienced teacher can impart. These teachers were often overwhelmed with the climate of their schools, both public and charter. Just maintaining a semblance of order and an environment for teaching and learning was difficult at best.*
>
> ***Then... TNTP and TFA suddenly shifted their focus. The Widget Effect was launched, a baseless document that claims all public schools ignore teacher effectiveness. ...Washington (TNTPP) then changed the curriculum to be a canned, scripted seminar where I had to have a timer so that I could keep "on script"...*** *This unrealistic, theory-heavy curriculum was as frustrating to the teachers as it was to me.*
>
> ***By the middle of that third year, I quit. It was a moral and ethical decision on my part. These teachers were no more qualified to face the incredibly challenging students they were teaching at the end of the year as they were in the beginning.*** [Emphasis added.]

Ironically, the "Widget Effect" attempts to create its own "widgets": Instructors dependent upon timers and scripts. Instead, it drives away the veteran teachers upon which TNTP training depends.

Aside from its effect of "scripting" its own TNTP training, the "goal" of the "Widget Effect" is to fire more teachers. Such a goal is hardly surprising when one considers the funders of the report:

> *...Provided by the **Robertson Foundation**, the **Bill & Melinda Gates Foundation** and the **Joyce Foundation**. Additional funding was provided by the **Carnegie Corporation** of New York, the Laura and John **Arnold Foundation**, the Charles and Helen **Schwab Foundation** and the **Walton Family Foundation**. We thank all of our funders for their generous support; however...*

And now for a great irony:

> *...we acknowledge that the findings and recommendations presented in this report are those of the The New Teacher Project alone **and do not necessarily reflect our funders' opinions or positions**.*[19] [Emphasis added.]

Translation: "You rich people bent on corporate reform funded a project biased towards corporate reform with an outcome that lauds corporate reform, but we just wanted to say that your corporate-reform bent and the associated corporate-reform big money you gave us had nothing to do with our finding in favor of corporate reform."[20]

TNTP also produced a report called "The Irreplaceables,"[21] which focuses on the need to retain "good" teachers, the definition of which is sketchy at best and is further diluted by potential data issues. Matt DiCarlo of the Shanker Institute highlights some of the classification issues with this limited, four-district sample:

> *...if you look at how they (TNTP) actually sorted teachers into categories, the label "irreplaceable," at least as I interpret it, seems inappropriate no matter how much data are available.*
>
> *For example, in "District B," it is teachers with at least one median growth percentile rank (e.g., in one subject) above 65 and none below 35, while in "District D," it is teachers with at least one statistically significant, positive percentile rank and none below the median. In "District C," teachers are coded as "irreplaceable" if they have at least one score significantly above average, and none significantly below average.*
>
> *I would characterize these (test-based) definitions as "probably above average"* (though *remember that teachers need only score highly in one subject—half/most of a teacher's estimates can be statistically average—and those in Districts B and C can actually have most of their point estimates below the mean/median—so long as one of them [e.g., one subject] is discernibly above*).
>
> *In other words, calling them "irreplaceable" seems, at best, an exaggeration.*[22] [Emphasis added.]

Thus, the inconsistent, watery defining of "stellar teaching" reduces "irreplaceable" to the "average"—and likely to the point where all would have been regarded as "effective" using the non-test-score-based teacher evaluation system that reformers scoff. It seems, then, that the "irreplaceables" of this study could be the "unfirables" of the "Widget Effect."

Note that the criteria for defining the approximate top 20% for the four districts in the "Irreplaceables" varies according to what it takes to define the top 20%. As such, the definition of "irreplaceable" is sample-dependent. By such reasoning, every school's top 20% is "irreplaceable"—just tailor the definition to suit whomever the top 20% happens to be at a given school.

Another serious flaw in this study is the application of imprecise criteria to define "irreplaceable" in the four districts. Thus, a teacher meeting the "irreplaceable" criteria could hover right around the mean ("average"). In other words, in "The Irreplaceables," TNTP unwittingly creates its own "widgets"—its own "interchangeables."

The very data that reformers worship can be— even for them— sadly unreliable. As DiCarlo cautiously observes in a footnote:

> *My guess is that TNTP predetermined that roughly the "top 20 percent" of teachers should be classified as "irreplaceable" in each of the four districts (perhaps in part to provide a sufficiently large sample to use their survey data), and then calibrated their definitions to produce that result.* **Yet—and remember I'm speculating here—the scores in some districts were so imprecisely-estimated that they couldn't achieve the 20 percent sub-sample without relaxing their definitions to the point where they (at least in my view) no longer reflected "irreplaceability."**[23] [Emphasis added.]

The report offers numerous suggestions for ridding schools of the low performers, whose lowest –20%% definitions are also sample-dependent: using buy outs; training administrators on how to "encourage" these low performers (based on test scores) how to voluntarily resign; giving principals ultimate power in hiring (and tacitly, firing), and streamlining the firing process. As the report insists:

> *Teachers who cannot teach as well as the average first-year teacher should be considered ineffective—unless they are first-year teachers. Those who fail to improve rapidly— within one year—should not remain in the classroom, and principals should be held accountable for making sure they don't.*[24]

Again, keep in mind the hypocrisy of Michelle Rhee's promoting this report. Keep in mind her own ineptness (and cruelty, and deceit) in the classroom as a "teacher" for three years. The irony here is that Rhee had no intention of "remaining in the classroom"—her goal was to run education from the outside, such as via creating pro-reform organizations like this TNTP.

According to the report, a chief way to retain the arguably-overhyped "miracle teachers": merit pay, of course. The teachers whose students score well on standardized tests (the ultimate measure of teacher "effectiveness") get more money:

> *State and district leaders should phase out quality-blind pay structures in favor of more flexible compensation systems that offer greater earnings potential for high performing teachers early in their careers. As a rule of thumb,* **we recommend that Irreplaceables be able to make a six-figure salary by the end of their sixth year of teaching** *(or the market equivalent in lower cost-of-living areas). To fund these raises, states and districts will need to reduce or phase out automatic salary increases for factors that have no proven connection to a teacher's success in the classroom, such as additional college course credits or advanced degrees. They will also need to reduce or phase out automatic increases for seniority. These transitions will be difficult, but districts cannot afford to*

award raises for ineffectiveness and still pay top teachers the salaries they deserve.[25] [Emphasis added.]

In order to raise my teaching salary to six figures, one or two teachers would have to be let go. I find this a sobering thought. And assuming the same student enrollment, my class sizes would have to at least double. Another sobering thought.

Given that teaching salaries are modest when compared with other professions requiring four-year college attendance,[26] it should come as no surprise that for career teachers, money is arguably not a primary motivating factor. Never mind that merit pay systems bespeak a business world competition that has never fared well in the more community-oriented setting of the traditional public school.[27,28]

Corporate reformers are in it for the money. Career teachers are not.

ANOTHER RHEE PROJECT: STUDENTSFIRST

StudentsFirst is a privatization scheme purportedly formed "in response to an increasing demand for a better education system in America,"[29] and I will draw from my work previously posted on my blog.[30] This supposedly "grassroots" organization is a thinly-disguised privatization machine:

> *Some of the country's key education activists and public officials are standing with StudentsFirst.* ***They have endorsed our policy agenda*** *and will speak on our behalf.*[31] [Emphasis added.]

Rhee then lists names like New York Mayor Bloomberg, former DC Mayor Adrian Fenty (he appointed Rhee as DC chancellor), former NYC Chancellor Joel Klein, and Colorado Lieutenant Governor Barbara O'Brien.

And what is "our policy agenda"?

> *Michelle Rhee, the former chancellor of the Washington, D.C. public schools, launched StudentsFirst in the fall of 2010 with the stated goal of raising $1 billion over five years. Among the reforms it advocates:* ***abolishing teacher tenure; permitting more teachers without formal education training to take charge of classrooms; evaluating teachers in large measure by their students' growth on standardized tests; and expanding charter schools, which are publicly funded but typically run by private corporations, including for-profit management firms.***[32] [Emphasis added.]

StudentsFirst complements the goals of TNTP's "Widget" and "Irreplaceables." And the money StudentsFirst vows to raise is certainly not from "grassroots" donors. The buy-in comes from politicians and hedge fund managers:

> *…Recent donors include* ***New York Mayor Michael Bloomberg*** *and* ***hedge fund managers David Tepper and Alan Fournier,*** *who have pledged substantial resources to a*

*StudentsFirst partner organization in New Jersey. The Laura and John **Arnold Foundation**, funded by hedge fund manager John Arnold* [also a former Enron trader], *has also pledged $20 million to Rhee's organization over five years, a donation that does not appear to be reflected in the IRS forms released on Monday.*[33]

Funny how interesting education has become to hedge fund managers and foundations wishing to direct the nation's agenda. And despite Rhee's unresolved participation in the DC cheating scandal, the Walton Foundation donated $8 million to StudentsFirst in April 2013.[34] Nevertheless, the goal that Rhee publicized on *Oprah*— of StudentsFirst's raising one billion in one year— has not come to pass; the organization only raised a mere $28.5 million (tongue in cheek here).[35]

No corporate reform machine would truly be transformed from velveteen to flesh without Broad money (as in TFA, Broad Superintendents Academy, and Harvard Graduate School of Education):

*An additional donor to StudentsFirst is **The Broad Foundation, the philanthropy run by Eli and Edythe Broad that puts billions into education reform** causes such as charter schools and parent unions. Erica Lepping, a Broad spokesperson, confirmed that one year ago, **the foundation contributed $500,000 in startup costs to StudentsFirst.** "We've been in discussions with them since, regarding **how we may be further able to support their work**," Lepping added in an email.*[36] [Emphasis added.]

How sweet to know that the Broads see a future in supporting StudentsFirst. And why wouldn't they? StudentsFirst is everything that good, true, and forthright education is not. To Eli Broad, public education is a "game" that needs to be "changed," and Rhee is just the person to do so:

Philanthropist Eli Broad says he "expects to be a major contributor [to Rhee's StudentsFirst]." "People supporting the status quo have spent hundreds of millions of dollars a year to maintain it," Broad says. "I think she'll be a game changer."[37]

Broad was right about Rhee's being a "game changer." Just consider the looming, unresolved cheating scandal under her watch as DC chancellor. (See Rhee chapter.) The new game is High Test Scores at Any Cost Without Speedy and Through Accountability.

Rhee wins. For now.

As a lobbying organization, StudentsFirst has the financial backing to infuse itself into state and district elections in order to endorse both candidates and ballot measures supporting its views.[38,39] The group is clear in the goals of election financing:

Accordingly, in choosing individual races, we considered three factors:
- *A candidate's commitment to reforming the shortcomings of the public education system with student-centric policies as expressed by the StudentsFirst policy agenda;*
- *Our potential impact in affecting the outcome of the race; and*

- *The impact of the race in promoting the cause of reform more broadly.*[40]

StudentsFirst is a well-funded privatization machine that inserts its influence into elections across the nation in an effort to promote an agenda bent on annihilating traditional public education. It portrays itself as bipartisan; however, leadership turnover in the organization over StudentsFirst's increasingly pro-Republican (and, in contrast, anti-Democrat) positions on issues such as collective bargaining and partisanship reveal otherwise.[41] In 2012, StudentsFirst supported 105 candidates. Ninety were Republicans.[42] Furthermore, most of Rhee's donor money comes from Republicans.[43]

Through StudentsFirst, Rhee inserts her traditional-public-school-killing, corporation-friendly education reform agenda into communities that wonder, frankly, why her group is there:

> *The national education reform advocacy group StudentsFirst will start running a radio spot in the Des Moines area this week (April 23, 2013) aimed at breaking a stalemate in the state's education reform debate.*
>
> *StudentsFirst is the nonprofit lobbying group formed by former Washington, D.C., schools chancellor Michelle Rhee.* **It's known for its support of legislation to tie teacher evaluations to student test scores and "trigger" legislation that allows parents to turn failing schools into charters, among other polices.**
>
> **It also was the single largest contributor to state legislative races in 2012, donating more than $317,000 to Statehouse candidates.** ...
>
> **"We continue to be mystified why a California-based group feels like it should get involved in Iowa education policy,"** *said Jean Hessburg, spokeswoman for the Iowa State Education Association, which represents about 34,000 Iowa teachers.*[44] [Emphasis added.]

StudentsFirst did not raise $28.5 million in 2012 to restrict their reform influence to the location of its national headquarters in California.[45]

In Tennessee, Rhee and StudentsFirst came to the aid of Representative John DeBerry, who was used to operating on a modest election budget and shaking lots of hands in an effort to earn votes. Rhee discovered that DeBerry is a democrat who happens to promote vouchers and charters, so she and StudentsFirst chipped in a mere $110,000 to assist with his re-election. DeBerry was amazed. He won re-election by a notable margin.[46]

As *New Republic* reporter Jeff Gao notes, Tennessee stands in awe of reformers and their money:

> *Ever since she resigned as chancellor of Washington, D.C. public schools in 2010 and started StudentsFirst,* **Rhee has raised millions of dollars from rich donors, which she funnels to local lawmakers who support her policies.** *Nowhere has her influence been felt more acutely than in Tennessee, where campaigns are a bargain and where*

legislators eager to amend the state's dismal record on education have made it a mecca for reformers. ...

In 2011–2012, her group spent $533,000 on over 60 local politicians, outspending the main teachers' union by a third and becoming Tennessee's biggest source of campaign money outside of the party PACs, according to election filings. ...The result has been a gush of education-reform money taking over the state's politics.

*"They've become like the gun lobby in Tennessee," a former aide to a top Nashville politician told me. "**Everybody is scared of the NRA. It's the same way with these education reform people.**" ...*

Rhee has said that pushing back at the teachers' unions was one of the reasons she founded StudentsFirst, *and the union-blaming that accompanied the bills in Tennessee echoed her rhetoric.*[47] [Emphasis added.]

Michelle Rhee is merely purchasing her own agenda wherever she can find it. StudentsFirst and its reform-bent millionaire and billionaire donors enable her to do so.

Democracy? So what?

Nevertheless, StudentsFirst money is not always able to purchase an election result. In February 2013, StudentsFirst funded three reform-minded individuals running for the Los Angeles Unified School District (LAUSD) board a total of $250,000. Monica Garcia was running for re-election as board president, and Kate Anderson and Antonio Garcia were running for first-time membership.[48] Monica Garcia was re-elected; however, voters placed the non-StudentsFirst-favored incumbent Steve Zimmer and newcomer Monica Ratliff in the two other seats.[49]

In addition to the StudentsFirst contribution, New York Mayor Bloomberg donated one million. Rhee's StudentsFirst matched the contribution of Eli Broad, a funder of Rhee's TNTP who, like Bloomberg,[50] is also known to attempt to influence school board results.[51]

The involvement of StudentsFirst and other major reformer money garnered a similar reaction to that in Iowa:

*"**This is just another example of outside 'reformers' trying to influence the outcome** of the Los Angeles school board races," Warren Fletcher, president of United Teachers Los Angeles, said in a statement. Voters "do not need outsiders deciding who is best to sit on the LAUSD Board of Education."*[52] [Emphasis added.]

Rhee makes her intention clear in pouring StudentsFirst money into a district in which she has no personal investment:

Rhee said her involvement in Los Angeles could advance school reform statewide.

"We think it's important that [LAUSD Superintendent] John Deasy be able to continue on the job to finish the work he started," she said.

Deasy is developing an evaluation system that incorporates the use of student standardized test scores as one measure of an instructor's effectiveness. Last week, he directed principals to count test results as 30% of an evaluation. He also has altered district rules so that layoffs are not based strictly on seniority.[53] [Emphasis added.]

Fortunately, StudentsFirst and the other reform-pushing financiers were not able to purchase all three seats. Sometimes reformers' raising "too much money" might be their undoing.[54]

Democracy still works. It is refreshing to know.

Perhaps one of the most brazen efforts of StudentsFirst involves its publishing a "State Policy Report Card" whereby it grades states based upon how well each is implementing the now-popular privatizer-favoring spectrum of anti-community-school, anti-teacher, and, ultimately, anti-student reforms. The so-called "report card" was released January 7, 2013, and was launched January 9, 2013, in a panel discussion by the American Enterprise Institute (AEI) and Fordham Institute. The panel included AEI's and the National Council for Teacher Quality's (NCTQ's) Frederick Hess, Fordham's Mike Petrilli, and Chiefs for Change emeritus member Eric Smith.[55]

Held accountable to no one themselves, reformers like Rhee love to grade those they view as below them.

Self-appointed grader Rhee and her StudentsFirst decided that no state deserved an A, which is actually encouraging since it means that Rhee's nightmarish utopia of reform has not been realized. This arrogant group gave 12 states a B or C, and most states, a D or F. Of course, reform-infested states, such as Louisiana and Florida, rated high (B), and "less reformy" states, like Iowa and Montana, "failed." In their abbreviated report, StudentsFirst tries to assure its readers that its goals are to "elevate the teaching profession," "empower parents with data and choice," and "spend wisely and govern well."[56]

Not everyone is buying it.

On the same day as the AEI/Fordham panel, the National Opportunity to Learn Campaign (NOLC), whose advisors include Anthony Cody of the Network for Public Education and Linda Darling-Hammond of Stanford University,[57] released its report entitled, *5 Ways Michelle Rhee's Report Puts Students Last.* The report offers this harsh critique of "Rhee's Report" in its opening:

*Rather than focus on issues facing students and families, **particularly those affected by unequal access to school resources,** the policy benchmarks in the new report reveal StudentsFirst's obsession with charter schools and de-professionalizing the teaching profession. The report pushes policies that are either untested or disproven—but happen to be welcome in the halls of right-wing think tanks and politicians. ...*

*States are given a clear choice in this report, and for that at least we can thank its authors: **either you care about students, or about StudentsFirst. There's little room for both.**[58] [Emphasis added.]*

The body of the NOLC report includes five reasons "why this State Report Card is a veritable wish list for privatization advocates and a recipe for failure for everyone else." Here is an abbreviated version:

1. *Ironically, it ignores the needs of students: Missing from this report card is any evaluation based on multiple success measures, including student graduation rates, a college ready curriculum, access to art and music classes, or learning benchmarks that will prepare students to be critical thinkers and leaders in their community.... **There is also little correlation between StudentsFirst's rankings and the graduation gap between Black and White students—a key indicator of whether a state's policies promote equity or erode it.**[59] [Emphasis added.]*

This last statement is indeed ironic since reformers like Rhee frequently cry about the need to "close the achievement gap." They also insist that effectiveness be quantified. Yet Rhee fails to combine these two ideas in her StudentsFirst report and consider "closing the graduation gap" as necessary for a higher state grade.

2. *It opposes personalized and student-centered learning: ...**Research has consistently found that the teacher-to-student ratio is an important variable** in ensuring that all students have an opportunity to learn. And for a report that wants to empower parents, **it's curious that they would reject small class size: it's something that parents consistently clamor for.**[60] [Emphasis added.]*

Reformers do not send their children to schools with high student-to-teacher ratios. However, they "advocate" such a position for "other people's children."

3. *It Argues That We Don't Have Enough Quality Teachers... While Advocating That We Lower the Bar for Teacher Preparation: ...It appears that StudentsFirst is more interested in applauding alternative certification for simply existing than alternative certification that's actually working. ...The report is opposed to any regulations as to where alternatively certified teachers are placed. Given that even by StudentsFirst's own standards **very few states can ensure quality alternative certification, why policymakers should allow them anywhere and everywhere is baffling. ...The very students who need fully certified, experienced teachers are the most are the ones least likely to have them.**[61] [Emphasis added.]*

This dual standard of "teacher quality" and "drive-thru teacher prep" is not unique to StudentsFirst. This same hypocrisy is promoted by the National Council on Teacher Quality (NCTQ), a group that advocates for the same reform agenda as StudentsFirst and that also takes it upon itself to grade entities (in NCTQ's case, traditional teacher training programs), all the while offering its own fast-track teacher certification via the American Board for Certification of Teacher Excellence (ABCTE) ("Become a certified teacher now for less than the cost of one college class!").[62,63]

Rhee is a former NCTQ advisory board member.

4. *[Rhee's Report Card] Continues the Disastrous High-Stakes Testing Drumbeat: StudentsFirst is adamant that both evaluations and teachers' salaries should be determined primarily (50%) on "objective measures of student growth," i.e. test scores. ...Up to a third of the school year in kindergarten is now spent taking standardized tests, not even counting all the prep time. ...The research shows how ineffective [that] test-based "value added" rating systems are. In March [2013], Phi Delta Kappan published a review of those systems,[64] showing just how dangerously inconsistent they can be—and pointing to more accurate solutions that can actually gauge what goes on in the classroom.[65]* [Emphasis added.]

One area in particular where StudentsFirst focuses its reform efforts involves the use of value-added measures for evaluating teacher "effectiveness." StudentsFirstNY even produced a television commercial played during coverage of the Newtown, Connecticut, school massacre, implying that grading teachers using test scores must be passed in order to "save" NY $30 million.[66] As the NOLC report implies, to corporate reformers, the sought outcome of administering standardized tests it to grade, whether it be students, teachers, schools, or states. However, since corporate reform places ultimate responsibility for student "success" on teachers, they regard value-added teacher evaluation as the principal means for "education cleansing."

Winning on this issue is so important to StudentsFirst that it will callously position a commercial ad amongst news of teachers and administrators being gunned down while protecting their students.[67]

It is through value-added teacher evaluation that pro-privatization groups like StudentsFirst are able to destroy teaching as a profession—an indispensable, foundational component to achieving their goal of privatizing public education nationwide and bringing the democratic ideal of American public education to its end.

For this reason, I will expend extra effort addressing this NOLC report point.

In their zeal to rip the traditional education tablecloth from the occupied table, reformers like Rhee refuse to acknowledge that value-added assessment has a number of problems. One major issue is the claim that value-added measurement is able to isolate the contribution of a single teacher to an individual student's learning and that this one-year-increment of learning can be represented in a single standardized test score. StudentsFirst offers to an unassuming public a "myths versus facts sheet" on value-added teacher evaluations.[68] Here is an example of what StudentsFirst terms a "myth" regarding value-added measurement:

Myth: Value-added measures fluctuate from year to year; basing evaluations on this measure of student growth is unfair and unreliable.

As Matt DiCarlo of the Shanker Institute observes:

Right off the bat, seeing the phrase "value-added measures fluctuate from year to year" in the "myths" column is pretty amazing. ... The "predictive power" of value-added—for instance, its stability over time—really cannot be called "high." On the whole, it tends to be quite modest. Also, just to be clear, the claim that value-added can predict "teacher effects on student achievement" is better-phrased as "value-added can predict itself." Let's not make it sound more grand than it is. ...Overall, there is a lot of simple human judgment involved here, and not much room for blanket statements.[69] [Emphasis added.]

Despite their mandated use, Louisiana's value-added teacher evaluations are erratic; the value-added outcome identifies a number of teachers as "ineffective" though their students score "advanced," "mastery," or "excellent" on the state tests. For these teachers, the value-added score is "pending further study."[70] The Louisiana Department of Education offered its own version of "myth versus fact" earlier this same school year in which it declared it a "myth" that teachers of high-achieving students could be penalized using value-added modeling.[71]

Here is a second StudentsFirst "myth" offering:

Myth: Evaluations that tie into personnel decisions—like compensation, hiring, and dismissal decisions—will make teachers want to collaborate less because they will feel like they are in competition with each other.

And DiCarlo's response:

Again, it's rather surprising to see the very real concern that using evaluations in high-stakes decisions may impede collaboration in the "myths" column. No matter what you think of these new systems, their impact on teacher teamwork and other types of behavioral outcomes is entirely uncertain, and very important. Relegating these concerns to the "myths" column is just odd.

Also, the "facts" here consist of a series of statements about what SF thinks new teacher evaluation systems should accomplish. For example, I have no doubt that "the goal [of new evaluations] is not to create unhealthy competition," but that doesn't mean it won't happen. Facts are supposed to be facts.[72] [Emphasis added.]

Those who advocate loudest for value-added modeling are those whose livelihoods are not subjected to it. In this regard, Michelle Rhee is at the front of foundation- and hedge-fund-supported line.

Now let us return to the NOLC report for its fifth and final point opposing the StudentsFirst state report cards:

5.   *It Advocates "Equal Funding" and "Equitable Access" for Charter Corpora-*
     tions and Private Schools, Not Students: ... *What concerns StudentsFirst in these*
     *two sections is **making sure that the non-profit and for-profit corporations that***
     run charter schools get every last penny of public money they can. *"Enable Equi-*
     table Access to Facilities" means charters should get first dibs at public prop-
     erty and pay at **or below** (emphasis theirs) market value for it. *Especially*
     in an age of school budget cuts, suggesting that charter corporations make off
     with public resources below market value is unconscionable. The report even
     promotes voucher programs (called "scholarships" in StudentsFirst parlance), **one**
     of the oldest ways to siphon public money into private hands. They insist that
     vouchers should provide a "tuition amount that is competitive with private
     school tuition. "[73] [Emphasis added except where noted.]

Imagine that: A model of school reform that is ChartersFirst and Vouchers-
First. To organizations like Rhee's, students become the casualties.

The promotion of privatization in education is not for the children.
The requirement that states effectively bankrupt their public school systems in favor of under-regulated privatization is undeniable evidence that
"the students" are being utterly disregarded in favor of the dollar. Charters
and vouchers fiscally destabilize American public education. "Alternative"
teacher certification becomes the "instant breakfast" of education—nothing of diligence, commitment, and substance—"just add water." Tying
career teacher jobs to student test scores via unstable value-added results
provides the excuse organizations like StudentsFirst must have in order to
continue to scapegoat the profession. This, in turn, affords those in Rhee's
camp endless opportunity to promote their reformerspeak "solution" of
ironically-debilitating "parent choice."

CHAPTER 17

DEMOCRATS FOR EDUCATION REFORM (DFER) AND EDUCATION REFORM NOW (ERN)

Corporate reform is primarily a Republican push. The American Legislative Exchange Council (ALEC) is arguably the major, overwhelmingly Republican force promoting education reform in all states. Even so, there are Democrats willing to forsake the party's pro-labor roots and declare themselves "for education reform" while continuing to call themselves Democrats.

Democrats for Education Reform (DFER) is a political action committee formed in 2005[1] to lobby for the corporate reform agenda from inside the party to outside:

> *Democrats for Education Reform (DFER) is a political action committee **whose mission is to encourage a more productive dialogue within the Democratic Party** on the need to fundamentally reform American public education. DFER operates on all levels of government to educate elected officials and support reform-minded candidates **for public office.**[2]* [Emphasis added.]

At least DFER doesn't call itself a "nonprofit." However, the DFER Statement of Purpose could belong to any number of pro-privatizing education groups for its use of worn-out, corporate reform language:

> *A first-rate system of public education is the cornerstone of a prosperous, free and just society, yet millions of American children today—particularly low-income and children of color—**are trapped in persistently failing schools** that are part of deeply dysfunctional school systems. These systems, once viewed romantically as avenues of opportunity for all, **have become captive to powerful, entrenched interests that too often put the demands of adults before the educational needs of children**....*
>
> *Both political parties have failed to address **the tragic decline of our system of public education**....*
>
> *Democrats for Education Reform aims to return the Democratic Party to its rightful place as **a champion of children**, first and foremost, in America's public education systems.*
>
> *We support leaders in our party who have the courage to **challenge a failing status quo** and who believe that **the severity of our nation's educational crisis demands that we tackle this problem using every possible tool at our disposal**.*
>
> *We believe that **reforming broken public school systems** cannot be accomplished by tinkering at the margins, but rather through **bold and revolutionary leadership**. This requires **opening up the traditional top-down monopoly of most school systems** and empowering all parents to access great schools for their children....*[3] [Emphasis added.]

"Opening up the traditional top-down monopoly" provides the best of hypocrisies when one considers the federal role in privatization. The ultimate example of "Democrats for education reform" lay in President Obama and US Secretary of Education Arne Duncan, both of whom are pushing privatization from the White House via their No Child Left Behind with a New Label, Race to the Top, with its mandates for states to both remove caps on charter schools and agree to implement the Common Core.

DFER decries the "traditional top-down monopoly" in favor of yet another top-down monopoly, that of mayoral control and other, single-individual-control arrangements, such as school principal control. As DFER declares on its "What We Stand For" webpage:

> *We support governance structures which hold leaders responsible, while giving them the tools to **effectuate change**. We believe in empowering mayors to lead urban school districts, **so that they can be held accountable by the electorate**.*
>
> *We support policies that allow school principals and their school communities to select their teams of educators, holding them accountable for student performance but allowing them flexibility **to exercise sound, professional judgment**.*[4] [Emphasis added.]

New York schools have been subjected to mayoral control since 2001 with the election of Michael Bloomberg and his appointment of Joel Klein. Under Bloomberg and Klein, charter schools are allowed to move in facilities with existing public schools; the competition for both facilities and students is often detrimental to the reform-disfavored community schools. Chicago has been under mayoral control since 1995. It is certainly no better for the arrangement. In July 2013, approximately 50 public schools are slated to close at the whim of Chicago Mayor Rahm Emanuel.[5] Here is an example of DFER's "empowering mayors to lead urban school districts":

> *Months of argument and anguish over **Mayor Rahm Emanuel's push for sweeping school closings came to a climax Wednesday as his hand-picked Board of Education voted to shut 49 elementary schools** and transfer thousands of children to new classroom settings.*[6] [Emphasis added.]

Eighteen years of mayoral control, and Chicago's schools are a chaotic wreck. DFER has no problem with closing schools and directly states as much:

> *We support policies which **stimulate the creation of new, accountable public schools and which simultaneously close down failing schools**.*[7]

Translation: "We support the endless school churn produced by closing traditional public schools in favor of privately-run charters that are able to set their own rules and that, as a whole, yield student test scores equal to or lower than the public schools they replace."[8]

Contrary to the reformer cry for "parental choice and empowerment," parents must fight hard for their limited victories where saving community schools are concerned. In July 2013, CTU filed on behalf of parents two lawsuits seeking to prevent closure of 49 Chicago schools. One lawsuit requests a year's delay prior to closing given schools; the other seeks to halt closures. Mayoral control has run roughshod over both parents and students—including special needs and minority students:

> *One lawsuit argues that CPS is violating the Americans with Disabilities Act by **failing to set up an orderly process of closings for special-needs children**. The second suit alleges racial discrimination, saying **the closings disproportionately affect African-American students, and argues that thousands of special-needs children will be destabilized by the closings.***
>
> ***More than 5,000 special education students are expected to be affected by this year's closings***.[9] [Emphasis added.]

Apparently, these lawsuits represent facers of "parent choice" not friendly to privatization and therefore not endorsed by DFER.

In addition to mayoral control and charter favoritism, DFER also supports vouchers and Common Core (CCSS):

> *We support mechanisms that* **allow parents to select excellent schools for their children, and where education dollars follow each child** *to their school.*

> *We support* **clearly-articulated national standards** *and expectations for core subject areas,* **while allowing states and local districts to determine how best to make sure that all students are reaching those standards.**[10] [Emphasis added.]

Interestingly, DFER sidesteps the notion that CCSS is "state-led"; the "standards" are a given. The role of the states is to implement the "national standards"—which states are coerced into doing if they accept RTTT money.

DFER = ALEC = Jeb Bush = Gates = Rhee....

A truly bipartisan force-feeding of the education privatization agenda.

As for finances, the money that officially flows into and out of DFER is modest by corporate reform donor standards; for 2006–2008, DFER contributions totaled $170,770; for 2008–2010, $184,133, and in 2012, $53,830.[11] Well-known donors include John and Laura Arnold of the Arnold Foundation; Teach for America alumnus and vice-chair of New York KIPP charters Whitney Tilson; director of Rockport Capital Peter Ackerman, and Gotham Capital founder Joel Greenblatt. Tilson is and Greenblatt was also on the DFER board.[12,13]

Five of DFER's 2013 board members are hedge-fund managers.[14]

It is interesting that the more famous reform-minded Democrats, such as Michelle Rhee, Michael Bloomberg, Joel Klein, Rahm Emanuel—and even Arne Duncan and Barack Obama—have not contributed to a group that seeks to advance their coveted agenda. DFER needs fundraising help. In June 2013, DFER named former New York State Senator Craig Johnson as chair of the DFER board. Johnson's principal task will be to "get the donor base engaged again."[15]

DFER Executive Director Joe Williams attributes the lagging DFER funding to the "education advocacy field [growing] more crowded."[16] Yet if ALEC membership is any indication, education reform is a Republican-run show, and the Republicans are not likely to donate money that could so obviously benefit their rival party. Democrats who draw huge Republican donations—Michelle Rhee being the most notable example—do not themselves contribute to DFER. In withholding their money, they evidence tacit support for being "more Republican than Democrat," which Rhee has been accused of for publicly allying herself with notable Republicans, including governors Rick Scott (Florida), John Kasitch (Ohio), Chris Christie (New Jersey), Mitch Daniels (Indiana), and Rick Snyder (Michigan).[17] It is not likely coincidence that in 2013, Rhee's StudentsFirst garnered an $8 million donation from the traditionally-Republican Walton Foundation.[18]

Johnson was selected as chairperson of the DFER board for his devotion to the corporate reform agenda, a position not commonly held by Democrats:

> *Johnson, who won his seat in 2007 in a Long Island district long dominated by Republicans,* **aligned with DFER on successful legislative efforts required to qualify for federal Race to the Top funding.**
>
> **The most notable was a revision to the Charter Schools Act that more than doubled the number of charter schools allowed to operate in the state.** *Snubbing pressure from his Democratic colleagues,* **Johnson "single-handedly" blocked an early version of the bill that would have banned school building co-locations and slowed down the authorizing process.**[19] [Emphasis added.]

Johnson is a DFER hero for pushing legislation that favors the likes of Eva Moskowitz's Success Academies that just happen to have been co-founded by DFER board member John Petry.[20]

Just because the notable reformer billionaires do not directly fund DFER, do not count them as missing on the fringes. For example, DFER board executive Joe Williams also heads another reform group, this one actually is classed as a "nonprofit," and it doesn't have the D-word in its title: Education Reform Now (ERN). Nevertheless, ERN is a Democratic entity[21] understood to be a "sister entity" to DFER.[22,23] All six DFER board members are hedge-fund managers.[24] Like DFER, ERN was also started in 2005. In its first year, ERN raised $92,000. By 2008, the sum rose to $1.28 million,[25] and by 2010, ERN contributions leapt to over $9.1 million.[26] The Broad Foundation is a contributor,[27] as is the Walton Foundation[28] ($1.1 million in 2011; $500,000 in 2012).

ERN enables hedge fund managers who wish to "quietly donate" to Democrats advancing the privatization agenda. In June 2008, Reverend Al Sharpton decided to join then-NYC Chancellor Joel Klein efforts to privatize public education. Upon publicizing the decision, ERN sent a $500,000 donation to Sharpton's National Action Network. Yet ERN was merely the funnel; the half million came from former NYC Chancellor Harold Levy's company, Plainfield Asset Management, a hedge fund located in Connecticut. By sending the money via ERN, a 501(c)3 nonprofit, Levy was able to claim the reform-purchasing money as a charitable donation.[29]

Everyone outside of traditional public education wins.

The nonprofit ERN also has a "political arm," Education Reform Now Advocacy Committee, a 501(c)4, or an organization allowed to attempt to influence legislation specific to social welfare.[30,31]

Looks like the big Republican money is available to DFER, after all—through its ERN back door. The fact that DFER has access to millions in

Republican funding in order to promote a predominately-Republican education reform agenda is not lost on the mainstream Democratic Party. At the 2013 California Democratic Convention, labor groups including the California Teachers Association and the California Federation of Teachers passed a resolution specifically condemning the actions of DFER and Rhee's StudentsFirst for their Republican-financed roles in the destruction of American public education:

> *Whereas, the reform initiatives of Students First, rely on destructive anti-educator policies that do nothing for students but blame educators and their unions for the ills of society, make testing the goal of education, shatter communities by closing their public schools, and see public schools as potential profit centers and children as measureable commodities; and*
>
> *Whereas, the political action committee, entitled Democrats for Education Reform is funded by corporations, Republican operatives and wealthy individuals dedicated to privatization and anti-educator initiatives, and not grassroots democrats or classroom educators; and*
>
> *Whereas, the billionaires funding Students First and Democrats for Education Reform are supporting candidates and local programs that would dismantle a free public education for every student in California and replace it with company run charter schools, non-credentialed teachers and unproven untested so-called "reforms";*
>
> *THEREFORE BE IT RESOLVED, that the California Democratic Party reaffirms its commitment to free accessible public schools for all which offer a fair, substantive opportunity to learn with educators who have the right to be represented by their union, bargain collectively and have a voice in the policies which affect their schools, classrooms and their students;*
>
> *BE IT FURTHER RESOLVED, that the California Democratic Party send this resolution to all elected Democratic leaders in California, publicize the corporate and Republican funding of these groups and work with the authors of this resolution to dispel the false reforms and support the real needs of the classroom: trained teachers, adequate funding, safe and clean facilities, diverse and stimulating curriculum and access to pre-school and higher education.*[32] [Emphasis added.]

The necessity of the California Democratic Party to pass such a resolution highlights an important point regarding the symbiosis between DFER and ERN. DFER must have the term "Democrat" in its title in order to lend the appearance of being endorsed by the Democratic Party and a legitimate organization so that its reform-minded members might infiltrate their own party with the reformer agenda. In addition, having the term "Democrat" in its title makes it easier for DFER to garner support from an unsuspecting Democratic public. (Mainline Democrats understand this potential for deception.[33]) However, the Democrats tend not to have the reform-minded billionaires among them. The reform-minded billionaires are chiefly Republican and will not write hefty checks to an organization that has "Democrat" in its title. Thus, one must create a second organization, one that does not include the term "Democrat" in its title so that Republic money might flow to Democrats who are pushing the signature-Republican reforms. Ironically, the absence of "Democrat" from the ERN title serves the same purpose as inclusion of "Democrat" in the DFER title: Appeal to a given audience.

How very chameleon of DFER/ERN.

DFER founding member Whitney Tilson has no intention of removing "Democrat" from the DFER name. Tilson even partially credits DFER for Duncan's appointment as US Secretary of Education. Here Tilson promotes the privatization agenda for "his" party:

> *I'm one of the founders of an upstart political organization, Democrats for Education Reform,* **that aims to move the Democratic Party (my party) to embrace genuine school reform,** *rather than being a major obstacle, which is, sadly, pretty much where it is today. ...***Thanks in part to our efforts, President Obama has been extraordinarily bold on this issue (moving the Democratic Party to embrace reform), starting with his selection of Arne Duncan as Secretary of Education.**[34] [Emphasis added.]

Tilson's reform involvements began with his joining Wendy Kopp in founding Teach for America (TFA) in 1989.[35] Many high-profile reformers launched their privatizing careers via TFA, including Michelle Rhee of StudentsFirst and Mike Feinberg and Dave Levin of KIPP charter schools. Their reform involvements continue to feed one another. For example, Tilson serves on the KIPP schools in the south Bronx. Also, Kopp sits on the Broad Foundation board, and Broad funds DFER complement, ERN.

There is also a connection between Rhee and DFER via ERN. Even though DFER publicly lauds StudentsFirst,[36] it is through ERN that DFER conducts business with Rhee's organization. In fact, according to ERN's 2010 990, ERN owed both StudentsFirst and Students for Education Reform (SFER) over $1.6 million.[37] SFER is supposed to be a "grassroots" student movement, but the fact that in 2010 DFER spent at least $1.6 million on StudentsFirst and SFER combined bespeaks a foundation- and hedge-funded "Astroturf reform."[38] Here is what ERN funding to SFER is purchasing:

> *In late November [2012], a small crowd of Columbia University and New York University students organized by Students for Education Reform (SFER) marched from the United Federation of Teachers (UFT) building in downtown Manhattan to the steps of the Department of Education building, demanding that public school teachers reach an agreement with the Bloomberg administration over new evaluation standards. Hanging in the balance is $450 million worth of state aid that will be withheld from city public schools by Governor Cuomo if a deal is not reached by January 17 [2013].* **Students sporting red and green Christmas hats called on teachers to "Make a deal!" and "Compromise!" in a spectacular show of misplaced activist spirit.**

> The "compromise" would place teachers at the mercy of a counterproductive test-based system, allowing up to 40 percent of their evaluative ratings to come from the standardized test scores *of their students. It's even worse than it sounds though, because* New York state requires that "teachers rated ineffective on student performance based on objective assessments must be rated ineffective overall," *as education historian Diane Ravitch explains,* "a teacher who does not raise test scores will be found ineffective overall, no matter how well he or she does with the remaining 60 percent...."[39]
> [Emphasis added.]

The article continues with information about well-intentioned-yet-misinformed students, one who naively thought that yielding to teacher evaluations based on test scores would make the $450 million available for materials in a student's art class. The student does not understand how destructive an evaluation so heavily dependent on test scores is to the healthy operation of schools. The narrowed, increasingly-high-stakes focus on the standardized test will swallow student (and teacher) creativity. Indeed, classes in the fine arts will likely be the first to go since such courses do not directly impact school wellbeing when the very life of a school is at the mercy of "data-driven" outcomes.

Like StudentsFirst, DFER and ERN are anti-union. It is sad that these organizations are able to manipulate the idealism of youth to an end that the youth do not fully comprehend. Consider this SFER student's response to *Nation* reporter George Joseph at the November 2012 New York rally:

> A participating NYU student named Danny told me, *"I'm in no way anti-union, I'm in no way anti-teacher. In fact, I don't even really like standardized testing."* When I asked him why he thought the UFT was not on board *with the proposed standards,* he shrugged.[40] [Emphasis added.]

DFER is not so innocent. In anticipation of the Chicago Teachers Strike in September 2012, DFER purchased radio airtime in order to "circulate ads that criticize the teachers' early strike vote. The ads argued it 'makes no sense' for teachers to push for a strike vote 'before they even see the deal' being offered."[41] As such, the DFER ads were slanted; in truth, negotiations between the Chicago Teachers Union and Chicago Public Schools followed a process, and once CTU President Karen Lewis realized that the negotiation would go no further, she acted on a vote that had to be conducted in advance of an actual strike. (See Chapter Nine.)

DFER's attack on the CTU was not reserved for the days prior to the strike. In May 2012, the school year in Chicago was coming to a tense end, and Illinois DFER Director Rebeca Nieves-Huffman did what reformers do when they wish to appear "grassroots": They take to the op/eds. In her May 4, 2012, letter in the *Chicago Sun-Times,* Nieves-Huffman's clear goal is to attack CTU:

> **For much of the last year,** *while parents, community leaders, and policymakers have been focused on bringing much-needed improvements to the Chicago Public Schools, the teachers union has been not-so-secretly planning to hold our city—and our school-children—hostage* **by calling for a strike.** *... It is a nuclear option for defiant union negotiators who don't get their way.*[42] [Emphasis added.]

There we have it: The problem is the stubborn, greedy union. And the reader can trust Nieves-Huffman since she belongs to an organization with "Democrat" in its name.

Nieves-Huffman continues by stating, "Strikes are extremely dangerous, which makes them effective as political tools."[43] Indeed, divesting teachers of their collective bargaining rights poses a different, more sinister set of dangers. In the absence of collective bargaining, education privatizers have free reign as they open under-regulated charter schools, spend public funds with little to no oversight, and hire and fire whomever and whenever they please, without any thought to teachers' possessing suitable credentials or having due process rights. One cannot successfully argue that such capriciousness is "good for the children." Yet Nieves-Huffman disregards these truths as she continues in her letter:

> *If the union follows through on its threats to walk next school year... Chicago and our students would suffer. It would certainly make for interesting conversation between public school parents when one parent can't send their child to school* **while another parent sends theirs off every morning to a public charter school (there are 110 public charter schools in the city with non-unionized teachers).** *...Chicago will be watching to see who is really putting children first.*[44] [Emphasis added.]

Nieves-Huffman promotes non-unionization of "public" charters as a benefit. In her op/ed, she does not disclose her extensive history in corporate reform, including her history in leading the charter movement. Nieves-Huffman is a former vice president of the National Association of Charter School Authorizers and former Associate Director for Recruitment and Selection of the KIPP Foundation. Nieves-Huffman is also involved with the education-reform-promoting Friedman Foundation and Aspen Institute.[45]

Like Nieves-Huffman, DFER leaders Joe Williams and Kevin Chavous are also featured reformers with the Friedman Foundation.[46,47] Furthermore, like Williams and Chavous, Nieves-Huffman has made a career of reforms that favor charters and oppose unions. She chooses not to inform the readers of her anti-union op/ed regarding this information.

DFER promotes mayoral control and insists that "accountability" be built in to such a system. Still, in the wake of the strike, DFER did not publicly consider that mayoral control put CPS in the position it was in and that a contributing factor involved the unabashed favoring of privately-run charters at the expense of the fiscally-starving community public schools.

In true corporate reformer style, DFER placed the blame for the entire situation on Chicago's teachers and especially on the union. In the game of privatization, unions rally the workers, and rallied workers can become quite the reckoning force—a force that interferes with management-directed profits. As such, one must not forget that the principal players on the boards of DFER and ERN are hedge fund managers. In education, hedge fund managers do not make money if the traditional public school thrives. They make money if it does not, if it is closed and replaced with privately-run charters. As Milwaukee journalist Barbara Miner observes:

> *...**The hedge fund crowd is comfortable with the charter way of doing business-over-whelmingly nonunion, which means that management gets to call all the shots;** a **guaranteed cash flow in the form of public dollars** per student; **minimal public oversight;** lots of data and test scores; and **an educational ideology based on a free-market model of schooling.** ...*

> ***Charter schools are the type of entrepreneurial initiative that "electrifies" hedge fund managers, according to Whitney Tilson,** a finance capitalist, founding member of Teach for America, and board member of the Knowledge Is Power Program (KIPP). (Tilson also sits on the DFER board.) **"With the state providing so much of the money, outside contributions are insanely well leveraged,"** he told the New York Times.*[48] [Emphasis added.]

Teacher strikes tend to interfere with all of that "insane leveraging" of philanthropy poured on top of public funding.

Another observation:

> *Take away the **Gates, Walton, and Broad** foundations, **Teach for America alumni, Democrats for Education Reform (DFER),** and a few essential hedge fund and investment managers, and the pro-corporate charter movement would shrink significantly.*[49] [Emphasis added.]

It is no secret who drives the corporate reform bus.

Consider also the following from *Forbes* magazine:

> *[2011] was a terrible year on the whole for hedge funds, but **the top 40 hedge fund earners still managed to make a combined $13.2 billion. This is what a bad year in the hedge fund industry looks like.**[50] [Emphasis added.]

In 2011, the "bad" year for hedge fund managers, DFER funder John Arnold ranked 9 out of 40. His earnings equaled $360 million.

Based upon DFER and ERN board membership, hedge fund managers favor corporate reform, where "empowerment" converts traditional public schools into charters. Unlike vouchers, which rely heavily on parent choice, charter schools become the "choice" that privatizers are able to maneuver with little to no need to negotiate with parents. With their overwhelming lack of public accountability, charter schools appeal to hedge fund managers, who are accustomed to directing their financial destinies behind a veil. Barbara Miner continues:

> *The minimal public transparency and oversight of charters is particularly in sync with the hedge fund culture.* **Infamous for their secrecy, hedge funds operate largely beyond public scrutiny.** *Their securities tend to be issued in "private offerings" that are not registered with the Securities and Exchange Commission, whose regulations were established in 1933 during the banking crises of the Great Depression.* **Nor are they required to make periodic reports under the Securities Exchange Act of 1934.** *And, to play the game, you have to be rich, with millions of dollars to invest. …*
>
> **Charter schools have also become a way to network and hobnob with elite powerbrokers and celebrities** *(who knows what deal might emerge from such networking)*—**all in the name of helping poor people.**[51] [Emphasis added.]

As to those "poor people," some selling of the charter "product" is still necessary. What better way to do so than via a sentimental film about how important winning a place in a charter school lottery is to these (exploited) parents and their children: *Waiting for Superman*. DFER has its place via the signature role-crossing of the well-positioned and amply-funded:

> *DFER is a national political action committee that promotes charter and other "school choice" options. The movie's (Waiting for Superman's) central narrative metaphor—highly emotional public lotteries—***turns out to have been perfected during a political strategy and public relations campaign engineered by Success Charter Network and DFER.** *A look at DFER and its relationship to Success Charter Network uncovers how the politics of charters operate in the real world rather than in the sanitized Hollywood version.*
>
> *First, there are the personal connections—***rich people rarely leave their fate to ping-pong balls and lotteries. John Petry, for instance, is on the boards of DFER, its non-profit arm, Education Reform Now, and the Success Charter Network. Joel Greenblatt is on the DFER board of advisors and is chair of the Success Charter Network board.**[52] [Emphasis added.]

In order to sell the film, the public needs to be primed to receive it. To this end, Success Charter Network and DFER promoted a public awareness campaign beginning in 2007 called Flooding the Zone, the primary goal of which was to mold a favorable public reception to charter schools even as charters in New York are allowed to overtake public school buildings still in use. Barbara Miner continues:

> **The strategy was to create a groundswell of publicity** *for the charter lotteries and to "flood the zone" in Harlem with pro-school choice messages.* **No effort was spared, with hundreds of thousands of leaflets, multiple mailings to families, ads at bus stops, posters, and literature drops. Lacking a membership base, DFER used "an army of**

*field workers, many high school students who were hired to blanket the neighborhood with materials." Success Charter Network coordinated the information and **DFER** coordinated the political rally.*

*A recent article in the New York Daily News reported that **Success Charter Network spent $1.3 million on marketing between 2007 and 2009, with most of that going to the leaflets, posters, and mailings that were part of the Flooding the Zone campaign.**[53]* [Emphasis added.]

Public relations at its finest—with no expense spared. Where hedge fund managers spare no expense know that the end goal involves profits.

Preferring to be behind the scenes, DFER's promotion of *Waiting for Superman* came through ERN and was dubbed "Done Waiting." Maura Walz of *Gotham Schools* notes:

> *The campaign, called "Done Waiting," represents one winner in the ongoing debate inside the education world about how to transform the attention the film into a coherent "call to action" for agitated movie-goers.*
>
> *The answer put forward by Education Reform Now, the group leading the "Done Waiting" campaign, is to **use the film as a springboard for making specific political changes.** The group's favored changes include **expanding charter schools and changing the way teachers are evaluated and granted tenure. Paid canvassers waiting outside movie theaters across the country hand movie-goers literature, direct them to a campaign-style web site, DoneWaiting.org, and encourage them to add their e-mail addresses to the group's mailing list.**[54]* [Emphasis added.]

DFER/ERN is invested in *Waiting for Superman*, but it is not for "parental empowerment." It is for money. DFER Executive Joe Williams makes his position clear in a May 2010 "summit" of New Schools Venture Fund:

> *I think charter schools should be paying advocacy organizations for their advocacy work out of their per pupil dollars. If you think of running a school as running a business, any sound business is going to allocate right off the bat a certain percentage of their funding towards lobbying, advocacy work.[55]* [Emphasis added.]

Not only should charter schools pay advocacy organizations (like ERN?)—that payment should be taken from the per-pupil funding. Forget the students. Think of the organizations that say they are for the students. They need that student funding.

If running a school is to be like running a business, then the first order of business is certainly not the student. It is turning a profit.

Williams could not have made his self-serving point any clearer.

As for the DFER "investment" in *Waiting for Superman:* The DFER and Success Academy shared goal is to drum up more business. More charter schools means higher profits. Nothing more.

DFER and sister ERN are yet another two in a very long line of organizations pushing the reform agenda onto America's schools. DFER is unique in its purporting via its name to represent Democrats, which necessitates the complement organization ERN. ERN allows wealthy, pro-reform Republicans to pour their millions into DFER while providing protection from a publicized "D" connection. Education reform could not thrive without Republican money.

Bipartisan. Education. Reform.

The DFER-ERN partnership makes this claim possible.

CHAPTER 18

NATIONAL COUNCIL ON TEACHER QUALITY (NCTQ), OR SO THEY SAY

In several of the preceding chapters, I have referred to the organization, NCTQ, or the National Council on Teacher Quality. (Indeed, much of the content of this chapter was first published on my blog, *deutsch29.wordpress.com.*) A number of the individuals actively and aggressively promoting the reformer agenda are or have been associated with NCTQ.

Reformers are excellent networkers. They sit on each other's organizational boards. They have common millionaire and billionaire funders. They publicly write and speak on each other's behalf, always in defense of the privatization agenda.

NCTQ is a reformer organization that has and continues to connect numerous well-funded and highly influential corporate reformers. It deserves its own chapter in this book.

THE NCTQ MISSION

NCTQ was founded in 2000 by the conservative Thomas B. Fordham Foundation as "a new entity to promote alternative certification and to break the

A Chronicle of Echoes: Who's Who in the Implosion of American Public Education,
pages 289–304.
Copyright © 2014 by Information Age Publishing

power of the hated ed schools." As former Fordham board member Diane Ravitch notes,

> We thought they (traditional teacher training programs) were too touchy-feely, too con-cerned about self-esteem and social justice and not concerned enough with basic skills and academics. In 1997, we had commissioned a Public Agenda study called "Different Drummers"; this study chided professors of education because they didn't care much about discipline and safety and were more concerned with how children learn rather than what they learned.[2]

Thus, NCTQ was created to alter traditional teacher training. In March 2013, its website byline noted that NCTQ "is committed to restructuring the teaching profession."[3] The byline was removed by July 2013; however, NCTQ continues to be undeniably biased in favor of corporate reform:

> Based in Washington, D.C., the National Council on Teacher Quality was founded in 2000 to provide **an alternative national voice** to existing teacher organizations **and to build the case for a comprehensive reform agenda that would challenge the current structure and regulation of the profession.**[4] [Emphasis added.]

In short, NCTQ pushes the now-popular privatization agenda, its most publicized vehicle being its annually-released report in which it rates the nation's traditional teacher training programs. In declaring itself "an alter-native national voice," NCTQ appears to be giving itself a credibility that it does not actually hold. NCTQ is not an accrediting body. It does not have the authority to grant or revoke official certification of teacher train-ing programs. In contrast, NCTQ is an advocacy group—one that actively promotes a given position or agenda. In true corporate reform fashion, NCTQ has clearly and repeatedly demonstrates its commitment to data and testing above all else that could possibly contribute to education "quality." This is the reformer ultimate end": the test score. NCTQ's original and only president, Kate Walsh, attested as much in 2011 before the Committee on Education and the Workforce.[5] On behalf of NCTQ, she offers ten sugges-tions to Congress concerning "teacher quality." I present them here, briefly stated:

1. Require data tracking systems that allow for value added measure-ment.
2. Develop performance-based teacher evaluation systems.
3. No more "highly qualified": Teacher demonstration of subject mat-ter as demonstrated on "rigorous content tests."
4. Ensure teacher content knowledge tests are rigorous.
5. Do not allow subject teachers to be generalists.

6. Develop a teacher quality index, including average ACT or SAT scores for a teacher's undergraduate institution. Publicly report teacher performance.
7. Remove barriers to alternate routes to teacher and principal certification.
8. Report value added data for teacher training programs.
9. Tie funding to increasing and retaining highly effective (based on student scores) teachers.
10. Do not equalize teacher salaries across schools.

Seven of the ten suggestions above depend upon test scores. One (point five) appears to argue for teacher training rigor; however, another (point seven) arguably counters the argument for teacher training rigor, as "alternate certification" could include unregulated, online degree purchase.

I read Walsh's statement before Congress; what I find amazing is the clearly-noted, perceived NCTQ entitlement to rate teacher training programs at both at public and private institutions and her offended surprise that many institutions decline to cooperate. NCTQ's unequivocal devotion to "disruptive innovation" and its partnership with fellow corporate reform promoter Mortimer Zuckerman's *US News and World Report* make NCTQ a biased review organization with the potential to nationally broadcast its slanted ratings of teacher training programs and damage such programs. No wonder that teacher training programs refuse to participate. Add to NCTQ's incredible bias and ability to nationally stigmatize programs the fact that it is not even a recognized postsecondary accrediting agency. NCTQ is a self-declared policeman of teacher training and is itself accountable to no auditing agency.

NCTQ maintains that it advocates for "rigor" in teacher training. Walsh is even willing to do so surreptitiously, via op/eds. And despite a call for accountability in traditional teacher training programs, NCTQ actually created its own "alternative," a short-order version of teacher certification, and one that is subjected to no NCTQ-type, highly publicized review: the American Board for Certification of Teacher Excellence (ABCTE). The link that connects these two concepts—the op/ed and ABCTE—is US Department of Education (USDOE) money.

KATE WALSH, THE OP/EDS, AND ABCTE

NCTQ President Kate Walsh is sold on the reformer agenda, enough to warrant this 2003–04 investigation by the US Inspector General (IG) regarding $677,318 in USDOE unsolicited grant money awarded to Oquirrh Institute and NCTQ. As the IG report notes:

*The purpose of this unsolicited grant was to **increase the American public's exposure and understanding of the research and full spectrum of ideas on teacher quality.** According to the grantees' monthly progress reports, **NCTQ was able to publish op-eds in 11 newspapers; however, we have been able to obtain copies of only three.** The three op-eds we reviewed focused on proposed changes in teacher reform and NCLB. **Each op-ed advocated a particular viewpoint and did not contain the required disclaimer.**[6]* [Emphasis added.]

Kate Walsh wrote all three op/eds.

*The op-eds can be construed as advocating a particular point of view. In the op-ed published in the Mobile Register, **Walsh states that the NCLB requirement that all teachers be rated "highly qualified" in the subjects they teach "is not overly demanding or unfair."** She later states "[t]he inability to reach consensus over these minimal* Similarly, *in the other two op-eds, Walsh advocated policy positions. In the op-ed published in the Grand Island Independent, **she advocated changes in teacher qualification requirements in Nebraska.** In the op-ed published in the Sacramento Bee, Walsh states: "[p]utting merit pay decisions in the hands of states or even school districts [sic] officials still will lead to excessively complicated formulas that suppress the potential benefits that merit pay could achieve."*

requirements signals a resistance, however unintended, to putting the needs of children first."

None of the op-eds we reviewed disclosed the role of the Department. Prior to the initial publication of the op-eds, a Department grants specialist reviewed a draft op-ed and reminded the grantee that the Department s regulations at 34 C.F.R. § 75.620 require a disclaimer on all grant publications. The grant specialist did not know why the published op-eds did not contain the disclaimer.[7] [Emphasis added.]

In her failure to disclose the grant funding behind her position, Walsh demonstrates intentional disregard for protocol:

*As these op/eds were published without the EDGAR (Education Department General Administrative Regulations) disclaimer, **the funds used to produce them may have resulted in an improper expenditure of grant funds. If all of the produced op-eds are similarly silent on the role of the Department, then all of the expenditures associated with goal one of the grant may have been improper.**[8]* [Emphasis added.]

In the IG summation, USDOE is exonerated:

*While three of the grants resulted in op-ed opinion pieces that did not include the disclaimer language required by the Education Department General Administrative Regulations (EDGAR) at 34 C.F.R. § 75.620, **we did not find evidence to conclude that the Department awarded these grants with an intent to influence public opinion through the undisclosed use of third party grantees.**[9]* [Emphasis added.]

It seems that Kate Walsh's NCTQ involvement in promoting a paid USDOE agenda is part of a much larger story involving former US Secretary of Education Rod Paige.[10]

And what is the big deal, anyway, for publishing a simple opinion letter and not disclosing the over-half-a-million dollars from which these op/eds were funded? I mean, can't Kate Walsh just write about what she believes in because she believes in it?

Sure, but not if she has accepted money to do so. In the latter case, Walsh had a duty to disclose, which she actively and intentionally ignored.

Concealing the funding behind the letters presents the illusion that no major organization (in this case, the USDOE) is promoting the messages. Instead, the op/eds deceptively appear to be "grassroots" when they are certainly not.

What Walsh did is illegal. The IG report said that NCTQ needed to return the money for failure to disclose the funding:

> **The disclaimer language required by EDGAR applies to any publication produced with grant funds.** *In the absence of the disclaimer language, the funds used to produce a publication may be an improper expenditure,* **requiring the Department to initiate appropriate recovery action. The three op-ed pieces appear to be such expenditures.**[11]
> [Emphasis added.]

As it turns out, $677,318 is a relatively small sum for NCTQ to return when one considers just how kind former US Secretary of Education Paige was to NCTQ with his "discretionary" funds. It seems that NCTQ accepted $6.25 million from Paige. In addition, NCTQ's fast-track teacher certification creation, ABCTE, was awarded $35 million to develop a computerized teacher certification test. The writer of the *Spokesman Review* piece previously cited notes, "Pass their $500 test and you can teach in Idaho."[12] The cost has since risen to $1995 and has been extended as a "state approved route to teacher certification" in Florida, Idaho, Mississippi, Missouri, New Hampshire, Nevada, Oklahoma, Pennsylvania, South Carolina, Tennessee, and Utah.[13]

Keep in mind that NCTQ was started because conservatives viewed traditional teacher training programs as lacking rigor. So, this is the NCTQ answer, created in 2001 with the help of $5 million in Paige money: ABCTE-buy-a-degree.[14]

Fortunately for Teach for America (TFA), NCTQ protestations of "academic rigor" also conveniently exclude this multi-million-dollar teacher temp agency and its five-week-trained "teachers."

Traditional teacher training requires NCTQ "regulation"; as for ABCTE and TFA—forget about it. Off the hook. Pardoned.

Corporate reform is replete with such double-standard hypocrisy.

Though the Fordham Foundation created NCTQ to address perceived shortcomings of teacher training, NCTQ was floundering even as it received what was questionable money in 2001[15] (the $5 million) from Paige: The $5 million awarded to NCTQ was done so despite proposal rejection by two of the three reviewers of the NCTQ[16] "unsolicited proposal to create a new national accreditation program for teachers" (ABCTE). Within two years, and by the time USDOE offered money to NCTQ that resulted in Walsh's op/eds, NCTQ had solidified its purpose as a corporate reform conduit. In fact, concurrent with the 2003–04 USDOE award of $677,318 connected to Walsh's op/eds, NCTQ/ABCTE received $17,902,700 in unsolicited grant money from USDOE.[17] The erratic manner in which Paige and USDOE awarded grant money resulted in this Government Accountability Office (GAO) audit and censure:

The Department of Education has the responsibility to ensure that when it makes discretionary grant awards it follows a transparent and fair process that results in awards to deserving eligible applicants.... However, Education based its decisions about the likely national significance and quality of proposals on information that varied greatly in detail and, as a result, sent applications forward for peer review that sometimes required extensive revisions. Without requiring a more uniform format for unsolicited proposals, OII may not have adequate information on which to base its screening decisions.

Regarding its competitive awards process, **the department has put in place management controls that, if followed, provide a reasonable assurance that awards are made appropriately....** *Furthermore,* **in the absence of such diligence, actions taken that benefit specific grantees, such as those we found in 2001 and 2002, could happen again.**

...Specifically, to improve the process for selecting and awarding grants based on unsolicited proposals, we are recommending that the Secretary develop a more systematic format to select unsolicited proposals for further consideration by peer reviewers....[18] [Emphasis added.]

So much exposure regarding NCTQ/ABCTE funding. In 2005, Kate Walsh resigned from the ABCTE board[19] in the wake of organizational instability:

Kathleen A. Madigan, the founding president of the American Board for Certification of Teacher Excellence, resigned last month. *Meanwhile, the Education Leaders Council, the conservative-leaning group of education officials that got the board started in 2001, has been labeled a "high-risk grantee"* for its handling of millions of dollars in federal grants.

Then, late last month (September 2005), Kate Walsh, the president of the National Council on Teacher Quality, quit the ABCTE board of directors.[20] [Emphasis added.]

The hypocrisy of attempting to hold teacher education accountable while promoting a flimsy, easy-to-purchase "alternative" certification would haunt

NCTQ in its 2011 efforts to join with Zuckerman's *US News and World Report* in a very public crusade to rate teacher prep programs. And well it should.[21]

ZUCKERMAN, WALSH, AND THE CLOSE-KNIT THAT IS REFORM

Kate Walsh and NCTQ did form a tight alliance with Mortimer Zuckerman and *US News and World Report*. Zuckerman's publication enables Walsh and NCTQ to discredit traditional teacher training in front of an international audience. However, the greater alliance involves more than Zuckerman and Walsh.

For reformers, no alliance is limited to two individuals. Just know that.

Mortimer Zuckerman, billionaire CEO and editor-in-chief of *US News and World Report* and owner/publisher of the *New York Daily News,* is recognized by Jeb Bush's Foundation for Excellence in Education (FEE) as a "reformer."[22] Zuckerman's own writing supports as much in a piece on the 2009 Cardozo High School rally in DC:

> *None of the speakers at the rally fell back on tired nostrums to excuse the poor performance of minority students or to justify the need for new spending.... Nor did anyone suggest that achievement tests were inherently unfair to minority students and should not be used under the No Child Left Behind Act to hold schools, principals, and teachers accountable for student performance.*[23] [Emphasis added.]

Thus, the CEO and editor-in-chief of *US News and World Report* has the same reformer bent as does Kate Walsh and her NCTQ. Like Zuckerman, Walsh is also a FEE-recognized "reformer."[24] Zuckerman also sits on the board of directors of the Fund for Public Schools, "public-private partnership" expressly designed for advancing New York education reform (i.e., privatization of public schools):

> *In 2002 Mayor Michael R. Bloomberg and Chancellor Joel I. Klein established public-private partnerships as a critical means of supporting public education reform.........
> The Fund is the primary vehicle for advancing these efforts.*[25] [Emphasis added.]

As to more tangling of the web: Bloomberg, whose education reform policies via appointees like Joel Klein clearly favor charter schools,[26] wants to fund his own charter schools,[27] paid for out of Bloomberg Philanthropies,[28] a group funded by the Gates Foundation– and on whose board of directors Jeb Bush sits.[29]

Gates also funds NCTQ.[30]

It's difficult to keep track of the financial back-scratching.

What is important to remember is that NCTQ is steeped in (undeniably fiscal) associations biased toward corporate reform.

As to the concept of ranking programs and publicizing the rankings, *US News and World Report* has been ranking colleges and hospitals for decades.[31]

Its college rankings have been criticized for the superficial nature of the data collected. As Kevin Carey of Education Sector notes in 2006:

> *The U.S. News rankings have become the nation's de facto higher education account-ability system.... **But the U.S. News ranking system is deeply flawed. Instead of focus-ing on the fundamental issues of how well colleges and universities educate their students and how well they prepare them to be successful after college, the magazine's rankings are almost entirely a function of three factors: fame, wealth, and exclusivity. They directly or indirectly account for 95 percent of a school's ranking....*[32] [Empha-sis added.]

Carey then takes the list of information *US News* collects on the colleges and universities and classifies it into one of four categories: fame, wealth, exclu-sivity, and quality. The only quality item is "graduation rate performance, predicted vs. actual."

None of the information collected by *US News* for its college and uni-versity rankings requires a site visit.[33] It appears that the same is true of its hospital rankings.[34]

> *The American Institutes for Research (AIR) has noted the shortcomings of using docu-ment reviews to measure teacher preparation program effectiveness. In its 2012 Evalu-ating the Effectiveness of Teacher Preparation Programs for Support and Accountabil-ity*[35] *report, AIR lists several challenges with using process measures to evaluate teacher preparation programs: **The research base of a document review is not robust enough to build assessment for accountability based on process measures; process measures do not always accurately capture what actually happens in preparation programs....*[36] [Emphasis added.]

This hyped-yet-empty NCTQ "rating" of teacher training programs proves that well-connected reformers lacking in solid education backgrounds and harboring suspicious, self-serving motives can publish whatever they like, proclaim it to be The Truth, and damage the reputations of those they declare to be Unfit.

In any research report, the funders and board members reveal impor-tant information regarding the potential biases in a report before one even reads the report. Of course, funders are able to hide their identities via anonymity. Only two national funders did so. Nevertheless, one can readily read the names of wealthy foundations more than willing to dole out big bucks all for the sake of privatizing public education, including the Arnold and Dell foundations, and—one of The Big Three in undermining public education—the Broad Foundation. Eli Broad is well known for his wishes to privatize. He wrote a detailed report in 2009 telling schools (not suggest-ing, but telling) what reforms one could expect to be in place by 2012. Sev-eral NCTQ members participated in the report, including NCTQ President Kate Walsh.[37]

In addition, Broad published a "manifesto," also in collaboration with several NCTQ advisory board members. Main points of the manifesto include inserting "talented" individuals from outside of the field of education into key education administration positions.[38]

The reformer world is a close-knit world. Nothing like having a common goal to destroy traditional public education. The very fact that Broad financed this NCTQ report is reason enough to doubt its fairness to traditional training programs.

Another Broad-funded program is the Harvard Graduate School of Education (HGSE),[39] offers a doctorate focused on corporate reform.[40] Partners for this amazingly "tuition-free degree "include NCTQ advisory board members Wendy Kopp (Teach for America) and Joel Klein (via Rupert Murdoch's News Corp/Wireless Generation). Also "partnering" is Mayor Bloomberg (New York State Department of Education).[41-43]

Notice how eerily complementary this 2011comment by HGSE teacher education director Katherine Mersdeth is to the oft-promoted, NCTQ dismal view of traditional teacher training programs:

> *The director of teacher education at the Harvard Graduate School of Education was quoted on a New York Times online forum as saying that **of the nation's 1,300 graduate teacher-training programs, only about 100 were doing a competent job.***
>
> **The rest "could be shut down tomorrow," said Harvard's Katherine Merseth.**[44] [Emphasis added.]

Why, NCTQ could have said those very same words.

Same sandbox; same language.

It gets better: The Broad Foundation also funds Jeb Bush's FEE,[45] which, you might recall, endorses both Walsh (NCTQ) and Zuckerman (*US News*).

Another major concern regarding the credibility of the NCTQ 2013 ratings is Rhode Island Commissioner of Education Deborah Gist's involvement on the technical panel. Gist is a member of Bush's Chiefs for Change.[46] She is also a graduate of the Broad Superintendents Academy,[47] one of those "talented" individuals outside of education positioned to make reform happen at any cost. Former-basketball-player-gone-US Secretary of Education Arne Duncan proclaimed himself as her endorser for a renewed term:

> *In a call of support for Gist, Duncan touted rising test scores and graduation rates as signs that the state is making progress. **Teachers and parents have been outspoken in their opposition to Gist. But Duncan defends her,** calling her collaborative. . . .* [48][Emphasis added.]

Never mind Gist's poor approval rating prior to her reappointment: 85% of teachers polled did not want her as education commissioner any longer:

*The survey of 402 [out of approximately 10,500] teachers shows **85% of those asked believe Gist's contract should not be renewed.** The poll also found that 73% of teachers find Gist to be "somewhat ineffective" or "infective" and another 82% feel less respected than they did when Gist was hired in 2009.*[49] [Emphasis added.]

Duncan took advice for Race to the Top criteria from Jeb Bush via Chiefs for Change.[50] Gist is a member of Chiefs for Change, and she is both reappointed as RI Commissioner of Education and a contributor to the fabulous work in biased reformer propaganda that is the NCTQ teacher training ratings report.

Never forget: The reformer world is a close-knit world.

PURGING THE WEBSITE

NCTQ has received much publicity due to its releasing of annual reports in which it judges teacher training programs using artifacts. In January through March 2013, I wrote a blog series on NCTQ. (Much of what is presented in this chapter comes directly from entries in my NCTQ series.[51,52]) At that time, NCTQ was very open in presenting its outspoken viewpoint on its website. At some point over the next several months, however, NCTQ cleaned up its website, arguably in an effort to protect itself from further scrutiny. Nevertheless, since NCTQ continues to slander teacher training programs in the same fashion as it did prior to neutralizing its website, there is no evidence that any of the removed content represents a change of position on the part of NCTQ. For this reason, I will present information that was once on the NCTQ website, prominently displayed. (I will even include the original links for the hidden content since a skilled tech person could possibly access "old" links.) Call it a historical exploration, if you like. Even though NCTQ would like to conceal its past via website reconstruction, erasing the past is only an option in science fiction.

Ironically, one of the removed NCTQ links was entitled, "The public has the right to know"; here NCTQ presented its argument for the need for "transparency" of teacher training programs. On this link, NCTQ purported, "We are keeping no secrets."[53]

I suppose that by July 2013, NCTQ decided that it had better "keep some secrets," after all.

Before its website alteration, NCTQ once offered two letters from universities refusing to participate as well as Walsh's letters of reply. Let us consider these two, now-hidden letters and Walsh's replies as president of NCTQ.

First, according to this letter, dated February 3, 2011, from the Association of American Universities (AAU) written to *US News and World Report* Editor Brian Kelly and copied to Kate Walsh on behalf of 36 teacher training programs, NCTQ is not transparent regarding its method of rating training programs. Furthermore, the ratings appear to be based upon the superficial evidence of course syllabi:

> *...The methodology for conducting a NCTQ review is not transparent. A review of documents from NCTQ reveals that judgments made about education schools and critical comments made by NCTQ lack supporting evidence or information on the methodology used to arrive at the ratings....*
>
> *Finally, and perhaps most importantly, the NCTQ evaluation did not assess what teachers know and can do, or whether what they do impacts student learning. Rather, judgments appear to be based on what content is included in syllabi gathered. It is not clear how the syllabi were reviewed, coded, or rated. Furthermore, there is little evidence given that the content NCTQ sought on syllabi affects teacher effectiveness.*[54] [Emphasis added.]

This leaning on the content of syllabi and other course artifacts in order to judge teacher training programs is supported by this request formerly on the NCTQ website as it pumps the public for such esoteric information in order to judge teacher training programs unwilling to volunteer to be judged:

> *In order to conduct our evaluation, NCTQ needs basic course materials from these institutions—the same materials students are routinely provided. We are primarily looking for certain course syllabi and materials relating to the student teaching program, such as student teaching handbooks.*
>
> *We are appealing to students on public and private campuses to help by sharing these basic materials in order that we can produce a fair and valid rating of program quality. We are paying stipends of $25 to $200 for the materials we need (much less than what many institutions are effectively charging).*[55] [Emphasis added.]

It certainly appears that NCTQ rates teacher training programs based upon superficial criteria.

In her response to AAU dated February 7, 2011, Kate Walsh makes the following statement:

> *We believe that the basic aspects of our methodology are quite transparent.*[56]

Transparent generalities yet hidden specifics. Walsh defends NCTQ transparency by concealing details.

Walsh says a lot in this letter without ever presenting the details of the NCTQ review process. Not once does she offer a detailed list, or a rubric, or reference a website link outlining the NCTQ review criteria and decision making process. Walsh writes about "refining a methodology over time," yet she presents no details. She simply refers AAU to "past reports."

Next, let us consider this telling admission in the same letter by Walsh:

> *We also are looking to implement a more transparent process so that anyone can see how we rated an institution.*[57]

Even though the stated purpose of NCTQ teacher training program ratings was that "the public has a right to know," they do not get details on the ratings of specific institutions. They get the outcome of the evaluation process. And in June 2013, the public also saw generalized graphs on specific grading criteria. However, the June 2013 report includes no detailed information on the specific criteria as such was applied to each institution.[58]

In her 2011 response, Walsh's very next sentence begins, "After our ratings are released…." What she is telling AAU is that they do not get to know in this letter, before committing to be reviewed, how they will be rated, but once the letter grade rating has been publicized, a program can challenge it, "using a section of our website as a public forum."

Walsh's bizarre justification for the NCTQ "process" continues:

> *As challenges accumulate, the public will be able to judge their merits,* given both the institutions assertions and NCTQ's response. *It will either become clear to the public (and to the institutions as well) that NCTQ is conducting fair and accurate assessments* or our credibility will be undermined and our work shut down. *We are confident that the former outcome will turn out to be the case.*[59] [Emphasis added.]

"As challenges accumulate"??

According to this 2011 correspondence, the public does not have access to the NCTQ evaluation criteria prior to letter grade release, but NCTQ deems the public "able to judge the merits" of subsequent challenges.

NCTQ is a corporate reform organization, and corporate reformers avoid fully disclosing themselves though they require it of the nonreformer education institutions with which they deal.

NCTQ is a corporate reform organization, and corporate reformers like to tell the public that they "have a right to know" even though the reformers never fully inform the public from the outset of a situation. In this case, the public does not know the exact criteria by which teacher training programs are being measured. How then can the public accurately evaluate the meaning of some NCTQ-assigned rating?

According to this 2011 correspondence, it cannot. NCTQ wants to assign ratings and leave the public to "take our word for it."

NCTQ holds all of the cards in this game of teacher training "transparency." They deal the cards as they wish, demanding the training programs to play the game and show their hand when told. They arrogantly insist that the training programs place their forced bets knowing that the deck is stacked. Once the hand is over, if the training programs feel cheated, they can complain, and NCTQ will rearrange the deck and present a constructed justification wholly at the mercy of a whimsical dealer. Take it or leave it.

Consider excerpts from this second letter, dated February 9, 2011, authored by three universities (in California, New York, and Maryland) unwilling to volunteer access to NCTQ review. The authors express concern regarding "insufficient detail… regarding the data to be collected, the methods for scoring, and the rater attributes" and "validity of conclusions." The authors also note, "It is essential that our institutions be able to review all key aspects of the methodology and data collection in advance."[60]

Regarding NCTQ's emphasis on forming judgments based upon syllabi, the authors state, "A focus on course syllabi and other program inputs is altogether inappropriate. Analyses are needed that represent the comprehensive types of evidence on program outcomes and impacts collected by programs."[61]

Finally, the authors address what appears to be NCTQ coercion if a program wishes to withdraw its participation: "Further, we object to the process used when institutions with to withdraw from the study. In the past, when institutions have sought to withdraw, frequently due to sound concerns, NCTQ has refused and indicated that if the institution does not comply, then results would be based on what they are able to find online and elsewhere. This is not an appropriate response."[62]

The authors close with, "Unless we have assurances by *March 15, 2011*, indicating that each of our concerns, which are similar to those expressed by all other major universities in the nation are addressed, we will urge all of our campuses *not* to participate in the survey."[63]

Though the letter was addressed to Brian Kelly, editor of *US News and World Report*, it was copied to NCTQ President Kate Walsh. I would like to offer one statement from her response, dated March 16, 2011 (hmmm.):

> *…The belief that participation in this process should be optional, if widely shared, reveals a gap between us that will be hard to close.*[64]

One thing is clear: NCTQ does not believe in voluntary review. NCTQ sees itself as entitled to review teacher training programs. It is not asking permission. NCTQ IS Mount Olympus. The arrogance is palpable.

The above letters were from a correspondence dated 2011. On its website in March 2013, NCTQ had posted standards, rationales, and indicators;[65] this rating information is dated February 2013.[66] Three notes regarding this information:

1) NCTQ offers no evidence of testing its own standards. NCTQ simply expects training programs and the public to trust what it calls its "well-honed methodology."[67] And yet, as I demonstrated in my review of the NCTQ advisory board,[68] most members have no experience as classroom teachers. This irony presents serious questions regarding the appropriateness of NCTQ as a qualified organization to rate teacher training programs, period, its conceited, "just trust us" standards aside.

2) From what is posted, the NCTQ ratings process remains "artifact dependent"; that is, it is possible to rate a teacher training program without

having a site visit. This idea is supported by NCTQ's website plea to the public to send in syllabi for programs that refuse to participate:

> *In order to conduct our evaluation, NCTQ needs basic course materials from these institutions—the same materials students are routinely provided. We are primarily looking for certain course syllabi and materials relating to the student teaching program, such as student teaching handbooks.*[69] [Emphasis added.]

There you have it: The artifact-dependent review.

The NCTQ shallow review "process" is further supported by summary information provided by NCTQ:

> *Drawing on seven years of research, NCTQ has developed a set of comprehensive standards covering **the most important aspects of teacher preparation.** These "nuts and bolts" represent the knowledge and skills new teachers need in order to be successful in the classroom. **By examining evidence—admissions standards, required course syllabi, textbooks, student teaching policy handbooks, and data showing program outcomes—**of what teacher preparation programs are demanding of their teacher candidates, **our review will reveal which programs are truly preparing** their future teachers for tomorrow's classrooms.*[70] [Emphasis added.]

No site visit is required for an NCTQ "review."

3) There is no clear connection between rating indicators and any means of scoring leading to the publicized ratings. This is very important; by offering the standards, rationales, and indicators, NCTQ offers the illusion of transparency. However, if NCTQ provides no clear connection between such indicators and the specific ratings it publicizes, the entire process

remains cryptic, with NCTQ holding the power to offer whatever grades it subjectively pleases. By extension, from the time of the writing of the 2011 correspondence above to the inclusion of standards information on the NCTQ website in March 2013, both the teacher training programs and the public remain uninformed about the NCTQ ratings process in its entirety.

The 2011 letters include concerns about the superficial nature of NCTQ teacher training program ratings. In 2013, ratings remain superficial. The 2011 letters include concerns regarding a lack of clarity in NCTQ rating criteria. In 2013, an important connection between NCTQ ratings indicators and actual rating calculations is missing from NCTQ's publicized ratings process information. The 2011 letters include concerns about being able to opt out of the ratings process. The March 2013 website offered no such option and instead included information indicating that nonparticipatory institutions will be pursued and rated without their consent. In short, NCTQ has not adequately addressed the 2011 concerns of university teacher training programs as of the original March 2013 writing.

YET ANOTHER NCTQ REVIEW

In June 2013, NCTQ released another report reviewing teacher training programs using artifacts and requiring no site visit. And once again, NCTQ, producer of the ABCTE, "do-it-yourself" teacher degree "for less than the cost of one college class,"[71] proclaimed US teacher training to be in dire straits:

> *There's no shortage of factors for America's educational decline: budget cutbacks, entrenched poverty, crowded classrooms, shorter school years, greater diversity of students than in other countries. The list seems endless.*
>
> *NCTQ's Teacher Prep Review has uncovered another cause, one that few would suspect: the colleges and universities producing America's traditionally prepared teachers.*
>
> *Through **an exhaustive and unprecedented examination** of how these schools operate, the Review finds they have become an **industry of mediocrity, churning out first-year teachers with classroom management skills and content knowledge inadequate to thrive in classrooms with ever-increasing ethnic and socioeconomic student diversity.**[72]* [Emphasis added.]

As to the "exhaustive and unprecedented examination": One would think that "exhaustive" includes site visits. Not according to NCTQ:

> *We have created the largest database on teacher preparation ever assembled, with information from thousands of **syllabi, textbooks, student teaching handbooks, student teacher observation instruments and other material.**[73]* [Emphasis added.]

NCTQ is obviously proud of its superficial judgment. It views itself as "making teacher preparation matter."

Not quite.

In June 2013, NCTQ offered a 117-page report[74] on its evaluating teacher training programs. I examined the three schools I attended for my degrees. For each, I saw an overall star rating. (All three rated one to two stars.) I saw no detailed report outlining the exact calculations for the ratings of these three (or for any) teacher training programs. I did see over a hundred pages of color-coded, multi-graphed hype obviously constructed to dazzle an unassuming public and injure traditional teacher training across the US.

Accountable to no one, NCTQ continues to demand as much out of college and university teacher training programs. In its suggestions to the public, NCTQ arrogance thrives:

> *Clearly, many consumers will, for the near future, be forced to choose between one- and two-star programs. In the meantime, consumers who cannot vote with their feet can do so with words. **Institutions should be required to answer the questions and concerns voiced by prospective teacher candidates, current teacher candidates and certainly tuition-paying, loan-burdened students and parents.** School districts can play a par-*

ticularly important role in this regard, **making it clear in their communications that they expect the institution's graduates to be better trained and to come from programs that have earned a high rating.**[75] [Emphasis added.]

Not a word on what the public should "demand" of the NCTQ-birthed ABCTE "instant" teacher. Such is in keeping with the reformer dual standard: Increased pressure on traditional public education; increased deregulation for privatizing entities.

NCTQ: SAME OLD SAME OLD

NCTQ might have erased details from its website, but as of July 2013, nothing has changed. NCTQ refuses to offer complete–"complete" being the key term here– detailed information regarding program review in advance of a program's committing to such review. Furthermore, the public in general is not provided with complete–again, the key word– details of the review, particularly details regarding how NCTQ arrives at each of its individual program ratings, though they are expected to trust the rating results of the review as such are broadcast nationally. Like many corporate reformer machines, NCTQ refers often to "transparency"; however, it is a selective, self-serving, incomplete transparency, which is really not transparency at all.

NCTQ believes that its corporate reform agenda is the mold into which teacher training programs should be forced. Thus, NCTQ enters the program evaluation process laden with bias, including the damaging belief that standardized test scores possess the power to define "quality" education.

CHAPTER 19

STAND FOR CHILDREN
(CRUSH THEIR TEACHERS)

In June 2010, Forbes published a piece entitled, "The Billionaire Mayor's Daughter Gets Her Own Nonprofit." It is an article about billionaire Michael Bloomberg's daughter, Emma, who in 2010 started the nonprofit Robin Hood Foundation, "a nonprofit that fights poverty by partnering with 240 nonprofits around [New York City.]" [1]

Emma is the daughter of a man who has had mayoral control of New York City's schools since 2001 and whose most amazing accomplishment has been to allow well-financed charter schools to move into occupied public school buildings, forcing a competition that favors the parasitic, often hedge-fund-financed charters.

By 2013, and not only does Billionaire Mayor's Daughter Emma have her own nonprofit; she is also the chair of another well-financed nonprofit, Stand for Children (SFC), whose board includes members freshly discussed in the KIPP chapter, Katherine Bradley, KIPP board member and chair of Washington regional Teach for America, and Michael Lomax, KIPP board member and CEO of the United Negro College Fund.

A Chronicle of Echoes: Who's Who in the Implosion of American Public Education,
pages 305–319.

SFC board members Katherine Bradley and Lisette Nieves also share a connection with TFA founder Wendy Kopp by way of the Woodrow Wilson School at Princeton University. Bradley is a 1986 alumnus; Kopp, a 1989 alumnus, and Nieves is a member of its advisory council.[2,3]

Another notable SFC board member is Don Washburn, former executive with Booz Allen Hamilton, the company for which technician Edward Snowden worked prior to his June 2013 leaking information about internet and phone tapping done to an unsuspecting American public by the America's own National Security Agency.[4] Snowden's revelations do not bode well for a president whose Race to the Top requires states to "implement a statewide longitudinal data system."[5]

Phil Handy is also on the SFC board, which brings Jeb Bush's influence into play; Handy was appointed by Bush as chair of the Florida State Board of Education (2001–07). Handy is also a board member of Jeb Bush's Foundation for Florida's Future, one of three Bush nonprofits that shares an address with a lobbying firm (see FEE and Chiefs for Change chapter). Like previously noted reformers Erik Hanushek and Chester Finn, Handy has ties to the reformer think tank Hoover Institution at Stanford University (see chapters on Hanushek and Finn).

It is not difficult to see from this board that SFC is yet another conduit for privatization of public education.

SFC was co-founded by board member Eliza Leighton and CEO Jonah Edelman in 1996. The organization has two components, SFC, the 501(c)4 (nonprofit advocacy) and SFC Leadership Center, the 501(c)3. As of 2013, the organization operates in ten states, Arizona, Colorado, Illinois, Indiana, Louisiana, Massachusetts, Oregon, Tennessee, Texas, and Washington.[6] Once working independent of one another, the various state organizations are now unified under one collective mission of education reform. In 2012, SFC published a document, "What We Stand For." I present some excerpts here. Though the language should read familiar by now, to the untrained eye, these ideas might appear uplifting and supportive. However, never forget the associations of those on the SFC board:

Consider first this general statement of purpose:

Educate and **empower parents,** *teachers, and community members* **to demand excellent schools.**

Advocate for effective local, state and national education policies and investments.

Ensure the policies and funding we advocate for reach classrooms and help students.

Elect courageous leaders who will stand up for our priorities.[7] [Emphasis added.]

SFC is a 501(c)4, which means that it is a lobbying group. Based upon the above statement, Stand for Children uses its financial resources to shape educational policy and to elect policymakers who endorse the education reform agenda. SFC will also push for implementation of its reform agenda. Notice again the reformer language (bolded):

> *Effective teachers and principals are the top two in-school factors impacting student achievement. Strong, well-supported teachers and principals can close the achievement gap, help underserved students stay on track, and impact students throughout their lives.* Ensuring every child has **a strong principal** leading their school and **effective teachers in every class, every year,** *requires a comprehensive approach to developing educators, including effective systems for:*
> * *training and preparation,*
> * *recruitment hiring, and placement,*
> * *mentoring and induction,*
> * *evaluation that is connected to well-designed professional support and development,*
> * **competitive compensation,** *and*
> * **retention of the strongest educators and dismissal of ineffective educators.**[8] [Emphasis added.]

If popular education reform ideas such as a top-down leadership model including "strong principals"; "competitive compensation," or merit pay, and "dismissal of ineffective educators," or value-added teacher evaluation sound like ideas straight from Bill Gates, it should come as no surprise that according to the Gates grants website, SFC's 501(c)3, SFC Leadership Center, has received just over $9 million from the Gates Foundation in the years from "2009 and before" to 2012.[9] It should also come as no surprise that SFC endorses the Common Core State Standards (CCSS). Consider this excerpt from the SFC mission document:

> **Quality instruction requires rigorous and aligned standards, curriculum and assessments.** *Standards must clearly outline what students have to know and be able to do at every grade level* **to be prepared for college** *and other training beyond high school. Curricula, instructional approaches, and learning tools* **must help students master these standards.** ... *State Superintendents and State Boards of Education* **must ensure high school graduation equals college readiness.**...[10] [Emphasis added.]

Though couched in generalities, the foundation exists to prime the public for SFC's endorsement of CCSS. On the SFC Washington website, the SFC position on CCSS is indisputable:

> *The Common Core State Standards, or "Common Core," is a set of* **high academic learning standards in math and English language arts** *that are designed to better prepare students for success in college, work, and life.*

> *Standards are benchmarks of* **what students should know and be able to do at every grade level.** *The Common Core standards were developed using international benchmarks and adopted by 46 states—unprecedented cooperation in our nation's history.*

> *At every grade level, parents will have a clear idea of what their child is expected to know and how they are really doing in school. Until now, every state had different learning standards. What a student was expected to learn depended on where they lived. Common Core fixes that and raises the bar for learning—an approach that will help all Washington students build the practical skills they need for success after high school.*[11]
> [Emphasis added in last two paragraphs.]

Such laudation betrays its sales pitch. CCSS was designed by education businesses, not by seasoned teachers (see chapter on David Coleman). Apparently such details are irrelevant. For over $9 million in Gates Foundation money, SFC cannot help but endorse What Bill Wants.

Another Gates Foundation recipient is the Aspen Institute, home of the Aspen Ideas Festival. Between January and July 2013, the Gates Foundation donated $5.7 million to Aspen; since "2009 and before," the total Gates funding for the Aspen Institute has been $49.6 million.

It makes one wonder if ideas really are for sale.

In 2011, SFC CEO Jonah Edelman spoke at the Aspen Ideas Festival. For 14 minutes Edelman details how he used SFC to position the legislation requiring Chicago teachers to have 75% agreement among their membership in order to strike. He also openly admits to mush of the education reform agenda hinted at in the 2012 SFC position statement.

Edelman's blunt, public admission of his shamelessly leveraging the SFC political machine to his advantage in Illinois politics is powerful, not only for SFC's involvement but also because Edelman's supporters connect to the White House. For its import in illustrating the gross abuse that is the political agenda of education privatization, I include much of the transcribed 14 minutes in this chapter. In short, this is exactly the nonsense that the American public needs to see in this book.

The transcription of Edelman's speech is from the *Parents Across America* website. Asides in the text are also provided by *Parents Across America* for clarification.

In this excerpt, Edelman begins by explaining his decision to move SFC into Illinois:

> *... when Bruce Rauner [apparently Chicago venture capitalist Bruce V. Rauner] ... asked,* **after seeing that we passed legislation in several states including Colorado,** *that we look at Illinois, I was skeptical.* **After interviewing 55 different folks in the landscape—the Speaker of the House, Senate President, minority leadership, education advocates ... I was very surprised to see that there was a tremendous political opening** *that I think Bruce wasn't even aware of.*[12] [Emphasis added.]

According to the 2010 SFC annual report, the Rauner Family Foundation—as in venture capitalist Bruce Rauner[13]—who Edelman credits with inviting SFC to Illinois—donated at least $250,000 to SFC.[14] In 2011, Rauner and his wife Diana donated between $100,000 and $250,000 to SFC.[15]

The Illinois Teachers Union decided to cut funding to Illinois Speaker of the House Michael Madigan over a pension reform bill. The union also publicized that it would cut union funding to any Democrat supporting the pension reform bill. This issue is key since funding Madigan to make up for lost funding from the teachers union is Edelman's means for leveraging power. Madigan is a Democrat, and SFC receives much funding from Gates and Walton (Republicans), so Edelman's supporting a Democratic Speaker was "questionable."

> ... *We [SFC] decided to get involved in midterm elections, which many advised us against doing. ... **My position was we had to be involved to show our capabilities, to build some clout. ... While there were a lot of folks, I think, who thought the Republicans were going to take over in Illinois, our analysis was that Madigan would still be speaker.** ... That wasn't what I think a lot of our colleagues wanted to hear.*[16] ... [Emphasis added.]

Despite Edelman's publicly aligning with (and receiving substantial funding from) Republicans, well-connected Democrats are still willing to invest in SFC's reform push. SFC received $150,000 from the Chicago-based Joyce Foundation in 2010 for the purpose of starting SFC Indiana.[17] Obama served as a Joyce Foundation board member from 1994 to 2002.[18]

Nevertheless, most of the money that SFC received in Illinois is connected to such powerful Democrats as Obama's 2008 campaign finance chief and billionaire Hyatt Hotel owner Penny Pritzker, whose fundraising efforts enabled SFC to go "from zero to more than $3 million"[19] in five months (by January 2011). Pritzker's interest in SFC apparently centered on its union-busting efforts. Pritzker also subsequently supported Rahm Emanuel for Chicago mayor.[20]

Edelman is certainly fulfilling his obligation to Pritzker: he is contributing to union busting. First, he must neutralize the union's financial pull over Madigan:

> So our [SFC's] analysis was he's (Madigan) still going to be in power, and as such the raw politics were that we should tilt toward him, *and so we interviewed 36 candidates in targeted races. ... I'm being quite blunt here.* **The individual candidates were essentially a vehicle to execute a political objective, which was to tilt toward Madigan.** *The press never picked up on it.* **We endorsed nine individuals—and six of them were Democrats, three Republicans—and tilted our money toward Madigan,** *who was expecting because of Bruce Rauner's leadership ... that all our money was going to go to Republicans.* **That was really an show of—indication to him that we could be a new partner to take the place of the Illinois Federation of Teachers. That was the point.** *Luckily, it never got covered that way. That wouldn't have worked well in Illinois—Madigan is not particularly well liked. And it did work.*[21] [Emphasis added.]

All reformers, whether Republican or Democrat, want the unions out of the way so that privatization can more easily flourish. With SFC having millions in funding (from both Republicans and Democrats) and establishing itself as a neutralizer to union bargaining power in the previous election, SFC is not in a position to reveal in undeniable detail what it attempts to soften in flowery reformer rhetoric in its 2012 position statement; Teacher employment tied to "performance" (student test scores) and principal carte blanche in hiring/firing:

> *After the election, Advance Illinois* **and Stand [for Children] had drafted a very bold proposal called Performance Counts. It tied tenure and layoffs to performance; it let principals hire who they choose; it streamlined dismissal of ineffective tenured teachers substantially—from two-plus years and $200 thousand-plus in legal fees on average to three to four months with very little likelihood of legal recourse. And most importantly, called for the reform of collective bargaining throughout the state,** *essentially proposing that school boards would be able to decide any disputed issue and impasse—so a very, very bold proposal for Illinois and* **one that six months earlier** *would have been unthinkable, undiscussable.*[22] [Emphasis added.]

Though they are of opposing political parties, both Gates and Pritzker agree with the teacher disenfranchisement behind SFC's "Performance Counts."

Madigan created the Education Reform Commission and asked Edelman's advice on committee membership:

> *And so in Aurora, Ill., in December [2010], out of nowhere, there were hearings on our proposal. In addition,* **we hired 11 lobbyists, including four of the absolute best insiders, and seven of the best minority lobbyists—preventing the unions from hiring them.** *We enlisted a state public affairs firm. We had tens of thousands of supporters. ...* **We raised $3 million for our political action committee. That's more money than either of the unions have in their political action committees.**[23] [Emphasis added.]

The Pritzker money—Pritzker, who helped Obama raise " the largest amount of campaign cash in history"[24] and who supported Obama Chief of Staff Emanuel for Chicago mayor.

This next excerpt reveals just how reform works: It is a "ramming down the throat" an agenda that serves the elite at the expense of the classroom teacher. Edelman's arrogance is undeniable in his delivery of how he "stuck it to" the union—the collective power of the classroom teacher to fight an obscenely-financed reformer attack:

> **And so essentially what we did in a very short period of time was shift the balance of power.** *And I can tell you* **there was a palpable sense of concern, if not shock, on the part of the teachers unions in Illinois** *that Speaker Madigan had changed allegiance and that we had clear political capability to potentially jam this proposal down their throats the same way pension reform had been jammed down their throats six months earlier. In fact, the pension reform was called Senate Bill 1946, and the unions started talking to each other about "we're not going to let ourselves be 1946 d again," using it as a verb.*[25] [Emphasis added.]

Edelman is proud of himself. He is "standing for children" by "jamming" legislation "down" teachers' "throats."

"Performance Counts" did not make it through the lame duck session. Thus, Edelman and others refocused their efforts on Chicago and formulate legislation designed to curtail union power by introducing "binding arbitration" or some process of negotiation that would in essence make it near impossible for the union membership to organize a strike.

In short, the Chicago Teachers Union (CTU) did not want to sacrifice the right to strike in lieu of "binding arbitration." So, Emanuel—formerly Obama's chief of staff and Chicago's mayor—Edelman, and others decide to set a high union membership vote threshold for the right to strike: 75%. In exchange for retaining the right to strike, CTU President Karen Lewis agrees to a longer school day and longer school year:

> *Rahm pushed it (the 75% strike threshold); [Senator] Kimberly Lightford pushed it;* **we'd done our homework—we knew that the highest threshold of any bargaining unit that had voted one way or the other on a collective bargaining agreement on a contract vote was 48.3%. The threshold that we were arguing for was three-quarters,** *so in effect* **they couldn't have the ability to strike even though the right was maintained.** *And so in the endgame, the Chicago Teachers Union took that deal,* **misunderstanding, probably not knowing the statistics about voting history—and the length of day and year was no longer bargainable in Chicago. ...**

> *So the Senate backed it 59–0, and then the Chicago Teachers Union leader started getting pushback from her membership for a deal that really probably wasn't from their perspective strategic.* **She (Lewis) backed off for a little while but the die had been cast—she had publicly been supportive—so we did some face-saving technical fixes in a separate bill**—*but the House approved it 112-1.* **And a liberal Democratic governor who was elected by public sector unions—that's not even debatable—in fact signed it and took credit for it.** *So we talk about a process that ends up achieving transformational change—***it's going to allow the new mayor and the new CEO [of Chicago schools] to lengthen the day and year as much as they want. The unions cannot strike in Chicago. They will never be able to muster the 75% threshold necessary to strike.**[26] [Emphasis added.]

Edelman shows his shortsightedness in two ways. First, he cannot resist bragging about his accomplishment in a very public forum, thereby revealing how he (and SFC) "play the reformer game" and informing all of the influential, connected people they fooled in the process as to their modus operandi. Second, he assumed that reform pressure could not solidify more than 75% of CTU's teachers in a vote to strike, and in September 2012, he was proved wrong.

Edelman's organization should be renamed based upon Edelman's revealed focus: Stand Against Classroom Teachers.

But it wasn't always this way.

Recall that the 2012 SFC position statement noted it was a "shared point of view to maximize our collective impact."[27] In July 2011, former SFC Oregon parent Susan Barrett decided to leave SFC because of the change from invested, grassroots reform to corporate reform. As Barrett writes in *Parents Across America:*

I recently stepped down as a volunteer co-leader of a Stand for Children (SFC) team in Portland Oregon, the headquarters of this organization. **Being a SFC member has meant fighting for the needs of children and better public schools for all students in this state. However, things have started changing here in Oregon, and I worry that SFC is headed down the path that disaffected parents, like me, identify as the corporate reform movement.** ...

SFC holds a special place for many activist parents and community members in Oregon. **You have to understand that they didn't storm into the state with millions of dollars to influence election outcomes like they did in Illinois. Here, they had far more humble beginnings.**

The organization was inspired by a Stand for Children Day Rally in 1996 in Washington, D.C. Marian Wright Edelman, founder and president of the Children's Defense Fund, enlisted the help of her son, Jonah Edelman, to help organize this event. With over 300,000 people attending, Jonah wanted to keep the spirit alive and continue to work on issues attendees were passionate about. He and a co-founder set up a home base in Oregon, **and worked on smaller issues with positive impact such as after-school program funding and emergency dental care for uninsured kids. Many parents like me who joined SFC a while back still remember how it was an organization fighting for the Portland Children's Levy, which provided funds for early childhood education, foster care, child abuse prevention programs, and a variety of other programs centered on children.**

Because this is part of the organization's history, it makes it that much harder to believe how much it has changed. *Parents and community members most likely do not know that* **SFC now has private equity investors and venture philanthropists on the board, making decisions for the organization** *as it grows new chapters. And, grow they will,* **as they have announced the need to hire a National Expansion Manager, having raised over a million dollars in funding from the Walton Foundation, and over three million dollars from the Gates Foundation.** ...

With SFC inspiring many of its members to run for school board seats, *and the funding it gives through its PAC, I worry we will lose a truly democratic discussion and action on education weighted in favor of corporate reforms.*[28] [Emphasis added.]

SFC has had both an infusion of reformer cash and the infection of the reformer agenda. In addition to the millions previously-mentioned from the Gates Foundation, both the Gates Family Foundation and Microsoft Corporation donated several thousand to SFC in 2010 and 2011. In 2010, the Walton Foundation donated $1.4 million to SFC.[29] In 2011, the amount to SFC was $1.1million;[30] in 2012, that amount decreased to $621,591.[31]

In July 2011, Edelman publicly apologized for the Aspen Ideas Festival video circulating and presenting his unfiltered view of his SFC accomplishments. Though Edelman apologizes for the attitude his words convey, he does not recant the corporate reform agenda SFC promotes. Edelman's seeming contrition is little more than an acknowledged necessity at knowing that a speech meant for the privatizing elite has been circulated among the affected masses.[32]

Edelman is a strategizing privatizer, and he is proud of it. In 2009, his involvement in Denver Public Schools (DPS) board elections stirred controversy, and rightly so. First of all, Edelman does not live in Colorado, yet he traveled to Colorado in an effort to recruit parental involvement in SFC Colorado—including involvement in school politics. Second, keep in mind that SFC is not only a nonprofit; it has SFC Leadership Center, its "advocacy" component—better known as a PAC. PACs do not travel across the country except to influence the political climate of region. Third, by 2009, SFC had already taken over $1.6 million in Gates Foundation money designated for "global policy and advocacy."[33]

At the center of Edelman's Colorado presence was his using the name of high-level DPS administrator Brad Jupp in emails soliciting help from DPS principals in identifying parents who might be interested in SFC involvement. Jupp denied knowledge of Edelman's name-dropping.

Edelman attempted to excuse himself by saying that using Jupp's name was an accident. Nevertheless, Edelman implies that he had Jupp's permission in saying, "…The intention there was simply to be direct about who referred us."[34] The questionable emails apparently were sent via the SRC Colorado director—who later resigned "for personal reasons."[35]

Concerns over Edelman's intentions were magnified by childhood connections he had to another DPS official, Superintendent Tom Boasberg—whose sister, Margaret, had been a member of the SFC national board (she resigned only one month prior, in September 2009).[36] Both Edelman and Boasberg maintain that Edelberg's predecessor, Michael Bennett, was Edelman's contact for coming to Colorado to begin a chapter of SFC and that the arrangement was made without Boasberg's involvement.[37,38] Nevertheless, SFC is a PAC, and as a PAC, it had an agenda to promote: In this case, influencing the election of the DPS board—Boasberg's "boss."[39] In response to the controversy over his presence in Denver and SFC's actions in promoting an agenda that includes promoting public school expansion, Boasberg attempts to convey an "I'm just here to help" neutrality:

*"I consider the school board race a pro and a con, frankly," Edelman said. **"The pro of it was there's an opportunity to help. It feels like there's an important race** where the*

involvement of parents and educators focused only on which candidates would be best for children would help … "[40] [Emphasis added.]

"It feels like this is an important race"—why? Why this race? The words "it feels" is an attempt to convey an innocent uncertainty, yet Edelman knows exactly why he and SFC are in Denver and what they are there to accomplish. Regarding its influence in the DPS board elections, SFC cannot help but brag on its 2011 990:

> *In Colorado, we helped maintain a 4-3 pro-reform majority on the Denver School Board by playing a key role in the election of two reform candidates. Played a significant role in the candidate recruitment process and reached 21,000 voters through phone banks and door to door canvassing during the campaign. We also worked to ensure the successful implementation of SB 191 by influencing the Colorado State Board of Education on the rules for implementing the teacher and principal evaluation system.*[41] [Emphasis added.]

Colorado's SB 191 "…requires that at least 50% of a teacher's evaluation is determined by the academic growth of the teacher's students…."[42] By July 2013, half of a Colorado teacher's evaluation was tied to "multiple measures," all of which are test scores.[43]

In addition to promoting teacher evaluation tied to student test scores in Colorado, SFC's 2011 990 indicates that it both "mobilized members in support of teacher effectiveness regulations" and "helped pass health benefits reform legislation" in Massachusetts. For this, SFC spent just over $800,000.[44] Still, not all "members" wished to be "mobilized" in lock-step to the privatization agenda. As one member of SFC Massachusetts candidly writes:

> *In 2009, I was a member of a local group of Stand for Children in Massachusetts. Even as a relatively new group, we had already successfully engaged in advocacy for new revenues for our local municipality. Late that summer, the Ed reform bill was being discussed by the Massachusetts legislature. We realized there were many provisions in that bill that we disagreed with, some with potentially negative consequences for funding for our local school district. What a rude awakening to learn that the Massachusetts chapter of Stand was supporting the bill and, in fact, pushing for measures that could hurt our local school district. We had formed our local group with the understanding that Stand would help us advocate for funding for public education as was their stated mission and now they were supporting measures that would adversely affect our funding and were also advocating for education policy changes. I was outraged and wondered how Stand which was purportedly a grassroots organization that democratically decided on which issues to pursue as a state could be supporting such legislation that was so unfriendly to public education.*
>
> *Someone I was complaining to advised me with that oft repeated cliché: Follow the money.*

*So I set about researching where Stand was getting their money from and who was governing the various boards. **Once I started uncovering that information for myself, I understood what had happened to Stand for Children. Their revenues were increasingly from individuals and organizations that had their own education reform agendas.** No wonder Stand for Children had changed from a grassroots organization that advocated for funding for public education **to the top-down "reform" policy driven organization they are today.**[45] [Emphasis added.]*

That SFC is willing to callously leverage its corporate reform position has already been proved by Edelman's own disclosure of his actions in Chicago in 2010–11. Edelman's maneuvering is also evident in its proposed 2012 Massachusetts SFC Ballot Initiative. In true Stand Against Classroom Teachers form, SFC's initiative would have sought to alter current law so that teacher experience would not matter in securing another position if a teacher were removed from a position due to school closing, layoff, or position cut. A teacher in such a position would have no guarantees of a job regardless of previous positive evaluation results. In signature SFC fashion, only evaluation results—from an unpiloted evaluation system—would be used in determining which teachers would be allowed to stay when force reduction became an issue. According to the Massachusetts Federation of Teachers, the teacher divesting under the SFC would have been profound:

*...The initiative gives a teacher **little or no ability to appeal a rating**, and **no ability to appeal a layoff decision**. This means that, in cases of staff reductions or school reorganizations, **a teacher could be effectively terminated based on alleged performance flaws—even minor ones—that the teacher has no opportunity to dispute or rectify.***

Current workplace protections—including the requirement that an employer show "just cause" before terminating an experienced teacher—exist so that teachers can advocate for educational quality without fear of retribution.

*But, **under the SFC initiative,** <u>one</u> **not-quite-perfect evaluation—which the teacher has no right to challenge—could cost an experienced, high-quality teacher his or her job in cases of staff reductions or school reorganizations.***

*Removing due process for teachers in this manner would have a chilling effect. It would **rob teachers of their power to speak their minds freely**, since doing so might result in a lower performance rating and a greater risk of job loss.*

*Particularly **vulnerable might be** higher-paid teachers, teachers with health issues, teachers with family obligations, **outspoken teachers, or politically active teachers.**[46]* [Emphasis added.]

Make no mistake whom SFC "stands for": The privatizers of traditional public education. SFC doesn't want the traditional classroom teacher to have any job security, as such interferes with the ability of hedge fund managers to assume control over public education. The SFC Initiative would have allowed an evaluation system to be imposed upon teachers in characteristic, reformer-lauded, top-down fashion.

SFC's goal in proposing the ballot initiative was to hold unions hostage to negotiate the SFC agenda of teacher seniority expunging and due process removal—more of Edelman's "ramming it down their throats." In June 2012, both teachers unions in Massachusetts conceded to SFC's push for legislation mandating the usual reformer-promoted teacher evaluation based in part on student test scores and removal of teacher seniority. The unions viewed the legislation as preferable to the stark mandates of the ballot initiative.[47]

This is SFC "leveraging": Use money and political clout to choke the life out of schools to which those with the money and clout do not send their own children, anyway.

SFC also makes another admission in pushing the teacher evaluation legislation in Massachusetts: Desire to create the statewide data reporting system,[48] a chief aim of Bill Gates,[49] who has donated $9 million to SFC.[50]

In bending to SFC's pressure, the Massachusetts Federation of Teachers offers this observation:

> *AFT Massachusetts said in its statement that it would neither support nor oppose the bill going forward. The union said while it had "deep reservations" about the bill, it judged the compromise to be "far less harmful to our Commonwealth's **first-in-the-nation schools** than the misguided ballot question."*[51] [Emphasis added.]

When it comes to putting public money in private pockets, no state is exempt, not even those who rank highest. Education historian Diane Ravitch offers this comment on SFC's seemingly nonsensical targeting of Massachusetts teachers:

> **Since Massachusetts leads the nation on the no-stakes federal tests called the National Assessment of Educational Progress, it seems difficult to understand how Stand for Children was able to mount a campaign against the state's teachers. But the national atmosphere is so poisonous towards teachers,** *that Stand must have latched onto the sentiment generated by the odious movie "Waiting for 'Superman'"* **and the public relations machine** *of those out to belittle teachers while pretending to care about teacher quality.*[52] [Emphasis added.]

As to the reformer-backed, anti-teacher "public relations machine," the SFC 990 is the place to read for SFC's self-perceived education reform "accomplishments" of its arm of that machine. Another example of SFC in action: It "helped pass SB 1 which mandates the development and piloting of various model evaluation systems across the state and ties teacher tenure and layoff decisions to teacher evaluation ratings" in Indiana. SFC had just arrived in Indiana in 2010; the Illinois-based Joyce Foundation gave SFC Oregon a $150,000 grant for its Indiana launch. Here is a summation of the Indiana teacher evaluation component of SB 1. The language is that of reform:

> *Eliminates the advisory board of the division of professional standards of the department of education. ...* **Establishes an annual staff performance evaluation that categorizes teachers as highly effective, effective, improvement necessary, or ineffective. Specifies that a teacher rated ineffective or improvement necessary may not receive a raise or increment for the following year.** *Repeals references to the advisory board and the existing staff performance evaluation provisions....*[53] [Emphasis added.]

In Indiana, teacher pay must be connected to the teacher evaluation, and the teacher evaluation must be determined in part by student test scores.[54] Moreover, student test scores will impact teacher compensation in 2014.[55] Fortunately for Indiana's teachers, after SB 1 was passed, Indiana gained a new state superintendent who is not a promoter of education reform, Glenda Ritz. Unlike her predecessor, Jeb-Bush-endorsed Tony Bennett, Ritz established a career in the classroom and was a National Board Certified Teacher.[56,57] Ritz has even gone so far as to scrap Bennett's proposed evaluation model, RISE, and she appears to be taking the sting out of the mandate that teachers be evaluated according to student test scores:

> *...***Ritz's vision is very different from Bennett's.** *Teacher quality is an area where she has deep expertise.* **And she's moved quickly to undo some of the supports he put into place for new evaluation system.**
>
> **For example, the Indiana Department of Education's online resources intended to guide administrators and teachers grappling with the new law have been dramatically overhauled.**
>
> **Gone is all reference to RISE, the state's model teacher evaluation system developed by Bennett's team** *that many expected would become the default model at most schools.*
> ...
>
> *One new link is to a video featuring Ritz speaking into the camera about evaluation and* **dropping another bombshell—that her staff plans to revise Bennett-created rules that would have assigned teachers ratings of 1 through 4 based on the ISTEP test score growth of their students** *that districts could use as part of their evaluations.*[58] [Emphasis added.]

In response to Ritz's anti-education-reform agenda of shackling teacher livelihood to student test scores, SFC Indiana Executive Director Justin Ohlemiller promotes the "for the children plus teachers want it" angle:

> *"We have to focus not only on the feedback but also the outcomes we are getting for our kids,"* [Ohlemiller] said. **"We hear from teachers that they want to be measured by outcomes. They are not afraid of that system. They invite it."**[59] [Emphasis added.]

If teachers "wanted " the Bennett system, they could have re-elected Bennett. Despite a Jeb-Bush infusion of cash from a Bennett fundraiser Bush held at his 2012 Foundation for Excellence in Education annual summit,[60] Bennett lost. Ritz won, and it was not due to her outspending reformer-financed Bennett, whose contributions, like those of SFC, included Walton money.[61]

In 2011, SFC spent $442,000 for "advocacy" in Texas.[62] Among other Texas SFC involvements, SFC takes credit for "ending 'last in-first out' retention practices through SB 8" in Texas, yet another state in which SFC's recent arrival marked immediately influencing teacher jobs.[63] Texas' SB 8, the focus of which is teaching furloughs and other means of salary reduction, is a fine example of just how destabilizing education reform can be to traditional public education. The full effect of the bill was delayed for a year due to its inability to override then-current teacher contract conditions. However, SB 8 was able to negatively impact Indiana teacher job security in 2012–13 as follows:

> *Although SB 8 leaves intact the state minimum salary schedule,* **the bill repeals a special salary floor in state law that has blocked rollback of state pay raises below the 2010–2011 level.** *... SB 8 allows a district to impose unpaid furloughs of up to six non-instructional days if the district's funding falls below its 2010–2011 level,* *as determined by the commissioner of education.* *...**Other forms of salary reduction of unspecified extent, such as percentage cuts, can be adopted without first showing that the district's funding falls below its 2010–2011 level.***[64] [Emphasis added.]

Under Texas' SB 8, teacher employment stability is at the mercy of the commissioner of education for certain parts of the law, including the determination that an unpaid furlough is needed. For other parts, teacher employment is controlled by the district. Such is true of the component for which SFC takes credit. As the Texas Federation of Teachers reports:

> **SB 8 repeals a long-established state law that has required terminations of continuing-contract teachers due to necessary reductions of personnel to be made in reverse order of seniority within each teaching field.** *The bill requires such layoffs in the future to be* **based on teacher appraisals and other factors established by the local school board. But please note: The school board thus retains the option of making seniority one of the primary considerations, along with appraisals, in determining the order of layoffs due to a necessary reduction of personnel.**[65] [Emphasis added.]

As such, a local school board in Texas is not allowed to ignore the teacher evaluations, but the board can still make seniority a component of teacher retention in the face of personnel reduction.

SFC's 2011 990 includes one more item worthy of note in this chapter. It happens to be SFC's most expensive political expenditure for the year—

over one million dollars. Discussion of this expenditure will bring the chapter full circle, a return to 2011 in Chicago:

> *In Illinois Stand members and staff helped pass SB 7 early in the year. We also helped defeat HB 3793 to stop a property tax bill that would have stripped hundreds of millions of dollars from public school funding.*[66] [Emphasis added.]

SFC opposition for HB 3793 did benefit tax-capped districts from losing additional revenue in their schools.[67] However, SFC has repeatedly demonstrated its drive to cripple teachers unions and divest teachers of employment rights and security by tying their livelihoods to faulty, punitive evaluation systems.

That was Edelman's goal in "trapping" Chicago Teachers Union in SB 7: The bill that requires a 75% union member vote to strike, and the agreement to both a longer school day and school year. Illinois' SB 7 was the end result of Edelman's political maneuvering to support House Speaker Madigan when the union stood against him on pension reform.

In July 2011, Edelman apologized, but not for his role in SB 7. Here is an excerpt from an apology he wrote as part of the comments to a Seattle Education blog that publicized his 14-minute Aspen gloat:

> *After watching the fourteen minute excerpt and then viewing the whole video of the hour-long session, I want to very sincerely apologize.*
>
> *My shorthand explanation in the excerpt of what brought about the passage of Senate Bill 7 had a slant and tone that doesn't reflect the more complex and reality of what went into this legislation, nor does it reflect my heart and point of view....*[68] [Emphasis added.]

Edelman is not sorry for SB 7. He is not sorry for his leveraging SFC against teachers. *It is what he does.* It is what SFC does. What Edelman's and SFC's actions reveal, over and over again, is that SFC is against the traditional classroom teacher.

Mr. Edelman: No apology replaces your repeated behavior.

I am a traditional classroom teacher, and I know what you are.

CHAPTER 20

BLACK ALLIANCE FOR EDUCATION OPTIONS (BAEO) AND PARENT REVOLUTION (PR)

Some reform organizations attempt to conceal their conservative Republican funding behind the holographic screen of Democratic grass roots. This is useful to privatization, for the nonpartisan appearance can disguise its ultimate greed. This chapter exposes two such deceptive organizations, the Black Alliance for Educational Options (BAEO) and Parent Revolution (PR). Both BAEO and PR have a Democratic face used to hide millions in Republican reformer money; both have a specific and calculated agenda, and both attempt to coerce unsuspecting parents to unwittingly fulfill the wishes of very wealthy in the noble name of parental empowerment.

BAEO

According to its mission statement, the Black Alliance for Educational Options (BAEO) supports "transformational education reform initiatives and parental choice policies that empower low-income and working-class Black families."[1] BAEO might appear to be a grass roots organization; however,

A Chronicle of Echoes: Who's Who in the Implosion of American Public Education,
pages 321–336.

from its very beginnings, BAEO was a billionaire-supported front for corporate reform.

Let us first consider the BAEO board of directors.

BAEO was co-founded in 1999[2] by former Milwaukee Schools Superintendent Howard Fuller,[3] who began the largest school voucher program in the nation. The "success" of the Milwaukee voucher program hinges on use of "intent to treat" analysis. That is, if a student ever accepted a voucher and graduated from high school, researchers credit the student's merely accepting the voucher as "proof" of voucher effectiveness. Thus, if a student accepts a voucher in the freshman year and returns to the community public school as a sophomore through senior and graduates, the researchers from the Walton-funded University of Arkansas' Department of Education Reform credit the student as a graduate associated with the voucher program.[4]

Fuller's wife and hedge-fund manager Deborah McGriff also co-founded BAEO.[5] McGriff is a partner of NewSchools Venture Fund, part of the Edison Schools family (as in Edison, the corporation that former Florida Governor Jeb Bush rescued using Florida teacher pension fund money— see Chiefs for Change chapter) offering "investment opportunities" in a portfolio of corporate-run charter school chains, including Match Charter Schools, Rocketship Education, Khan Academy. GSV Asset Management report credits McGriff's NewSchools Venture Fund as having "helped to create the charter management organization market."[6]

NewSchools Venture Fund is supported by a number of obviously pro-privatizing foundations, including Broad, Gates, and Walton, Carnegie, Casey, and Dell, and reform-friendly individuals including Rupert Murdoch of Wireless Generation and Reed Hastings of Netflix.[7]

Other BAEO board members include hedge-fund managers Mashea Ashton, Daryl Cobb, and Kevin Hinton; executive director of the Pennsylvania branch of Rhee's StudentsFirst, Dawn Chavous, and Association of Christian Schools Director Vernard Gant, who appears to be the only board member not connected to infusions of reformer cash except for his sitting on the BAEO board.[8]

BAEO promotes itself as a "grassroots" organization. Not true. In Washington, DC, in 2000, Howard Fuller announced formation of BAEO and its agenda of vouchers, charters, and public-private partnerships during a National Press Club broadcast. Fuller founded the Marquette University College of Education's Institute for the Transformation of Learning in 1995; BAEO hails from this Institute, which boasts of receiving $14 million in grants "from local and national foundations for working across systems to reform K-12 education in Milwaukee and nationally."[9] BAEO was bankrolled from its inception; following Fuller's announcement of BAEO formation, the organization began running newspaper ads and then commercials in order to "change the face" of the predominately-Republican voucher movement to one that the public would identify with as "the great civil rights issue of our time" or "the civil rights issue of this century" (ironically, a phrase promoted by Bush in 2002[10] and McCain in 2008[11]). As People for the American Way Foundation notes:

> *Almost immediately after formation, BAEO began running print ads in several na-tional newspapers, including the Washington Post, Washington Times, and New York Times, and over a dozen community newspapers with predominantly black readership. The ads feature young African American students and their parents repeating BAEO's mantra, "Parental school choice is widespread—unless you're poor." Designed to put a new face on what has traditionally been a largely white Republican movement, the ads' objective, Fuller explained, "is to change the face of [the voucher] movement."[12]* [Emphasis added.]

This is not grass roots; this is a well-funded, calculated, orchestrated politi-cal maneuver to attempt to market a "choice" that doesn't disappear but that has never thrived: vouchers.

In order to reach an influential audience, BAEO targeted DC legislators and press via radio and television ads following the November 2000 elec-tion. BAEO orchestrated a second ad campaign wave several months later, from April to June 2001. Not everyone was taken in with the content of the ads; rather, some were with wondering about the origin of money enabling waves of sophisticated media blitzes:

> *…Andre Hornsby, president of the National Alliance of Black School Educators in Washington, disagrees [that BAEO is a harbinger of things to come]. "This is America, and they [the BAEO] have a right to present any view they choose to present, but the truth should be told about who they are and who is financing this campaign," Dr. Hornsby says. "What they really represent is the views of a conservative think tank."*
>
> *Hornsby and some other blacks say BAEO—which admits freely that it accepts gener-ous funding from a number of largely white, conservative foundations—is being used by conservatives to put a black face on a white movement.[13]* [Emphasis added]

Upon realizing that his talks given nationwide on vouchers appealed to a predominately white audience, Fuller admits "need[ing] to change the complexion of these rooms (meetings for those interested in vouchers)."[14]

BAEO has a product to sell: school "choice." Though it advocates for a broad array of "choice" options— charters, magnets, open enrollment in public schools, and even home schooling—BAEO's chief goal is the "publicly financed private school voucher for low-income parents in ur-ban settings."[15] In 2001, when it was paying handsomely for its multi-tiered voucher marketing ads, BAEO registered only 1000 members. But it was not the membership that supported BAEO from inception; the money for these ads came from financial support of the Bradley, Walton, and Friedman Foundations. Hornsby finds unsettling the involvement of these very wealthy promoters of corporate reform. Notice Fuller's perspective:

> *"Are the parents financing this [advertising] campaign?" [Hornsby] asks of the current media blitz,* **which according to some reports is costing $3-million, although BAEO will say only that funding for it tops $1.2 million.** *"If not, who is?"*
>
> **But Fuller insists such questions are not important.**[16] [Emphasis added.]

On the contrary, funding is important. As it turns out, the 2001 media ads cost over $4.3 million. Too, a $900,000 grant from the Walton Foundation started BAEO.[17] However, Fuller did not announce the direct connection between the Walton-funded $900,000 operating budget[18] and the BAEO formal launch in DC in 2000. BAEO has operated on a calculated, foundation-financed privatization agenda from Day One. Nevertheless, BAEO's website attempts to promote the idea that BAEO began as a grass roots movement that grew over time:

> *In March 1999, the Institute for the Transformation of Learning (ITL) at Marquette University convened the First Annual Symposium, a meeting of 150 Black people in Milwaukee, Wisconsin, to discuss parental choice and the educational challenges facing disadvantaged Black families in America. At that time, the charter school movement was growing, and parental choice was gaining currency among progressive policymakers and at the grassroots....*
>
> *The Second Annual Symposium, hosted again by ITL, drew approximately 350 attendees, 90 of whom met subsequently to continue organizing BAEO. At this meeting, participants reviewed the first draft of the organization's bylaws and elected Dr. Howard Fuller as President of the Board (the title was later changed to Chair of the Board). A 29-member board formed and met for the first time on June 17, 2000. The organization officially launched with a press conference at the National Press Club in Washington, DC, on August 24, 2000.*
>
> *BAEO* **has grown to become** *the preeminent national organization....*[19] [Emphasis added.]

BAEO didn't need to "grow"; through foundation cash, it was almost immediately engaged in a national media blitz. Whereas the details of the first two paragraphs may well be accurate, the deception lay in BAEO's omission of its immediate and profound infusion of reformer money.

Fuller has accepted money from the Bradley and Walton Foundations, hardly known for supporting anything that might promote "a civil rights issue." As the New Jersey Education Association observes in 2004:

> *Ironically, the Bradley and Walton foundations have spent hundreds of millions of dollars opposing affirmative action, civil rights, and equal educational opportunity through front organizations, ballot initiatives, and other like-minded foundations.*

> *In 1994, the Bradley Foundation **paid Charles Murray $1 million to write The Bell Curve...**, the controversial book that claimed blacks were genetically incapable of learning at high levels, making its subsequent support of BAEO all the more cynical—and all the more deserving of closer scrutiny.*

> *In 2002, President Bush gushed: "The Bradley Foundation has always been willing to seek different solutions. **They've been willing to challenge the status quo.** And the foundation has not only been kind and generous with its donations, the foundation also has been willing to help people think anew."*[20] [Emphasis added.]

Money makes corporate reform appear both nonpartisan and nonsensical by revealing a common ultimate motive: greed. Corporate reform is all about making money via a fronted agenda of "choice."

There is a reason that Milwaukee-based BAEO moved to DC: To leverage its power.[21] Walton and Bradley money enabled BAEO to increase its leverage, right up to the Oval Office. From 2002–04, BAEO received over one million dollars in US Department of Education (USDOE) grant money for a

> *"**multi-layered media campaign**" that would "utilize direct mail, radio, newspaper, the Internet and direct engagement techniques." Further, [BAEO] hoped to contact eligible parents and community leaders "a minimum of three times... **about the benefits of NCLB.** In addition... "BAEO also hopes to continue to change the conversation about parental choice **by positively influencing individuals who are resisting parental choice options and getting them to reconsider their outlook.**"*

> *...All of the products, which were designed to reach families in Dallas, Detroit, Milwaukee and Philadelphia, provided information to eligible parents regarding their rights to 1) **know if their child's school has been designated "in need of improvement";** 2) **transfer their child to another school;** and 3) get supplemental education services for their child, such as free tutoring. All of the materials were informational; **none of them contained the required disclaimer.**[22] [Emphasis added.]*

Not only did BAEO receive substantial USDOE money; BAEO used that money to finance ads promoting the USDOE agenda without informing the public that the USDOE paid for the ads. This is illegal, for it raises the possibility that the USDOE distributed this grant money with the intent of covertly promoting the NCLB agenda. The 2005 Office of Inspector General (OIG) report quoted above did not find that the USDOE issued the money with the intent that BAEO should omit the required disclaimer from its ads. However, as is evident from the tenor of the report and the frequency with which disclaimer omission occurs, OIG is concerned about the seriousness of such appearances.

BAEO markets education reform. BAEO is in the education reform business.

Consider also the BAEO board—chiefly comprised of hedge-fund managers. Such is not the mark of "homegrown" reform. Neither is the presence of the billionaire foundations that continue to support BAEO's reformer agenda. From 2009–12, the Walton Foundation donated almost $3.4 million to BAEO.[23-26] The Gates Foundation donated $4 million from "2009 and before" and an additional $350,000 in 2011–12.[27]

Given so much Gates money, one should expect BAEO to heartily endorse the unpiloted, corporate-created, politically-promoted Common Core State Standards (CCSS):

> *The standards were designed by a diverse group of teachers, experts, parents, and school administrators. The purpose of the standards is to outline **exactly what skills and knowledge students should obtain** at each step in their academic instruction in order to be prepared for college and career. **This will ensure that both educators and parents understand what the student should learn as they progress through the educational system.***
>
> ***CCSSI will be a state driven effort.** State adoption of the standards is voluntary and each state has flexibility in determining how to implement the standards in their state. Although a state adopts the standards, each state will determine its own curriculum. The **standards are intended to set clear expectations on what all students should learn, however, each state must determine the best way for their students to reach the academic goals set by CCSSI.**[28] [Emphasis added.]*

BAEO's promotion of CCSS incorrectly assures readers that CCSS is "state driven" and "developed" by "teachers" (listed first). In contrast, the federal government was active in both CCSS development and promotion (see chapter on David Coleman and Frederick Hess.), and the BAEO promo makes no mention of CCSS "architect" David Coleman, or College Board, or ACT as being overwhelmingly represented at the CCSS drafting table. In addition, BAEO is doing a sales job on its readers; no one has evidence that CCSS "ensures" anything or that CCSS "skills and knowledge" are "exactly" what students need to learn. Finally, BAEO appears to have no issue with these untested "standards" also having mandated CCSS exams, mysteriously developed by Someone and not created until after Race to the Top (RTTT)-coerced, CCSS adoption by most states.

Gates will be pleased.

Given the millions BAEO has taken from billionaire Republicans with a clear privatization agenda, even those with an established history of funding projects evidencing anti-African-American sentiment,[29] I find incredible irony in this statement by Kevin Campbell, BAEO President, on advertising the 2013 BAEO Symposium:

We cannot have an America where people with money are the only people who get to choose how and where their children are educated.[30]

What we have is an America where people with money are fast becoming the only people who get to choose how and where the majority of children—"other people's children"—are educated.

The White billionaires are the choosers for all of America, and they are choosing to put public school money into both their own and their cronies' private pockets. In taking their money, BAEO becomes their accomplice.

PARENT REVOLUTION

Parent Revolution (PR) is yet another in the long line of pro-privatization organizations to present a homegrown veneer over the corporately-funded education reform agenda. PR's specialty is in convincing parents to "take over" community schools via the "parent trigger" legislation active in many states. Once PR gathers enough parent signatures for the "take over," parents then learn that they just handed their community schools over to privately-run charters. And the parents have no control over reversing the decision. They have been tricked into believing they had control when they were only being used to deliver control to privatizers. For this reason, "parent trigger" has earned the nickname "parent tricker."

In December 2010, the American Legislative Exchange Council (ALEC) featured parent trigger model legislation at its States and Nation Policy Summit in Washington, DC. The sponsor of the model legislation was Mark Oestreich of the Heartland Institute in Chicago, one of many conservative think tanks promoting privatization of the public sector. One of Heartland's donors is the Charles Koch Foundation[31] —as in the Koch brothers—as in long-time funders and supporters of ALEC.[32] Other Heartland funders include Bill Gates' Microsoft Corporation, the Bradley Foundation, and the Friedman Foundation.[33]

In its 2010 DC meeting, ALEC introduced Heartland Institute as a "new member" of the education task force. Here is what Oestreich was promoting for ALEC to adopt and push through statehouses around the country:

> *The Parent Trigger places democratic control into the hands of parents at school level. Parents can, with a simple majority, opt to usher in one of three choice-based options of reform: (1) transforming their school into a charter school, (2) supplying students from that school with a 75 percent per pupil cost voucher, or (3) closing the school.*[34]

According to the Parent Trigger proposed model, the "choice" parents have is to gather the signatures of over half of the parents/guardians of students currently attending or who would yield from feeder schools in order to invoke one of the three choices above. It is important to note that if parents opt for charter takeover, parents have limited control over what charter operator will run the school or how that charter operator will operate.

The parent trigger model legislation is pro-privatization; as such, it does not allow parents to petition to deliver a charter school back to its former school board. In addition, if the parents choose the option to close the school and no other schools are within "reasonable proximity" to the close school, then the "option" becomes the voucher option. Finally, incoming students to the "triggered" school automatically qualify for vouchers to attend private schools.[35]

Parent trigger has a number of contingencies designed to benefit privatizers.

Although promoted to be adopted as ALEC model legislation, the parent trigger originated in California with a group called the Los Angeles Parents Union, whose web address is parentrevolution.com, and whose leader is Ben Austin. Austin was already in the privatization business associated with Green Dot Charter Schools. In January 2010, the parent trigger barely passed the California legislature (by one vote in each branch) in an effort to garner Race to the Top money.[36] However, the positioning of the Los Angeles Parent Union/Parent Revolution was happening in the years prior to passage of California's parent trigger legislation.

Before being connected with PR, Austin was associated with Green Dot charters. Indeed, via Green Dot, Austin takes credit for "transforming" Locke High School, "the worst school in Los Angeles into a college preparatory model of reform."[37] In 2006, Eli Broad announced that he would invest $10.5 million in Steve Barr's Green Dot Education Project.[38] Sadly, Locke High School became a casualty to Barr's amply-funded "experiment." Austin was able to benefit from Locke's undoing. In 2007, Austin was paid $95,000 by Green Dot for "consulting"[39] If a "model of reform" involves dividing a school into several smaller schools, closing and reopening these smaller schools multiple times, and finally putting some but not all back together into one school again, all inside of five years, the yes, Locke is a "model of reform."[40] Teacher and administrator turnover at this "model" is astounding, with only a handful of teachers remaining through multiple years and no original, 2008 administrators remaining. The overwhelming majority of teachers are temporary teachers hailing from Teach for America (TFA).[41] This is what billionaire money buys.

PR/ Los Angeles Parent Union was the brainchild of Green Dot charters; according to its 2008 990, the organization was formed in 2007. On the 2007 990 for the Los Angeles Parent Union, the address listed is 350 South Figouroa Street, Los Angeles—the same address as Green Dot Educational Project (charters). Green Dot Executive Director and CEO Steve Barr is listed as the Los Angeles Parent Union president, and Green Dot CEO Marco Petruzzi is listed as a Los Angeles Parent Union member. Ten other individuals are listed, and all twelve (including Barr and Petruzzi) use 350 South Figueroa Street, Los Angeles, as their address. On the 2007

Green Dot 990, Green Dot board member Steve Barr earns $215,467 in his position as Green Dot executive director/CEO; Petruzzi earns $204,022 as CEO.[42]

There's more.

On the 2008 990 forms of both Green Dot and Los Angeles Parent Union/ PR (PR was not listed as a name until 2008), the two groups continue to share a common address: 350 South Figueroa Street in Los Angeles.[43] On the 2008 PR 990, Steve Barr is listed as the "principal officer."[44] That same year, Steve Barr was paid $198,855 as a Green Dot board member—not as executive director/CEO. In the listing of board members and employees, the title next to Barr's name is written in all caps—BOARD MEMBER—as though it were written another way first and later changed. And oddly enough, Barr is the only "board member" working 40 hours a week and earning a salary.[45]

The fishiness continues on the 2008 PR 990: Even though the "principal officer" is Steve Barr, the signature on the 2008 Parent Revolution 990 is Ben Austin's. He signed with the title, "executive director," and he dated the form August 10, 2009. At some point between the typing of Steve Barr's name at the top of the form as "principal officer" and the signing of Austin's name at the bottom of the same form, Austin "became" executive director.[46]

Wait. There is still more.

On its 2009 990, PR has both a new principal officer and a new address: Ben Austin; 315 West Ninth Street, Los Angeles. And yet, as recorded on the 2007 Green Dot 990, Austin's home address is in Beverly Hills. Since Austin was listed as an independent consultant with Green Dot, Green Dot was required to include Austin's home address on its 2007 990. As of 2013, Austin was still registered as living in Beverly Hills, California.

Austin is not a Los Angeles parent. Austin was on the Green Dot payroll before he assumed Green Dot Executive Barr's position as "principal officer" of the Los Angeles-based Parent Revolution.

So much for the "Los Angeles 'parent' union." PR is nothing more than Green Dot prefabrication. What money there is to be made for charters if one can pass legislation "empowering" parents to hand over their neighborhood schools to charter operators! And what if this new "grass roots prefab," the Los Angeles Parent Union, could be handed over to someone already credited with "turning around" the "worst school in Los Angeles"?

In its promoting California's parent trigger before an ALEC audience, Heartland Institute members emphasize that this model legislation originated "from the left":

> *The Parent Trigger concept is the creation of the Los Angeles Parents Union, a group of self-described progressives led by Ben Austin, a Democrat.... The Parent Trigger is unique. Unlike most reform proposals based on empowering parents, the Parent Trig-*

ger originates from activists on the political left, not from the center-right coalition.[47] [Emphasis added.]

Apparently, Heartland believes that part of the "selling power" of the parent trigger is its appearing to originate with Democrats. Yet in 2009, Broad had already given $50,000 to the Los Angeles Parent Union,[48] and Walton had already donated $100,000. In 2010, Walton increased its donation to $500,000;[49] also in 2010, Gates donated $700,250, and Broad, $787,000[50] The Republican money was already overwhelmingly behind the Democratic, "grass roots" front.

In 2007, the Los Angeles Parent Union received $323,343 in "gifts, grants, and contributions."[51] In 2008, the amount was around the same: $343,860. However, in 2009, contributions almost doubled: $651,208.[52]

And then came the jump.

In 2010, on its 990, the Los Angeles Parent Union reported $3.7 million in contributions.[53]

California now had a parent trigger law in effect. Time to get to work.

Many parents of students at Desert Trails Elementary in Aledanto, California, thought that signing a petition for "parent takeover" of their school would result in better options for their children and their community. There to stir the issue and collect the signatures was PR. As Sephanie Simon of Reuters reports in March 2012:

> *Desert Trails Elementary School in the impoverished town of Adelanto, California, has been failing local kids for years. More than half the students can't pass state math or reading tests.*
>
> *On Tuesday, the school board will discuss a radical fix: **a parent takeover of the school**.*
> ...
>
> ***A 2010 California law permits parents at the state's worst public schools to band together and effectively wrest control from the district. The parents can enact dramatic changes, such as firing teachers, ousting the principal, or converting the school into a charter institution run by a private management company.*** *...*
>
> *A determined group of Desert Trails parents is leading the charge, **with substantial help from a well-funded activist group, Parent Revolution**. The trigger advocates say they have collected signatures from a majority of families **in support of closing down the school this summer and reopening it as a charter school in the fall, to be run by a partnership of parents, teachers and the school district.***[54] [Emphasis added.]

It sounds so promising, so empowering—parents taking over. In reality, only a handful of parents—with "substantial help" from an organization receiving millions from those with a clear agenda to privatize—orchestrated the takeover. In 2013, PR's website included the Big Three in Republican reformer money: the Gates, Walton, and Broad Foundations.[55] Gates contributed almost $1 million dollars to the Los Angeles Parent Union in 2012, and Walton increased its donation to $1.2 million in 2011 and to $2.5 million in 2012. Such ample financing allows Parent Revolution to rent a house in the locale where it focuses its efforts.[56] It needs a local headquarters, and renting a house as opposed to an office building does lend an appearance of "homegrown" to so much corporate funding.

I wonder if any of the parents signing the petition for "takeover" understood exactly whose money provided the "substantial help." And I wonder how many knew the details of the 2010 Parent Trigger Law—and just how little "parent empowerment" there would be once the charter moved in. Simon includes some of these details in her article:

> *One chain of charter schools heavily backed by [Gates, Broad, and Walton] foundation money, for instance, is* **Green Dot—which founded the predecessor to Parent Revolution.** *Many of the 14 Green Dot charter schools in California have shown impressive academic progress,* **but all still fall below the state median on standardized test scores. Half rank lower—many far lower—than Desert Trails. Nationally, studies suggest that charter schools rarely outperform regular public schools of similar demographics.**[57] [Emphasis added.]

Parent Revolution promises parents that they are "here to support you." Those supporting the trigger say that they don't intent to convert all schools into charters—which is technically true since vouchers are part of the package, as well.

Not to worry: Parent Revolution members are also willing to work with other groups—such as StudentsFirst. And they are even willing to cross party lines and work with former Florida Governor Jeb Bush in promoting parent trigger in Florida.[58] (Appearance is important; like BAEO, the group takes Republican money but retains its Democratic face.)

By October 2012, the fight continued for Desert Trails Parent Union (sounds a lot like a transplant of the fabricated Los Angeles Parent Union) to take control of their local school and turn it over to a charter operator. That's right. "Take control" and "turn over." The only control is in the parent's writing the signature on the petition. And here is the crux of the matter:

> *Influential groups like Parent Revolution and StudentsFirst have been lobbying for the cause and searching for parents to test out the fledgling laws. The legislation's supporters are pouncing on the chance to use "Won't Back Down," which is financed by conservative billionaire Philip Anschutz's Walden Media, to popularize the parent-trigger policy.*[59] [Emphasis added.]

Parent Revolution is using these parents for their own ends—money in hedge-fund pockets. Groups like StudentsFirst are there to help, and Rhee is happy to promote the glamorized propaganda film, *Won't Back Down*, in an effort to incite parents against their community schools.

Despite its famous cast, including Maggie Gyllenhaal, Viola Davis, Holly Hunter, and Rosie Perez, *Won't Back Down* was a box office failure—worst film opening ever.[60]

It could be that parents do not want to seize control of their schools only to hand control over to a charter operator. However, Parent Revolution wants them to, and so, Parent Revolution will spend its millions to claim success. Austin does not see *Won't Back Down* for the propagandistic failure that it was. In fact, he even paints parent trigger as a "movement" despite the fact that two years have passed since parent trigger became a law in California and no school had been "taken over" by "empowered" parents:

> *"Usually a movie like this comes out long after a social movement and documents it through the eyes of the hero," said Ben Austin, founder of Parent Revolution and former Clinton White House adviser.* **"But this movie is coming out in the almost embryonic stage of the movement, and will sort of become part of the movement.** *We see it, frankly,* **as just another powerful organizational tool** *to educate parents about their rights."*[61] [Emphasis added.]

The very day that Austin's comment was printed in the Huffington Post, *the* Post *published its article about* Won't Back Down *scoring worst opening weekend ever.*

> *No time to stop and think that the film's poor reception might actually complement the public's disinterest in a parent trigger law that was two years old and had never been utilized. It isn't like Parent Revolution had not been trying:*

> *Parent Revolution's first attempt—in 2010 at McKinley Elementary in Compton, Calif.—ultimately died in court. The charter operator picked by Parent Revolution still managed to get approval to open a school close to McKinley,* **but less than one-fifth of McKinley parents moved their children there.**[62] [Emphasis added.]

Parent Revolution even recruited two of the Desert Trails Parent Union members to travel and promote the film, with Parent Revolution covering the cost of the trips.[63]

As for Desert Trails Elementary, the Parent Union members approached the school board with a list of demands that could not be fulfilled absent additional funding, including requiring that all teachers have a masters degree and reducing all class sizes. As leverage, of course, the Parent Union had its petitions—two different petitions.

Here is where the "parent tricker" comes to bear:

> **The parent union had parents sign two petitions**—*one for those reforms (the reforms demanded at the school board meeting)* **and another to convert Desert Trails into a charter school.** *The plan was to use the charter school petition as leverage to negotiate*

*with district officials to get more parent control and new teacher contracts, **but the charter school petition was the only one ever submitted to the district.**...*

*Some parents said they felt betrayed and confused by the two-petition strategy. They
claimed **they'd been told that signing the petition meant their children would get new
technology like iPads**, cleaner bathrooms and extended school days, **but did not expect
teachers to lose their jobs as the school turned charter.***[64] [Emphasis added.]

Parents who wanted out of the situation were not allowed to rescind their
signatures despite the fact that there were two competing petitions. In July
2012, a San Bernardino Superior Court judge ruled that the parent trigger
law does not allow for rescinding signatures.[65] Due to resistance, another
Superior Court ruling was required in order to enforce proceeding with
the charter takeover. In October 2012, those parents who signed for charter
takeover were the ones who were able to vote on which charter school operator could come take over the school. Ben Austin calls this "taking back
power."[66]

Only the petition signers were allowed to vote on a ballot with only two
choices for charter operators. The parents did not select the operators; on
the contrary, the operators selected Desert Trails.

An US Inspector General's audit released in September 2012 indicated
that California charters were grossly under-regulated by the US Department of Education.[67] Given that a California charter company started Parent Revolution, it appears illogical to believe that Parent Revolution would
have informed Desert Trails parents of the differences in oversight between
local community schools and charters. In fact, the wording of the 2010 parent trigger law (amazingly called the Parent Empowerment Act) does not
allow for open and frank discussion by of the problems of parent trigger
since such might be determined to "impede the signature gathering process." Los Angeles Unified School Board member Steve Zimmer wants to
introduce a change to the parent trigger law so that parents might be informed of both the advantages and disadvantages of proceeding with the
parent trigger petition.[68,69]

In January 2013, the Aledanto School Board approved the parent vote to
have the selected charter operator, LaVerne Elementary Preparatory Academy, assume control of Desert Trails Elementary.[70]

In the end, it was not a majority of parents of returning Desert Trails
Elementary students who voted to fire teachers and administration and
hand over the school to a charter operator. As to the actual "empowering"
vote: 286 parents signed the petition seeking charter takeover. Over 100 of
those parents were no longer affiliated with Desert Trails due to a change
of school year from the time the petition was signed to the time the vote
was taken. That left 180 parents eligible to cast a vote to decide upon the

charter operator. In the end, only 53 parents chose to vote—18.5% of those who originally signed to bring the issue to a vote in the first place.[71]

The 127 parents who chose not to vote must not have seen a choice that empowered them on the ballot.

As to the 53 voters: Something is terribly wrong with this scenario if so few parents are deciding the fate of a public school that they do not own to begin with.

As for the leader of the Desert Trails Parent Union, Doreen Diaz: she landed a job with Parent Revolution. Spokesman David Phelps sees no conflict of interest in such an arrangement:

> *In February [2012],* **after the Adelanto Elementary School District voted to approve the group's parent trigger petition, Diaz was hired by Parent Revolution** *as one of their community organizers, Phelps said.*
>
> *"She went through the normal interview process and application. She stepped down from any position in DTPU when she knew she was going to apply," he said.*
>
> **"I think it's to our benefit to have parents who have been involved in efforts with us who tell us they'd like to be full-time organizers** *be able to go on the ground with other parents at other schools, knowing the likely challenges that may come up."*[72] [Emphasis added.]

Diaz just spent over six months pushing the parent trigger. She was the local public face for the Parent Revolution's first success at forcing what they call "parent choice" even when parents decided they wanted out. As a result, the group that benefits from her push is able to promote itself as successful. But hiring Diaz was not Parent Revolution's idea; she "told them" she wanted to be paid from Parent Revolution's billionaire-supported education reform coffer.

Parent trigger legislation barely passed in California, where it was promoted as part of a package to attempt to secure RTTT funding. Other states have resisted the trigger, including Colorado, Georgia, Oklahoma,[73] and even Jeb Bush's Florida, where Bush really wants the trigger legislation to pass.[74] By 2013, only seven states had passed Parent Trigger legislation: California, Connecticut, Indiana, Louisiana, Mississippi, Ohio, and Texas.[75]

PR's second "victory" was in their home base of Los Angeles and involved the removal of Weigand Elementary School Principal Irma Cobian, by parent petition via the parent trigger law. In this case, the parent leader, Llury Garcia, desired to take charge by ousting only Cobian and retaining the faculty. However, in an amazing display of loyalty, 21 out of 22 teachers requested transfers from Weigand upon learning of Cobian's dismissal. As one might expect, the petition to remove Cobian was PR-orchestrated:

> *Parent leader Llury Garcia said that* **although her second-grade daughter has done fairly well at Weigand, Cobian was inaccessible and rude.** *She and other petition backers* **were assisted by Parent Revolution,** *a Los Angeles nonprofit* **that lobbied for the parent trigger law and is aiding overhaul efforts at several other Los Angeles campuses.**[76] [Emphasis added.]

Cobian was working to improve Weigand, and her efforts were lauded by LAUSD administration:

> *Los Angeles Unified Supt. John Deasy* **praised a plan developed by Cobian and her team to turn around the struggling campus**—*where most students test below grade level in reading and math—calling it a "well-organized program for accelerated student achievement."* **He thanked Cobian for her commitment and hard work.**[77] [Emphasis added.]

Cobian had a school improvement plan that was working. She had the help and support of her faculty. She had the endorsement of her superintendent. And yet none of that matters when a heavily-funded privatization group can take a law that it promoted and use it to manipulate pettiness into career termination.

In a sad commentary on who is really in charge of the parent trigger, parents voted to move forward on the school improvement plan formulated by the principal they just fired. According to accounts at Desert Trails Elementary, PR showed up with its own people sporting PR t-shirts and infiltrating the campus with the clear goal to incite a "revolution."[78] Garcia might have been the leader, but she was not the one in charge.

As for Cobian's careful school improvement plan: Garcia never read it. Nevertheless, that doesn't stop her from having an opinion already acknowledged to be rooted in ignorance:

> **This week, parents voted to accept Cobian's turnaround plan as the next step forward.** *Although a Parent Revolution statement quoted Garcia as saying that parents "spent several months carefully reviewing" the plan,* **she told The Times last week that she had never read it and disagreed with key elements, such as its focus on reading and writing.**[79] [Emphasis added.]

The vote is irrelevant given that Cobian and virtually the entire faculty are leaving Weigand. The school will be a different school, and not likely for the better: PR effectively ousted Weigand's faculty community, and constructive teaching communities require time and nurturing to build.

By methodically spreading discord, PR destroys school communities. On its website, PR portrays itself as working alongside parent groups that PR itself did not foster. The website is craftily written so as to convey the idea that the "parent unions" are just "happening,": "roughly a dozen chapters have formed...."[80] Yet for all of its well-designed web links, PR has little to show for its efforts at privatizing. The parent trigger law has been around since

2010, and the seven states with parent trigger laws are not yielding school takeovers one must hope for when promoting parent trigger legislation. What is more, the word is spreading regarding the tactics PR uses to insert itself into an unsuspecting school community for the purpose of promoting charters and vouchers. As a result, parents are choosing—to reject PR for the corporate front that it is.

CHAPTER 21

KNOWLEDGE IS POWER PROGRAM (KIPP): WHAT MONEY CANNOT SEEM TO DO

In 1994, two former Teach for America graduates, Michael Feinberg and Dave Levin, founded the Knowledge is Power Program (KIPP), one of the largest charter school chains in the United States.[1] Feinberg and Levin each taught for three years (1991–1994)[2,3] on a few weeks of crash-course, TFA training; then, as many reformers do, they decided leadership in education was the business for them. They began small; Feinberg established KIPP Academy in Houston, and Levin, KIPP Academy in New York. By 2000, Feinberg and Levin were receiving funding from Donald and Doris Fisher (Fisher Foundation; Gap, Inc.).[4] Don and Doris Fisher co-founded the KIPP Foundation to fund KIPP schools.[5]

As one might expect, the Fishers are well represented on the KIPP board of directors, where they keep company with Carrie Walton Penner (Walton Foundation), Mark Nunnely of Bain Capital, Michael Lomax of the United Negro College Fund, Reed Hastings of NetFlix, and Katherine Bradley of CityBridge and Washington regional board of TFA, among others.[6]

A Chronicle of Echoes: Who's Who in the Implosion of American Public Education,
pages 337–352.

The Fishers were the financial springboard for KIPP, as a 2009 *Gotham Schools* article notes:

> *The Fishers have given KIPP over $50 million since the network began with two schools in 2000, funding initiatives aimed at replicating the original schools around the country, such as principal training programs and professional development for teachers.*[7] [Emphasis added.]

Enter the KIPP "Fisher Fellows": The Fisher Fellowship enables the franchising of KIPP by financially supporting for a one year internship individuals who wish to become "founding principals" of KIPP charters. KIPP also has a Miles Family Fellowship to pay for the year-long training of KIPP grade-level chairs, department chairs, and lead teachers.[8]

Incredible cash flowed into KIPP for charter replication. We live in a time in which billionaires have decided that privatizing public education is their "cause." This philanthropy bankrolling enables two young men with minimal experience in teaching and no experience in education administration to "start a business" that just happens to be a chain of schools.

In 2011 and 2012, KIPP Chicago received $75,000[9,10] from the Joyce Foundation, an Illinois-based foundation whose influence extends to the Oval Office. President Obama was on the Joyce Foundation board of directors from 1994 to 2002,[11,12] and he has made removing the charter school caps a requirement for Race to the Top (RTTT) funding. The Joyce Foundation's interest in advancing charters is extends to at least 1997.[13] Here is a noteworthy coincidence: Even though KIPP Chicago had been in existence since 2003,[14] it was not until post-RTTT that KIPP Chicago began receiving Joyce Foundation contributions.

Before becoming president and instituting RTTT, Obama had already intervened for KIPP Chicago. In 2008, at the request of the *Chicago Sun-Times*, then-Illinois Senator Obama agreed to publicize all of the earmark requests he made since becoming senator in 2005. Included among them was this one, made in 2006 for KIPP Chicago:

> *Obama requested $200,000 For the Knowledge Is Power Program's (KIPP) Ascend Charter School in Chicago. In 2006, Obama requested $200,000 For the Knowledge Is Power Program (KIPP) to support the KIPP Ascend Charter School in Chicago. The KIPP Ascend Charter School, which opened in the summer of 2003, is modeled on the two original KIPP Academies and has grown to serve the fifth through eighth grade in middle school. KIPP schools are tuition-free, open enrollment, college prep public middle schools, and the students are accepted regardless of prior academic record or socioeconomic background. 100 percent of KIPP Ascend students are African American or Latino, 90 percent qualify for the free and reduced meal program. In order to continue serving students in this high-need community and maintain their stellar student achievement record, $200,000 in federal funding is needed to help ensure that these talented students in Chicago are able to continue on the path to college and life-long suc-*

cess. [Obama Request Letter To Senate Appropriations Subcommittee on Labor, Health, Education, 4/5/06][15][Emphasis added.]

"Tuition-free" is a chameleon term; in reality, "tuition-free" means that the families do not pay directly for the school; however, as a "public" charter school, this KIPP school siphons money from the community school budget. Thus, Obama earmarked $200,000 for a school already positioned to choke the financial life out of area community schools.

Obama's actions make it obvious that for KIPP, the favoritism does not stop with its philanthropic edge. KIPP abounds in both charitable donations as well as a privileged padding of public funds. According to a 2011 analysis of department of education databases, Western Michigan researcher Gary Miron and others found that KIPP schools receive more public funding per student than did either traditional public schools or other charter schools. In 2007–08, the average public disbursement for KIPP students was $12,731 per pupil, when the average disbursement for traditional public school students was $11,960 per child and the average for other charter school students, $9,579 per student. The department of education data included no explanation for the additional funding to KIPP.[16]

As for federal funding, KIPP also beats the competitors. Based upon the 2007–08 federal dataset of school finance for 25 KIPP schools and corresponding local districts, KIPP's per-student federal allotment was $1,779, a larger amount than was paid to corresponding local districts ($1,332), the nationwide charter district average ($949) or the national average in general ($922).[17]

Finally, as to private contributions, Miron reports the following:

> *None of the 12 KIPP districts reported any private revenues in the NCES finance survey; however,* **a separate analysis of these districts' 990 tax forms for 2007–08 revealed large sums of private contributions.** *Per-pupil contributions for the 11 KIPP districts that we could include in this analysis equaled* **an average of $5,760, much more than the $1,000 to $1,500 additional per-pupil revenue KIPP estimates is necessary for their program. Two KIPP districts or groups received more than $10,000 per pupil in private revenues.**[18] [Emphasis added.]

KIPP has clearly outpaced both traditional public schools and its charter counterparts in the funding that it has available per student:

> *Combining public and private sources of revenue,* **KIPP received, on average, $18,491 per pupil in 2007–08. This is $6,500 more per pupil than what the local school districts received in revenues.**[19] [Emphasis added.]

There is more to "power" than "knowledge." In 2011, *Democratic Underground* blogger "Madfloridian" reflects upon the apparent fiscal favoritism KIPP experiences:

> *It would be interesting to know in what other years KIPP received more mon-*
> *ey than public schools and other charters.* **It is odd that could happen at all.**
> **We know that KIPP and TFA are among the largest recipients of federal education**
> **money. What is not so well known is that the founder of TFA is the wife of a head of**
> **the KIPP charters** (Richard Barth). *And many do not realize that* **last year they each**
> **got 50 million from the DOE** (US Department of Education).[20]

Madfloridian is citing a *New York Times* article reporting on the 2010 US-DOE Investing in Innovation Grant money:

> *Teach for America, the nonprofit group that recruits elite college students to teach*
> *in public schools,* **and the KIPP Foundation, which runs a nationwide network**
> **of charter schools, were big winners** *in a $650 million federal grant competition*
> *known as Investing in Innovation, the Department of Education said Wednesday.*
> **Each group won $50 million.** ...
>
> *The $650 million was given out in awards of three levels.* **The four largest awards of**
> **nearly $50 million each went to groups proposing to greatly expand programs, like**
> **Teach for America and the KIPP charters, that the department viewed has having**
> **been proved successful.**[21]

There is a slant to these incredibly large awards, one that illustrates how money leads to money:

> **In order to qualify for the awards, all the winning groups must obtain 20 percent**
> **matching pledges from foundations or other private sector donors** *by Sept. 8, the de-*
> *partment said.* **Each of the groups that won $50 million, for instance, must persuade**
> **private donors to give an additional $10 million to support their projects.**[22] [Em-
> phasis added.]

The privatization edge. Groups advancing the USDOE-endorsed educa-tion reform agenda tend to be those already connected to foundation and hedge-fund money. KIPP is receiving larger sums of public money for its students than are traditional public schools and other charters, and it is infusing its schools with incredible sums of private contributions. For ex-ample, based upon KIPP 990 information on the internet, contributions and grants to KIPP DC in 2007 was $6.2 million, and in 2008, rose to $15.2 million.[23] KIPP LA (Los Angeles) exceeded $12 million in 2009 and $16 million in 2010.[24] In 2009, KIPP Austin received over $11 million in contri-butions and grants; in 2010, the sum rose to over $14 million.[25]

In a May 2012, the National Education Policy Center (NEPC) produced a study of schools in New York, Ohio, and Texas. The researchers make the following observations concerning KIPP NY spending:

> *...The Green Dot School reported spending $552 to $870 more per pupil than similar*
> *NYC BOE schools. Spending in Achievement First schools and Success Academies was*
> *comparable to that of NYC BOE schools.* **By contrast, the city's KIPP academies spent**

nearly $4,000 per pupil more, on average, than comparable city public schools. Since the average spending per pupil was some $12,000 to $14,000 citywide, the nearly $4,000 difference for the KIPP academies means they spend about 30% more than comparable public schools.

... KIPP schools... on average have relatively low special education populations but in many cases have per-pupil spending levels similar to or higher than NYC public schools with much higher special education populations.[26] [Emphasis added.]

KIPP NYC schools not only tend to have lower special education representation; KIPP in general tends to have fewer students with disabilities and fewer English language learners. As noted in Miron's 2011 study, the resulting student homogeneity provides a fiscal edge for KIPP over the schools that tend to serve special populations: traditional public schools:

The findings in our report show that [in KIPP schools] students with disabilities and students classified as English language learners are greatly underrepresented. The relative absence of students with disabilities and English language learners results in more homogenous classrooms. Secondly, in both traditional public schools and KIPP schools, the additional costs for these students—especially students with moderate or severe disabilities—is typically not fully funded, and therefore some of the costs for regular education is devoted to students requiring additional remediation. Because traditional public schools have a higher proportion of students with disabilities, and a higher concentration of students with severe and moderate disabilities, the burden of having to subsidize their education falls more heavily on them.[27] [Emphasis added.]

The absence of special needs students in KIPP schools contributes to its favorable financial leveraging nationally, especially when compared to non-philanthropic-supported, traditional public schools. The philanthropy KIPP enjoys is astounding. As is true of KIPP NY schools, KIPP Central Ohio stands out among charter schools for its high rate of private contributions:

...Most IRS filings on Ohio charter schools report very low private contribution rates on their IRS 990s, with the bulk of revenue generated via government grants and program service revenues. Only a select handful of Ohio charters reported any substantive private revenue. KIPP Central Ohio... generated over 30% of its revenue from private gifts in 2010.[28] [Emphasis added.]

The trademark ample funding continues for KIPP's Texas schools, both as concerns per pupil spending and district-level operating costs:

...KIPP Austin, Dallas and San Antonio schools... spent from $750 to $1,700 more per pupil than similar traditional public schools, or about 11% to just over 25% of the average $6,500. ...KIPP Houston middle schools consistently outspent other middle schools in Houston, but KIPP Houston also operates lower schools whose spending is more in line with Houston public elementary schools.

> *Based on IRS filings for the KIPP [Texas] networks, total expenditures per network pu-pil for KIPP schools* **exceeded traditional public school spending by $4,000 to nearly $6,500 per pupil.** *This finding seems consistent with Gronberg, Taylor and Jansens' finding*[29] **that some KIPP academies had raised as much as $11,000 per pupil in philanthropic giving,** *during the same time frame examined here. ...*

> *KIPP regional (district) level expenditures* **remained substantially greater than tradi-tional public schools in the same city when determined by their IRS 990 filings.** *In this case, KIPP expenditures* **ranged from nearly $5,000 per pupil more to over $7,000 per pupil more than traditional public school site operating expenditures...—or ap-proximately twice the average spending of traditional public schools.**[30] [Emphasis added.]

KIPP has money, and KIPP spends money. The question is whether all of this reformer money is yielding the superior outcomes that reformers val-ue. KIPP prides itself on its proliferation, its "no excuses" philosophy and extensive school day and year, and what it considers as proof of its success—its college graduation rates. The KIPP Academy Houston website offers this information regarding the school's history, philosophy, and success:

> **KIPP, the Knowledge Is Power Program,** *is on a mission to develop in underserved students the academic skills, intellectual habits, and qualities of character necessary to succeed at all levels of pre-kindergarten through 12th grade, college, and the competi-tive world beyond. Finishing its second decade, KIPP has become a national leader in the movement to provide all children with access to an excellent education. KIPP was founded in Houston in 1994* **and has grown to 142 public schools in 20 states and DC serving nearly 50,000 children. Houston is KIPP's largest region, with 22 public schools serving over 10,000 students and an additional 1,000 alumni in college and beyond.** *While only 8 percent of students from low-income communities across the nation graduate from college,* **KIPPsters boast a 47 percent college graduation rate, tracking from 8**[th] **grade.**

> *As we teach our students, there are no shortcuts on the path to college graduation. Students achieve their dreams by following two important rules: Work hard. Be nice. KIPPsters work hard by spending more time on task than many of their peers.* **They are in class from 7:30 a.m. to 5:00 p.m. Monday through Friday and have extra learning opportunities during weekends and summers.**[31] [Emphasis added.]

Hard work. Determination. An overwhelming amount of money spent per pupil. The result: A college graduation rate that on the surface appears to be quite the feat.

On the surface.

As reported by Gary Miron and others in 2011, KIPP has an attrition rate of 30% between sixth and eighth grade.[32] This means that almost one in three KIPP students who make it to sixth grade will not make it to ninth grade. Furthermore, 40% of African American males leave KIPP between sixth and eighth grades. To consider this latter stat another way: Of every five African American boys who enroll at a KIPP school, only three will stay to reach ninth grade.[33]

This purging of the ranks makes any statistic based on eighth grade and beyond suspect.

Varied statistics are available regarding KIPP's college graduation rates. In the KIPP Houston excerpt above, KIPP claims a 47% graduation rate "tracking from eighth grade." Yet this same stat is not available in either the 2011 or 2012 information promoted by KIPP in 2011 in the media and in its own 2012 reports. An April 2011 *Houston Chronicle* article reports that 33% of the 209 KIPP students—70 students—from both Houston and New York who were tracked from eighth grade earned a bachelors degree by ten years later. If one considers associate degrees and bachelors degrees for the Houston students alone, the completion rate in ten years past eighth grade is 40%.[34] Feinberg was quoted in the article, so he must have been aware of the 33% statistic.

The 2012 KIPP MA annual report states, "36% of students who attend KIPP graduate from college."[35] On the KIPP MA website, KIPP indicates that the 36% is a nationwide statistic.[36] There is no other qualifying information for this statistic.

KIPP boasts that its primarily low-income student body is graduating college at a much higher rate than are low-income students in general. Only 8.3% of low-income students in their mid-20s have college degrees.[37,38] However, this statistic is not adjusted to reflect the high attrition that occurs prior to eighth grade. This is an important point; if 30% of students drop prior to measuring the eighth-to-twelfth-grade statistic, then the rate is based on a maximum of 70% of KIPP students who have stayed at KIPP since sixth grade. For those students who do graduate from KIPP, KIPP has attempted to raise its college completion statistic by spending money on supports for its students beyond their time at KIPP. Consider what KIPP advertises in its 2012 MA annual report as available college supports for KIPP alumni via the KIPP Through College (KTC) program:

> *KTC not only supports students on their journey to college, **but also directly supports them through college graduation** by: Mentoring alumni; assisting with college course selection and advising on majors; providing social and emotional support; offering financial aid guidance; assisting with career planning; helping students prepare and build a resume; connecting alumni with other KIPPsters in college throughout the country; parent workshops.*[39] [Emphasis added.]

The amount of money KIPP devotes to its students beyond high school cannot be matched by the American public education system. KIPP wants to raise its college completion statistics. And yet, their efforts do not parallel the need as reported in this December 2012 *My San Antonio* article:

*Spotting a shortcoming in its otherwise stellar statistics, leaders of KIPP charter schools plan to use **a three-year, $3.3 million grant [provided by the global consulting company Accenture] to improve their students' odds of graduating from college**. ...*

*Some quit college to work full time because **their families are struggling**, while others drop out because **they are homesick** or **can no longer afford tuition**. ...*

*In Houston, **every 10th-grader and 11th-grader at a KIPP school will receive training and mentoring**. The curriculum, expected to launch in late January, will help students **build their resumes, succeed in interviews and sharpen other college and career skills, such as time management and presentation skills.***

*As part of the program, KIPP Houston will attempt to **place 160 high-schoolers in summer internships**, and KIPP graduates now attending the University of Houston and the University of Texas at San Antonio will be provided with **resume and career-development resources**.[40] [Emphasis added.]*

KIPP has over $3 million dollars to spend on raising its college graduation rates. Reported reasons for students' dropping out have nothing to do with needed mentoring or lacking time management skills. The students have family issues at home. They miss home. They can't afford the college bill.

KIPP has the solution: Help them to write better resumes.

No matter how many millions are spent, if the spending does not meet the need, the spending is a waste.

Perhaps what is most important is the image of success rather than actual success. KIPP uses statistics to promote the image of success. Aside from its citing college completion rates, KIPP cites even more impressive-appearing percentages of student who graduate and who enroll in college. Consider these statistics advertised on the KIPP website:

Nationally, over 93 percent of those who completed eighth grade at KIPP have graduated from high school and over 83 percent have gone on to college.[41] [Emphasis added.]

A brief word regarding "college attendance": It means little aside from college completion. KIPP has already advertised its college completion rates tracked from those KIPPsters who make it to eighth grade as approximately 36% in the ten years beyond eighth grade. Given the amount of money KIPP spends on its pupils both as KIPP students and beyond, 36% college completion in the six years beyond high school graduation is lukewarm at best.

Whenever one reads of an amazing KIPP statistic, one should factor in KIPP student attrition. Though KIPP tries to combat it with lofty statistics, KIPP has experienced an ongoing public battle regarding its high attrition rates. A 2011 Western Michigan University study shows that KIPP loses approximately 15% of its students from each grade cohorts each year.[42] Results of a three-year study of KIPP conducted by *Mathematica* found KIPP attrition to be 37% over three years, comparable to the public schools it used for comparison. The Western Michigan study notes that those leaving KIPP are likely to be low-performing students who likely return to the local community school. Here KIPP has another advantage: That of not replacing students once lost. And yet, KIPP is able to keep the money it received for children no longer on its roles. As the 2011 Western Michigan KIPP study notes:

> *The departure of low-performing students helps KIPP improve its aggregate results. **Unlike local school districts, KIPP is not replacing the students who are leaving.** When a student returns to a traditional public school after the autumn head count, **KIPP retains most or all of the money** (the amount depends on the particular state) allocated for educating that student during that school year. **Traditional public schools do not typically benefit in the same way when they experience attrition, since vacancies are typically filled by other mobile students, even in mid-year.**[43]* [Emphasis added.]

When a student leaves KIPP, that student likely returns to the local school. When a student leaves the local school, that student is not likely to then enroll in KIPP. Traditional public schools are always at the bottom of the order, and as such, it is the traditional public school that is likely to enroll students leaving charter schools. In his open letter to KIPP founders Feinberg and Levin in November 2012, fellow TFA alumnus Gary Rubinstein states as much:

> *In a speech that Mike made which I saw on YouTube he said that this was a better attrition rate than the neighborhood schools. I think this is misleading. **The neighborhood schools take the kids who leave the charters, though charters generally don't get the kids who leave the neighborhood schools.** I'm going to write something very obvious here, yet something that is not often said: **Not every school is a good fit for every kid. And this is true for KIPP also. There are some kids who, for various reasons, aren't able—or willing—to do what it takes to get through KIPP.** Now this isn't something to be ashamed of, but it is a reality that the politicians and other ed 'reformers' who seem to love nothing more than shutting down schools to make space for more charters are not willing to admit.[44]* [Emphasis added.]

As to the claims of high graduation rates, Rubinstein confronts KIPP founders Michael Feinberg and Dave Levin regarding their failure to acknowledge student attrition as a factor in KIPP's seemingly phenomenal graduation rates:

> *KIPP publishes an annual report which gives the attrition rate for each of their schools. They say that the rate is around 10%, which doesn't sound that bad **until you realize that this is 10% per year so nearly 40% of students who start as 5th graders don't graduate as 8th graders. This doesn't mean that KIPP is not a good thing. It just means that it is not good enough to justify the school closings across the country and***

the witch hunts for the ineffective teachers who are managing to get good principal evaluations despite their low value-added scores.[45] [Emphasis added.]

In not disclosing the KIPP attrition rate in connection with advertising their "stellar" graduation rates, Feinberg and Levin are not being honest with the public. The truth is that many who begin as KIPP students will not graduate from KIPP.

Rubinstein also challenges KIPP on another sly manner that it reports "success": That of "college readiness." In a KIPP NYC College Prep High School newsletter, KIPP boasts a "72% of the KIPP students were ready for college." As it turns out, KIPP used the definition of "college ready" that the New York Department of Education (NYDOE) used: a 75 % on English regents test and an 80% on math Regents. What Rubinstein takes issue with is the "conversion table" NYDOE uses to "convert" a 59% on math Regents "into" an 80%. Furthermore, Rubinstein considers a 75% on English Regents as "not that impressive." Rubinstein concludes,

> *I guess the point is that **like other words that have gotten new definitions in education** like 'reform', 'accountability', 'value', 'choice', 'graduation rate', 'high performing', 'failing' and a whole bunch of others, **we can add 'college ready' as an expression that really doesn't mean what it implies.***[46] [Emphasis added.]

> *Another questionable KIPP factor concerns KIPP salaries and benefits. For all of the millions KIPP receives in combined charitable contributions and public funding (mostly charitable contributions), KIPP does not pay its employees accordingly. In his 2011 KIPP study, Miron reports the following:*

> **When spending on salaries is examined on a district-by-district basis, 11 of 12 KIPP districts spend less per pupil on salaries. The same pattern emerges when examining employee benefits.** *Eleven of the 12 KIPP districts spend less on employee benefits than do their host districts.* **KIPP also spends less per pupil on special education teachers' salaries than does any other comparison group. The finding likely reflects the fact that KIPP enrolls fewer students with disabilities, particularly students with moderate or severe disabilities.**[47] [Emphasis added.]

What further underscores the issue of low salaries is the fact that KIPP schools have longer school days and longer school years that do their host districts. Aside from salary issues, this heightened time commitment certainly can place additional stress on both faculty and students—and the extended school schedule does not necessarily translate into improved student achievement. As *EdWeek* observes regarding the 2013 *Mathematica* study on KIPP:

> **KIPP students spend an average of nine hours per day, for 192 days each year, in school, compared to 6.6 hours per day, for 180 days, for traditional public schools.** *In addition, KIPP students spend an extra 35–53 minutes on homework each night than*

students not enrolled in KIPP. **But the study also found that having a longer school day doesn't always correlate with greater achievement. In fact, the KIPP schools with the longest school days actually had slightly lower achievement than KIPP schools with shorter days.** *Researchers found that the element most strongly associated with higher achievement was more time spent on core-subject areas.*[48] [Emphasis added.]

As one might expect from a school environment that requires long hours of its staff, both turnover and potential burnout are higher at KIPP than at traditional public schools. Also from *EdWeek*:

*One area of concern could be the amount of teacher turnover in KIPP schools and potentially overworked principals.... The [Mathematica] study found teacher turnover in KIPP schools to occur at slightly higher rates than traditional public schools (**21 percent compared to 15 percent**). **KIPP principals in the study reported working an average of 74 hours per week on work-related activities—an average of 12 hours per day, six days per week.***

Those findings raise concerns about **"how replicable this model is** *in terms of going to scale given the high demands [on teachers and principals,]" said [Jeffrey] Henig [a professor of political science and education at Teachers College, Columbia University].*

*"When the economy [is] tough, it might be easier to get young college grads .... **but they may find that it's harder to keep filling the bucket in terms of teachers and principals.***"[49] [Emphasis added.]

In its 2012 Report Card, KIPP reports, "74% of teachers returned last year." Below that, KIPP clarifies, "68% returned to their position." Finally, below that, KIPP adds, "6% moved into a non-teaching position at KIPP or now teach at another KIPP school."[50] Curiously, KIPP also offers retention information on its schools, but only for locations with more than one KIPP school. For locations with individual schools, KIPP does report the number of teachers at the school but chooses to provide no information regarding teacher turnover regardless of the fact that the schools have been open for several years. Below is a list of percentages of teachers returning to their position for 12 KIPP districts:

KIPP Austin (five schools), 60% returned to their position.
KIPP Chicago (two schools), 67%
KIPP Denver (three schools), 43%
KIPP DC (nine schools), 67%
KIPP Houston (20 schools), 65%
KIPP New Orleans (nine schools), 66%
KIPP NYC (eight schools), 81%
KIPP San Antonio (three schools), 76%
KIPP Albany (one school), no information reported.
KIPP Central Ohio (one school), no information reported.

KIPP Kansas City (one school), no information reported.

KIPP Tulsa (one school), no information reported.

What these percentages mean is that from one year to the next (presumably 2010–11 to 2011–12 since this is KIPP's 2012 report card), approximately two thirds of KIPP teachers returned. This means that approximately one third did not return. It also appears that KIPP's overall statistic for teachers "returning to their position" omits districts with a single school.

KIPP teacher turnover certainly is influenced by its employing one third of its teachers from TFA, whose five-to-six-week, crash-course-trained recruits typically plan to stay for only two years. On its website, KIPP advertises that 33% of its teachers are "TFA alumni."[51] However, TFA teachers are not known for their remaining in the teaching profession. A 2007 *Phi Delta Kappan* study indicated that fewer than 12% of three TFA cohorts (2000–02) planned to make teaching a lifelong career.[52] The fact that KIPP employs so many TFAers is an expected and convenient arrangement given that TFA founder Wendy Kopp is married to KIPP CEO Richard Barth. In his discussing problems of KIPP teacher turnover, Barth does not include the obvious issue that 33% of KIPP's teachers—TFA teachers, be they "alumni" or not—are temporary by design.[53]

If teachers are not certified, if they have not invested time in pursuing education as a formal and intentional profession, they are less likely to remain as teachers. The 2007 *Phi Delta Kappan* TFA study concludes as much; Of the proportion of those TFAers who expressed a commitment to teaching, 71% of that group who were education majors remained in the classroom longer than four years; of the sample as a whole, only 35.5% stayed four years.

The issue of non-certification could also be problematic for KIPP education quality. KIPP's "Frequently Asked Questions" (FAQ) includes this one regarding its teachers: "What is the experience and background of the typical KIPP teacher?" Here is the response:

KIPP teachers are the heart and soul of KIPP schools. There are currently more than 2,800 KIPP teachers nationwide, and each shares the fundamental belief that all children can and will learn.

KIPP teachers are a diverse group, including experienced teachers who have worked in schools serving underserved students, new teachers who are just beginning their careers and career changers who are entering the classroom after succeeding in another profession.

Across our network, nearly 38 percent of our teachers are African-American or Latino, about 33 percent are Teach For America alumni, and more than 32 percent hold master's degrees.[54]

Note that KIPP requires no formal teacher training; KIPP requires no teacher certification, and, based upon the information written above, KIPP requires no college degree. A KIPP teacher can be formally trained in education; a KIPP teacher can hold advanced degrees, but these are descriptives, not professional standards.

Consider yet another KIPP FAQ: "What are the requirements for teaching at a KIPP school?" Again, formal teacher credentialing is not an indisputable mandate; recall that KIPP is "franchise education":

> *KIPP school is a belief in a very simple concept: that we will do whatever it takes to help each and every student develop the character and academic skills necessary for them to lead self-sufficient, successful and happy lives.*

> *KIPP schools comply with any applicable state and federal laws, and **certification requirements for charter school teachers vary by state. While many KIPP schools look for candidates with at least two years of prior teaching experience, several also have programs designed specifically for those new to teaching.***

> *Each KIPP school is managed locally, and hiring decisions are made at the level of the individual school. **For more information about the requirements to teach at a specific KIPP school,** please visit our School Directory to access an individual school's website. **Please note that to be considered for a teaching position at a KIPP school, you must have legal authorization to work in the United States.**[55] [Emphasis added.]*

"New to teaching" does not necessarily mean one who just graduated from a four-year college or university with a degree in education from an accredited teacher training program. It could mean one of those "career changers" mentioned in the previous FAQ and who has no background in education. It could even mean someone who holds only a high school diploma.[56] It could also mean TFA recruits who are in their first or second years in the classroom founded upon one summer of training. "Requirements" vary by school. Indeed, the only non-negotiable point in this "requirements" section involves having US citizenship or a work visa.

Where there is no true professional standard, there need be no professional treatment. There need be no competitive salary, nor renewable teaching contract. There need be no due process rights. There need be no required planning period nor any mandated breaks during the day. There need be no limits to the types and number of duties assigned. There need be no consideration of when the workday ends and personal life begins.

If professionalism is erased, teachers become disenfranchised servants to the whims of their top-down, data-driven employers.

I would like to close this KIPP chapter with excerpts from the experiences of three people associated with KIPP: A student, a teacher, and a visitor. The first is a former KIPP NYC middle school student who required special education services that KIPP did not provide. In the full interview (written in Leonie Haimson's *Class Size Matters* blog), this child and her mother discuss a number of difficulties the child faced as a KIPP student. The excerpt I have reproduced concerns KIPP's "no excuses" discipline policy and student and teacher attrition:

> *I had to sit like this. [demonstrates]* **It's called S.L.A.N.T.: Sit straight. Listen. Ask a question. Nod your head. Track. Track is, if the teacher is going that way you have to...** *[demonstrates]* **follow...** **If you didn't do that, they'll yell at you: "You're supposed to be looking at me!"** *[points to demerit sheet]* **"No SLANTing." They'll put that on there.**

> **If I got into an argument with a teacher, I would have to stand outside the classroom on the black line, holding my notebook out.** *[Stands up and demonstrates, holding arms out]* *I would have to stand there until they decided to come out.* **For 20 minutes, 30 minutes, sometimes they'll forget you're out there and you'll be there the whole period –an hour and forty minutes standing.** *if you have necklaces you have to tuck them away so they can't see them—or else* **they'll have you write four pages of a sentence about KIPP—"I must follow the rules of the KIPP Academy" or "I must not talk" for four pages.**

> *They would have us stand on the black line for as many minutes as they felt was right for what I did.* **I would never get my homework during that hour when I was outside on the line. And I'd ask for the homework, they'd be like "I'll give it to you later". And the next day I would come in without homework and it goes directly on my paycheck** *[the demerit system].* ...

> **I noticed that a lot of kids left.** *In 5th grade, there were about 50 students. 6th grade, I came back and there were 30. 7th grade: 20. About 10 of them were held back and a lot of them left.*

> **A lot of the teachers left too. When I got to 6th grade, the 5th grade teachers had all changed. By the time I got to 8th grade, there were only about four teachers left that I knew.** *And now it's all new teachers.* **None of them are there that I went to school with.** ...

> *At KIPP, I would wake up sick, every single day. Except on Sunday, 'cause that day I didn't have to go to school.* **All the students called KIPP the "Kids in Prison Program."**[57] [Emphasis added.]

After reading this child's story, I better understand KIPP student attrition. Those who stay apparently must master a system of discipline reminiscent of the military or of prison. Since KIPP schools are "franchised," and since KIPP trains its principals and other school leaders via its own "fellows" program, it seems that this rigid, overly-authoritative method of discipline might be more the rule than the exception. I cannot know. What I do know is that the experience this child had at the hands of adults supposed to be nurturing her and investing in her education is inexcusable. As a teacher,

I feel compelled to apologize to her and her mother on behalf of the true teaching profession.

In the comments section of Haimson's post, a KIPP teacher had this information to offer regarding her experiences as a KIPP teacher. Her words are equally sobering:

> *I was a teacher at a KIPP school for 1 /1/2 years. (Not in NYC) It was the most horrible experience of my life.* **The teachers and students are literally in school for 11 hours a day. You basically have no personal life as it is all about KIPP.** *The school has a cult like mentality with chants, rituals, and an obsessive focus on "being nice, work hard, get into college".* **I saw numerous teachers experience nervous breakdowns** *from the extreme pressure and harassment of administration.* **There was a 50% turnover for staff each year. They made me chaperone a week-long trip** *to another city to visit colleges. I had to sleep in the same room as the students.* **(They do NOT pay anywhere near what would be expected from a district school.)** *KIPP also* **made me go door to door in one of the most dangerous neighborhoods on (sp)the city that I worked in to recruit students.** *The most crazy thing I witnessed was at* **a KIPP summer seminar that had KIPP teachers from throughout the United States** *present. One of the main speakers asked the audience of KIPP teachers to stand up if they were* **first year teachers. About 30%** *of the audience stood up. Then they asked teachers* **with 2–5 years of experience** *to stand up. At that time* **60% of the teachers stood up.** *Then they asked teachers* **with 5–10 years experience** *to stand up and* **10% stood up.** *Then they asked teachers with* **more than 10 years of experience** *to stand up. At that time* **I WAS STANDING WITH 2 OTHER TEACHERS OUT OF AN AUDIENCE OF 500 TEACHERS!** [58][Emphasis added.]

Gary Rubinstein visited the KIPP high school in New York, and his account focuses on another yet another, broader issue: That of KIPP's seeming academic "averageness" and the repercussions traditional public education is experiencing because it is not as "stellar" as what is really "average" KIPP:

> **Most of the teaching, I should stress, was not 'bad.' The issue I have is that the teaching would need to be spectacular to satisfy me. Schools are getting closed all around the country,** *20 in New York City, 20 in Washington D.C., 30 in Philadelphia, 50 in Chicago.* **When politicians are asked why they are doing this they generally point to a charter school, often a KIPP, which 'proves' that all you need are 'highly effective' teachers and all students will excel.** *This KIPP is the only KIPP High School in New York City so all the students from their middle schools filter into this school. They will have their own multimillion dollar new building next year, paid for with money that I believe could have been better spent elsewhere.*

> **What was strange was that the teachers and administrators who I spoke to, who were quite nice to me, were completely oblivious to the ed reform context in which they teach.** *Maybe they were in denial about it,* **but it is pretty clear that kids, teachers, and schools are being punished all over the place for failing to live up to how great a school like this KIPP is supposed to be. I'd love it if a KIPP teacher would come out and say "Please stop shutting down schools and using me as the justification for**

it." *It seems to me that* **the whole charter school movement, at which KIPP is at the forefront, has benefited the small percent of students who make it through the KIPP program**—*they have a lot of attrition*—*and also benefits 'the adults' like the teachers and the administrators there, but* **that benefit has come at a much much larger cost, the destruction of neighborhood schools and displacement of unwanted students.** *All in all, it is a large net negative, though it needn't be.* **With more honesty about what they are, and are not, accomplishing at KIPP and other charter schools, we could improve public schools rather than obliterate them.**[59] [Emphasis added.]

Operating a public school—a traditional public school—is not easy. KIPP knows as much firsthand from its failed attempt to "turn around" the "failing" Cole Middle School in Denver. KIPP assumed control of the school in 2004 and made promises it did not fulfill. KIPP bailed in 2007 and excused its breaking its promises by stating that it could not find the right principal. Thus, KIPP placed blame for their failure on an individual who did not exist.[60]

Even so, KIPP schools are considered the "cutting edge" of charters. They are well financed above and beyond their counterparts. They promote a "no excuses" philosophy that they are careful to mold into an image of success before the public. They have the reputation for getting low-income children to and through college. Yet as this chapter reveals, the KIPP gloss has its cracks upon closer scrutiny. First and foremost, its discipline practices and teacher turnover need addressing. Next, as Rubinstein suggests, KIPP needs to confess its undecorated, unshaped, honest achievements (and shortcomings) to a policymakers willing to continue to close community schools in order to achieve what is really the KIPP mirage. As KIPP's experience in Denver reveals, KIPP needs those public schools; it cannot successfully take charge of them, for where would the many who decide to leave KIPP go?

CHAPTER 22

THE ASPEN AND PAHARA INSTITUTES: ADVANCING PRIVATIZATION IN FINE STYLE

Throughout the course of this book, I have alluded to a number of institutes to which reformers belong, including the Fordham Institute, the Hoover Institute, the American Enterprise Institute, the Heartland Institute, and the Aspen Institute. These institutes are also referred to as "think tanks"; they express a certain scholarly aim or objective and conduct and promote research on given topics. Institutes are often funded by gifts, grants, and contributions.

With the growing power of education reform, institutes have become a vehicle for writing and disseminating research—often nothing more than propaganda—for the purpose of advancing the aims of privatization. Many institutes also offer consortia and other formalized opportunities for members to meet and exchange ideas. Whereas the exchange of ideas can be a healthy scholarly objective, in the face of education privatization, such meetings also provide increased opportunity for privatizers to organize and solidify their objectives of destroying American public education.

A Chronicle of Echoes: Who's Who in the Implosion of American Public Education,
pages 353–368.
353

Though a number of institutes push to privatize American public education, I would like to focus on the roles of a particular institute and its recent offshoot in destroying the community school: the Aspen and Pahara Institutes. Investigation of these two institutes will leave readers with both general knowledge of institutes and their power in advancing privatization.

THE ASPEN INSTITUTE

The Aspen Institute for Humanistic Studies (now known only as the Aspen Institute) was founded in 1949 by Chicago millionaire Walter Paepke, who envisioned a society for the exchange of ideas where its members "might sit together and debate great books."[1] Paepke chose as his locale what was then the quiet mining town of Aspen, Colorado. Original organizers of the Institute included Paepke, his wife, Elizabeth, and his brother-in-law, Paul; University of Colorado President Robert Maynard, and philosopher Mortimer Adler.[2] Over the decades, the Aspen Institute grew into a "synthesis of elite leadership, commerce, politics, and the arts that emerged from the big ideas and open markets of mid-century University of Chicago."[3]

By 1981, the Institute expanded to include "a headquarters in New York City, a 2000-acre estate on Chesapeake Bay, and conference centers in Hawaii, Berlin, and Tokyo."[4] In the late-1970s, early 1980s, the Institute also sold its property in Aspen and relocated 100 miles southeast to Crestone. An Aspen Institute trustee donated the new property, and the Institute's promoting sales of nearby property also owned by the trustee caused a stir; while Aspen's promoting sales of the adjacent property was not illegal, many Institute members and former trustees viewed the promotion as improper for a nonprofit. Indeed, even Paepke's widow and trustee emeritus Elizabeth was shocked at learning of the board's decision to leave Aspen. Then-president of the Institute, Joseph Slater, said that the move was necessary in order to foster institute expansion: "The institute could not be sustained, either financially or intellectually, in Aspen alone."[5]

Years earlier, Paepke's locating the Institute in Aspen caused property values to soar. When Pepke died in 1960, he left his Aspen holdings to the Institute. Institute Chairman Anderson eventually sold the Aspen land for $5.9 million in 1979, enabling the Institute to not only pay off its debts but also start an endowment. The Aspen Institute's operating budget was $1 million in 1969; it rose to $10 million by 1981. As part of the sale arrangement, the Institute continued to lease the land "so it could keep some of its programs in Aspen."[6] The Institute did relocate in part to Crestone, Colorado; in 1990, the Aspen Institute sold its Crestone land to Colorado College.[7]

Over the past several decades, the Institute has indeed expanded:

The Aspen Institute is an educational and policy studies organization based in Washington, DC. Its mission is to foster leadership based on enduring values and to provide a nonpartisan venue for dealing with critical issues. The Institute has campuses in As-pen, Colorado, and on the Wye River on Maryland's Eastern Shore. It also maintains offices in New York City and has an international network of partners.

The Aspen Institute does this primarily in four ways:

Seminars, *which help participants reflect on what they think makes a good society, thereby deepening knowledge, broadening perspectives and enhancing their capacity to solve the problems leaders face.*

Young-leader fellowships around the globe, *which bring a selected class of proven lead-ers together for an intense multi-year program and commitment. The fellows become better leaders and apply their skills to significant challenges.*

Policy programs, *which serve as nonpartisan forums for analysis, consensus building, and problem solving on a wide variety of issues.*

Public conferences and events, *which provide a commons for people to share ideas.*[8]
[Emphasis added.]

Aspen Institute's substantial growth is reflected in its finances. In 2011, the Institute recorded $74 million in total expenses—leaving the organization with net assets totaling $158 million.[9]

The success of the Institute is also evident in its week-long Aspen Ideas Festival, an academic conference started in 2005. Similar in format to other education conventions, the Festival offers educational exchanges including tutorials, seminars, and panel discussions.[10] Topics include global issues, domestic issues, education, the environment, science, technology, health, the arts, the economy, and society.[11] Notable speakers and moderators have included Madeline Albright, Steve Case, Howard Gardner, Annie Lennox, Yo-yo Ma, and Diane Ravitch.[12,13]

Though an established institute offering discussion on a variety of topics affecting our nation and world, the Aspen Institute is not immune to the influence of the privatization agenda. From 2010 to 2013, the Gates Foun-dation donated $15.8 million to the Aspen Institute; for the years "2009 and before" as designated on the Gates website, Gates donated $33.4 million, for a grand total of just over $49 million in Gates money given to the Aspen Institute. Of that total, $8.4 million is designated for the issue of "college ready"; $670,000, designated for "postsecondary success" and $5.5 million, for "global policy and advocacy" in the "US program."[14]

That much money is bound to influence the exchange of ideas.

In February 2007, the Aspen Institute's Commission on No Child Left Behind (NCLB) released a report, *Beyond NCLB: Fulfilling the Promise of Our Nation's Children.* The Commission offered a number of recommendations, including that states be required to create and utilize value-added measures of teacher effectiveness in order to determine whether or not teachers were "highly qualified"; that principals be given the right to refuse transfer into their school a teacher not designated "highly qualified"; that the definition of Adequate Yearly Progress (AYP) be modified to include student test scores, and that schools be held accountable for closing the achievement gap, as evidenced in graduation rates, by 2014.[15]

A particularly noteworthy recommendation involves the Commission suggested linking standards and assessments to a common scale to allow for comparisons among states—and requiring "high-quality longitudinal data systems that permit the tracking of student achievement over time" and that "such systems be in place no more than four years after the enactment of reauthorized NCLB."[16]

As part of the 2013 Aspen Ideas Festival, speakers Turnaround for Children CEO Pamela Cantor, Aspen Institute Vice President Ross Wiener, and US Department of Education (USDOE) Acting Deputy Secretary for Innovation and Improvement Jim Shelton offered a presentation entitled, *Ready to Learn? Ready to Teach?*, in which they purport that Common Core "sets a high and necessary bar." Ross Wiener, also director of the Education and Society program at the Institute, begins this session by stating the purpose is to discuss "what it is going to take to make sure that our kids are ready to meet the new high standards and expectations that we have laid out for students in our public schools."[17] This is not meant to be a discussion of why Gates and others are pushing a set of untested standards nationwide, nor is it meant to be a place to consider halting the implementation of this secretly-formed, unproven, costly "non-curriculum."

Note also that the USDOE is present for this CCSS promotion in the form of Jim Shelton.

The Aspen Institute connections to key individuals in corporate reform abounds. Institute President Walter Isaacson is the former chairman and CEO of CNN and editor of *Time*.[18] Isaacson's Aspen Institute salary was $800,000 in 2007[19] and $841,511 by 2011.[20] He was also the co-founder and chair of the board of the national-level Teach for America (TFA), called Teach for All; in February 2013, Wendy Kopp assumed the role of Teach for All chair, and Isaacson continues as chair emeritus.[21,22] He is from New Orleans, where TFA abounds. Even though Isaacson's Aspen Institute bio advertises TFA as "recruit[ing] college graduates to teach in underserved communities,"[23] TFA now has an established reputation of placing itself in competition with traditionally-trained teachers for teaching jobs in communities without teacher shortages. Even in "underserved" communities, TFA's presence is questionable since TFAers are temporary; their presence introduces a constant turnover in the districts where they work,[24] and TFA requires districts to pay a fee—between $2000 and $5000—for each TFA teacher above the teacher's salary.[25]

Reformer paths are tightly interwoven. In 2009, the Eli and Edythe Broad Foundation donated $1.2 million to TFA in New Orleans.[26] Kopp sits on the Broad board, as does her husband, KIPP CEO Richard Barth.

Kopp and Barth were both Aspen Institute speakers in 2011.[27] Eli Broad was a speaker in 2013, as was Broad board member and former US Secretary of Education Margaret Spellings.

In a rare recent Aspen Ideas Festival session in which both sides of the debate over education reform was presented between education historian and former USDOE Assistant Secretary of Education Diane Ravitch and Kopp in 2011, Kopp declared that everyone should "see for yourself, study for yourself... New Orleans."[28] Wendy Kopp promotes New Orleans as a model of reform. TFA is making millions in New Orleans. In 2013, former TFAer, Broad-Academy-graduate and Superintendent John White and the state education board chose to give $1.2 million to TFA in Louisiana.[29]

As for former TFAer Richard Barth's KIPP, in the 2011 Aspen Ideas Festival presentation entitled, *Schools for the Future*, Wiener introduces him as one of "three educators who are really at the vanguard of innovation in pursuing excellence in public education." With Barth is John Danner, co-founder of Rocketship Education and founding director of KIPP Nashville. The third member on the panel with Barth is Joel Rose, former TFAer and founder of School for One, which he "pitch[ed]... to Joel Klein... to get it off the ground...."[30]

Wiener introduces Barth also as a NewSchools Venture Fund fellow—as in NewSchools Venture Fund, the hedge fund where BAEO co-founder Deborah McGriff is partner. He also mentions that Barth was a director with Edison Education, the company that Jeb Bush bailed out using Florida teacher pension money.[31] In 2007–08, the Institute donated just under $1 million to NewSchools Venture Fund. In 2007, it also invested $9.1 million in hedge funds.[32,33]

None of these additional facts surface in Wiener's introduction of these three "innovative" individuals. Wiener does mention "the reach that they (these education entrepreneurs) have in their later pursuits."[34] As previously noted in this book, KIPP has an incredibly high cash infusion, a notable attrition rate, and questionable discipline practices. Such qualities should not land KIPP's CEO a place as a featured speaker at an international conference.

Former New York City Chancellor and charter school promoter Joel Klein was also featured at Aspen, in 2013. Klein resigned as NYC Chancellor in 2010 to begin working for Rupert Murdoch's Amplify. Murdoch views education as a market—a view shared by the likes of Gates, Kopp, Barth, and other "innovative education entrepreneurs," including Klein:

*[In 2010], News Corp. paid **$360 million for 90% of Wireless Generation, a New York-based maker of software and other tools to help schools evaluate and monitor***

student performance and devise instruction accordingly. The acquisition came shortly after News Corp. announced the hiring of Joel Klein, former New York City Schools Chancellor, to oversee education initiatives.

Mr. Murdoch has described Wireless Generation as a gateway to a kindergarten-through-12th grade education market he says is worth about $500 billion a year in the U.S. alone. People familiar with News Corp.'s thinking have said the company, which also owns The Wall Street Journal, could make other smaller acquisitions but that Wireless Generation likely will be the foundation of its initiative.[35] [Emphasis added.]

The Aspen Institute Commission on NCLB recommended that NCLB require teachers to be evaluated using student test scores. President Obama's Race to the Top (RTTT) does exactly that. The Commission also suggested a "Common Core" –like standard, complete with assessments.

In March 2013, Murdoch's Amplify won the $12.5 million contract to develop Common Core (CCSS) "assessment tools."[36] It just so happens that Klein, along with Vice Chairman of the holding company, Roll Global, Lynda Resnick; US House of Representatives Majority Leader Eric Cantor, and Los Angeles Unified School District (LAUSD) Superintendent John Deasy, is promoting CCSS as a "seismic shift in our schools" and even as a "revolution." The 2013 Institute panel discussion on the issue includes the following sales pitch:

The world is changing and the American education system hasn't kept pace. Experts from across the ideological spectrum agree that we must dramatically retool education in this country—but the question is how? Forty-five states and the District of Columbia have now agreed to a seismic shift in the teaching of language arts and math by embracing the Common Core State Standards. Join us for a special forum moderated by education philanthropist Lynda Resnick to hear from some of the nation's leading experts in education and workforce development as they discuss the hard work of creating a paradigm shift in how we equip our children for a radically changing global economy.[37] [Emphasis added.]

In truth, this "embracing" of CCSS is more of a forced acceptance for states wishing to gain RTTT money. CCSS adoption is a federal requirement for RTTT funding. So many proponents of CCSS pitch them as "voluntary"; however, there is a power differential at play when federal funding is held hostage to CCSS "volunteering."

Joel Klein is hardly a "leading education expert." He is a lawyer who was appointed as NYC chancellor.

If a hospital appoints a computer technician as head surgeon, does that make him one? How about a literature professor appointed as chief electrical engineer? Or an interior designer appointed as political analyst?

At the 2010 Institute, Klein was available to discuss "the learning ecosystem" and its connection to "education innovation." Klein has a single month of teaching to his credit,[38] and he was asked to speak as an expert on the ways that digital media "will change learning for generations to come."[39] Never mind that in 2010 he changed to the business of selling digital media and that his boss has an eye on profits:

> *The educational division of the media conglomerate News Corp., called Amplify, unveiled a new digital tablet this week [March 8, 2013] at the SXSW tech conference in Austin, Texas, **intended to serve millions of schoolchildren and their teachers across the country.***
>
> *Amplify promises the tablet will simplify administrative chores for teachers, enable shy children to participate more readily in discussions, and allow students to complete coursework at their own pace while drawing upon carefully selected online research resources.*
>
> ***News Corp. chairman and CEO Rupert Murdoch views the digital tablet as part of a push to modernize the educational system. But he has another goal in mind as well. The media mogul is counting on future revenues from his educational branch to help shore up the finances of his newspaper and publishing division as it is split off later this year from the conglomerate's vast holdings in television and entertainment.***[40]
> [Emphasis added.]

The opportunity for billionaire Murdoch's "education-related" profits continues in his joining with billionaire reformer Gates and other philanthropies to form the inBloom data "cloud," a place to store student data (for a fee)—and whether parents want the data stored or not.[41] This data storing mandate is in line with the 2007 Aspen Institute Commission on NCLB's suggesting that the federal government require states to store data for tracking student achievement by no later than four years following NCLB reauthorization.[42]

There are a number of highly profitable components to CCSS. Aside from the mandated data storing and student assessments, there is quite the market for materials to "assist" teachers with implementing CCSS, right down to the lesson plans (see Coleman chapter).

Another notable connection to Klein via the Aspen Institute is former Secretary of State Condoleeza Rice, who is a member of the Aspen Institute Board of Trustees.[43] In 2012, Klein and Rice co-authored the Council on Foreign Relations report, *US Education Reform and National Security*, famous for its declaring that our national security is threatened by our education system—and implying that unless schools improve—unless student scores rise on international tests—the United States would be at risk on several fronts:

> ***"Educational failure puts the United States' future economic prosperity, global position, and physical safety at risk,"*** *warns the Task Force, chaired by **Joel I. Klein**, former head of New York City public schools, and **Condoleezza Rice**, former U.S. secretary of*

state. ***The country "will not be able to keep pace—much less lead—globally unless it moves to fix the problems it has allowed to fester for too long,"*** *argues the Task Force.*

*The report notes that while the United States invests more in K-12 public education than many other developed countries, its **students are ill prepared to compete with their global peers.** According to the results of the 2009 Program for International Student Assessment (PISA), an international assessment that measures the performance of 15-year-olds in reading, mathematics, and science every three years, U.S. students rank fourteenth in reading, twenty-fifth in math, and seventeenth in science compared to students in other industrialized countries.*[44] [Emphasis added.]

It is quite a jump in logic to believe that "low" international test scores translate into a national security threat. Historically, the United States has not scored well on international tests. Now, however, those in high profile positions are obsessing over those scores, for in corporate reform, the test score is the magical measure to guarantee a prosperous and protected country. I wonder if Klein and Rice stopped to think of where our nation will be in ten or twenty years if creativity and ingenuity are replaced with test prep—or with forced standardization via CCSS.

Given that Gates has invested almost $50 million in the Aspen institute, and given that Gates wants CCSS, it seems only logical that the Aspen Ideas Festival should strongly endorse and market CCSS. There is no finer example of such marketing of both CCSS as well as other Gates-approved reforms than through the actions of American Federation of Teachers (AFT) President Randi Weingarten. In 2012, Weingarten spoke at the Aspen Ideas festival; the title of her presentation was, *Can Teacher Unions Be Partners in Reforming Schools in the 21ˢᵗ Century?* Serving as moderator was Walter Isaacson, then chair of the international branch of TFA, Teach for All. Weingarten begins with strategically-placed mention of her own teacher training. (Based upon the New York State Education teacher certification files, Weingarten held a string of temporary certificates from 1991 to 1996, at which time she was issued a permanent certificate.[45] Weingarten advertises her teaching experience as lasting from 1991 to 1997,[46] which means she quit almost immediately following certification. In an October 26, 2013, email, Weingarten confirmed her teaching experience: "…I taught for 6 years, mostly part-time with 1 or 2 or 3 classes and one semester full time….") She continues with discussion of the differences in quality of teacher training institutions around the US. Weingarten observes that even though there are some good teacher training programs, there are also some poor quality programs. Of course, the great irony is that she is having this discussion with a TFA executive. Not only does TFA train its recruits for only weeks; it also trains recruits for temporary teaching assignments. Yet Weingarten identifies with Isaacson's offering "alternatives" to traditionally certified teachers. Weingarten says she wants rigor in the teaching profession and even advocates for a "teacher bar exam," yet she cannot seem to confront the situational irony before her in the form of Walter Isaacson.[47]

Weingarten's position is similar to that of the National Council for Teacher Quality (NCTQ), which criticizes traditional teacher training programs for their lack of quality, all the while promoting its own "alternative certification" that it advertises as "costing less than one college class" (see NCTQ chapter). The similar message is no surprise given that both NCTQ and AFT receive substantial, reform-minded philanthropic funding.

The promotional summary for Weingarten's session includes the phrase, "helping to develop and promote the common core standards."[48] However, teachers were not present from the outset of CCSS "development"; CCSS was almost exclusively drafted by two testing companies, College Board and ACT; one education no profit, Achieve, Inc, and David Coleman's Student Achievement Partners—David Coleman, who later became president of College Board. Further along in the process, AFT was allowed to contribute. (See Coleman chapter.) Thus, more of AFT's time and effort has been to the promoting of CCSS than to the development of the standards.

A national delegation of teachers did not write CCSS.

As her 2012 Aspen Ideas Festival session summation indicates, Weingarten does promote CCSS. She works very hard to convince teachers to accept that they have a vested interest in these chiefly-testing-company-education-nonprofit-drafted standards. She believes in CCSS and has even served on the US Department of Education's Excellence in Equity Commission, a commission that not only formally endorsed the standards but also urged Duncan to actively promote them. In its February 2013 report to US Secretary of Education Arne Duncan, Weingarten and others made this recommendation:

> ...*Federal, state and local entities should be working together* **to give all students full access to the Common Core State Standards** *now being implemented in so many jurisdictions.*[49] [Emphasis added.]

This committee recommended to the US secretary of education to actively promote a set of untested and supposedly "voluntary" standards. He has publicly followed their suggestion.[50]

The Aspen Ideas Festival abounds with individuals "actively promoting" CCSS as well as other showcased privatizing reforms, such as tying teacher employment and pay to student test scores, utilizing "temporary" teachers while calling for more rigor in traditional teacher training, and promoting charter schools and digital learning. As to the active campaign for AFT to promote CCSS, one need only consider finances. The distillation of modern education reform always reveals money. In January 2009, the Gates Foundation gave AFT its first million in Gates grant money. Coincidentally, in 2009, AFT began its "innovation fund," offering grants "to cultivate and invest in bold, teacher-driven ideas for school improvement." In 2012, Gates published the AFT grant notice on its *Impatient Optimist* website. The goal of the grants is to "bring teacher voice to the Common Core"[51]

Such a statement implies that "teacher voice" was not already present.

The 2012 article on the Innovation Fund reads like a marketing brochure:

> *The AFT believes that the promise of these college-and career-ready standards will only be realized if educators have the tools they need to make them a reality in every classroom.* **Unfortunately, in the recent past, efforts to set academic standards fell short because they swiftly moved into assessments, bypassing teachers and students.** *(Read the AFT's 2011 resolution in support of the Common Core here [link in article].)*[52] [Emphasis added.]

If teachers created CCSS, how can they be "bypassed" by them? Simple: Teachers did not create the standards, and teachers will not create the assessments.

All that is left is the daily lesson.

For that, AFT, via Gates financing, is here to help.

In 2010, AFT received one of two of its largest contributions from Gates: $4 million. That same year, Gates also paid for the AFT conference, and Weingarten invited Gates to be the featured speaker at the AFT convention. Gates' speech includes a number of factual errors, not the least of which is this one that places total responsibility for student success squarely on the classroom teacher:

> **There is an expanding body of evidence that says the single most decisive factor in student achievement is excellent teaching.**[53] [Emphasis added.]

The problem is that the statement's incorrectness will not be appraised by all who quote it as What Bill Gates Said. This is what Gates promotes, and, well, he buys organizations and functions, including AFT and the Aspen Ideas Festival, so it must be true.

Gates continues his 2010 AFT speech by promoting RTTT as "bringing crucial new funding" to schools. He does not mention the overwhelming costs of instituting RTTT required "reforms"—including CCSS.[54]

AFT's largest Gates contribution to date came in 2012, in the amount of $4.4 million. By then AFT had formally endorsed CCSS.[55] In 2013, Weingarten co-authored an article with Vicky Philips of the Gates Foundation—the same Vicky Phillips who co-authored a statement officially announcing CCSS four months before it was completed (see Coleman chapter). In their article, they come closer to the truth of teacher influence than did Gates in his 2010 AFT speech:

While many factors outside school affect children's achievement, research shows that teaching matters more than anything else schools can do.[56] [Emphasis added.]

Weingarten and Phillips neglect to add just how influential those ""factors outside of school" are. Truth is, the influence upon the school environment of factors external to school is difficult to assess. The original Organization for Economic Cooperation and Development (OECD) study misquoted above states, "…of the variables that are open to policy influence… 'teacher quality' is the single most important school variable influencing achievement."[57] The OECD study does not state that influencing "teacher quality" will override the influence of factors external to the school, including abilities, attitudes, and family and community background.[58] Constructing a teacher evaluation system that implies otherwise aligns teachers for failure.

The focus of the Weingarten/Phillips article is teacher evaluation. CCSS makes its appearance in Point Five: Align Teacher Development and Evaluation to the Common Core State Standards. CCSS usefulness is assumed; it's a given. CCSS works. It's just a matter of teaching teachers how to "do" CCSS.[59]

AFT supports teacher evaluation based upon student test scores (note: Weingarten withdrew her support of value-added modeling [VAM] in December 2013), and it supports CCSS. In total, AFT received $11.3 million in Gates Foundation funding up to July 2013. In Weingarten's 2012 Aspen Ideas Festival presentation, Isaacson comments, "We have two great teachers unions in the United States, the American Federation of Teachers, which [Weingarten] leads, and the National Education Association (NEA), which… has not been quite as open to, 'Let's think about new ideas.'"[60]

That was 2012.

In July 2013, NEA publicly and formally endorsed CCSS. They had been "on board" since 2009 but had withheld any open commitment. NEA also voted to endorse AFT's moratorium on CCSS tests—a postponement of the standardized tests until teachers have time to adjust to CCSS.[61]

Gates money flowed to NEA accordingly: Before NEA publicized its support for CCSS, the Gates Foundation had donated $1 million across several years (2009 to 2012). However, in 2013—the year that NEA openly endorsed CCSS—Gates donated $6.3 million to NEA.[62]

$49 million to the Aspen Institute.

$11.3 million to AFT.

$7.3 million to NEA.

Gates is purchasing his version of education reform.

Promoting his well-financed personal view of education reform, Gates himself has participated in Aspen Ideas Festival discussions. In 2010, the topic was the newly-released charter school promotional film, *Waiting for Superman*. This was not a discussion in support of the community school; this was a discussion aimed at replacing the community school with corporate-run charters billed as the solution to the ills of traditional public school. On the panel with Gates was Geoffrey Canada, CEO of the amply-funded Harlem Children's Zone, who is known for (wrongly) boasting of a 100% graduation rate[63] and who twice "fired" an entire eighth grade class for not having sufficient test scores.[64] Also on the panel was *Waiting for Superman* director Davis Guggenheim, film producer Leslie Chilcott, and chief Washington correspondent of CBS News Bob Schieffer.

In short, the film focuses on the lives of several Harlem students and their families, all of whom have decided to vie for one of a limited number of student seats in a charter school for the upcoming school year. The film culminates in the families' attending the public lottery to draw for the lucky students who are able to leave their terrible community schools behind for a bright, new life as a charter school student. Some students are selected, and some are not. The film is interspersed with brief interview segments from Gates, Canada, Weingarten, and others.

What is not explored is that the two featured charter networks in the film, Canada's Harlem Children's Zone and Eva Moskowitz's Success Charter Network, both regularly benefit handsomely from hedge fund managers, an advantage that no traditional public school experiences. Moskowitz has hired two hedge fund managers, Jon Petry and Joel Greenblatt, to recruit others:

> *John Petry and Joel Greenblatt, who are partners in the hedge fund Gotham Capital, had an agenda:* **to identify new [hedge fund manager] candidates to join their Success Charter Network**, *a cause they embrace with all the fervor of social reformers. ...*

> *Boards [of each Success Academy school]* **agree to donate or raise $1.3 million to subsidize their school for the first three years.** *...*

> *Charters have attracted benefactors from many fields. But it is impossible to ignore that in New York,* **hedge funds are at the movement's epicenter.**[65] [Emphasis added.]

As for Canada, he receives millions from Goldman Sachs and invests heavily in hedge funds:

> **Following** *Waiting for Superman, where its founder Geoffrey Canada emerged as the most charismatic and eloquent of those featured,* **Harlem Children's Zone received millions—including $20 million from Goldman Sachs in mid-September. New York City is also contributing $60 million toward a $100 million new school.**

But there are also those who will make money off of Harlem Children's Zone.

> **The organization had net assets of $194 million listed on its 2008 nonprofit tax report.** *Almost $15 million was in savings and temporary investments,* **and another $128 million was invested at a hedge fund.** *Given that most hedge funds operate on what is known as a 2–20 fee structure (a 2 percent management fee and a 20 percent*

take of any profits), **some lucky hedge fund will make millions of dollars off of Harlem Children's Zone in any given year.**[66] [Emphasis added.]

In the corporate reformer's mind, hedge fund managers, whose focus is on scoring a fat profit, will save education. The undisguised truth is that since community public schools yield no profit, hedge fund managers do not invest in them.

Waiting for Superman also portrays teachers unions as the villains who keep inadequate teachers in their jobs. This is an interesting take on unions especially since AFT President Randi Weingarten invited Gates to speak at the AFT convention in 2010. Nevertheless, in *Waiting for Superman*, Weingarten is set up to be the "problem" and Canada, who fires classes of children whose test scores embarrass his board, is positioned to be the "solution."

In the Aspen panel discussion of the film, Canada had a standing ovation upon his entrance to the stage.[67]

Weingarten is not part of the panel.

Guggenheim bills his film as being "about schools that aren't working."[68] Instead of entering those schools and speaking with teachers, students and administration to discover why (or even if) these schools "aren't working," Guggenheim focuses on the hedge-fund-financed route, never investigating in any depth what life in the charters is really like. Had he done so, he might have discovered Moskowitz's forcing public schools out of their buildings, or Canada's "firing" classes of students.

In discussing his involvement in education reform, Gates speaks of the need to be "pulled down to the truth."[69] What is sad for Gates and destructive for traditional public education in America is that Gates believes he now knows "the truth" and is sure of it enough to throw his millions behind it.

Though likely the most generous for having donated multiple millions to the Aspen Institute, Gates is not the only education-reform-minded philanthropist ever featured as a speaker at the Aspen Ideas Festival. Another influential name in education reform is Eli Broad, who has appeared several times at the Festival. In 2008, Broad was part of a panel promoting "what the nation needs to do to help all young Americans compete in the global economy."[70] On this panel with Broad is Barbara Byrd Bennett, Chicago Schools CEO who closed approximately 50 Chicago public schools under the directive of Chicago Mayor Rahm Emanuel in 2013.[71] In 2012, Broad discussed the same issue—global economy and the stakes associated with education.[72] "What the nation needs" certainly is not the mass closure of its community schools. "The nation" doesn't "need" to promote teaching as a temporary stop for TFAers before they embark on their "real" careers,[73] neither does it "need" well financed charters to be placed into competition with neighborhood schools,[74] nor does it "need" to "train" non-educators and place them into superintendent positions via a non-accredited "super-intendents academy.[75]

In 2009, Broad interviewed then-DC Chancellor Michelle Rhee regarding "turning around" schools. Rhee continues to be plagued by issues of test impropriety during her time as chancellor (see Rhee chapter).[76] Broad was also on a panel in 2009 to discuss *Ideas that Work: Can Charter Schools Transform Urban Education*[77]

Same reformer ideas, different years.

No reform-minded institute would be complete if it had Gates and Broad but lacked even one Walton. As it so happens, in 2009, Rob Walton, son of WalMart founder Sam Walton and chairman of the board of WalMart, spoke at the Aspen Ideas Festival. Unfortunately, there is no record of what he said.[78] Nevertheless, one might assume that Walton spoke about that on which he and his family are willing to spend their money. According to the Walton Foundation 2009 990, the Waltons loaned $5 million interest-free to Brighter Choice charters for the purpose of "financing charter schools." They also extended to Brighter Choice a $10 million, interest-free credit line for ten years (2004–14) to "support construction financing." Pacific Charter School Development also garnered a nine-year (2005–14), interest-free loan of $3.75 million for "construction of charter school facilities" and a second, nine-year, interest-free loan (2009–18) for $10 million. Other recipients of these millions in interest-free loans include the California Charter School Association, Building Hope Charters, IFF Charter Schools, the Local Initiatives Support Corporation, E-stem Public Charter Schools, and Excellent Education Development. The grand total of interest-free loans for charter school development as recorded on the Walton Foundation 2009 tax form is an astounding $72.75 million.

Among its numerous charter school grants, the Walton Foundation donated $2 million to the DC Public Charter School Fund, $13 million to the Charter Fund, $1.8 million to Great Schools, $3.9 million to KIPP, $1.6 million to the Michigan Association of Public School Academies, $1.6 million to the National Association of Charter School Authorizers, $1.2 million to the New York Charter Schools Association, $1.3 million to the Success Charter Network.[79]

In 2009, the Walton Foundation also donated $3.5 million to the New Teacher Project, $4 million to the NewSchools Venture Fund, and $7.2 million to TFA, with an additional $1 million for TFA Arkansas.[80]

Since its inception in 2005, the Aspen Ideas festival has had thousands of speakers and moderators at its conferences. Among their ranks are many more influential, education-reform-minded individuals about whom I could have written. However, from the few represented in these pages, one realizes that discussions of education at the Aspen Ideas Festival clearly favor privatization.

THE PAHARA INSTITUTE

The Pahara Institute has the same goal as does Broad's Superintendents Academy: the positioning of reform-minded individuals in education leadership for the express advancement of the privatization agenda. Just as the Aspen Institute is led by one associated with TFA, so is the Pahara Institute. Furthermore, as is true of the Aspen Institute, the Pahara Institute also has connections to NewSchools Venture Fund:

> *Earlier in [Pahara Institute founder Kim Smith's] career she served as a founding team member at Teach For America…. After completing her M.B.A. at Stanford University, she co-founded and led NewSchools Venture Fund, a philanthropy focused on transforming public education through social entrepreneurship….*[81]

The Pahara Institute has only three board members, one of whom is Reed Hastings of Netflix.[82] The Pahara team includes those with associating with TFA, founding charter schools, independently consulting expressly focused on reform, advocating, and "increasing community engagement."[83]

Pahara wants to find and train reform-minded leaders:

> **To achieve educational excellence and equity** *at the same time and to live up to our aspirations as a democratic society,* **we must make bold improvements to our public schools** *so that every child in America has access to the tools and skills he or she needs to be successful in life.*

> *The Pahara Institute seeks to strengthen the movement for educational excellence and equity by:*
> - *helping to* **develop and sustain experienced, innovative leaders**
> - **identifying and developing the next generation of leaders**
> - **better connecting leaders** *across the field, and across traditional silos and stakeholder groups*
> - *Our work is to support exceptional, innovative leaders* **who bring urgency** *and dedication to* **ensuring that all our children have access to an excellent public school.**[84] [Emphasis added.]

In order to bring about these "bold" reforms via leadership development, Pahara offers two programs, the Pahara-Aspen Education Fellowship, and the Aspen Teacher Leader Fellowship. The Education fellows are trained in cohorts of approximately 20 over the course of two years on how to "usher in" the agenda of education reform.[85] The Teacher Leader Fellowship does not require a cohort though it also takes two years to complete. One difference between the two fellowships is that the Teacher Leader is to "strengthen the teaching profession and the capacity of educators to improve student achievement."[86] Thus, the latter focuses more on test score outcomes.

Once the participants complete their Pahara programs, they return to their communities and spread the message of education reform. A number of these individuals start their own education businesses.[87]

Some notable Pahara Fellows include NewSchools Venture fund partner Deborah McGriff; Foundation for Excellence in Education Chief Executive Officer Patricia Levesque, Rhode Island Commissioner Deborah Gist, Gates Foundation deputy Director Don Shalvey, Office of the Secretary of Education Senior Program Advisor Brad Jupp, New Schools for New Orleans CEO Neerav Kingsland, Colorado State Senator Michael Johnston, Denver Schools Superintendent Tom Boasberg, Louisiana Association of Public Charter Schools Executive Director Caroline Roemer Shirley, and Former Gates Foundation executive and current College Board Policy, Advocacy, and Government Relations Chief Stefanie Sanford.[88]

The list continues; even though Pahara Institute has only formally begun in 2012, the program for fellows has been around since 2007, under different names: the Pahara-Aspen Fellowship, and the Aspen-NewSchools Fellowship.[89]

With the new name came a fresh infusion of Gates money; in 2012, Gates designated $2 million to Pahara for "strategic partnerships."[90]

That is exactly what Pahara offers: Indoctrination in education reform for those who do not already possess the bent, and strategic placing of these networked reformers in positions of leadership, both traditional and newly-contrived.

Gates wants education reform. He has the bankroll to make it happen. A powerful, Gates-bankrolled vehicle is the Aspen Institute—with the added, longer-term investment opportunity provided by Pahara indoctrination, should one so choose.

It makes one wonder if all reformer roads lead back to Bill Gates.

CHAPTER 23

THE BIG THREE FOUNDATIONS: GATES, WALTON, AND BROAD

In this age of the philanthropic vogue to promote education reform, foundation contributions for the express purpose of privatizing public education abound. As such, a number of wealthy foundations are actively involved in driving the reform. Surely investigation of them all could make yet another book, and an interesting one, at that. For example, there is the Arnold Foundation, whose founder, John Arnold, a former Enron trader who managed to walk away from the infamous scandal unscathed, establish a hedge fund, and retire at 38 years old worth $3.5 billion.[1] There is also the Bradley Foundation, a current supporter of the Black Alliance for Education Options (BAEO) that years earlier funded Charles Murray's racist book, *The Bell Curve*, which promotes racial inferiority of blacks, a book that provided the Bradley's fuel to promote their version of welfare reform.[2] And there is also the David Koch Foundation, whose namesake founder donated millions to medical and cancer research[3] but who has the reputation for not tipping working class individuals who regularly perform special services for him.[4]

Interesting stories abound.

A Chronicle of Echoes: Who's Who in the Implosion of American Public Education, pages 369–385.
369

Nevertheless, for the sake of space, this chapter focuses on those considered the Big Three foundations forcefully promoting the education reform movement: the Bill and Melinda Gates Foundation, the Walton Family Foundation, and the Eli and Edythe Broad Foundation. As the content of the previous chapters attests, these three foundations are ubiquitous in modern education reform. And while there are many contributors to the current purchase of the basic democratic institution of public education, the vast wealth and influence provided by these three foundations amply fuels the vehicle of nationwide education privatization.

THE BILL AND MELINDA GATES FOUNDATION

The Bill and Melinda Gates Foundation (the Gates Foundation) is the "largest transparently operated foundation in the world."[5] As of 2013, the Foundation is worth $36.4 billion and has paid $26.1 billion in grants since its inception.[6] Gates Foundation board member and business magnate Warren Buffet donated his first $1.6 billion to the foundation in 2006 and continues to donate between $1.25 and $1.8 billion each year.[7] The Gates Foundation website records foundation activity from 1997,[8] though the current version of the foundation hails from the William H. Gates Foundation, created in 1994 with a focus on reproductive and child health and directed by Gates' father. In 2000, the William H. Gates Foundation merged with the Gates Learning Foundation to create what is now the Bill and Melinda Gates Foundation,[9] with a world headquarters that opened in Seattle in 2011.[10] In 2008, Bill Gates retired from Microsoft to work full time with the Gates Foundation.[11]

Once Gates was with the Foundation full time, his push for the corporate reforming focus on teacher training, evaluation, and compensation began. Hence the 2009 declaration on the Gates Foundation timeline:

Investment of $290 Million in Four Communities Across U.S.

*We announce **an investment of $290 million in four communities** across the U.S., **supporting bold, ambitious plans to transform the way schools recruit, develop, reward, and keep teachers.**[12] [Emphasis added.]*

Gates added to the above "investment" an additional $45 million component known as the Measuring Effective Teaching (MET) study. The goal of both grants was to evaluate teachers using student test scores and pay teachers based upon the "value-added" outcomes rather than upon credentials or experience. As for the "initiative," four school systems were awarded multi-million-dollar grants for three years to begin this "initiative": Hillsborough County Schools (Florida), Memphis City Schools, The College-Ready Promise (Los Angeles), and Pittsburgh Public Schools. Beyond three years, the districts were expected to assume the cost for continuing this "pay for performance" model:

> *Each of these partners will develop and implement new approaches, strategies, and policies, including adopting better measures of teacher effectiveness that include growth in student achievement and college readiness; using those measures to boost teacher development, training, and support;* **tying tenure decisions more closely to teacher effectiveness measures and rewarding highly effective teachers through new career and compensation** *opportunities that keep them in the classroom; strengthening school leadership; and* **providing incentives for the most effective teachers** *to work in the highest-need schools and classrooms.*[13] [Emphasis added.]

As noted in the previous chapter on the Aspen Institute, Gates once again promotes a misreading of the results of the OECD study on influences on student achievement, thereby placing responsibility for student outcomes squarely on their teachers:

> *"Decades of research and our own grant making provide clear evidence* **that supports the growing consensus among policymakers and parents alike that teachers matter most when it comes to student achievement,** *" said Vicky L. Phillips, Director of Education, College-Ready, at the [Gates] foundation.*[14] [Emphasis added.]

In an effort to establish the use of student test scores as a means of evaluating teachers, Gates conducted its MET study over the course of two years. He painted MET as "a real opportunity for teachers to inform the national discussion on educational reform."[15] In 2013, Gates officially concluded that teachers are best evaluated using a combination of student test scores, observations and student surveys. This global declaration cannot account for the established lack of accuracy and stability in value-added results;[16,17] it cannot account for the increased cost on school districts to sustain this so-called "performance" model,[18–20] it ignores that fact that merit pay has never worked in public education,[21] and it does not account for the limited number of courses that have standardized tests, thereby seriously limiting the subjects that could be included in the study. As for the last issue, that's okay: Gates will tell the nation how to proceed on that issue:

> **Many teachers do not have state test data for their students** *because the tests are given only in a limited number of disciplines. In Pittsburgh, only about 35 to 40 percent of teachers have state test scores that can be used for evaluation.*
>
> **In a phone news conference, Vicki Phillips, director of education, College Ready— U.S. Program for the foundation, said more work needs to be done on that question.**
>
> **"I think you'll hear us have more to say about it going forward,"** *she said.*[22] [Emphasis added.]

Time to move forward on Gates' evaluation system because he said so and he has the billions.

Gates assumes that higher student test scores automatically translate into increased learning. He has yet to investigate the impact of test prep marketing upon both student test scores and translatable, real-world functioning.

Also absent from Gates' investigations is any in-depth study on the impact of placing teacher jobs on student test scores and its relationship to the nation's two most famous cheating scandals in Atlanta and DC.

The MET study was not the first major insertion of Gates and his money into the American education process. Conspicuously absent from the Gates website timeline is Gates' disruptive failure for "small schools." In 2000, Gates decided that breaking large, urban high schools into smaller units would benefit students since "research" showed that dropout rates tended to be higher at large, urban high schools. Gates determined that the anonymity and impersonal atmosphere of the larger high schools must be the problem, along with lower expectations.[23,24] Thus, Gates decided to solve the problem himself by offering millions to districts willing to have their larger high schools chopped into components and labeled "small schools."

In July 1999, Gates hired former-businessman-gone-superintendent Tom Vander Ark to become director of the new Gates Education Initiative,[25] which had a budget of $350 million over three years to devote to "educational programs."[26] In hiring Vander Ark, Gates commends the controversial superintendent on the test scores of his former district.[27] What he fails to mention is Vander Ark's top-down controlling of the district and his alienating scores of teachers and administrators by forcing numerous reforms upon them.[28]

In his role as Gates Education Initiative director, Vander Ark parroted the Gates view that small schools were The Solution:

> *"We believe that large, comprehensive schools don't work for most students, particularly poor kids of color in urban centers," Vander Ark said. Despite "outrageously high" dropout rates, he added, "we continue to build these large schools that don't work."*[29]

That was in 2000. By 2006, the millions invested did not yield the stellar results that Gates just knew would happen.[30]

The *Seattle Times* article excerpt below refers to small schools as an "experiment." That they were, and one perpetrated by Gates and then abandoned:

> **The experiment—an attempt to downsize the American high school—has proven less successful than hoped.**

> **The changes were often so divisive—and the academic results so mixed—*that the Gates Foundation has stopped always pushing small as a first step* in improving big high schools.**[31] [Emphasis added.]

Gates was "pushing" small schools onto districts. Gates wants reform, and he has the billions to make it happen. If "it" doesn't work, Gates still has his billions and can move on to the next "cutting edge" reform.

He can even erase the botched-reform embarrassment by excluding it from the timeline on his website.

Notice how Vander Ark attempts to sound scientific about the failure of this multi-million-dollar, school-destroying, Gates-"pushed" venture:

> *"We looked at good schools, and they were autonomous,* **and made the hypothesis that autonomous was an important ingredient**,*" said Tom Vander Ark, the foundation's outgoing executive director of education giving.* **"But there were problems with that hypothesis** ... *and I think we know today that* **what struggling schools need more than autonomy is guidance.** *"*[32] [Emphasis added.]

Now the talk of "hypothesis"—after the destruction is done. Gates did not carefully examine the situation before he plunged in with his millions. He was too quick to declare that small schools could and should be replicated:

The Small Schools Solution: combining rigor and relationships

Small high schools (ideally 400 students or fewer) can provide a personalized learning environment where every student has an adult advocate.

Students in small schools feel less alienated and tend to be more actively engaged in school activities.

Students in small schools are far less likely to experience physical danger, loss of property and the demoralizing effects of vandalism.

Students in small schools in New York had higher graduation rates and lower drop-out rates than their peers in larger schools.

Students in small schools in Chicago had dropout rates one-third lower than students attending big schools.

Small schools show the most promise for raising achievement levels of disadvantaged students and students of color.

Small schools create professional learning communities where teachers have the opportunity to work collectively to improve their skills and curriculum.[33] [Emphasis added.]

Incidentally, the excerpt above comes from a one-page document authored by the Gates Foundation and entitled, *Making the Case for Small Schools—The Facts.*

Gates did not bother to closely examine the New York and Chicago situations. If he had, he would have learned that the New York, small schools "success" involved serious statistical manipulation[34] and that in Chicago, small school success was unique to the school's situation and could not be manufactured.[35]

Professor of Public Affairs Frumkin says that Gates' philanthropy is different because it is "grounded in data." [36] However, as Gates has illustrated with his "small schools" idea, it is possible not only to read studies and draw faulty conclusions from them but also to spend millions and drag unsuspecting communities into chaos based in misplaced, zealous error.

There is a callous element to Gates' decision to abandon the small schools effort without assisting the districts he affected in some type of reconstruction effort. Moreover, this situation between Vander Ark and an unsuspecting district leader illustrates the sinister exploitation that occurs when the billionaire philanthropist decides he wants out but is not willing to openly admit his failure. This scenario could be entitled, "Left Holding the Bag":

> *It should have been a happy occasion.*
>
> *Tom Vander Ark, the executive director of education for the Bill & Melinda Gates Foundation, had come to town in the summer of 2003 to finalize the details of a prestigious $17 million grant to create 50 new small high schools in Milwaukee. The foundation had been impressed with the wide variety of schools in the city, and the seemingly unanimous commitment of public and private school leaders to the new project. **Optimism was high, both in Milwaukee and across the nation, that the fabled wealth of Bill Gates could help accomplish change in the thorny field of education.***
>
> *But as Dan Grego drove Vander Ark back to General Mitchell International Airport, he was struck by his passenger's reserve. Grego, a 30-year veteran of alternative education, had been chosen to lead the initiative in Milwaukee. He had fond hopes of ending the longtime war between public education and voucher advocates, and radically altering the traditional organizational model for high schools. **He found himself waiting for something momentous, some words of wisdom from Vander Ark, a former business executive and former school superintendent who was now running this new national education project. But between the monotonous whining and whooshing of the I-94 traffic, Vander Ark wasn't saying much.***
>
> *Finally, just as he was leaving the car, he offered a rather ambiguous benediction. "I guess," Vander Ark said with a chuckle, "you just got yourself in for a helluva five years."*
>
> *Grego was taken aback. "It felt a little chilling," he recalls. ...*
>
> *Today, some seven years later, the extraordinary $2 billion initiative—which created 2,600 new small schools in 45 states and the District of Columbia—has been ditched by Gates and his foundation. School districts across the nation were left disrupted, with some charging that Gates had abandoned the successful good schools he created and **Gates citing statistics showing the project failed. Gates has now moved on to***

*funding a completely different approach involving teacher education, **and Vander Ark no longer works with the foundation.***[37] [Emphasis added.]

Reformers don't fail. They just transition to the next bold initiative.

Bill Gates really wants the Common Core State Standards (CCSS); he is spending millions to bring it to pass, and not always directly. Education writer Valerie Strauss of the *Washington Post* has documented $150 million in grants paid by the Gates foundation to support organizations that, in turn, support CCSS.[38] Gates is clear on the intent of the grants; all that one must do to verify the connection is type the keyword "common core" into the Gates grants search engine.[39] What is interesting is the timing of the Gates money transfers. For example, in 2010, the Gates Foundation donated $1 million to the Kentucky Department of Education, the same board that voted to adopt CCSS in June 2010.[40] In July 2010, Pennsylvania did the same, and in 2010, the Pennsylvania Department of Education scored $1 million from Gates. And not only boards of education are reaping the benefits of Gates money for publicly endorsing CCSS. In July 2013, the National Education Association (NEA) formally endorsed CCSS; it just so happens that NEA garnered it largest infusion of Gates money ever by far in 2013: $6.3 million.[41]

Some of the Gates endorsement is even less obvious, for it comes in the form of seemingly grass-roots format: the op/ed. Consider, for example, a letter in the opinion pages of Pennsylvania's *Patriot News*. The letter's authors, Joan Benso, CEO of Pennsylvania Partnerships for Children (PPC), and David Patti, CEO of the Pennsylvania Business Council (PBC), promote CCSS as the solution for Pennsylvania:

> *In simple terms, the Pennsylvania Common Core Standards will help give our students, parents and all taxpayers **assurance that the resources we put into education are truly preparing our graduates** for the challenges they will face beyond high school—whether that means joining the workforce, enlisting in the military or pursuing a postsecondary degree. ...*
>
> *Those who say we should abandon state standards don't have **a workable alternative. Abandoning the Common Core really means stranding the commonwealth's students on an island of academic mediocrity and lost opportunities.** Our students, parents, employers and taxpayers deserve better.*[42] [Emphasis added.]

Benso and Patti have no solid evidence that CCSS will work, yet they assure readers that CCSS will offer "assurance" of student preparedness. They see CCSS as "workable" and tell the public that CCSS must be the standards since the public has no "alternative." Even though they both include name and affiliation with their letter, they do not include the fact that Gates gave PPC $240,000 in 2013 and PBC's education foundation $257,000 in 2012 expressly for supporting CCSS.[43] Furthermore, even though the PBC education foundation notes on its webpage that it conducts no lobbying,[44] that does not prevent PBC for lobbying on behalf of its foundation.

If Pennsylvania had already adopted CCSS in 2010, why a letter in May 2013 lauding CCSS? The truth is that a number of states were considering dropping CCSS,[45–47] and Pennsylvania was one of them.[48] Some states adopting CCSS had elected to drop the CCSS assessments.[49,50] Others continued to struggle with problems plaguing the CCSS assessment process.[51] In 2013, US Secretary of Education Arne Duncan even told newspaper editors how to report on CCSS, offering an "impassioned defense" for the supposedly state-led program.[52]

Gates wants CCSS. For all of his talk of basing reforms "in research," Gates does not insist upon a piloting of CCSS. No one does. They broadcast that CCSS is founded on research, but when asked to produce the research, they do not. (See Coleman chapter.)

The most important component of CCSS research should have been pilot testing of the entire CCSS process—preparation, implementation, and assessment included. No such pilot study exists, yet Gates is spending millions to promote CCSS nationwide.

Why?

I think it has to do with the longitudinal gathering of data on students. CCSS requires the gathering of student personal data—data that could be invaluable to those in business.[53] Gates and other powerful individuals, such as news mogul Rupert Murdoch, want this information, and information—more so than even money—is power.

In October 2012, Gates invested $16.8 million for startup costs in establishing the data storing "cloud," inBloom, as a nonprofit.[54] InBloom's nonprofit status allows wealthy businesses to "donate" to it and receive tax breaks for doing so.

Gates and others say that using inBloom to establish the Shared Learning Collaborative (SLC) is only to "free up data to personalize k-12 education."[55] Forget privacy rights; parental permission has been intentionally disregarded in this "philanthropic" process of "improving the nation's children." Gates and inBloom say it is up to states to decide regarding procedures for opting out; however, states can (and have) said there will be no opting out.[56]

What should have happened in the first place is parental "opting in" to data sharing via inBloom. However, it is the states that have "opted in" without asking parents, and they have done so by signing on to the amply-Gates-funded CCSS.

Individuals and organizations are fighting this publicized personal data heist, including Leonie Haimson's New-York-based Class Size Matters. Haimson urges others to become involved against inBloom:

*inBloom Inc. is a non-profit organization, funded by the Bill &Melinda Gates Foundation and the Carnegie Corporation of New York, **to the tune of $100 million**. Its website says it was created to help states and districts "record student information, administer tests, analyze performance, train teachers and share lesson plans to support personalized learning."*

The data about individual students are stored on a cloud run by Amazon.com, with an operating system created by Wireless/Amplify, a subsidiary of News Corporation. inBloom plans to share the data with for-profit vendors *as well as non-profits* **with state and district consent.** ...

I believe parents, advocates and concerned citizens should urge their legislators, their school boards and state education officials to pull all student data out of inBloom as soon as possible. The risks of sharing this data with vendors far outweigh the potential benefits. *A sample letter, which also asks school boards to hold a public meeting and disclose what their current data sharing practices are, is posted here [link to letter].*[57] [Emphasis added.]

One sure way to remove data from inBloom is for states to opt out of CCSS. If states drop CCSS, imagine how much personal information on students will be lost to greedy individuals wishing to manipulate people—possibly even holding individuals hostage to the threatened release of the personal details of their lives—in order to score some serious cash.

In 2010, Bill and Melinda Gates and Warren Buffet formally challenged America's wealthiest citizens to contribute to philanthropic charities.[58] In the case of education reform, this outpouring of wealth has not only crippled the functioning of the local school system; it also places individual privacy of American citizens in jeopardy as such is relinquished to the whims of the wealthy.

THE WALTON FAMILY FOUNDATION

In writing about their foundation, the Waltons pen themselves as nothing if not benevolent:

*When Sam and Helen Walton launched their modest retail business in 1962, **one of their goals was to increase opportunity and improve the lives of others along the way. This guiding principle has played a major role in the phenomenal growth of their small enterprise into a global retail leader [WalMart].** This principle—to the benefit of deserving people and inspiring projects around the world—**also drives the philanthropic mission of the Walton Family Foundation.**[59] [Emphasis added.]*

The Walton Family Foundation is founded and run by the Walton family, named in 2011 "the richest family in the world" for the members' combined worth of $93 billion.[60] The Walton Family Foundation has a board of directors completely comprised of Waltons, a group of six of Sam Walton's children and grandchildren.[61]

The Waltons' riches come from their retail chain, Walmart. Whereas the Walton Family Foundation website proclaims that its "guiding principle" involves "improv[ing] the lives of others," WalMart has been cited for violating child labor laws,[62] including conducting business with a company in violation of child labor.[63] WalMart has also used prison labor to build a distribution center in place of paying a living wage to local construction workers,[64] and they have been found using forced prison labor to grow produce.[65] Known for a curious absence of any unionizing among any employees at its 4000-plus stores nationwide,[66] WalMart pays its workers a wage low enough to force many to seek public assistance[67,68] This saves money for WalMart while placing the burden for its workers' health benefits onto the taxpayer. Finally, WalMart has been investigated in connection with bribery of Mexican officials, an issue documented in emails as far back as 2005.[69]

The Waltons' values as evidenced in their questionable business practices carries over into the education initiatives that the Walton Foundation supports. Consider this statement, part of the Walton Foundation's vision statement for "empowering parents with quality school choices and information":

> *Our core strategy is to infuse competitive pressure into the nation's K-12 education system by increasing the quantity and quality of school choices available to parents, especially in low-income communities.*
>
> *When all families are empowered to choose from among several quality school options, all schools will be fully motivated to provide the best possible education. Better school performance leads, in turn, to higher student achievement, lower dropout rates and greater numbers of students entering and completing college.*[70] [Emphasis added.]

Market competition. Pressure produces results. However, one cannot have any unions in the way to force the price to rise. Thus, the Walton Foundation supports organizations that "shape public policy" in ways that promote the "market competition" in the form of charters, vouchers, temporary teachers not requiring health and retirement benefits—chief among them TFA—and pressure to produce via teacher evaluations tied to student test scores.

The irony in the Walton Foundation's stating that its spending is to "empower all families" is that its retail chain pays its employees poorly enough to require public assistance yet a WalMart employee union is glaringly absent. This hypocrisy is not lost on the Chicago Teachers Union in the face of WalMart's "staged" community meetings in the wake of almost 50 school closings planned for 2013 and thousands of teacher layoffs besides:

> *Ironically, one of the things shown repeatedly to improve academic performance is improving the economic situation for children and their families. **While the Walton family likes to talk about how they value all children, Walmart,** which the family controls*

roughly half of, **continues to keep many of its associates in poverty, with low wages, poor benefits** *and the kinds of unpredictable schedules that make parenting even more difficult.* **If the Waltons were truly concerned about lifting all boats, they could start with something directly under their control—living wages for 1.3 million Walmart workers in the United States alone.**

In the ideal Walton world, schools would compete against each other for students, resources, and test scores. But there's a problem: When there is a competition with winners and losers, there are inevitably losers. Chicago parents don't want their children to be on the losing team in the Walton-engineered competition.[71] [Emphasis added.]

In 2012, the Walton Foundation spent more than $158 million on corporate reform initiatives, including those to shape public policy, create "schools of choice," and aid reformers in their controlling existing schools, their choice investment for existing school control being TFA.[72]

In shaping public policy, the Walton Foundation openly acknowledges its "strategy" of supporting groups that advocate for charters, vouchers, and open enrollment (both within and across districts). In 2012, the Walton Foundation spent $61 million to alter public policy in favor of privatization.[73] Its recipients included Ben Austin's Parent Revolution (also known as the Los Angeles Parent Union) ($2.5 million). Rhee's StudentsFirst ($2 million), Eva Moskowitz' Success Academy Charters ($1 million), the Newark Charter Schools Fund ($1.9 million), Howard Fuller's Black Alliance for Educational Options (BAEO) ($1.1 million), Deborah McGriff's NewSchools Venture Fund ($1.1 million), the Pahara Institute ($500,000), and Chester Finn's Fordham Institute ($650,000).[74]

None of the Walton money is awarded to organizations advocating on behalf of the traditional classroom teacher—and especially not teachers unions.

An interesting 2012 Walton Foundation grantee under the category of shaping public policy in favor of education reform is National Public Radio (NPR), for $1.4 million. If the Waltons' goal was to slant NPR coverage in favor of education reform, that does not appear to have worked. NPR continues to publish stories not palatable to the hardened reformer, including those about states backing out of CCSS assessments; those questioning charter school student superiority, and those discussing the possibility that CCSS will be test-driven.[75]

The Walton Foundation also donated $325,000 to the University of Arkansas Foundation. In addition, the Waltons fund the University of Arkansas Department of Education Reform, a department known for its "independent evaluation" of the Milwaukee voucher program.[76] Of course, the voucher program is declared a success despite the high numbers of students who accept vouchers yet decide to return to their local schools.[77,78]

Most 2012 Walton Foundation Funding ($73 million) was spent on the development and establishment of charter schools. Given the Waltons' extreme anti-union stance, the appeal of charter schools is expected. Unlike traditional public schools, most charter schools have no unions. Those charter school teachers desiring union representation are at the mercy of the charter school board to negotiate a deal with the union.[79] Charter school teachers are at the mercy of their employers and often work longer hours, including longer school days and years.[80,81] Charter school teachers can be fired without notice—and not even in person.[82] They also are not guaranteed health and retirement benefits.[83–85] And charter school teachers do not necessarily need to be certified teachers—a perk for charter school owners and boards desiring to keep costs at a minimum.[86,87]

In short, charter schools appeal to the established Walton stinginess toward the average worker.

In 2012, the Walton Foundation donated $14.9 million to the Charter Fund, otherwise known as the Charter School Growth Fund, a nonprofit founded in 2005,[88] designed to offer start-up funding for "high performing" charter schools—those that yield high student test scores.[89] (Gates also regularly donates to the Charter Fund, $23 million between 2010 and 2013.)[90] It is a bit of comedy, then, to note that the Waltons also donated $2 million to the Charter School Growth Fund in Louisiana; in 2012, the Recovery School District (RSD) in New Orleans was comprised of 59 charter schools (83%), and it has the distinction of being one of the lowest performing districts in the state.[91,92] The humor continues in that a 2012 featured Walton Foundation grant involves the somewhat-unified application process for attending New Orleans' open enrollment schools, the OneApp, a cumbersome application whereby most of the choices are RSD schools that are labeled "failing" by the state's own criteria.[93]

As a part of "school choice," the Walton Foundation also supports vouchers. As such, with the assistance of the Walton Foundation, the late John Walton created the Children's Scholarship Fund, expressly designed to fund vouchers to private schools for low-income, public school students attending "failing" schools. In 2012, the Walton Foundation donated $8.2 million to the fund.[94,95]

Scholarship recipients cannot choose to use their money to attend another public school. This is private money for private schools.

Of that $73 million devoted in 2012 to school choice options, the Foundation's favored charter organization is KIPP, garnering $8.4 million in Walton funding for 2012. KIPP's President, Richard Barth, is the husband of the founder of another Walton-favored reform organization, TFA. It is Wendy Kopp who envisioned public school classrooms churning with the constant rotation of slightly-trained, TFA temporary teachers, those who do not stay around long enough to join unions and require pensions.

The Waltons like a low bottom line. The Waltons like TFA. They spend most of the money designated as being for "existing schools" on TFA, and they are straightforward with their reasons: Spending to "improve existing schools" is to establish reformer presence in those schools. Walton wants TFA to magnify its reformer impact via proliferation in all schools, whether traditional, charter, or private:

> *Improve Existing Schools.* **Helps reformers** *respond constructively to* **increased competition.** *The foundation focuses on improving teacher effectiveness and* **addressing weaknesses in the governance, management and instructional performance of traditional, public charter and private schools.**
>
> *Example grantee: Teach For America, which received $49.5 million [to date].* This *investment will* **allow Teach For America to double the size of its teaching corps over** *five years.*[96] [Emphasis added.]

The Waltons' goal in inserting its billions into American education was to create competition. Now that it has created the competition, it wants to amply fund the winners. Based on Walton dollars spent, TFA is the Waltons' chosen winner. In 2012, the Walton Foundation spent $23.6 million on "improving existing schools." Though the list of recipients includes 18 organizations, TFA was given almost half of the total: $11.4 million.[97]

The Waltons have the money. They get to weight the outcome.

THE ELI AND EDYTHE BROAD FOUNDATION

Eli Broad is the only CEO to found two Fortune 500 companies in varied industries, the Kaufman and Broad Home Corporation (KB Home) (housing) and SunAmerica/AIG (insurance).[98] In 1999, Broad sold his stock in SunAmerica/AIG in order to fund the Eli and Edythe Broad Foundation (Broad Foundation), with 2013 assets of 2.5 billion.[99,100] The Broad Foundation has funded biomedical research (science), the arts, and education.[101,102]

Broad refers to his efforts in education reform as "the biggest time-suck" for people being "resistant to change."[103]

Like the Waltons, Broad wants to introduce competition into education. But first, he offers a colorful declaration of the Urgency of the Situation:

> *Jobs are leaving this country and American employers say that students today lack the basic skills to do even the simplest jobs. Without dramatic changes, the U.S. economy will continue to suffer, crime will go up and* **our children won't be able to find a job or afford a house.** *Education is an issue that affects our national strength and security.* **If we do not create dramatically new opportunities to educate our youth, our standard of living will decline, our democracy will be at risk and we will continue to fall behind as other countries surpass us.**[104] [Emphasis added.]

"Jobs leaving this country" has more to do with that coveted cheaper bottom line so many corporations worship and little to do with uneducated youth. In fact, the jobs "leave" because employers do not want to pay more expensive Americans. This works counter to Broad's argument for the need to improve student achievement, which would make students more skilled and therefore expensive for companies to afford. "Our children not being able to find a job or afford a house" is undeniably impacted by corporate outsourcing.

There is abundant hypocrisy in Broad's assertions. Does he not realize that reformer efforts to undermine the teaching profession, to close schools and disrupt communities, is causing teachers and other school- and district-level personnel to lose jobs and not afford houses? Does he not realize that his and other billionaire reformer efforts are weakening the economy and causing the standard of living for thousands of community school employees to decline? Does he not realize that the narrow focus on test scores will culminate in a less-educated generation for their having lost valuable instruction time on test prep and test completion?

Apparently not.

The obsession with international test scores has reformers like Broad believing that the US is being "surpassed." In discussing the Rothstein and Carnoy reanalysis of international test scores,[105] educational historian Diane Ravitch observes the following:

> *In every nation, students from the most affluent homes are at the top of the test scores, and students from the poorest homes are at the bottom. In other words, there is an "achievement gap" based on social class in every nation.*

> *[Rothstein and Carnoy] point out that the big assessment programs—PISA (Programme for International Student Assessment) and TIMSS (Trends in International Mathematics and Science Study)—do not consistently disaggregate by social class, which creates "findings" that are misleading and inaccurate.*

> *Rothstein and Carnoy note that American policymakers have been disaggregating by income and other measures since No Child Left Behind was passed, yet they gullibly accept international test score data without insisting on the same kind of disaggregation.*

> *In other words, we know that a school where most of the students live in affluent, college-educated families will get higher test scores than a school in an impoverished neighborhood. But we don't ask the same questions when we look at international testing data.*[106] [Emphasis added.]

Broad is not making the poverty-test score connection:

> *We focus on improving **urban school districts** because they serve one of every four American children. **These districts are currently among the most under-performing and*

represent the greatest opportunity to dramatically improve student achievement.[107] [Emphasis added.]

Instead of focusing his philanthropy on combating the issues students bring with them to school and which therefore impact the school environment, including community poverty, Broad, a businessman, decided upon a top-down approach to school reform, one that culminated in his Broad Center, featuring his Broad Superintendents Academy:

> *We didn't know anything about curriculum, so we started looking at governance and management. **With rare exceptions, people become school superintendents without any training in management, finance, systems. So I said, Why don't we create an academy to train superintendents?***[108] [Emphasis added.]

In this 2013 interview for the magazine *Inc.*, Broad portrays his Superintendents Academy as simply training in business. However, what he fails to include in the discussion is the fact that he believes and promotes the view that school leaders need not have education backgrounds. This view he shares with an organization he amply supports, TFA. In fact, TFA founder Wendy Kopp sits on the Broad board.

There is something about intelligent, rotating labor that appeals to both Walton and Broad. However, Broad travels further with the TFA mission to have former TFAers become "talented leaders" who, like an entitled bloodline, are placed in key positions of educational leadership. Broad will enroll them in his unaccredited Superintendents Academy so that they might "graduate" and perpetrate reform in school districts and states across the country. As a matter of fact, Louisiana has one of these fine former TFAers-become-Broad-trained-superintendents in the form of John White. White is a remarkable man who in his position as superintendent has performed at his reformer best in a number of ways, including forming clandestine arrangements for data sharing via inBloom;[109,110] denying then finally admitting to inflated school letter grades;[111] attempting to talk school boards into laundering student funds to his voucher program;[112] refusing to perform site visits to the state-run charter schools at the legislative auditor's urging,[113] and donating $1.2 million to TFA in 2013 alone.[114]

One need not be TFA alum in order to "qualify" for the Broad Superintendents Academy. One only needs to be "talented," as Broad makes clear in his 2003 *Better Leaders for Better Schools: A Manifesto*:

> *We should **create alternative pathways for school and school system administrators...** **so that managerial talent from all sectors can more easily make the transition into public education.** Rather than create bureaucratic barriers to entry, **we should focus on strategic recruitment....**[115] [Emphasis added.]

Let us consider some examples of what this "strategic recruitment" has produced by way of "talented superintendents" from Broad's academy. There is Jean-Claude Brizard,[116] who was superintendent in Chicago and was forced out as part of the negotiations to settle the Chicago teachers strike in 2012 (see second Chicago Connection chapter). There is also Chris Cerf,[117] whose floundering Edison schools former Florida governor Jeb Bush enabled to go private using Florida teacher pension money.[118] In Los Angeles, Broad-trained John Deasy[119] openly defies his employer, the Los Angeles school board by ignoring the resolutions they pass and following the ones they don't. His response is, "...They can't stop me...."[120] Next is Rhode Island Commissioner Deborah Gist,[12] whose popularity was so low among teachers that US Secretary of Education Arne Duncan inserted himself into her contract renewal in 2013. (A sort of "save the reformer" moment from one to one.) (See Chiefs for Change chapter.)

This is Broad leadership. This is what will save our country from impending international embarrassment and threat.

These three reformers have overlapping interests, and so, their contributions overlap accordingly, especially as concerns charter schools. For example, as was true of the Gates and Walton Foundations, the Broad Foundation also contributes to the Charter Fund ($1.4 million in 2011).[122] Also, as is true of the Waltons, Broad favors TFA. In 2011, Broad awarded $12.4 million to TFA, including $10 million earmarked for "establishing an endowment."[123] A third example is Green Dot charters, the launch for Austin's Parent Revolution: One of Broad's largest contributions in 2011 was to Green Dot Charters in Los Angeles ($1.3 million). Gates also donated to Green Dot in 2011 ($5.7 million),[124] as did Walton ($500,000). Next is KIPP: A favorite of the Waltons', KIPP also garnered serious funding from Broad in 2011: $2.1 million.[125] Major funding from Gates to KIPP did not come until 2012, when Gates donated $1.1 million for "technology innovation," including "capturing and sharing knowledge in and outside the KIPP network."[126] And now, to Moskowitz' Success Charter Network: In addition to its 2012 Walton funding, Success Charter Network drew $1.3 million in Broad money in 2011. Finally, NewSchools Venture Fund appears to always draw huge reformer money; Broad donated $1.5 million to the Venture in 2011. NewSchools is a sort of one-stop shop for those interested in dabbling in the charter school business. Given that the Big Three all donate to the Venture, business must be good.[127]

Let us now consider other Broad investments. A popular venue for reformer advanced degrees is the Harvard Graduate School of Education. Coincidentally, in 2011, Broad donated almost $1 million to Harvard University, with $125,000 earmarked for the Graduate School of Education's Education Leadership doctorate,[128] designed to "effect systemic change."[129]

In keeping with the desire to grade teacher training programs, in 2011, Broad awarded the National Council on Teacher Quality (NCTQ) $500,000 for "developing a report card on the quality of schools of education."[130] Broad's own makeshift academy for superintendents escaped scrutiny by NCTQ. Reformer academies must not be the NCTQ focus since such are already on the "right" side of privatization. Gates donated $2.9 million to NCTQ in 2011 so that NCTQ might "continue its transformative work."[131]

In addition the Broad Center, there is the 2002-established Broad Prize, a $1 million annual award to the school district best exemplifying the wonders of reform. The seniors in the winning district also receive up to $20,000 each in scholarship money toward attendance in two- or four-year degree programs. This is a generous offering. Unfortunately, the criteria for achieving the award involves the typical reform agenda focus on test scores.[132] The Broad Prize Review Board includes a number of reformers previously discussed in this book, including Erik Hanushek, Frederick Hess, Patricia Levesque, and Deborah McGriff.[133] The Co-CEO of TFA, Elisa Beard, also sits on this board. There is also a Broad Prize Selection Jury, including former Secretary of State Condoleeza Rice, former Secretary of Education Rod Paige, former Secretary of Education Margaret Spellings, and United Negro College Fund CEO Michael Lomax.[134]

The intent of the Broad prize is noble. The focus on the reformer agenda is misguided.

As is true for all three billionaires represented in this chapter, as well as the numerous other billionaires and millionaires whose philanthropy is driving the education reform movement, Broad money is smothering the democratic institution of the community public school. In spending so much money to raise test scores, billionaire reformers are inadvertently cheapening American education, making it little more than scoring high numbers on tests, a skill that is increasingly separated from genuine learning as focus upon it intensifies.

CHAPTER 24

THE AMERICAN LEGISLATIVE EXCHANGE COUNCIL (ALEC)

Manipulating the Nation State by State

If the education reform movement were reduced to a single organization, that organization would be the American Legislative Exchange Council (ALEC). ALEC has existed for decades and is omnipresent in reformer circles, yet this colossal engine for privatization has managed to elude exposure until 2012. Though it might seem incredulous, through its membership, ALEC is present in every chapter in this book. Make no mistake: Privatization belongs to ALEC.

ALEC was formally organized in September 1973 in Chicago, Illinois,[1] and received its 501(c)3, "nonprofit" designation in 1977.[2] ALEC describes itself as, "a nonpartisan membership association for conservative state lawmakers who shared a common belief in limited government, free markets, federalism, and individual liberty."[3] Founders include Illinois Representative Henry Hyde; "Moral Majority" founder Paul Weyrich, and 1968 Reagan campaigner Lou Barnett.[4] Other ALEC formative-years members included Robert Kasten, Tommy Thompson, John Kasich, John Engler, Terry Brans-

A Chronicle of Echoes: Who's Who in the Implosion of American Public Education,
pages 387–402.
Copyright © 2014 by Information Age Publishing
387

tad, "all of whom moved on to become governors or members of Congress."[5] The ALEC roster also included state senators John Buckley and Jesse Helms, and state representatives Phil Crane and Jack Kemp.

From inception, ALEC was powerful. And for the most part, it kept its business to itself.

In April 2012, the public interest group, Common Cause, had just released information about a mammoth lobbying group that somehow had maintained a low profile for decades under the guise of a nonprofit (its official registration) but that had been lobbying extensively for conservative legislation in a number of areas, including education. On April 20, 2012, Common Cause officially filed a whistleblower complaint on ALEC with the IRS alleging that even though as a nonprofit ALEC was allowed to spend a maximum of five percent of its money on lobbying activity, ALEC's primary mission was that of lobbying, and that is where most of its spending was (and is) directed.[6]

According to documents released as part of the Freedom of Information (FOIA) and Public Records Acts (PRA), what Common Cause reveals as ALEC's "scheme"[7] was exposed before a disbelieving public. In short, what ALEC does is bring together corporations and legislators, compose or endorse what it considers as proposed "model" legislation (that which is designed to yield profits for the corporations), vote by ALEC Task Force committee to "adopt" the model legislation, then instruct legislators on how to pass the legislation in their respective statehouses.

This is a pretty sweet deal for the corporations, who foot most of the bill for ALEC (and exercise most of the say in what proposed "model bills" become officially ALEC-endorsed). This is what ALEC means in calling itself "conservative"—avoiding government regulation of corporate activity so that what is public money might become corporate profits. The arrangement also benefits ALEC legislators, who now not only have the "support" of the corporations that have profited from the passage of ALEC legislation but also get to take credit for the legislation.

In the weeks following ALEC's public exposure, a number of corporations and other organizations began to drop their memberships in ALEC. Among them was WalMart, the Bill and Melinda Gates Foundation, Johnson and Johnson, McDonalds, Coca-Cola, Wendy's, the National Board for Professional Teaching Standards, Scantron, and National Association of Charter School Authorizers.[8,9] Legislative members also left ALEC; most of these belonged to the minority, Democratic ALEC membership.[10]

Even though the revealing of ALEC's inner workings in general was enough for some of its membership to flee, the stronger catalyst was the publicizing of the involvements of one of ALEC's committees, the Public Safety and Elections Task Force. This was the task force responsible for promoting voter suppression legislation and gun laws favoring gun retailers—not the least of which was WalMart. (WalMart's interest in ALEC is no surprise given ALEC's promoting legislation favoring union-busting,[11] the repeal of minimum wages,[12] and repealing paid sick day requirements.)[13,14]

Exposed was the fact that the ALEC Public Safety and Elections Task Force originated bills aimed at suppressing certain groups of voters at the polls by requiring photo IDs in order to vote.[15] Such legislation is likely to impact certain subpopulations—such as those who tend to exert less power in society in general, including the elderly, the less educated, and the poor—in other words, those who are less likely to benefit from a system that caters to corporations. Those promoting the voter ID laws insisted that these would reduce voter fraud. However, "voter fraud" could not be substantiated as a legitimate problem at the polls.[16]

ALEC-member flight in spring 2012 was arguably prompted most by one particular piece of the highly controversial legislation promoted in the ALEC Public Safety and Elections Task Force: its model legislation based upon Florida's Stand Your Ground Law, passed in 2005. On February 26, 2012, an unarmed 17-year-old male, Trayvon Martin, was fatally wounded by shooter George Zimmerman, who decided he had the right to shoot Martin based upon Stand Your Ground, a law that has resulted in a number of deaths of unarmed individuals.[17] The ALEC version is called the Castle Doctrine Act:

> **This act authorizes the use of force, including deadly force,** *against an intruder or attacker in a dwelling, residence, or vehicle under specified circumstances.*
>
> **It further creates a presumption that a reasonable fear of death or great bodily harm exists under these specific circumstances, and declares that a person has no duty to retreat and has the right to stand his or her ground and meet force with force if the person is in a place where he or she has a right to be and the force is necessary to prevent death, great bodily harm, or the commission of a forcible felony.**
>
> **Finally, the act provides immunity from civil prosecution or civil action for using deadly force,** *defines the term "criminal prosecution," and authorizes law enforcement agencies to investigate the use of deadly force* **while prohibiting the agencies from arresting a person in these circumstances unless the agency determines that there is probable cause that the force the person used was unlawful.**[18] [Emphasis added.]

The National Rifle Association (NRA) introduced this bill to ALEC[19] and is a frequent sponsor of ALEC model legislation.[20] ALEC legislation is designed to benefit its corporate members—and one that stands to benefit from gun sales is WalMart. Citing Common Cause,[21] Bill Moyer reports on the Stand your Ground-Walmart connection:

> *The citizen's advocacy group Common Cause has an explanation as to why it believes ALEC, which mostly promotes corporate interests, has campaigned for Stand Your Ground laws nationwide.* **The National Rifle Association is a longtime funder of**

> *ALEC. The NRA pushed for the Florida bill's passage and one of its lobbyists then asked a closed-door meeting of ALEC's Criminal Justice Task Force to use the law as a template for other state legislatures. At the time, that task force was co-chaired by Walmart, America's largest seller of guns and ammunition.* In September 2005, the bill was adopted by ALEC's board of directors.
>
> *Since then, more than two dozen states have passed laws based on Stand Your Ground (also known as the Castle Doctrine).*[22] [Emphasis added.]

ALEC is about money, and ALEC corporations, such as Walmart, are about money. There is no other reason for corporations to invest so heavily in the "nonprofit" ALEC.

On April 17, 2012, ALEC publicized that it was disbanding its Public Safety and Elections Task Force.[23] Nevertheless, it still had a May 2012 task force meeting at its convention in Charlotte, North Carolina. In the task force mail-out (sent to task force members on April 6, prior to the ALEC announcement of disbanding), the task force materials both announce its upcoming "exciting agenda" and note, as is true of prior task force mailouts,[24] "the future of the Task Force will be driven by our membership, the political climate, and the top policy issues of the day."[25] On the day of its announcement to disband, the organization credited for forcing the disbandment, Color of Change, referred to ALEC's announcement as a "PR stunt":

> *ALEC has spent years promoting voter suppression laws, Kill at Will bills, and other policies that hurt Black and other marginalized communities. **They have done this with the support of some of America's biggest corporations,** including AT&T, Johnson & Johnson and State Farm.*
>
> *ALEC's latest statement is nothing more than a PR stunt **aimed at diverting attention from its agenda,** which has done serious damage to our communities. ...**Shutting down one task force does not provide justice to the millions of Americans whose lives are impacted by these dangerous and discriminatory laws courtesy of ALEC and its corporate backers.***[26] [Emphasis added.]

By July 2013, ALEC's original statement of Public Safety and Elections Task Force disbandment has been removed from its website. Coincidentally, ALEC advertises its added, Justice Performance Project,[27] which includes the promotion of model legislation "to protect from unjust punishment under vague or ambiguous criminal offenses... where the law has heretofore clearly and expressly set forth the criminal intent... requirements."[28]

ALEC actively promotes its legislation. And to some legislators, ALEC's offering model legislation appeared to be neutral and welcome—at first. This legislator reflects upon ALEC's attempts to enlist him as an "ALEC legislator":

*When I received my first ALEC booklet [after paying $100 to become an ALEC legisla- tive member], **I thought they were just another independent legislative source** and the "American Legislative Exchange Council" didn't sound very sinister. We (legislators in general) were already familiar with the National Conference of State Legislatures that has been a positive source of information and ALEC seemed to be one and the same.*

*I eventually found out that ALEC is like the house guest that never leaves. At first you're glad to see them, **but as time progresses you wonder what their motives are** for sticking around. They initially provided legislators with some good legal concepts **but then over time they became a Trojan Horse working their way into the law-making process with an agenda that isn't exactly pro-people.**[29]* [Emphasis added.]

In its whistleblower IRS complaint, Common Cause details the methods ALEC uses to convert its model legislation into law. The ALEC insistence that the federal government not interfere with state affairs offers a thinly-veiled hypocrisy for ALEC's powerful orchestrating of model bill passage in legislatures nationwide.

A chief means of advancing ALEC legislation is the task force. On its website, ALEC credits the task force idea to President Reagan's 1981 forma-tion of his National Task Force on Federalism. ALEC members were heavily involved in this Federalism task force. As a result, ALEC members devel-oped seven other task forces to work with the Reagan administration on policy development. ALEC involvement resulted in its own report entitled *Reagan and the States*, which ALEC distributed *en masse*. When the Reagan administration's *A Nation at Risk* was produced in 1983, ALEC was there to spread its own interpretation:

*...A two-part report on Education **which laid the blame for the nation's educational decline squarely where it belonged-on centralization, declining values, and an in- creasingly liberal social agenda that had pervaded schools since the 1960s-and which offered such "radical" ideas as a voucher system, merit pay for teachers and higher academic and behavioral standards for students** as possible solutions to the problems.[30]* [Emphasis added.]

The birth of the corporate reform agenda.

In 1986, ALEC formally organized its own task forces, the goal being, "to develop policy covering virtually every responsibility of state government."[31] Originally, the task forces were "clearinghouses for ideas"; however, post-Reagan, ALEC admits shifting the task force focus to that of "freestanding think tanks and model bill movers."[32] ALEC brags that it is responsible for "close to 1,000 bills, based at least in part on ALEC Model Legislation"[34] each year.

ALEC is running America via its state-level legislation. Corporations are running ALEC via their substantial funding. Therefore, corporations are running American via their money.

ALEC has eight task forces: Civil Justice; Commerce, Insurance, and Economic Development; Communications and Technology; Education; Energy, Environment, and Agriculture; Health and Human Services; International Relations; Justice Performance Project, and Tax and Fiscal Policy. Each task force has both public and private sector membership, and each sector has a chair. Each task force also has a director. Thirty-five days prior to each convention, task force members receive via email what is known as a "35-day mailout" of the model legislation to be discussed and voted on by the task force at the convention. Once model legislation is approved by the task force, it becomes available to ALEC members to promote (and take credit for) in their own states.[35]

What legislative members learn all too well is that ALEC has no intention of providing model legislation and leaving its legislative members to decide whether or not to promote it.

ALEC plans to be in touch, overwhelmingly so.

In addition to its model legislation, ALEC sends its legislative members "issue alerts"[36] via email. These issue alerts inform ALEC legislators of the "official" ALEC position on the legislation presented in their respective statehouses. The emails also offer legislators a few quick reasons for supporting or not supporting given legislation.

ALEC does not leave the thinking up to its legislators. It tells them what to think.

These "definitely lobbying" issue alert emails are generated by the varied ALEC task forces, whose private sector members have at least the same influence on the task force as do the legislative members.[37] However, the bulk of ALEC money is generated from its corporate members. Legislative membership is $100 for two years.[38] In stark contrast, corporate members can choose from among three levels of membership: $7,000, $12,000, or $25,000. As such, corporate members pay for their level of clout in ALEC.[39] One cannot pretend that this has no bearing upon the voting power of legislators versus corporate members and ultimately upon the issues ALEC promotes. The Stand Your Ground legislation-Walmart connection is evidence of the influence of money upon the legislation ALEC promotes.

A third means of ALEC's controlling the legislators involves its sending them "talking points"[40] regarding current legislative discussions. ALEC leaves nothing to independent legislator thought; one could be completely uninformed on the true depth of an issue yet prepared with an ALEC "Cliff's Notes" talking points email and hold a conversation on an issue and sound both fully informed and intellectually astute. The "talking points" email approaches an issue from a variety of angles and provides short-list arguments that favor the ALEC position on an issue.

The only problem is that if too many legislators use these talking points, they begin to sound like parrots mimicking some human being who has left the room.

The task force model bills, the issue alerts, the talking points.... One might think that would be enough ALEC smothering in the corporate-legislative relationship. But there's more. ALEC also offers prefabricated press releases for legislators to use in the promotion of recently-passed ALEC legislation (or recently-repealed, non-ALEC legislation). The legislator must remember, however, to write his or her name in the places where the model release indicates, "insert legislator." No kidding. Consider this excerpt from a model ALEC press release on Obamacare repeal:

> **LOCATION (Date)—[Legislator], [insert any leadership or health committee assignments]**, commends the US House of Representatives for its repeal of ObamaCare and is ready to move forward with legislation at the state level to further protect the citizens of [insert state] from the overreaching arms of the federal government. [41]

Note the situational irony in ALEC's pushing its views on legislators in [insert state] and not even leaving it to these legislators to think on their own to object to the "overreaching arms of the federal government."

In joining ALEC, legislators have only exchanged one set of arms for another.

The ALEC control isn't over yet. Next come the bill tracking documents. As Common Cause reports in its April 2012 letter to the IRS:

> ALEC spends resources preparing and researching the legislative process in anticipation (and as a result) of its lobbying. ALEC tracks its approved legislation when it is introduced in state legislatures, and makes contacts with state legislators about the bills. ALEC's spreadsheets identify where legislators have introduced bills substantially similar to ALEC legislation. The tracking documents include specific details about the bills (for example, the bill number and its sponsor) and their status. **The sole purpose of this bill tracking and communication with legislators is to "influence legislation."**[42][Emphasis added.]

The houseguest who just won't leave.

It is worth noting that ALEC's overwhelming contact with its legislators was not possible in the decades preceding internet technology. The fact that information can so easily be disseminated to millions within fractions of a second has monumentally accelerated the travel of news worldwide, enabling ALEC to be efficiently and effectively informed of local, national and international events. The internet also enables ALEC to rapidly insert its agenda into multiple legislative offices with an ease unimaginable in 1973, the year ALEC was formed.

The availability of a sophisticated internet makes ALEC machinations possible. ALEC must be able to readily force (and enforce) its privatization agenda upon legislators who are no longer gathered at one conference but who have gone home to work in their local environs.

The internet is ALEC's daily tie to statehouses nationwide.

Yet there must be a willing human being at the other end of the ALEC-approved electronic communications. ALEC needs its legislative members to be the pigeons homing its corporation-fattening legislation. Imagine how tiresome it is for the legislator attempting to exercise independent thought to be constantly bombarded by ALEC directives. Therefore, ALEC must make this relationship worth the legislators' time. One means of doing so involves offering legislators corporate-sponsored "scholarships" to its extravagant conventions.[43] This way, the ALEC meeting becomes for legislators what the Center for Media and Democracy terms, "the corporate-funded vacation":

> **ALEC's annual meetings and task force summits are usually held in vacation spots** *like New Orleans and at swank resorts like the Westin Kierland Resort in Scottsdale, Arizona. Most state legislators only work part-time and earn, on average, about $46,000 a year,* **so for many politicians these destinations and resorts would be unaffordable. Lucky for ALEC legislators, ALEC's corporate members bankroll** *their flights, hotel rooms, and meals.*

> **As a further incentive to attend ALEC meetings, elected officials are encouraged to bring their families,** *and offered subsidized childcare for kids six months and older called "Kids Congress."*[44] [Emphasis added.]

One might wonder how ALEC is able to use corporate money to fund legislator conference attendance. For one, this activity was hidden from public view for years, so people in general were not aware that it was occurring. Too, as the Center for Media and Democracy points out, there are ways around what should be the illegal funding of public officials by private companies; these involve passing the corporate funds through ALEC's "scholarship fund":

> *...***By calling this spending a "scholarship" and filtering it through a bank account designated as the "ALEC scholarship fund,"** *corporations have, so far, been* **maneuvering around laws** *designed to limit improper influence. ...*

> *Many state ethics and lobbying laws prohibit gifts like hotel rooms and plane tickets if they come from lobbyists or organizations that employ lobbyists in the state. However,* **some legislators have managed to write an explicit exception for ALEC or similar organizations into their state laws.**[45]

> *Ethics boards in other states have sanctioned the scholarships* **on the grounds that the check** <u>officially</u> **comes from ALEC.**[46,47] [Bolding added.]

In short, the ALEC-approved[48] corporate donations (likely from a corporation's lobbyist)[49] are laundered through ALEC's "scholarship fund" so that legislators' trips are "technically" funded by the nonprofit ALEC, not corporations. Ethics committees are apparently shortsighted enough to not investigate exactly who is funding the "scholarship fund."

If there were any doubt that corporations fund legislators' ALEC travels, consider this email excerpt from a thank-you note from a legislator to an ALEC corporation as originally publicized by the Center for Media and Democracy:

> *"Because of your help and others like you, the trip to ALEC was made possible for our legislators," writes Ohio State Chair John Adams to AT&T lobbyist Bob Blazer, in an August 26, 2010, letter obtained through open records requests. "Thank you also to AT&T for their generous contribution [and sponsorship of the Ohio Night event!]"*[50,51]

Whereas it includes some information that the public is able to view regarding ALEC corporate involvement, the ALEC website downplays ALEC corporations' extreme involvement. For example, the ALEC board of directors is comprised entirely of legislators.[52] ALEC also has its state chairmen— also legislators.[53] It does offer a view of its "Private Enterprise Advisory Council,"[54] yet this group is not nearly as large as the number of legislators showcased in the board of directors and state chairs. ALEC offers examples of its model legislation; what it does not offer is information concerning the degree to which corporate America is financing the legislation.[55]

In the 1980s when ALEC was working for the Reagan administration, one of its early attempts to disseminate its views centered upon the area of education reform. In the decades to follow, ALEC established its Education Task Force, now undeniably dedicated to cementing its education privatization agenda nationwide through the guise of "state-led" initiatives.

Through its freedom of information requests, Common Cause has made available to the public seven ALEC Education Task Force 35-Day mailouts related to ALEC meetings scheduled from August 2010 to May 2012. The volume of proposed model legislation in these mailouts surely exceeds that of a single chapter; thus, I will offer here select components of ALEC's models. In the end, I promise that readers will have a grounded sense of the corporate-driven wonder that is ALEC.

In October 2010, Education Task Force Director David Myslinski sent task force members a 35-day mailout prior to ALEC's annual meeting in Washington, DC. The mailout included four proposed model bills, including the *A-Plus Literacy Act*, amendments to the *Open Enrollment Act*, the *Resolution in Support of Private Sector Colleges and Universities*, and the *Parent Trigger Act*. Sometimes ALEC model bill titles do not betray the intent of the bill. The *A-Plus Literacy Act* is an omnibus bill comprised of three other ALEC model bills, the *Alternative Teacher Certification Act*, the *Great Schools Tax Credit*

Program Act, and the *Special Needs Scholarship Program Act.* ALEC introduces this Florida-inspired bill by crediting Florida's National Assessment of Educational Progress (NAEP) scores—but only focusing on subgroups:

> *The A-Plus Literacy Act is inspired by a comprehensive set of K–12 reforms*
>
> *implemented by Florida lawmakers in 1999, and supplemented over the next decade.* **As a result of these reforms, Florida's scores on the highly respected National Assessment of Educational Progress (NAEP) have soared for all major student subgroups.** *All 50 states began taking the NAEP exams in 2003, and since that point, Florida students have made the most gains. In 2009, Florida's Hispanic students outscored or tied 31 statewide averages on 4th-grade reading, and their African-American students outscored or tied eight statewide averages.*[56] [Emphasis added.]

Compare the sales pitch above to this 2011 *Orlando Sentinel* article on Florida's NAEP scores:

> **Florida made no gains on the latest round of national math and reading tests** *and, therefore, little progress toward its goal of being among top state performers by 2015, according to exam scores released this morning. ...*
>
> *On the National Assessment of Educational Progress tests in math and reading given earlier this year,* **Florida's fourth and eighth graders—the two groups tested—showed no significant change from two years ago.**
>
> *Fourth graders were still ahead of the national average in reading and at the mean in math. Eighth graders scored at about the national average in reading and below it in math.*
>
> **On both NAEP tests and in both grades, however, Florida was well below top-performing states.**[57] [Emphasis added.]

The content of the Sentinel article does not bode well for ALEC's promoting Florida education reforms in other states. The ALEC slant is vital to effectively marketing the Bush-endorsed reforms. Bush is a name brand at ALEC. The truth about his so-named "success" is irrelevant.

In true ALEC fashion, the organization continues in promoting the A-Plus Literacy Act by instructing legislators on how to promote the bill:

> *This bill is written as an omnibus education reform act.* **Some may find it most useful to introduce as an omnibus bill, but others may prefer to introduce separate measures depending upon legislative dynamics. Regardless of the number of bills introduced, it is suggested that lawmakers pursue the full package of reforms.** *High quality research evaluations have found significant gains associated with several different reform elements, but working in concert, these elements can radically improved academic achievement for all students.*[58] [Emphasis added.]

In sum, this omnibus bill is designed to peddle Florida reforms: School and district report cards; financial rewards to schools for good or improving school grades; vouchers; alternative teacher certification; social promotion ban, school and teacher bonuses for Advanced Placement. Jeb Bush's Florida reform success is illusory. Test scores are unimpressive unless spun. Florida tests are rotated, and the resulting, contingent school letter grades mean little. The social promotion ban is a bust. Vouchers have never flourished. Neither has merit pay. (See chapters on Bush.) Yet Bush is powerful among ALEC ranks, so his reforms, packaged under a catchy name, are promoted via 30 pages of ALEC proposed model legislation, including more ALEC suggestions:

> *In the current economic climate, it may prove challenging for states to provide additional funding for school improvement. Furthermore, many legislators may justifiably believe that their states already provide too much funding to district schools already.*
>
> *If however your state can successfully establish a rigorous A-F grading system, at that point you may want to condition a large portion of any future funding increases through the recognition program.*[59] [Emphasis added.]

Pay for performance based upon letter grades. The business world invades the schoolhouse.

There is no denying that Jeb Bush is an influential ALEC member. For example, he is connected to the 2010 ALEC meeting in DC in at least three ways. First, Bush's Foundation for Excellence in Education's (FEE) annual summit was held in DC in 2010 immediately preceding the ALEC meeting, conveniently enabling FEE summit attendees to attend both conferences.[60,61] Second, the education task force materials for ALEC's DC meeting feature Florida education reforms and explicitly refer ALEC members to FEE for assistance with Florida-type educational reform. The excerpt below comes from the 2010 education task force mailout:

> *In passing their comprehensive, linked reforms beginning in 1999, Florida lawmakers embraced a comprehensive, multifaceted approach to improving academic achievement focused on early childhood literacy as the gateway to learning.*
>
> *The central Florida reform involved increasing transparency: assigning all schools and districts a letter grade of A, B, C, D, or F. The other reform elements combined to spur improvement as well. Parental choice programs for children attending failing schools, low-income students and children with disabilities gave potential exit power for the least advantaged children. A strong charter school law and virtual education statutes provide universally available options. Florida embraced far-reaching alternative teacher certification paths to improve teacher quality, and curtailed the social promotion of children.*

> *Florida lawmakers have continued to update their reforms over time.* **Those interested in the latest policy innovations in Florida can contact the Foundation for Excellence in Education. The Foundation can assist with technical issues, provide sample rules created by the Florida State Board of Education and other assistance.**[62] [Emphasis added.]

A third connection between ALEC and Jeb Bush involves ALEC Education Task Force Director Myslinski—who left his position at ALEC for one with Jeb Bush's FEE. In fact, it was Myslinski who announced that ALEC voted to oppose its own model legislation against CCSS. Here is an excerpt from his November 19, 2012, announcement on the FEE website, including an excerpt from his FEE bio:

> *Over the weekend, the American Legislative Exchange Council (ALEC) rejected an anti-Common Core bill, thus completing its 18-month exploration of the Common Core State Standards.* **This action reaffirmed ALEC's position that states should be in charge of their education standards and supports the option for states to freely adopt Common Core.**
>
> *By rejecting the bill,* **which would have tied the hands of state legislators,** *ALEC made clear its support of states raising student expectations through higher standards—working in consort with other states or working independently. This position is laid out in ALEC's current Resolution Opposing Federal Intrusion in State Education Content Standards.* **The decision to work together to improve academic standards is a choice all 50 states have freely made, with 46 states adopting Common Core so far, and four states choosing not to adopt the standards.** ...
>
> **Dave (Myslinski)** *serves as the* **State Policy Director for Digital Learning Now! at the Foundation for Excellence in Education. He previously has served as the Education Task Force Director at the American Legislative Exchange Council** *where he focused on digital learning, K-12 education reform, and higher education.*[63] [Emphasis added.]

Myslinski puts the federalism spin on his announcement to make it appear that ALEC is not allowing federal intrusion. What Myslinski does not address is that the federal government is requiring CCSS as a condition for states to receive Race to the Top money.

The original ALEC model resolution opposing CCSS was part of the education task force's 35-day mailout to its members on July 1, 2011, preceding the ALEC annual meeting to be held in New Orleans in August 2011. The sponsor of the model bill was Jonathan Butcher of the Goldwater Institute, named for its founder, the late Senator Barry Goldwater. Located in Phoenix, Arizona, the current Goldwater Institute has the reputation for operating like a mini-ALEC. According to her 1999 interview with Tony Ortega of the *Phoenix New Times News*, Goldwater's widow, Susan, commented that Goldwater did not approve of the direction the Goldwater Institute was assuming: "What he (Barry Goldwater) didn't like was seeing it turn into a special-interest, big-business lobbying group." Susan Goldwater continues by saying that Goldwater was "nervous about charter schools... about what they would do to the public schools."[64]

Though Goldwater considered rescinding use of his name from the institute that bore it, he never did,[65] and now Goldwater is synonymous for ALEC. And ALEC is anti-federal-government interference. Thus it only makes sense that a model resolution placing educational responsibility into local jurisdiction would readily pass—except that there are so many corporations that stand to benefit from CCSS, one can understand the quandary.

Given ALEC's penchant for replacing federal control with its own control over states, its rejecting a set of educational standards that the Obama administration has mandated to be adopted by states wishing to receive RTTT funding is an anticipated ALEC course of action. Even if its motives are suspect, ALEC's resolution is sound. Here it is, reproduced in its entirety as it was written in the 2011 ALEC Education Task Force 35-Day Mailout dated July 1, 2011:

Resolution Opposing the Implementation of the Common Core State

Standards Initiative

Model Resolution

WHEREAS, *high student performance and closing the achievement gap is fundamentally linked to an overall reform of our public education system through a strong system of accountability and transparency* **built on state standards,** *and*

WHEREAS, *the responsibility for* **the education of each child of this nation primarily lies with parents, supported by locally elected school boards and state governments,** *and*

WHEREAS, *common standards have resulted in increased decision making on issues of state and local significance* **without the input of state and local stakeholders,** *and*

WHEREAS, no empirical evidence indicates that centralized education standards necessarily result in higher student achievement, *and*

WHEREAS, special interest groups can expose the vulnerability of the centralized decision making that governs common standards and lower the standards' rigor and quality to suit their priorities, *and*

WHEREAS, *adoption of the Common Core standards* **would force several states to lower their standards,** *and*

WHEREAS, *the* **National Assessment of Educational Progress national test already exists and allows comparisons of academic achievement to be made across the states, without the necessity of imposing national standards, curricula or assessments,** *and*

WHEREAS, imposing a set of national standards is likely to lead to the imposition of a national curriculum and national assessment upon the various states, a clear violation of the Elementary Secondary Education Act, and

WHEREAS, claims from the Common Core Initiative that the Common Core will not dictate what teachers teach in the classroom are refuted by language in the standards as written, and

WHEREAS, common standards will continue to lessen the ability for local stakeholders to innovate and continue to make improvements over time, and

WHEREAS, when no less than 22 states face budget shortfalls and Race to the Top funding for states is limited, $350 million for consortia to develop new assessments aligned with the Common Core standards will not cover the entire cost of overhauling state accountability systems, which includes implementation of standards and testing and associated professional development and curriculum restructuring, and

WHEREAS, local education officials, school leaders, teachers, and parents were not included in the discussion, evaluation and preparation of the standards that would affect students in this state.

NOW, THEREFORE, BE IT RESOLVED that the {legislative body} of the state of {name of state} rejects any policies and procedures that would be incumbent on the state based on the Common Core State Standards Initiative.[66] [Emphasis added excepting bolded, capped words.]

In the October 27, 2011 ALEC Education Task Force 35-Day Mailout for the Scottsdale, AZ, meeting in November/December 2011, ALEC added an option to convert the resolution into a statute:

The State Board of Education may not adopt, and the State Department of Education may not implement, the Common Core State Standards developed by the Common Core State Standards Initiative. Any actions taken to adopt or implement the Common Core State Standards as of the effective date of this section are void ab initio. Neither this nor any other statewide education standards may be adopted or implemented without the approval of the Legislature.[67]

If ALEC had ever made sense, if even for selfish motives, it was with this resolution opposing CCSS. Local stakeholders did not offer any substantive input into CCSS. Too, CCSS has not been tested, and the possibilities for special interest groups to influence CCSS direction abound. The language of CCSS intrudes upon the art of teaching. The list continues.

Why did ALEC not vote to approve this resolution?

They did. Then Jeb stepped in.

In the Scottsdale mailout, Education Task Force members were instructed to read several articles in order to prepare for discussion on the issue. (I know, ironic—ALEC wants to promote discussion on CCSS while at the same time directing legislators on what exactly they should read as "homework.")

Here is the list:

Articles in Support for the Common Core State Standards Initiative:

Five Myths About the Common Core State Standards, By Robert Rothman

FACT SHEET: The Common Core State Standards

The Wall Street Journal: "The Case for Common Educational Standards", By Jeb Bush and Joel Klein

Articles in Opposition to the Common Core State Standards Initiative:

Jay P. Greene's Testimony before the US House Subcommittee on Early Education, Elementary, and Secondary Education

National Review: "Standardizing Mediocrity: Why national standards won't fix American Education", By Lindsey Burke and Jennifer A. Marshall

Pioneer Institute: "Common Core's Standards Still Don't Make the Grade:

Why Massachusetts and California Academic Destinies", By Sandra Stotsky and Ze'ev Wurman[68] [Emphasis added.]

If ALEC was encouraging its members to read on both sides of an issue, that could only mean that ALEC members were divided on the issue. The dilemma is clear: CCSS violates ALEC's oft-professed allegiance to federalism, yet CCSS offers incredible opportunity for profits for its corporations.

Note that one of the articles assigned to legislators to read in support of CCSS is co-authored by Jeb Bush and Joel Klein.

In Scottsdale, on December 1, 2011, as noted in meeting minutes included in the April 2012 mailout for the May 2012 ALEC meeting in Charlotte, North Carolina, the ALEC Education Task Force members voted to approve the resolution opposing CCSS and promote it as ALEC-endorsed, model legislation:

> *The second bill the Education Task Force members considered was the* Comprehensive Legislative Package Opposing the Common Core State Standards Initiative, *cosponsored by Jonathan Butcher of Goldwater Institute and Emmett McGroarty of American Principles Project. After discussion, the legislation passed both the public sector with 14 Yeas, 6 Nays, and the private sector with 9 Yeas, and 4 Nays.* The Comprehensive Legislative Package Opposing the Common Core State Standards Initiative *was approved.*[69]

The outcome appears to be clear enough: Resolution approved.

Stay tuned.

In the same mailout information that included the vote for ALEC to officially oppose CCSS, Wireless Generation was announced as a new member to ALEC's Education Task Force (May 2012). Also announced was a new task force director[70]— former director, David Myslinski, left to go work for Jeb Bush.

Jeb Bush was clearly in favor of CCSS. He co-authored with former New York City Chancellor Joel Klein an article about his position—one that Education Task Force legislators were required to read.

Joel Klein now works for Amplify, owned by Rupert Murdoch, who also owns Wireless Generation.

In March 2013, Murdoch's Amplify was awarded the contract to develop the CCSS assessments.[71]

As for Wireless Generation, it built the operating system for the Gates- and Carnegie-funded data storage cloud, inBloom.[72]

Rupert Murdoch stands to benefit immensely from CCSS, both for its assessment and data collection requirements.

CCSS must happen.

Jeb Bush stepped in to save the day.[73] Keep in mind that the "final vote" for ALEC to officially approve of a model resolution opposing CCSS had been taken and recorded in ALEC minutes in December 2011.

FEE Executive Director Patricia Levesque issued an email on November 20, 2012, offering verbatim the announcement that former ALEC director and current FEE state policy director for Bush's Digital Learning Now! David Myslinski publicized a day earlier and cited previously in this chapter. Levesque's email begins as follows:

> *After an 18-month exploration of Common Core State Standards, the American Legislative Exchange Council (ALEC) came to a final vote over the weekend, rejecting a bill opposing Common Core.*[74]

This must be the "final final vote"—the one that favors Murdoch profits for both data collection and assessment—and the one that Jeb Bush wanted all along.

At least now we need not wonder what would happen if ALEC had to choose between federalism and materialism. Materialism, one; federalism, zero.

But then, ALEC has always worked hard to put money in its corporate members' pockets. And in this age in which those with a lust for power fully comprehend the need for information control, ALEC will always find an obscenely wealthy patron willing to reward it for voting—and—when necessary—voting again.

CONCLUSION: WHERE TO FROM HERE?

My goal in writing this book was to expose the implosive designs upon American public education of self-designated "reformers." By way of their destructive ploys, the individuals and organizations represented herein are systematically placing dynamite into the education structure, and in the name of the bold and urgent, they cause schools, districts, states, and, ultimately, our country to collapse upon themselves. If our nation is currently at risk because of the state of American education, it is the result of corporate reform deception and greed, of the push for the test score to grade all and of underfunding while demanding more out of the traditional public school.

Now it is time for the readers of this book to make their own demands of the corporate reformers. I have exposed their wiles. I have documented their sleights of fact, their deal-making, their lack of substance behind their echoes of public education failure and privatization solution. Take my work and run with it. Actively register your dissatisfaction with would-be corporate reform succubus "solutions." Go to the news networks, the legislative sessions, the school board meetings. Go to the polls. If you believe you are

A Chronicle of Echoes: Who's Who in the Implosion of American Public Education,
pages 403–404.

not being heard, invite a friend and go again. And again. And again. Boycott the tests. Take back your schools. They belong to you, the public.

Stymie the implosion.

Silence the echoes.

ENDNOTES

CHAPTER 1

1. Schneider, M. (2013, February 3). NCTQ letter grades and the reformer agenda: Part IX. [Web log post]. Retrieved from http://deutsch29.word-press.com/2013/02/03/nctq-letter-grades-and-the-reformer-agenda-part-ix/

2. Medina, J. (2009, August 7). N.Y. Senate renews mayor's power to run schools. *New York Times*. Retrieved from http://www.nytimes.com/2009/08/07/nyregion/07control.html?_r=0

3. Cramer, P. (2013, February 14). Bloomberg shifts tone n school reforms in last annual address. Retrieved from http://gothamschools.org/2013/02/14/bloomberg-shifts-tone-on-school-reforms-in-last-annual-address/

4. Gonen, Y. (2013, March 5). Classy Mike wants to fund own schools. *New York Post*. Retrieved from http://www.nypost.com/p/news/local/classy_mike_wants_to_fund_own_schools_diqABEWjf27KqU66a75vwI

5. Matthews, K. (2012, August 13). Joel Klein, former New York City schools chief, touts News Corp. tablet computer education enture. *Huffington Post*. Retrieved from http://www.huffingtonpost.com/2012/08/13/former-nyc-schools-chief-_0_n_1773271.html

A Chronicle of Echoes: Who's Who in the Implosion of American Public Education,
pages 405–493.
Copyright © 2014 by Information Age Publishing
All rights of reproduction in any form reserved.

6.   Bloomberg, M. (2002, July 30). Letter to Honorable Richard Mills on behalf of Joel Klein. *New York Times.* Retrieved from http://graphics8.nytimes.com/packages/pdf/kleinapplication.pdf

7.   Otterman, S. (2010, November 10). New York Schools chancellor ends 8-year run. *New York Times.* Retrieved from http://www.nytimes.com/2010/11/10/nyregion/10klein.html?ref=joeliklein

8.   See 2.

9.   *United States of America vs. Microsoft Corporation.* (1999, November 5). Findings of fact for civil action no. 98-1232 (TPJ). Retrieved April23, 2013, from http://www.webcitation.org/query?id=1298665666970544

10.   Cringely, R. (2004, April 8). The once and future king: Now the only way Microsoft can die is by suicide. Retrieved from http://www.pbs.org/cringely/pulpit/2004/pulpit_20040408_000808.html

11.   Jenkins, G., & Bing, R. (2007). Microsoft's monopoly: Anti-competitive behavior, predatory tactics, and the failure of governmental will. Retrieved from   http://journals.cluteonline.com/index.php/JBER/article/viewArticle/2508

12.   CNN. (2000, September 19). US antitrust chief resigns. Retrieved from http://cnnfn.cnn.com/2000/09/19/news/klein/

13.   Indiana State Government. (n.d.). Chancellor Joel Klein background materials. Retrieved on April 23, 2013, from http://www.in.gov/edroundtable/files/5Chancellor_Joel_Klein_Background_Materials.pdf

14.   Broad Foundation and Fordham Institute (2003, May). Better leaders for America's schools: A manifesto. Retrieved from http://www.broadeducation.org/asset/1128-betterleadersforamericasschools.pdf

15.   Eli Broad. (n.d.). *Huffington Post.* Retrieved from http://www.huffingtonpost.com/eli-broad/

16.   Educators for All. (2012, March 8). Why schools fail, or what if failing schools... aren't? Retrieved April 23, 2013, from http://educatorsforall.org/blog/2012/3/8/why-schools-fail-or-what-if-failing-schoolsarent.html

17.   Rothstein, R. (2012, October 11). Joel Klein's misleading autobiography. Retrieved from http://prospect.org/article/joel-kleins-misleading-autobiography

18.   Klein, J., & Rice, C. (2012). Task force report: US education reform and national security. Retrieved from http://www.cfr.org/united-states/us-education-reform-national-security/p27618

19.   Friedman, G. (2013, January 8). US national security hinges on the middle class. Retrieved from http://www.speroforum.com/a/UHFRIGAMIE6/73446-US-national-security-hinges-on-crisis-of-Americas-middle-class

20.–23. See 17.

24.   Rothstein, R. (2012, October 12). Expose: Former NYC school chancellor Joel Klein is not telling the whole truth about his personal history. Retrieved from http://www.alternet.org/education/expose-former-nyc-school-chancellor-joel-klein-not-telling-whole-truth-about-his-personal?page=0%2C1

25.   Orlich, D., & Gifford, G. (2006, October 20). Test scores, poverty, and ethnicity: The new American dilemma. Retrieved from http://www.cha. wa.gov/?q=files/Highstakestesting_poverty_ethnicity.pdf

26.   Strauss, V. (2010, December 9). How poverty affected US Pisa scores. [Web log post]. *Washington Post*. Retrieved from http://voices.washingtonpost. com/answer-sheet/research/how-poverty-affected-us-pisa-s.html

27.–30.   StudentsFirstNY. (n.d.). About us. Retrieved from http://www.studentsfirst-ny.org/index.cfm?objectid=19788100-EC1D-11E1-9930000C296BA163

31.   Hill, P. T., Campbell, C., & Gross, B. (2012). *Strife and Progress: Portfolio Strategies for Managing Urban Schools*. Washington, D.C.: Brookings Institute Press. Retrieved from http://books.google.com/books?id=QqTyaf6IMOY C&pg=PA111&lpg=PA111&dq=joel+klein+andres+alonso&source=bl&ots =kZNde2k74r&sig=Oa-3whhBYZGwuTPEzb5O9P3kmXk&hl=en&sa=X&e i=OEd3Ueu1JpHA9QSJpYHQCw&ved=0CFwQ6AEwBzgK#v=onepage&q= joel%20klein%20andres%20alonso&f=false

32.   Monohan, R. (2012, May 12). Joel Klein tight with charter school lobbyists, emails show. *New York Daily News*. Retrieved from http://www.nydailynews. com/new-york/joel-klein-tight-charter-school-lobbyists-emails-shows-article-1.1076974

33.   Vanacore, A. (2012, July 2). Report: Emails reveal damage control effort by John White, Jindal officials over voucher program. *Times-Picayune*. Retrieved from http://www.nola.com/education/index.ssf/2012/07/report_emails_reveal_damage_co.html

34.   Aswell, T. (2013, February 19). It took the threat of a lawsuit, but John White did respond to Louisiana Voice's multiple public records requests—sort of. [Web log post]. Retrieved from http://louisianavoice.com/2013/02/19/ it-took-the-threat-of-a-lawsuit-but-john-white-did-respond-to-louisianavoic-es-multiple-public-records-requests-sort-of/

35.   Benckini, K. (2012, March 7). Grasmick didn't need driver; why does Alonso? *Baltimore Sun*. Retrieved from http://articles.baltimoresun.com/2012-03-07/news/bs-ed-grasmick-alonso-driver-20120307_1_nancy-grasmick-driver-state-schools-superintendent

36.   Green, Erica. (2012, March 1). City schools pay $14 million overtime in four years. *Baltimore Sun*. Retrieved from http://articles.baltimoresun. com/2012-03-01/news/bs-md-ci-schools-overtime-20120301_1_ralph-askins-neil-duke-tisha-edwards

37.   Baltimore spends $500,000 to renovate school offices. (2012, April 27). *WBAL-TV*. Retrieved from http://www.wbaltv.com/news/mary-land/education/Baltimore-spends-500-000-to-renovate-school-offices/-/9379316/12149668/-/95iqkk/-/index.html

38.   Matthews, J. (n.d.) Andres Alonso failed stewardship. *Baltimore Times*. Retrieved April 25, 2013, from http://baltimoretimes-online.com/index. php?option=com_content&view=article&id=1429:andres-alonsos-failed-stewardship-&catid=104:jayne-matthews&Itemid=486

39.   Byrne, J., Ahmed-Ullah, N., & Sobol, R. (2012, October 12). Brizard out as CPS chief: "We agreed it's best." *Chicago Tribune*. Retrieved from http:// articles.chicagotribune.com/2012-10-12/news/chi-jean-claude-brizard-

out-as-cps-head-20121011_1_jean-claude-brizard-chicago-teachers-union-chief-education-officer

40.   Rossi, R., & Janssen, K. (n.d.). Rahm Emanuel names Jean-Claude Brizard new Chicago school CEO. *Sun Times*. Retrieved from http://www.suntimes.com/news/metro/4897090-418/rahm-emanuel-to-name-new-yorks-jean-claude-brizard-new-chicago-schools-chief.html

41.   Cramer, P. (2009, June 8). Garth Harries to leave city for New Haven schools at end of year. Retrieved from http://gothamschools.org/2009/06/08/garth-harries-to-leave-city-for-new-haven-schools-at-end-of-year/

42.   Bailey, M. (2011, May 13). City secretly plans school's for-profit takeover. *New Haven Independent*. Retrieved from http://www.newhavenindependent.org/index.php/archives/entry/ch_co._takeover_nears/

43.–44.   Neufeld, S. (2012, November 29). Newark's school turnaround strategy changes course. *Hechinger Report*. Retrieved from http://hechingerreport.org/content/newarks-school-turnaround-strategy-changes-course_10451/

45.   Mooney, J. (2012, February 6). Rough start for Newark super's school reorganization strategy. *NJ Spotlight*. Retrieved from http://www.njspotlight.com/stories/12/0205/2035/

46.   Wallack, T. (2000, November 2). Covad CEO forced out of his job. *San Francisco Chronicle*. Retrieved from http://www.sfgate.com/business/article/Covad-CEO-Forced-Out-Of-His-Job-2730600.php

47.   Arp, C. (2011, June 10). For the first time, new principal academy CEO was once a principal. Retrieved from http://gothamschools.org/2011/06/10/for-first-time-new-principal-academy-ceo-was-once-a-principal/

48.   Haimson, L. (2008, July 9). Joel Klein devises a plan in which he can stay in power... forever! [Web log post]. Retrieved from http://nycpublicschoolparents.blogspot.com/2008/07/joel-klein-devises-plan-in-which-he-can.html

49.   Gootman, E. (2009, May 26). Principals younger and freer, but raise doubts in the schools. *New York Times*. Retrieved from http://www.nytimes.com/2009/05/26/nyregion/26principals.html?pagewanted=all&_r=0

50.   Chapman, B. (2010, October 22). Principal writes memo full of typos—parents and teachers give him an 'F.' *New York Daily News*. Retrieved from http://www.nydailynews.com/new-york/principal-writes-memo-full-typos-parents-teachers-give-f-article-1.188871

51.   Chapman, B., Fanelli, J. (2010, October 23). Writing-challenged principal Andrew Buck stands behind his idiotic letter. *New York Daily News*. Retrieved from   http://www.nydailynews.com/new-york/education/writing-challenged-principal-andrew-buck-stands-behind-idiotic-letter-article-1.191750

52.   See 50.

53.   [Excerpts from the letter principal Andrew Buck emailed to teachers]. (2010, October 16). Retrieved from https://docs.google.com/viewer?a=v&pid=sites&srcid=ZGVmYXVsdGRvbWFpbnxueWWRuZG9j3xneDoyMTdjY2M3ZWQzOWJlNDA0&pli=1

54.   Chapman, B. (2010, October 29). Daily News finds principal's bad writing is least of school's woes as sex, violence plague it also. *New York Daily News*. Retrieved from http://www.nydailynews.com/new-york/education/

daily-news-finds-principal-bad-writing-school-woes-sex-violence-plague-article-1.186571

55. Chapman, B. (2011, May 31). Pleeze help: Writing-challenged Brooklyn principal Andrew Buck asking parents, teacher for support. *New York Daily News.* Retrieved from http://www.nydailynews.com/new-york/education/pleeze-writing-challenged-brooklyn-principal-andrew-buck-parents-teachers-support-article-1.142526

56. Chapman, B. (2011, July 2). 'Least trustworthy' principal in New York City public schools finally fired from post. *New York Daily News.* Retrieved from http://www.nydailynews.com/new-york/brooklyn/least-trustworthy-principal-new-york-city-public-schools-finally-fired-brooklyn-post-article-1.157094

57. Smith, H. (2005). District-wide reform. Interview with Joel Klein, chancellor (2002-   present), New York City Department of Education. *PBS.* Retrieved from   http://www.pbs.org/makingschoolswork/dwr/ny/klein.html

58. Herszenhorn, D. (2003, September 17). New York schools get $51.2 million from Gates. *New York Times.* Retrieved from http://www.nytimes.com/2003/09/17/education/17CND-SCHOO.html

59. Epstein, M. (2013, February 21). Small schools: Miracle or mirage? [Web log post]. *Huffington Post.* Retrieved from http://www.huffingtonpost.com/marc-epstein/small-schools-miracle-or_b_2641400.html

60. Robinson, G. (NYC's school closing gambit leaves students behind. [Web log post]. *Huffington Post.* Retrieved from http://www.huffingtonpost.com/gail-robinson/nycs-school-closing-gambi_b_1644758.html

61. See 7.

62. Rupert Murdoch, Joel Klein, and New York City schools. (n.d.). Retrieved on April 24, 2013, from http://www.edwize.org/rupert-murdoch-joel-klein-and- new-york-city-schools

63. Dicker, F., & Campanile, C. (2011, February 11). Ad 'merits' a look. *New York Post.* Retrieved from http://www.nypost.com/p/news/local/ad_merits_look_EYQnRDn2WYP7jcCLFEfpSL

64. Quigley, B. (2010, May 3). Education Reform Now's hedge fund buddies. [Web log post]. Retrieved from http://blogs.artvoice.com/avdaily/2010/05/03/education-reform-nows-hedge-fund-buddies/

65.–66. McClelland, E. (2012, September 20). Rahm's post-strike ad paid for by ed reform group. [Web log post]. *NBC Chicago.* Retrieved from http://www.nbcchicago.com/blogs/ward-room/Rahms-Post-Strike-Paid-For-By-Ed-Reform-Group-170513836.html

67. Phillips, A. (2011, May 4). City to review $4.5 million contract with Wireless Generation. Retrieved from http://gothamschools.org/2011/05/04/city-plans-to-give-1-5-million-contract-to-wireless-generation/

68. Quillen, I. (2011, June 10). Klein, Wireless Generation questioned again in NYC media. [Web log post]. Retrieved from http://blogs.edweek.org/edweek/DigitalEducation/2011/06/klein_wireless_generation_ques.html

69.   Jilani, Z. (2011, July 14). Mired in scandal, News Corp seeks New York state's signoff for $27 million no-bid contract. Retrieved from http://think-progress.org/politics/2011/07/14/268598/news-corp-911-contract/

70.   *See 7.*

71.–72. *Santos, F. (2010, November 24). News Corp, after hiring Klein, buys technology partner in a city schools project. New York Times. Retrieved from* http://www.nytimes.com/2010/11/24/nyregion/24newscorp.html?_r=1&partner=rss&emc=rss

73.   Schools Chancellor Joel I. Klein announces selection of IBM to develop achievement reporting system for educators and parents. (2004, March 5). Retrieved from http://www-03.ibm.com/press/us/en/pressrelease/21183.wss

74.   Liu, J. (2012, January 23). Audit report in brief (Achievement Reporting and Innovation System [ARIS]). Retrieved from the New York City Bureau of Audit website, http://www.comptroller.nyc.gov/bureaus/audit/audits_2012/1-23-12_7I11-118A.shtm/

75.   Cramer, P. (2012, January 23). Liu: City hasn't gotten sufficient bang from ARIS's $83m buck. Retrieved from http://gothamschools.org/2012/01/23/liu-city-hasnt-gotten-sufficient-bang-from-ariss-83m-buck/

76.   Monahan, R. (2012, January 16). Liu clobbers no-bid deal for Klein co. *New York Daily News.* Retrieved from http://www.nydailynews.com/news/liu-clobbers-no-bid-deal-klein-article-1.1007246

77.   Colvin, J., & Zimmer, A. (2012, July 30). City's $80m student data system to be replaced by state portal. Retrieved from http://www.dnainfo.com/new-york/20120730/new-york-city/citys-80m-student-data-system-be-replaced-by-state-portal

78.–80. Murphy, J. (2006, November 21). Contract killer: Laughs and legal threats. Retrieved April 25, 2913, in full text from http://www.parentadvocates.org/nicecontent/dsp_printable.cfm?articleID=7231

81.–82. Gootman, E., & Herszenhorn, D. (2007, February 3). Consultants draw fire in bus woes. *New York Times.* Retrieved from http://www.nytimes.com/2007/02/03/nyregion/03bus.html?pagewanted=all&_r=0

83.   Lazarowitz, E. (2009, February 7). Joel Klein under fire admits bus bungle. *New York Daily News.* Retrieved from http://www.nydailynews.com/new-york/education/joel-klein-fire-admits-bus-bungle-article-1.390640

84.   http://www.nysun.com/new-york/consulting-firm-aiding-the-city-may-see-its/44770/

85.   Brown, A. (n.d.). Bad math at the RSD. *Tribune Talk.* Retrieved from http://www.tribunetalk.com/?p=4513

86.   Turgue, B. (2012, March 8). Alvarez and Marsal hired for cheating probe. [Web log post]. *Washington Post.* Retrieved from http://www.washington-post.com/blogs/dc-schools-insider/post/alvarez-and-marsal-hired-for-cheating-probe/2012/03/08/gIQAJ5m00R_blog.html

87.   Merrow, J. (2013, April 25). Penetrating the smokescreen. [Web log post]. Retrieved from http://takingnote.learningmatters.tv/?p=6332

88.   See 86.

CHAPTER 2

1.–2.   Eva Moskowitz. (n.d.). *Wikipedia*. Retrieved April 29, 2013, from, http://en.wikipedia.org/wiki/Eva_Moskowitz

3.   Success Academies. (n.d.). Our leaders. Retrieved April 29, 2013, from http://www.successacademies.org/page.cfm?p=301

4.   Chapman, B. (2013, September 23). With the threat of an unsupportive mayor on the horizon, charter schools shamelessly send students to protest di Blasio's plan. *New York Daily News*. Retrieved from http://www.nydailynews.com/news/election/charters-send-kids-march-blaz-plan-article-1.1465408

5.–10.   [Email exchange between Eva Moskowitz and Joel Klein, August 2006 to July 2009.] Retrieved from https://docs.google.com/viewer?a=v&pid=sites&srcid=ZGVmYXVsdGRvbWFpbnxueWRuZG9j3xneDoyMjFlOTliYmVlNjUxMmIw

11.   Winerip, M. (2011, April 25). Charter school space: Free of rent, maybe, but not of hurdles. *New York Times*. Retrieved from http://www.nytimes.com/2011/04/25/nyregion/charter-schools-face-hurdles-in-offer-of-free-space.html?pagewanted=all

12.   Success Academies. (n.d.). Success Academy Bronx 2. Retrieved April 29, 2013, from http://www.successacademies.org/page.cfm?p=730

13.   See 11.

14.   New York City Schools. (n.d.). Patrick Sullivan, Manhattan representative. Retrieved from http://schools.nyc.gov/AboutUs/leadership/PEP/members/PatrickSullivan.htm

15.   Gonzalez, J. (2009, June 3). Students at PS 123 in Harlem are pushed aside for charter school expansion. *New York Daily News*. Retrieved from http://www.nydailynews.com/new-york/education/students-ps-123-harlem-pushed-charter-school-expansion-article-1.373060

16.   See 14.

17.–18.   New York City Schools. (2012, June 27). Regulation of the chancellor: Parent associations and the schools. Retrieved from http://schools.nyc.gov/NR/rdonlyres/EBEFFD82-30D5-4B91-9F9A-6A07B0D0F2D6/0/A660.pdf

19.–20.   See 5.

21.   See 15.

22.–23.   See 5.

24.   Gonzalez, J. (2010, February 25). Moskowitz asks Klein to expand charters; dept. of education closes school to make room. *New York Daily News*. Retrieved from http://www.nydailynews.com/new-york/education/moskowitz-asks-klein-expand-charters-dept-education-closes-schools-room-article-1.173883

25.   See 5.

26.   See 15.

27.–30.   See 5.

31.   Hernandez, J. (2009, March 25). Suit challenges city plan to replace three schools. *New York Times*. Retrieved from http://www.nytimes.com/2009/03/25/education/25charter.html?_r=0

32.–33. See 5.

34. See 31.

35.–36. *Grinage et al. vs. NYC School Board* (2009, March 24). [Case filed with the Supreme Court of the State of New York, County of New York]. Retrieved from http://www.nyclu.org/files/CEC_Suit_03.24.09.PDF

37.–38. See 5.

39.–40. Cramer, P., & Green, E. (2009, April 2). DOE dropping school closure plan that drew UFT, parent lawsuit. Retrieved from http://gothamschools. org/2009/04/02/doe-dropping-school-closure-plan-that-drew-uft-parent-lawsuit/

41. The patron saint (and scourge) of lost schools.(n.d.). *New York Magazine.* Retrieved from http://nymag.com/nymag/features/65614/index3.html

42. See 39.

43.–45. See 5.

46. Eva Moskowitz's sin. (2013, April 27). *New York Post.* Retrieved from http://www.nypost.com/p/news/opinion/editorials/eva_moskowitz_sin_aJ723ceJmugMitdfh7R0EJ

47. See 41.

48. See 46.

49. See 41.

50.–51. Smith, K. (2011, August 27). Talking out of school. Retrieved from http://www.successacademies.org/page.cfm?p=585

52. See 5.

53. See 50.

54. See 5.

55. New York City Government. (2011, March 2). Youth and Community Development: Intent to award. *City record, 138*(41) 421-422. Retrieved from http://www.nyc.gov/html/dcas/downloads/pdf/cityrecord/cityre-cord-3-2-11.pdf

56. Boys and Girls Harbor Inc. Parents Community. (n.d.). NYC DYCD and Boys and Girls Harbor Inc.: Appeal and stop budget cuts for NYC after-school boys and girls harbor. Retrieved from https://www.change.org/petitions/nyc-dycd-and-boys-girls-harbor-inc-appeal-stop-budget-cuts-for-nyc-afterschool-boys-girls-harbor

57. NYC Youth Funders . (2011, July 14). State of youth services in NYC in 2011: Challenging times and strategic responses. Retrieved from http://www.nycyouthfunders.org/docs/nycyf_summary_20110714.pdf

58. Gonzalez, J. (2011, July 27). Success Charter Network has been just that for Eva Moskowitz but not for public schools. *New York Daily News.* Retrieved from http://www.nydailynews.com/new-york/success-charter-network-eva-moskowitz-public-schools-article-1.159481

59. Kamenetz, A. (2013, January 30). Invasion of the charter schools. *Village Voice.* Retrieved from http://www.villagevoice.com/2013-01-30/news/Eva-Moskowitz-Bloomberg-Charter-Schools/full/

60. Solomon, S. (2013, February 20). Eva Moskowitz's Success Academy aims to open six new charter schools in 2013. Retrieved from http://www.

dnainfo.com/new-york/20130220/lower-east-side/eva-moskowitz-success-academy-aims-open-7-new-charter-schools-2014

61. Gonzalez, J. (2012, June 25). Eva Moskowitz's Success Academy Schools network rolling in money but still wants 50% increase in management fees from state. *New York Daily News*. Retrieved from http://www.nydailynews.com/new-york/eva-moskowitz-success-academy-charter-schools-disproportionate-share-state-education-money-article-1.1101668

62. Gordon, A. (2013, May 23). Scene last night: Loeb, Christie, Tepper, Singer, Bommer (1). *Business Week*. Retrieved from http://www.businessweek.com/news/2013-05-23/scene-last-night-loeb-christie-jones-tepper-singer-bommer

63.–64. Lestch, C. (2013, January 14). New Success Academy charter school headed by Eva Moskowitz to open in the Bronx with little parent say. *New York Daily News*. Retrieved from http://www.nydailynews.com/new-york/bronx/success-academy-charter-network-open-school-bronx-article-1.1236356

65. Ravitch, D. (2011, January 13). Myth of charter schools. *New York Books*. Retrieved from http://www.nybooks.com/articles/archives/2010/nov/11/myth-charter-schools/?pagination=false

66. See 62.

67.–68. Akaqi, K. (2013, February 20). At Bronx closure hearing, an apology and pleas for more space. Retrieved from http://gothamschools.org/2013/02/20/at-bronx-closure-hearing-an-apology-and-pleas-for-more-space/#more-100150

69. Success Academy Bronx 3. (n.d.). Retrieved April 30, 2013, from the Success Academies website, http://www.successacademies.org/page.cfm?p=762

70.–71. Long-Middleton, M. (2011, November 15). Opposition continues to mount against Success Academy Cobble Hill. Retrieved from http://carrollgardens.patch.com/groups/schools/p/school-fo-international-studies-pta-meeting-strong-op523e68f70c

72. Success Academies. (n.d.). Success Academy Cobble Hill. Retrieved April 29, 2013, from http://www.successacademies.org/page.cfm?p=734

73. Louis, E. (2010, October 17). The next charter school war: Eva Moskowitz is ready to expand into a wealthier, whiter nabes. *New York Daily News*. Retrieved from http://www.nydailynews.com/opinion/charter-school-war-eva-moskowitz-ready-expand-wealthier-whiter-nabes-article-1.192921#ixzz2SOPFNAo8

74. See 59.

75. Decker, G. (2012, June 13). Moskowitz to authorizers: Reject high-need enrollment targets. Retrieved from http://gothamschools.org/2012/06/13/moskowitz-to-authorizers-reject-high-need-enrollment-targets/

76. Success Academies. (n.d.). Success Academy Upper West. Retrieved April 30, 2013, from http://www.successacademies.org/page.cfm?p=732

CHAPTER 3

1. Schneider, M. (2013, January 31). NCTQ letter grades and the reformer agenda: part VII. [Web log post]. Retrieved from http://deutsch29.wordpress.com/2013/01/31/nctq-letter-grades-and-the-reformer-agenda-part-vii/

2. Park Cities, Texas. (2013, June 22). *Wikipedia.* Retrieved from http://en.wikipedia.org/wiki/Park_Cities,_Texas

3. George, B., Mayer, D., & McLean, A. (2007, April 11). Wendy Kopp and Teach for America (A). Retrieved from http://www.kiyoshikurokawa.com/jp/files/teachforamerica1.pdf

4. Stockdale, N. (2011, September 23). Point person: Our Q&A with Teach for America founder Wendy Kopp. *Dallas News.* Retrieved from http://www.dallasnews.com/opinion/sunday-commentary/20110923-point-person-our-qa-with-teach-for-america-founder-wendy-kopp.ece

5. Statistics for Highland Park High School—Dallas, Texas. Retrieved May 12, 2013, from http://www.schools-data.com/schools/HIGHLAND-PARK-HS-DALLAS.html

6. Statistics for Highland Park High School in Dallas, Texas. Retrieved May 12, 2013, from http://www.city-data.com/school/highland-park-high-school-tx.html

7. See 5.

8. Parsa, Amir. (1987, April 24). Growth, success mark 19 years at publication. *The Daily Princetonian, 111*(56), 1.

9.–10. Friedman, Tracy, & Parsa, Amir. (1987, April 22). Business Today fabricates own "letters to the editor"; Publisher says magazine will revise policy. *The Daily Princetonian, 111*(54), 1.

11.–12. Parsa, Amir. (1987, April, 24). Growth, success mark 19 years at publication. *The Daily Princetonian, 111*(56), 1.

13.–14. Goodman, Jack. (1988, February, 16). Don't look back. *The Daily Princetonian, 112*(12), 6.

15. Gentin, Pierre. (1987, April 24). Ethics purveyor. Opinions/editorials. *The Daily Princetonian, 111*(56), 10.

16. Kopp, Wendy. (1987, April, 24). Basic tenets. Opinions/editorials. *The Daily Princetonian, 111*(56), 10.

17. Cooke, Janet. (1988, January 18). Shapiro: We were just watching: New prez Hal caught. *Princeton Post*, 6.

18. [Advertisement.] (1988, November 18). *The Daily Princetonian, 112*(115), 9.

19. Brill, Steven. 2011. *Class Warfare.* New York: Simon and Schuster. Pg. 54.

20. See 3.

21. Romero, D. (1993, March 25). A thesis come true the concept of Wendy Kopp's senior paper: Give bright college grads some instruction, then send them to teach in the inner city. After graduation, she started Teach for America. *Philadelphia Inquirer.* Retrieved from http://articles.philly.com/1993-03-25/living/25951233_1_teacher-program-college-grads-thesis

22.   Kopp named MHC commencement speaker. (2007, April 24). Retrieved from http://www.mtholyoke.edu/news/stories/5187646

23.   Tan, R. (n.d.). Thesis sparks thriving teacher corps. Retrieved from http://www.princeton.edu/pr/pwb/01/0521/9a.shtml

24.   Teach for America. (n.d.). Our history. Retrieved May 12, 2013, from https://www.teachforamerica.org/our-organization/our-history

25.   *See 23.*

26.   See 3.

27.   Robin, C. (2013, March 11). Wendy Kopp, Princeton Tory. [Web log post]. Retrieved from http://coreyrobin.com/2013/03/11/wendy-kopp-princeton-tory/

28.   Strauss, V. (2012, October 22). How Teach for America became powerful. [Web log post]. *Washington Post.* Retrieved from http://www.washingtonpost.com/blogs/answer-sheet/wp/2012/10/22/how-teach-for-america-became-powerful-2/

29.   See 3.

30.   Tourangeau, M. (n.d.). Teach for America. Retrieved from http://learningtogive.org/papers/paper161.html

31.–32. See 3.

33.–34. Darling-Hammond, L. (1994, September). Who will speak for the children? *Phi Delta Kappan,* 21-34. Retrieved from http://www.trincoll.edu/depts/educ/Resources/DarlingHammond.PDF

35.   Heilig, J., Cole, H., & Springel, M. (2011, June 10). Alternative certification and Teach for America: The search for high-quality teachers. [Galley]. Retrieved from http://ows.edb.utexas.edu/sites/default/files/users/jvh/2%20-%20Heilig%20-%20Galley.pdf

36.   See 21.

37.   See 34.

38.   See 3.

39.   Teach for America, (n.d.). Research. Retrieved May 12, 2013, from http://www.teachforamerica.org/our-organization/research

40.   Darling-Hammond, L., Holtzman, D., Gatlin, S., & Heilig, J. (n.d.). Does teacher preparation matter? Retrieved from http://www.stanford.edu/~ldh/publications/LDH-teacher-certification-april2005.pdf

41.   Simon, S. (2012, August 16). Has Teach for America betrayed its mission? *Chicago Tribune.* Retrieved from http://articles.chicagotribune.com/2012-08-16/news/sns-rt-us-usa-education-teachforamerica-bre87f05o-20120815_1_tfa-seasoned-teachers-recruits

42.   Teach for America 2001 Form 990. Retrieved from http://207.153.189.83/EINS/133541913/133541913_2001_00a68706.PDF

43.   Teach for America 2005 Form 990. Retrieved from http://207.153.189.83/EINS/133541913/133541913_2005_03A673F0.PDF

44.   Teach for America 2010 Form 990. Retrieved from http://207.153.189.83/EINS/133541913/133541913_2010_08746967.PDF

45.   Fairbanks, A. (2011, July 27). Walton Family Foundations gifts Teach for America $49.5 million. *Huffington Post.* Retrieved from http://www.

huffingtonpost.com/2011/07/27/walton-foundation-teach-for-america-walmart_n_910615.html

46. See 28.

47. Strauss, V. (2012, October 1). What is Wendy Kopp talking about? [Web log post]. *Washington Post.* Retrieved from http://www.washingtonpost.com/blogs/answer-sheet/post/what-is-wendy-kopp-talking-about/2012/10/01/b4437b60-0b6f-11e2-bb5e-492c0d30bff6_blog.html

48. See 21.

49. See 24.

50. See 28.

51. Wendy Kopp: 1991 fellow. (n.d.). Retrieved from http://www.echoinggreen.org/fellows/wendy-kopp

52. Brill, Steven. 2011. *Class Warfare.* New York: Simon and Schuster. Pg. 54.

53. Donors. (n.d.). Retrieved May 12, 2013, from the Teach for America website, http://www.teachforamerica.org/support-us/donors

54. ALEC Corporations (2013, August 6). Retrieved from h t t p : / / w w w . sourcewatch.org/index.php/ALEC_Corporations

55. ALEC documents. (n.d.). Retrieved May 13, 2013, from http:// www.commoncause.org/site/pp.asp?c=dkLNK1MQIwG&b=8097075

56. Ravitch, D. (2013, January 30). Walton Foundation awards $158 million for privatization. [Web log post]. Retrieved from http://dianeravitch.net/2013/01/30/14815/

57. Gose, B. (2007). Back to school. Retrieved from the Social Impact Exchange website, http://www.socialimpactexchange.org/sites/www.socialimpactexchange.org/files/publications/Back%20to%20School_0.pdf

58. Taylor, D. (2010, May 25). Teach for American cashing in on ed reform? [Web log post]. Retrieved from http://seattleducation2010.wordpress.com/2012/05/25/teach-for-america-cashing-in-on-ed-reform/

59. Broad Center. (n.d.). Broad Center board. Retrieved May 13, 2013, from http://www.broadcenter.org/about/board.html

60. Taylor, D. (2912, February 21). A look at Race to the Top. [Web log post]. Retrieved from http://seattleducation2010.wordpress.com/2012/02/21/a-look-at-race-to-the-top/

61. Brown, J., Gutstein, E., & Lipman, P. (2009, May 29). Arne Duncan and the Chicago success story: Myth or reality? Retrieved from h t t p : / / www.commondreams.org/view/2009/05/29-10

62. Taylor, D. (2011, February 4). Why I am not a defender of the status quo in education—because the status quo is failed ed reforms. [Web log post]. Retrieved from http://seattleducation2010.wordpress.com/2011/02/04/why-i-am-not-a-defender-of-the-status-quo-in-education-because-the-status-quo-is-failed-ed-reforms/

63. Broad Foundation. (n.d.). All current investments. Retrieved from http://www.broadeducation.org/investments/current_investments/investments_all.html

64. Ravitch, D. (2012, October 3). The ultimate insult to Louisiana teachers. [Web log post]. Retrieved from http://dianeravitch.net/2012/10/03/the-ultimate-insult-to-louisiana-teachers/

65.   Hannah Dietsch [Biography]. (n.d.). Retrieved May 13, 2013, from http://www.linkedin.com/pub/hannah-dietsch/4/3b3/b02

66.   Broad Center. (n.d.). Hannah Dietsch: The Broad residency class of 2008-10. Retrieved May 13, 2013, from http://www.broadcenter.org/residency/network/profile/hannah-dietsch

67.   See 65.

68.   Teach for America. (n.d.). Teach for America school leadership initiative. Retrieved May 13, 2013, from http://www.teachforamerica.org/assets/documents/HGSE.CPS.Overview.pdf

69.–70.   Graduate school and employer partnerships. (n.d.). Retrieved May 13, 2013, from http://www.teachforamerica.org/why-teach-for-america/compensation-and-benefits/graduate-school-and-employer-partnerships/

71.–72.   Blanchard, O. (2013, September 23). I quit Teach for America. *Atlantic.* Retrieved from http://m.theatlantic.com/education/archive/2013/09/i-quit-teach-for-america/279724/

73.   Schneider, M. (2013, August 7). Kira Orange-Jones, TFA promotion, and LDOE TFA contracts [Web log post]. Retrieved from http://deutsch29.wordpress.com/2013/08/07/kira-orange-jones-tfa-promotion-and-ldoe-tfa-contracts/

74.   See.69.

75.   Barker, K. (2012, August, 18). How nonprofits spend millions on elections and call it public welfare. Retrieved from http://www.propublica.org/article/how-nonprofits-spend-millions-on-elections-and-call-it-public-welfare

76.   Leadership for Educational Equity. (n.d.). [Log –in page]. Retrieved from the website, https://educationalequity.org/login?auth_msg=needed&back=http%3a%2f%2feducationalequity.org%2fwork%2fwhat%2f

77.   Cersonsky, J. (2012, October 24). Teach for America's deep bench. Retrieved from http://prospect.org/article/teach-america%E2%80%99s-deep-bench

78.–79.   University of Colorado, Denver. (n.d.). Doctor of Education, Leadership for Educational Equity. [Degree program]. Retrieved from http://www.ucdenver.edu/academics/colleges/SchoolOfEducation/Academics/Doctorate/Pages/EdD.aspx

80.   Heilig, J., Williams, A., McNeil, L., & Lee, C. (n.d.). Is choice a panacea? An analysis of black secondary student attrition from KIPP, other privately operated charters, and urban districts. *Berkley Review of Education, 2*(2), 153-178. Retrieved from http://escholarship.org/uc/item/0vs9d4fr

81.   Rubinstein, G. (2011, October 31). Why I did TFA and why you shouldn't. [Web log post]. Retrieved from http://garyrubinstein.teachforus.org/2011/10/31/why-i-did-tfa-and-why-you-shouldnt/

82.–84.   Strauss, V. (2013, February 28). It's time for TFA to fold—former TFAer. [Web log post]. *Washington Post.* Retrieved from http://www.washingtonpost.com/blogs/answer-sheet/wp/2013/02/28/its-time-for-teach-for-america-to-fold-former-tfaer/

85.   Wendy Kopp to step down as Teach for America CEO. (2013, February 15). Retrieved from http://foundationcenter.org/pnd/news/story.jhtml?id=410300002

86.–87.   Teach for America. (2013, February 13). Teach for America founder voted chair of the board. Retrieved from http://www.teachforamerica.org/press-room/press-releases/2013/teach-america-founder-voted-chair-board

88.   Teach for All. (2013). Locations and programs. Retrieved from http://www.teachforall.org/network_locations.html

CHAPTER 4

1.   Cuban, L. (2013, May 16). Kiss Michelle Rhee goodbye. [Web log post]. Retrieved from http://larrycuban.wordpress.com/2013/05/16/kiss-mi-chelle-rhee-goodbye/

2.   Schneider, M. (2013, February 2). NCTQ letter grades and the reformer agenda: Part VIII. [Web log post]. Retrieved from http://deutsch29.word-press.com/2013/02/02/nctq-letter-grades-and-the-reformer-agenda-part-viii/

3.   *Brandenburg, G. (2011, January 31). The Rhee miracle examined again by co-hort. [Web log post]. Retrieved from http://gfbrandenburg.wordpress.com/2011/01/31/the-rhee-miracle-examined-again-by-cohort/*

4.   *Brandenburg, G. (2011, January 30). Answers to the latest quiz on the Baltimore Rhee miracle. [Web log post]. Retrieved from http://gfbrandenburg.word-press.com/2011/01/30/answers-to-the-latest-quiz-on-the-baltimore-rhee-miracle/*

5.   *Smith, K. (2003). The Ideology of Education: The Commonwealth, the Market, and America's Schools. Albany, NY: State University of New York Press. Retrieved from* http://books.google.com/books?id=LN0DMjzlHeUC&pg=PA138&lpg=PA138&dq=tesseract+edison&source=bl&ots=3DkEjVIH4p&sig=I1IQOdf_4dG2tqO2SUwI2TBhov4&hl=en&sa=X&ei=yqqiUfvQE4OG9gSPz4DgAw&ved=0CEUQ6AEwBA#v=onepage&q=tesseract%20edison&f=false

6.   Williams, L., & Leak, L. (1995). The UMBC evaluation of the Tesseract program in Baltimore City. Retrieved from http://www.eric.ed.gov/ERICWeb-Portal/search/detailmini.jsp?_nfpb=true&_&ERICExtSearch_SearchValue_0=ED390170&ERICExtSearch_SearchType_0=no&accno=ED390170

7.   *See 4.*

8.   *Brandenburg, G. (2011, January). Cohort effects at Harlem Park. [Web log post]. Retrieved from* http://gfbrandenburg.files.wordpress.com/2011/01/co-hort-effects-at-harlem-park-jpg.jpg

9.   *Brandenburg, G.(2013, February 18). The lies by which Saint Michelle built her brand [Harlem Park category]. [Web log posts]. Retrieved from* http://gfbran-denburg.wordpress.com/tag/harlem-park/

10.   *Schools nominee fails to validate success. (2007, June 28). Washington Times. Retrieved from* http://www.washingtontimes.com/news/2007/jun/28/schools-nominee-fails-to-validate-success/?page=all

11.   *Schemo, D. (2007, June 20). Recruited to rescue Washington's schools. New York Times. Retrieved from* http://www.nytimes.com/2007/06/20/education/20face.html?ref=michellerhee

12.   *Michelle A. Rhee, founder and CEO of StudentsFirst. (n.d.). Retrieved from* http://www.studentsfirst.org/pages/about-michelle-rhee

13. *See 11.*
14. *See 10.*
15. *Schneider, M. (2013, January 25). My commentary t the miracle classroom solution: TFA. [Web log post]. Retrieved from* http://deutsch29.wordpress.com/2013/01/25/my-commentary-to-the-miracle-classroom-solution-tfa/
16. *See 11.*
17. Jaffe, H. (2007, September 1). Can Michelle Rhee save DC schools? *Washingtonian.* Retrieved from http://www.washingtonian.com/articles/people/can-michelle-rhee-save-dc-schools/#
18. See 11.
19. *See 17.*
20. *Naison, M. (n.d.). Why Teach for America is not welcome in my classroom. Retrieved from* http://www.laprogressive.com/teach-america/
21. See 2.
22.–24. *Turque, B. (2010, August 13). Michelle Rhee, first year teacher. Washington Post. Retrieved from* http://voices.washingtonpost.com/dcschools/2010/08/michelle_rhee_first-year_teach.html
25. See 17.
26.–27. See 1.
28. Michelle Rhee invites reporters to film her as she fires a principal. (2012, May 22). Retrieved from http://www.democraticunderground.com/1002714439
29. Public Education Reform Amendment Act of 2007. Enrolled original. Codification District of Columbia original code, 2001 edition. West Group publisher. Retrieved at http://0361050.netsolhost.com/pdfs/DC%20Public%20Education%20Reform%20Act%20of%202007%201.pdf
30. See 17.
31. Moroney, T., & Young, J. (2010, October 13). Michelle Rhee quits as Washington, D.C., schools chief amid clash with teachers. *Bloomberg.* Retrieved from http://www.bloomberg.com/news/2010-10-13/michelle-rhee-is-said-to-step-down-as-washington-d-c-schools-chancellor.html
32. See 17.
33.–34. Turque, B. (2011, February 8). Rhee's firing of 75 D.C. teachers in 2008 was improper, arbitor says. *Washington Post.* Retrieved from http://www.washingtonpost.com/wp-dyn/content/article/2011/02/08/AR2011020804813.html
35. Turque, B. (2009, June 18). About 250 D.C. teachers are given pink slips. *Washington Post.* Retrieved from http://www.washingtonpost.com/wp-dyn/content/article/2009/06/18/AR2009061803844.html
36. Turque, B., & Brown, E. (2009, October 2). D.C. schools lay off more than 220 teachers, lose 300 guards. *Washington Post.* Retrieved from http://www.washingtonpost.com/wp-dyn/content/article/2009/10/02/AR2009100202289.html?sid=ST2009100501506
37. Somerby, B. (2013, January 14). Peddling Rhee: The post won't stop. [Web log post]. Retrieved from http://dailyhowler.blogspot.com/2013/01/peddling-rhee-post-wont-stop.html

38.   Banchero, S. (2010, July 24). Teachers lose jobs over test scores. Retrieved from http://online.wsj.com/article/SB1000142405274870424900457538 5500484438266.html

39.   http://www.washingtonpost.com/wp-dyn/content/article/2011/02/08/AR2011020804813.html

40.   See 33.

41.   Gillum, J., & Bello, M. (2011, March 28). When standardized test scores sailed in D.C., were the gains real? *USA Today*. Retrieved from http://usatoday30.usatoday.com/news/education/2011-03-28-1Aschooltesting28_CV_N.htm

42.   District of Columbia Public Schools. (n.d.). Noyes education campus. Retrieved from http://profiles.dcps.dc.gov/Noyes+Education+Campus

43.–44. Brandenburg, G. (2013, January 10). More data on the fraud that Rhee and Henderson and Duncan insist never happened at Noyes and elsewhere. [Web log post]. Retrieved from http://gfbrandenburg.wordpress.com/2013/01/10/more-data-on-the-fraud-that-rhee-and-henderson-and-duncan-insist-never-happened-at-noyes-and-elsewhere/

45.–47. See 41.

48–49. [Public records request for electronic communications between two D.C. education agencies regarding testing investigations, and correspondence between *USA Today* and D.C. Public Schools]. (2008, November 20, to 2011, April 27). Retrieved from http://www.documentcloud.org/documents/73991-day-three-documents#document/p100/a13043

50.   Turque, B. (2011, May 21). DCPS leaves consultant Caveon's toolbox shut in test cheating allegation inquiry. [Web log post]. *Washington Post*. Retrieved from http://www.washingtonpost.com/blogs/dc-schools-insider/post/dcps-leaves-consultant-caveons-toolbox-shut-in-test-cheating-allegation-inquiry/2011/05/21/AF889i9G_blog.html

51.–53. See 49.

54.   Bello, M., & Gillum, J. (2011, March 29). D.C. officials to review high rates of erasures on school tests. *USA Today*. Retrieved from http://usatoday30.usatoday.com/news/education/2011-03-29-dcschools29_ST_N.htm

55.   *Adell Cothorne vs. District of Columbia*. (2011, May 2). Case number 1:11-cv-00819-RLW. Retrieved from http://learningmatters.tv/pdfs/cothorne-v-district-of-columbia.pdf

56.   Turque, B. (2011, June 20). Ex-Noyes principal Wayne Ryan resigns. [Web log post]. *Washington Post*. Retrieved from http://www.washingtonpost.com/blogs/dc-schools-insider/post/ex-noyes-principal-wayne-ryan-resigns/2011/06/20/AG58v9cH_blog.html

57.   See 48.

58.   See 55.

59.   Michelle Rhee's education reform record: total failure and corruption (Meet Adell Cothorne). (2013, February 6). Retrieved from http://www.democraticunderground.com/10022320579

60.   See 55.

61.   See 48.

62.–66.   Merrow, J. (2013, January 9). Meet Adell Cothorne. [Web log post]' Retrieved from http://takingnote.learningmatters.tv/?p=6070

67.   See 55.

68.   See 62.

69.   See 43.

70.   See 62.

71.   See 55.

72.   Scott, N. (2013, May 23). John Merrow's growing restlessness on Rhee cheating scandal sparks Rhee scrutiny. [Web log post]. Retrieved from http://ednotesonline.blogspot.com/2013/05/john-merrows-growing-relentlessness-on.html#comment-form

73.   Merrow, J. (2013, April 18). Who created "Michell Rhee"? [Web log post]. Retrieved from http://takingnote.learningmatters.tv/?p=6316

74.   The education of Michelle Rhee. (2013, January 8). [Video interview]. *PBS.* Retrieved from http://www.pbs.org/wgbh/pages/frontline/education-of-michelle-rhee/

75.   Turque, B. (2010, March 22). Katherine Bradley funding Dunn deal. *Washington Post.* Retrieved from http://voices.washingtonpost.com/dc-schools/2010/03/katherine_bradley_funding_dunn.html

76.   Ward, J. (2012, September 2). Democratic split over education reform tested by Hollywood movie. *Huffington Post.* Retrieved from http://www.huffingtonpost.com/2012/09/02/dnc-education-reform_n_1850089.html

77.   Williams, P. (2013, April 20). Michelle Rhee creators: PBS' John Merrow omits major contributors. Retrieved June 1, 2013, from http://potterwilliamsreport.com/2013/04/20/michelle-rhee-creators-pbs-john-merrow-omits-major-contributors.aspx

78.   Merrow, J. (2013, May 15). Michelle Rhee and the Washington Post. [Web log post]. Retrieved from http://takingnote.learningmatters.tv/?p=6374

79.   Merrow, J. (2013, April 25). Penetrating the smokescreen. [Web log post]. Retrieved from http://takingnote.learningmatters.tv/?p=6332

80.   Merrow, J. (2013, January 15). The missing memo. [Web log post]. Retrieved from http://takingnote.learningmatters.tv/?p=6108

81.   [D.C. schools "missing" erasure study memo]. (2009, Jan 30). Retrieved from http://learningmatters.tv/pdfs/memo.pdf

82.   Toppo, G. (2013, April 11). Memo warns of rampant cheating in D.C. public schools. *USA Today.* Retrieved from http://www.usatoday.com/story/news/nation/2013/04/11/memo-washington-dc-schools-cheating/2074473/

83.   See 79.

CHAPTER 5

1.   Hoover Institute. (n.d.). Mission statement. Retrieved from http://www.hoover.org/about/mission-statement

2.   American Legislative Exchange Council. (n.d.). About ALEC. Retrieved from http://www.alec.org/about-alec/

3.   Texas Schools Project news (n.d.). Retrieved from http://www.utdallas.edu/research/tsp-erc/news.html#class_size

4.   GreatSchools awarded $20 million to enable kids to get to college. (2008, November 10). *Businesswire.* Retrieved from http://www.businesswire.com/news/home/20081110005395/en/GreatSchools-Awarded-20-Million-Enable-Kids-College

5.   GreatSchools. (n.d.). Frequently asked questions. Retrieved from http://www.greatschools.org/about/gsFaq.page

6.   Hanushek, E. (2013, March 7). Curriculum vitae. Retrieved from http://hanushek.stanford.edu/sites/default/files/cv%20_%20Eric%20A.%20Hanushek.pdf

7.   Equity and Excellence Commission. (2013, February 2). For each and every child: A strategy for education equity and excellence. Retrieved from http://www2.ed.gov/about/bdscomm/list/eec/equity-excellence-commission-report.pdf

8.   Foundation for Excellence in Education. (n.d.).Eric Hanushek [Biography]. Retrieved from http://excelined.org/team/eric-hanushek/

9.–13.   Hanushek, Eric A. (1968). The Education of Negroes and Whites. Doctoral thesis, Massachusetts Institute of Technology. 150 pages.

14.–17. Hanushek, E. (1999). Evidence on class size. In S. Mayer and P. Peterson (Eds.), *Earning and Learning: How Schools matter.* Washington, DC: Brookings Institution Press, 131-168. Retrieved from http://hanushek.stanford.edu/sites/default/files/publications/Hanushek%201999%20Evidence1onCLassSize.pdf

18.   Hanushek, E. (1999). Evidence on class size. In S. Mayer and P. Peterson (Eds.), *Earning and Learning: How Schools matter.* Washington, DC: Brookings Institution Press, 131-168. Retrieved from http://hanushek.stanford.edu/publications/evidence-class-size

19.   See 9.

20.–25. Hanushek, E. (1986, September). The economics of schooling: Production and efficiency in public schools. *Journal of Economic Literature, 24*(3), 1141-1177. Retrieved from http://www.albany.edu/faculty/schen/old/Hanushek1986.pdf

26.–28. Baker, B. (2012). Revisiting that age-old question: Does money matter in education? Retrieved from http://www.shankerinstitute.org/images/doesmoneymatter_final.pdf

29.   Baker, B.D., Farrie, D., Sciarra, D., Coley, R., (2010) Is School Funding Fair. Retrieved from www.schoolfundingfairness.org

30.   See 26.

31.–33. *Hoke vs. State* memorandum of decision. (2000, October). Retrieved from http://www.schoolfunding.info/states/nc/HOKEI.PDF

34.   See 26.

35.   Hoover, T., & Bartels, L. (2011, December 9). Denver court decision in education suit says Colorado is underfunding by billions. *Denver Post.* Retrieved from http://www.denverpost.com/breakingnews/ci_19511537

36.–37. Stanley, D. (2013, May 28). State wins Lobato vs. Colorado; Co. Supreme Court finds financing system complies with constitution. *The Denver Chan-*

nel. Retrieved from http://www.thedenverchannel.com/news/local-news/colorado-supreme-court-finds-school-financing-system-complies-with-state-constitution

38.   *Lobato vs. State* Findings of fact and conclusions of law. (2011, December 9). Case number 2005CV4794. [Litigation.] Retrieved from http://www.courts.state.co.us/Media/Opinion_Docs/05CV4794%20Lobato%20v.%20Colorado.pdf

39.–40. Glass, G. (2012, March 15). Eric Hanushek testifies in school finance cases. Retrieved from http://ed2worlds.blogspot.com/2012/03/eric-hanushek-testifies-in-school.html

41.   Pallas, A. (2011, December 6). Throwing students at classrooms. Retrieved from http://eyeoned.org/content/throwing-students-at-classrooms_286/

42.   See 39.

43.–44. See 38.

45.   Partners. (n.d.). Retrieved from the GreatSchools website, http://www.greatschools.org/about/partnerOpportunities.page

46.   GreatSchools. (n.d.). GreatSchools ratings FAQ. Retrieved from http://www.greatschools.org/find-a-school/defining-your-ideal/2423-ratings.gs

47.   GreatSchools. (n.d.). How important is class size? Retrieved from the GreatSchools website, http://www.greatschools.org/find-a-school/defining-your-ideal/174-class-size.gs?page=3

48.–49. Gee, A. (n.d.). Making the most of larger class sizes. Retrieved from http://www.greatschools.org/improvement/quality-teaching/1516-making-the-most-of-larger-class-sizes.gs

50.   Bridgeland, J., DiIulio, J, & Morison, K. (2006, March). The silent epidemic: Perspectives of high school dropouts. Retrieved from http://www.ignitelearning.com/pdf/TheSilentEpidemic3-06FINAL.pdf

51.   See 48.

52.   See 20.

53.   See 48.

CHAPTER 6

1.   Williams, L. (1988, January 7). Washington's doctor debunks foul play. Retrieved from http://docs.newsbank.com/openurl?ctx_ver=z39.88-2004&rft_id=info:sid/iw.newsbank.com:NewsBank:CSTB&rft_val_format=info:ofi/fmt:kev:mtx:ctx&rft_dat=0EB36DABC60075D3&svc_dat=InfoWeb:aggregated5&req_dat=AA98CDC331574F0ABEAFF732B33DC0B2

2.   Johnson, D. (1988, December 6). Daley entering Chicago contest for mayoralty. *New York Times.* Retrieved from http://www.nytimes.com/1988/12/06/us/daley-entering-chicago-contest-for-mayoralty.html

3.   Brief history of Chicago Board of Education. (n.d.). Retrieved June 13, 2013, from http://www.google.com/url?sa=t&rct=j&q=chicago%2Bschool%2Breform%2Bact%2Bof%2B1988&source=web&cd=15&ved=0CEUQFjAEOAo&url=http%3A%2F%2Filraiseyourhand.org%2Fsites%2Filraiseyourhand.org%2Ffiles%2FBrief%2520History%25

20of%2520Chicago%2520Board%2520of%2520Education.doc&ei=LWe7
UaPOLoiG9gTsmoDIDQ&usg=AFQjCNE7BH8KC7SR8RA1vo3L6LjoVN7
4ow

4. Zmuda, M., & Simpson, D. (2013, April 8). Continuing the rubber stamp city council: Chicago City Council report #6, June 8, 2011—February 13, 2013. Retrieved from http://www.uic.edu/depts/pols/ChicagoPolitics/City_Council_Report_April2013

5. Heard, J. (1996, February 4). Tough love: Paul Vallas' job is to teach the Chicago Public Schools a lesson in discipline (page 6). *Chicago Tribune.* Retrieved from http://articles.chicagotribune.com/1996-02-04/features/9602040209_1_paul-vallas-chicago-schools-new-schools/6

6. Richard Daley. (n.d.). Retrieved June 13, 2013, from http://www.answers.com/topic/richard-m-daley

7. See 3.

8. Haney, Leviis, "The 1995 Chicago School Reform Amendatory Act and the Cps Ceo: A Historical Examination of the Administration of Ceos Paul Vallas and Arne Duncan" (2011). *Dissertations.* Paper 62. Retrieved from http://ecommons.luc.edu/luc_diss/62

9. Heard, J. (1996, February 4). Tough love: Paul Vallas' job is to teach the Chicago Public Schools a lesson in discipline (page 3). *Chicago Tribune.* Retrieved from http://articles.chicagotribune.com/1996-02-04/features/9602040209_1_paul-vallas-chicago-schools-new-schools/3

10. Heard, J. (1996, February 4). Tough love: Paul Vallas' job is to teach the Chicago Public Schools a lesson in discipline (page 2). *Chicago Tribune.* Retrieved from http://articles.chicagotribune.com/1996-02- 04/features/9602040209_1_paul-vallas-chicago-schools-new-schools/2

11. See 5.

12. Heard, J. (1996, February 4). Tough love: Paul Vallas' job is to teach the Chicago Public Schools a lesson in discipline (page 5). *Chicago Tribune.* Retrieved from http://articles.chicagotribune.com/1996-02-04/features/9602040209_1_paul-vallas-chicago-schools-new-schools/5

13. Heard, J. (1996, February 4). Tough love: Paul Vallas' job is to teach the Chicago Public Schools a lesson in discipline (page 4). *Chicago Tribune.* Retrieved from http://articles.chicagotribune.com/1996-02-04/features/9602040209_1_paul-vallas-chicago-schools-new-schools/4

14. Heard, J. (1995, September 28). Schools crisis plan gets unruly welcome. *Chicago Tribune.* Retrieved from http://articles.chicagotribune.com/1995-09-28/news/9509280186_1_councils-intervention-plan-school-leaders

15. See 12.

16.–17. Haynes, V. (1995, August 14). Proposed budget has pupil focus. *Chicago Tribune.* Retrieved from http://articles.chicagotribune.com/1995-08-14/news/9508140160_1_violent-students-dropout-rate-vallas

18. See 12.

19. Heard, J. (1996, February 4). Tough love: Paul Vallas' job is to teach the Chicago Public Schools a lesson in discipline (page 7). *Chicago Tribune.* Retrieved from http://articles.chicagotribune.com/1996-02-04/features/9602040209_1_paul-vallas-chicago-schools-new-schools/7

20.   Martinez, M., & Poe, J. (1996, June 4). Chicago grade schools pull off test turnaround. *Chicago Tribune*. Retrieved from http://articles.chicago-tribune.com/1996-06-04/news/9606040240_1_elementary-schools-paul-vallas-test-scores

21.   Jacob, B. (2003, Winter). High stakes in Chicago: Are Chicago's rising test scores genuine? Retrieved from http://educationnext.org/high-stakesinchicago/

22.   Terry, Don. (1996, October 1). One fifth of schools put on proba-tion in Chicago. *New York Times*. Retrieved from http://www.nytimes.com/1996/10/01/us/one-fifth-of-schools-put-on-probation-in-chicago.html

23.   Herold, B. (2003, Spring). Looking for lessons from Chicago about promotion, retention. Retrieved from http://thenotebook.org/spring-2003/03912/looking-lessons-chicago-about-promotion-retention

24.   See 20.

25.–26. 2000 news briefs. (n.d.). Retrieved from the Catalyst Chicago website, http://www.catalyst-chicago.org/node/18741

27.   Poe, J. (1997, May 23). Test scores soar at city schools on probation. *Chicago Tribune*. Retrieved from http://articles.chicagotribune.com/1997-05-23/news/9705230188_1_test-scores-elementary-schools-high-school-students-scores

28.–31. Designs for Change.(2001, March). Chicago test score research shows that school-level initiative brings the largest sustained reading gains: Evidence indicates the need for "phase three" of Chicago school reform. Retrieved from http://www.designsforchange.org/pdfs/ITBS0401.pdf

32.   Washburn, G. (2001, February 16). Schools told to think 'outside the box.' *Chicago Tribune*. Retrieved from http://articles.chicagotribune.com/2001-02-16/news/0102160172_1_paul-vallas-school-reform-students-reading-abilities

33.   See 28.

34.–35. See 25.

36.–37. Martinez, M., & Poe, J. (1998, May 7). Kids who flunk twice give city schools big test. *Chicago Tribune*. Retrieved from http://articles.chicagotribune.com/1998-05-07/news/9805070187_1_social-promotions-iowa-tests-8th-graders

38.   Jimerson, S. R. (1999). On the failure of failure: Examining the association between early grade retention and education and employment outcomes during late adolescence. *Journal of School Psychology, 37*(3), 243–272. Re-trieved from http://education.ucsb.edu/jimerson/NEW%20retention/Publications/JSP_FailureFailure1999.pdf

39.   Jimerson, S.R., Ferguson, P., Whipple, A.D., Anderson, G.E., & Dalton, M.J. (2002). Exploring the association between grade retention and dropout: A longitudinal study examining socio-emotional, behavioral, and achieve-ment characteristics of retained students. *California School Psychologist, 7*, 51-62. Retrieved from http://www.education.ucsb.edu/jimerson/reten-tion/CSP_RetentionDropout2002.pdf

40.   Xia, C., Glennie, E. (2005, January). Cost-benefit analysis of grade reten-
        tion. Part two. Retrieved from the Center for Child and Family (Duke
        University) website, http://www.childandfamilypolicy.duke.edu/pdfs/
        pubpres/FlawedStrategy_PartTwo.pdf
41.   See 36.
42.–43. Martinez, M. (1998, May 9). Vallas says he, Daley agree on flunking kids.
        Chicago Tribune. Retrieved from http://articles.chicagotribune.com/1998-
        05-09/news/9805090035_1_flunk-paul-vallas-mayor-richard-daley
44.   Martinez, M. (1998, June 21). A painful steady climb. *Chicago Tri-
        bune*. Retrieved from http://articles.chicagotribune.com/1998-06-21/
        news/9806210146_1_elementary-school-improvement-chicago-public-
        schools-education-side
45.–46. Martinez, M. (1998, August 22). Schools hold firm as 1,300 fail twice. *Chi-
        cago Tribune*. Retrieved from http://articles.chicagotribune.com/1998-08-
        22/news/9808220195_1_social-promotions-summer-school-school-board
47.   Martinez, M. (1999, May 17). Schools won't hold back pupils flunking
        3rd time. *Chicago Tribune*. Retrieved from http://articles.chicagotribune.
        com/1999-05-17/news/9905170158_1_social-promotions-6th-graders-stu-
        dent
48.–49. Martinez, M.(2000, August 24). First day push to go to school comes up
        short. *Chicago Tribune*. Retrieved from http://articles.chicagotribune.
        com/2000-08-24/news/0008240253_1_back-to-school-year-round-chica-
        go-mayor-richard-daley
50.–51. Martinez, M. & Strzalka, D. (2000, August 25). Daley not taking any ex-
        cuses for first-day truancy. *Chicago Tribune*. Retrieved from http://articles.
        chicagotribune.com/2000-08-25/news/0008250378_1_magnet-programs-
        magnet-schools-9th-graders
52.   See 25.
53.   See 32.
54.   Kass, J. (2001, June 7). Vallas stuck neck out for schools, only to get axed.
        Chicago Tribune. Retrieved from http://articles.chicagotribune.com/2001-
        06-07/news/0106070207_1_paul-vallas-mayor-richard-daley-chicago-pub-
        lic-schools
55.–56. Martinez, M. (2001, June 3). New teachers union chief poised to pounce.
        Chicago Tribune. Retrieved from http://articles.chicagotribune.com/2001-
        06-03/news/0106030288_1_first-teachers-strike-chicago-teachers-union-
        board

CHAPTER 7

1.   Mre, J. (2001, June 25). Duncan and Daley. [Photo]. *Chicago Tribune*. Re-
        trieved from http://www.chicagotribune.com/ct-081216duncandaley-
        photo,0,147145.photo
2.   Arne Duncan, U.S. Secretary of Education. Biography. (n.d.). Retrieved
        from the U.S. Department of Education website, http://www2.ed.gov/
        news/staff/bios/duncan.html

3.   Ariel Investments. (n.d.). Ariel education initiative. Retrieved June 12, 2013, from http://www.arielinvestments.com/ariel-education-initiative/
4.   Ariel Investments. (n.d.). Investment curriculum. Retrieved June 12, 2013, from http://www.arielinvestments.com/investment-curriculum/
5.   Ariel Investments. (n.d.). A night with John W. Rogers, Jr. Retrieved June 12, 2013, from http://www.arielinvestments.com/historymakers/
6.   Reform before the storm: Chicago Public Schools timeline. (2012, November). *Chicago Magazine*. Retrieved from http://www.chicagomag.com/Chicago-Magazine/November-2012/Reform-Before-the-Storm-Chicago-Public-Schools-Timeline/
7.   Harvard Graduate School of Education. (2009, September). Will Obama's choice change education in America (2009, September). Retrieved from http://www.gse.harvard.edu/news-impact/2009/09/will-obamas-choice-change-education-in-america/
8.   School search results.(n.d.). Retrieved June 12, 2013, from the Chicago Public Schools website, http://www.cps.edu/Schools/Find_a_school/Pages/SchoolSearchResults.aspx?Type=1&Filter=CPSSchoolGrade%3dElementary+school%3bCPSSchoolType%3dCharter
9.–10. Mr. Rogers' neighborhood. (n.d.). Retrieved June 12, 2013, from http://www.smartmoney.com/invest/funds/mr-rogers-neighborhood-12405/
11.   See 8.
12.   See 4.
13.   Arne Duncan. (2013, August 10). Retrieved from http://en.wikipedia.org/wiki/Arne_Duncan
14.   See 7.
15.   See 2.
16.   See 5.
17.   See 9.
18.   See 7.
19.   Arne Duncan, Secretary of Education (since January 2009). (n.d.). *Washington Post*. Retrieved from http://www.washingtonpost.com/politics/arne-duncan/gIQAqFMc9O_topic.html
20.   See 2.
21.   Pickert, K. (2008, December 17). 2-minute bio: Education Secretary: Arne Duncan. Retrieved from http://www.time.com/time/politics/article/0,8599,1867011,00.html
22.   O'Shea, J. (2009, January 7). 10 things you didn't know about Arne Duncan. *US News and World Report*. Retrieved from http://www.usnews.com/news/obama/articles/2009/01/07/10-things-you-didnt-know-about-arne-duncan
23.   Vallas steps down as schools chief. (2001, June 7). Retrieved from the metropolitan   Planning Council website, http://www.metroplanning.org/news-events/article/2938
24.   See 7.
25.   See 2.

26. Renaissance 2010. (n.d.). Retrieved from the Chicago Public Schools website, http://www.cps.edu/PROGRAMS/DISTRICTINITIATIVES/Pages/Renaissance2010.aspx

27. Toppo, G. (2009, July 12). Chicago schools report contradicts Obama and Duncan. *USA Today*. Retrieved from http://usatoday30.usatoday.com/news/education/2009-07-12-chicagoschools13_N.htm

28.–29. Still left behind. (n.d.). Retrieved June 12, 2013, from http://www.civic-committee.org/Still%20Left%20Behind%20v2.pdf

30. Obama taps Arne Duncan for education post. (2009, June 18). Retrieved June 12, 2013, from http://www.cbsnews.com/stories/2008/12/16/politics/main4671087.shtml

31. See 27.

32. See 30.

33.–35. Vevea, B. (2013, May 8). CPS wants to close first Renaissance schools. Retrieved from http://www.wbez.org/news/education/cps-wants-close-first-renaissance-schools-107072

36. Race to the Top; The Wrap-up and supporting data. (n.d.). Retrieved from http://racetotop.com/

37. Race to the Top. (2013, May 23). *Wikipedia*. Retrieved from http://en.wikipedia.org/wiki/Race_to_the_Top

38. US Department of Education. (n.d.). Race to the Top: Phase 1 final results. Retrieved June 12, 2013, from http://www2.ed.gov/programs/racetothetop/phase1-applications/score-summary.pdf

39. US Department of Education. (n.d.). Race to the Top: Phase 2 final results. Retrieved June 12, 2013, from http://www2.ed.gov/programs/racetothetop/phase2-applications/summary.pdf

40. Darling-Hammond, L. (2008, October). [Resume]. Retrieved from http://stanford.edu/~ldh/resume.html

41. Ayers, B. (n.d.). President Obama: Replace Arne Duncan with Linda Darling-Hammond. [Petition]. Retrieved from http://petitions.moveon.org/sign/president-obama-replace-1.fb23?source=s.icn.fb&r_by=6240309

42. See 30.

CHAPTER 8

1. Rahm Emanuel. (2013, August 8). *Wikipedia*. Retrieved from http://en.wikipedia.org/wiki/Rahm_Emanuel

2. Corley, C. (2011, May 13). In Chicago, a political dynasty nears its end. [Interview]. Retrieved from http://www.npr.org/templates/transcript/transcript.php?storyId=136240147

3. Allison, B. (2009, March 26). Freddie Mac records exempt from FOIA. Retrieved from http://reporting.sunlightfoundation.com/2009/freddie-mac-records-exempt-from-foia/

4.–5. Office of Federal Housing Enterprise Oversight. (2003, December). Report of the special examination of Freddie Mac. *ABC News*. Retrieved from http://abcnews.go.com/images/Blotter/specialreport122003.pdf

6. Secter, B., & Zajac, A. (2009, March 26). Freddie Mac scandals began during Emanuel's watch. Retrieved from http://www.chicagotribune.com/news/local/chi-rahm-emanuelmar26,0,1946702.story

7. Zorn, E. (2011, January 10). From the archives: Rahm Emanuel, Freddie Mac and the big buck years. [Web log post]. *Chicago Tribune.* Retrieved from http://blogs.chicagotribune.com/news_columnists_ezorn/2011/01/from-the-archives-rahm-emanuel-freddie-mac-and-the-big-bucks-years.html

8. Emanuel resigns as Obama chief of staff, eyes Chicago mayoral race. (2010, October 1). *Fox news.* Retrieved from http://www.foxnews.com/politics/2010/10/01/rahm-expected-leave-white-house-chicago-mayor-run/

9. Richard M. Daley. (2013, August 12). *Wikipedia.* Retrieved from http://en.wikipedia.org/wiki/Richard_M._Daley

10. Rahm Emanuel plans big changes for Chicago schools. (2011, April 20). *Huffington Post.* Retrieved from http://www.huffingtonpost.com/2011/04/20/rahm-emanuel-chicago-schools_n_851294.html

11.–12. Mack, K., & Ahmed-Ullah, N. (2011, April 14). Chicago teachers union tweaks Emanuel. *Chicago Tribune.* Retrieved from http://articles.chicagotribune.com/2011-04-14/news/ct-met-rahm-chicago-teachers-union-20110414_1_mayor-elect-school-day-chicago-teachers-union

13. Ahmed-Ullah, N. ((2011, April 18). CPS leadership announced. *Chicago Tribune.* Retrieved from http://articles.chicagotribune.com/2011-04-18/news/ct-met-emanuel-schools-leaders-0419-20110418_1_chief-education-officer-cps-leadership-school-reform

14. Nocera, J. (2012, September 11). In Chicago, it's a mess, all right. *New York Times.* Retrieved from http://www.nytimes.com/2012/09/11/opinion/nocera-in-chicago-its-a-mess-all-right.html?_r=0

15. Rochester teachers union "no confidence" vote in Jean-Claude Brizard. Retrieved June 15, 2013, from http://rochesterhomepage.net/fulltext?nxd_id=232966

16. Chicago Public Schools CEO Ron Huberman to resign. (2010, November 3). Retrieved from the Chicago Public Schools website, http://www.cps.edu/News/Press_releases/Pages/11_03_2010_PR1.aspx

17. Ahmed, A., & Lightly, T. (2010, January 10). Chicago Public Schools CEO Ron Huberman has not one, but two cars paid for by you. *Chicago Tribune.* Retrieved from http://articles.chicagotribune.com/2010-01-10/news/1001090218_1_paul-vallas-chicago-public-schools-school-district/2

18. Terry Mazany, chief executive officer, Chicago Public Schools. (2011, January 10). Retrieved from the Chicago Public Schools website, http://www.cps.edu/About_CPS/At-a-glance/Pages/TerryMazany.aspx

19.–20. See 14.

21. Ahmed-Ullah, N. (2011, August 3). Emanuel still pushing longer school day. *Chicago Tribune.* Retrieved from http://articles.chicagotribune.com/2011-08-03/news/ct-met-back-to-school-pols-0803-20110803_1_school-day-contract-negotiations-teachers-and-other-union

22.   Ahmed-Ullah, N., & Hood, J. (2011, August 26). Teachers union says no to 2 percent raise for longer days. *Chicago Tribune*. Retrieved from http://articles.chicagotribune.com/2011-08-26/news/ct-met-teachers-rejecti-offer-0826-20110826_1_president-karen-lewis-school-day-teachers-union

23.   Hood, J., & Rado, D. (2011, September 13). CPS' school day not that much shorter than those in some suburban districts. *Chicago Tribune*. Retrieved from http://articles.chicagotribune.com/2011-09-13/news/ct-met-timeinschool-20110913_1_cps-school-day-districts

24.   Ahmed-Ullah, N. (2011, August 10). Schools CEO, teachers union head discuss longer school day. *Chicago Tribune*. Retrieved from http://articles.chicagotribune.com/2011-08-10/news/ct-met-cps-longerday09-20110810_1_school-day-days-districtwide-teachers-union

25.   See 23.

26.   Hood, J., & Ahmed-Ullah, N. (2011, October 24). CPS considers giving charter schools added perks for longer school day. *Chicago Tribune*. Retrieved from http://articles.chicagotribune.com/2011-10-24/news/chi-cps-considers-giving-charter-schools-added-perks-for-longer-school-day-20111024_1_andrew-broy-charter-schools-school-day

27.   Ahmed-Ullah, N. (2012, March 6). Longer school day subject of dueling forums. *Chicago Tribune*. Retrieved from http://articles.chicagotribune.com/2012-03-06/news/ct-met-cps-longer-day-20120306_1_school-day-community-forum-cps-officials

28.   Ahmed-Ullah, N. (2012, April 24). Brizard hopes funds for longer school day give principals more autonomy. *Chicago Tribune*. Retrieved from http://articles.chicagotribune.com/2012-04-24/news/ct-met-cps-principal-budgets-20120424_1_brizard-school-day-clarice-berry

29.   Lemon, M. (2010, Spring). General assembly passes Performance Evaluation reform Act of 2010. Retrieved from the Ottosen-Britz website, http://www.ottosenlaw.com/article.asp?a=516

30.–32. Kumashiro, K. (2012, March 26). Misconceptions and realities about teacher and principal evaluation. [Open letter]. Retrieved from http://dl.dropboxusercontent.com/u/2561000/OpenLetterCPSTeacherEval-Signers3.23.12.pdf

33.   A report card for teachers. (2012, April 5). *Chicago Tribune*. Retrieved from http://articles.chicagotribune.com/2012-04-05/opinion/ct-edit-perform-0405-20120405_1_teacher-evaluations-evaluation-system-chicago-teachers

34.   Fischer, J.D. (2006, Fall). Implications of recent research on student evaluations of teaching. *Montana Professor, 17*(1). Retrieved from http://mtprof.msun.edu/Fall2006/fischer.html

35.   See 33.

36.–37. Ahmed-Ullah, N. (2012, April 1). Schools, union far apart on salary negotiations. *Chicago Tribune*. Retrieved from http://articles.chicagotribune.com/2012-04-01/news/ct-met-cps-teacher-aftermath-20120401_1_jesse-sharkey-cps-teacher-evaluations

38.   Ahmed-Ullah, N. (2012, April 3). Chicago Teachers Union say polls show support for a strike. *Chicago Tribune*. Retrieved from http://articles.chi-

cagotribune.com/2012-04-03/news/ct-met-cps-union-strike-20120404_1_polls-show-support-strike-ctu

39. Ahmed-ULlah, N. (2012, May 11). Chicago teachers conduct 'dry run' for strike vote. *Chicago Tribune.* Retrieved from http://articles.chicagotribune.com/2012-05-11/news/ct-met-cps-union-poll-20120511_1_strike-vote-contract-proposal-union-poll

40. Ahmed-Ullah, N. (2012, May 23). School reform groups urge not strike for Chicago. *Chicago Tribune.* Retrieved from http://articles.chicagotribune.com/2012-05-23/news/chi-school-reform-groups-urge-no-strike-for-chicago-20120523_1_education-reform-strike-vote-groups

41. Ahmed-Ullah, N., & Hood, J. (2012, June 6). Chicago teachers line up to vote on strike authorization. *Chicago Tribune.* Retrieved from http://articles.chicagotribune.com/2012-06-06/news/chi-teachers-take-strike-authorization-vote-today-20120606_1_strike-authorization-jesse-sharkey-chicago-teachers-union

42. Ahmed-Ullah, N., & Hood, J. (2012, June 11). CTU: Nearly 90 percent of teachers vote to authorize strike. *Chicago Tribune.* Retrieved from http://articles.chicagotribune.com/2012-06-11/news/chi-ctu-chicago-teachers-vote-to-authorize-strike-20120611_1_teachers-vote-strike-next-fall-ctu-president-karen-lewis

43. Moran, T. (2012, August 28). Chicago teachers say they'll strike for the kids. Retrieved from http://www.labornotes.org/2012/08/chicago-teachers-say-theyll-strike-kids

44. Sustar, L. (2012, August 31). Chicago teachers draw a line. [Web log post]. Retrieved from http://www.indypendent.org/2012/08/31/chicago-teachers-draw-line

45. Chicago public teachers stage historic strike in clash with Mayor Rahm Emanuel on education reforms. [Video and interview]. Retrieved from http://www.democracynow.org/2012/9/10/chicago_public_teachers_stage_historic_strike

46.–48. Layton, L., Wallsten, P., & Turque, B. (2012, September 11). Chicago teachers strike places Obama at odds with key part of political base. *Washington Post.* Retrieved from http://articles.washingtonpost.com/2012-09-11/politics/35497511_1_democrats-for-education-reform-president-obama-teachers

49. Soave, R. (2012, September 17). Obama keeps distance from Chicago teachers' strike. *Daily Caller.* Retrieved from http://dailycaller.com/2012/09/17/obama-keeps-distance-from-chicago-teachers-strike/

50. Resmovits, J. (2012, October 11). Chicago teachers strike contract leaves education issues unresolved. *Huffington Post.* Retrieved from http://www.huffingtonpost.com/2012/10/11/chicago-teachers-strike-contract_n_1959129.html

51. Judge declines to expedite hearing in Chicago teacher strike. (2012, September 17). [Web log post]. *NBC News.* Retrieved from http://usnews.nbcnews.com/_news/2012/09/17/13915011-judge-declines-to-expedite-hearing-in-chicago-teacher-strike

52.–53. Kelleher, J., & Kirby, A. (2012, September 17). Emanuel's court bid to end strike stalls, teachers call it "vindictive." *Reuters*. Retrieved from http://www.reuters.com/article/2012/09/17/us-usa-chicago-schools-idUS-BRE88E0IV20120917

54. Welch, W., & Bello, M. (2012, September 18). Chicago teachers vote to return to classroom. *USA Today*. Retrieved from http://usatoday30.usatoday.com/news/nation/story/2012/09/18/chicago-teachers-are-suspending-seven-day-strike/57799352/1

55. See 50.

56.–57. See 44.

58.–60. See 50.

61. See 44.

62. See 43.

63. Spielman, F., & Rossi, R. (2012, October 11). CPS boss Jean-Claude Brizard out by "mutual agreement." *Chicago Sun Times*. Retrieved from http://www.suntimes.com/news/cityhall/15699019-418/chicago-public-schools-ceo-jean-claude-brizard-out-by-mutual-agreement.html

64. See 50.

65. Ahmed-Ullah, N. (2012, November 20). Teachers union chief slams 'top down' reform. *Chicago Tribune*. Retrieved from http://articles.chicagotribune.com/2012-11-20/news/ct-met-ctu-president-speaks-20121121_1_school-closings-charter-schools-union-president-karen-lewis

66. See 49.

67. Ahmed-Ullah, N., & Chase, J. (2012, December 19). Document shows Emanuel administration had detailed school closing plans. *Chicago Tribune*. Retrieved from http://articles.chicagotribune.com/2012-12-19/news/ct-met-school-closings-1217-20121219_1_ceo-barbara-byrd-bennett-school-actions-school-leaders

68. Ahmed-Ullah, N., & Long, R. (2012, November 28). General assembly to vote on extending school closings announcement. *Chicago Tribune*. Retrieved from http://articles.chicagotribune.com/2012-11-28/news/ct-met-cps-state-school-bill-20121128_1_school-closings-byrd-bennett-school-district

69. Ahmed-Ullah, N, & Chase, J. (2013, February 14). Anxiety grows as CPS releases preliminary school closings list. *Chicago Tribune*. Retrieved from http://articles.chicagotribune.com/2013-02-14/news/chi-129-on-new-chicago-schools-closing-list-20130213_1_commission-on-school-utilization-barbara-byrd-bennett-dwayne-truss

70.–73. Ahmed-Ullah, N. (2013, March 16). School closings to test CPS chief. *Chicago Tribune*. Retrieved from http://articles.chicagotribune.com/2013-03-16/news/ct-met-cps-byrd-bennett-20130301_1_closings-barbara-byrd-bennett-community-action-councils

74. Reaction to school closings [Photo gallery]. (2013, April 9). *Chicago Tribune*. Retrieved from, http://galleries.apps.chicagotribune.com/chi-130321-cps-school-closings-pictures/

75. See 70.

76.   Ravitch, D. (2013, June 21). Major rally today in Chicago to protest budget cuts. [Web log post]. Retrieved from http://dianeravitch. net/2013/06/21/major-rally-today-in-chicago-to-protest-budget-cuts/

CHAPTER 9

1.   Williams, D. (1996, October 1). Fear jump-starts school improvement. Retrieved from http://www.catalyst-chicago.org/news/2005/07/25/fear-jump-starts-school-improvement

2.   Illinois governor, Democratic primary election. (2002). Retrieved from http://www.ourcampaigns.com/RaceDetail.html?RaceID=6435

3.   Davey, M. (2011, December 8). Blagojevich sentenced to 14 years in prison. *New York Times.* Retrieved from http://www.nytimes.com/2011/12/08/ us/blagojevich-expresses-remorse-in-courtroom-speech.html?_r=0

4.   Hartocollis, A. (2002, July 10). Search for new chancellor loses a leading candidate. *New York Times.* Retrieved from http://www.nytimes. com/2002/07/10/nyregion/search-for-new-chancellor-loses-a-leading-candidate.html

5.   Bishop, T. (2001, November 15). Pennsylvania prepares privatization of Philadelphia public schools. Retrieved from http://www.wsws.org/en/articles/2001/11/phil-n15.html

6.–7.   Clowes, G. (1998, June 1). Philadelphia schools face state takeover. Retrieved from http://news.heartland.org/newspaper-article/1998/06/01/philadelphia-schools-face-state-takeover

8.–9.   See 5.

10.   Tom Ridge heads Office of Homeland Security. (2001, October 8). Retrieved from http://pittsburgh.about.com/library/weekly/aa100801a.htm

11.   See 5.

12.   Mezzacappa, D. (2000, June 5). Phila. Schools chief Hornbeck plans to resign. *Philadelphia Inquirer.* Retrieved from http://articles.philly.com/2000-06-05/news/25603149_1_david-hornbeck-schools-open-next-year-city-school-system

13.–14. See 5.

15.   Edison Schools, Inc. (2001, September 26). 2001 annual report. Retrieved from http://media.corporate-ir.net/media_files/NSD/edsn/reports/edsn_ar_01.pdf

16.–18. See 5.

19.   National Briefing | Mid-Atlantic: Pennsylvania: Snub For Edison Schools. (2002, July 27). *New York Times.* Retrieved from http://www.nytimes.com/2002/07/27/us/national-briefing-mid-atlantic-pennsylvania-snub-for-edison-schools.html?ref=paulgvallas

20.   National Briefing | Mid-Atlantic: Pennsylvania: Philadelphia Schools Plan. (2002, August 24). *New York Times.* Retrieved from http://www.nytimes.com/2002/08/24/us/national-briefing-mid-atlantic-pennsylvania-philadelphia-schools-plan.html?ref=paulgvallas

21.   Philadelphia plans to cut fees to school operators. (2003, May 24). *New York Times*. Retrieved from http://www.nytimes.com/2003/05/24/us/philadelphia-plans-to-cut-fees-to-school-operators.html?ref=paulgvallas

22.–24.   Graham, K. (2006, December 12). Of deficits and dropout rates Council quizzed Paul Vallas and Mayor Street about efforts to solve school district troubles. Philadelphia Inquirer. Retrieved from   http://articles.philly.com/2006-12-12/news/25398676_1_paul-vallas-dropout-rate-fund-balance

25.   Mezzacappa, D. (2008, Spring). The Vallas effect. *Education Next,8*(2). Retrieved from http://educationnext.org/the-vallas-effect/

26.   Congressman Brady comments on Paul Vallas' resignation. (2007, April 30). *Philadelphia Inquirer.* Retrieved from http://pdn.philly.com/nm_contest/prarchive/20070412_Brady_on_vallas_resignation.html

27.   Consulting agreement between the School District of Philadelphia and Paul Vallas. (2006, September 23). *Philadelphia Inquirer.* Retrieved from http://www.phila.gov/mayor/school/Paul%20Vallas'%20Contract.pdf

28.   Moser, W. (2013, June 20). How did Chicago's public schools get in such a huge financial hole? *Chicago Magazine*. Retrieved from http://www.chicagomag.com/Chicago-Magazine/The-312/June-2013/Chicago-Public-Schools-Pension-Bomb/

29.   Grotto, J. (2010, November 16). Politicians helped bring Chicago's public pension funds to the brink of insolvency. *Chicago Tribune*. Retrieved from http://articles.chicagotribune.com/2010-11-16/news/ct-met-pensions-deals-20101116_1_pension-crisis-state-pension-debt-retirement-funds/3

30.   School District of Philadelphia 2002-2012 PSSA results. [Graphs]. Retrieved   from   https://thenotebook.org/sites/default/files/Charts%20-%20School%20District%20of%20Philadelphia%202012%20PSSA%20Test%20Results%20Press_Release-2.pdf

31.   Poverty in the United States: Frequently asked questions. (n.d.). Retrieved from the National Poverty Center website, http://www.npc.umich.edu/poverty/#5

32.–33.   See 30.

34.   Neild, R., & Balfanz, R. (2006). Unfulfilled promise: The dimensions and characteristics of Philadelphia's dropout crisis, 2000-2005. Retrieved from   http://www.cof.org/files/Documents/Conferences/2008Summit/Site%20Session%20Multiple%20Pathways%208.pdf

35.–36.   Herold, B., & Mezzacappa, D. (2012, August 16). Scores plunge in many schools targeted in cheating probe; early grades did poorly. [Web log post]. Retrieved from http://thenotebook.org/blog/125072/big-test-scores-drops-schools-targeted-cheating-probe-and-early-grades

37.   Socalar, P. (2007, Spring). TerraNova scores reach plateau. Retrieved from http://thenotebook.org/spring-2007/0747/terranova-scores-reach-plateau

38.   Carr, S. (2008, June 9). Recovery School District Superintendent Paul Vallas aims for long-term stability. *Times Picayune*. Retrieved from http://www.nola.com/news/index.ssf/2008/06/recovery_school_district_super.html

CHAPTER 10

1.–2.   Cowen Institute for Public Education Initiatives. (2012). Transforming public education in New Orleans: The Recovery School District, 2003–2011. Retrieved from http://www.coweninstitute.com/wp-content/up-loads/2011/12/History-of-the-RSD-Report-2011.pdf

3.   Thevenot, B. (2005, April 13). Besieged Amato calls it quits. Retrieved from http://parentadvocates.org/nicecontent/dsp_printable.cfm?articleID=5878

4.   Robelen, E. (2005, November 4). Louisiana eyes plan to let state control New Orleans schools. Retrieved from http://www.edweek.org/ew/articles/2005/11/04/11louisiana.h25.html

5.   Toppo, G. (2006, June 11). New Orleans Schools aim higher. *USA Today.* Retrieved from http://usatoday30.usatoday.com/news/education/2006-06-11-parish-schools_x.htm

6.   Louisiana Public Square. (2010). Charter schools in Louisiana. Retrieved from http://beta.lpb.org/images/lps_uploads/lps201009charter.pdf

7.–8.   Weil, D. (2009, December 15). Teachers unions and charter schools: Taking Race to the Top money and starving public schools, their teachers and students. *Daily Censored.* Retrieved from http://www.dailycensored.com/teachers-unions-and-charter-schools-taking-race-to-the-top-money-and-starving-public-schools-their-teachers-and-students/

9.   New Orleans Tourism Marketing Corporation. (n.d.). New Orleans facts pre-Katrina. Retrieved from the website, http://www.neworleansonline.com/pr/releases/releases/New%20Orleans%20Facts%20Pre%20Katrina.pdf

10.   Carr, S. (2008, June 9). Recovery School District Superintendent Paul Vallas aims for long-term stability. *Times Picayune.* Retrieved from http://www.nola.com/news/index.ssf/2008/06/recovery_school_district_super.html

11.–12. Scheets, G. (2007, May 2). Jarvis to leave school district post. *Times Picayune.* Retrieved from http://blog.nola.com/topnews/2007/05/jarvis_to_leave_school_distric.html

13.   How did Chicago's public schools get into such a huge financial hole? (2013, June 20). *Chicago Magazine.* Retrieved from http://www.chicagomag.com/Chicago-Magazine/The-312/June-2013/Chicago-Public-Schools-Pension-Bomb/

14.   Pastorek, Paul G.–Adams and Reese. [Address.] (n.d.). Retrieved June 26, 2013, from http://businessfinder.nola.com/pastorek-paul-g-adams-and-reese-llp-new-orleans-la.html

15.   ALEC law firms. (2012, August 22). Retrieved from http://www.sourcewatch.org/index.php/ALEC_Law_Firms

16.   Toppo, G. (2008, August 26). Superintendent of New Orleans watched by other city schools. *USA Today.* Retrieved from http://usatoday30.usatoday.com/news/education/2008-08-26-new-orleans-superintendent_N.htm

17.   Tough, P. (2008, August 17). A teachable moment. *New York Times.* Retrieved from http://www.nytimes.com/2008/08/17/magazine/17NewOrleans-t.html?_r=3&pagewanted=all&

18.   See 16.

19.   Moller, J. (2009, November 23). RSD Superintendent Paul Vallas used state car on 31 out-of-state trips. *Times Picayune*. Retrieved from http://www.nola.com/politics/index.ssf/2009/11/rsd_superintendent_paul_vallas.html

20.   See 16.

21.   Schneider, M. (2013, January 25). In case you missed it, you didn't miss much. Retrieved from http://deutsch29.wordpress.com/2013/01/25/in-case-you-missed-it-you-really-didnt-miss-much/

22.   Mike. (2010, October 24). Charter schools, test scores, and skimming the cream. [Web log post]. Retrieved from http://scienceblogs.com/mikethemadbiologist/2010/10/24/charter-schools-test-scores-an/

23.   See 6.

24.   Ferguson, B. (2011, July). Dumping kids out—The misuse of charter schools in New Orleans, Part 1. Retrieved from http://www.researchonreforms.org/html/documents/DumpingKidsOut.pdf

25.–28. Hatfield, C. (2011, April 1). Have RSD schools really improved significantly since 2005? Retrieved from http://www.researchonreforms.org/documents/HaveRSDSchoolsReallyImprovedSignificantlySince2005_000.pdf

29.   New RSD leader given $281,000 pay package. (2011, May 4). [Web log post]. Retrieved from http://neworleanscitybusiness.com/blog/2011/05/04/new-rsd-leader-given-281000-pay-package/

30.   Sanders, R. (n.d.). Legislative audit cites fiscal mismanagement of Recovery School District [Paper]. Retrieved from http://www.researchonreforms.org/html/commentary/researchpapers/Legislative%20Audit%20Cites%20Fiscal%20Mismanagement%20of%20Recovery%20School%20District.pdf

31.   Dreilinger, D. (2013, April 8). Audit questions $6.1 million in costs on $105 million Recovery School District building project. *Times Picayune*. Retrieved from http://www.nola.com/education/index.ssf/2013/04/audit_questions_61_million_in.html

32.   Purpera, D. (2010, December 29). Recovery School District, Department of Education, State of Louisiana, Louisiana legislative auditor management letter. Retrieved from http://www.coweninstitute.com/wp-content/uploads/2010/05/RSD09-10.pdf

33.   Purpera, D. (2012, January 18). Recovery School District, Department of Education, State of Louisiana, Louisiana legislative auditor management letter. Retrieved from http://app1.lla.state.la.us/PublicReports.nsf/F00CAD2B2AAC142D86257989006984E2/$FILE/00025879.pdf

34.   Carr, S. (2010, February 20). Haiti rebuilding effort draws on expertise of RSD Superintendent Paul Vallas. *Times Picayune*. Retrieved from http://www.nola.com/politics/index.ssf/2010/02/haiti_rebuilding_effort_draws.html

35.   Fattah to team up with first lady of Haiti, Paul Vallas to rebuild education in Haiti. (2010, March 11). *PR Newswire*. Retrieved from http://www.prnewswire.com/news-releases/fattah-to-team-up-with-first-lady-of-haiti-paul-vallas-to-rebuild-education-in-haiti-87381132.html

36. Paul Vallas: Not running for Chicago mayor, developing school model for Haiti. (2010, February 15). *Huffington Post*. Retrieved from http://www.huffingtonpost.com/2010/02/15/paul-vallas-not-running-f_n_462620.html

37. Williams, J. (2010, December 9). RSD superintendent Vallas not working full schedule because of disaster work. *The Lens*. Retrieved from http://thelensnola.org/2010/12/09/vallas-time-away/

38. Schmidt, G. (2011, July 17). Protests grow in Chile as Vallas' 'Chicago boys' bring UAS corporate reform to S. America four decades after the first round of free-market fascism under Vallas predecessor Augusto Pinochet. Retrieved from http://www.substancenews.net/articles.php?page=2439

39. Dessoff, A. (2012, July/August). Paul Vallas for sale. Retrieved from http://www.districtadministration.com/article/paul-vallas-sale

40. Tepfer, D., & Lambeck, L. (2012, February 28). Supreme Court voids take-over of schools. *Connecticut Post*. Retrieved from http://www.ctpost.com/news/article/Supreme-Court-voids-takeover-of-schools-3367832.php

41. –42. Lambeck, L. (2011, December 20). National education reformer to lead Bridgeport. *Connecticut Post*. Retrieved from http://www.ctpost.com/news/article/National-education-reformer-to-lead-Bridgeport-2415319.php

43.–44. Lambeck, L. (2013, April 1). Vallas being sued over certification. [Web log post]. *Connecticut News*. Retrieved from http://blog.ctnews.com/education/2013/04/01/vallas-being-sued-over-certification/

45.–46. Pelto, J. (2013, June 21). Right on schedule: Pryor waives certification requirement for Vallas. [Web log post]. Retrieved from http://jonathanpelto.com/2013/06/21/right-on-schedule-pryor-waives-certification-requirement-for-vallas/

47. Pelto, J. (2013, June 22). Bridgeport board of education schedules emergency vote Monday to formally make Vallas permanent superintendent. [Web log post]. Retrieved from http://jonathanpelto.com/2013/06/22/bridgeport-board-of-education-schedules-emergency-vote-monday-to-formally-make-vallas-permanent-superintendent/

48. Tepfer, D. (2013, July 10). Court orders Vallas out, but he's not packing yet. *Connecticut Post*. Retrieved from http://www.ctpost.com/local/article/Court-orders-Vallas-out-but-he-s-not-packing-yet-4657834.php

49. Tepfer, D. (2013, June 7). Critics dispute Vallas qualifications. *Connecticut Post*. Retrieved from http://www.ctpost.com/local/article/Critics-dispute-Vallas-qualifications-4587721.php

50. Court rules Bridgeport superintendent Paul Vallas can stay on the job. [Video]. (2013, July 26). *Connecticut News 12*. Retrieved from http://connecticut.news12.com/news/court-rules-bridgeport-superintendent-paul-vallas-can-stay-on-the-job-1.5772852

51. Pelto, J. (2013, February 8). Vallas is not the only Bridgeport board of education employee out consulting. [Web log post]. Retrieved from http://jonathanpelto.com/2013/02/08/vallas-is-not-the-only-bridgeport-board-of-education-employee-out-consulting/

52.   Pelto, J. (2012, April 25). And the answer is: MORE standardized testing—Hooray! [Web log post]. Retrieved from http://jonathanpelto. com/2012/04/25/and-the-answer-is-more-standardized-testing-hooray/

53.   Sprinkles. (2013, May 16). School turnaround genius Paul Vallas leaves a trail of destruction in Bridgeport. [Web log post]. Retrieved from http:// www.dailykos.com/story/2013/05/16/1209666/-School-turnaround-genius-Paul-Vallas-leaves-a-trail-of-destruction

54.   Connecticut Education Association. (2013, May 21). Rogue Bridgeport schools superintendent sued by teachers union. Retrieved from http:// thecontributor.com/breaking-teacher-union-files-lawsuit-against-bridgeport-school-superintendent

CHAPTER 11

1.   Goldstein, D. (2012, September 19). The schoolmaster. *The Atlantic.* Retrieved from http://www.theatlantic.com/magazine/archive/2012/10/ the-schoolmaster/309091/

2.   Gewertz, C. (2013, March 13). Common-core test take up to 10 hours. Retrieved from http://www.edweek.org/ew/articles/2013/03/13/24parcc. h32.html

3.–5.   Common core state standards for English language arts, and literacy in history,/social studies, science, and technical subjects. Retrieved from http://www.corestandards.org/assets/CCSSI_ELA%20Standards.pdf

6.   Coleman, D. (2011, April 28). Bringing the common core to life. [Transcript]. Retrieved from http://usny.nysed.gov/rttt/docs/bringingthecommoncoretolife/fulltranscript.pdf

7.–8.   A teacher says "No!" to common core state standards. (2012, March 4). [Web log post]. Retrieved from http://seattleducation2010.wordpress. com/2012/03/04/a-teacher-says-no-to-common-core-standards/

9.   Sandra Stotsky on the mediocrity of the common core ELA standards. (2011, April 17). Retrieved from http://parentsacrossamerica.org/sandra-stotsky-on-the-mediocrity-of-the-common-core-ela-standards/

10.   Sandra Stotsky's testimony before Indiana senate education committee. (2012, January 23). Retrieved from http://hoosiersagainstcommoncore. com/sandra-stotskys-testimony-before-indiana-senate-education-commitee/

11.–12. See 9.

13.   Phillips, V., & Wong, C. (2010, February). *Phi Delta Kappan, 91*(5), 37–42. Retrieved from http://bswpservicelearningandinquiry.wikispaces.com/ file/view/CCSS_article_for_WS%5B1%5D.pdf

14.   Schneider, M. (2013, October 14). The Common Core memorandum of understanding: What a story. [Web log post]. Retrieved from http:// deutsch29.wordpress.com/2013/10/14/the-common-core-memorandum-of-understanding-what-a-story/

15.   Gallagher, M. (2013, May 12). Two moms vs. common core. *National Review.* Retrieved from http://www.nationalreview.com/article/347973/ two-moms-vs-common-core

16. James Milgram testimony before Indiana senate education committee. (2012, January 23). Retrieved from http://hoosiersagainstcommoncore. com/james-milgram-testimony-to-the-indiana-senate-committee/

17. Common Core State Standards Initiative. (n.d.). Frequently asked questions. Retrieved from http://www.corestandards.org/resources/frequently-asked-questions

18.–19. See 1.

20. McGraw Hill. (n.d.). Common core solutions. Retrieved from http://www. commoncoresolutions.com/resources.php

21. See 17.

22. See 14.

23. See 6.

24. Schneider, M. (2013, May 30). Hart, Weingarten, and power point deception. [Web log post]. Retrieved from http://deutsch29.wordpress. com/2013/05/30/hart-weingarten-and-power-point-deception/

25. See 6.

26. National Governors Association. (2009, July 1). Common core state standards development work group and feedback group announced. Retrieved from http://www.nga.org/cms/home/news-room/news-releases/ page_2009/col2-content/main-content-list/title_common-core-state-standards-development-work-group-and-feedback-group-announced.html

27. Innes, R. (2013, June 10). Innes' testimony on common core transparency. Retrieved from http://www.bipps.org/innes-testimony-on-common-core-transparency/

28. See 26.

29. See 9.

30. See 10.

31. See 14.

32. stlgretchen. (2013, June). Straight from David Coleman's mouth about common core: he's making the educational decisions for all children. [Transcript]. [web log post]. Retrieved from http://www.missourieducationwatchdog.com/2013/06/straight-from-david-colemans-mouth.html

33. See 17.

34. See 1.

35. National PTA. (n.d.). Parent's guide to student success. (n.d.). Retrieved from http://pta.org/parents/content.cfm?ItemNumber=2583

36.–37. Hernandez, J., & Baker, A. (2013, April 19). Common core testing spurs protest and tears. *New York Times.* Retrieved from http://www.nytimes. com/2013/04/19/education/common-core-testing-spurs-outrage-and-protest-among-parents.html?_r=0

38. President of College Board: I convinced the governors. (2013, June 17). [Video web log post]. Retrieved from http://whatiscommoncore.wordpress.com/2013/06/17/president-of-college-board-i-convinced-the-governors/

39. See 1.

40. Strauss, V. (2013, June 25). Arne Duncan tells newspaper editors how to report on common core. [Web log post]. *Washington Post.* Retrieved from

http://www.washingtonpost.com/blogs/answer-sheet/wp/2013/06/25/arne-duncan-tells-newspaper-editors-how-to-report-on-common-core/

41. US Department of Education. (n.d.). Elementary and Secondary Education Subpart 2: Other provisions. Retrieved from http://www2.ed.gov/policy/elsec/leg/esea02/pg112.html

42.–43. Common Core State Standards Initiative. (n.d.). English language arts standards, reading: Informational text, grade 9–10. Retrieved from http://www.corestandards.org/ELA-Literacy/RI/9-10

44. See 13.

45. See 17.

46.–47. Lewin, Tamar. (2012, May 16). Backer of common core school curriculum is chosen to lead College Board. *New York Times.* Retrieved from http://www.nytimes.com/2012/05/16/education/david-coleman-to-lead-college-board.html?_r=0

48. CreditCards.com. (2011, April 28). What you're worth on the black market. *MSN Money.* Retrieved from http://money.msn.com/identity-theft/what-you-are-worth-on-black-market-credit-cards

49. Ellis, R. (2005, June 21). Thieves create internet black market for identity theft. *NBC News.* Retrieved from http://www.nbcnews.com/id/8307418/ns/nbc_nightly_news_with_brian_williams/t/thieves-create-internet-black-market-identity-theft/

50.–51. Cushing, T. (2013, February 13). Texas DMV sells personal information to hundreds of companies; drivers not allowed to opt-out. *Techdirt.* Retrieved from http://www.techdirt.com/articles/20130212/21285321958/texas-dmv-sells-personal-information-to-hundreds-companies-drivers-not-allowed-to-opt-out.shtml

52.–58. See 32.

CHAPTER 12

1. Board of directors. (n.d.). Retrieved July 7, 2013, from the NCTQ website, http://www.nctq.org/about/board.jsp

2. Thomas B. Fordham Institute. (2013, June 27). *Wikipedia.* Retrieved from http://en.wikipedia.org/wiki/Thomas_B._Fordham_Foundation

3. Chester E. Finn, Jr. (n.d.). Retrieved from http://www.hoover.org/fellows/10338

4. Thomas B. Fordham Institute. (n.d.). About us. Retrieved from http://www.edexcellence.net/about-us/

5. Thomas B. Fordham. (n.d.). Board of trustees. Retrieved from http://www.edexcellence.net/about-us/board-of-trustees.html

6. Schneider, M. (2013, March 18). NCTQ's varicose reform. [Web log post]. Retrieved from http://deutsch29.wordpress.com/2013/03/18/nctqs-varicose-reform/

7. National Council on Teacher Quality. (n.d.). About. Retrieved July 7, 2013, from http://www.nctq.org/about/

8. National Council on Teacher Quality. (n.d.). Advisory board. Retrieved July 7, 2013, from http://www.nctq.org/about/advisoryBoard.jsp

9. Thomas B. Fordham Institute. (n.d.). Partners. Retrieved from http://www.edexcellence.net/about-us/partners.html
10. National Council on Teacher Quality. (n.d.). Funders. Retrieved July 7, 2013, from http://www.nctq.org/about/funders.jsp
11. Thomas B. Fordham Institute. (n.d.). Standards-based reforms. Retrieved from http://www.edexcellence.net/policy-priorities/standards-based-reforms/
12. See 9.
13.–15. Finn, C. (2013, May 29). The GOP and the Common Core. Retrieved from http://www.hoover.org/publications/defining-ideas/article/147681
16. Thomas B. Fordham Institute. (n.d.). Quality choices. Retrieved from http://www.edexcellence.net/policy-priorities/quality-choices/
17. Finn, C. (n.d.). The selective-admission quandary. [Web log post]. Retrieved from http://www.edexcellence.net/commentary/education-gadfly-weekly/2013/may-30/the-selective-admission-quandary.html
18. Finn, C. (2011, July 29). Is the charter-school movement stuck in a rut? Retrieved from http://educationnext.org/is-the-charter-school-movement-stuck-in-a-rut/
19. Carr, S. (2009, September 11). National charter advocate says he's opposed to selective admissions during talk in New Orleans. *Times Picayune*. Retrieved from http://www.nola.com/education/index.ssf/2009/09/national_charter_advocate_spea.html
20. Schneider, M. (2013, July 5). New Orleans parental choice and the oneapp. [Web log post]. Retrieved from http://deutsch29.wordpress.com/2013/07/05/new-orleans-parental-choice-and-the-walton-funded-oneapp/
21. Finn, Chester E., Jr. (2008). *Troublemaker*. Princeton, NJ: Princeton University Press.
22. See 20.
23. See 21.
24. Schneider, M. (2013, April 2). In Ravitch's defense: Milwaukee voucher study found wanting. [Web log post]. Retrieved from http://deutsch29.wordpress.com/2013/04/02/in-ravitchs-defense-milwaukee-voucher-study-found-wanting/
25. Finn, C., & Horn, M. (2013, Winter). Can digital learning transform education? Retrieved from http://educationnext.org/files/ednext_20131_forum.pdf
26. Schneider, M. (2013, May 12). I am Louisiana course choice, and I enroll without parental consent. [Web log post]. Retrieved from http://deutsch29.wordpress.com/2013/05/12/i-am-louisiana-course-choice-and-i-enroll-without-parental-consent/
27.–28. See 25.
29. Schneider, M. (2013, May 22). Louisiana charter school audit reveals faux accountability. [Web log post]. Retrieved from http://deutsch29.wordpress.com/2013/05/22/louisiana-charter-school-audit-reveals-faux-accountability/

30.   Mann, R. (2013, July 7). Where is state voucher money going? *Times Pica-yune*. Retrieved from http://www.nola.com/opinions/index.ssf/2013/07/where_is_state_voucher_money_a.html

31.   Welborn, V., & Nash-Wood, M. (2013, May 13). Some La. Students were signed up for course choice without their knowledge. *The Town Talk*. Retrieved from http://www.thetowntalk.com/article/20130513/NEWS01/305130012/Some-La-students-were-signed-up-Course-Choice-without-their-knowledge

32.   FastPath Learning. (n.d.). Dr. Rod Paige, Chairman of the board. Retrieved from http://fastpathlearning.com/recommendation/dr-rod-paige

33.–34.   Aswell, T. (2013, May 20). More sordid details emerging in apparent fraud-ulent course choice registrations in three northwest Louisiana parishes. [Web log post]. Retrieved from http://louisianavoice.com/2013/05/20/more-sordid-details-emerging-in-apparent-fraudulent-course-choice-regis-trations-in-three-northwest-louisiana-parishes/

35.–36.   Sentell, W. (2013, June 16). State rethinks course choice. *Baton Rouge Advo-cate*. Retrieved from http://theadvocate.com/home/6241659-125/state-rethinks-course-choice

37.   Thomas B. Fordham Institute. (n.d.). A reform-driven system. Retrieved from http://www.edexcellence.net/policy-priorities/a-reform-driven-sys-tem/

38.   Harvard Graduate School of Education. (n.d.). Teacher education pro-gram. Retrieved from http://www.gse.harvard.edu/academics/masters/tep/description/tac.html

39.   Frederick Hess, scholar, author, and speaker [Biography]. (n.d.). Re-trieved from http://www.linkedin.com/pub/frederick-hess/10/403/209

40.   Thomas B. Fordham Institute. (n.d.). Marci Kanstorom, Ph.D., senior edi-tor [Biography]. Retrieved from http://www.edexcellence.net/about-us/fordham-staff/marci-kanstoroom-phd.html

41.   University of Arkansas. (n.d.). Jay P. Greene, Ph.D., Endowed chair and head of the department of education reform [Biography]. Retrieved from http://edre.uark.edu/2474.htm

42.   Terry Moe (n.d.). Retrieved from the Department of political science, Stanford University website, http://politicalscience.stanford.edu/faculty/terry-moe

43.   John Chubb. (n.d.). Retrieved from the EducationNext website, http://educationnext.org/author/jchubb/

44.   Mezzacappa, D. (2006, April 18). Market forces: Professor Paul Peter-son's influential protégés. Retrieved from http://www.educationsector.org/publications/market-forces-professor-paul-petersons-influential-prot%C3%A9g%C3%A9s

45.–47.   EducationNext. (n.d.). About. Retrieved from http://educationnext.org/sub/about/

48.   Hess, F, (2013, June 19). AA playbook for the common core'ites, part i. *Education Next*. Retrieved from http://educationnext.org/a-playbook-for-the-common-coreites-part-i/

49.–52.   Hess, F, (2013, June 19). AA playbook for the common core'ites, part ii. *Education Next*. Retrieved from http://educationnext.org/a-playbook-for-the-common-coreites-part-2/

53.   Broad prize review board. (n.d.). Retrieved from http://broadprize.org/about/decision_makers/review_board.html

54.   Broad Center. (n.d.). Board of directors. Retrieved from http://www.broadcenter.org/who-we-are/board-of-directors/

55.   Higgins, M., Robison, W., Weiner, J., & Hess, F. (2011, Summer). Creating a corps of change agents. *Education Next*. Retrieved from http://educationnext.org/creating-a-corps-of-change-agents/

56.   Broad Foundation and Thomas B. Fordham Institute. (2003, May). Better leaders for better schools: A manifesto. Retrieved from http://www.broadeducation.org/asset/1128-betterleadersforamericasschools.pdf

57.–58.   Schneider, M. (2013, January 30). NCTQ letter grades and the reformer agenda, part vi. [Web log post]. Retrieved from http://deutsch29.wordpress.com/2013/01/30/nctq-letter-grades-and-the-reformer-agenda-part-vi/

59.   See 56.

60.   Schneider, M. (2013, January 30). NCTQ letter grades and the reformer agenda, part vii. [Web log post]. Retrieved from http://deutsch29.wordpress.com/2013/01/31/nctq-letter-grades-and-the-reformer-agenda-part-vii/

61.   Eidler, S. (2013, January 2). Deferring six figures on Wall Street for teacher's salary. *New York Times*. Retrieved from http://dealbook.nytimes.com/2013/01/02/deferring-six-figures-on-wall-street-for-teachers-salary/

62.   See 56.

63.–65.   See 57.

66.–67.   Hess, F. (2013, January 16). Cage-busting leadership. [Video]. Retrieved from http://www.youtube.com/watch?v=aZHaZ6xQ6C0

CHAPTER 13

1.   Hawkins, B. (2011, April 26). Jeb Bush touts school reforms to Capitol's supportive GOP, skeptical DFL. Retrieved from http://www.minnpost.com/learning-curve/2011/04/jeb-bush-touts-florida-school-reforms-capitols-supportive-gop-skeptical-dfl

2.   Wing, N. (2012, November 27). Jeb Bush huddles with group of former White House officials in Washington: Report. *Huffington Post*. Retrieved from http://www.huffingtonpost.com/2012/11/27/jeb-bush-white-house_n_2197124.html

3.   Crowley, C. (2013, March 10). Jeb Bush for president in 2016? [Web log post.] Retrieved from http://sotu.blogs.cnn.com/2013/03/10/jeb-bush-for-president-in-2016/

4.   Backgrounder. (n.d.). Retrieved from http://www.in.gov/edroundtable/files/Education_Reform_in_Florida_(COMPLETE).pdf

5.–6.   About us. (n.d.). Retrieved from Foundation for Florida's Future website, http://www.foundationforfloridasfuture.org/Pages/About_Us.aspx

7.   Jeb Bush: The Once and Future Reformer. (n.d.). [Web log post]. Retrieved from http://stateimpact.npr.org/florida/tag/jeb-bush/

8.   Jeb Bush likes Race to the Top, too. (2009, July 24). [Web log post]. Retrieved from http://www.tampabay.com/blogs/gradebook/content/jeb-bush-likes-race-top-too

9.   Peterson, P. (n.d.). The A+ plan. Retrieved from http://media.hoover.org/sites/default/files/documents/ktf_florida_book_49.pdf

10.   Ladner, M., & Lips, D. (2009, January 7). How "No Child Left Behind" threatens Florida's successful education reforms. Retrieved from http://www.heritage.org/research/reports/2009/01/how-no-child-left-behind-threatens-floridas-successful-education-reforms

11.   See 1.

12.   Schneider, M. (2013, March 21). Like spokes to a hub: Chiefs for Change in Bush's service. [Web log post.] Retrieved from http://deutsch29.word-press.com/2013/03/21/like-spokes-to-a-hub-chiefs-for-change-in-bushs-service/

13.   See 7.

14.   Gabriel, T. (2011, April 26). Jeb Bush leads broad push for education change with Florida. *New York Times*. Retrieved from http://www.nytimes.com/2011/04/27/education/27bush.html?_r=0

15.   Foundation for Florida's Future. (n.d.). School grades FAQs. Retrieved from http://www.foundationforfloridasfuture.org/Images/FCAT%20Results%20Graphics/SchoolGradesFAQs.pdf

16.   See 9.

17.–18. See 15.

19.   Florida Department of Education (2011, July). 2011 guide to calculating school grades: Technical assistance paper. Retrieved from http://school-grades.fldoe.org/pdf/1011/SchoolGradesTAP2011.pdf

20.   See 9.

21.   Florida Department of Education (2012, June). 2012 guide to calculating school grades: Technical assistance paper. Retrieved from http://school-grades.fldoe.org/pdf/1112/SchoolGradesTAP2012.pdf

22.   Isensee, L., & Vasquez, M. (2012, July 23). State forgot part of formula in calculation, revises grades for nearly 50 South Florida schools. *Miami Herald*. Retrieved from http://www.miamiherald.com/2012/07/23/2908074/miami-dade-to-see-grades-revised.html

23.–24. Fund Education Now! (2012). High-stakes testing. Retrieved from http://www.fundeducationnow.org/resource-room/high-stakes-testing/

25.   Ward, K. (2010, August 30). 'Inflated' FCAT writing scores p ad school grades. Retrieved from http://www.sunshinestatenews.com/story/inflated-fcat-writing-scores-pad-school-grades

26.   High stakes testing resistance spreads across Florida. (2012, June 30). *Bradenton Times*. Retrieved from http://www.thebradentontimes.com/news/2012/06/30/schools_and_education/high_stakes_testing_resistance_spreads_across_florida/

27.   See 9.

28. Weber, D. (2001, December 4). Lawmakers decry school reading loophole. *Orlando Sentinel*. Retrieved from http://articles.orlandosentinel.com/2001-12-04/news/0112040071_1_loophole-fourth-graders-social-promotion

29.–30. Greene, J., & Winters, M. (2004, December). An evaluation of Florida's program to end social promotion. Retrieved on April 10, 2013, from http://www.manhattan-institute.org/html/ewp_07.htm

31. See 14.

32. See 5.

33. Simon, S. (2012, November 27). Jeb Bush, with cash and clout, pushes contentious school reforms. *Reuters*. Retrieved from http://www.reuters.com/article/2012/11/27/usa-education-bush-foundation-idUSL1E8MR08N20121127

34. Winters, M. (2012, Fall). Florida defeats the skeptics. Retrieved from http://educationnext.org/florida-defeats-the-skeptics/

35. Bush, J. (1999, September 23). An A+ plan for education. Retrieved from http://www.icasinc.org/1999/1999l/1999ljeb.html

36. Floroda Education Association (n.d.). Senate Bill 736: How will it affect me? Frequently asked questions. Retrieved from http://feaweb.org/senate-bill-736-how-will-it-affect-me

37. Bush, J. (2012, September 14). Reforming education. *Chicago Tribune*. Retrieved from http://articles.chicagotribune.com/2012-09-14/news/ct-perspec-0914-jeb-20120914_1_chicago-teachers-union-teachers-strike-worst-teachers

38.–39. Florida Department of Education. (2011). Senate Bill 736. Retrieved from http://www.fldoe.org/GR/Bill_Summary/2011/SB736.pdf

40. Strauss, V. (2012, December 6). Florida bungles teacher evaluation results. [Web log post]. *Washington Post*. Retrieved from http://www.washingtonpost.com/blogs/answer-sheet/wp/2012/12/06/florida-bungles-teacher-evaluation-results/

41.–42. Krueger, C., Sokol, M., Solochek, J., & Valentine, D. (2012, December 5). State botches release of new data on teacher evaluations. *Tampa Bay Times*. Retrieved from http://www.tampabay.com/news/education/teachers/state-botches-release-of-new-data-on-teacher-evaluations/1264717?utm_source=dlvr.it&utm_medium=twitter

43.–44. O'Donnell, C., & Russon, G. (2012, December 5). State: Almost half of local teachers 'highly effective.' *Herald Tribune*. Retrieved from http://www.heraldtribune.com/article/20121205/ARTICLE/121209819

45. Larrabee, B. (2013, January 31). Florida teacher evaluation system: Concerns mounting over future of new teacher evaluation. Retrieved from http://www.wptv.com/dpp/news/state/florida-teacher-evaluation-system-concerns-mounting-over-future-of-new-teacher-evaluation-system

46. Dixon, M. (2013, January 29). Don Gaetz: Florida teacher evaluation not working. [Web log post.] *Florida Times-Union*. Retrieved from http://jacksonville.com/opinion/blog/403455/matt-dixon/2013-01-29/don-gaetz-florida-teacher-evaluation-not-working

47.   Florida Department of Education. (n.d.). Educator certification. Retrieved on April 10, 2013, from http://www.fldoe.org/edcert/level3.asp

48.   American Board for Certification of Teacher Excellence. (n.d.). About us. Retrieved from http://abcte.org/about-us/

49.   United States Government Accountability Office. (2006, February). Discretionary grants: Further tightening of education's procedures for making awards could improve transparency and accountability. Retrieved from http://www.gao.gov/new.items/d06268.pdf

50.   Schneider, M. (2013, March 18). NCTQ's varicose reform. [Web log post]. Retrieved from http://deutsch29.wordpress.com/2013/03/18/nctqs-varicose-reform/

51.   NCTQ's defense of the ABCTE teaching credential. (n.d.). Retrieved on March 18, 2013, from the NCTQ website, http://www.nctq.org/p/tqb/printStory.jsp?id=502

52.   US Department of Education Office of Inspector General. (2006, January). The Education Leaders Council's drawdown and expenditure of federal reports: Final audit report. Retrieved from http://www2.ed.gov/about/offices/list/oig/auditreports/a03f0010.pdf

53.   Keller, B. (2005, October 19). Upheaval hits teacher credentialing board. Retrieved from http://www.edweek.org/ew/articles/2005/10/19/08abcte.h25.html

54.   American Board for Certification of Teacher Excellence. (n.d.). Homepage. Retrieved from American Board of Certification of Teacher Excellence website, http://abcte.org/

55.–56. American Board for Certification of Teacher Excellence. (n.d.). American Board teacher certification courses. Retrieved from American Board of Certification of Teacher Excellence website, http://abcte.org/certification/courses/

57.   Madison, L. (2012, August 30). Jeb Bush: America's future depends upon better education. *CBS News*. Retrieved from http://www.cbsnews.com/8301-503544_162-57503951-503544/jeb-bush-americas-future-depends-on-better-education/

58.   Florida Department of Education Bureau of Research and Evaluation. (2010, January). Critical teacher shortage areas: Florida public schools. Retrieved from the Florida Department of Education website, http://www.fldoe.org/arm/pdf/ctsa1112.pdf

59.   American Board for Certification of Teacher Excellence. (n.d.). Become a teacher in Florida. Retrieved from American Board of Certification of Teacher Excellence website, http://abcte.org/teach/florida/

60.   Special education teacher job description; Part 1. (n.d.). Retrieved from http://job-descriptions.careerplanner.com/Special-Education-Teachers-Secondary-School.cfm

61.   Florida House of Representatives. (n.d.). 2010-11 education fact sheet. Retrieved from http://www.myfloridahouse.gov/FileStores/Web/HouseContent/Approved/Web%20Site/education_fact_sheets/2011/documents/2010 1%20Alternative%20Teacher%20Certification.3.pdf

CHAPTER 14

1.   Hogan, L.(2013, January 29). Jeb Bush urges charter school expansion in state. Retrieved from http://www.arkansasonline.com/news/2013/jan/29/jeb-bush-urges-charter-school-expansion-state/

2.   Fang, L. (2013, January 30). Emails show Jeb Bush foundation lobbied for businesses, including one tied to Bush. [Web log post.] The Nation. Retrieved from http://www.thenation.com/blog/172551/e-mails-show-jeb-bush-foundation-lobbied-businesses-including-one-tied-bush#

3.   National Council on Teacher Quality. (n.d.) Advisory board members. Retrieved on March 8, 2013, from http://www.nctq.org/p/about/advisory.jsp

4.   Schneider, M. (2013, March 5). New Orleans Recovery School District: The lie unveiled. [Web log post]. Retrieved from http://deutsch29.wordpress.com/2013/03/05/new-orleans-recovery-school-district-the-lie-unveiled/

5.   Schneider, M. (2013, March 25). Arizona education: A pocket-lining, conflict-of-interest mecca. http://deutsch29.wordpress.com/2013/03/25/arizona-education-a-pocket-lining-conflict-of-interest-mecca/

6.   Florida Charter Schools. (n.d.). 1996 charter school statutes. Retrieved on April 10, 2013, from http://www.floridacharterschools.org/global/downloads/1996CharterSchoolStatutes.pdf

7.   Bush, J., & Fair, T. (n.d.). A new lease on learning: Florida's first charter school. Retrieved from http://heartland.org/sites/all/modules/custom/heartland_migration/files/pdfs/1880.pdf

8.   Collie, T. (1997, December 21). Jeb Bush is feeling charter school heat. Retrieved from http://articles.sun-sentinel.com/1997-12-21/news/9712200102_1_charter-schools-bush-s-political-aspirations-schools-and-vouchers

9.   Moore, P. (2008, Mach 13). The death of Florida's first charter school. [Web log post]. Retrieved from http://normsnotes2.blogspot.com/2008/03/death-of-floridas-first-charter-school.html

10.–11. S. Davis and Associates, P.A. (2007). Liberty Schools Charter School Project, Inc.: A charter school and component unit of the Miami-Dade County District School Board financial statements for the years ended June 30, 2007 and 2006. Retrieved from http://mca.dadeschools.net/CBO-CharterDocs0708/CS4.pdf

12.   Meyer, P. (2012, Fall). Advice for education reformers: Be bold! Retrieved from http://educationnext.org/advice-for-education-reformers-be-bold/

13.   McGrory, K., & Hiaasen, S. (2011, December 16). Charter schools enrolling low number of poor students. Miami Herald. Retrieved from http://www.miamiherald.com/2011/12/16/2548465/charters-schools-enrolling-low.html

14.   Florida Department of Education. (2012, January 1). Charter school report. Retrieved from the Florida Department of Education website, http://www.fldoe.org/fefp/pdf/CharterSchoolReport-ch2011-232.pdf

15.   Kennedy, J. (2013, April 4). Florida House bolsters charter school growth, over teacher, union objections. Palm Beach Post. Retrieved from http://

www.palmbeachpost.com/news/news/state-regional-govt-politics/florida-house-bolsters-charter-school-growth-over-/nXC8T/

16. See 6.

17. See 13.

18.–19. McGrory, K., & Hiaasen, S. (2011, December 14). Academica: Florida's richest charter school management firm. Miami Herald. Retrieved from http://www.miamiherald.com/2011/12/13/v-fullstory/2545377/academica-florida-richest-charter.html

20. See 15.

21. McClure, V., & Shanklin, M. (n.d.). Risky choices: Many charters prove poor options. Orlando Sentinel. Retrieved from http://www.orlandosentinel.com/orl-special-charterschools-part1,0,5859445.htmlpage

22. Weber, D. (2011, July 16). Florida charter schools' many F's give ammunition to critics. Orlando Sentinel. Retrieved from http://articles.orlandosentinel.com/2011-07-16/news/os-charter-schools-fail-071711-20110716_1_charter-schools-imani-charter-traditional-schools

23. O'Connor, J. (2012, July 12). The good news and bad news about 2012 Florida charter school grades. Retrieved from http://stateimpact.npr.org/florida/2012/07/12/the-good-news-and-bad-news-about-2012-florida-charter-school-grades/

24. See 21.

25. Roth, L. (2012, December 1). Sentinel watchdog: Failed charter school paid principal's husband $460 k. Orlando Sentinel. Retrieved from http://articles.orlandosentinel.com/2012-12-01/features/os-northstar-charter-high-husband-20121201_1_charter-school-schools-use-public-money-state-auditor?pagewanted=all

26.–27. US Department of Education Office of Inspector General. (2012, September). The Office of Innovation and Improvement's oversight and monitoring of the charter schools program's planning and implementation grants. Retrieved from http://www2.ed.gov/about/offices/list/oig/auditreports/fy2012/a02l0002.pdf

28. McGrory, K. (2013, March 26). Jeb Bush's education foundation 'debunks myths' about contentious parent-trigger proposal. [Web log post]. Tampa Bay Tribune. Retrieved from http://www.tampabay.com/blogs/the-buzz-florida-politics/jeb-bushs-education-foundation-debunks-myths-about-contentious/2111273

29. See 15.

30. Bush, J. (1999, September 23). An A+ plan for education. Retrieved from http://www.icasinc.org/1999/1999l/1999ljeb.html

31. National Education Association. (n.d.). Florida court rules voucher program unconstitutional. Retrieved from the National Education Association website, http://www.nea.org/home/17938.htm

32. Dillon, S. (2006, January 6). Florida Supreme Court blocks school vouchers. New York Times. Retrieved from http://www.nytimes.com/2006/01/06/national/06florida.html?_r=0

33. Bush vs. Holmes. (2006, January 5). Supreme Court of Florida, summary for case number SC04-2323. Retrieved from http://www.floridasuprem-

ecourt.org/pub_info/summaries/briefs/04/04-2323/Filed_01-05-2006_Opinion.pdf

34. Fund Education Now! (n.d.). Voucher school programs. Retrieved from Fund Education Now! website, http://www.fundeducationnow.org/resource-room/voucher-school-programs/

35. Harding, A., & Pinkham, P. (2010, October 31). Concerns raised over Florida's Corporate Income Tax Credit Scholarship program. Florida Times-Union. Retrieved from http://jacksonville.com/news/metro/2010-10-31/story/concerns-raised-over-scholarship-program#ixzz2Q2BBUMhd

36. Florida Department of Education. (2004, April). A parent and teacher guide to Section 504: Frequently asked questions. Retrieved from http://sss.usf.edu/resources/format/memos/2004/04_064att.pdf

37. Florida Department of Education Office of Independent Education and Parental Choice. (n.d.) Eligibility requirements. Retrieved from http://www.floridaschoolchoice.org/Information/McKay/eligibility.asp

38. Kidder, K. (2013, April 7). Is public funding of private schools constitutional? [Opinion.] Gainesville Sun. Retrieved from http://www.gainesville.com/article/20130407/OPINION03/130409700?p=2&tc=pg

39. Garcia-Roberts, G. (2011, June 23). McKay Scholarship program sparks a cottage industry of fraud and chaos. Miami New Times. Retrieved from http://www.miaminewtimes.com/2011-06-23/news/mckay-scholarship-program-sparks-a-cottage-industry-of-fraud-and-chaos/

40. Strauss, S. (2011, March 4). Reports of school voucher fraud and accountability problems from around the country. [Web log post]. Retrieved from http://pachurchesadvocacy.org/weblog/?p=7571

41. Bogus students, fake curriculums, ghost schools: Florida's voucher fraud is probed. (2011, October 4). [Web log post]. Retrieved from http://flaglerlive.com/29041/florida-voucher-fraud/

42. See 35.

43. See 38.

44. Bush, J. (2013, January 31). Students should have the choice of digital schools. [We log post]. Retrieved from http://schoolsofthought.blogs.cnn.com/2013/01/31/jeb-bush-students-should-have-the-choice-of-digital-schools/?hpt=hp_c3

45. Amos, J. (2010, December 1). Digital Learning Now! Governors Jeb Bush and Bob Wise announce the 10 elements of high quality digital learning. Retrieved from the Alliance for Excellent Education website, http://www.all4ed.org/press_room/press_releases/12012010

46. Foundation for Excellence in Education (n.d.) Digital Learning Now. Retrieved on April 10, 2013 from http://excelined.org/Pages/Programs/Excellence_in_Action/Digital_Learning_Now.aspx

47. Alliance for Excellent Education. (2010, December 1). 10 elements of high quality digital learning. Retrieved from the Alliance for Excellent Education website, http://www.all4ed.org/publication_material/reports/10ElementsDLC

48.   Bush, J., & Wise, B. (2010, December 1). 10 elements of high quality digital learning. Retrieved from http://www.all4ed.org/files/10ElementsDLC.pdf

49.   Horn, M. (2010, December 2). Digital Learning Now! launches with recommendations for educational transformation. Forbes. Retrieved from http://www.forbes.com/sites/michaelhorn/2010/12/02/digital-learning-now-launches-with-recommendations-for-educational-transformation/

50.   Beuerman, J. (2011, October 25). Governors Bush and Wise announce blueprint for digital education initiative. Pelican Post. Retrieved from http://www.thepelicanpost.org/2011/10/25/governors-bush-and-wise-announce-blueprint-for-digital-education-initiative/

51.   American Legislative Exchange Council. (2011, September 16). Resolution adopting the 10 elements of high-quality digital learning for k-12. Retrieved from the American Legislative Exchange Council website, http://www.alec.org/model-legislation/resolution-adopting-the-10-elements-of-high-quality-digital-learning-for-k-12/

52.   Digital learning. (n.d.) 2012 Florida statutes. Retrieved from the Florida legislature website, http://www.leg.state.fl.us/statutes/index.cfm?App_mode=Display_Statute&Search_String=&URL=1000-1099/1002/Sections/1002.321.html

53.   ressy10. (2012, September 9). Florida Virtual School (FLVS) Part I. [Web log post]. Retrieved from http://www.dailykos.com/story/2012/09/09/1128525/-Florida-Virtual-School-FLVS-Part-I

54.   Aaronson, T., & O'Connor, J. (2012, September 11). State investigating virtual schools provider K12. Retrieved from http://fcir.org/2012/09/11/state-investigating-virtual-schools-provider-k12/

55.   Sikes, B. (2013, January 1). What will happen to FLDOE investigation of K12 Inc. when Tony Bennett arrives? [Web log post]. Retrieved from http://bobsidlethoughtsandmusings.wordpress.com/2013/01/01/what-will-happen-to-fldoe-investigation-of-k12-inc-when-tony-bennett-arrives/

56.   Cavanagh, S. (2013, March 5). K12 Inc. reaches tentative settlement in investor lawsuit. [Web log post]. Retrieved from http://blogs.edweek.org/edweek/marketplacek12/2013/03/k12_reaches_settlement_in_investor_lawsuit.html

57.   Catalanetto, R., & Sokol, M. (2012, January 7). Success of Florida Virtual School is difficult to measure. Tampa Bay Times. Retrieved from http://www.tampabay.com/news/education/k12/success-of-florida-virtual-school-is-difficult-to-measure/1209497

58.   Fang, L. (2011, November 16). How online learning companies bought America's schools. The Nation. Retrieved from http://www.thenation.com/article/164651/how-online-learning-companies-bought-americas-schools

59.   Florida Legislature. (2012). The Florida virtual school: 2012 Florida statutes. Retrieved from http://www.leg.state.fl.us/statutes/index.cfm?App_mode=Display_Statute&Search_String=&URL=1000-1099/1002/Sections/1002.37.html

60.   See 57.

61.   See 58.

62.   See 49.

63.   Larrabee, B. (2013, March 28). Florida Virtual School likely to face major budget cuts. West Orlando News. Retrieved from http://westorlandonews. com/2013/03/28/florida-virtual-school-likely-to-face-major-budget-cuts/

64.   See 58.

65.   Pearson and Florida Virtual School announce agreement. (2010, November 17). Retrieved from the Pearson website, http://www.pearsoned. com/pearson-and-florida-virtual-school-announce-agreement/#.UW4L-RYko7Mw

66.   See 56.

67.   Catalanetto, R. (2012, February 13). Florida Virtual School's revenues falling short of expectations. Tampa Bay Times. Retrieved from http://www. tampabay.com/news/education/k12/florida-virtual-schools-revenues-falling-short-of-expectations/1215320

68.   Sikes, B. (2012, February 14). Florida Virtual School's curious business plan and even more curious supporters. [Web log post]. Retrieved from http://bobsidlethoughtsandmusings.wordpress.com/2012/02/14/florida-virtual-schools-curious-business-plan-and-even-more-curious-supporters/

69.   Ash, K. (2013, March 21). Digital Learning Now! grades states on ed-tech policies. [Web log post]. Retrieved from http://blogs.edweek.org/edweek/DigitalEducation/2013/03/digital_learning_now_grades_st.html

CHAPTER 15

1.   Jeb Bush. (2013, August 16). *Wikipedia*. Retrieved from http://en.wikipedia. org/wiki/Jeb_Bush

2.–4.   Foundation for Excellence in Education. (n.d.). About us. Retrieved from the website, http://excelined.org/about-us/

5.–6.   Myslinski, D. (2010, October 28). 35-day mailing, American Legislative Exchange Council education task force. Retrieved from http://www.commoncause.org/atf/cf/%7BFB3C17E2-CDD1-4DF6-92BE-BD4429893665%7D/ ed_35daymailing-dc.pdf

7.–8.   O'Connor, J. (2012, May 31). How Jeb Bush stood up to ALEC for national education standards. Retrieved from http://stateimpact.npr.org/ florida/2012/05/31/how-jeb-bush-stood-up-to-alec-for-national-education-standards/

9.   Reformer profiles. (n.d.). Retrieved from the Foundation for Excellence in Education website, http://excelined.org/policy-library/reformer-profiles/

10.   Myslinski, D. (2012, November 19). ALEC vote rejects anti-common core resolution. [Web log post]. Retrieved from http://excelined. org/2012/11/alec-vote-rejects-anti-common-core-resolution/

11.   Publius, G. (2012, April 11). Gates foundation drops ALEC (but why was Bill Gates funding it?). [Web log post]. Retrieved from http://america-

blog.com/2012/04/gates-foundation-drops-alec-but-why-was-bill-gates-funding-it.html

12.   Bill and Melinda Gates Foundation. (n.d.). Foundation for Excellence in Education [Grant funding database]. Retrieved from http://www.gatesfoundation.org/How-We-Work/Quick-Links/Grants-Database#q/k=foundation%20for%20excellence%20in%20education

13.   Foundation for Excellence in Education. (n.d.). Reformer profiles. Retrieved from http://excelined.org/policy-library/reformer-profiles/

14.   Foundation for Excellence in Education. (n.d.). National summit. Retrieved from http://excelined.org/national-summit/

15.   Foundation for Excellence in Education. (n.d.). Meet the sponsors. Retrieved from http://excelined.org/national-summit/meet-the-sponsors/

16.–17. See 14.

18.   Foundation for Excellence in Education. (n.d.). 2010 agenda. Retrieved from http://excelined.org/national-summit/2010-agenda/

19.   See 5.

20.   College Board. (n.d.). College Board names Dr. Stefanie Sanford as chief of policy, advocacy, and government relations [Press release]. Retrieved from http://press.collegeboard.org/releases/2012/college-board-names-dr-stefanie-sanford-chief-policy-advocacy-and-government-relations

21.   See 18.

22.   [Emails between the Foundation for Excellence in Education and varied state education officials]. (2011-12). Retrieved March 20, 2013, from In the Public Interest website, http://www.inthepublicinterest.org/node/2747

23.   See 18.

24.   March, W. (2013, March 3). Jeb Bush's education foundation under fire for lobbying for laws that benefit corporate donors. *Huffington Post*. Retrieved from http://www.huffingtonpost.com/2013/03/03/jeb-bush-education-foundation_n_2802536.html

25.   Ravitch, D. (2013, March 17). Rupert Murdoch wins contract to develop common core tests. [Web log post]. Retrieved from http://dianeravitch.net/2013/03/17/rupert-murdoch-wins-contract-to-develop-common-core-tests/

26.   See 24.

27.   Ellenberg, J. (2013, August 2). The case of the missing zeroes. *Slate*. Retrieved from http://www.slate.com/articles/news_and_politics/do_the_math/2013/08/tony_bennett_education_an_astonishing_act_of_statistical_chutzpah_in_the.html

28.   Patricia Levesque. (n.d.). Retrieved from the Foundation for Excellence in Education website, http://excelined.org/team/patricia-levesque/

29.   Chiefs for Change. (n.d.). Donate. Retrieved July 11, 2013, from http://chiefsforchange.org/donate/

30.   Foundation for Excellence in Education. (n.d.). Contact. Retrieved July 11, 2013, from http://excelined.org/about-us/contact/

31.   Foundation for Florida's Future. (n.d.). Contact. Retrieved July 11, 2013, from http://www.foundationforfloridasfuture.org/Contact.aspx

32. Meridian Strategies. (n.d.). Contact information. Retrieved July 11, 2013, from http://www.meridianstrategiesllc.com/

33. See 24.

34. Miller, S. (2013, March 6). Following criticism, Jeb Bush's lobbyist withdraws state registration. Retrieved from http://fcir.org/2013/03/06/following-criticism-jeb-bushs-lobbyist-withdraws-state-registration/

35. Schneider, M. (2013, March 21). Like spokes to a hub: Chiefs for Change in Bush's service. [Web log post]. Retrieved from http://deutsch29.wordpress.com/2013/03/21/like-spokes-to-a-hub-chiefs-for-change-in-bushs-service/

36. Gabriel, T. (2011, April 26). Jeb Bush leads broad push for education change with 'Florida formula.' *New York Times*. Retrieved from http://www.nytimes.com/2011/04/27/education/27bush.html?_r=0

37. Chiefs for Change. (n.d.). Members. Retrieved March 20, 2013, from http://chiefsforchange.org/members-page/

38. See 5.

39. Ujifusa, A. (2012, November 7). Tony Bennett says Common Core in jeopardy in Indiana. *Education Week*. Retrieved from http://blogs.edweek.org/edweek/state_edwatch/2012/11/tony_bennett_says_common_core_in_jeopardy_in_indiana.html

40. See 36.

41. Florida education commissioner choice: Tony Bennett, outgoing Indiana schools chief. (2012, December 12). *Huffington Post*. Retrieved from http://www.huffingtonpost.com/2012/12/12/florida-education-commissioner-tony-bennett_n_2287884.html

42. LoBianco, T. (2013, July 29). AP exclusive: GOP donor's school grade changed. Retrieved from http://bigstory.ap.org/article/ap-exclusive-gop-donors-school-grade-changed

43. McGrory, K., & Solochek, J. (2013, August 1). Tony Bennett resigns as Florida education commissioner. *Tampa Bay Times*. Retrieved from http://www.tampabay.com/news/education/k12/florida-education-commissioner-tony-bennett-expected-to-resign-today/2134254

44. [Emails between the Foundation for Excellence in Education and varied state education officials]. (2011-12). Retrieved March 20, 2013, from In the Public Interest document cloud, http://www.documentcloud.org/documents/559602-me-response-october-2011.html

45. Sentell, W. (2012, October). Races for BESE seats heat up. *Baton Rouge Advocate*. Retrieved from http://theadvocate.com/home/1003929-79/story.html

46. Cunningham-Cook, M. (2012, October 17). Why do some of America's wealthiest individuals have fingers in Louisiana's education system? *The Nation*. Retrieved from http://www.thenation.com/article/170649/why-do-some-americas-wealthiest-individuals-have-fingers-louisianas-education-system

47. ALEC law firms [Listing]. (2012, August 22). Retrieved from http://www.sourcewatch.org/index.php/ALEC_Law_Firms

48. Paul G. Pastorek, Adams and Reese. (n.d.). *Times Picayune*. Retrieved from http://businessfinder.nola.com/pastorek-paul-g-adams-and-reese-llp-new-orleans-la.html

49. Paul Pastorek. (n.d.). Retrieved July 11, 2013, from the Chiefs for Change website, http://chiefsforchange.org/members/paul-pastorek/

50. Schneider, M. (2013, March 5). New Orleans Recovery School District: The lie unveiled. [Web log post]. Retrieved from http://deutsch29.wordpress.com/2013/03/05/new-orleans-recovery-school-district-the-lie-unveiled/

51. Schneider, M. (2013, May 22). Louisiana charter school audit reveals faux accountability. [Web log post]. Retrieved from http://deutsch29.wordpress.com/2013/05/22/louisiana-charter-school-audit-reveals-faux-accountability/

52. Schneider, M. (2013, June 29). RSD's watered-down, incremental miracle and continued fiscal embarrassment. [Web log post]. Retrieved from http://deutsch29.wordpress.com/2013/06/29/rsds-watered-down-incremental-miracle-and-continued-fiscal-embarrassment/

53. Schneider, M. (2013, July 10). John White: I'll just tell them reforms are working. [Web log post]. Retrieved from http://deutsch29.wordpress.com/2013/07/10/john-white-ill-just-tell-them-reforms-are-working/

54. *Ross, R. (2011, April 11). Louisiana dropout rate falls 31 percent. Pelican Post. Retrieved from* http://www.thepelicanpost.org/2011/04/11/louisiana-dropout-rate-falls-31-percent/

55. *Vanacore, A. (2011, May 10). State superintendent of education Paul Pastorek resigning. Times Picayune. Retrieved from* http://www.nola.com/education/index.ssf/2011/05/state_superintendent_of_educat_1.html

56. *Aswell, T. (2011, April 22). Education superintendent Paul Pastorek learns a lesson in humility. [Web log post]. Retrieved from* http://louisianavoice.com/2011/04/22/education-superintendent-paul-pastorek-learns-a-lesson-in-humility

57. See 44.

58. PARCC, the non-profit. (2013, March 13). [Web log post]. Retrieved from http://okeducationtruths.wordpress.com/2013/03/13/parcc-the-non-profit/

59. Ravitch, D. (2013, March 17). Is this the ALEC group for testing common core? [Web log post]. Retrieved from http://dianeravitch.net/2013/03/17/is-this-the-alec-group-for-testing-common-core/

60.–62. See 44.

63. See 2.

64. Woodard, C. (2013, March 8). LePage to host education reformers. *Maine Sunday Telegram*. Retrieved from http://www.pressherald.com/politics/maine-will-host-florida-education-reformers_2013-03-08.html

65. Corso, E. (2011, March 17). The problem with Skanderra. *NMPolitics.net*. Retrieved from http://www.nmpolitics.net/index/2011/03/the-problem-with-skandera/

66. Haussamen, H. (2010, December 21). Martinez picks Florida reformer to be education secretary. *NMPolitics.net*. Retrieved from http://www.nmpoli-

tics.net/index/2010/12/martinez-picks-florida-reformer-to-be-education-secretary/

67.   Will Skandera ever get a confirmation hearing? (2012, February 2). *Capitol Report New Mexico*. Retrieved from http://www.capitolreportnewmexico. com/2012/02/will-skandera-ever-get-a-confirmation-hearing/

68.   Ravitch, D. (2013, March 4). Will Jeb Bush's deputy be confirmed as state commissioner in New Mexico? [Web log post]. Retrieved from http://dianeravitch.net/2013/03/04/will-jeb-bushs-deputy-be-confirmed-as-state-commissioner-in-new-mexico/

69.   Horwath, J. (2013, March 6). Hannah Skandera's jet-setting tenure at PED. *Santa Fe Reporter*. Retrieved from http://www.sfreporter.com/santafe/article-7284-ped-crossing.html

70.   Skandera testimony to Congress on behalf of expanding virtual industry's access to Federal Funds. (2013, March 11). Retrieved from http://www.scribd.com/doc/129729274/Skandera-Testimony-to-Congress-on-Behalf-of-Expanding-Virtual-Industry-s-Access-to-Federal-Funds

71.   [Emails between the Foundation for Excellence in Education and varied state education officials]. (2011-12). Retrieved March 20, 2013, from https://s3.amazonaws.com/s3.documentcloud.org/documents/558541/12-033-documents-8.pdf

72.   Fang, L. (2011, December 5). How online learning companies bought America's schools. *The Nation*. Retrieved from http://www.thenation. com/article/164651/how-online-learning-companies-bought-americas-schools

73.   See 71.

74.   See 69.

75.   See 71.

76.   Chiefs for Change. (n.d.). Hanna Skandera. Retrieved March 20, 2013, from http://chiefsforchange.org/members/hanna-skandera/

77.   Nikolewski, R. (2013, March 10). Editorial: An education in politics. Retrieved from http://newmexico.watchdog.org/17185/editorial-an-education-in-politics/

78.   Educational Testing Service. (n.d.). Tests and products. Retrieved July 11, 2013, from http://www.ets.org/tests_products

79.   Strauss, Valerie. (2013, January 30). Emails link Bush foundation corporations and education officials. [Web log post]. *Washington Post*. Retrieved from http://www.washingtonpost.com/blogs/answer-sheet/wp/2013/01/30/e-mails-link-bush-foundation-corporations-and-education-officials/

80.   [Emails between the Foundation for Excellence in Education and varied state education officials]. (2011-12). Retrieved March 20, 2013, from In the Public Interest document cloud, http://www.documentcloud.org/documents/559710-itpi-107.html

81.   Rhode Island Department of Education. (2012, June 22). [Rhode Island commissioner field memos]. Retrieved March 20, 2013, from http://www. ride.ri.gov/commissioner/fieldmemos/Field%20memo%206-22-12.pdf

82.   See 78.

83. Huntley, H. (2003, September 26). Legislators, teachers balk at deal for Edison Schools. *St. Petersburg Times*. Retrieved from http://www.sptimes. com/2003/09/26/Business/Legislators__teachers.shtml

84. JerseyJazzman. (2011, January 2). The Chris Cerf story, part i. [Web log post]. Retrieved from http://jerseyjazzman.blogspot.com/2011/01/chris-cerf-story-part-i.html

85. Ravitch, D. (2013, March 8). Kevin Huffman's zombie policies. [Web log post]. Retrieved from http://dianeravitch.net/2013/03/08/16128/

86. Foundation for Excellence in Education. (n.d.). 2010 agenda. Retrieved from http://excelined.org/national-summit/2012-agenda/

87. Strauss, V. (2011, May 8). Leading mathematician debunks 'value-added.' [Web log post]. *Washington Post*. Retrieved from http://www.washington-post.com/blogs/answer-sheet/post/leading-mathematician-debunks-value-added/2011/05/08/AFb999UG_blog.html

88.–89. Gonzalez, T. (2012, July 17). TN education reform hits bump in teacher evaluation. *WBIR-10*. Retrieved from http://www.wbir.com/news/article/226990/0/TN-education-reform-hits-bump-in-teacher-evaluation

90. Schneider, M. (2013, January 25). VAM explanation for legislators. [Web log post]. Retrieved from http://deutsch29.wordpress.com/2013/01/25/25/

91. Bundegaard, C. (2013, January 14). Bush touts TN reforms while Haslam talks voucher bill. *WKRN*. Retrieved from http://www.wkrn.com/story/20586177/bush-touts-tn-reforms-while-haslam-talks-voucher-bill

92. Fingeroot, L. (2013, February 28). TN education commissioner Kevin Huffman says charters can serve better. *Tennessean*. Retrieved March 20, 2013, from http://www.tennessean.com/article/20130228/NEWS04/302280045/TN-Education-Commissioner-Kevin-Huffman-says-charters-can-serve-better

93. [Emails between the Foundation for Excellence in Education and varied state education officials]. (2011-12). Retrieved March 20, 2013, from In the Public Interest document cloud, https://www.documentcloud.org/documents/560847-re-fw-reaction-pours-in-on-nclb-waiver-announcem.html#search/p1/Sec.%20Duncan%20called

94.–95. [Emails between the Foundation for Excellence in Education and varied state education officials]. (2011-12). Retrieved March 20, 2013, from In the Public Interest document cloud, https://www.documentcloud.org/documents/560947-waiver-request-from-oklahoma-0001.html#search/p1/I%20was%20asked%20by%20my

96. Sikes, B. (2013, February 18). Another Bush Chief for Change, another misinformation campaign. [Web log post]. Retrieved from http://bobsidlethoughtsandmusings.wordpress.com/2013/02/18/another-bush-chief-for-change-another-misinformation-campaign/

97. Chiefs for Change. (n.d.). Gerard Robinson [Biography]. Retrieved August 27, 2013, from http://chiefsforchange.org/members/gerard-robinson/

98. Larrabee, B. (2012, July 31). Embattled education commissioner Gerard Robinson resigns. *Miami Herald*. Retrieved from http://www.miamiherald.com/2012/07/31/2923731/embattled-education-commissioner.html

99.   Postal, L. (2011, December 8). FCAT scoring likely to get even tougher. *Orlando Sentinel*. Retrieved from http://articles.orlandosentinel.com/2011-12-08/features/os-fcat-scores-commissioner-20111208_1_fcat-reading-section-test-scores

100. Sikes, B. (2012, May 17). How Gerard Robinson is taking the FCAT bullet for Jeb Bush. [Web log post]. Retrieved from http://bobsidlethoughtsand-musings.wordpress.com/2012/05/17/how-gerard-robinson-is-taking-the-fcat-bullet-for-jeb-bush/

101. Smith, E. (2012, April 4). Building on the values of No Child Left Behind. [Web log post]. *Huffington Post*. Retrieved from http://www.huffington-post.com/eric-smith/no-child-left-behind_b_1403453.html

102. Solochek, J. (2012, April 4). Former commissioner Eric Smith lands at Bush institute. *Tampa Bay Times*. Retrieved from http://www.tampabay.com/blogs/gradebook/content/former-commissioner-eric-smith-lands-bush-institute

CHAPTER 16

1.–2. TNTP. (n.d.). Our history. Retrieved from http://tntp.org/about-tntp/our-history

3.   TNTP. (n.d.). Teaching fellows. Retrieved from http://tntp.org/what-we-do/training/teaching-fellows

4.   TNTP. (n.d.). How to apply. Retrieved from http://tntp.org/become-a-teacher/how-to-apply

5.–6. TNTP. (n.d.). TNTP academy. Retrieved from http://tntp.org/what-we-do/training/tntp-academy

7.   TNTP. (n.d.). Our board. Retrieved from http://tntp.org/about-tntp/our-board

8.   Education Trust. (n.d.). Funders. Retrieved from http://www.edtrust.org/dc/about/funders

9.   TNTP. (n.d.). Our funding model. Retrieved from http://tntp.org/about-tntp/our-funding-model

10.   Orlich, D., & Gifford, G. (2006, October 20). Test scores, poverty, and ethnicity: The new American dilemma. Retrieved from http://www.cha.wa.gov/?q=files/Highstakestesting_poverty_ethnicity.pdf

11.   US Department of Education. (2011, November 30). More than 40% of low-income schools don't get a fair share of state and local funds, Department of Education research finds. Retrieved from http://www.ed.gov/news/press-releases/more-40-low-income-schools-dont-get-fair-share-state-and-local-funds-department-

12.   Haycock, K. (2004, October 6). Funding gap states shortchange poor and minority students of education dollars. Retrieved from http://www.edtrust.org/dc/press-room/press-release/funding-gap-states-shortchange-poor-minority-students-of-education-dolla

13.   TNTP. (n.d.). About. Retrieved from http://tntp.org/about-tntp

14.   http://garyrubinstein.teachforus.org/2012/11/11/tntp-releases-odd-report-about-progress-in-d-c/

15.   See 9.

16.   US Department of Education. (2013, August 26). Investing in Innovation fund (I3). Retrieved from http://www2.ed.gov/programs/innovation/index.html

17.   Weisberg, D., Sexton, S., Mulhern, J., & Keeling, D. (2009). The widget effect. Retrieved from http://www.ride.ri.gov/Portals/0/Uploads/Documents/Teachers-and-Administrators-Excellent-Educators/Educator-Evaluation/Education-Eval-Main-Page/TheWidgetEffect-execsummary.pdf

18.   Merrow, J. (2009, June 18). Understanding the widget effect. [Web log post]. Retrieved from http://learningmatters.tv/blog/news-desk/understanding-the-widget-effect/2059/

19.   [Re: TNTP and NCTQ: Enemies of teachers]. (2012, January 25). Retrieved from http://groups.yahoo.com/group/nyceducationnews/message/42630

20.   Schneider, M. (2013, February 2). NCTQ letter grades and the reformer agenda, part viii. [Web log post]. Retrieved from http://deutsch29.wordpress.com/2013/02/02/nctq-letter-grades-and-the-reformer-agenda-part-viii/

21.   TNTP. (2012). The irreplaceables. Retrieved from http://tntp.org/assets/documents/TNTP_Irreplaceables_2012.pdf

22.–23.   Strauss, V. (2012, August 1). How do you identify 'irreplaceable' teachers? [Web log post]. *Washington Post*. Retrieved from http://www.washingtonpost.com/blogs/answer-sheet/post/how-do-you-identify-irreplaceable-teachers/2012/08/01/gJQAsC5OPX_blog.html

24.–25.   See 21.

26.   Eggers, D., & Calegari, N. (2011, May 1). The high cost of low teacher salaries. *New York Times*. Retrieved from http://www.nytimes.com/2011/05/01/opinion/01eggers.html?_r=0

27.   Ravitch, D. (2012, August 6). What scholars say about merit pay. [Web log post]. Retrieved from http://dianeravitch.net/2012/08/06/what-scholars-say-about-merit-pay/

28.   The 'Irreplaceables'; Another flawed report from TNTP. (2012, July). [Web log post]. Retrieved from http://thediariesofalawstudent.blogspot.com/2012/07/the-another-flawed-report-from-tntp.html

29.   About StudentsFirst. (n.d.). Retrieved from http://www.studentsfirst.org/pages/about-students-first

30.   See 20.

31.   Support for StudentsFirst. (n.d.). Retrieved from http://www.studentsfirst.org/policy-agenda/entry/support-for-studentsfirst-policy-agenda

32.   Simon, S. (2012, June 26). National education reform group's spending shown. *Reuters*. Retrieved from http://www.reuters.com/article/2012/06/26/us-usa-education-reform-studentsfirst-idUSBRE85O1CN20120626

33.   Simon, S. (2012, June 25). StudentsFirst spending: National education reform group's partial tax records released. *Huffington Post*. Retrieved from http://www.huffingtonpost.com/2012/06/25/corrected-national-educat_n_1626053.html

34. Blume, H. (2013, April 30). Walton foundation gives $8 million to StudentsFirst. Los Angeles Times. Retrieved from http://www.latimes.com/local/lanow/la-me-ln-walton-8-million-studentsfirst-20130429,0,3488400.story

35. Resmovits, J. (2013, July 2). Michelle Rhee's StudentsFirst missed its fundraising goal, tax documents reveal. *Huffington Post.* Retrieved from http://www.huffingtonpost.com/2013/07/02/michelle-rhee-studentsfirst_n_3535480.html?utm_hp_ref=politics

36. Resmovits, J. (2012, February 24). Michelle Rhee's backers include Obama bundler billionaire, big Romney backer. Huffington Post. Retrieved from http://www.huffingtonpost.com/2012/02/24/michelle-rhees-backers-in_n_1300146.html

37. Chu, J. (2011, January 12). Michelle Rhee wants to spend $1 billion fixing education. Fast Company. Retrieved from http://www.fastcompany.com/1715178/michelle-rhee-wants-spend-1-billion-fixing-education

38. *Butrymowicz, S. (2012, November 4). New player jumps into state elections to push education overhaul. Hechinger Report. Retrieved from http://hechingerreport.org/content/new-player-jumps-into-state-elections-to-push-education-overhaul_10164/*

39. See 33.

40. StudentsFirst electoral activity in 2012. (2012, November 8). Retrieved from http://www.studentsfirst.org/press/entry/studentsfirst-electoral-activity-in-2012

41. Resmovits, J. (2013, January 4). Michelle Rhee's StudentsFirst group loses top democrats, hires new president. *Huffington Post.* Retrieved from http://www.huffingtonpost.com/2013/01/04/michelle-rhees-studentsfirst_n_2411484.html

42. Clawson, L. (2013, April 26). StudentsFirst's Tennessee reformer of the year coauthored anti-gay bill. Retrieved from http://www.dailykos.com/story/2013/04/26/1204987/-StudentsFirst-s-Tennessee-reformer-of-the-year-coauthored-anti-gay-bill#

43. Guo, J. (2013, July 8). Reforming Michelle Rhee. *New Republic.* Retrieved from http://www.newrepublic.com/article/113204/michelle-rhee-tennessee-studentsfirst-floods-school-races#

44. Wiser, M. (2013, April 23). Education group tries to jumpstart debate. *WBIR-10.* Retrieved from http://qctimes.com/news/state-and-regional/iowa/article_3c0773b8-6092-5bac-aa56-a569eb072df7.html

45. Contact. (n.d.). Retrieved from the StudentsFirst website, http://www.studentsfirst.org/page/s/contact

46.–47. See 43.

48. Blume, H. (2013, February 20). Michelle Rhee group donates $250,000 to candidates in LAUSD races. *Los Angeles Times.* Retrieved from http://articles.latimes.com/2013/feb/20/local/la-me-0221-school-board-20130221

49. Los Angeles Unified School District (2013). (n.d.).Retrieved July 19, 2013, from http://ballotpedia.org/wiki/index.php/Los_Angeles_Unified_School_District_elections_(2013)

50.   Cunningham-Cook, M. (2012, October 17). Why do some of America's wealthiest individuals have their fingers in Louisiana's education system? *The Nation.* Retrieved from http://www.thenation.com/article/170649/why-do-some-americas-wealthiest-individuals-have-fingers-louisianas-education-system

51.   Ohanian, S. (2013, February 10). The resistance: Casting a broad net of influence. [Web log post.] Retrieved from http://www.susanohanian.org/show_commentary.php?id=333

52.–53. See 48.

54.   Magee, M. (2005, May 1). Departing schools chief hailed nationwide, yet reviled by many in S.D. *U-T San Diego.* Retrieved from http://legacy.ut-sandiego.com/news/education/20050501-9999-1n1bersin.html

55.   State of education, state policy report card 2013. (n.d.). Retrieved from the StudentsFirst website, http://www.studentsfirst.org/pages/state-of-education-state-policy-report-card-2013

56.   State policy report card executive summary. (2013). Retrieved from the StudentsFirst website, http://www.studentsfirst.org/page/-/docs/sprc2013/2013_SF_SPRC_Executive_Summary.pdf

57.   National Opportunity to Learn Campaign. (n.d.). Advisory board. Retrieved from http://www.otlcampaign.org/content/otl-advisory-board

58.–61. Five ways Michelle Rhee's Report puts students last. (2013, January 9). [Web log post]. Retrieved from http://www.otlcampaign.org/blog/2013/01/09/5-ways-michelle-rhee's-report-puts-students-last

62.   Homepage. (n.d.). Retrieved from the American Board for Certification of Teacher Excellence website, http://abcte.org/

63.   Schneider, M. (2013, March 18). NCTQ's varicose reform. [Web log post]. Retrieved from http://deutsch29.wordpress.com/2013/03/18/nctqs-varicose-reform/

64.   Darling-Hammond, L., Amrein-Beardsley, A., Haerte, E., & Rothstein, J. (2012, March). Evaluating teacher evaluation. *Phi Delta Kappan,93*(6), 8–15. Retrieved from http://www.otlcampaign.org/sites/default/files/resources/evaluating-teacher-evaluation-ldh.pdf

65.   See 58.

66.   New TV ad: Teachers and parents urge union leaders and city officials to agree on teacher evaluations. (2012, December 5). [Television ad]. Retrieved from http://www.studentsfirstny.org/index.cfm?objectid=DD317E30-3F2E-11E2-8E3B000C296BA163

67.   Ravitch, D. (2012, December 19). StudentsFirst attacks union in NYC. [Web log post]. Retrieved from http://dianeravitch.net/2012/12/19/studentsfirst-attacks-union-in-nyc/

68.   http://www.studentsfirst.org/policy/entry/myths-v-facts-educator-evaluations

69.   DiCarlo, M. (2013, April 8). On teacher evaluations, between myth and fact lies truth. [Web log post]. Retrieved from http://shankerblog.org/?p=8093

70.   COMPASS frequently asked questions. (2013, July 8). Retrieved from the Louisiana Believes website, http://www.louisianabelieves.com/docs/teaching/compass-process-faq-june-27.pdf?sfvrsn=4

71.   COMPASS myth vs. fact. (n.d.). Retrieved July 19, 2013, from the Louisiana Believes website, http://www.louisianabelieves.com/docs/teaching/myth-vs-fact—compass.pdf?sfvrsn=2

72.   See 69.

73.   See 58.

CHAPTER 17

1.   DFER images. (n.d.). Retrieved July 16, 2013, from http://images.nictusa.com/cgi-bin/fecgifpdf/

2.   About. (n.d.). Retrieved from the DFER website, http://www.dfer.org/about/

3.   Principles. (n.d.). Retrieved from the DFER website, http://www.dfer.org/about/principles/

4.   What we stand for. (n.d.). Retrieved from the DFER website, http://www.dfer.org/about/standfor

5.–6.   Ahmed-Ullah, N., Chase, J. & Sector, B. (2013, May 23). CPS approves largest school closure in Chicago's history. *Chicago Tribune.* Retrieved from http://articles.chicagotribune.com/2013-05-23/news/chi-chicago-school-closings-20130522_1_chicago-teachers-union-byrd-bennett-one-high-school-program

7.   See 4.

8.   Charter school achievement: Hype vs. evidence. (2010). Retrieved from the Education Justice website, http://www.educationjustice.org/newsletters/nlej_iss21_art5_detail_CharterSchoolAchievement.htm

9.   Ahmed-Ullah, N. (2013, July 16). Hearings today on lawsuits against CPS school closings. *Chicago Tribune.* Retrieved from http://www.chicagotribune.com/news/education/ct-met-cps-federal-hearing-20130715,0,7690800.story

10.   See 4.

11.   Democrats for Education reform contributors. (n.d.). Retrieved from http://www.opensecrets.org/pacs/pacgave2.php?cmte=C00417733&cycle=2010

12.   Hirsch, M. (2010, December 16). Who are democrats for Education Reform? Retrieved from http://www.uft.org/feature-stories/who-are-democrats-education-reform

13.–14. Democrats for Education Reform. (n.d.). Board of directors. Retrieved from http://www.dfer.org/list/about/board/

15.–16. Decker, G. (2013, June 25). Ex-state senator picked to lead DFER's New York fundraising. Retrieved from http://gothamschools.org/tag/democrats-for-education-reform/

17.   Ravitch, D. (2012, April 18). I don't understand Michelle Rhee. Retrieved from https://www.commondreams.org/view/2012/04/18-11

18.   Solomon, B. (2012, October 23). WalMart heir donates to Obama PAC, defying rest of billionaire family. *Forbes.* Retrieved from http://www.forbes.

com/sites/briansolomon/2012/10/23/wal-mart-heir-donates-to-obama-pac-defying-rest-of-billionaire-family/

19. See 15.

20. See 12.

21.   Education Reform Now. (n.d.). Activities. Retrieved from http://www.edreformnow.org/about/activities/

22. See 12.

23. Gmstein. (2013, May 22). "Democrat" runs for lasing city council. [Web log post]. Retrieved from http://bloggingformichigan.com/2013/05/22/democrat-runs-for-lansing-city-council/

24. See 21.

25. Education Reform Now. (n.d.). Retrieved from the DFER Watch website, http://dferwatch.wordpress.com/connections-2/education-reform-now-inc-2/

26. Libby, K. (2012, January 9). Education Now's 2010 IRS 990 form. Retrieved from http://dferwatch.wordpress.com/2012/01/09/education-reform-nows-2010-irs-990-form/

27. Broad Foundation. (n.d.). All current investments. Retrieved from http://www.broadeducation.org/investments/current_investments/investments_all.html

28. Walton Family Foundation. (2011). Education reform grant list. Retrieved from http://waltonfamilyfoundation.org/2011-education-reform-grant-list

29. Gonzalez, J. (2009, March 31). Rev. Al Sharpton's $500G link to education reform. *New York Daily News*. Retrieved from http://www.nydailynews.com/news/rev-al-sharpton-500g-link-education-reform-article-1.359635

30. 26 USC 501: Exemption from tax on corporations, certain trusts. (n.d.). Retrieved from http://www.law.cornell.edu/uscode/26/501(c)(4)(A).html

31. See 25.

32. Persephone's mother. (2013, April 14). California Dem's resolving not to be suckered by corporate "reformers." [Web log post]. Retrieved from http://persephonesmother.wordpress.com/2013/04/14/california-dems-resolving-not-to-be-suckered-by-corporate-reformers/

33. [Letter from Eric Bauman, Chair, Los Angeles County Democratic party, to Kevin Chavous, Chair, Democrats for Education Reform]. (2012, May 1). Retrieved from http://www.lacdp.org/wp-content/uploads/2012/05/LACDP-2012-DFER-Cease-Desist-Final.pdf

34. Tillson, W. (n.d.). Democrats for Education Reform. Retrieved from http://www.arightdenied.org/democrats-for-education-reform/

35. A Right Denied. (n.d.). About. Retrieved from http://www.arightdenied.org/about/

36. StudentsFirst. (n.d.). About. Retrieved from http://www.studentsfirst.org/pages/about-students-first

37. DFER. (2012, January 16). [Amended 2010 IRS form 990]. Retrieved from http://dferwatch.files.wordpress.com/2012/06/ern-form-990-2010-amended.pdf

38.–40. Joseph, G., & StudentNation. (2013, January 11). Astroturf activism: Who is behind Students for Education Reform? [Web log post]. *The Nation*. Retrieved from http://www.thenation.com/blog/172174/astroturf-activism-who-behind-students-education-reform#axzz2ZB5ZSSzq

41. Chicago teachers strike: Teachers union begins strike authorization vote Wednesday (VIDEO). (2012, June 6). Retrieved from, http://www.dfer.org/2012/06/chicago_teacher_1.php

42.–44. Horn, J. (2012, May 7). Corporate Party Continues Propaganda Campaign Against Chicago Teachers Union and Chicago's real public school teachers... Who is Rebecca Nieves-Huffman, Chicago's latest teacher bashing pundit? Retrieved from http://www.substancenews.net/articles.php?page=3241

45.   Friedman Foundation. (n.d.). Rebeca Nieves-Huffman [Biography]. Retrieved from http://www.edchoice.org/Foundation-Services/Speakers/Rebeca-Nieves-Huffman.aspx

46. Friedman Foundation. (n.d.). Joe Williams [Biography]. Retrieved from http://www.edchoice.org/Foundation-Services/Speakers/Joe-Williams.aspx

47. Friedman Foundation. (n.d.). Kevin P. Chavous [Biography]. Retrieved from http://www.edchoice.org/Foundation-Services/Speakers/Kevin-P–Chavous.aspx

48.–49. See 17.

50. Vardi, N. (2012, March 1). Ray Dalio tops 2011 hedge fund earnings. *Forbes*. Retrieved from http://www.forbes.com/lists/2012/hedge-fund-managers-12_land.html

51.–53. See 17.

54. Walz, M. (2010, September 28). Canvassers urge "Superman" audience to join fight. Retrieved from http://www.dfer.org/2010/09/canvassers_urge.php

55. Barkan, J. (2012, Spring). Hired guns on astroturf: How to buy and sell school reform. *Dissent Magazine*. Retrieved from http://www.dissentmagazine.org/article/hired-guns-on-astroturfhow-to-buy-and-sell-school-reform

CHAPTER 18

1. Public Agenda. (1997, October 22). Professors of education: It's how you learn, not what you learn that's most important. Retrieved from http://www.publicagenda.org/press-releases/professors-education-its-how-you-learn-not-what-you-learn-thats-most-important

2. Ravitch, D. (2012, May 23). What is NCTQ? [Web log post]. Retrieved from http://dianeravitch.net/2012/05/23/what-is-nctq/

3. National Council on Teacher Quality. (n.d.). [Website byline]. Retrieved March 18, 2013, from the NCTQ website, http://www.nctq.org/p/

4. National Council on Teacher Quality. (n.d.). About. Retrieved March 18, 2013, from http://www.nctq.org/about/

5.   Walsh, K. (2011, July 27). Education reforms: Exploring teacher quality initiatives. Retrieved from http://edworkforce.house.gov/uploaded-files/07.27.11_walsh.pdf

6.–9.   Horn, J. (2005, September 6). More corruption at ED. [Web log post]. Retrieved from http://www.schoolsmatter.info/2005/09/more-corruption-at-ed.html

10.   November Coalition. (2005, January 10). People shouldn't pay for fake news. Retrieved from http://www.november.org/stayinfo/breaking3/FakeNewsOpEd.html

11.   See 6.

12.   Orlich, D. (2005, February 5). Follow the money, taxpayers. [Letter to the editor]. *Spokesman Review.* Retrieved from http://news.google.com/newspapers?id=V2hWAAAAIBAJ&sjid=7PIDAAAAIBAJ&pg=4907,2619535&dq=national-council-on-teacher-quality&hl=en

13.   American Board for Certification of Teacher Excellence. (n.d.). Teach. Retrieved from http://abcte.org/teach/

14.–15. See 2.

16.–18. United States Government Accountability Office. (2006, February). Discretionary Grants: Further tightening of Education's procedures for making awards could improve transparency and accountability. [Report]. Retrieved from http://www.gao.gov/new.items/d06268.pdf

19.   Source Watch. (2011, April 11). National Council on Teacher Quality. Retrieved from http://www.sourcewatch.org/index.php?title=National_Council_on_Teacher_Quality

20.   Keller, B. (2005, October 19). Upheaval hits teacher credentialing board. Retrieved from http://www.edweek.org/ew/articles/2005/10/19/08abcte.h25.html

21.   Taylor, D. (2011, January 23). Kate Walsh the NCTQ, and US News and World Report. [Web log post]. Retrieved from http://seattleducation2010.wordpress.com/2011/01/23/kate-walsh-nctq-and-us-news-world-report/

22.   Foundation for Excellence in Education. (n.d.). Mortimer Zuckerman [Biography]. Retrieved from http://excelined.org/team/mortimer-zuckerman/

23.   Zuckerman, M. (2009, February 2). Education reform consensus grows on fixing urban schools. *US News and World Report.* Retrieved from http://lwindy.org/files/EducationReformConsensusGrows.pdf

24.   Foundation for Excellence in Education. (n.d.). Kate Walsh [Biography]. Retrieved from http://excelined.org/team/kate-walsh/

25.   Fund for Public Schools.(n.d.). Board and officers. Retrieved from https://www.fundforpublicschools.org/leadership

26.   Goodman, A. (2010, February 25). Juan Gonzalez: Eva Moskowitz has special access to schools chancellor Klein. [Interview]. Retrieved from http://www.democracynow.org/2010/2/25/juan_gonzalez_eva_moskowitz_has_special

27.   Gonen, Y. (2013, March 5). Classy Mike wants to fund own schools. *New York Post.* Retrieved from http://www.nypost.com/p/news/local/classy_mike_wants_to_fund_own_schools_diqABEWjf27KqU66a75vwI

28. Bloomberg. (n.d.). Our partners. Retrieved from http://www.bloomberg. org/#about/our-partners

29. Bloomberg. (n.d.). Board of directors. Retrieved from http://www.bloom- berg.org/#about/board-of-directors

30. National Council on Teacher Quality. (n.d.). Funders. Retrieved March 18, 2013, from http://www.nctq.org/p/about/funders.jsp

31. *US News and World Report.* (2013, August 8). *Wikipedia.* Retrieved from http://en.wikipedia.org/wiki/U.S._News_%26_World_Report

32.–33. Carey, K. (2006, September). College rankings reformed: The case for a new order in higher education. *Education Sector Reports.* Retrieved from http://www.educationsector.org/usr_doc/CollegeRankingsReformed. pdf

34. Comarow, A. (2008, July 10). A look inside the hospital rankings. *US News and World Report.* Retrieved from http://health.usnews.com/health-news/ best-hospitals/articles/2008/07/10/a-look-inside-the-hospital-rankings

35. Coggshall, J., Bivona, L., & Reschly, D. (2012, August). Evaluating the ef- fectiveness of teacher preparation programs for support and accountabil- ity. [Report]. Retrieved from http://hub.mspnet.org/index.cfm/25224

36. American Association of Colleges for Teacher Education. (2013, June 20). NCTQ review of nation's education schools deceives, misinforms public. [Press release]. Retrieved from http://aacte.org/news-room/press-releas- es/nctq-review-of-nations-education-schools-deceives-misinforms-public. html

37. Coalition for Student Achievement. (2009, April). Smart options: Invest- ing the recovery funds for student success. Retrieved from http://www. broadeducation.org/asset/429-arrasmartoptions.pdf

38. Schneider, M. (2013, February 8). NCTQ letter grades and the reformer agenda, part xi. [Web log post]. Retrieved from http://deutsch29.word- press.com/2013/02/08/nctq-letter-grades-and-the-reformer-agenda-part- xi/

39. Broad Education. (n.d.). Current investments. Retrieved from http:// www.broadeducation.org/investments/current_investments/invest- ments_all.html

40. Harvard University Graduate School of Education. (2009, September 15). Harvard University to offer groundbreaking doctoral program for education leaders. Retrieved from http://www.gse.harvard.edu/news- impact/2009/09/harvard-university-to-offer-groundbreaking-doctoral- program-for-education-leaders/

41. Harvard University Graduate School of Education. (n.d.). Partners. Re- trieved from http://www.gse.harvard.edu/academics/doctorate/edld/ partners.html

42. See 40.

43. National Council on Teacher Quality. (n.d.). Advisory board. Retrieved from http://www.nctq.org/p/about/advisory.jsp

44. Prepped teachers goal of reform. (2011, October 12). *Times Lead- er.* Retrieved July 15, 2013, from http://archives.timesleader.

com/2011_18/2011_10_12_Prepped_teachers_goal_of_reform_-editorial.html

45.   See 39.

46.   Schneider, M. (2013, March 21). Like spokes to a hub: Chiefs for Change in Bush's service. [Web log post]. Retrieved from http://deutsch29.wordpress.com/2013/03/21/like-spokes-to-a-hub-chiefs-for-change-in-bushs-service/

47.   Broad Superintendents Academy. (n.d.). Featured profiles: Deborah Gist. Retrieved from http://www.broadcenter.org/academy/network/profile/featured-deborah-gist

48.   Welch, C. (2013, June 4). U.S. education secretary defends RI Commissioner Gist. *Rhode Island Public Radio.* Retrieved from http://ripr.org/post/us-education-secretary-defends-ri-commissioner-gist

49.   McGowan, D. (2013, April 30). Union poll finds little support for Education Commissioner Deborah Gist. *WPRI.com.* Retrieved from http://www.wpri.com/dpp/news/local_news/mcgowan/union-poll-finds-little-support-for-education-commissioner-deborah-gist

50.   See 46.

51.   Schneider, M. (2013, February 20). Part xvii: Grading the NCTQ advisory board. [Web log post]. Retrieved from http://deutsch29.wordpress.com/2013/02/20/part-xvii-grading-the-nctq-advisory-board/

52.   Schneider, M. (2013, March 18). NCTQ's varicose reform. [Web log post]. Retrieved from http://deutsch29.wordpress.com/2013/03/18/nctqs-varicose-reform/

53.   National Council on Teacher Quality. (n.d.). Right to know. Retrieved March 18, 2013, from http://www.nctq.org/righttoknow/

54.   American Association of Universities. (2011, February 3). [Letter to *US News and World Report* Editor Brian Kelly and copied to NCTQ President Kate Walsh]. Retrieved March 18, 2013, from the NCTQ website, http://www.nctq.org/edschoolreports/national/docs/letters/AAU_Letter.pdf

55.   See 53.

56.–57.   Walsh, K. (2011, February 7). [Letter to American Association of Universities]. Retrieved March 18, 2013, from the NCTQ website, http://www.nctq.org/edschoolreports/national/docs/letters/AAU_NCTQ_Response.pdf

58.   National Council on Teacher Quality. (2013). Teacher Prep Review. [Report]. Retrieved from http://nctq.org/dmsView/Teacher_Prep_Review_2013_Report

59.   See 56.

60.–63.   California State, University of Maryland, State University of New York. (2011, February 7). [Letter to *US News and World Report* Editor Brian Kelly and copied to NCTQ President Kate Walsh]. Retrieved March 18, 2013, from the NCTQ website, http://www.nctq.org/edschoolreports/national/docs/letters/CalState_UMD_SUNY_Letter.pdf

64.   Walsh, K. (2011, March 16). [Letter to California State, University of Maryland, State University of New York]. Retrieved March 18, 2013, from the NCTQ website, http://www.nctq.org/edschoolreports/national/docs/letters/CalState_UMD_SUNY_NCTQ_Response.pdf

65. National Council on Teacher Quality. (n.d.). Standards, rationales, and indicators. Retrieved March 18, 2013, from http://www.nctq.org/standardsDisplay.do

66. National Council on Teacher Quality. (n.d.). Standards, rationales, and indicators. Retrieved March 18, 2013, from http://www.nctq.org/standardsDisplay.do?include=I

67. National Council on Teacher Quality. (n.d.). "Well-honed methodology." Retrieved March 18, 2013, from http://www.nctq.org/p/edschools/approach.jsp

68. See 51.

69. See 53.

70. See 65.

71. American Board for Certification of Teacher Excellence. (n.d.). Retrieved from http://abcte.org/

72.–75. See 58.

CHAPTER 19

1. Kumar, J. (2010, June 21). The billionaire mayor's daughter. *Forbes*. Retrieved from http://www.forbes.com/2010/06/21/billionaire-heiress-interview-michael-bloomberg-emma.html

2. Stand for Children. (n.d.). Board of directors. Retrieved from http://stand.org/national/about/board-directors

3. Knowledge is Power Program. (n.d.). Board of directors. Retrieved from http://www.kipp.org/about-kipp/the-kipp-foundation/board-of-directors

4. Bennett, D., & Riley, M. (2013, June 20). Booz Allen, the world's most profitable spy organization. *Bloomberg Businessweek*. Retrieved from http://www.businessweek.com/articles/2013-06-20/booz-allen-the-worlds-most-profitable-spy-organization

5. U.S. Department of Education. (2009, November). Race to the Top program executive summary. [Report]. Retrieved from http://www2.ed.gov/programs/racetothetop/executive-summary.pdf

6. Stand for Children. (n.d.). [Website]. Retrieved from http://stand.org/

7.–8. Stand for Children Leadership Center. (n.d.). What we stand for. Retrieved from http://standleadershipcenter.org/sites/standleadershipcenter.org/files/media/WWSF%20Point%20of%20View.pdf

9. Bill and Melinda Gates Foundation. (2005–2013). Awarded grants: Stand for Children. [Database search result]. Retrieved from http://www.gatesfoundation.org/How-We-Work/Quick-Links/Grants-Database#q/k=stand%20for%20children

10. See 7.

11. Stand for Children. (n.d.). Common core. Retrieved from http://stand.org/washington/action/common-core

12. Grannan, C. (2011, July 12). Jonah Edelman on outfoxing teachers' unions: Transcribed remarks. [Web log post]. Retrieved from http://

parentsacrossamerica.org/jonah-edelman-on-outfoxing-teachers-unions-transcribed-remarks/

13.   Rauner Family Foundation. (n.d.). [Tax exempt status]. Retrieved from http://501c3lookup.org/THE_RAUNER_FAMILY_FOUNDATION/

14.   Stand for Children. (2010). Annual report. [Report]. Retrieved from http://stand.org/sites/default/files/National/Documents/STANDFOR-CHILDREN_ANNUALREPORT_2010.pdf

15.   Stand for Children. (2007, June 12). Annual report. [Report]. Retrieved from http://stand.org/sites/default/files/National/Final%20Annual%20Report%20070612.pdf

16.   See 12.

17.   Joyce Foundation. (2010). Education grants. Retrieved from http://www.joycefdn.org/ar/2010/education-grants.html

18.   Discover the Networks. (n.d.). Funder profile: Joyce Foundation. Retrieved from http://www.discoverthenetworks.org/funderprofile.asp?fndid=5310

19.–20.   Schmidt, G. (2011, January 22). Emanuel's billionaire donors also bankrolling 'Stand for Children', pushing union-busting organizations in Illinois. *Substance News*. Retrieved from http://www.substancenews.net/articles.php?page=1948

21.–23.   See 12.

24.   See 19.

25.–26.   See 12.

27.   See 7.

28.   Barrett, S. (2011, July 8). Stand for Children: A hometown perspective of its evolution. [Web log post]. Retrieved from http://parentsacrossamerica.org/stand-for-children-a-hometown-perspective-of-its-evolution/

29.   Walton Family Foundation. (2010). Education grants. Retrieved from http://waltonfamilyfoundation.org/about/2010-grants-report#education

30.   Walton Family Foundation. (2011). Education reform grant list. Retrieved from http://waltonfamilyfoundation.org/2011-education-reform-grant-list

31.   See 29.

32.   Guzzardi, W (2011, July 12). Jonah Edelman on Illinois school reform: Stand for Children head talks political maneuvers. *Huffington Post*. Retrieved from http://www.huffingtonpost.com/2011/07/12/jonah-edelman-on-illinois_n_896512.html

33.   See 9.

34.   Mitchell, N. (2009, October 20). The controversy over 'Stand': A closer look. *EdNews Colorado*. Retrieved from http://www.ednewscolorado.org/news/education-news/the-furor-over-stand-a-closer-look

35.   Meyer, J. (2009, September 29). A tipping point for DPS schools. *Denver Post*. Retrieved from http://www.denverpost.com/frontpage/ci_13441129

36.   Augden, E. (2011, September 8). Stand for Children: Advocates for kids or corporations? Retrieved from http://defensedenver.com/2011/09/stand-for-children-advocates-for-kids-or-corporations/

37.   See 34.

38.–39.   See 35.

40. See 34.

41. Stand for Children, Inc. (2011). [IRS Form 990]. Retrieved from http://
     stand.org/sites/default/files/National/Documents/2011%20Stand%20
     C4%20Form%20990%20PUBLIC%20DISCLOSURE%20COPY.pdf

42. Colorado Senate Bill 191 updated summary. (2010, May 21). Retrieved
     July 19, 2013, from http://www.coloradoea.org/Libraries/General_Docu-
     ments/SB_191_Updated_Summary_May_21_2010.sflb.ashx

43. Colorado Department of Education (n.d.). State model evaluation system
     for teachers. Retrieved from http://www.cde.state.co.us/EducatorEffec-
     tiveness/SMES-Teacher.asp

44. See 41.

45. YourName (2012, April 25). Introduction: Stand for Children influences
     on agenda. Retrieved from http://commonground.tiddlyspot.com/

46.   AFT Colorado. (2012, February). Stand for Children ballot initiative:
     harmful to students, unfair to teachers. [Bulletin]. Retrieved from http://
     tagboston.org/wp-content/uploads/2012/02/Stand-Fact-Sheet-AFT.pdf

47.–48. Salsberg, B. (2012, June 20). 2 Mass. Unions drop opposition to teach-
     ers bill. *Boston.com.* Retrieved from http://www.boston.com/news/educa-
     tion/articles/2012/06/20/2_mass_unions_drop_opposition_to_teach-
     ers_bill/

49. Posel, S. (2013, March 19). Gates Foundation funds data mining project
     to dumb down students. Retrieved from http://www.occupycorporat-
     ism.com/gates-foundation-funds-data-mining-project-to-dumb-down-stu-
     dents/

50. See 9.

51. See 47.

52. Ravitch, D. (2012, June 14). Stand for Children does not stand for pub-
     lic education. [Web log post]. Retrieved from http://dianeravitch.
     net/2012/06/14/stand-for-children-does-not-stand-for-public-education/

53. Indiana State Government. (2011, February 16). Indiana Senate Bill 1. Re-
     trieved from http://www.in.gov/legislative/bills/2011/SB/SB0001.1.html

54. Moxley, E. (2012, August 20). Five things to know about Indiana's
     teacher evaluation law. *StateImpact.* http://stateimpact.npr.org/indi-
     ana/2012/08/20/five-things-to-know-about-indianas-teacher-evaluation-
     law/

55. Elliot, S., & Butrymowicz, S. (2013, June 28). Ritz is changing the game on
     teacher evaluation. *Indianapolis Star.* Retrieved from http://www.indystar.
     com/article/20130628/EXCLUSIVE05/306280006/Ritz-changing-game-
     teacher-evaluation

56. Glenda Ritz. (2013, July 10). *Ballotpedia.* Retrieved from http://ballotpe-
     dia.org/wiki/index.php/Glenda_Ritz

57.–58. Elliot, S., & Butrymowicz, S. (2013, July 1). Indiana's new education chief
     is changing the game on teacher evaluation. *Hechinger Report.* Retrieved
     from http://hechingerreport.org/content/indianas-new-education-chief-
     is-changing-the-game-on-teacher-evaluation_12416/

59. See 55.

60. March, W. (2013, March 3). Jeb Bush's education foundation under fire for lobbying for laws that benefit corporate donors. *Huffington Post*. Retrieved from http://www.huffingtonpost.com/2013/03/03/jeb-bush-education-foundation_n_2802536.html

61. Stokes, K. (2012, August 2). Interactive map: Who's giving money in the campaign for state superintendent. *StateImpact*. Retrieved from http://stateimpact.npr.org/indiana/2012/08/02/interactive-map-whos-giving-money-in-the-campaign-for-state-superintendent/

62.–63. See 41.

64.–65. Texas AFT. (n.d.). SB 8 watch: FAQ (frequently asked questions) on legislation. Retrieved from http://tx.aft.org/about-us/sb-8-watch-faq-legislation

66. See 41.

67. Illinois federation of Teachers. (n.d.). HB 3793 will further reduce revenue, harm students. [Bulletin]. Retrieved from http://action.aft.org/c/493/p/dia/action/public/?action_KEY=3066

68. Edelman, J. (2011, July 10). Re: Stand for Children stands for the rich and powerful. [Web log comment]. Retrieved from http://seattleducation2010.wordpress.com/2011/07/09/stand-for-children-stands-for-the-rich-and-the-powerful/

CHAPTER 20

1. Black Alliance for Educational Options (n.d.). Our mission and core values. Retrieved from http://www.baeo.org/?ns_ref=14&id=5457

2. Black Alliance for Educational Options. (n.d.). Organizational history. Retrieved from http://www.baeo.org/?ns_ref=14&id=5458

3. Howard Fuller [Biography]. (n.d.). Retrieved from http://activistcash.com/person/3736-howard-fuller/

4. Schneider, M. (2013, April 2). In Ravitch's defense: Milwaukee voucher study found wanting [Web log post]. Retrieved from http://deutsch29.wordpress.com/2013/04/02/in-ravitchs-defense-milwaukee-voucher-study-found-wanting/

5. National Academy of Engineering. (n.d.). Deborah McGriff biography. Retrieved from http://www.nae.edu/Projects/24591/engineeringink12-symposium/15871.aspx

6.–7. Schneider, M. (2013, February 8). NCTQ letter grades and the reformer agenda, part xi [Web log post]. Retrieved from http://deutsch29.wordpress.com/2013/02/08/nctq-letter-grades-and-the-reformer-agenda-part-xi/

8. Black Alliance for Educational Options. (n.d.). Board of directors. Retrieved from http://www.baeo.org/?ns_ref=14&id=5660

9. Marquette University. (n.d.). Research center and clinics. Retrieved from http://www.marquette.edu/education/centers_clinics/institute-for-the-transformation-of-learning.shtml

10. Bush calls education 'civil rights issue of our time.' (2002, January 19). *CNN*. Retrieved from http://articles.cnn.com/2002-01-19/politics/bush.

democrats.radio_1_education-overhaul-education-secretary-rod-paige-bush-and-congressional-republicans?_s=PM:ALLPOLITICS

11. McCain, J. (2008, September 4). John McCain's Acceptance Speech [Transcript]. *NPR.* Retrieved from http://www.npr.org/templates/story/story.php?storyId=94302894

12. People for the American Way Foundation. (2003, July). Community voice or captive of the right? Black Alliance for Educational Options [Report]. Retrieved from http://www.pfaw.org/sites/default/files/file_237.pdf

13.–14. Coeyman, M. (2001, July 10). Vouchers get a boost from Black Alliance. Christian Science Monitor. Retrieved from http://www.csmonitor.com/2001/0710/p19s1.html

15. Pedroni, T.C. (2007). *Market Movements: African American Involvement in School Voucher Reform.* New York: Taylor and Francis Group. Retrieved from http://books.google.com/books?id=5uo_VSlBJ7oC&pg=PA58&lpg=PA-58&dq=BAEO+walton+900000+2000&source=bl&ots=HwbK2REX0A&sig=-OC_NRXqqyAr52M5mXx1vjhdYvE&hl=en&sa=X&ei=kYzsUcLMKpDc8wS1oIHoBA&ved=0CCoQ6AEwAA#v=onepage&q&f=false

16. See 13.

17. http://www.njea.org/issues-and-political-action/vouchers/vouchers-series/fronting-for-the-movement

18. See 15.

19. See 4.

20.–21. See 17.

22. Office of Inspector General. (2005, September). Review of Department Identified Contracts and Grants for Public Relations Services: Final Inspection Report ED-OIG/I13-F0012 [Report]. Retrieved from http://www.google.com/url?sa=t&rct=j&q=%E2%80%9Cmulti-layered%20media%20campaign%E2%80%9D%20that%20would%20%E2%80%9Cutilize%20direct%20mail%2C%20radio%2C%20newspaper%2C%20the%20Internet%20and%20direct%20engagement%20techniques.%E2%80%9D%20&source=web&cd=1&ved=0CCsQFjAA&url=http%3A%2F%2Fwww.ed.gov%2Fabout%2Foffices%2Flist%2Foig%2Faireports%2Fi13f0012.doc&ei=ZfQnUpcolPj2BIjigaAG&usg=AFQjCNGKh3BlH9e7XYr3kFbs1eEu8FlNQg&bvm=bv.51773540,d.eWU

23. Walton Family Foundation. (2009). 2009 grants [Listing]. Retrieved from http://waltonfamilyfoundation.org/about/2009-grants#1

24. Walton Family Foundation. (2010). 2010 grants report, education [Report]. Retrieved from http://waltonfamilyfoundation.org/about/2010-grants-report#education

25. Walton Family Foundation. (2011). 2011 grants report, education [Report]. Retrieved from http://waltonfamilyfoundation.org/about/2011-grant-report#education

26. Walton Family Foundation. (2012). 2012 grants report, education [Report]. Retrieved from http://waltonfamilyfoundation.org/about/2012-grant-report#education

27. Bill and Melinda Gates Foundation. (2013). Grants [Database]. Retrieved from http://www.gatesfoundation.org/How-We-Work/Quick-Links/

Grants-Database#q/k=black%20alliance%20for%20educational%20options

28. Black Alliance for Educational options. (n.d.). The Common Core State Standards Initiative: BAEO policy analysis. Retrieved from http://www.baeo.org/?ns_ref=14&id=5459

29. See 15.

30. Black Alliance for Educational Options. (2013, January 20). BAEO Symposium 2013 [Video]. Retrieved from http://www.youtube.com/watch?v=fleR6bgH61E

31. http://thinkprogress.org/wp-content/uploads/2012/02/1-15-2012-2012-Fundraising-Plan.pdf

32. Rayfield J. (2013, February 1). Koch brothers donated big to ALEC, Heartland Institute. *Salon.* Retrieved from http://www.salon.com/2013/02/01/koch_brothers_donated_big_to_alec_heartland_institute/

33. See 31.

34.–36. Myslinski, D. (2010, October 28). American Legislative Exchange Council 35-day mailing, education task force meeting [Model legislation]. Retrieved from http://www.commoncause.org/atf/cf/%7BFB3C17E2-CDD1-4DF6-92BE-BD4429893665%7D/ed_35daymailing-dc.pdf

37. Parent Revolution. (n.d.). Ben Austin [Biography]. Retrieved from http://www.parentrevolution.org/our-staff#ben-austin

38. Lewis, J. (2006, December 7). The secret of his success. *LA Weekly.* Retrieved from http://www.laweekly.com/2006-12-07/news/the-secret-of-his-success/

39. Green Dot Educational Project. (2007). [IRS Form 990]. Retrieved from http://www.scribd.com/doc/65811566/Green-Dot-Eductational-Project-AKA-Green-Dot-Public-Schools-2007-Form-990

40.–41. Ravitch, D. (2013, June 5). The inside story of the Green Dot charter schools [Web log post]. Retrieved from http://dianeravitch.net/2013/06/05/the-inside-story-of-the-green-dot-charter-schools/

42. See 39.

43. Green Dot Educational Project. (2008). [IRS Form 990]. Retrieved from http://www.scribd.com/doc/65811613/Green-Dot-Eductational-Project-AKA-Green-Dot-Public-Schools-2008-Form-990

44. Los Angeles Parents Union. (2008). [IRS Form 990]. Retrieved from http://www.scribd.com/doc/65809661/Los-Angeles-Parents-Union-DBA-LAPU-or-Parent-Revolution-2008-Form-990

45. See 43.

46. See 44.

47. See 34.

48. Eli and Edythe Broad Foundation. (2009). [IRS Form 990]. Retrieved from http://www.scribd.com/doc/65818733/The-Eli-and-Edythe-Broad-Foundation-AKA-The-Broad-Foundation-2009-Form-990-PF

49. See 24.

50. Los Angeles Parents Union. (2010). [IRS Form 990]. Retrieved from http://www.scribd.com/doc/83962507/Los-Angeles-Parents-Union-DBA-LAPU-or-Parent-Revolution-2010-Form-990-Part-1

51.   Los Angeles Parents Union. (2007). [IRS Form 990]. Retrieved from http://www.scribd.com/doc/65809565/Los-Angeles-Parents-Union-DBA-LAPU-or-Parent-Revolution-2007-Form-990

52.   Los Angeles Parents Union. (2009). [IRS Form 990]. Retrieved from http://www.scribd.com/doc/65322146/Los-Angeles-Parents-Union-DBA-LAPU-or-Parent-Revolution-2009-Form-990

53.   See 50.

54.   Simon, S. (2012, March 20). Desert Trails Elementary parents seek to control of failing Aledanto, California school in high-stakes U.S. education reform [Corrected article]. Retrieved from http://www.huffingtonpost.com/2012/03/19/corrected-hostile-takeove_n_1365925.html

55.   Parent Revolution. (n.d.). Our funders. Retrieved from http://www.parentrevolution.org/content/our-funders

56.   Yarbrough, B. (2013, May 23). Parent trigger leader alleges organizers promised parents pay. *San Bernardino County Sun.* Retrieved from http://www.sbsun.com/news/ci_23317024/parent-trigger-leader-alleges-organizers-promised-parents-pay

57.–58. See 54.

59.   Lindstrom, N. (2012, October 3). 'Won't back Down' Inspiration: Struggling Desert Trails Elementary School in Aledanto waging bitter fight, no tidy Hollywood ending. *Huffington Post.* Retrieved from http://www.huffingtonpost.com/2012/10/03/wont-back-down-inspiratio_n_1935876.html

60.   Sieczkowski, C. (2012, October 3). 'Won't Back Down' box office is the worst opening ever. *Huffington Post.* Retrieved from http://www.huffingtonpost.com/2012/10/03/wont-back-down-box-office_n_1935527.html

61.–62. See 59.

63.   See 56.

64.   See 59.

65.   Watanabe, T. (2012, July 24). Ruling supports Aledanto charter school effort. *Los Angeles Times.* Retrieved from http://articles.latimes.com/2012/jul/24/local/la-me-parent-trigger-20120724

66.   Lindstrom, N. (2012, October 16). First "parent trigger" moves to a crucial vote after court ruling. *Hechinger Report.* Retrieved from http://hechingerreport.org/content/parent-trigger-moves-to-a-crucial-vote-after-court-ruling_9939/

67.   Office of Inspector General. (2012, September). Office of Innovation and Improvement's oversight and monitoring of the charter schools program's planning and implementation grants: Final Audit Report ED-OIG/A02-L0002 [Report]. Retrieved from http://deutsch29.files.wordpress.com/2013/05/us-dept-of-ed-charter-audit1.pdf

68.   Ravitch, D. (2013, June 14). The Unfairness of the parent trigger [Web log post]. Retrieved from http://dianeravitch.net/2013/06/14/the-unfairness-of-the-parent-trigger/

69.   Ravitch, D. (2013, June 14). Steve Zimmer proposes safety lock for parent trigger [Web log post]. http://dianeravitch.net/2013/06/14/steve-zimmer-proposes-safety-lock-for-parent-trigger/

70. High desert charter school first success for parent trigger law. (2013, January 8). [Web log post]. *Los Angeles Times.* Retrieved from http://latimesblogs.latimes.com/lanow/2013/01/mojave-desert-parents-made-history-tuesday-by-becoming-the-first-group-in-california-to-successfully-use-the-states-lan.html

71. Lindstrom, N. (2012, October 3). Desert Trails Elementary School parents choose new charter operator in first ever 'parent trigger.' *Huffington Post.* Retrieved from http://www.huffingtonpost.com/2012/10/19/desert-trails-elementary-_n_1987283.html

72. See 63.

73. Litvinov, A. (2013, April 2). Parents press lawmakers to abandon "parent trigger" in three more states. Retrieved from http://educationvotes.nea.org/2013/04/02/parents-press-lawmakers-to-abandon-parent-trigger-in-three-more-states/

74. Ravitch, D. (2013, April 30). Breaking news: Florida parents beat trigger again [Web log post]. Retrieved from http://dianeravitch.net/2013/04/30/breaking-news-florida-parents-beat-trigger-again/

75. Lu, A. (2013, July 1). Parents revolt against failing schools. Stateline. Retrieved from http://www.pewstates.org/projects/stateline/headlines/parents-revolt-against-failing-schools-85899487344

76.–77. Watanabe, T. (2013, May 24). Popular principal's dismissal leaves a south L.A. school divided. *Los Angeles Times.* Retrieved from http://articles.latimes.com/2013/may/24/local/la-me-weigand-20130525

78. Davis, T. (2013, March 13). Parent trigger—false promises, divided communities, and disrupted young lives [Video]. Retrieved from http://www.youtube.com/watch?v=HtTGMqHYaJk

79. See 76.

80. Parent Revolution. (n.d.). Chapter organizing efforts. Retrieved from http://parentrevolution.org/content/chapter-organizing-efforts

CHAPTER 21

1. Time for a test. (2009, June 11). *Economist.* Retrieved from http://www.economist.com/node/13832483

2. Society for Entrepreneurship and Education. (2009). David Levin [Biographical sketch]. Retrieved from http://www.tc.columbia.edu/students/seae/DavidLevin.html

3. Knowledge is Power Program. (n.d.). Board of directors. Retrieved from http://www.kipp.org/about-kipp/the-kipp-foundation/board-of-directors

4. The history of KIPP. (n.d.). Retrieved from http://www.kipp.org/about-kipp/history

5. The KIPP foundation. (n.d.). Retrieved from http://www.kipp.org/about-kipp/the-kipp-foundation

6. Board of directors. (n.d.). Retrieved from the KIPP website, http://www.kipp.org/about-kipp/the-kipp-foundation/board-of-directors

7. Green, E., & Cramer, P. (2009, February 17). KIPP charter school funders are major Republican party donors. *Gotham Schools*. Retrieved from http://gothamschools.org/2009/02/17/kipp-charter-school-funders-are-major-republican-party-donors/

8. KIPP school leader fellowships: Fisher fellowship. (n.d.). Retrieved from http://www.kipp.org/kipp-school-leadership-fellowships#Fisher

9. Joyce Foundation. (2011). 2011 annual report [Report]. Retrieved from http://ar2011.joycefdn.org/

10. Joyce Foundation (2012). Education grantees [Report]. Retrieved from http://www.joycefdn.org/programs/education/education-grantees/

11. Vogel, K. (2008, April 19). Obama linked to gun control efforts. *Politico*. Retrieved from http://www.politico.com/news/stories/0408/9722.html

12. Horn, S. (2013, July 9). Chicago school closings and the Joyce Foundation: The Obama connection. *MintPress News*. Retrieved from http://www.mintpressnews.com/a-closer-look-at-the-joyce-foundation-shows-obamas-ties-to-chicago-school-privatizations/164972/

13. Joyce Foundation. (n.d.). Annual reports [Listing]. Retrieved from http://www.joycefdn.org/about/annual-reports/

14. KIPP Chicago. (n.d.). About KIPP Chicago schools. Retrieved from http://www.kippchicago.org/about

15. Sweet, L. (2008, March 13). Sweet scoop: Obama, after initial refusal, releases all earmark requests. Read them here. UPDATES [Web log post]. Retrieved from http://blogs.suntimes.com/sweet/2008/03/sweet_scoop_obama_after_initia.html

16.–19. Miron, G., Urschel, J., & Saxton, N. (2011, March). What makes KIPP work? A study of student characteristics, attrition, and school finance [Paper]. Retrieved from http://www.edweek.org/media/kippstudy.pdf

20. Madfloridian. (2011, April 7). KIPP charters got more federal money than public schools. Also higher attrition rate helps scores? [Web log post]. Retrieved from http://journals.democraticunderground.com/madfloridian/7540

21. Dillon, S. (2010, August 5). Education department deals out big awards. *New York Times*. Retrieved from http://www.nytimes.com/2010/08/05/education/05grants.html

22. See 21.

23. KIPP DC. (2010). [IRS Form 990]. Retrieved from https://bulk.resource.org/irs.gov/eo/2010_06_EO/74-2974642_990_200906.pdf

24. KIPP LA Schools. (2010). [IRS Form 990]. Retrieved from http://www.kippla.org/about/documents/12010KIPPLAtaxreturns.PDF

25. KIPP Austin Public Schools, Inc. (2010). [IRS Form 990]. Retrieved from https://bulk.resource.org/irs.gov/eo/2012_06_EO/01-0639602_990_201108.pdf

26. Baker, B., Libby, K., & Wiley, K. (2012, May). Spending by the major charter management organizations: Comparing charter school and local public district financial resources in New York, Ohio, and Texas [Policy brief]. *National Education Policy Center*. Retrieved from http://greatlakescenter.org/docs/Policy_Briefs/Baker_CharterSpending.pdf

27.–28. See 16.

29.   Gronberg, T., Jansen, D. & Taylor, L. (2012, April). The relative efficacy of charter schools: A cost frontier approach. *Economics of Education Review, 31*(2), 302-317. Retrieved from http://www.sciencedirect.com/science/article/pii/S027277571100104X

30.   See 26.

31.   KIPP Houston. (n.d.). About. Retrieved from http://kipphouston.org/about

32.–33. See 16.

34.   Radcliffe, J. (2011, April 28). KIPP college grad rates draw both praise and concern. *Houston Chronicle.* Retrieved from http://www.chron.com/news/houston-texas/article/KIPP-college-grad-rates-draw-both-praise-and-1692194.php

35.   KIPP MA. (2012). Annual report [Report]. Retrieved from http://issuu.com/kippma/docs/kippma_fy2012_final?e=4293621/2713038

36.   KIPP MA. (n.d.). Results. Retrieved from http://www.kippma.org/kippma-results.php

37.   See 34.

38.   See 31.

39.   See 35.

40.   Radcliffe, J. (2012, December 24). KIPP struggles to see its graduates through college. *MySA.* Retrieved from http://www.mysanantonio.com/news/education/article/KIPP-struggles-to-see-its-graduates-through-4144370.php

41.   KIPP. (n.d.). Students. Retrieved from http://kipp.org/about-kipp/students

42.–43. See 16.

44.–45. Rubinstein, G. (2012, November 26). Open letters to reformers I know, part 2: Dave Levin and Mike Feinberg [Web log post]. Retrieved from http://garyrubinstein.teachforus.org/2012/11/26/open-letters-to-reformers-i-know-part-2-dave-levin-and-mike-feinberg/

46.   *Rubinstein, G. (2012, November 22). Ready or not... [Web log post]. Retrieved from* http://garyrubinstein.teachforus.org/2012/11/22/ready-or-not/

47.   See 16.

48.–49. Ash, K. (2013, February 27). Education Week—"KIPP schools boost academic performance, study finds." Retrieved from http://www.kipp.org/news/education-week-kipp-schools-boost-academic-performance-study-finds

50.   KIPP. (2012). 2012 report card [Report]. Retrieved from http://on.kipp.org/15pSbsC

51.   KIPP. (n.d.). Frequently asked questions. Retrieved from http://www.kipp.org/faq

52.   Donaldson, M. & Johnson, S. (2011, October 4). TFA teachers: How long do they teach? Why do they leave? Retrieved from http://www.edweek.org/ew/articles/2011/10/04/kappan_donaldson.html

53.   See 48.

54.–55. See 51.

56. Texas Education Agency. (n.d.). Charter schools—Employees FAQs [Listing]. Retrieved from http://www.tea.state.tx.us/index2. aspx?id=2986#FAQ 1

57.–58. Haimson, L. (2012, March 22). "At KIPP, I would wake up sick, every single day" [Web log post]. Retrieved from http://nycpublicschoolparents. blogspot.com/2012/03/at-kipp-i-would-wake-up-sick-every.html

59. Rubinstein, G. (2013, April 10). Teacher quality at KIPP [Web log post]. Retrieved from http://garyrubinstein.teachforus.org/2013/04/10/teacher-quality-at-kipp/

60. Sherry, A. (2007, January 12). Cole charter school set for closure. *Denver Post*. http://www.denverpost.com/sportscolumnists/ci_4997813

CHAPTER 22

1. Schnmidt, W. (1981, December 12). Some questions Aspen Institute tie to resort sales. *New York Times*. Retrieved from http://www.nytimes. com/1981/12/13/us/some-question-aspen-institute-tie-to-resort-sales. html?pagewanted=1

2.–3. Moser, W. (2012, June 27). Walter Paepke, Founder of Aspen Institute and Chicago patron of mid-century modernism [Web log post]. *Chicago Magazine*. Retrieved from http://www.chicagomag.com/Chicago-Magazine/ The-312/June-2012/Walter-Paepcke-Founder-of-the-Aspen-Institute-and-Chicago-Patron-of-Mid-Century-Modernism/

4,- 6. See 1.

7. Baca Grande. (n.d.). Retrieved from the Colorado Collehe website, http://www.coloradocollege.edu/offices/dean/the-baca-grande/

8. Aspen Institute. (n.d.). Mission. Retrieved from http://www.aspeninstitute.org/about/mission

9. Aspen Institute. (2011). [IRS Form 990]. Retrieved from http://207.153.189.83/EINS/840399006/840399006_2011_08a5ccae. PDF

10. Aspen Ideas Festival. (2013, August 21). *Wikipedia*. Retrieved from http:// en.wikipedia.org/wiki/Aspen_Ideas_Festival

11. Aspen Ideas Festival. (2013). History and highlights. Retrieved from http://www.aspenideas.org/festival/about

12. Aspen Ideas Festival. (2013). Speakers and moderators. Retrieved from http://www.aspenideas.org/speakers?festival=2013

13. Aspen Ideas Festival. (2011). Speakers and moderators. Retrieved from http://www.aspenideas.org/speakers?festival=2011

14. Bill and Melinda Gates Foundation. (n.d.). Aspen Institute [Database entry]. Retrieved from http://www.gatesfoundation.org/How-We-Work/ Quick-Links/Grants-Database#q/k=aspen%20institute

15.–16. Untitled, unpublished summary of the Aspen Institute Commission on No Child Left Behind. Retrieved from http://www.principals.org/portals/0/ content/55265.pdf

17. Cantor, P., Wiener, R., & Shelton, J. (2013). Ready to learn? Ready to teach? [Video]. Retrieved from http://www.aspenideas.org/session/ready-learn-ready-teach

18. Aspen Institute. (n.d.). About Walter Isaacson. Retrieved from http://www.aspeninstitute.org/about/about-walter-isaacson

19. Aspen Institute. (2007). [IRS Form 990]. Retrieved from http://207.153.189.83/EINS/840399006/840399006_2007_04A623A9.PDF

20. See 9.

21. See 18.

22. Isaacson, W. (2013, February 13). Outgoing board chair Walter Isaacson announces leadership transition [Web log post]. Retrieved from http://www.teachforamerica.org/blog/outgoing-board-chair-walter-isaacson-announces-leadership-transition

23. See 18.

24. Strauss, V. (2013, February 28). It's time for Teach for America to fold—former TFAer [Web log post]. *Washington Post*. Retrieved from http://www.washingtonpost.com/blogs/answer-sheet/wp/2013/02/28/its-time-for-teach-for-america-to-fold-former-tfaer/

25. Simon, S. (2012, August 16). Has Teach for America betrayed its mission? *Reuters*. Retrieved from http://www.reuters.com/article/2012/08/16/us-usa-education-teachforamerica-idUSBRE87F05O20120816

26. Eli and Edythe Broad Foundation. (2009). [IRS Form 990]. Retrieved from http://www.scribd.com/doc/65818733/The-Eli-and-Edythe-Broad-Foundation-AKA-The-Broad-Foundation-2009-Form-990-PF

27. See 13.

28. Aspen Ideas Festival. (2011). Kopp and Ravitch: What does real reform require? [Video]. Retrieved from http://fora.tv/2011/06/29/Kopp_and_Ravitch_What_Does_Real_Reform_Require

29. Sentell, W. (2013, June 27). Teach for America aid sparks heated arguments. *Baton Rouge Advocate*. Retrieved from http://theadvocate.com/home/6356299-125/teacher-aid-sparks-heated-arguments

30. Barth, R., Rose, J., & Wiener, R. (2011). Schools for the future [Video]. Retrieved from http://www.aspenideas.org/session/schools-future

31. Haimson, L. (2011, March 14). Chris Cerf, there you go again! [Web log post]. Retrieved from http://www.huffingtonpost.com/leonie-haimson/chris-cerf-there-you-go-a_b_835180.html

32. See 19.

33. Aspen Institute. (2008). [IRS Form 990]. Retrieved from http://207.153.189.83/EINS/840399006/840399006_2008_0579AA51.PDF

34. See 30.

35. Adams, R. (2011, May 24). Murdoch says schools miss out on tech revolution. *Wall Street Journal*. Retrieved from http://online.wsj.com/article/SB10001424052702304066504576343231249392742.html

36. Cavanagh, S. (2013, March 14). Amplify Insight wins contract from Common-Core testing consortium [Web log post]. Retrieved from http://

blogs.edweek.org/edweek/marketplacek12/2013/03/amplify_insight_
wins_contract_from_common_core_testing_consortium.html

37.   Resnick, L., Klein, J., Cantor, E., & Deasy, J. (2013). A seismic shift in our
        schools: College prep, career readiness, and the Common Core revolu-
        tion. [Video]. Retrieved from http://www.aspenideas.org/session/seis-
        mic-shift-our-schools-college-prep-career-readiness-and-common-core-rev-
        olution

38.   Scott, N. (2013, July 1). Joel Klein teaching resume: Sept/Oct 1968 during
        teacher strike–was Klein a scab? [Web log post]. Retrieved from http://
        ednotesonline.blogspot.com/2013/07/joel-klein-teaching-resume-sep-
        toct-1968.html

39.   Gardner, H., Klein, J., & Yowell, C. (2010). What is a learning ecosystem
        and how does it advance educational innovation? [Video]. Retrieved from
        http://www.aspenideas.org/session/what-learning-ecosystem-and-how-
        does-it-advance-educational-innovation

40.   Folkinflik, D. (2013, March 8). News Corp. education tablet:
        For the love of learning? *NPR*. Retrieved from http://www.npr.
        org/2013/03/08/173766828/news-corp-education-tablet-for-the-love-of-
        learning

41.   Rugh, P. (2013, April 29). Exposed: How Murdoch, Bill Gates, and big
        corporations are data mining our schools. Retrieved from http://www.oc-
        cupy.com/article/exposed-how-murdoch-bill-gates-and-big-corporations-
        are-data-mining-our-schools

42.   See 15.

43.   Aspen Institute. (n.d.). Condoleeza Rice [Biography]. Retrieved from
        http://www.aspeninstitute.org/people/condoleezza-rice

44.   Klein, J., & Rice, C. (2012). U.S. education reform and national security
        [Overview]. Retrieved from http://www.cfr.org/united-states/us-educa-
        tion-reform-national-security/p27618

45.   New York State Department of Education. (n.d.). [Teacher certification
        portal]. Retrieved from http://eservices.nysed.gov/teach/certhelp/Cp-
        PersonSearchExternal.jsp

46.   American Federation of Teachers.(2013, May 10). AFT President Randi
        Weingarten [Biography]. Retrieved from http://www.aft.org/about/lead-
        ership/president.cfm

47.–48. Weingarten, R., & Isaacson, W. (2012). Can teacher unions be partners
        in reforming schools in the 21st century? [Video]. Retrieved from http://
        www.aspenideas.org/session/can-teacher-unions-be-partners-reforming-
        schools-21st-century#bc-9155=1861036574001

49.   Equity and Excellence Commission. (2013, February 2). For each and ev-
        ery child: A strategy for education equity and excellence [Report]. Re-
        trieved from http://www2.ed.gov/about/bdscomm/list/eec/equity-ex-
        cellence-commission-report.pdf

50.   Layton, L. (2013, June 25). Common Core foes spreading misinformation,
        Duncan says. *Washington Post*. Retrieved from http://www.washingtonpost.
        com/local/education/common-core-foes-spreading-misinformation-

duncan-says/2013/06/25/332e9574-ddc8-11e2-948c-d644453cf169_story. html

51.–52. Bradley, A. (2012, September 20). The AFT innovation fund brings teacher voice to 'common core.' Retrieved from http://www.impatientoptimists. org/Posts/2012/09/The-AFT-and-the-Common-Core

53.–54. Schmidt, G. (2010, July 11). 'Just because you're rich doesn't mean you're smart...' (Gerald Bracey)... How Bill Gates received a totalitarians' welcome to the AFT national convention on July 10, 2010 and the complete text of the speech he delivered. *Substance News*. Retrieved from http:// www.substancenews.net/articles.php?page=1529

55. American Federation of Teachers. (2011, May 19). Recommendations of the AFT ad-hoc committee on standards rollout [Declaration]. Retrieved from http://www.aft.org/pdfs/teachers/reso_commoncorestandards.pdf

56. Phillips, V., & Weingarten, R. (2013, March 25). Six steps to effective teacher development and evaluation. *New Republic*. Retrieved from http://www. newrepublic.com/article/112746/gates-foundation-sponsored-effective-teaching#

57.–58. Hammatt, N. (2013, June 8). Why schools "fail," or what if "failing schools" aren't? [Web log post]. Retrieved from http://exploringeducation. blogspot.com/2013/06/v-behaviorurldefaultvmlo.html

59. See 55.

60. See 46.

61. Gewertz, C. (2013, April 30). Teachers' union president: halt all high stakes linked to Common Core [Web log post]. *Education Week*. Retrieved from http://blogs.edweek.org/edweek/curriculum/2013/04/halt_high_stakes_linked_to_common_core.html

62. Bill and Melinda Gates Foundation. (n.d.). NEA foundation [Database entry]. Retrieved from http://www.gatesfoundation.org/How-We-Work/ Quick-Links/Grants-Database#q/k=NEA%20foundation

63. Rubinstein, G. (2013, May 12). Canada's legendary TED talk lie [Web log post]. Retrieved from http://garyrubinstein.teachforus.org/2013/05/12/ canadas-legend-ary-ted-talk-lie/

64. Ravitch, D. (2013, May 13). Geoffrey Canada, just tell the truth [Web log post]. Retrieved from http://dianeravitch.net/2013/05/13/geoffrey-canada-just-tell-the-truth/

65. Hass, N. (2009, December 6). Scholarly investments. *New York Times*. Retrieved from http://www.nytimes.com/2009/12/06/fashion/06charter. html?_r=0&sq=Scholarly Investments&st=cse&adxnnl=1&scp=1&pagewan ted=1&adxnnlx=1374726266-1gjWyXaMmCaqhrJacoQFAA

66. Miner, B. (2010, October 20). Ultimate $uperpower: Supersized dollars drive *Waiting for Superman* agenda. *Not Waiting for Superman*. Retrieved from http://www.notwaitingforsuperman.org/Articles/20101020-Miner-UltimateSuperpower

67.–69. Canada, G., Chilcott, L., Gates, B., Guggenheim, D., & Schieffer, B. (2010). Waiting for Superman [Video]. Retrieved from http://www.aspenideas. org/session/waiting-superman

70. Broad, E., Byrd-Bennett, B., Gardner, H., Rotherham, A., & Schmidt, W. (2008). Competing globally? Reforming America's education [Video]. Retrieved from http://www.aspenideas.org/session/competing-globally-reforming-americas-education

71. Ahmed-Ullah, N., Chase, J., & Secter, B. (2013, May 23). CPS approves largest school closure in Chicago's history. *Chicago Tribune*. Retrieved from http://articles.chicagotribune.com/2013-05-23/news/chi-chicago-school-closings-20130522_1_chicago-teachers-union-byrd-bennett-one-high-school-program

72. Broad, E., & Friedman, T. (2012). Lessons in education [Video]. Retrieved from http://www.aspenideas.org/session/lessons-education

73.–74. Broad Foundation Education. (n.d.). All current investments [Listing]. Retrieved from http://www.broadeducation.org/investments/current_investments/investments_all.html

75. Broad Center. (n.d.). Borad superintendents academy. Retrieved from http://www.broadcenter.org/academy/

76. Rhee, M. (n.d.). Transforming the system [Video interview]. Retrieved July 25, 2013, from http://www.aspenideas.org/session/transforming-system-interview-michelle-rhee

77. http://www.aspenideas.org/session/ideas-work-can-charter-schools-transform-urban-education

78. Walton, R. (2009). Speaker [Listing]. Retrieved July 25, 2013, from http://www.aspenideas.org/speaker/rob-walton

79.–80. Walton Family Foundation. (2009). [IRS Form 990]. Retrieved from http://www.scribd.com/doc/65818585/Walton-Family-Foundation-Inc-2009-Form-990-PF

81. Pahara Institute. (n.d.). Our team [Biographical listing]. Retrieved from http://pahara.org/about-us/our-team/

82. Pahara Institute. (n.d.). Board of directors. Retrieved from http://pahara.org/about-us/board-of-directors/

83. See 80.

84. Pahara Institute. (n.d.). About us. Retrieved from http://pahara.org/about-us/

85.–86. Pahara Institute. (n.d.). Program details. Retrieved from http://pahara.org/our-work/pahara-aspen-education-fellowship/program-details/

87. Pahara Institute. (2012). Our fellows [Listing]. Retrieved from http://pahara.org/our-work/aspen-teacher-leader-fellowship/our-fellows/

88. Pahara Institute. (2013). Our fellows [Listing]. Retrieved from http://pahara.org/our-work/pahara-aspen-education-fellowship/ourfellows/

89. See 83.

90. See 14.

CHAPTER 23

1. Bradford, H. (2012, May 3). John Arnold, hedge fund manager and former Enron trader, retires at 38 years old with $3.5 billion. *Huffington Post*.

Retrieved from http://www.huffingtonpost.com/2012/05/03/john-arnold-enron-retires_n_1475574.html

2.   Workers World. (1997). [Bradley funding for Charles Murray's book, *The Bell Curve*]. Retrieved July 26, 2013, from http://www.workers.org/ww/1997/bradley.html

3.   Koch Family Foundations and Philanthropy. (n.d.). David H. Koch charitable foundation and personal philanthropy. Retrieved from http://www.kochfamilyfoundations.org/FoundationsDHK.asp

4.   Weller, S. (2013, May 24). David Koch: Just as bad as I thought, only cheaper [Web log post]. Retrieved from http://www.washingtonpost.com/blogs/she-the-people/wp/2013/05/24/david-koch-just-as-bad-as-i-thought-only-cheaper/

5.   Bill and Melinda Gates Foundation. (2013, September 8). *Wikipedia*. Retrieved from http://en.wikipedia.org/wiki/Bill_%26_Melinda_Gates_Foundation

6.–7.   Bill and Melinda Gates Foundation. (n.d.). Foundation facts sheet. Retrieved from http://www.gatesfoundation.org/Who-We-Are/General-Information/Foundation-Factsheet

8.   Bill and Melinda Gates Foundation. (n.d.). History. Retrieved from http://www.gatesfoundation.org/Who-We-Are/General-Information/History

9.   Bill and Melinda Gates Foundation. (n.d.). William H. Gates, Sr. [Biography]. Retrieved from http://www.gatesfoundation.org/who-we-are/general-information/leadership/management-committee/william-h-gates-sr

10.–12.   See 8.

13.–15.   Bill and Melinda Gates Foundation. (2009, November). Foundation commits $335 million to promote effective teaching and raise student achievement [Press release]. Retrieved from http://www.gatesfoundation.org/Media-Center/Press-Releases/2009/11/Foundation-Commits-$335-Million-to-Promote-Effective-Teaching-and-Raise-Student-Achievement

16.   Strauss, V. (2011, May 8). Leading mathematician debunks 'value-added' [Web log post]. Retrieved from http://www.washingtonpost.com/blogs/answer-sheet/post/leading-mathematician-debunks-value-added/2011/05/08/AFb999UG_blog.html

17.   Schneider, M. (2013, January 25). VAM explanation for legislators [Web log post]. Retrieved from http://deutsch29.wordpress.com/2013/01/25/25/

18.   Sokol, M. (2012, May 1). Hillsborough school board member Stacy White blasts Gates initiative. *Tampa Bay Times*. Retrieved from http://www.tampabay.com/news/education/k12/hillsborough-school-board-member-stacy-white-blasts-gates-initiative/1227901

19.   Fensterwald, J. (2011, October 24). Charters launch in-depth evals. Retrieved from http://toped.svefoundation.org/2011/10/24/charters-experiment-with-evaluations/

20.   Roberts, J. (2011, October 30). Memphis schools grapple with maintaining Gates reforms after money runs out. *Commercial Appeal*. Retrieved from http://www.commercialappeal.com/news/2011/oct/30/mcs-eyes-future-of-gates-effort/

21. Strauss, V. (2010, September 29). Ravitch: The long, failed history of merit pay and how the Ed Department ignores it [Web log post]. Retrieved from http://voices.washingtonpost.com/answer-sheet/diane-ravitch/ravitch-merit-pays-long-unsucc.html

22. Chute, E. (2013, January 9). Gates Foundation airs model to evaluate teachers. *Pittsburgh Post-Gazette.* Retrieved from http://www.post-gazette.com/stories/news/education/gates-foundation-airs-model-to-evaluate-teachers-669579/

23. Bill and Melinda Gates Foundation. (n.d.). Making the case for small schools—the facts [Paper]. Retrieved from http://www.washingtonsmall-schools.org/makingthecase.pdf

24. Groves, M. (2000, November 16). Gates Foundation giving $37 million to small schools. *Los Angeles Times.* Retrieved from http://articles.latimes.com/2000/nov/16/news/mn-52877

25. Pemberton-Butler, L. (1999, May 6). Vander Ark's exit no surprise. *Seattle Times.* Retrieved from http://community.seattletimes.nwsource.com/archive/?date=19990506&slug=2959089

26. See 24.

27. Bill and Melinda Gates Foundation. (1999, May). Gates learning foundation selects education initiative director [Press release]. Retrieved from http://www.gatesfoundation.org/Media-Center/Press-Releases/1999/05/Tom-Vander-Ark-Education-Initiative-Director

28. Schneider, M. (2013, March 15). Tom Vander Ark and the business of education [Web log post]. Retrieved from http://deutsch29.wordpress.com/2013/03/15/tom-vander-ark-and-the-business-of-education/

29. See 24.

30. Ravitch, D. (2008, November 18). Gates and his silver bullet. *Forbes.* Retrieved from http://www.forbes.com/2008/11/18/gates-foundation-schools-oped-cx_dr_1119ravitch.html

31.–32. Shaw, L. (2006, November 5). Foundation's small-schools experiment has yet to yield big results. *Seattle Times.* Retrieved from http://seattletimes.com/html/localnews/2003348701_gates05m.html

33. See 23.

34. Chaz. (2013, February 25). Bill Gates is wrong, the New York City small schools do not work [Web log post]. Retrieved from http://chaz11.blogspot.com/2013/02/bill-gates-is-wrong-new-york-city-small.html

35. Lipman, P. (2013). *The New Political Economy of Urban Education.* New York: Taylor and Francis. Retrieved from http://books.google.com/books?id=VRa_20-M2OYC&printsec=frontcover#v=onepage&q&f=false

36. Gralla, P. (2008, June 23). Gates' historical legacy may focus more on philanthropy than on Microsoft. *Computerworld.* Retrieved from http://www.computerworld.com/s/article/9101858/Gates_historical_legacy_may_focus_more_on_philanthropy_than_on_Microsoft?taxonomyId=125&pageNumber=2

37. Rondy, J. (2011, November 24). The human cost [Web log post]. Retrieved from http://www.susanohanian.org/outrage_fetch.php?id=887

38.   Strauss, V. (2013, May 12). Gates gives $150 million in grants for Common Core Standards [Web log post]. Retrieved from http://www.washington-post.com/blogs/answer-sheet/wp/2013/05/12/gates-gives-150-million-in-grants-for-common-core-standards/

39.   Bill and Melinda Gates Foundation (n.d.). Common core [database search result]. Retrieved from http://www.gatesfoundation.org/How-We-Work/Quick-Links/Grants-Database#q/k=Common%20Core

40.   Kentucky curriculum documents. (2013, march 25). [Curriculum documents]. Retrieved from http://kate.murraystate.edu/resources/pdre-source/49/

41.   Bill and Melinda Gates Foundation. (n.d.). NEA [database search result]. Retrieved from http://www.gatesfoundation.org/How-We-Work/Quick-Links/Grants-Database#q/k=NEA

42.   Benso, J., & Patti, D. (2013, may 5). Common core standards will prepare kids for success: As I see it [Opinion editorial]. Retrieved from http://www.pennlive.com/opinion/index.ssf/2013/05/common_core_stan-dards_will_prepare_kids_for_success_as_i_see_it.html

43.   Bill and Melinda Gates Foundation. (n.d.). Pennsylvania common core [Database search result]. Retrieved from http://www.gatesfoundation.org/How-We-Work/Quick-Links/Grants-Database#q/k=pennsylvania%20common%20core

44.   Pennsylvania Business Council (n.d.). Education foundation research summits. Retrieved July 25, 2013, from http://www.pegweb.org/pbc-ed-foundation-research-summits

45.   Pullman, J. (2013, July 18). Top FL lawmakers to Tony Bennett: Drop national Common Core tests. *Heartlander.* Retrieved from http://news.heart-land.org/newspaper-article/2013/07/18/top-fla-lawmakers-tony-bennett-drop-national-common-core-tests

46.   DeMillo, A. (2013, July 23). Opponents ask Arkansas to drop Common Core school standards. *Arkansas Business.* Retrieved from http://www.ar-kansasbusiness.com/article/93667/opponents-ask-arkansas-to-drop-com-mon-core-school-standards

47.   Neher, J. (2013, March 20). State lawmakers consider dropping Common Core standards for schools. *Michigan Radio.* Retrieved from http://www.michiganradio.org/post/state-lawmakers-consider-dropping-common-core-standards-schools

48.   White, J. (2013, July 9). Penn. To consider Common Core repeal. *Heart-lander.* Retrieved from http://news.heartland.org/newspaper-arti-cle/2013/07/09/penn-consider-common-core-repeal

49.   Jones, W. (2013, July 22). Georgia sticking with nationwide Common Core curriculum but will write own exams, governor says. *Florida Times-Union.* Retrieved from http://jacksonville.com/news/georgia/2013-07-22/sto-ry/georgia-sticking-nationwide-common-core-curriculum-will-write-own

50.   Layton, L. (2013, July 23). Georgia, Oklahoma say Common Core tests are too costly and decide not to adopt them. *Washington Post.* Retrieved from http://www.washingtonpost.com/local/education/georgia-oklahoma-

say-common-core-tests-are-too-costly/2013/07/23/e95b312e-f3c9-11e2-aa2e-4088616498b4_story.html

51. Ujifusa, A. (2013, May 6). Kentucky Common-Core testing snafus upset lawmakers [Web log post]. *Education Week*. Retrieved from http://blogs.edweek.org/edweek/state_edwatch/2013/05/kentucky_common_core_test_scoring_altered_lawmakers_upset.html

52. Strauss, V. (2013, June 25). Arne Duncan tells newspaper editors how to report on Common Core [Web log post]. Retrieved from http://www.washingtonpost.com/blogs/answer-sheet/wp/2013/06/25/arne-duncan-tells-newspaper-editors-how-to-report-on-common-core/

53. Sauer, M. (2013, April 25). Data mining students through Common Core. *New American*. Retrieved from http://www.thenewamerican.com/culture/education/item/15213-data-mining-students-through-common-core

54. Bill and Melinda Gates Foundation. (n.d.). inBloom, Inc. [Database search result]. Retrieved from http://www.gatesfoundation.org/How-We-Work/Quick-Links/Grants-Database/Grants/2012/10/OPP1070519

55. Heussner, K. (2013, February 5). Gates Foundation-backed inBloom frees up data to personalize k12 education [Web log post]. Retrieved from http://gigaom.com/2013/02/05/gates-foundation-backed-inbloom-frees-up-data-to-personalize-k-12-education/

56.–57. Haimson, L. (2013, July 23). Parent sounds alarm on student privacy [Web log post]. Retrieved from http://www.wnyc.org/blogs/schoolbook/2013/jul/23/what-you-need-know-about-inbloom-student-database/

58. See 8.

59. Walton Family Foundation. (n.d.). About. Retrieved from http://www.waltonfamilyfoundation.org/about

60. Said, S. (2011, September 22). The richest family in the world 2011—worth $93 billion. *Richest*. Retrieved from http://www.therichest.com/world/richest-family/

61. Walton Family Foundation, Inc. (2011). [IRS Form 990 PF]. Retrieved from https://bulk.resource.org/irs.gov/eo/2012_11_PF/13-3441466_990PF_201112.pdf

62.–63. Greenhouse, S. (2004, January 13). In-house audit says Wal-Mart violated labor laws. *New York Times*. Retrieved from http://www.nytimes.com/2004/01/13/us/in-house-audit-says-wal-mart-violated-labor-laws.html

64. National coalition calls Wal-Mart to account. (2005, December). *Union Labor News*. Retrieved from http://scfl.org/uln.php?ulnid=1124

65. Law, V. (2011, June 24). Martori Farms: Abusive conditions at a key Wal-Mart supplier. *Truthout*. Retrieved from http://truth-out.org/news/item/1808:martori-farms-abusive-conditions-at-a-key-walmart-supplier

66. Dickinson, J. (2013, June 5). Walmart's war against unions—and the U.S. laws that make it possible [Web log post]. *Huffington Post*. Retrieved from http://www.huffingtonpost.com/julie-b-gutman/walmart-labor-laws_b_3390994.html

67. Meyerson, H. (2013, July 18). Wal-Mart's low wages are a threat to Americans' standard of living [Editorial]. *Investor's Business Daily*. Retrieved

from   http://news.investors.com/ibd-editorials-on-the-left/071813-664297-walmart-low-wage-policy-impoverishes-its-own-workers.htm

68.   Fox, E. (2013, June 4). Wal-Mart's low wages cost taxpayers. *CNN Money*. Retrieved from http://money.cnn.com/2013/06/04/news/companies/walmart-medicaid/index.html

69.   Fox, E. (2013, January 10). Wal-Mart knew about Mexico bribery in 2005, say lawmakers. *CNN Money*. Retrieved from http://money.cnn.com/2013/01/10/news/companies/walmart-investigation/index.html

70.   Walton Family Foundation. (2012). 2012 grant report [Report]. Retrieved from http://wff.cotcdn.rockfishhosting.com/documents/76022f5d-f9e0-44aa-929c-1c2e26f219ac.pdf

71.   Ravitch, D. (2013, April 18). Walton Family Foundation supporting mass school closings in Chicago [Web log post]. Retrieved from http://dianeravitch.net/2013/04/18/walton-family-foundation-supporting-mass-school-closings-in-chicago/

72.   See 70.

73.–74. Walton Family Foundation. (2012). 2012 grant report: Education [Report]. Retrieved from http://waltonfamilyfoundation.org/about/2012-grant-report#education

75.   The twenty-first century teacher [News hub]. *NPR*. Retrieved July 26, 2013, from http://www.the21stcenturyteacher.com/npr

76.   Smith, D., & Brantley, M. (2005, July 8). Conservative think-tanker to head UA school-reform operation. *Arkansas Times*. Retrieved from http://www.arktimes.com/arkansas/conservative-think-tanker-to-head-ua-school-reform-operation/Content?oid=867264

77.   Brantley, M. (2013, March 30). School vouchers don't work [Web log post]. *Arkansas Times*. Retrieved from http://www.arktimes.com/ArkansasBlog/archives/2013/03/30/school-vouchers-dont-work

78.   Schneider, M. (2013, April 2). In Ravitch's defense: Milwaukee voucher study found wanting [Web log post]. Retrieved from http://deutsch29.wordpress.com/2013/04/02/in-ravitchs-defense-milwaukee-voucher-study-found-wanting/

79.   Phillips, A. (2010, July 22). Union demands charter school reinstate fired teachers. *Gotham Schools*. Retrieved from http://gothamschools.org/2010/07/22/union-demands-charter-school-reinstate-fired-teachers/

80.   National Alliance for Public Charter Schools. (n.d.). What are public charter schools? Retrieved from http://www.publiccharters.org/About-Charter-Schools/What-are-Charter-Schools003F.aspx

81.   KIPP. (n.d.). Frequently asked questions. Retrieved from http://www.kipp.org/faq

82.   See 79.

83.   Blume, H. (2009, April 30). Charter school staff face dilemma on benefits. *Los Angeles Times*. Retrieved from http://articles.latimes.com/2009/apr/30/local/me-benefits30

84.   Williams, J. (2012, November 28). Teachers face tough choices as charter schools drop pensions. *Lens*. Retrieved from http://thelensnola.

org/2012/11/28/rising-costs-drive-charter-schools-to-drop-out-of-state-pension-system/

85.   Pullman, J. (2012, February 10). IRS regulation could threaten charter school teachers' pensions. *Heartlander*. Retrieved from http://news.heart-land.org/newspaper-article/2012/02/10/irs-regulation-could-threaten-charter-school-teachers-pensions

86.   Pennsylvania department of Education. (1997, June 12). Summary of charter school legislation. Retrieved from http://www.portal.state.pa.us/portal/server.pt/community/charter_school_regulations/7359/summa-ry_of_charter_school_legislation/508170

87.   KIPP. (n.d.). Questions about teaching in KIPP schools. Retrieved from http://www.kipp.org/about-kipp/faq/#teaching

88.   GuideStar. (n.d.). Charter Fund, Inc., Charter School Growth Fund [Database search result]. Retrieved from http://www.guidestar.org/organiza-tions/05-0620063/charter-fund-charter-school-growth-fund.aspx

89.   Charter School Growth Fund. (n.d.). Our investment strategy. Retrieved from http://chartergrowthfund.org/invest-with-us/our-investment-strate-gy/

90.   Bill and Melinda Gates Foundation. (n.d.). Charter fund [Database search result]. Retrieved from http://www.gatesfoundation.org/How-We-Work/Quick-Links/Grants-Database#q/k=charter%20fund

91.   Schneider, M. (2013, March 5). New Orleans Recovery School District: The lie unveiled [Web log post]. Retrieved from http://deutsch29.wordpress.com/2013/03/05/new-orleans-recovery-school-district-the-lie-unveiled/

92.   Schneider, M. (2013, June 29). RSD's watered-down, incremental mira-cle and continued fiscal embarrassment [Web log post]. Retrieved from http://deutsch29.wordpress.com/2013/06/29/rsds-watered-down-incre-mental-miracle-and-continued-fiscal-embarrassment/

93.   Schneider, M. (2013, July 5). New Orleans parental choice and the Walton-funded OneApp [Web log post]. Retrieved from http://deutsch29.word-press.com/2013/07/05/new-orleans-parental-choice-and-the-walton-funded-oneapp/

94.   Children's Scholarship Fund. (n.d.). Our founders: Built on a strong foundation. Retrieved from http://www.scholarshipfund.org/drupal1/founders

95.–97. See 73.

98.   Broad Foundations. (n.d.). Eli and Edythe Broad [Biography]. Retrieved from http://www.broadfoundation.org/about_broads.html

99.   Lacter, M. (2013, February 5). Eli Broad: A most unreasonable man. *Inc.* Retrieved from http://www.inc.com/magazine/201302/mark-lacter/eli-broad-a-most-unreasonable-man.html

100.–101. See 98.

102.–103. See 99.

104.   Broad Foundation Education. (n.d.). Mission and overview. Retrieved from http://www.broadeducation.org/about/overview.html

105.   Carnoy, M., & Rothstein, R. (2013, January 15). International tests show achievement gaps in all countries, with big gains for U.S. disadvantaged

students [Web log post]. *Economic Policy Institute*. Retrieved from http://www.epi.org/blog/international-tests-achievement-gaps-gains-american-students/

106. Ravitch, D. (2013, January 25). Good news: Major re-analysis of international tests [Web log post]. Retrieved from http://dianeravitch.net/2013/01/25/good-news-major-re-analysis-of-international-tests/

107. See 104.

108. See 99.

109. Schneider, M. (2013, April 22). John White and inBloom: It ain't over, folks [Web log post]. Retrieved from http://deutsch29.wordpress.com/2013/04/22/john-white-and-inbloom-it-aint-over-folks/

110. Schneider, M. (2013, April 19). John White's hidden memorandum of understanding with inBloom [Web log post]. Retrieved from http://deutsch29.wordpress.com/2013/04/19/john-whites-hidden-memorandum-of-understanding-with-inbloom/

111. Schneider, M. (2013, July 10). John White: "I'll just tell them reforms are working" [Web log post]. Retrieved from http://deutsch29.wordpress.com/2013/07/10/john-white-ill-just-tell-them-reforms-are-working/

112. Schneider, M. (2013, March 1). John White's voucher laundering scheme [Web log post]. Retrieved from http://deutsch29.wordpress.com/2013/03/01/john-whites-voucher-laundering-scheme/

113. Schneider, M. (2013, May 22). Louisiana charter school audit reveals faux-accountability [Web log post]. Retrieved from http://deutsch29.wordpress.com/2013/05/22/louisiana-charter-school-audit-reveals-faux-accountability/

114. Sentell, W. (2013, June 27). Teach for America aid sparks heated arguments *Baton Rouge Advocate*. Retrieved from http://theadvocate.com/home/6356299-125/teacher-aid-sparks-heated-arguments

115. Broad Foundation and Thomas B. Fordham Institute. (2003, May). Better leaders for America's schools: A manifesto [Paper]. Retrieved from http://www.broadeducation.org/asset/1128-betterleadersforamericasschools.pdf

116. Broad Center. (n.d.). Jean-Claude Brizard [Biography]. Retrieved from http://www.broadcenter.org//network/profile/jean-claude-brizard

117. Broad Center. (n.d.). Christopher Cerf. [Biography]. Retrieved from http://www.broadcenter.org//network/profile/christopher-cerf

118. Haimson, L. (2011, March 14). Chris Cerf, there you go again! [Web log post]. *Huffington Post*. Retrieved from http://www.huffingtonpost.com/leonie-haimson/chris-cerf-there-you-go-a_b_835180.html

119. Broad Center. (n.d.). John Deasy. [Biography]. Retrieved from http://www.broadcenter.org//network/profile/john-deasy

120. Aron, H. (2013, June 20). Defiant Deasy says he'll push targeted spending plan anyway. *LA School Report*. Retrieved from http://laschoolreport.com/defiant-deasy-says-hell-continue-to-push-local-spending-plan/

121. Broad Center. (n.d.). Deborah Gist. [Biography]. Retrieved from http://www.broadcenter.org//network/profile/deborah-gist

122.–123. Eli and Edythe Broad Foundation. (2011). [IRS Form 990 PF]. Retrieved from http://207.153.189.83/EINS/954686318/954686318_2011_08bfc 7d1.PDF

124. Bill and Melinda Gates Foundation. (n.d.). Green dot [Database search result]. http://www.gatesfoundation.org/How-We-Work/Quick-Links/ Grants-Database#q/k=green%20dot

125. See 122.

126. Bill and Melinda Gates Foundation. (n.d.). KIPP Foundation [Database search result]. http://www.gatesfoundation.org/How-We-Work/Quick-Links/Grants-Database/Grants/2012/11/OPP1070481

127.–128. See 122.

129. Harvard Graduate School of Education. (n.d.). Doctor of education leadership [Degree program description]. Retrieved from http://www.gse. harvard.edu/academics/doctorate/edld/

130. See 122.

131. Bill and Melinda Gates Foundation. (n.d.). National Council on Teacher Quality [Database search result]. http://www.gatesfoundation.org/How-We-Work/Quick-Links/Grants-Database/Grants/2011/10/OPP1033849

132. Broad Prize for Urban Education. (n.d.). Overview. Retrieved from http:// www.broadprize.org/about/overview.html

133. Broad Prize for Urban Education. (n.d.). Broad prize review board. Retrieved from http://www.broadprize.org/about/decision_makers/review_board.html

134. Broad Prize for Urban Education. (n.d.). Broad prize selection jury. Retrieved from http://www.broadprize.org/about/decision_makers/selection_jury.html

CHAPTER 24

1. American Legislative Exchange Council. (n.d.). History. Retrieved from http://www.alec.org/about-alec/history/

2. ALEC Watch. (n.d.). Chapter Six—A brief history: ALEC's formation, growth, and transformation. *Corporate America's Trojan Horse in the States: The Untold Story Behind the American Legislative Exchange Council* [Report]. Retrieved from http://www.alecwatch.org/chaptersix.html

3.–5. See 1.

6.–7. Common Cause. (2012, April 20). IRS whistleblower letter on ALEC [Letter]. Retrieved from http://www.commoncause.org/site/ pp.asp?c=dkLNK1MQIwG&b=8060297

8. Strasser, A. (2012, June 12). BREAKING: Johnson and Johnson drops ALEC. *ThinkProgress*. Retrieved from http://thinkprogress.org/justice/2012/06/12/498620/breaking-johnson-johnson-drops-alec/

9. Shakir, F. (2012, April 9). Bill and Melinda Gates Foundation withdraws support from ALEC. *ThinkProgress*. Retrieved from http://thinkprogress. org/justice/2012/04/09/461217/bill-melinda-gates-foundation-withdraws-support-from-alec/

10. Millhiser, I. (2012, May 18). BREAKING: Eleven more lawmakers drop ALEC. *ThinkProgress.* Retrieved from http://thinkprogress.org/justice/2012/05/18/486883/breaking-eleven-more-lawmakers-drop-alec/

11. Fang, L. (2011, March 4). David Koch claims he doesn't 'directly' support Wisconsin Gov. Scott Walker. *ThinkProgress.* Retrieved from http://thinkprogress.org/politics/2011/03/04/148632/david-koch-walker/

12. Alec Exposed. (n.d.). Starting (minimum) wage repeal act [Model legislation]. Retrieved from http://www.alecexposed.org/w/images/3/34/1E10-Starting_%28Minimum%29_Wage_Repeal_Act_Exposed.pdf

13. Jilani, Z. (2011, October 19). Corporate front group ALEC pushing for repeal of paid sick day laws nationwide. *ThinkProgress.* Retrieved from http://thinkprogress.org/economy/2011/10/19/347793/alec-repeal-sick-days/

14. See 10.

15.–16. Kremer, J. (2012, August 29). Voter photo identification laws and ALEC [Web log post]. Retrieved from http://www.huffingtonpost.com/jerry-kremer/voter-photo-identificatio_b_1836990.html

17. Wilce, R. (2013, June 26). Seven faces of NRA/ALEC-approved "stand your ground" law. *PR Watch.* Retrieved from http://www.prwatch.org/news/2013/06/11384/seven-faces-nraalec-approved-stand-your-ground-law

18. ALEC Exposed. (n.d.). Castle doctrine act [Model legislation]. Retrieved from http://alecexposed.org/w/images/7/7e/7J2-Castle_Doctrine_Act_Exposed.PDF

19. See 17.

20. O'Brien, C. (2011, October 27). Public Safety and Elections task force—35 day mailing [Model legislation]. Retrieved from http://www.commoncause.org/atf/cf/%7BFB3C17E2-CDD1-4DF6-92BE-BD4429893665%7D/PSE%20AZ%2035-day_mailing.pdf

21. Surgey, M. (2012, March 23). Fact sheet: ALEC, the NRA, the castle doctrine, and Trayvon Martin [Web log post]. Retrieved from http://www.commonblog.com/2012/03/23/fact-sheet-alec-the-nra-the-castle-doctrine-and-trayvon-martin/

22. Feeney, L. (2012, March 28). What does Walmart have to do with Trayvon Martin? *Moyers and Company.* Retrieved from http://billmoyers.com/2012/03/28/what-does-walmart-have-to-do-with-trayvon-martin/

23. Keyes, S. (2012, April 17). PROGRESSIVE VICTORY: ALEC ends its guns and voter suppression task force. *ThinkProgress.* Retrieved from http://thinkprogress.org/justice/2012/04/17/465775/alec-retreat-non-economic-issues/

24. O'Brien, C. (2011, March 31). Public Safety and Elections task force—35 day mailing [Model legislation]. Retrieved from http://www.commoncause.org/atf/cf/%7BFB3C17E2-CDD1-4DF6-92BE-BD4429893665%7D/pseupdated_35-daymailing%20Ohio.pdf

25. O'Brien, C. (2012, April 6). Public Safety and Elections task force—35 day mailing [Model legislation]. Retrieved from http://www.commoncause.org/atf/cf/%7BFB3C17E2-CDD1-4DF6-92BE-BD4429893665%7D/35_day_mailing_pse_stfs2012.pdf

26. Robinson, R. (2012, April 17). ColorOfChange responds to ALEC announcement that it will end its task force that dealt with non-economic issues. Retrieved from http://colorofchange.org/press/releases/2012/4/17/colorofchange-responds-alec-announcement-it-will-e/

27. American Legislative Exchange Council. (n.d.). Justice performance project. Retrieved from http://www.alec.org/task-forces/justice-performance-project/

28. See 15.

29. American Legislative Exchange Council. (n.d.). Criminal intent protection act [Model legislation]. Retrieved from http://www.alec.org/model-legislation/criminal-intent-protection-act/

30.–34. See 1.

35. See 25.

36. ALEC's Public Safety and Elections task Force. (2011, February 15). Issue alert [Bulletin]. Retrieved from (http://www.commoncause.org/atf/cf/%7Bfb3c17e2-cdd1-4df6-92be-bd4429893665%7D/1-ALEC_IssueAlerts.PDF

37. O'Brien, C. (2011, June 30). Public Safety and Elections task force—35 day mailing [Model legislation]. Retrieved from http://www.commoncause.org/atf/cf/%7BFB3C17E2-CDD1-4DF6-92BE-BD4429893665%7D/pse_35-day_mailing_2011_annual_meeting%20new%20orleans.pdf

38. American Legislative Exchange Council. (n.d.). Join ALEC online. Retrieved July 28, 2013, from http://www.alec.org/membership/legislative-membership/join-alec-online/

39. American Legislative Exchange Council. (n.d.). Private sector membership. Retrieved July 28, 2013, from http://www.alec.org/membership/private-sector-membership/

40. American Legislative Exchange Council. (n.d.). Talking points, AZ HB 2423. Retrieved from http://www.commoncause.org/atf/cf/%7Bfb3c17e2-cdd1-4df6-92be-bd4429893665%7D/2-ALEC_Talking_Points_Examples.PDF

41. American Legislative Exchange Council. (n.d.). Press release [Template]. Retrieved from http://www.commoncause.org/atf/cf/%7Bfb3c17e2-cdd1-4df6-92be-bd4429893665%7D/3-ALEC_ObamaCare_Press_Release.PDF

42. See 6. http://www.commoncause.org/site/pp.asp?c=dkLNK1MQIwG&b=8060297

43.–44. Fischer, B. (2012, May 7). A CMD special report: ALEC's "scholarship" scheme helps corporations fund legislator trips. *PR Watch*. Retrieved from http://prwatch.org/news/2012/05/11443/cmd-special-report-alecs-scholarship-scheme-helps-corporations-fund-legislator-tr

45. Terkel, A. (2012, April 26). ALEC has special exemption in South Carolina's lobbying law. *Huffington Post*. Retrieved from http://www.huffingtonpost.com/2012/04/26/alec-south-carolina-lobbying-exemption_n_1455861.html

46. North Carolina General Assembly Legislative Ethics Committee. (2007, June 20). Published edited advisory opinion of the Legislative Ethics Com-

mittee [Document number AO-E-07-0009]. Retrieved from http://www.ethicscommission.nc.gov/library/pdfs/AOs/PDFs/aoE070009.pdf

47. See 43.
48. American Legislative Exchange Council. (2007, December 31). Bylaws. Retrieved from http://www.prwatch.org/files/ALEC_bylaws.pdf
49. See 43.
50. http://www.prwatch.org/files/AT&T.pdf
51. See 43.
52. American Legislarive Exchange Council. (n.d.). Board of directors. Retrieved July 28, 2013, from http://www.alec.org/about-alec/board-of-directors/
53. American Legislative Exchange Council. (n.d.). State chairmen. Retrieved July 28, 2013, from http://www.alec.org/about-alec/state-chairmen/
54. American Legislative Exchange Council. (n.d.). Private enterprise advisory council. Retrieved July 28, 2013, from http://www.alec.org/about-alec/private-enterprise-advisory-council/
55. American Legislative Exchange Council. (n.d.). Task forces: Education. Retrieved from http://www.alec.org/task-forces/education/
56. See 25.
57. Postal, L. (2011, November 1). Florida's NAEP scores fall short of Race to the Top goals. *Orlando Sentinel*. Retrieved from http://articles.orlandosentinel.com/2011-11-01/features/os-florida-naep-scores-20111101_1_reading-scores-math-scores-scores-for-black-students
58.–59. See 25.
60. Foundation for Excellence in Education. (2010). Summit agenda. Retrieved from http://excelined.org/national-summit/2010-agenda/
61.–62. See 25.
63. Myslinski, D. (2012, November 19). ALEC vote rejects anti-Common Core resolution [Web log post]. Retrieved from http://excelined.org/2012/11/alec-vote-rejects-anti-common-core-resolution/
64.–65. Ortega, T. (1999, May 13). Think tank warfare. *Phoenix New Times News*. Retrieved from http://www.phoenixnewtimes.com/1999-05-13/news/think-tank-warfare/
66. Myslinski, D. (2011, July 1). ALEC Education task force 35-day mailing. Retrieved from http://www.commoncause.org/atf/cf/%7BFB3C17E2-CDD1-4DF6-92BE-BD4429893665%7D/education_35-day_mailing%20-%20new%20orleans.pdf
67.–68. See 20.
69.–70. See 25.
71. Ravitch, D, (2013, March 17). Rupert Murdoch wins contract to develop Common Core tests [Web log post]. Retrieved from http://dianeravitch.net/2013/03/17/rupert-murdoch-wins-contract-to-develop-common-core-tests/
72. Haimson, L. (2013, March 14). Student education data collecting initiative inBloom puts sensitive information at risk. *New York Daily News*. Retrieved from http://www.nydailynews.com/new-york/inbloom-education-data-cloud-jeopardizes-lives-new-york-students-article-1.1288189

73.   O'Connor, J. (2012, May 31). How Jeb Bush stood up to ALEC for national education standards. *State Impact*. Retrieved from http://stateimpact.npr.org/florida/2012/05/31/how-jeb-bush-stood-up-to-alec-for-national-education-standards/

74.   Levesque, P. (2012, November 20). Re: ALEC vote rejects anti-Common Core resolution [Email]. Retrieved from http://groups.yahoo.com/group/nyceducationnews/message/48902

CPSIA information can be obtained at www.ICGtesting.com
Printed in the USA
BVOW01s1046080514

352811BV00004B/40/P